Cultural Implications of Knowledge Sharing, Management and Transfer:

Identifying Competitive Advantage

Deogratias Harorimana
Southampton Solent University, UK

T0321686

A volume in the Advances in Knowledge Acquisition, Transfer, and Management (AKATM) Book Series

Director of Editorial Content:	Kristin Klinger
Senior Managing Editor:	Jamie Snavely
Assistant Managing Editor:	Michael Brehm
Publishing Assistant:	Sean Woznicki
Typesetter:	Michael Brehm
Cover Design:	Lisa Tosheff

Published in the United States of America by
Information Science Reference (an imprint of IGI Global)
701 E. Chocolate Avenue
Hershey PA 17033
Tel: 717-533-8845
Fax: 717-533-8661
E-mail: cust@igi-global.com
Web site: http://www.igi-global.com

Library of Congress Cataloging-in-Publication Data

Cultural implications of knowledge sharing, management and transfer : identifying competitive advantage / Deogratias Harorimana, editor.
    p. cm.
  Includes bibliographical references and index.
  Summary: "This book illustrates, compares, and discusses models, perspectives, and approaches involved in the distribution, administration, and transmission of knowledge across organizations"--Provided by publisher.
  ISBN 978-1-60566-790-4 (hbk. : alk. paper) -- ISBN 978-1-60566-791-1 (ebook : alk. paper) 1. Knowledge management. 2. Knowledge management--Social aspects. I. Harorimana, Deogratias, 1972-
  HD30.2.C85 2010
  658.4'038--dc22
                                        2009021683

This book is published in the IGI Global book series Advances in Knowledge Acquisition, Transfer, and Management (AKATM) Book Series (ISSN: 2326-7607; eISSN: 2326-7615)

British Cataloguing in Publication Data
A Cataloguing in Publication record for this book is available from the British Library.

All work contributed to this book is new, previously-unpublished material. The views expressed in this book are those of the authors, but not necessarily of the publisher.

Advances in Knowledge Acquisition, Transfer, and Management (AKATM) Book Series

Murray E. Jennex
San Diego State University, USA

ISSN: 2326-7607
EISSN: 2326-7615

MISSION

Organizations and businesses continue to utilize knowledge management practices in order to streamline processes and procedures. The emergence of web technologies has provided new methods of information usage and knowledge sharing. The **Advances in Knowledge Acquisition, Transfer, and Management (AKATM) Book Series** brings together research on emerging technologies and its effect on information systems and knowledge society.AKATM will provide researchers, students, practitioners, and industry leaders with highlights on the knowledge management discipline, including technology support issues and knowledge representation.

COVERAGE

- Cognitive Theories
- Cultural Impacts
- Information and Communication Systems
- Knowledge Acquisition and Transfer Processes
- Knowledge Management Strategy
- Knowledge Sharing
- Organizational Learning
- Organizational Memory
- Small and Medium Enterprises
- Virtual Communities

IGI Global is currently accepting manuscripts for publication within this series. To submit a proposal for a volume in this series, please contact our Acquisition Editors at Acquisitions@igi-global.com or visit: http://www.igi-global.com/publish/.

Titles in this Series

For a list of additional titles in this series, please visit: www.igi-global.com

www.igi-global.com

701 E. Chocolate Ave., Hershey, PA 17033
Order online at www.igi-global.com or call 717-533-8845 x100
To place a standing order for titles released in this series, contact: cust@igi-global.com
Mon-Fri 8:00 am - 5:00 pm (est) or fax 24 hours a day 717-533-8661

Josune Saenz, *University of Deusto, Spain*
Annette Dunham, *University of Canterbury, New Zealand*
Beate Klingenberg, *Marist College, Poughkeepsie, USA*
Helen Rotherhberg, *Marist College, USA*
Stavros T. Ponis , *National Technical University Athens, Greece*
Laura Zapata Cantú, *Tecnológico de Monterrey-Campus, Mexico*
Stavros T. Ponis, *National Technical University Athens, Greece*
Annette Dunham, *University of Canterbury, New Zealand*
Epaminondas Koronis, *Mediterranean University College, Greece*
Jianzhong Hong, *Lappeenranta University of Technology, Finland*
Pete Bond, *Learning Futures Consulting, UK*
Hanna Timonen, *Helsinki University of Technology, Finland*
Claire Seaman, *Queen Margaret University, UK*
Nekane Aramburu, *University of Deusto, Spain*
Graeme Smith, *Ordinance Survey, UK*
Frank Land, *London School of Economics, UK*
Vilma Vuori, *Tampere University of Technology, Finland*

Table of Contents

Detailed Table of Contents

Section 1

The first section focuses on a careful and purposeful survey of the topic under study. This section provides a foundation for further debate in the book.

Chapter 1
Exploring the Knowledge Management Landscape: A Critical Review of Existing
Knowledge Management Frameworks 1

> *Stavros T. Ponis, National Technical University Athens, Greece*
> *George Vagenas, National Technical University Athens, Greece*
> *Epaminondas Koronis, University of Warwick, UK*

Relevant literature suggests that the field of knowledge management (KM) at the service of contemporary organizations is characterized by a plethora of diverse frameworks. However, none of these frameworks has achieved such a wide acceptance so as to be conceived as a standard. In fact, practice proves that each research or consultant group follows its own approach while many initiatives are based on custom approaches, developed each time from scratch, or even worse do not follow a structured method at all. In this chapter the authors attempt to go deeper by proposing a classification of knowledge management frameworks based on their macroscopic characteristics followed by their evaluation against a set of predetermined content elements that a complete approach should possess. The main result propagated from our critique is a common understanding of current theoretical and practical shortcomings of the field and the specification of a consistent set of course of actions and guidelines for researchers and practitioners engaged in knowledge management and its applications.

Chapter 2

Markus Haag, University of Bedfordshire, UK
Yanqing Duan, University of Bedfordshire, UK
Brian Mathews, University of Bedfordshire, UK

The concept of culture and its relationship with Nonaka's SECI model, a widely used model of organizational knowledge creation, is discussed in this chapter. Culture, in various forms, is argued to impact on the SECI model and the model itself is embedded in a certain context. This context determines the characteristics of the knowledge creation modes as described by SECI and therefore makes the model either more, or less, pertinent in a given context. This is regardless of whether that context is primarily determined by national culture, organizational culture or other factors. Differences in emphases in a given contextual environment on either tacit or explicit knowledge also impacts on knowledge creation as defined by SECI. Finally, it is emphasized that being conscious of the cultural situatedness of the SECI model can lead to a more adequate use of the model for organizational knowledge creation.

Chapter 3

Knowledge, Culture, and Cultural Impact on Knowledge Management:

Deogratias Harorimana, Southampton Solent University, UK

This author of this chapter provides advice to knowledge managers in relation to managing, cultural impact on the knowledge management activities. The author provides an opportunity to discuss issues and challenges before providing practical lessons for researchers and practitionners in this domain. The author introduces ingredients for further debates that continue to emerge from within knowledge management communities. The author has identified the broad nuts and bolts encountered by managers who find themselves faced by high costs of breaking cultural barriers. The chapter offers the advice into how those problems can be overcome. From an academic perspective, the author argues that successful knowledge creation and management comes from the combination of the two schools –social and technological thoughts. The chapter argues that current organizational practices of strong emphasis on team work and ability to use technologies dominate business operations and as a result, it is equaly important to unblock human factors that are likely to hinder people's interaction as it is to keep to a minimum physical barriers and systems that may impede this exercise. Organisational systems may include the reporting relationships and lack of social interactions opportunities.

Chapter 4

Caroline Kamau, Southampton Solent University, UK

Impression management is a powerful psychological phenomenon with much unexplored potential in corporate settings. Employees or corporations can deploy impression management strategies in order to manipulate others' perceptions of them. Cultural knowledge is powerful capital in impression management, yet this has not been sufficiently explored in previous literature. This chapter argues that impression-motivated employees or corporations need to perform a three-step knowledge audit: (i) knowing what their impression deficits are; (ii) knowing what impression management strategy is needed to address that deficit, based on the taxonomy of impression management strategies tabulated here; (iii) knowing what societal (e.g., collectivist culture or individualist culture) or organization-specific cultural adjustments are needed. A cultural knowledge base can thus be created through cross-cultural training of and knowledge transfer by expatriates. Multinational corporations can also benefit from utilising the knowledge presented in this chapter in their international public relations efforts.

Chapter 5

Christian-Andreas Schumann, University of Applied Sciences Zwickau, Germany
Claudia Tittmann, University of Applied Sciences Zwickau, Germany

The currently developing knowledge society needs high quality knowledge bases with wide-spreading knowledge sources. Because of the complexity of knowledge, they organize in knowledge networks. In addition, the intellectual capital of organizational units influences more and more the market value of organizations and companies. Thus, it is a challenging question to look at how intellectual capital can be developed and measured from tacit knowledge, and which factors of trust, risk, and compliance influence this. This chapter will describe the approach of knowledge nodes, the small components of knowledge networks, and their processes and their influence onto the value of knowledge networks.

Chapter 6

Peter L. Bond, Learning Futures Consulting, UK

This chapter raises difficult questions regarding the validity and motive for prolonging current forms of economic development and competition in the face of the much heralded global environmental crisis threatened by humankind's success as a species. In response, a living systems theoretical framework is introduced for managing technology, innovation, knowledge, cultural and, ultimately, economic change. It is suggested that the framework provides many elements of a possible new paradigm for cultural change that closes the gap between the social and natural sciences. It will demonstrate the possibilities of developing new forms of explanation and new techniques for organisation and economic development from a synthesis of knowledge management and new philosophical, sociological, anthropological, and, distinctively, biological perspectives of technology. The new framework will effectively reconcile the practices of technology, knowledge and cultural change management.

Section 2

The second section of this book provides a much more detailed discussion, together with examples of applied models and frameworks. It is a rich section for those who are interested in uncovering cultural implications sector by sector, region by region, or country by country, and more importantly, those examples which relate to specific industry practices such as higher education KM versus business KM cultures, or KM in hospitals and in multinational organisations.

In today's world, where uncertainty and the rapidity of technological changes predominate, companies need to generate and adopt knowledge continuously in order to build a sustainable competitive advantage. In this context, analyzing the collaborative relationships existing between the university and firms is relevant. The aim of this chapter is to explore the role of the university as a generator and disseminator of knowledge, as well as the difficulties it faces in making the results of its research available to the business world. The collaboration efforts between the academic and business worlds are assessed in order to ultimately propose the review of teaching, continuing education, and consulting as knowledge dissemination channels. This research project has been conducted in the context of a Mexican university. Besides the findings of the current and future research projects, the matter of the question is the redefinition of the university and its role in society. In business schools in particular, the pending issue is to discuss the basic aim of academic research in management.

Knowledge management is a set of purposeful activities led by management in order to enable and support generation, storage, transfer and application of knowledge within an organization so as to create value and improve the organization's effectiveness. The effectiveness of these activities is in a large part dependent on organizational culture, which can support or impede the two-way social process of learning and knowledge sharing between individuals, groups, organizations, and artifacts. This chapter discusses the fundamentals of organizational culture and knowledge management, their definitions, components, and processes. Specifically, the study presented is focused on how different types of organizational culture, as defined by the competing values framework, might be related to the iterative processes of knowledge generation, storage, transfer, and application in higher education.

Chapter 9

This study analyses best practices of knowledge strategies in hospitals considering the implementation of medical protocols. Protocols are research products originated from the based-on-evidence medicine. Knowledge strategy depends on specific organizational context that can be expressed by its barriers and enablers. Eight hospitals were studied in the state of Rio Grande do Sul, Brazil, involving multi-disciplinary teams of the cardiology services which are acknowledged as the area of expertise with more implemented protocols. The same protocols are available in all investigated hospitals and are implemented by different practices in daily activities. A formal structure for the promotion of the organizational context is proposed in relation to the protocol implementation. The following factors were found as critical for the promotion of knowledge strategies' best practices in hospitals: a common language for sharing information among different professionals; the knowledge gap as a corporate vision, and the particular hole of information technology.

Chapter 10

This chapter investigates the strategies used by hospitality businesses in the Northern Territory (NT) of Australia to remain competitive in the face of high rates of staff turnover. The authors suggest it could be beneficial to foster a symbiotic relationship between staff and knowledge retention with an explicit focus on the social aspects of managing knowledge in a hospitality environment. The authors propose a knowledge mobilization or flow strategy to complement staff and knowledge retention strategies. Creating and sustaining a competitive advantage through knowledge management (KM) practices that recognize the industry's specific context and allow it to compete for customers and staff in the global marketplace is imperative for the NT hospitality sector. The proposed strategy could make hospitality businesses more adaptable in the face of staff turnover and more flexible by fostering a context that nurtures the mobilization or flow of disparate and person specific knowledge. This chapter describes and critically reviews what is known about staff turnover in hospitality, the case study destination and its hospitality sector. Semi-structured interviews with 13 managers of hospitality businesses and representatives of industry organizations and the destination marketing organization (DMO) in the NT revealed current and desired strategies for managing turnover as well as how turnover affects relationships, knowledge management and idea generation.

Chapter 11

This chapter considers both the role that knowledge transfer may have in family businesses and the different manners in which knowledge transfer may take place within this diverse environment. The economic, social and community importance of family businesses within Scotland is considered, alongside the different manner in which family businesses commonly operate and the implications for knowledge transfer. The importance of knowledge transfer in the creation of competitive advantage within a family business environment and the relatively limited nature of research in this area are explored, highlighting the need for further research both to support the on-going development of a strategy for family businesses in Scotland and to facilitate future development of high quality knowledge transfer. Key to all of this, however, is an increased understanding of what is meant by knowledge transfer and the breadth of ways in which it happens.

Annette H. Dunham, University of Canterbury, New Zealand
Christopher D.B. Burt, University of Canterbury, New Zealand

Organizational memory, the knowledge gained from organizational experience, has significant potential for competitive advantage. Many authors in the knowledge management and human resource management literatures consider mentoring to be a particularly effective method of transferring organizational memory. In addition, older workers are often considered ideal mentors in organizations because of their experience and alleged willingness to pass on their knowledge to less experienced employees. There is an associated assumption that these workers also anticipate and experience positive outcomes when mentoring others. This chapter considers whether these assumptions hold up in the workplaces of the 21st century, particularly within Western countries. Individualistic cultural norms and some discriminatory practices towards older workers, along with a changing career contract that no longer guarantees employment in one organization for life, may discourage knowledge sharing in organizations. This chapter discusses the constraints and motivations that may operate when older experienced workers consider mentoring others. It considers relevant global and organizational cultural characteristics that may influence mentoring to transfer knowledge, and accordingly suggests strategies for those eager to capitalise on the knowledge experienced employees possess.

Section 3

The last section analyses theoretical and practical perspectives of, and provides some examples of, failed/successful projects where, essentially, culture was perceived as a central factor to knowledge creation, sharing and transfer.

Helen N. Rothberg, Marist College, USA
Beate Klingenberg, Marist College, USA

Responding to increasingly competitive environments, it has become commonplace for multinationals to enter into cross-border partnerships, ventures and alliances to gain know-how, manage costs and grow revenue. The results from these activities however, have not always delivered on their promise. Part of the reason lies in the challenges of transferring knowledge compounded by an international setting. The degree of difficulty in knowledge transfer increases for multinational managers and their counterparts because cultural differences influence information processing, management styles and sense making. In addition, most knowledge transfer projects do not take the time to allow partners to develop the rapport and trust pivotal for project commitment and successful learning to occur. This chapter explores a failed knowledge transfer project between two distinct cultures and, using literature on cross-cultural knowledge transfer and communication theory as well as anecdotes from the actual process, offers a process for creating and engaging a more successful design.

Chapter 14

Jianzhong Hong, Lappeenranta University of Technology, Finland
Johanna Heikkinen, Lappeenranta University of Technology, Finland
Mia Salila, Lappeenranta University of Technology, Finland

Recent studies on university–industry collaboration have paid a growing attention to complementary knowledge interaction, which is of crucial importance for networked learning and knowledge co-creation needed in today's rapidly changing markets and for gaining global competitiveness. The existent studies concentrate on the transfer of knowledge from the university to the company, and the impact of culture is examined with a focus on fundamentally different cultures between two types of organizations (i.e., between universities and firms). The studies, however, remain highly fragmented in cultural exploration on one level, and are primarily concerned with one-way technology and knowledge transfer. Research on more interactive knowledge interaction and collaborative knowledge creation and especially in the Chinese context is seriously lacking. This chapter explores university–industry knowledge interaction in a broad sense, focusing on the development of a conceptual view on the understanding and analysis of the cultural impact in the Chinese MNC context. The chapter is an early work in process and it is theoretical in nature. It clarifies and elaborates key concepts and perspectives, and suggests implications for future research and practice regarding effective knowledge co-creation involving dissimilar cultures.

Chapter 15

Josune Sáenz, University of Deusto, Spain
Nekane Aramburu, University of Deusto, Spain
Olga Rivera, University of Deusto, Spain

The aim of this chapter is to analyze the degree of influence of different organizational enablers (i.e., "structural capital") on knowledge sharing, as well as the influence of the latter and other structural capital components on innovation capability, both from a theoretical and empirical perspective. Additionally, the relevance of different innovation capability dimensions (i.e., ideation, project management, and timeliness and cost efficiency) on business competitiveness will be examined. For these relationships to be tested, an empirical study has been carried out among Spanish manufacturing firms with more than 50 employees and with R&D activities. To this end, a questionnaire has been designed and submitted to the CEOs of the companies making up the target population of the research. Structural equation modelling (SEM) based on partial least squares (PLS) has then been applied in order to test the main hypotheses of the research.

This chapter argues the case for a proactive process to facilitate knowledge creation between universities and small to medium size enterprises (SMEs). Cultural issues dictating reticence of engagement are discussed as well as the inhibitors that prevent the free interchange of knowledge. The chapter shows how reticence can be overcome by serving the needs of both parties and how knowledge created through successful interaction can be measured. The knowledge creation process itself is analysed in the context of Nonaka's SECI model. The chapter concludes with recommendations for the reader on areas for public investment to enhance the knowledge transfer process and provides lessons learned for the measurement of knowledge transfer at these interfaces. The outcomes are of value to those interested in the continuing applicability of Nonaka's work outside of the heavy industrial context as well as to those interested in the traditional problems associated with knowledge transfer between universities and SMEs.

Foreword

Knowledge management is still young enough to be seen as fashionable. As Kalling and Styhre (2003) have pointed out: 'knowledge in organizations is not a new thing; knowledge management is.' There is of course no domain of human activity in which knowledge of some sort is not created, shared or transferred. Conceived as it is today as a critical organizational resource, knowledge is seen to reside in collections of heterogeneous knowledge assets that are socially complex and generally inimitable. Bound up with this is an abiding recognition – or at least assumption – that 'the ability to constantly create new knowledge and convert it into value-creating innovation is a decisive ingredient in the success of every company' (Bukh *et al*, 2005). From this notion it follows – or rather it is frequently argued - that astute exploitation of organizational knowledge - alias knowledge management - leads to superior corporate performance, (sustained) competitive advantage and even ascension on '"the Slope of Enlightenment" to the "Plateau of Productivity"' (Ruggles and Hotshouse, 1999; original emphasis).

But awkwardly it can be very difficult to identify causal relationships between exploiting knowledge assets and hard results (Christensen, 2003). At best there may only be 'a minor correlation between knowledge management and the company's bottom line' (Christensen, 2003, citing Lucier and Torsilieri, 2001). Despite that limitation, KM has become 'a broad field with explosive growth' (Kärreman et al., 2005), bringing with it 'new terminology' in companies, consultancy and research (Bukh et al., 2005a)

One of the key questions about knowledge management is of course this: are we really talking about management in terms of organization and coordination as opposed to mere processing? Dixon (2000) has argued that 'the term "knowledge management" has unwanted implications. The "management" part implies that this is something Management is in charge of, when what is wanted is that everyone in an organization be involved in the exchange as well as the generation of knowledge' (original emphasis). In a similar vein Alvesson and Kärreman (2001) have noted that knowledge is 'a concept far too loose, ambiguous, and rich and pointing in far too many directions' to be managed i.e. organized, co-ordinated, controlled.

One must surely conclude that strictly speaking knowledge cannot be managed. One might even facetiously say that there has been a failure on the part of the KM community to manage knowledge management! Thus it really behooves the KM community to tackle this issue, if the domain is to realize its full potential in the everyday operations of organizations of every kind and, incidentally, find for itself firmer footing on the agenda of business schools.

This may sound a strange thing to say. Some will counter by saying that every year we see an endless stream of books and articles on KM as well as regular practitioner events, academic conferences and scores of websites, all of which attest to the development of KM as practice and object of academic investigation. This is indeed true, but yet in many ways KM is still in its infancy, and possibly for a not immediately obvious reason: there is persistent vagueness about the nature of tacit knowledge as an organizational resource and as an influence on human behaviour in the workplace, whether that workplace happens to a car production line, an advertising agency or one's company's Asia headquarters in Shanghai. Tacit knowledge is, as it were, KM's lost continent.

Just about everyone in the KM field subscribes to the view that there is something special about tacit knowledge. It has been hailed as 'the key to sustainable competitive advantage' (Burton-Jones, 1999), a 'reservoir of wisdom' (Baumard, 1999) and even a form of Holy Grail of admittedly exaggerated efficacy (Styhre, 2003). Yet, when we look at standard range of books on KM, it is striking fact that tacit knowledge receives amazingly little attention. This does not, of course, apply to the writings of Nonaka and several of his collaborators, to whom the role of tacit knowledge is central to knowledge creation – or rather, Japanese-style knowledge creation (Glisby and Holden, 2002). It is in fact possible to come across books on KM and find no indexed reference to tacit knowledge whatsoever. In other words, tacit knowledge just gets lip-service.

Invisible, intangible, inchoate and elusive, tacit knowledge is by definition hard to investigate or specify. To add to the messiness, any formal description of tacit knowledge automatically converts it a different state of being, namely explicit knowledge. At best one can refer to tacit knowledge in elliptical ways; which is, as they say, bad science. Even so it seems that we can all agree on three things

1. tacit knowledge, for all its indefinability, is an influence in its own right on relationships involving the creation, sharing and transfer of knowledge
2. its effects, which are invariably situation-specific, cannot be easily quantified or measured.
3. the carrier of tacit knowledge is human language in its oral mode.

Faced with conundrums like that, we might be inclined to concede defeat, continue paying lip-service, and decide to focus our energies on understanding KM with virtually exclusive reference to explicit knowledge: in other words, stay in the comfort zone. But what if it could be demonstrated that tacit knowledge is a significantly wider influence on human relationships within and between organizations than is usually thought?

In a book I am currently co-authoring a multi-country case-based book on tacit knowledge, we cite some remarkable data (Holden and Glisby, 2009). With three sets of small samples at our disposal we have established that some 60 fully qualified scientists and engineers working in the technical domains in industries diverse as engine management systems, software design and petroleum engineering variously devote 30-70% of their professional time handling tacit knowledge, *once they understand what the term tacit knowledge connotes.* Hitherto they had thought of themselves as handling only explicit knowledge to carry out their jobs in scientific consultancy, technical sales or advanced manufacturing.

In a separate case my co-author and myself interviewed a British engineer, who had years of experience the design and manufacture of car engines. In 2003 he joined the UK subsidiary of a major Japanese MNC in the automotive sector. At that time he estimated that 'only 20%' of his job content was connected with handling tacit knowledge - again, once he appreciated what the term meant. In the intervening six years he has risen in stature in the company and holds a key role in mediating European know-how to the company headquarters in Japan. In this enhanced capacity he is holding regular meeting in Japan and Europe with senior Japanese technical and strategic managers. The fact that he must communicate his hard knowledge into Japan-based networks requires him to be immensely skilled in cross-cultural behaviour and communication. He now estimates that *80%* of his job content is connected with handling tacit knowledge.

All this is illuminating. If even technically trained people – nominal users of explicit knowledge *par excellence* – are spending, say, a minimum of 30% of their professional time engaging with tacit knowledge, do their employers realise this? Almost certainly not. Of particular interest is the fact that the tacit knowledge they have handling *has been learnt on the job* and only a small proportion of it is retained as a resource in the company. I should perhaps have mentioned earlier that the 60 scientists and engineers mentioned above were all taking a part-time MBA course at the Technical University of Vienna in the period 2007-2009. Approximately half the entire group of 60 were Austrian, the remainder mainly from East and Central European countries.

Many of them, like the UK engineer, operate professionally in various countries. In other words, they are accumulating their tacit knowledge from several (national) cultural contexts. This suggests that one should perhaps not just consider tacit knowledge to be an organizational resource, but a product of cross-cultural professional interactions. That is precisely the topic that my co-author and myself are currently exploring, and we are beginning to see not only tacit knowledge but also knowledge management from new and unusual perspectives. We can certainly endorse the conviction that 'knowledge management depends on how knowledge is perceived' (Christensen et al., 2005) with the important qualifying rider: 'from particular cultural vantage points.' In short, in our investigations culture is emerging as a facet of tacit knowledge in its own right, but it is no easy task to specify that most complex relationship.

Burton-Jones (1999) has written that tacit knowledge is 'less manageable' than explicit knowledge. That is hardly a felicitous way of putting it, but what these instances about scientists and engineers tell us is that tacit knowledge has a very strong claim to be a management issue. For that and other reasons we have dared to write that 'the world needs all the help it can get to understand tacit knowledge' (Holden and Glisby, 2009). We do not mean that smugly, but as a necessity for the practical running of international businesses and for the furtherance of KM studies in business schools and universities.

This book, edited by Deogratias Harorimana, does a service to the KM community by focusing on the forms of cultural impacts on the creation and sharing of knowledge from multiple standpoints. The editor is right to describe the themes addressed in this book as constituting 'a complex, but exciting debate.' At the present time this debate largely focuses on establishing causal links between KM and competitive advantage. But we are living in an era in which blind – discredited - competitive capitalism will have to be replaced by systems to underpin what Bartholemew and Adler (1996) have called 'cross-cultural collaborative learning.' This means that KM community no longer has the luxury to keep culture at bay as an awkward outlier, but must build factors to do culture's impact on knowledge creation, sharing and implementation into the general KM equation. It is not just the sustainability of organizations that is at stake here, but that of the very planet itself.

Nigel Holden
Director, Institute of International Business, University of Central Lancashire, UK

Nigel Holden *obtained his PhD from Manchester Business School in 1986 and has held professorial appointments in Denmark, Germany and the UK. He has been Professor of Cross-cultural Management at Lancashire Business School of the University of Central Lancashire, UK, since 2006. Internationally recognized in his field, he is author of the landmark book Cross-cultural management: A knowledge management perspective and numerous articles and chapters on culture and knowledge management. He is currently preparing a case-based book on tacit knowledge in firms' international networks. He has given over 100 invited lectures and keynote addresses to academic and professional audiences in several European countries, Japan, Taiwan, China, USA and Russia. . In April 2009 he was appointed as a member of an International Expert Group on Nuclear Knowledge Management by the UN's International Atomic Energy Agency.*

REFERENCES

Alvesson, M. and Kärreman, D. (2001). Odd couple: making sense of the curious concept of knowledge management. Journal of Management Studies. Vol. 38. No. 7, pp. 995-1018.

Bartholomew, S.and Adler, N. (1996). Building networks and crossing borders: the dynamics of knowledge generation in at a transnational world. In: Joynt, P. and Warner, M. (eds). *Managng across cultures: Issues and perspectives.* London: International Thompson, pp. 7-32.

Baumard, P. (1999). *Tacit knowledge in organizations.* London: Sage Publications.

Bukh, P. N., Skovvang, K. S. and Mouritsen, J. (2005) New economy, new theory or new practice? In:. Bukh, P. N., Skovvang, K. S. and Mouritsen, J. (2005). *Knowledge management and intellectual capital: Establishing a field of practice.* London: Palgrave MacMillan, pp. 1- 14.

Burton-Jones, A. (1999). *Knowledge capitalism: Business, work and learning in the new economy.* Oxford: Oxford University Press.

Christensen, K. S., Bukh, P. K. and Mouritsen, J. (2005). New economy, new theory – or new practice? In: Bukh, P. K., Christensen, K. S. and Mouritsen, J. (eds.). *Knowledge management and intellectual capital: Establishing a field of practice.* London: Palgrave Macmillan.

Christensen, P. H. (2003). *Knowledge management: Perspectives and pitfalls.* Copenhagen: Copenhagen Business School Press.

Dixon, N. (2000). *Common knowledge: How companies thrive by sharing what they know.* Boston, MA.: Harvard Business School Publishing.

Glisby, M. and Holden, N. J. (2002). Contextual constraints in knowledge management theory: the cultural embeddedness of Nonaka's knowledge-creating company. *Knowledge and Process Management.* Vol. 10. No. 2, 1-8.

Holden, N. J. (2002*). Cross-cultural management: a knowledge management perspective.* Harlow: Financial Times/Prentice Hall, pp. 328.

Holden, N. J. and Glibsy, M. (2009, forthcoming). *International business networks: tacit knowledge for competitive advantage.* Copenhagen: Copenhagen Business School Press.

Kalling, T. and Styhre, A. (2003). *Knowledge sharing in organizations.* Copenhagen: Copenhagen Business School Press.

Kärreman, D., Alvesson, M. and Blom, M. (2005). In: Bukh, P. N., Skovvang, K. S. and Mouritsen, J. *Knowledge management and intellectual capital: Establishing a field of practice.* London: Palgrave MacMillan, pp. 124 – 148.

Lucier, C. E. and Torsilieri, J. D. (2001). Can knowledge management deliver bottom-line results? In: Nonaka, I. and Teece, D. (eds.). *Managing industrial knowledge: Creation, transfer and utilization.* London: Sage.

Ruggles, R. (1999). Gaining the knowledge advantage. In: Ruggles, R. and Holthouse, D. (1999). *The knowledge advantage: 14 visionaries define market place success in the new economy.* Dover, NH.: Capstone, pp. 1-19.

Styhre, A. (1003). *Understanding knowledge management: Critical and postmodern perspectives.* Copenhagen: Copenhagen Business School Press.

Preface

When the editor embarked on his long and ambitious study on *Cultural Implications of Knowledge Sharing, Management and Transfer: Identifying Competitive Advantage* he had no idea how such a complex but exciting debate would evolve and spread so fast across the world of scholars and knowledge management practitioners. Of course this was never going to be a road without an end - as many readers may have thought - however the editor had no idea of just how far one of the (arguably) newest and yet most controversial research topics – the implications of culture on knowledge management – would take us. Thanks to many high quality contributions from eleven countries including the USA, UK, Greece, Germany, Brazil, Mexico, Slovenia, Australia,   New Zealand, Finland and Spain the book was able to fulfil its aims and objectives.

The problem of managing knowledge is, essentially, influenced by human behaviour and how humans interact with systems and tools. The challenge becomes clear from the outset. What happens with contextual factors that cannot be documented? How do we drive the process of managing and transferring tacit knowledge which is accepted to be context-dependent and is best transferred through experiential learning and personal involvement in the activity (Polanyi 1966)? To be managed, Garavelli et al. (2002) argues that knowledge needs to be retrieved from some source, processed, and then distributed to users who may need it.

As Bollisani (2008) argues, a rapid glance at the knowledge management literature is enough to highlight several problematic aspects that make the topic of knowledge sharing and transfer a challenging terrain for both the researcher and the practice. Bollisani (2008) found that an essential problem results from the extreme variety of situations to which the issue of knowledge sharing can be related. What we have is a myriad of knowledge sharing activities happening continuously but in disparate contexts. This is true even when these problems are not explicitly identified and recognised. For example, an inter-personal communication is an exchange of knowledge, but also economic transactions between two trading firms can be seen as (or involve) sharing of knowledge. Even two computers exchanging messages are, to some extent, part of a kind of knowledge sharing. What is more, one can speak of knowledge sharing even when there is someone that communicates a message to a broad audience: a television programme is a process of knowledge sharing, and so is the publication of a book or a Website.

The first challenge of defining knowledge management and its processes are highlighted within this preface stage – we lack a consensus on distinctive, familiar terms within knowledge management communities. For example we have researchers and practitioners who are referring to, in this book and elsewhere, knowledge sharing, knowledge transfer, and knowledge exchange when they all actually mean the same thing. In this preface, we will just speak of knowledge sharing, but we will more generally mean all the terms previously indicated.

In addition, knowledge sharing is a process that involves various elements (the knowledge objects exchanged, the sources and receivers, the carrier or medium, the mechanisms used, the transfer of practices, and so on). Thus, a researcher can decide to centre his or her analysis on one specific element, or to include different variables or factors, or to focus on the intertwined relationships among all these.

Due to these complications, the characterising aspects, implications and practical questions relating to knowledge sharing are many. Here, we explicitly focus on the perspectives adopted by researchers whose main field is that of KM. The contributors to this book were asked to explain their viewpoints, to elucidate their research methods and interpretative models, to debate the findings of their studies with the purpose of clarifying and contributing to the state of our knowledge on this issue, and to discuss the prospective fields of study. In particular, they were invited to provide insights into some open questions that we briefly recall below.

Cultural Implications for Knowledge Sharing Processes

The book invited contributors to consider two aspects, the first being how do people and organisations exchange knowledge? There was an open window of questioning based on the differences between interpersonal and organisational culture. Knowledge sharing between organisations is, or involves, knowledge sharing among individuals; hence, understanding interpersonal culture and the role it plays in knowledge sharing had to be addressed. The relationships among interpersonal and organisational cultures and how they impact knowledge sharing as a process require a conceptualisation that has not been achieved yet and the literature often focuses on specific aspects or specific practical cases. Here, contributors provide a well founded model of the mechanisms and rules that are employed for knowledge sharing through debate to demonstrate how culture (and context) influences the nature or type of knowledge sharing activities specified within the debates. It was therefore necessary for authors to demonstrate the competitive advantage – if any – of knowledge sharing practices.

Competitive Advantage

It is now recognised that knowledge has no value if it cannot be used for commercial ends (Cohen and Levinthal, 1990). Where knowledge sharing takes place, there is an element of trust and mutual benefit that is attached to it (Pinch *et al*, 2003) but also in addition, organisational knowledge is valued for being the sole source of competitive advantage (Harorimana, 2007). The motivation of knowledge sharing, and the competitive advantage the players attach to this activity is another subject of debate within KM and a central theme of this book as well. The successful practice shows that KM initiatives that do not account for the motivations of participants, or their cultural background of understanding in knowledge sharing, are likely to fail (Cumming and Teng, 2003). There is thus the need to explain the factors that can facilitate and hinder the personal participation in a process of knowledge exchange. Motivation can be seen from different viewpoints and based on various conceptual references. Bollisani (2008) argues that motivation can be related to various but intertwined concepts, such as the personal utility (i.e., knowledge is exchanged to solve a problem or accomplish a task), the economic value (knowledge is considered as good source of income), or the social motivation (knowledge sharing because people belong to a particular culture, a particular context, or are co-located, to mention but a few). The difference between personal or organisational competitive advantage is clarified herein.

Systems Interaction

We are experiencing a series of debates in the role various cultures play in influencing KM outcomes. We are also observing an emergence of journals of cultural knowledge management. While this trend is a welcome development, we are left with lack of synthesis of current understanding around how culture impacts on social relationships in the knowledge sharing arena. Hot issues in the KM literature are, for example, the cultural distance between players or the trustworthy climate that facilitates the sharing of knowledge. Another burning issue is the most appropriate organisational system that fosters a culture of knowledge creation and sharing. Not all organisational systems support a culture of engagement, people interaction and knowledge sharing. The structure and nature of the organisational system of interpersonal or inter-organisational relationships and the distinct roles performed by the various players are thus an essential focus of analysis. There is rich and significant literature on knowledge management systems and, more generally, on the use of ICT applications for supporting knowledge exchange between individuals and/or organisations. However, technology is not the universal remedy for any problem of knowledge exchange. Here, various models and references are often drawn from a multiplicity of disciplines and fields (see for example, Malhotra, 2000). In this climate, the KM community requires a concerted effort to provide the appropriate mechanism within which cultural influence is recognised without over-burdening businesses that are looking to maximise returns on their investment in knowledge sharing projects.

Organisational vs. Interpersonal Culture

A common element in many KM research frameworks and models (included in the models discussed above) is that of organisational culture. For the most part, it is assumed that technology plays a key role in the processes involved in KM. Contributors have demonstrated that KM is shaped by three important perspectives: namely (a) information-based, (b) technology-based, and (c) culture-based. The last of these perspectives highlights the importance of organisational culture in the KM process. Moreover, what is observed from several studies is that not all KM processes require high investment in technology. More importantly, successful use of the technology is often dependent on the incorporation of KM behaviour into the organisational culture. That is, the organisational culture as defined by Schein (1990:111) where culture is: "…a) a pattern of basic assumptions, (b) invented, discovered, or developed by a given group, (c) as it learns to cope with its problems of external adaptation and internal integration, d) that has worked well enough to be considered valid and, therefore e) is to be taught to new members as the f) correct way to perceive, think, and feel in relation to those problems," and where Wilkins and Dyer (1988) suggest that culture "is [composed] of the values, competencies, and beliefs of a group of people that strongly influence whether and how organizational strategies are implemented (p. 522)." In this book contributors focused on defining culture in the context of KM and theoretical frameworks are still required.

Aims of the Book

Cultural Implications of Knowledge Sharing, Management and Transfer: Identifying Competitive Advantage gathers contributions by scholars from different but related disciplines. It illustrates, compares, and discusses models, perspectives, and approaches that are helpful to understanding current research on this topic. Contributions came from different viewpoints and depict possible trajectories of future development.

This book has emerged to provide a "common interface" for the meeting of scholars and practitioners who are interested in how culture shapes knowledge creation, sharing, management and transfer activities. This was an important platform for the communication between different disciplines and areas, with the hope that this "cross-fertilisation" can help to overcome the limitations of the single viewpoint.

The assumption was that a systematic comparison and discussion of different but converging models and approaches was essential in creating the foundations of a common language and agreed conceptual framework allowing for the exchange of findings and ideas. The editor recognises that in such a multi-disciplinary project there will always be risks, since it involves different disciplines and academic approaches that can be too distant (and sometimes individualistic). However, the nature of current studies on *Cultural Implications of Knowledge Sharing, Management and Transfer* makes the effort valuable and necessary.

Target Audience

This book is the exciting result of the input of many experts from both academics and business practitioners. This book will help those readers who are interested in developing a broad picture of the current research on the topic seen from different viewpoints, and enable them to recognise the possible trajectories of future developments. It will provide for those seeking to build a common set of concepts, terms, references, and approaches in disciplinary areas that are sometimes too distant from one another.

In that regard, the principal target audience for this book consists of scholars and researchers in knowledge management and related fields. It is also a useful tool for those conducting research into cultural implications for human behaviour in the workplace. The book is also written to provide "food for thought" for future research; however, practitioners might identify foundations for new ideas in a dynamic environment such as how to manage culture complexities in their businesses and learning how to minimise the costs and risks associated with managing knowledge in a culturally rich (diverse) environment. Graduate and post-graduate students would also find this book to be a useful reference resource.

Structure of the Book and Contributions

This book is made up of 16 chapters which were divided into three sections. The first section focuses on a careful and purposeful survey of the topic under study. This section provides a foundation for further debate in the book. To set the scene of this debate, Stavros Ponis, George Vagena and Epaminondas Koroni conduct a long journey within KM through their "Critical Evaluation of Existing Knowledge Management Frameworks." They review different frameworks that have been applied by and to the KM research and practitioner communities. To further feed the reader's interest, the authors outline shortcomings and limitations that have been found so far in the literature. Their contribution however can never be underestimated; the authors have carefully evaluated and proposed the ways in which challenges they identified can be overcome. In their study, they help the reader to discover how literature on knowledge management at the service of contemporary organisations is characterised by a plethora of diverse frameworks and approaches. Within many of those frameworks not even a single one achieved such a wide acceptance so as to be conceived as a standard. That said, they argue that practice proves that each research or consultant group follows its own approach while many initiatives are based on custom approaches, developed each time from scratch; or even worse do not follow a structured method at all. In this chapter they dig deeper into proposing a complete checklist for evaluating existing frameworks against a set of predetermined elements that a KM approach should possess.

Peter Bond, in "Toward a living systems framework for unifying technology and knowledge management, organizational, cultural and economic change," engages in much deeper analysis of the KM and the economic case for its existence. Bond proposes a theoretical framework for managing technology, innovation, knowledge, cultural and, ultimately, economic change. In the chapter, Bond suggests a framework with a possible new paradigm for cultural change that closes the gap between the social and natural sciences, and he demonstrates the possibilities of developing new forms of explanation and new techniques for organisational and economic development from a synthesis of knowledge management. The new framework he proposes will, effectively, reconcile the practices of technology, knowledge and cultural change management.

As has been a familiar observation of those researching KM, It is rare to see literature on knowledge creation, sharing and transfer that ignores Nonaka and Takeuchi's (1995) model, widely known as the SECI model by the KM community. This model however was criticised for its lack of flexibility and lack of responsiveness to cultural changes (see Harorimana, 2008; Gourlay, 2006, 2007). The third chapter "The Impact of Culture on the application of the SECI Model," by **Markus Haag, Yanqing Duan and Brian Mathews**, takes a closer look into this model. Haag *et al* concluded that culture, in various forms, impacts on the SECI model and that the model itself was embedded in a certain context. This context determines the characteristics of the knowledge creation modes as described by the SECI model and therefore makes the model either more, or less, pertinent in a given context. They also add that this is regardless of whether that context is primarily determined by national culture, organisational culture or other factors. What they demonstrate here is that differences in emphasis in a given contextual environment on either tacit or explicit knowledge also impacts on knowledge creation as defined by the SECI model. They identify the competitive advantage by arguing that, being conscious of the cultural location of the SECI model can lead to a more adequate application of the model for organisational knowledge creation.

To extend on their debate **Deogratias Harorimana**, in "Knowledge, Culture, and Cultural Impact on Knowledge Management," provides useful hints and advice to those researching into how culture influences KM research activities and application. The author identified the nuts and bolts of the issue encountered by managers who find themselves faced by high costs of breaking cultural barriers, and offers advice on how those problems can be overcome. From an academic perspective, the author argues that successful knowledge creation and management comes from the combination of the two schools of thought, social and technological. He further shows that current organisational practices that place a strong emphasis on team work and ability to use technologies dominate business operations and, as a result, it is equally important to unblock human factors that are likely to hinder people's interaction as it is to keep to minimum physical barriers and systems that may impede human interaction.

The next chapter, by **Dr. Caroline Kamau**, builds on the previous one and complements probably the least explored element of human kind from a KM point of view. Through the chapter "Strategising Impression Management in Corporations: Cultural Knowledge as Capital" Kamau argues that impression management is a powerful psychological phenomenon with, as yet, much unexplored potential by KM and management researchers in general. However, there is a sticking point here in that employees or corporations can deploy impression management strategies in order to manipulate others' perceptions of them. Furthermore, Kamau's work shows that the issue of managing one's impressions has much to do with cultural knowledge. Cultural knowledge is powerful capital in impression management, yet this has not been sufficiently explored in previous literature. She argues that impression-motivated employees or corporations need to perform a three-step knowledge audit. Kamau argues that cultural knowledge can facilitate implementation of cross-cultural training and knowledge transfer by expatriates' nationals as well as be used to the benefits of multinational corporations that are seeking to move into new and emerging markets.

As KM becomes more complicated, academics continue to debate about the best mechanism to be used to enable fast transfer and sharing of knowledge while at the same time maintaining the aspect of "control" of their competitive advantage. In the next chapter of this section, **Christian-Andreas Schumann and Claudia Tittmann**, in their contribution "Potential for externalizing and measuring of tacit knowledge within knowledge nodes in the context of knowledge networks," continue the debate arguing that currently knowledge networks represent the best mechanism to widely transferring knowledge from the source. Their argument is that there are complexities attached to sharing and transferring knowledge as this is the intellectual capital of organisations which tends to influence more and more the market value of organisations and companies. Their investigations into how intellectual capital can be developed and measured identified the factors that influence effective knowledge transfer and sharing through networks. They argue that trust, risk, and compliance influence the value network as well as activities of knowledge transfer through networks.

The second section of this book provides a much more detailed discussion, together with examples of applied models and frameworks. It is a rich section for those who are interested in uncovering cultural implications sector by sector, region by region, or country by country, and more importantly, those examples which relate to specific industry practices such as higher education KM versus business KM cultures, or KM in hospitals and in multinational organisations.

José Louis Pineda, Laura Esther Zapata and Jacobo Ramírez, in their chapter "Strengthening knowledge transfer between the university and enterprise: A conceptual model for collaboration," analysed the collaborative relationships existing between the university and the firm and explored the role of the university as a generator and disseminator of knowledge, as well as the difficulties it faces in making the results of its research available to the business world. Their study shows that the collaborative efforts between the academic and business worlds require an urgent review so that universities do not continue as they have always done, but that, rather, they should shift their cultural way of working to become knowledge dissemination channels. This chapter reports on a research project conducted in the context of a Mexican higher education system. Their findings represent the ongoing and widespread view within developed countries' universities that there is a need to redefine the university and its role in society.

The above chapter is further added to by contributions from a Slovenian higher education perspective where **Roberto Biloslavo and Mojca Prevodnik** analysed the impact of organisational culture on knowledge management in higher education. This chapter discusses the fundamentals of organisational culture within knowledge management from a university's perspective and demonstrates that different types of organisational culture, as defined by the competing values framework, might be related to the iterative processes of knowledge generation, storage, transfer, and application in higher education.

Considering KM and cultural implications in hospital organisation, **Cláudio Reis Gonçalo and Jacques Edison Jacques** present "Best practices of Knowledge Strategy in Hospitals: a contextual perspective based on the implementation of medical protocols." They argue that knowledge strategy depends on a specific organisational context that can be expressed by its barriers and enablers. They reported findings from eight hospitals in the state of Rio Grande do Sul, Brazil. Their study involved multi-disciplinary teams. Gonçalo and Jacques recommend a formal structure for the promotion of the organisational context in relation to the protocol implementation. They identified as critical for the promotion of knowledge strategies' best practices in hospitals a common language for sharing information among different professionals; the knowledge gap as a corporate vision, and particularly the gap of information technology.

From a hospitality industry perspective, **Kalotina Chalkiti and Dean Carson**, in their chapter "Knowledge Cultures, Competitive Advantage and Staff Turnover in Hospitality in Australia's Northern Territory," investigated the strategies used by hospitality businesses in the Northern Territories (NT) of Australia to remain competitive in the face of high rates of staff turnover. Chalkiti and Carson recommend that it is necessary and beneficial to foster a symbiotic relationship between staff and knowledge retention with an explicit focus on the social aspects of managing knowledge in a hospitality environment. They propose a knowledge mobilisation or flow strategy to complement staff and knowledge retention strategies and identify the competitive advantage through knowledge management (KM) practices that recognise the industry's specific context and allow it to compete for customers and staff in the global marketplace within the NT hospitality sector.

A further contribution to understanding the implications of knowledge and its context within which it is shared/transferred was presented in **Claire Seaman and Stuart Graham's** chapter, "Creating Competitive Advantage in Scottish Family Businesses: Managing, Sharing and Transferring the Knowledge". This chapter considered both the role that knowledge transfer may have in family businesses and the different manners in which knowledge transfer may take place within this diverse environment. The economic, social and community importance of family businesses within Scotland was considered, alongside the different manner in which family businesses commonly operate and the implications for knowledge transfer. Seaman and Graham identified the importance of knowledge transfer in the creation of competitive advantage within a family business environment, and highlight the need for further research both to support the ongoing development of a strategy for family businesses in Scotland and to facilitate future development of high quality knowledge transfer. They conclude that there is a need to understand knowledge transfer, and the context within which it takes place, as well as its breadth.

Annette H. Dunham and Christopher Burt, in their chapter "Mentoring and the Transfer of Organizational Memory within the Context of an Aging Workforce: Cultural Implications for Competitive Advantage," found that the knowledge gained from organisational experience has significant potential for competitive advantage. The authors argue that due to individualistic cultural norms and some discriminatory practices towards older workers, along with the nature of a changing career contract that no longer guarantees employment in one organisation for life, these represent obstacles and discourage knowledge sharing in organisations. They discussed constraints and motivations that exist when employees are older, or when experienced workers consider mentoring others. This chapter considers relevant global and organisational cultural characteristics that may influence mentoring to transfer knowledge, and accordingly suggests strategies for those eager to capitalise on the knowledge that experienced employees possess.

The last section analyses theoretical and practical perspectives of, and provides some examples of, failed/successful projects where, essentially, culture was perceived as a central factor to knowledge creation, sharing and transfer. **Beate Klingenberg and Helen Rothberg**, in their chapter "Learning before Doing: Theoretical Perspective and Practical Lessons from a Failed Cross-Border Knowledge Transfer Initiative," explored a failed knowledge transfer project between two distinct cultures and, using literature on cross-cultural knowledge transfer and communication theory as well as anecdotes from the actual process, offer a process for creating and engaging in a more successful design. They found that there are challenges to transferring knowledge compounded by an international setting, and that the degree of difficulty in knowledge transfer increases for multinational managers and their counterparts because cultural differences influence information processing, management styles and sense making. Furthermore, they argued that multinational business relationships do not take the time to allow partners to develop the necessary rapport and trust pivotal for project commitment and successful learning to occur due to pressure to respond to increasingly competitive environments

Jianzhong Hong, Johanna Heikkinen, and Mia Salila, in "The Impact of Culture on University–Industry Knowledge Interaction in the Chinese MNC Context," built on the fact that recent studies on university–industry collaboration paid growing attention to complementary knowledge interaction - which is of importance for networking, learning and knowledge co-creation. Within this chapter, Hong, Heikkinen and Salila explore university–industry knowledge interaction in a broad sense, focusing on the development of a conceptual view on the understanding and analysis of the cultural impact in the Chinese Multi National Company context. The chapter clarifies and elaborates on key concepts and perspectives, and suggests implications for future research and practice regarding effective knowledge co-creation involving dissimilar cultures.

In "Exploring the Links between Structural Capital, Knowledge Sharing, Innovation Capability and Business Competitiveness," **Josune Sáenz, Nekane Aramburu and Olga Rivera** analysed the degree of influence of different organisational enablers (i.e., "structural capital") on knowledge sharing, as well as the influence of the latter and other structural capital components on innovation capability, both from a theoretical and empirical perspective. They analysed a set of relationships between innovation capability dimensions (i.e., ideation, project management, and timeliness and cost efficiency) and business competitiveness. Their study was based on Spanish manufacturing firms with more than 50 employees and with R&D activities. The chapter provides conclusions on structural equation modelling (SEM) based on partial least squares (PLS)

Finally, this book concludes with an exciting work contributed by **Elly Philpott and John Beaumont-Kerridge.** In "Overcoming reticence to aid knowledge creation between universities and business-a case reviewed" the authors argue the case for a proactive process to facilitate knowledge creation between universities and small to medium size enterprises (SMEs). They identify and discusses cultural issues that lead to reticence of engagement, in addition to inhibitors that prevent the free interchange of knowledge. Philpott and Beaumont-Kerridge show how reticence can be overcome by serving the needs of both parties who are engaged in knowledge creating and sharing activities and how knowledge created through successful interaction can be measured. They conclude with recommendations for the reader on areas for public investment to enhance the knowledge transfer process and provide lessons learned for the measurement of knowledge transfer at these interfaces. The outcomes from the authors' contributions are particularly useful to those interested in the continuing applicability of Nonaka and Takeuchi's work outside of the heavy industrial context as well as those interested in the traditional problems associated with knowledge transfer between universities and SMEs.

CONCLUSION

The contributions gathered and presented in this book are a reflection of the ways culture has been considered - or at the very least - how it is perceived by knowledge management researchers and practitioners. This book was an exciting journey to follow the search for how mergers and new business ventures handle the trickiest questions when it comes to facing cultural diversity and its impact on business interactions.

There were also sticky questions to deal with given the new approach to knowledge management research and practice that is being discussed herein. Those were, what culture is and what is knowledge? And, how do these relate to one another? Considering debates held therein, I am inclined to believe that knowledge is about the process of gathering information, and placing it in the cultural context of a given situation at hand in order to acquire meaningful usage.

That leads me even into the more serious debate of what constitutes knowledge and how can it be created. Of course my answer is that it is the *context* that creates knowledge. Models that respond to culture and context at the same time are more likely to fit the purpose. The purpose was: How can I transfer or share knowledge I have for the benefit of myself, the company and/or my colleagues? Nonaka and Takeuchi (1995) were good at linking together all these aspects – personal engagements (socialisation); contextualising personal level engagements by involving the expression of tacit knowledge and its conversion into comprehensible forms that are easier to understand (externalisation), the process of taking ownership, and make knowledge part of one's daily life and activities (internalisation). Internalisation requires individuals to identify relevant knowledge within the organisation's explicit knowledge, embrace it as their own, and incorporate it into their own knowledge base through, for example, on-the-job training. Finally, the combination of the tacit knowledge, its context and how this is converted into visible outputs, in actions such as clear communication, diffusion, integration, and systemisation of one's knowledge to the rest of the peers to contribute to knowledge at the group level as well as at the organisational level.

In this book, however, we have seen many people following several models. The overwhelming message from the book is that there is no single definition of culture, knowledge and a suitable model. There are equally as many frameworks as there are models and definitions of cultures, as well as knowledge transfer and management methods.

The use of Nonaka and Takeuchi's (1995) model underestimates other research models in the literature. The purpose of this section however is not to discuss models (I will happily leave this to my experts' contributions). What is interesting to me here is the diversity of approaches and diversification of debates, and how all have pulled together to demonstrate that, in each of their contributions, there are significant implications for culture and how it influences knowledge transfer outcomes.

Essential Tools for Cultural Change, Knowledge Sharing for Greater Competitiveness

There are key elements that are generally accepted as key for gaining competitive advantage. These are:

- **Effective and ongoing trainings:** Employees need to stay responsive to modern practices and new tools.
- **Effective communication:** Employees as individuals need to be constantly informed of what is affecting them, their organisation and the entire community. While cultural practices in some countries may allow employees to challenge or question their managers about changes within a company, there are countries where questioning your superior is not acceptable. That however does not make employees happier - they like to be informed and/or consulted regardless of which culture they operate within. Managing impressions of employee over managing them is probably the most exciting way to get everyone's behaviours committed to their jobs and engaging one another in a way that stimulates mutual support, effective knowledge sharing and ownership of business goals.
- **Rewards to positive behaviours:** Without the benefit of a culture that recognises, encourages, and rewards KM activities, consistent performance of KM activities will not occur.

Interaction and collaboration among employees is important when attempting to transmit tacit knowledge between individuals or convert tacit knowledge into explicit knowledge, thereby transforming it from the individual to the organisational level. Contributors in this book view culture as an important asset because it shapes assumptions and influences priorities about what knowledge is worth sharing and defines relationships between individual and organisational knowledge by creating the context. The context sets up a positive environment for social interaction. Culture all around determines how knowledge will be shared in particular situations and it shapes the processes by which new knowledge is created, legitimized, and distributed in organisations.

REAL GAPS POSING REAL CHALLENGES FOR FUTURE THOUGHTS

Systems and Technologies and Cultural Challenge

In this book, there is probably an astringent view that absence of technology does not prevent KM activity – it just means that KM activity must be accomplished in different ways. This is true in cross border communication where language may be a barrier to exchange within the context of the environment. Sophisticated software applications and other technology may help in knowledge management, but are certainly not a requirement. Highly organised and intellectually stimulating processes are more important. These processes require that the organisational culture values, encourages, and rewards KM behaviour.

Cultural Diversity of Organisations

It is also true in virtual interactions as well as within distant two-way relationships such as university/industry relationships – both of which are very different in culture. For example, commercial businesses have sufficient technology to assist them in creating, sharing and documenting knowledge which many universities may not have or they do not even need. This is because universities have been, traditionally, good generators of knowledge, but at a point the majority of them have not been commercially driven and they rarely justify economically their investment in research and teaching.

In our 21st century knowledge driven economies, Knowledge residing in universities has become economically important, the challenge which remains, is the alignment of university cultures to that of actively financially driven businesses.

Another rather surprising element of this book is the reflection on how cultural implications of knowledge sharing could be easily overlooked at the individual level. Like much research into KM, there is a general trend that suggests that once we mention culture in business, people only think about organisational culture and rarely come to realize how each of the units involved (one plus one) add up to a whole (the organisation). There are several studies that were conducted in the area of organisational culture (Davenport and Prusak, 1998; Grover and Davenport, 2001; Gold, Malhotra and Segars, 2001; Karlsen and Gottschalk, 2004) but there are far fewer that studied the individual's culture. What is known is that amongst those factors that lead to successful knowledge creation and transfer appear culture, training, top-management support, technology infrastructure, knowledge infrastructure, knowledge sharing, and knowledge transfer. These studies underline the importance of culture (Davenport and Prusak, 1998).

The Changes in Human Behaviour

This work points out the view that changes can only happen by successfully changing the mind-sets and behaviours of individuals – indeed, organisational culture can provide a supportive environment for people's change, but people must be ready and able to change too. Organisations with highly flexible, adaptable workforces are best placed to successfully learn new things, share knowledge with far less worries and engage in open, frank communication. It is therefore now accepted that changing human behaviour will be the key to effecting organisational knowledge sharing, and adapting innovative ways of working.

Adaptability to the Organisational Environment of the Day

As we debate cultural implications on knowledge transfer, it is necessary to think about human nature and high levels of flexibility required in today's workforce. As I am writing this book, when the world economy is in meltdown, the unpredictable economic downturn is affecting everyone (including knowledge workers), and businesses are looking at every possible avenue to protect their investments, it is absolutely necessary that this book is not lost within the "nonsense" of knowledgeable technologies which are not able to save the planet from such economic catastrophes. It is necessary, however, to recognise that everything we are experiencing in managing these changes is posing difficult questions for managers, on how they can get people to do what they want them to do and how they can overcome resistance to change. These are very serious questions which hit right at the heart of all types of businesses - universities, private companies, public sector institutions to name but a few.

REFERENCES

Bollisani, E. (Ed.). (2008). *Building the knowledge society on the Internet: Sharing and exchanging knowledge in networked environments*. Hershey, PA: Information Science Reference.

Cohen, W., & Levinthal, D. (1990). Absorptive capacity: A new perspective on learning and innovation. *Administrative Science Quarterly, 35*(1), 128-152.

Cummings, J. L., & Teng, B. S. (2003). Transferring R&D knowledge – the key factors affecting knowledge transfer success. *Journal of Engineering and Technology Management, 20*(1), 39-68.

Davenport, T. H., & Prusak, L. (1998). *Working knowledge: How organizations manage what they know*. Boston: Harvard Business School Press.

Garavelli, A. C., Gorgoglione, M., & Scozzi, B. (2002). Managing knowledge transfer by knowledge technologies. *Technovation, 22*(5), 269-279.

Gold, A. H., Malhotra, A., & Segars, A. H. (2001). Knowledge management: An organizational capabilities perspective. *Journal of Management Systems, 18*(1), 185-214.

Gourlay, S. N. (2006). Towards conceptual clarity concerning 'tacit knowledge': A review of empirical studies. *Knowledge Management Research and Practice, 4*(1), 60-69.

Gourlay, S. N. (2007). An activity centered framework for knowledge management. In C. McInerney & R. Day (Eds.), *Rethinking knowledge management: From knowledge management to knowledge processes. Information science and knowledge management, 12*, 21-64.

Grover, V., & Davenport, T. H. (2001). General Perspectives on knowledge management: Fostering a research agenda. *Journal of Management Information Systems, 18*(1), 5-21.

Harorimana, D. (2007). Boundary spanners and networks of knowledge: Developing a knowledge creation and transfer model. In D. Remenyi (Ed.), *Proceedings of the Academic Conferences International*, Reading (pp. 430-435).

Harorimana, D. (2008). Leading Firms as knowledge gatekeepers in a networked environment. In E. Bollisani (Ed.), *Building the knowledge society on the Internet: Sharing and exchanging knowledge in networked environments* (pp. 260-281). Hershey, PA: Information Science Reference.

Karlsen, J. T., & Gottschalk, P. (2004). Factors affecting knowledge transfer in IT projects. *Engineering Management Journal, 16*(1), 3-10.

Malhotra, Y. (2000). Knowledge management and new organization forms: A framework for business model innovation. *Information Resources Management Journal, 13*(1), 5-15.

Nonaka, I., &Takeuchi, H. (1995). *The knowledge-creating company*. New York: Oxford University Press.

Pinch, S., Henry, N., Jenkins, M., & Tallman, S. (2003). From 'industrial districts' to 'knowledge clusters': A model of knowledge dissemination and competitive advantage in industrial agglomerations. *Journal of Economic Geography, 3*, 373-388.

Polanyi, M. (1966). *The tacit dimension*. London: Routledge and Kegan Paul.

Schein, E. H. (1990). Organizational culture. *American Psychologist, 45*(2), 109-119.

Wilkins, A. L., & Dyer, W. G. (1988). Toward culturally sensitive theories of culture change. *The Academy of Management Review, 13*(4), 522-533.

Acknowledgment

Knowing is a reality of powerful influence to our lives,
Knowledge is the most precious treasure one may have,
Discovery is the last thing we think about and we know little how to realise it
If we knew, we would all start and complete at once

This book is such a journey and let me acknowledge the following precious people who made it possible....

My beloved family,
My beloved Cecilia, Fiona, Becky, and, Jessica
My Dad and Mum who educated me but left me to explore this world;
My all contributors and all those who worked so hard and contributed so much to make this book a reality;
All my reviewers, editors,
My friends and fellows at Southampton Solent University;
My fellow Staff at the Rwanda Development Board;

All I dedicate this book to you!

Deogratias Harorimana
Southampton Solent University, UK

Section 1

Chapter 1
Exploring the Knowledge Management Landscape:
A Critical Review of Existing Knowledge Management Frameworks

Stavros T. Ponis
National Technical University Athens, Greece

George Vagenas
National Technical University Athens, Greece

Epaminondas Koronis
University of Warwick, UK

ABSTRACT

Relevant literature suggests that the field of knowledge management (KM) at the service of contemporary organizations is characterized by a plethora of diverse frameworks. However, none of these frameworks has achieved such a wide acceptance so as to be conceived as a standard. In fact, practice proves that each research or consultant group follows its own approach while many initiatives are based on custom approaches, developed each time from scratch, or even worse do not follow a structured method at all. In this chapter the authors attempt to go deeper by proposing a classification of knowledge management frameworks based on their macroscopic characteristics followed by their evaluation against a set of predetermined content elements that a complete approach should possess. The main result propagated from their critique is a common understanding of current theoretical and practical shortcomings of the field and the specification of a consistent set of course of actions and guidelines for researchers and practitioners engaged in knowledge management and its applications.

DOI: 10.4018/978-1-60566-790-4.ch001

INTRODUCTION

Back in 1987, Robert Solow was awarded a Nobel Prize in economics for identifying the main sources of growth, capital and labor. Since then the global socioeconomic scene has dramatically changed, leading researchers such as Krugman (1991) and Lucas (1993) to propose that in addition to traditional production factors, knowledge has also become a vital source of growth. Along this evolution path organizations are not becoming more labor, material or capital-intensive, but more knowledge intensive (Drucker, 1993), thus giving rise to a brand new economy labeled as the knowledge economy.

Surprisingly, despite the wide acceptance and the proliferating implementations of Knowledge Management (KM), many organizations have failed to realize its expected results. These failures and shortcomings form the ground for severe criticism, which cannot be easily overlooked. In our view, overcoming current deficiencies requires the design and development of a solid architecture integrating methods, processes, tools, knowledge resources and technologies capable of supporting Knowledge Management in a holistic fashion. In other words, in order to take the field a step further, it has to be structured, through the development of a comprehensive and practical approach. Otherwise, the field's "progress is nothing but a fortunate combination of circumstances, research is fumbling in the dark, and dissemination of knowledge is a cumbersome process" (Vatter, 1947).

This need has already been recognized drawing the attention of researchers coming from a variety of disciplines, including Organizational Science, Strategy and Management Science, as well as Information Systems. As a result, there have been several efforts at developing frameworks, varying in scope and nature, trying to understand and describe the Knowledge Management phenomena. Despite, or maybe because of, this multicultural attention, a consensus regarding Knowledge Management has not been achieved yet. Such a deficiency is widely accepted and is summarized by Spender (2003) who states that, "as we look at the literature it is immediately clear that it is neither homogeneous nor well integrated. There is no single set of terms or even theoretical constructs".

The aim of this chapter is to investigate the current understanding of the discipline by analyzing and critically evaluating existing frameworks. In doing so, we first explore the concept and definitions of Knowledge Management in an effort to set the boundaries of the field. Moving to the core of the chapter the benefits and limitations of standardization are discussed, and a short description of some of the most well cited approaches is provided. Finally existing approaches are critically evaluated in order to understand current theoretical and practical shortcomings of the field and set a roadmap towards the development of an improved approach, supporting the successful adoption and assimilation of Knowledge Management in contemporary organizations.

BACKGROUND

Summarizing the concepts and processes which Knowledge Management entails in a few lines has proved to be a rather difficult task. As Quintas et. al (1997) pointed out "it is difficult to scope and define this disparate and emergent field and understand the processes involved to determine programmes and interventions". Some even claim that the term is rather an unfortunate one since it implies the painless control of knowledge, which is largely unstructured, in the same way that structured organizational facets are managed (Cloete & Snyman, 2003). However, in order to provide a complete specification of the term, a categorization and analysis of existing definitions is mandatory and will be presented in the remainder of this section.

A thorough reading of the definitions reveals that numerous perspectives exist. For one thing, some authors view *Knowledge Management* from a social and humanistic point of view, focusing on the management of the human factor. On the other side, IT focused approaches disregard organizational aspects, which are considered 'soft', in favor of 'hard' ones mostly in the form of IT tools and technologies. Some authors quite disagree with the latter approach such as Peters, (1992) who argues that the crux of the issue is not the supportive Information Technology. Adopting a much broader perspective other researchers focus their attention on the management of *Intellectual Capital* consisting of knowledge resources, and including among others human and IT resources. However, advocates of this view often adopt a mechanistic standpoint equalizing knowledge resources with ordinary corporate recourses despite their inherent discrepancies. Another popular approach is the view of Knowledge Management as a sum of knowledge processes. Under this scope activities that can be performed on knowledge are thoroughly analyzed, in an effort to effectively

Table 1. A categorization of knowledge management definitions

Reference	Definition of Knowledge Management
Human Capital	
Stuart, 1996	Efforts intended to retain, analyze and organize employee expertise, making it easily available anywhere, anytime, ideally and ultimately to improve the bottom line. (Mentioned in (Chai, 1998)).
Brooking, 1997	KM is the activity which is concerned with strategy and tactics to manage human centered assets.
Information Technology	
Frappaulo & Toms, 1997	KM is a toolset for the automation of deductive or inherent relationships between information objects, users and processes.
Allee, 1997	Technology and interior structure of a firm which can help people rethink the knowledge in the organization and help people communicate.
Intellectual Capital	
Sveiby, 1997	The art of creating value from an organization's intangible assets.
Bukowitz & Williams, 1999	Knowledge Management is the process by which the organization generates wealth from its knowledge or intellectual capital…
Rosemann, 2000	Knowledge Management seeks to deal with the problem of leveraging knowledge resources in an organization.
Knowledge Management processes	
Wiig, 1997	KM focuses on facilitating and managing knowledge related activities such as creation, capture, transformation and use.
Weggeman, 1997	KM deals with organizing and controlling the operational processes in the knowledge value chain in the most efficient way.
Smirnov et. al, 2004	Knowledge has to be delivered in the right context to the right person, in the right time for the right purpose. These activities called Knowledge Logistics (KL) (similar definitions: (Holsapple & Joshi, 1999; O'Dell & Grayston, 1998; Petrash, 1996).
Holistic nature of Knowledge Management	
Taylor et al., 1997	Powerful environmental forces are reshaping the world of the manager of the 21st century. These forces call for a fundamental shift in organization process and human resource strategy. This is Knowledge Management.
Quintas et. al, 1997	Knowledge management is the process of critically managing knowledge to meet existing needs, to identify and exploit existing and acquired knowledge assets and to develop new opportunities.
Holsapple & Joshi, 2004	Knowledge Management is an entity's systematic and deliberate efforts to expand, cultivate, and apply available knowledge in ways that add value to the entity, in the sense of positive results in accomplishing its objectives or fulfilling its purpose.

incorporate them in business practice and value adding processes. Finally, there are those that view Knowledge Management in an integrated manner and provide holistic descriptions that set this new paradigm in the broader business content.

Having identified the diversity of scopes inherent in all definitions harnessed from literature, in Table 1, we attempt a summary of some of the most representative and well cited definitions categorized under a 'scope' perspective.

On this profusion of definitions Scarborough (1996) comments: "the sprawling and eclectic literature and the ambiguity and definitional problems ... allow different groups to project their own interests and concerns onto it". As a consequence, "there is still no universally accepted definition for Knowledge Management" (Tsui, 2000) and the term is loosely used to refer to a range of organizational practices, and in some extreme situations to mere IT solutions.

In the context of this study Knowledge Management can be defined as the systematic and planned organizational practice that aims to create an internal environment that fosters knowledge in support of the value adding activities. The ultimate goal is to increase individual effectiveness and corporate competitiveness and performance.

The focal point of the above definition is that Knowledge Management is an organizational practice rather than a mere toolbox of techniques and IT solutions (McLoughlin & Thorpe, 1993). As such it has to be aligned with the corporate environment and strategy in order to support specific business goals and impact operational performance. More specifically, it is essential that Knowledge Management is managed not in isolation, but in coordination with other corporate activities, reflecting the fundamental view that it is certainly not a goal to itself.

STANDARDIZATION AND KNOWLEDGE MANAGEMENT

The overall aim of *standardization* is to facilitate the international exchange of goods and services, and thus provide benefits in the sphere of intellectual, scientific, technological and economic activity (ISO, 2007). However, standardization does not provide benefits on its own, unless it is based on real needs. So, is there a real need for standardization in the field? In search of an answer, the pros and cons of standardization and particularly in Knowledge Management have to be investigated.

On the one hand, the *benefits of standardization* in Knowledge Management can be summarized as follows (Weber et. al, 2002):

- The process of standardization provides transparency by achieving a common understanding and a common terminology for all involved parties (academic and business institutions).
- Standardized approaches that will prevail, like common approaches to processes, technologies and strategies, will bring the benefits of Knowledge Management to a broader circle of users, than the existing abundance of approaches.
- Standardization will allow the use of a validated common terminology that can ease communication in the field, both between practitioners and researchers.
- Standardization provides the fundamental base for the development of highly creative and at the same time fast and cost effective, customized solutions.
- Finally, standardized approaches can support educational and research causes. Frameworks enable the easier comprehension of the discipline by providing solid theoretical foundations supported by to researchers and practitioners that aim to study and develop the Knowledge Management field.

Besides the above, there are also two additional arguments in favor of standardization in Knowledge Management. With standardized approaches experience from past initiatives and evidence about the application of methods and software can be captured systematically. At the same time, the evaluation of success or failure in comparison to other similar efforts can also be promoted (Wildner et. al, 2007).

On the other hand, the arguments that speak against a standardized Knowledge Management approach mainly include the following (Weber et. al, 2002):

- A sound standardization effort can be a lengthy process and as a result standards run the risk of lagging behind current practice requirements. This has to do with the compromising nature of standardization and the need to reach a broad level of consensus.
- Standardization can only achieve its purpose if a critical mass of users of the elaborated standards is achieved.
- The question, what is a logic and yet adequate degree of standardization for a soft subject like Knowledge Management, is not an easy one.
- Last but not least, standardization is largely seen as a barrier for human creativity, innovation and flexibility. All of them constitute major Knowledge Management aspects and pursuits.

In this chapter we stand favorably behind the standardization of Knowledge Management domain. Despite the difficulties and shortcomings mentioned above, it seems that the proper use of standardization can provide considerable advantages. This assumption is amplified by the results standardization efforts have achieved in other disciplines such as Operations Management, Business Process Management and IT design and development. However, when considering the eclectic and subjective nature of Knowledge Management it becomes debatable whether standardization can achieve the same results. The soft nature of the field is the main reason that Weber et al. (2002) proposes the term *common approaches* instead of *standards* in order to describe approaches that the majority of the community agrees on, but do not necessarily comply with the strict requirements of a standard. We believe that this is a fair compromise.

OVERVIEW OF KNOWLEDGE MANAGEMENT FRAMEWORKS

Despite the above, ongoing debate, it seems that the potential benefits of standardization are already widely accepted, as there have been several efforts at developing more or less structured frameworks trying to understand and describe the Knowledge Management phenomenon. This section aims to identify the major approaches in the field, analyze them and bring to light, based on that analysis, existing shortcomings and limitations that restrain Knowledge Management application in contemporary enterprises.

Before proceeding, it is considered essential to clarify the term framework. A *framework* can be seen as a structure that provides elements, ideas and guidance in support of a topic area (Popper, 1994). Narrowing the scope a *Knowledge Management framework* relates the various components of Knowledge Management, providing a schematic picture of the interdependencies of these various aspects and helping to position projects and activities in the business field (CEN, 2004a).

The first step towards the identification of existing frameworks and approaches was an extensive keyword search through the Web (utilizing established search engines and specialized data bases).

The process of identifying and selecting existing Frameworks & Approaches is presented in a diagrammatic form in Figure 1.

Figure 1. The process of identifying and selecting existing frameworks & approaches

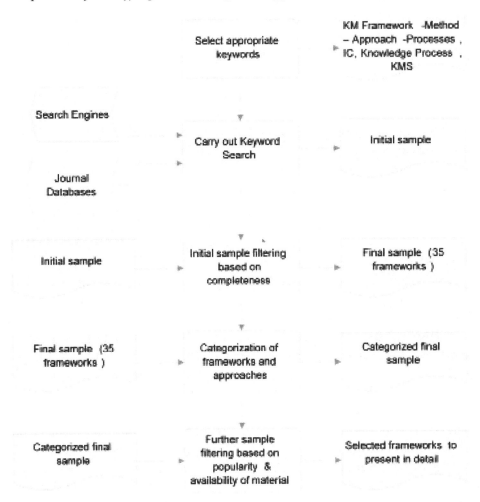

The keywords used for this purpose included, *KM Framework, KM Method, KM Approach, Intellectual Capital, KM Process(es), Knowledge Process(es) and Knowledge Management System(s)*.

The result was a great number of publications and resources that were downsized in numbers by keeping only the publications describing complete research works on frameworks and approaches. At the same time the references of the initial sample of publications were investigated, enriching the original sample with even more publications, again keeping those describing complete frame-

works and approaches. This selection process led to a final sample, of 34 frameworks, that were analyzed in detail.

After a primary analysis of the above frameworks the diversity of existing approaches was more than evident, avowing that Knowledge Management is a medley of numerous perspectives. In tight accordance to our previously used categorization of definitions, we then organized the approaches found in literature into three large categories, depending on their focus on *Intellectual Capital (IC), Information Technology (IT) and Processes*. Finally, *Holistic* approaches trying to integrate the above perspectives constitute a fourth category on their own. It has to be stressed out that assigning a framework to a specific category isn't always that simple. Approaches do exist that while focusing on a specific component they do so in a complete and thus "holistic" way taking into consideration most of the related organizational aspects. However, such approaches are not

Table 2. A categorization of kKnowledge management frameworks

Framework	Category
1. The Framework of Knowledge Management stages (van der Spek & Spijkervet, 1997)	Holistic
2. The Framework of Core Capabilities and Knowledge Building (Barton, 1995)	Holistic
3. The Process Oriented KM approach (Remus, 2002)	Holistic
4. The KPMG Knowledge Management framework (Alavi, 1997)	Holistic
5. The Knowledge Management event chain (Despres & Chauvel, 1999)	Process
6. The Value Platform (Petrash, 1996)	IC
7. The Intangible Assets Monitor (Sveiby, 1997)	IC
8. The Skandia Navigator (Edvinsson & Malone, 1997)	IC
9. The Intellectual Capital of the Firm (Sullivan, 1998)	IC
10. The CommonKADS methodology (Schreiber et. al, 1999)	IT
11. The OVUM system architecture (Woods & Sheina, 1999)	IT
12. The OMIS Success Model (Jennex et. al, 1998)	IT
13. The Knowledge Creating Company (Nonaka & Takeuchi, 1995).	Process
14. The Building Blocks of Knowledge Management (Probst et. al, 1997).	Process
15. The Movement of Knowledge in the I-Space (Boisot, 1987).	Process
16. The Knowledge Chain Model (Holsapple & Singh, 2001).	Process
17. Knowledge Management Process Model (Kucza, 2001).	Process
18. The Knowledge Management process framework (Bukowitz & William, 2000).	Process
19. The Knowledge Life Cycle (McElroy, 2002).	Process
20. The Three Pillars of Knowledge Management (Wiig, 1993).	Holistic
21. The Model of Organizational Knowledge Management (Andersen, A., & APQC, 1996).	Holistic
22. The Framework of Intellectual Capital Management (Huang, 1997).	IC
23. The Tasks of Knowledge Management (Allweyer, 1998).	Process
24. The Ernst and Young KM Method (Woods & Sheina, 1999).	Holistic
25. The Knowledge Value Chain (Weggeman, 1997)	Holistic
26. The Fraunhofer IPK Reference Model for KM (Heisig, 2000).	Holistic
27. The MITRE KM model (Taylor Small & Tatalias, 2000).	Holistic
28. Knowledge Management Maturity Model (Ehms & Langen, 2003).	Holistic
29. The „le manageur" Knowledge Management framework (Menon et. al, 1998)	Holistic
30. The EKMF KM Framework (Weber et. al, 2002).	Holistic
31. The Know-Net Approach (Mentzas et. al, 2003).	Holistic
32. The European Knowledge Management Framework (CEN, 2004a).	Holistic
33. The Process Model of Rastogi (2000).	Process
34. The Process Model of Tannembaum & Alliger (2000)	Process

considered as holistic since their intention is to describe a specific construct of the Knowledge Management edifice. Table 2 summarizes the frameworks that were analyzed and assigns them to the categories identified.

Having thoroughly investigated literature in search of available Knowledge Management frameworks and approaches we came down with, what seems to be, a rather exhaustive list that needs to be narrowed down based on hard criteria such as popularity and applicability. We do that in an attempt to help the reader to separate the wheat from the chaff and thus provide him with a clearer view of the current situation regarding existing frameworks and their application in contemporary organizations. Furthermore, such categorization will significantly help the organization of our critique presented in the next sections of this chapter. So, in the remainder of this section some of the most prominent frameworks of each of the above categories are described in more detail. These approaches were chosen based on their popularity (cited most frequently and having a high rank in search engine results – both indicators were qualitatively evaluated), while the availability of sufficient material in order to soundly describe and evaluate them, was also an influencing factor. Finally, Table 3 briefly describes some additional well cited frameworks and approaches that were investigated, thus contributing significantly to the completeness of our study.

THE INTANGIBLE ASSETS MONITOR

According to the IAM the *Total Market Value* of a company consists of its visible equity and three kinds of Intangible Assets namely, external structures, internal structures, and employee competence. *External structures* represent external flows (inflows or outflows) of knowledge with customers or suppliers and include customer and supplier relationships, brand names, trademarks,

and the general company's image. *Internal structures* represent flows of knowledge within an organization and include patents, concepts, models, computer and administrative systems, as well as organizational culture. Finally, *Employee competence* consists of skills and knowledge bases of individuals within an organization.

The *Intangible Assets Monitor* (IAM) (Sveiby, 1997; Sveiby, 1998) comprises a method for measuring the *Intangible Assets* of a company and attempts to redefine the firm from a knowledge perspective. In essence it proposes a number of relevant indicators for measuring Intangible Assets and a presentation format which allows the easier interpretation of results.

The Skandia Navigator

The *Skandia Navigator* was developed at the Swedish financial services company Skandia by a team led by Leif Edvinsson (Edvinsson & Malone, 1997), and was refined by Roos et al. (1997), whose Model gave a strategic perspective to the framework. The Skandia Navigator is a management reporting system for evaluating both the hard and the soft assets of an organization. The tool adopts a holistic view of performance measurement and goal achievement that helps managers guide the company into the future (Malone, 1997). This chronological sequence leading to the future is also evident in the organization of the proposed Navigator along five focus areas. The *financial focus area*, which emphasizes on the company's past performance; the *human, customer, and the process focus areas* reflecting current performance; and the *renewal and development focus areas* determining future performance.

The Skandia Navigator focuses on both financial and non-financial aspects of a company in order to measure in an improved way the total *Market Value* of a firm which is considered equal to its *Financial Capital* plus its *Intellectual Capital* (Luu et. al, 2001). In order to successfully measure

Table 3. An overview of knowledge management approaches

Categories of Knowledge Management Approaches and Frameworks
Intellectual Capital (IC)
• *The Value Platform (Petrash, 1996)*
The value platform model involves three types of organizational resources that are referred to as IC: human, organizational, and customer capital. The model recognizes that relationships among the three major types of IC lead to financial outcomes, and that maximizing the interrelationships among the three kinds intellectual capital increases the organization's value creating space.
• *The Intellectual Capital of the Firm (Sullivan, 1998)*
The IC of the firm is a model that divides IC into human capital and intellectual assets. Human capital, which creates values, is tacit by nature and lies in people. Intellectual assets, from which value can be extracted, represent the codified, tangible knowledge owned by a company. Finally, intellectual assets that are legally protected are referred to by the legal term intellectual property.
Information Technology
• *The OMIS Success Model (Jennex et. al, 1998)*
OMIS Success Model allows the measurement of a system that is thought to be an Organizational Memory system, along five blocks. The first block of the model defines the system quality in terms of the characteristics of the OMIS. The second, information quality, defines how good the system is in terms of its output. The third, information use, refers to the utilization of the outputs of the system, while the final two blocks try to evaluate the system in terms of individual and organizational impacts.
Knowledge Management processes
• *The Knowledge Management Process Model (Kucza, 2001)*
The Knowledge Management process model can be separated into two major parts: the co-ordination processes and the operational processes. The co-ordination processes represent the management tasks related to Knowledge Management (analyze, define, plan, and effect) and they are structured into a cycle, named the Knowledge Management Pr2imer that supports continuous improvement. The operational processes (Identification of Needs for Knowledge, Sharing of Knowledge, Knowledge Collection and Storage, Knowledge Update and Creation of Knowledge) present the processes of actually carrying out Knowledge Management and are interconnected with knowledge flows and activity/activation flows.
• *The Knowledge Life Cycle (McElroy, 2002)*
McElroy's model assumes that knowledge exits only after it has been produced, and after this it can be captured, codified and shared. The KLC model divides the Knowledge Creation Process in two big processes, Knowledge Production, a process synonymous with organizational learning, during which new organizational knowledge is created, and Knowledge Integration, that allows the sharing and distribution of knowledge. The most important aspect of this model is that it introduces two new concepts, the Demand Side and Supply Side and addresses the issue of a balance between these two sides.
• *The Tasks of Knowledge Management (Allweyer, 1998)*
The three level framework (Knowledge Management processes, business component and knowledge processing) considers Knowledge Management activities as an integral part of existing business processes. The approach aims to the description of required and used knowledge as well as generated and documented knowledge. The approach claims to support the structuring of knowledge into categories and the construction of a knowledge map, by using pictograms, in order to locate who knows what inside the organization.
Holistic nature of Knowledge Management
• *The Three Pillars of Knowledge Management (Wiig, 1993)*
Wiig's Knowledge Management framework is composed of three pillars that represent the major functions needed to manage knowledge. The pillars are based on a broad understanding of knowledge creation, manifestation, use, and transfer. The first pillar is concerned with exploring knowledge and its adequacy, the second pillar involves appraising and evaluating the value of knowledge and knowledge-related activities, while the third pillar focuses on governing Knowledge Management activities.
• *The Model of Organizational Knowledge Management (Andersen, A., & APQC, 1996)*
The APQC model identifies seven processes (create, identify, collect, adapt, organize, apply, and share) that can operate on an organization's knowledge and four organizational enablers (leadership, measurement, culture, and technology) that facilitate the workings of the Knowledge Management processes.
• *The Fraunhofer IPK Reference Model for Knowledge Management (Heisig, 2000)*
The Fraunhofer IPK reference model, intends to integrate Knowledge Management into daily business process. Business processes are seen as the application fields of knowledge, integrating the knowledge domains and providing context. The core activities of Knowledge Management (create, store, distribute, and apply) form a cycle and relate to the specific business processes, while measures within the six design areas (process organization, information technology, leadership, corporate culture, HRM and control) are also provided.

continued on following page

Table 3. continued

Categories of Knowledge Management Approaches and Frameworks
• *The MITRE Knowledge Management model (Taylor Small & Tatalias, 2000)*
The MITRE model provides a holistic approach to Knowledge Management, viewing it from a two dimensional perspective. The first dimension consists of the activities that are critical to knowledge creation and innovation (exchange, capture, re-use and internalization of knowledge). The second dimension consists of the elements that enable or influence the knowledge creation activities (strategy, measurement, policy, process and technology).

Figure 2. Skandia Intellectual Capital Index –Adapted from (Edvinsson & Malone, 1997)

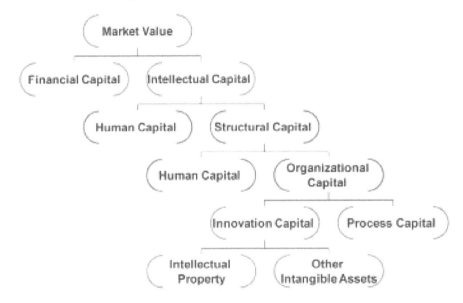

IC the Navigator includes a detailed description of its diverse components, as shown in the Figure 2.

Human capital is defined as the knowledge, skills and competencies that employees possess and is considered as the source of innovation and renewal. *Structural capital* consists of the IC that remains in the firm when employees retire, and encompasses the organizational capability to leverage IC. *Customer capital* is concerned with an enterprise's relationships with its customers. *Organizational capital* consists of an enterprise's systematized and packaged competencies, along with the systems for leveraging the company's innovative strength and value-creating capability. *Innovation capital* is the renewal strength of a company, expressed as intellectual property. *Process capital* is the combination of value-creating and

non value-creating processes. And finally, *Intellectual property* consists of patents, trademarks, copyrights, designs and other specifications, while *other intangible assets* mainly refer to culture. For each of the above IC dimensions the Navigator proposes specific measures (164 measures, of which 91 intellectually based and 73 financial) that should be selected ad hoc from the respective business unit managers.

The CommonKADS Methodology

The *CommonKADS methodology* (Schreiber et. al, 1999) is the leading methodology for the development of knowledge systems as tools to support knowledge intensive tasks. The CommonKADS methodology is a *top-down* knowledge engineering approach (Breuker & Van de Velde, 1994) based on the assumption that knowledge has a stable internal structure that is analyzable by distinguishing specific knowledge types and roles. As a result it proposes to concentrate on the conceptual structure of knowledge before proceeding to the programming details.

According to CommonKads, Knowledge Management, like any other managerial task is assigned with the achievement of specific organizational goals through the planning and implementation of targeted actions. More specifically, Knowledge Management consists of a cyclic exertion of three main activities: conceptualize (identify knowledge, analyze strengths and weaknesses), reflect (identify improvements, plan changes) and act (implement changes, monitor improvements). The final activity is about the application of the designed changes at the Knowledge Object Level which is defined by three objects: (i) *agents* as persons or software that process (ii) *knowledge assets* and participate in (iii) *business processes.*

Based on the above assumptions CommonKADS enables the discovery of opportunities and bottlenecks in how organizations develop, distribute and apply their knowledge resources, through a detailed analysis of knowledge-intensive tasks and processes. In support of this task it provides a detailed description of the *process* to be followed during the development of a knowledge based system, the necessary *roles* (knowledge provider, knowledge engineer/analyst, knowledge system developer, knowledge user, project manager, knowledge manager) and supplies the knowledge engineer and developer with a set of ready to use *model templates*, which can be configured, refined and filled during the design and development project.

The OVUM System Architecture

The OVUM system architecture (Woods & Sheina, 1999) is one of the most complete and descriptive IT models for Knowledge Manage-

ment, and has been slightly refined by (Lawton, 2001). A careful examination of the architecture reveals that it is not about a single technology but instead is a collection of indexing, classification, and information-retrieval technologies that are bundled together to provide a complete solution. Key underpinning technologies include content and workflow management, which organize knowledge and direct it to workers who can benefit from it; search functionalities enabling the easier retrieval of relevant information; and collaboration services which help workers share their knowledge.

The lowest layers of the architecture aim at managing sources of explicit knowledge that is articulated in the form of knowledge items such as documents or database records. In support of this layer typical tools such as database management systems and word processors are used. In order to make these disparate sources of information available to the higher layers, a web based infrastructure consisting of intranet and internet technologies that integrate information and enable content management is proposed. For the purpose of better organization of knowledge items according to the specific context of each enterprise, a corporate taxonomy (knowledge map) is suggested. This corporate taxonomy can provide the contextual base for the targeted provision of the system's knowledge services, which consist of classification and collaboration services. Finally, a knowledge portal that feeds the systems services for use by different knowledge intensive business processes such as Competitive Intelligence and Product Development, completes the stack of the proposed technological tools and solutions.

The Knowledge Creating Company

Nonaka and Takeuchi (1995) developed a highly theoretical model in order to describe and finally support the flow of organizational knowledge towards innovation and new knowledge creation. Their model is based on the constant interaction between two modes of knowledge, tacit and explicit (Hedlund & Nonaka, 1993), a distinction which has its origins in the work of Michael Polanyi (Polanyi, 1967). *Tacit* is knowledge that has a personal quality that makes it hard to formalize and communicate, while, *explicit* knowledge refers to knowledge that can be communicated in a formal systematic language (Wilson, 1996).

This interaction is called *Knowledge Conversion* and corresponds to four processes; socialization, externalization, combination and internalization of knowledge. This continuous and dynamic interaction between tacit and explicit knowledge takes place at the *individual*, *group* and *organizational level*, forming a *Knowledge Spiral* that underlies the five phase knowledge creation process (Nonaka & Takeuchi, 1995) (Von Krogh, 1998). The knowledge spriral is related to five enabling conditions namely intention, autonomy, fluctuation and creative chaos, redundancy, and finally requisite variety (Von Krogh et. al, 2000). From an organizational perspective the authors adopt a middle-up-down management model positioning middle managers in the heart of the knowledge creation process. In fact middle managers are characterized as the most powerful "*knowledge activists*", mainly because of their position at the intersection of the vertical and horizontal flows of information within a company.

The Knowledge Chain Model

The knowledge chain model (Holsapple & Singh, 2001) is based on a descriptive framework developed via a Delphi-study involving an international panel of prominent practitioners and academics (Joshi, 1998). The framework identifies five major *knowledge manipulation activities* that occur in various patterns within *Knowledge Management episodes* and four major *managerial influences* that affect the knowledge manipulation activities. Respectively, these form the five primary and four secondary activities in the knowledge chain model (Table 4). According to the authors, this set

of interrelated activities appears to be common across diverse organizations, and thus should be a major concern of a *Chief Knowledge Officer (CKO)*. The knowledge chain model is further decomposed since both primary and secondary activities involve sub-activities, in the form of actual business actions that instantiate the high level processes of the model (Holsapple & Joshi, 2004; Holsapple & Joshi, 2005).

The Building Blocks of Knowledge Management

Probst's *Building Blocks of Knowledge Management* (Probst et. al, 1997) represents activities that are directly knowledge related, and their arrangement in the model forms two cycles. An *inner cycle* consisting of the building blocks of identification, acquisition, development, distribution, preservation, and use of knowledge and an *outer cycle* consisting of all these activities plus goal setting and measurement (Figure 3). An important aspect of the outer cycle is the feedback flow, which clarifies the importance of measurement in order to focus on goal oriented interventions.

In detail the building blocks of Knowledge Management include:

- *Knowledge goals* show the way for Knowledge Management activities, determining which capabilities should be built on which level (Normative, Strategic, Operational)
- *Knowledge identification* aims at increasing internal and external knowledge transparency so as to know what knowledge and expertise exist both inside and outside the organization. Knowledge maps, personal contacts and discussions are proposed for this step.
- *Knowledge acquisition* refers to the attainment of critical capabilities from the external knowledge environment (knowledge markets) whether as an investment in

Table 4. Activities in the knowledge chain model

Activities in the Knowledge Chain Model	
Primary Activities in the Knowledge Chain Model	
Knowledge acquisition	Acquiring knowledge from external sources and making it suitable for subsequent use.
Knowledge selection	Selecting needed knowledge from internal sources and making it suitable for subsequent use.
Knowledge generation	Producing knowledge by either discovery or derivation from existing knowledge.
Knowledge internalization	Altering the state of an organization's knowledge resources by distributing and storing acquired, selected, or generated knowledge.
Knowledge externalization	Embedding knowledge into organizational outputs for release into the environment.
Secondary Activities in the Knowledge Chain Model	
Knowledge leadership	Establishing conditions that enable and facilitate the fruitful conduct of Knowledge Management.
Knowledge coordination	Managing dependencies among primary activities to ensure that proper processes and resources are brought to bear and adequately at appropriate times.
Knowledge control	Ensuring that needed knowledge processors and resources are available in sufficient quality and quantity and up to security requirements.
Knowledge measurement	Assessing values of knowledge resources, knowledge processors, their results and their deployment.

the future (potential knowledge) or as an investment in the present (directly usable knowledge).

- *Knowledge development* consists of all the management activities intended to produce new internal or external knowledge on both the individual (creativity and systematic problem solving) and the collective level (openness, communication, learning dynamics).
- *Knowledge distribution* refers to making knowledge available and usable across the

whole organization, by answering critical questions such as: Who should know what, to what level of detail, and how can the organization support the processes of knowledge distribution?

- *Knowledge use*, meaning the productive deployment of organizational knowledge in the production process, is considered as the ultimate purpose of Knowledge Management.
- *Knowledge preservation* aims to prevent the loss of valuable expertise, leading to "collective amnesia", by ensuring its suitable storage, and regular incorporation into the knowledge base.
- *Knowledge measurement* presents the biggest challenge in the field. In order to achieve it, Probst proposes the use of knowledge oriented cultural analysis and capability balance sheets, while also pointing out the need to link measurement to the organization's normative, strategic, and operational dimensions.

Figure 3. The building blocks of knowledge management - Adapted from (Probst et. al, 1997)

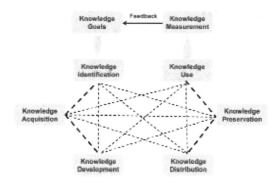

The Know-Net Approach

The Know-Net approach (Mentzas et. al, 2003) is a complete proposal consisting of a holistic framework, an implementation guide and an intranet based tool.

The *Know-Net framework* is comprised of three basic building blocks. The first one analyzes the business related Knowledge Assets of a company, which fall into three, dynamically interwove categories: the *human knowledge assets*, which generate organizational capabilities; the *structural knowledge assets*, which generalize human capabilities; and the *market knowledge assets*, which gauge the products and services of the company. The second building block of the framework is the *Knowledge Networking Levels* (individual level; team level; organizational level; and inter-organizational level), whose interdependencies facilitate the leveraging and flow of knowledge assets. Finally the third one refers to the *Knowledge Management Infrastructure*, which should be established within a company, in order to facilitate knowledge leveraging initiatives. The four components of the proposed infrastructure include *strategy* (values and mission), *organizational structure*, *processes* (acquisition, organization, sharing, use and creation of knowledge assets), and *systems*.

As for the implementation guide, named as the *Know-Net method*, it is designed as a supportive tool for the design, development, and deployment of a holistic Knowledge Management infrastructure that is aligned with business strategy, facilitates planning the required organizational changes, and shows ways to evaluate the impact of the initiative on the overall performance of the organization. Figure 4 presents in short the Know-Net Method

The European Guide to Good Practice In Knowledge Management

The European Guide to Good Practice in Knowledge Management has been developed by a Project Team reporting to the European Committee for Standardization within the context of a Workshop on Knowledge Management. The guide comprises of five main components (booklets), which are adjusted to the *Small and Medium-Sized Enterprises (SMEs)* specific business environment and include:

1. The *KM Framework*, which sets the overall context for Knowledge Management at both the organizational and personal level (CEN, 2004a).
2. The *Culture and Knowledge Management* component, which explains how to create the right cultural environment for introducing Knowledge Management (CEN, 2004b).
3. A guide to *implementing Knowledge Management in SMEs*, which provides a project management methodology to help

Figure 4. The know-net method - Adapted from (Mentzas et. al, 2003)

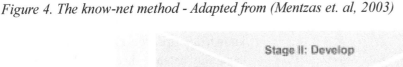

SMEs (and other organizations), get started (CEN, 2004c).

4. The *Measuring* component, which helps organizations assess their progress (CEN, 2004d).

5. *A Knowledge Management Terminology* index, which summarizes the key terms and concepts of the approach (CEN, 2004e).

The *European Knowledge Management Framework* (CEN, 2004a) is based on empirical research and practical experience in this field from all over Europe and the rest of the world and is designed to promote a common European understanding, show the value of Knowledge Management and help organizations towards its successful implementation. According to the authors, the Framework should be considered as a starting point for developing an organization-specific framework that best serves the needs of each particular organization. The Framework considers three layers as most important, the business focus, the core knowledge activities and the Knowledge Management enablers.

The second cornerstone of the European Guide to Good Practice in Knowledge Management is the *Project Management structure*, which aims at gradually introducing Knowledge Management through a set of small projects, concentrating upon carefully focused steps. This project management structure is adapted to the SMEs' needs and comprises of five phases (CEN, 2004c): *Setting up a Knowledge Management Project, Assessment, Development, Implementation, Evaluation/ Sustainability*. In order to measure the success of such an initiative the European Guide to Good Practice in Knowledge Management proposes the *Measurement* component according to which value can be added and thus measured in five dimensions, namely Financial, Innovation, Processes, Clients, Human. These five dimensions are directly related to Intellectual Capital (IC) which according to the guide includes Human Capital (HC), Structural Capital (SC), and Customer Capital (CC).

ANALYSIS OF KNOWLEDGE MANAGEMENT FRAMEWORKS

As it has become evident from the previous sections, the scientific field of Knowledge Management is characterized by a plethora of diverse frameworks and approaches. However, none of these efforts has achieved such a wide acceptance so as to be conceived as a standard. In fact, practice proves that each research or consultant group follows its own approach while many initiatives are based on custom approaches, developed each time from scratch, or even worse do not follow a structured method at all (Jennex, 2005).

In an effort to understand the above situation, existing frameworks are to be placed under the microscope in order to reveal and question their concepts and underlying assumptions. In doing so, the first step is to summarize and categorize the general, macroscopic aspects of each of the nine thoroughly described approaches along the following dimensions:

- *Background* refers to the intellectual antecedents of each framework. The identified intellectual roots or influences include economics, sociology, engineering and informatics, (see also Prusak, 2001)
- *Approach* describes the frameworks perspective on knowledge and its management recognizing the codification, the personalization and the integrative approach as the alternative options. In short, the codification approach views knowledge as an object, emphasizing on the reuse of explicit knowledge and business intelligence, while the personalization approach views knowledge as a dynamic and humanistic value, emphasizing on innovation through tacit knowledge creation and learning (Hansen et. al, 1999). Finally, the integrative view attempts to incorporate aspects and thus benefits of both previous approaches.

- *Intention* is about the descriptive or prescriptive nature of a framework. Descriptive frameworks attempt to characterize the nature of a phenomenon, whereas prescriptive frameworks prescribe methodologies to be followed (Holsapple & Joshi, 1999).
- *Scope* refers to whether a framework is holistic or partial. According to Weber holistic frameworks describe and combine all major aspects of Knowledge Management and explain their particular role and interrelations, while, explanatory frameworks explain certain facets, providing a small sub theory in itself (Weber et. al, 2002).

The above characteristics are useful for classification and epistemological reasons, examining existing frameworks from a rather theoretical perspective. However, the crux of the issue lies in the actual content and the practical implications of each approach. This very same speculation seems to interest many authors like Ilgen (2001), who proposes four major requirements for successful Knowledge Management approaches. According to Ilgen (2001), a primal requirement is the *clarity of terminology*, which is a problematic issue partly due to the multi-faceted nature of knowledge. An equally important issue is the *holistic and pragmatic* character of approaches. A successful approach has to consider all aspects and constructs of Knowledge Management (holistic), while at the same time be pragmatic, by offering practical tools that assist its implementation. Moving further on, the results of Knowledge Management have to be *measurable*, justifying in this way its contribution to organizational success. Finally, the requirements of *particular business sectors* have to be taken under consideration, as for example the knowledge reality of a consulting organization is expected to significantly differ from that of a manufacturing enterprise.

In an attempt to go deeper and effectively evaluate existing frameworks in terms of their content the following components are identified as the major elements that a complete Knowledge Management approach should consider, based on the requirements stressed out in the above paragraph.

- *Situational Factors*: The rationale behind having a set of parameters which correspond to specific business characteristics is that, there are few, if any, universal principles that describe the Knowledge Management discipline. This does not mean that we cannot make valid general descriptions but that concepts, tools, and guidelines must always be adjusted to reflect situational conditions.
- *Strategy*: Aims to define the organizational knowledge status and needs as well as the Knowledge Management goals to be pursued.
- *Organizational structure*: Describes the necessary knowledge oriented organizational structure that implements and supports Knowledge Management within a company. This component should provide for the identification of both the required *knowledge roles*, in terms of knowledge responsibilities and duties assigned to existing and typical working positions, and the additional *organizational roles,* which correspond to new working positions that participate in the company's organizational chart and are exclusively commissioned with Knowledge Management responsibilities.
- *Processes*: The process component includes the *knowledge processes* (knowledge life cycle), meaning the stages through which knowledge moves during its life time, as well as, the *Knowledge Management processes* which refer to typical business processes that direct and manage the implementation and enactment of Knowledge Management.

- *Knowledge*: This component aims to provide for the identification and analysis of the existing and required knowledge portfolio, in terms of its structure, key attributes and linkages to business processes.
- *Technology*: Describes the technological infrastructure required to support the identified Knowledge Management tasks and in this way enable the implementation of a Knowledge Management initiative.
- *Measurement*: The measurement component aims to quantify Knowledge Management's outcomes as well as its impact on organizational performance (McInerney, 2002).
- *Guidelines and Tools*: Refers to the provision of practical guidelines and supportive tools (technological or not) that can direct the real life application of an approach in time and cost effective way.

Tables 5 and 6 summarize the different approaches, described in previous sections, according to the evaluation criteria specified above. More specifically, Table 5 reviews the general or macroscopic characteristics of each approach, while Table 6 evaluates the completeness of each approach. Focusing in Table 6, its rows represent the different approaches, and its columns represent the identified indispensible constructs of a framework. Each cell of Table 6 is filled with three value types: "+"," o", and " -". The value "+" means that the approach includes the aspect under consideration, describing it in sufficient detail (structure, behavior, relations etc.). The value "o" means that the framework of the corresponding column identifies the respective construct but does not provide many details about it. Finally, the value "-" means that the specific construct is completely absent. It has to be mentioned that the evaluation is based on the literature mentioned in the corresponding

Table 5. General /Macroscopic characteristics of knowledge management approaches

Frameworks	Framework's Attributes			
	Background	Approach	Intention	Scope
Intangible Assets Monitor	Economics	Codification	Descriptive	Explanatory
The Skandia Navigator	Economics	Codification	Descriptive	Explanatory
The CommonKADS methodology	Informatics, engineering	Codification	Prescriptive	Explanatory
The OVUM System Architecture	Informatics	Codification	Descriptive	Explanatory
The Building Blocks of KM	Economics, informatics	Integrative	Descriptive	Explanatory
The Knowledge Creating Company	Economics, sociology	Integrative	Descriptive	Explanatory
The knowledge Value Chain	Economics, informatics	Integrative	Descriptive	Explanatory
The Know-net solution	Economics, informatics, sociology, engineering	Integrative	Prescriptive	Holistic
European Guide to Good Practice in Knowledge Management	Economics, informatics, sociology	Integrative	Prescriptive	Holistic

Table 6. Content evaluation of knowledge management approaches

Frameworks	Identified Constructs							
	Situational Factors	Strategy	Org Structure	Process	Knowledge	Technology	Measurement	Guidelines & Tools
Intangible Assets Monitor	-	-	-	-	o	-	+	+
The Skandia Navigator	-	-	-	-	o	-	+	+
The CommonKADS methodology	-	o	+	+	+	+	o	+
The KM IT Architecture	-	-	-	-	-	+	-	-
The Building Blocks of KM	-	o	-	+	-	o	o	-
The Knowledge Creating Company	-	o	o	o	o	o	-	-
The knowledge Value Chain	-	o	-	+	-	o	o	-
The Know-net solution	-	+	o	+	+	+	+	+
European Guide to Good Practice in Knowledge Management	-	+	o	+	+	o	o	o

sections. As a result, potential additional publications, extending the approaches analyzed, are not taken under consideration.

The most striking evidence emerging from this analysis is the *diverse nature of the examined frameworks*. All of them attempt to explain the same business practice but they do so from diametrically opposed viewing angles. For instance, the Skandia Navigator focuses on the description and measurement a company's Intellectual Capital while the Building Blocks of Knowledge Management, almost don't mention the issue and engage in the analysis of the major Knowledge Management processes. In our opinion, this lack of coordination which leads to the identified standardization deficit has its roots in the partial and particular character of most of the existing approaches. The nature of these approaches constrains them *on only a few of the Knowledge Management aspects* disregard-

ing in this way their existent interrelations with other constructs.

Another interesting finding is that *most of the examined approaches adopt a rather mechanistic view* treating knowledge as a commodity that can be manipulated and quantified. However, although making such a simplifying assumption may be useful, if not necessary, in order to pragmatically address such an issue and develop standardized approaches, completely disregarding the social aspects of knowledge, can result in over-simplistic arguments (Alvesson & Willmott, 1992; Gergen, 1991). What is required is the meaningful combination of both technical and human aspects, since the two approaches are not contradictory, but rather the two different sides of the same coin. This integration is a primary goal for holistic approaches which according to the preceding analysis seem to achieve it, at least to some extent.

Probably the most important remark is that most approaches *do not adequately provide for their implementation*. The operational aspects of Knowledge Management are not clearly addressed and there is a lack of implementation models that could guide the application of the approaches. This crucial shortcoming can be further deconstructed to the following largely unfulfilled requirements:

- No framework identifies any business parameters that could describe the context in which the application of a particular approach is promising and the adjustments that have to be made according to the users' needs.
- Existing approaches exclude the strategic issues related to Knowledge Management or disparage their importance.
- Existing approaches do not provide a clear statement of the potential benefits from their application and lack measures for evaluating their success or failure.
- Finally, while many approaches describe the process component of Knowledge Management, its organizational counterpart is insufficiently addressed. One can find little information about the required organizational structures in support of Knowledge Management (descriptions of roles and working positions, assignment in the organizational chart, etc.) and as a result it is no surprise that Knowledge Management processes cannot be well integrated as part of the job.

CONCLUSION

As the previous analysis suggests Knowledge Management literature is fragmented and characterized by strong fluctuations, creating a 'misty landscape', especially for the professionals of the field. Under these circumstances, one of the most important contributions of this chapter is considered to be that it can serve as a quick reference of the most widely known approaches and frameworks of the field. This could prove useful both for practitioners and researchers alike, since they can easily gain the insights of each approach described in the chapter. In this way practitioners can select the approach that fits better to their organization in terms of culture, perception and structure, while researchers can find a quick overview of the field and guide their research based on existing gaps and shortcomings.

In closure, the chapter raises one of the most important issues for the future development of the domain, the need for some degree of standardization or in other words for achieving a consensus on a widely accepted approach that could effectively guide practice and refute existing criticism. The necessity of common approaches is also evident in the abundance of available frameworks, demonstrating the anxiety of many researchers to provide the field with a structured approach. As for the feasibility of such a goal, the section discussing the pros and cons of standardization in Knowledge Management suggests that despite the indisputably existing difficulties and with the required compromises both in the requirements of standards and the theoretical complexities of the domain, a standardized approach can be achieved.

FUTURE RESEARCH DIRECTION

Over the past decade, the Knowledge Management field has received considerable attention from researchers and practitioners. Despite this attention and the definite consequent progress, there is still no well-integrated framework that could foster broad adoption and successful implementations. A possible explanation for this lag is that existing approaches are immature, if compared to other fields', such as software engineering or process engineering, implying that there is room for a more encompassing, unifying generic framework, capable to provide answers to fundamental questions, such as:

- What is the goal of implementing Knowledge Management?
- Which are the required processes, organizational structures, IT systems in order to achieve this goal?
- How can the above infrastructure be put in practice?
- How do business parameters affect the design and implementation of Knowledge Management?
- Which are the expected results and how can they be measured?

The answers to these questions should constitute the basic guidelines for every successful approach to Knowledge Management initiatives in contemporary organizations. Spasmodic, ad hoc approaches and segmented efforts towards addressing organizational knowledge needs may be sometimes successful in a sole case company basis, but apart from being extremely sort sighted and egocentric, they are doomed not to last. If not for Knowledge Management to become the next 'urban legend' of enterprise practice, the next soon to be forgotten hype, researchers and practitioners should join forces towards a common and widely accepted approach that will establish the discipline and justify related efforts in the decision making level of contemporary organizations. Towards this direction, we have already started a research venture for developing a methodology focused in supporting the implementation of Knowledge Management initiatives and embedding the leveraging of knowledge into everyday business activity, through helpful tools and practical guidelines.

REFERENCES

Alavi, M. (1997). *KPMG Peat Marwick U.S.: One giant brain.* Boston: Harvard Business School.

Allee, V. (1997). *The knowledge evolution: Expanding organizational intelligence.* Boston: Butterworth-Heinemann.

Allweyer, T. (1998). Modellbaslertess wissensmanagement. *IM Information Management and Consulting, 13*(1), 37–45.

Alvesson, M., & Willmott, H. (1992). *Critical management studies. London.* London: Sage.

Andersen, A., & The American Productivity and Quality Center. (1996). *The knowledge management assessment tool* [white paper].

Barton, L. D. (1995). *Wellsprings of knowledge.* Boston: Harvard Business School Press.

Boisot, M. (1987). *Information and organisations: The manager as anthropologist.* London: Fontana/Collins.

Breuker, J., & Van de Velde, W. (1994). *CommonKADS library for expertise modelling: Reusable problem solving components.* Amsterdam: IOS Press.

Brooking, A. (1997). The management of intellectual capital. *Journal of Long Range Planning, 30*(3), 364–365. doi:10.1016/S0024-6301(97)80911-9

Bukowitz, W., & Williams, R. (1999). *The knowledge management fieldbook.* Pearson Education Limited.

Bukowitz, W. R., & William, R. L. (2000). *The knowledge management fieldbook.* London: Prentice Hall.

CEN. (2004a). *European guide to good practice in knowledge management - part 1: Knowledge management framework.* CEN Workshop Agreement, European Committee For Standardization, Management Centre.

CEN. (2004b). *European guide to good practice in knowledge management - part 2: Organizational culture.* CEN Workshop Agreement, European Committee For Standardization, Management Centre.

CEN. (2004c). *European guide to good practice in knowledge management - part 3: SME implementation.* CEN Workshop Agreement, European Committee For Standardization, Management Centre.

CEN. (2004d). *European guide to good practice in knowledge management - part 4: Guidelines for measuring KM.* CEN Workshop Agreement, European Committee For Standardization, Management Centre.

CEN. (2004e). *European guide to good practice in knowledge management - part 5: KM terminology.* CEN Workshop Agreement, European Committee for Standardization, Management Centre.

Chai, K. H. (1998). *Managing knowledge in organizations: A literature review and a preliminary conceptual model* (Working paper series). Cambridge, UK: Cambridge University, Manufacturing and Management Center, Engineering Department, Cambridge.

Cloete, M., & Snyman, R. (2003). The enterprise portal: Is it knowledge management. *Aslib Proceedings, 55*(4), 234–242. doi:10.1108/00012530310486593

Despres, C., & Chauvel, D. (1999). Knowledge management(s). *Journal of Knowledge Management, 3*(2), 110–120. doi:10.1108/13673279910275567

Drucker, P. (1993). *Post-capitalist society.* New York: Harper Business.

Drucker, P. (2001). *The essential Drucker: Selections from the management works of Peter F. Drucker.* New York: Harper Business.

Edvinsson, L., & Malone, M. (1997). *Intellectual capital: Realizing your company's true value by finding its hidden brainpower.* New York: Harper Business.

Ehms, K., & Langen, M. (2003). *Holistic development of knowledge management with KMMM.* Positioning Paper on Workshop Bewertung von Wissensmanagement projekten.

Frappaulo, C., & Toms, W. (1997). Knowledge management: From terra incognita to terra firma. In J. W. Cortada & J. A. Woods (Eds.), *The knowledge management yearbook 1999–2000.* Boston: Butterworth Heinemann.

Gergen, J. (1991). *The saturated self.* New York: Basic Books.

Hansen, M., Nohria, N., & Tierney, T. (1999). What's your strategy for managing knowledge? *Harvard Business Review,* (March–April): 106–116.

Hedlund, G., & Nonaka, I. (1993). Models of knowledge management in the West and Japan. In B. Lorange, B. Chakravarthy, J. Roos, & H. Van de Ven (Eds.), *Implementing strategic processes, change, learning and cooperation.* London: Macmillan.

Heisig, P. (2000). Process modelling for knowledge management. In *Proceedings of the EKAW Workshop on Common Approaches on Knowledge Management, 12th International Conference on Knowledge Engineering and Knowledge Management.*

Holsapple, C. W., & Joshi, K. D. (1999). Description and analysis of existing knowledge management frameworks. In *Proceedings of the 32nd Hawaii International Conference on System Sciences.*

Holsapple, C. W., & Joshi, K. D. (1999). Knowledge selection: Concepts, issues, and technologies. In J. Liebowitz (Ed.), *Handbook on knowledge management.* Boca Raton, FL: CRC Press.

Holsapple, C. W., & Joshi, K. D. (2004). A formal knowledge management ontology: Conduct, activities, resources, and influences. *Journal of the American Society for Information Science and Technology, 55*(7), 593–612. doi:10.1002/asi.20007

Holsapple, C. W., & Joshi, K. D. (2004). Exploring primary activities of the knowledge chain. *Knowledge and Process Management, 11*(3), 155–174. doi:10.1002/kpm.200

Holsapple, C. W., & Joshi, K. D. (2004). A formal knowledge management ontology: Conduct, activities, resources, and influences. *Journal of the American Society for Information Science and Technology, 55*(7), 593–612. doi:10.1002/asi.20007

Holsapple, C. W., & Joshi, K. D. (2005). Exploring secondary activities of the knowledge chain. *Knowledge and Process Management, 12*(1), 3–31. doi:10.1002/kpm.219

Holsapple, C. W., & Singh, M. (2001). The knowledge chain model: Activities for competitiveness. *Expert Systems with Applications, 20*, 77–98. doi:10.1016/S0957-4174(00)00050-6

Huang, K. T. (1997). Capitalizing collective knowledge for winning, execution and teamwork. *Journal of Knowledge Management, 1*(2). doi:10.1108/EUM0000000004590

Ilgen, A. (2001). *Wissensmanagement im großanlagenbau. Ganzheitlicher ansatz und empirische prüfung.* Wiesbaden, Germany: Deutscher Universitätsverlag.

ISO. (2007). *Discover ISO - who standards benefit.* Retrieved December 2007, from http://www.iso.org

Jennex, M. (Ed.). (2005). *Case studies in knowledge management.* Hershey, PA: Idea Group Publishing.

Jennex, M., Olfman, L., & Pituma, P. (1998). An organizational memory information systems success model: An extension of DeLone and McLean's I/S success model. In *Proceedings of the 31st Annual Hawaii International Conference on System Sciences.*

Kankanhalli, A., & Tan, B. C. (2004). A review of metrics for knowledge management systems and knowledge management initiatives. In *Proceedings of the 37th Hawaii International Conference on System Sciences.*

Kim, Y. G., Yu, S. H., & Lee, J. H. (2003). Knowledge strategy planning: Methodology and case. *Expert Systems with Applications, 24*, 295–307. doi:10.1016/S0957-4174(02)00158-6

Krugman, P. (1991). Increasing returns and economic geography. *The Journal of Political Economy, 99*(3), 483–499. doi:10.1086/261763

Kucza, T. (2001). *Knowledge management process model.* Technical Research Centre of Finland, Finland: VTT Publications 455.

Lawton, G. (2001). Knowledge management: Ready for prime time? *IEEE Computer, 34*(2), 12–14.

Lucas, R. (1993). Making a miracle. *Econometrica, 61*(2), 251–272. doi:10.2307/2951551

Luu, N., Wykes, J., Williams, P., & Weir, T. (2001). *Invisible value: The case for measuring and reporting intellectual capital.* Canberra, Australia: Commonwealth of Australia, Department of Industry Science and Resources.

Maier, R. (2002). *Knowledge management systems: Information and communication technologies for knowledge management.* Berlin, Germany: Springer-Verlag.

Maier, R. (2002). State-of-practice of knowledge management systems: Results of an empirical study. *Upgrade, 3*(1), 15–23.

Maier, R., & Remus, U. (2003). Implementing process-oriented knowledge management strategies. *Journal of Knowledge Management, 7*(4), 62–74. doi:10.1108/13673270310492958

Malone, M. (1997). New metrics for a new age. *Forbes Magazine, 7*.

Marwick, A. (2001). Knowledge management technology. *IBM Systems Journal, 40*(4).

McAdam, R., & Reid, R. (2001). SME and large organization perceptions of knowledge management: comparisons and contrasts. *Journal of Knowledge Management, 5*(3), 231–241. doi:10.1108/13673270110400870

McElroy, M. (2002). *The new knowledge management, complexity, learning, and sustainable innovation.* Burlington, England: Butterworth-Heineman.

McInerney, C. (2002). Hot topics: Knowledge management – a practice still defining itself. *Bulletin of the American Society for Information Science, 28*(3), 14–15. doi:10.1002/bult.235

McLoughlin, H., & Thorpe, R. (1993). Action learning - a paradigm in emergence: The problems facing a challenge to traditional management education and development. *British Journal of Management, 4*, 19–27. doi:10.1111/j.1467-8551.1993.tb00158.x

Menon, A., Dekker, R., Oosterhof, J., & Oppelland, H. (1998). *Creating tomorrow's business: Managing knowledge.* Rotterdam, The Netherlands: Learning Center for Strategy and Entrepreneurship „le manageur".

Mentzas, G., Apostolou, D., Abecker, A., & Young, R. (2003). *Knowledge asset management: Beyond the process-centred and product-centred approaches.* London: Spinger-Verlag.

Nonaka, I., & Takeuchi, K. (1995). *The knowledge creating company: How Japanese companies create the dynamics of innovation.* Oxford, UK: Oxford University Press.

O'Dell, C., & Grayston, C. J. (1998). *If only we knew what we best know: The transfer of internal knowledge and best practice.* New York: The Free Press.

Peters, T. (1992). *Liberation management.* New York: Pan Books.

Petrash, G. (1996). Dow's Journey to a Knowledge Value Management Culture. *European Management Journal, 14*(4), 365–373. doi:10.1016/0263-2373(96)00023-0

Polanyi, M. (1967). *The tacit dimension.* New York: Doubleday.

Popper, K. (1994). *The myth of the framework: In defence of science and rationality.* London: Routledge.

Probst, G., Raub, S., & Romhard, K. (1997). *Wissen managen.* Wiesbaden, Germany: Gabler Verlag.

Prusak, L. (2001). Where did knowledge management come from? *IBM Systems Journal, 40*(4).

Quintas, P., Lefrere, P., & Jones, G. (1997). Knowledge management: A strategic agenda. *Journal of Long Range Planning, 30*(3), 385–391. doi:10.1016/S0024-6301(97)90252-1

Rastogi, P. N. (2000). Knowledge management and intellectual capital - the new virtuous reality of competitiveness. *Human Systems Management, 19*(1), 15–39.

Remus, U. (2002). *Prozessorientiertes wissensmanagement. Konzepte und modellierung.* Unpublished doctoral dissertation, Universitat Regensburg, Wirtschaftswissenschaftliche Fakultät.

Roos, J., Roos, G., Edvinsson, L., & Dragonetti, N. (1997). *Intellectual capital: Navigating in the new business landscape.* London: Macmillan Press.

Rosemann, M. a. (2000). Structuring and modeling knowledge in the context of enterprise resource planning. In *Proceedings of the Pacific Asia Conference on Information Systems,* Hong Kong, China.

Scarborough, H. (1996). *Business process redesign: The knowledge dimension.* Retrieved from http://bprc.warwick.ac.uk/rc-rep-8.1

Schreiber, G. A., de Hoog, R., Shadbolt, N., Van de Velde, W., & Wielinga, B. (1999). *Knowledge engineering and management: The CommonKADS methodology.* Cambridge, MA: The MIT Press.

Smirnov, A., Pashkin, M., Chilov, N., & Levashova, T. (2004). Knowledge logistics in information grid environment. *Future Generation Computer Systems, 20,* 61–79. doi:10.1016/S0167-739X(03)00165-1

Smirnov, A., Pashkin, M., Chilov, N., & Levashova, T. (2004). Knowledge logistics in information grid environment. *Future Generation Computer Systems, 20,* 61–79. doi:10.1016/S0167-739X(03)00165-1

Spender, J. C. (2003). Knowledge fields: Some post 9/11 thoughts about the knowledge-based theory of firm. In C. W. Holsapple (Ed.), *Handbook on knowledge management—knowledge matters* (pp. 59–71). Berlin, Germany: Springer-Verlag.

Sullivan, P. H. (1998). *Profiting from intellectual capital: Extracting Value from innovation.* New York: John Wiley & Sons.

Sveiby, K. (1997). *The new organizational wealth.* San Francisco: Berrett-Koehler.

Sveiby, K. (1998). Intellectual capital: thinking ahead. *Australian CPA, June,* 18-22.

Tannenbaum, S., & Alliger, G. (2000). *Knowledge management: Clarifying the key issues.* Paper presented at the IHRIM.

Taylor, (1997)... *International Journal of Technology Management, 11*(3), 385–391.

Taylor Small, C., & Tatalias, J. (2000). *Knowledge management model guides KM process.* Retrieved April 7, 2002, from http://www.mitre.org/news/the_edge/april_00/small.html

Tiwana, A. (2000). *The knowledge management toolkit: Practical techniques for building a knowledge management system.* Upper Saddle River, NJ: Prentice Hall.

Tsui, E. (2000). Exploring the KM toolbox. *Knowledge Management, 4*(2), 11–14.

van der Spek, R., & Spijkervet, A. (1997). Knowledge management: Dealing intelligently with knowledge. In J. Liebowitz & L. Wilcox (Eds.), *Knowledge management and its intergrative elements.* New York: CRC Press.

Vatter, W. J. (1947). *The fund theory of accounting and its implications for financial reports.* Chicago, IL: The University of Chicago Press.

Von Krogh, G. (1998). Care in knowledge creation. *California Management Review, 40*(3).

Von Krogh, G., Ichijo, K., & Nonaka, I. (2000). *Enabling knowledge creation.* Oxford, UK: Oxford University Press.

Weber, F., Wunram, M., Kemp, J., Pudlatz, M., & Bredehorst, B. (2002). Standardisation in knowledge management – towards a common KM framework in Europe. In *Towards Common Approaches & Standards in KM, Proceedings of the UNICOM Seminar,* London.

Weggeman, M. (1997). *Kennismanagement, inrichting es besturing vas kennisintensieve organisaties.* Schiedam, The Netherlands: Scriptum management.

Wiig, K. M. (1993). *Knowledge management foundations.* Arlington, VA: Schema Press.

Wiig, K. M. (1997). Knowledge management: Where did it come from and where will it go? *Expert Systems with Applications, 13*(1), 1–14. doi:10.1016/S0957-4174(97)00018-3

Wildner, S., Lehner, F., & Lehmann, H. (2007). Holistic approaches and standardisation as measures for broader adoption of KM in practice. In B. Martin & D. Remenyi (Ed.), *ECKM 2007 8th European Conference on Knowledge Management 2007, Volume Two* (pp. 1107-1114). Academic Conferences Limited.

Wilson, D. A. (1996). *Managing knowledge.* Oxford, UK: Butterworth Heinnmann.

Wilson, T. (2002). The nonsense of knowledge management. *Information Research, 8*(1).

Woods, E., & Sheina, M. (1999). *Knowledge management: Building the collaborative enterprise* (Report). London: Ovum Ltd.

ADDITIONAL READING

Bolisani, E. (Ed.). (2008). *Building the knowledge society on the Internet: Making value from information exchange.* Hershey, PA: Information Science Reference Collison, C., & Parcell, G. (2005). *Learning to fly: Practical knowledge management from leading and learning organizations.* UK: Capstone

Zack, M. H. (1999). Competing on knowledge. In *2000 handbook of business strategy* (pp. 81-88). New York: Faulkner & Gray.

Chapter 2
The Impact of Culture on the Application of the SECI Model

Markus Haag
University of Bedfordshire, UK

Yanqing Duan
University of Bedfordshire, UK

Brian Mathews
University of Bedfordshire, UK

ABSTRACT

The concept of culture and its relationship with Nonaka's SECI model, a widely used model of organizational knowledge creation, is discussed in this chapter. Culture, in various forms, is argued to impact on the SECI model and the model itself is embedded in a certain context. This context determines the characteristics of the knowledge creation modes as described by SECI and therefore makes the model either more, or less, pertinent in a given context. This is regardless of whether that context is primarily determined by national culture, organizational culture or other factors. Differences in emphases in a given contextual environment on either tacit or explicit knowledge also impacts on knowledge creation as defined by SECI. Finally, it is emphasized that being conscious of the cultural situatedness of the SECI model can lead to a more adequate use of the model for organizational knowledge creation.

INTRODUCTION

The objective of this chapter is to explore how the SECI model is influenced by, and relates to, the concept of culture at various levels. Cultural phenomena such as value orientations, and national, organizational, and other levels of culture arguably have an impact on the SECI model. Our main premise is that the SECI model – as other models

DOI: 10.4018/978-1-60566-790-4.ch002

and theories – was conceived in a particular cultural and value context. Thus, context shapes the model and determines how it can be applied in a different context, e.g. in a different culture, in a different organization or in a different department or team.

Knowledge and the ability to create new knowledge, share it and use it in organizational processes and routines is of paramount importance in order for organizations to survive in an increasingly competitive global marketplace (Nonaka & Toyama, 2003). In addition to sharing and applying existing knowledge, one of the key activities companies have to engage in is the creation of new knowledge through organizational learning (Argyris & Schön, 1978, 1996). Senge (2006) also emphasized the importance for organizations to engage constantly in learning.

Organizational knowledge creation has often been described using the SECI model (Socialization, Externalization, Combination, Internalization), first developed by Nonaka in 1991, and expanded and adapted further by, for example, Nonaka (1994), Nonaka & Takeuchi (1995), von Krogh, Ichijo & Nonaka (2000), and Takeuchi & Nonaka (2004). It is suggested here that it is worthwhile investigating this model from the point of view of culture in order to try to understand the model better and to make it more applicable and relevant across a wide variety of contexts. Furthermore, it is important to note that research into knowledge management has mostly been conducted in the Western world, particularly the USA, and therefore has a Western cultural bias to it (Pauleen, 2007). Applying a model which stems from a non-Western context can help to gain a fresh and different perspective on knowledge creation.

In order to discuss the cultural situatedness of the SECI model, we will start by addressing problems of defining the concepts of culture and values. Culture should not only be thought of as being primarily national, but one should also take other levels of culture into account as well. Then, the dichotomy of tacit and explicit knowledge, which is a central element of the SECI model, will be discussed and the SECI model itself described. It will be suggested that knowledge management itself and its tools and methods are determined and shaped by culture and a given situational context. The universal applicability of the SECI model and the impact of culture and context on knowledge creation and the SECI model and its applications in a business setting will be discussed. Focusing on three main levels of culture, rather than giving an exhaustive account of the many potential aspects of culture, we will explore a)

the national level using two of Hofstede's (1980, 1994) dimensions, b) organizational culture using two management practices of KEYS, a tool for assessing the climate for creativity in an organization (Amabile, Conti, Coon, Lazenby & Herron, 1996), and c) the individual-level values using two values of the Schwartz Value Survey (Schwartz, 1992, 1994). By way of example, we illustrate a range of potential impacts these three levels of culture can have on applying the SECI model in a business context. Finally, conclusions and suggestions for further research are given.

CULTURE AND VALUES

This section introduces the concept of culture, highlighting the importance of taking into account several levels of culture and provides a deliberately broad definition of culture for the purposes of this chapter. The concept of values will briefly be discussed since it is closely related to culture.

Arguably, culture determines behaviour in all areas of life. Behaviour does not take place in a vacuum, but is contextualized and situated in the concrete life-world of individuals (Lave & Wenger, 1991). There is a considerable number of cultural aspects that have been identified as influencing knowledge management (e.g. Ardichvili, Maurer, Li, Wentling & Stuedemann, 2006; Bhagat, Kedia, Harveston & Triandis, 2002; Carr-Chellman, 2005; Michailova & Hutchings, 2006; Yamazaki, 2005). All of these define culture as national culture. However, it is suggested here that *national* culture only accounts for some variations in behaviour across people, and that a more individualized and contextualized notion of culture is desirable. For example, Hofstede & Hofstede (2005) distinguish between six levels of culture: national, regional/ethnic/religious/ linguistic, gender, generation, social class and organizational or corporate. We suggest that all of these, depending on the situation and context, have the potential to determine behaviour to various degrees. In other words, in a particular situation gender differences could have a greater impact on the interaction and communication of people than differences in national culture. In turn, this means that it would be desirable to take into account all levels of culture as they are potentially important. Nevertheless, there appears to be no consensus on the relative impact or importance of the various levels of culture and so we therefore argue that it is counter-productive to provide a rank order as this would prevent having an open-minded and unbiased view of those levels of culture which are deemed to be less important in the hierarchy.

A substantial number of cultural value dimensions have been used to investigate the impact of national culture on behaviour, with Hofstede's dimensions arguably the most widely used (Hofstede, 1980, 1994; Hofstede & Hofstede, 2005). Nevertheless, as culture is such a complex and dynamic concept, these dimensions have often attracted criticism. Hofstede's dimensions have been criticized as not necessarily being exhaustive representations of national culture and not fully representing the wide variety of national cultures around the world (Schwartz, 1994). Furthermore, Schwartz (1994) criticizes that the IBM employees used in Hofstede's sample are not adequately representing the general population. Furthermore, Voronov & Singer (2002) voice criticism of the arguably most widely employed dimension of Hofstede, individualism-collectivism (Hofstede, 1994), concerning the reliability to distinguish cultures and describe them. Nevertheless, as Hofstede's dimensions have been widely applied world-wide (cf. Triandis, 1995) and are generally known to managers and entrepreneurs, this set of dimensions was chosen here to illustrate national culture and its relationship to knowledge creation. Some of the other cultural models that describe and categorize cultures are the value dimensions by Trompenaars (Trompenaars & Hampden-Turner, 1997), Hall's (1976) high context/low context distinction, among others.

It is not in the scope of this chapter to discuss and compare specific cultural values in depth. However, it is important to understand the concept of culture in general and the role of values in cross-cultural research and practice. For the purpose of this chapter culture is defined by using the broad definition by Hofstede & Hofstede (2005): [culture is] "the collective programming of the mind that distinguishes the members of one group or category of people from others" (p. 4). It is necessary to explain two notions of this definition, namely 'collective' and 'programming of the mind'. 'Collective' is a joint and shared experience of life within a particular social context shared with a particular group of people. Such a group of people can be the family, friends, colleagues, acquaintances, people from the same geographical region, people from the same country – other groupings are also possible. 'Programming of the mind' can be described as the whole of an individual's experiences in life that are interrelated and define her personal ideals, moral concepts and how things should be done.

The concept of values has been extensively used in researching and comparing behaviour across cultures. Rokeach (1973) states that a value is something that is personally or socially preferable. This distinction between personally preferable and socially preferable suggests that values are both held at an individual level and at a social/group/cultural level – hence the importance of taking into account both the concept of culture and values, rather than focusing on one concept only. One of the more well-known definitions of value orientations is Kluckhohn and Strodtbeck's (1961):

Value orientations are complex but definitely patterned (rank-ordered) principles, resulting from the transactional interplay of three analytically distinguishable elements of the evaluative process–the cognitive, the affective, and the directive elements–which give order and direction to the ever-flowing stream of human acts and thoughts as these relate to the solution of "common human problems". (Kluckhohn & Strodtbeck, 1961, p. 341)

After having introduced the first main topic area, culture and values, we will now move on to the second topic area and provide an overview of the concept of knowledge and the SECI model.

KNOWLEDGE AND THE SECI MODEL

The categorization of knowledge into tacit and explicit knowledge is only one of a large number of possible categorizations. We have to restrict our discussion to the tacit-explicit distinction, but the interested reader is referred to Lee, Foo & Goh (2006) who provide a discussion of several different types of knowledge, such as knowledge as an object or as a process, among others. In order to understand properly the functioning of the SECI model it is essential to know where these concepts come from, what they mean and, in particular, how they are used by Nonaka & Takeuchi (1995) in the context of SECI.

Tacit knowledge is considered to be a "cultural, emotional, and cognitive background, of which we are only marginally aware" (Stenmark, 2001, p. 10). Nonaka & Konno (1998) argue that there are two dimensions of tacit knowledge: a technical dimension which involves personal skills and is referred to as know-how, and a cognitive dimension which "consists of beliefs, ideals, values, schemata, and mental models which are deeply ingrained in us and which we often take for granted" (p. 42).

According to Nonaka (1991), explicit knowledge is knowledge that can be expressed, codified, stored in databases or as text in books or articles, transferred, shared and managed by knowledge management tools. In contrast, Nonaka (1991) defines tacit knowledge as highly personal, hard to formalize and, as a consequence, difficult to

communicate, transfer or share. He suggests that tacit knowledge is deeply linked and only relevant in a specific context (Nonaka, 1991). As culture is arguably one of the prime determinants of context, tacit knowledge itself is shaped by culture as well, be it the national cultural background of the employees or the organizational culture of the firm. He goes on to say that tacit knowledge consists of both technical skills or know-how and of taken-for-granted mental models and beliefs (Nonaka, 1991).

It is important to note that Nonaka (1991) does not regard tacit and explicit knowledge as opposed, separate and mutually exclusive, but as mutually complementary entities. In other words, knowledge is *not* either completely tacit nor completely explicit. This is in line with Johnson, Lorenz & Lundvall (2002) who suggest that tacit knowledge and explicit knowledge should be regarded as being complementary rather than in contradiction with each other. Knowledge at the extreme explicit side of the continuum should therefore be called information rather than knowledge as it does not require a particular context and situation to be given meaning. For example, a verbalized account of the specifications of a machine may be called information even if there is no concrete context or *ba* present. If these specifications are read by an engineer, made sense of and used to assemble this machine, we do have a concrete context and *ba* and the information becomes knowledge. Therefore, when applying the SECI model or when modelling knowledge creation and conversion processes using the model, one should be aware that in some situations or contexts, there is a strong emphasis on the explicit end of the knowledge type continuum, whereas in other contexts the emphasis is on the tacit end.

Hildreth & Kimble (2002) criticize the Externalization phase of SECI arguing that, if tacit knowledge cannot be articulated, then it cannot be made explicit, i.e. externalized. They propose a duality of knowledge in which all knowledge is both 'hard' and 'soft' (more explicit rather than tacit and more tacit rather than explicit) at the same time, with a varying degree of hardness and softness (Hildreth & Kimble, 2002). This seems to be a useful way of avoiding the mutual exclusiveness of tacit and explicit knowledge in which the two types of knowledge are seen as being at the extreme ends of a continuum. Tsoukas (2003) argues that they are "not the two ends of a continuum but the two sides of the same coin: even the most explicit kind of knowledge is underlain by tacit knowledge" (p. 425). Furthermore, externalizing or making explicit of fully tacit knowledge is by definition not only not possible, but not necessary – as Tsoukas (2003) suggests that it is essential "to find new ways of talking, fresh forms of interacting, and novel ways of distinguishing and connecting" (p. 426) rather than externalize tacit knowledge.

Socialization is defined as a "process of sharing experiences and thereby creating tacit knowledge such as shared mental models and technical skills" (Nonaka & Takeuchi, 1995, p. 62). In this mode, knowledge is acquired mainly by observation, imitation and learning by doing, similar to an apprenticeship (Nickols, 2000). Let us take the example of learning how to ride a bicycle. It is essential for the learner to observe how somebody rides a bicycle. This gives the learner an initial idea how to do it herself. This is the conversion process from tacit knowledge to tacit knowledge.

Externalization as a knowledge conversion mode is "typically seen in the process of concept creation and is triggered by dialogue or collective reflection" (Nonaka & Takeuchi, 1995, p. 64). The person who already knows how to ride a bike can explain it to the learner via dialogue, for example, explaining the importance of keeping balance. This is the conversion process from tacit knowledge to explicit knowledge.

Combination as a knowledge conversion mode "involves combining different bodies of explicit knowledge" (Nonaka & Takeuchi, 1995, p. 67). This is done by individuals exchanging and combining this knowledge in the forms such as documents. Combining texts about how to ride a bike with drawings that illustrate it is one example. This is the conversion process from explicit to explicit knowledge.

Internalization is defined as the process in which knowledge becomes valuable when "[it] is internalized in individuals' tacit knowledge bases through shared mental models or technical know-how" (Nonaka, Toyama & Byosière, 2001, p. 497), and it is closely related to learning by doing (Nonaka & Takeuchi, 1995). Practising riding a bike will give the learner more and more confidence and she will be in control of the bike more and more. Thus, knowledge and skills become embedded into an individual's mind and are used by her in daily routines in a specific context. This is the conversion process from explicit to tacit knowledge.

Nonaka & Konno (1998) introduced the concept of *ba*, which they consider "to be a shared space that serves as a foundation for knowledge creation" (p. 40). *Ba* is the place and cultural context for learning according to Lave & Wenger's (1991) notion of 'situated learning', thus making it a suitable concept for investigating learning processes. Nonaka & Konno (1998) also argue that *ba* provides "a platform for advancing individual and/or collective knowledge" (p. 40).

The terms of the four *ba* are as follows: originating *ba* for the Socialization mode, interacting *ba* for the Externalization mode, cyber *ba* for the Combination mode, and exercising *ba* for the Internalization mode. However, other terms have been used for the Externalization mode, namely dialoguing *ba* and for the Combination mode, namely Systemizing *ba*. All four *ba* are briefly defined here:

In the originating *ba* of the Socialization mode, tacit knowledge is being shared. It is a context where feelings, emotions and mental models are shared and it relies heavily on direct face-to-face interaction. It is also a place from where trust among peers can develop (Nonaka, Toyama & Byosière, 2001).

In the interacting *ba* or dialoguing *ba* of the Externalization mode, "individuals' mental models and skills are converted into common terms and concepts" (Nonaka, Toyama & Byosière, 2001, p. 500) through dialogue and reflection.

Systemizing *ba* or cyber *ba* of the Combination mode is virtual rather than set in real time and space and it is where new explicit knowledge is created through combining elements of other explicit knowledge. It can be facilitated by information technology and online collaborative environments and particularly involves group-to-group interaction (Nonaka, Toyama & Byosière, 2001).

Finally, exercising *ba* of the Internalization mode relies on "continuous learning and self-refinement through on-the-job training or peripheral and active participation" (Nonaka, Toyama & Byosière, 2001, p. 501).

Figure 1 shows the four SECI modes and their corresponding *ba*.

In addition to the level of the four SECI modes and the corresponding *ba*, the model was further expanded and enriched by the concept of knowledge assets. Nonaka, Toyama & Byosière (2001) defined assets as "firm-specific resources that are indispensable to the creation of values for the firm, and many researchers today agree that knowledge is precisely such an asset" (p. 501). They categorize knowledge assets into four groups: experiential knowledge assets are shared tacit knowledge through joint experiences such as individual skills and know-how. Conceptual knowledge assets, then, are "explicit knowledge articulated as concepts through images, symbols, and language" (Nonaka, Toyama & Byosière, 2001, p. 502) such as brand equity, product designs or product concepts. Systemic knowledge assets are explicit knowledge in the form of documents, patents, licenses, manuals, etc., and are therefore transferable relatively easily. Finally, they identi-

Figure 1. SECI modes and corresponding ba (Adapted from Nonaka & Konno, 1998, p. 46)

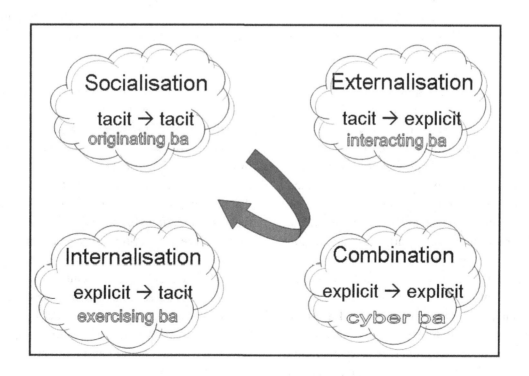

fied so-called routine knowledge assets, which are "tacit knowledge that is routinized and embedded within the actions and practices of an organization" (Nonaka, Toyama & Byosière, 2001, p. 502). Organizational culture, routines and know-how of the day-to-day work fall into this category.

The SECI model is popular and widely used by researchers into knowledge management and knowledge creation, but there are few reports by practitioners of how they applied the model and its four modes. However, this is not necessarily a weakness of the model itself, but suggests that the concepts involved in the model may be difficult to apply and research. This chapter cannot provide a thorough critical evaluation of the SECI model, but for criticism concerning the empirical basis of the model, the reader is referred to Gourlay (2004). We believe that the strength of the SECI model is that it brings together a wide variety of important concepts in knowledge creation: the two types of knowledge – tacit and explicit –, *ba* as the context of knowledge creation, and the four modes of knowledge conversion. It is also a process model thereby outlining what actually *happens* in knowledge creation rather than only describing what is involved. This focus on processes is a prerequisite for individuals to understand knowledge creation and their own role in it.

The more abstract additions to SECI, such as *ba*, make the model even more challenging to implement and use in an organization. There are no ready-made guidelines on how to model concrete processes of knowledge creation and conversion within an organization onto one of the four modes of SECI. In our opinion, however, the distinction between tacit and explicit knowledge and the emphasis on the importance of interaction between these two types of knowledge are very helpful for organizations as they are encouraged to try to establish an inventory of their knowledge (What tacit and explicit knowledge do we have?) as well as emphasize the importance of the knowledge conversion processes, often involving interpersonal interaction (What happens with our

knowledge and how is this mirrored by the four modes?).

We also suggest that a 'pre-mode' to the four SECI modes, not being part of the knowledge creation spiral itself but acting as a place for an explicit analysis of culture at various levels prior to exploring the various knowledge conversion modes is useful for organizations as they are thus more aware of cultural influences on knowledge creation so that they can take actions and possibly adopt the SECI model or create sub-models.

In 2003 Nonaka & Toyama incorporated dialectic thinking into the SECI model. They see "knowledge creation as a dialectical process, in which various contradictions are synthesized through dynamic interactions among individuals, the organization, and the environment" (Nonaka & Toyama, 2003, p. 2). This conceptual addition to the model points further to the importance of culture when it comes to applying SECI and to the constituting characteristic of context for knowledge creation. Nonaka & Toyama (2003) themselves note that "the same reality can be viewed differently depending on from which angle (context) one sees it" (p. 3). Furthermore, it is important to note here that knowledge is not created within one's mind totally detached from the environment, but by an individual's "actions and interactions with the environment" (Nonaka & Toyama, 2003, p. 4).

As we have seen, culture is an important determinant and creator of this context – *ba* is co-created by culture. It is important to note that culture does not need to be a separate aspect of the model, but that the idea of a 'pre-mode' which advocates that members of an organization or team should first analyze how culture influences knowledge creation and conversion within the particular context they are in. The insights gained by this 'pre-mode' enables one to better understand how the four knowledge conversion modes operate in a particular situation and context and, consequently, how knowledge creation and innovation can be more effectively fostered and facilitated.

CULTURAL SITUATEDNESS OF KNOWLEDGE MANAGEMENT AND THE SECI MODEL

After having introduced all the relevant concepts in the previous section, we will explore a range of the cross-cultural differences in knowledge management. Then, the cultural origin of the SECI model will be described and its universal applicability discussed.

Culture and Knowledge Management

On an epistemological level, Nisbett, Peng, Choi & Norenzayan (2001) suggest that the differences that exist among cultures have an influence on theories of knowledge and on what can be labelled as knowledge and also determine cognitive processes (Nisbett, 2003). Nisbett et al. (2001) suggest therefore that "the cognitive processes triggered by a given situation may not be so universal as generally supposed, or so divorced from content, or so independent of the particular character of thought that distinguishes one human group from another" (p. 307). In an experiment reported in Nisbett (2003), people from Asian and Western cultures had to decide which two of the three words 'panda', 'monkey' and 'banana' should be grouped together. Most Asians linked monkey with banana, most Westerners linked panda with monkey. This suggests that Westerners are more likely to perceive the world in categories (pandas and monkeys are both animals), whereas Asians are more likely emphasize relationships (monkeys eat bananas). In a heterogeneous team consisting of members of several cultures, these cognitive differences can have both advantages and disadvantages. On the one hand, perceiving the world in different ways presumably hampers interaction and communication within a team as obstacles are being created by different ways of thinking. On the other hand, bringing different styles of thinking and perception into a team can potentially lead to finding more than one possible solution to a problem or to increased creativity and innovation through a mutual challenge of one's own ways of thinking and working.

These differences in cognitive processes are important to note here, as differences in cognition are based on different tacit background knowledge (Viale & Pozzali, 2007) and will affect how knowledge is regarded, which in turn affects knowledge management and knowledge creation.

Zhu (2004) claims that knowledge management is not a universal concept, but argues that it is essential to jointly construct and share cross-cultural contexts for knowledge management to be successful. He posits that knowledge management "will benefit not from a universal concept, but from an interactionist strategy that facilitates the construction, connection and sharing of cross-cultural contexts, through which cultural differences and diversity are important sources for [knowledge management] competence rather than obstacles to be overcome" (p. 67). The suggestion that knowledge management is not a universal concept is supported by Begoña Lloria (2008). In her categorization, she distinguishes between models that fall into a knowledge-based theory of the firm, intellectual capital models which are primarily European, knowledge creation models which are primarily Japanese and knowledge management models which are primarily from the USA and are further sub-divided into models from an academic and from a consultancy perspective (Begoña Lloria, 2008). This suggests that the SECI model as a model of knowledge creation is indeed situated in a particular context and may be used differently in other contexts.

Being part of a community of practice (Wenger, 1998) in a shared context (Lave & Wenger, 1991) facilitates direct interaction with, or observation of, peers and is therefore an effective way of tapping into the tacit knowledge of others. The concept of 'communities of practice' (Wenger, 1998) provides further evidence of the situatedness and highly contextualized nature of knowledge management in general and organizational learning in particular.

Wenger (2004) defines communities of practice as "social structures that focus on knowledge and explicitly enable the management of knowledge to be placed in the hands of practitioners" (p. 2). *Ba* and communities of practice are thus related concepts. However, there are some differences that are worthwhile mentioning here:

While a community of practice is a place where the members learn knowledge that is embedded in the community, ba is a place where new knowledge is created. While a community of practice has an identity and its boundary is firmly set by the task, culture, and history of the community, the boundary of ba is fluid and can be changed quickly, as it is set by the participants. While the membership of a community is fairly stable, and it takes time for a new participant to learn about the community to become a full participant, the membership of ba is not fixed; participants come and go. Ba is created, functions, and disappears according to need. Whereas members of a community of practice belong to the community, participants of ba relate to the ba. Ba has a 'here and now' quality as does an emerging relationship, and is constantly moving as the contexts of participants and/or the membership of ba change. While learning occurs in any community of practice, ba needs energy to become an active ba where knowledge is created. (Nonaka & Toyama, 2003, p. 7)

Various levels of culture shape a community of practice. For example, organizational cultural characteristics as to what style of interaction between employee and superordinate is acceptable are mirrored in the – largely implicit – rules of communicating within a particular community of practice. Belonging to different professional cultures can cause problems in the communication with others in a community of practice: in preparing a product launch, marketing professionals emphasize other aspects of that product than engineers would do. We argue that it is essential that the members of a community of practice are aware of the impact of various levels of culture on the implicit rules and characteristics of the community. Culture at its various levels, the particular context of the 'here and now' in which the community is embedded and the characteristics of the individual community members all make up the communities of practice culture.

Discussion of the Universal Applicability of the SECI Model

It is argued that the SECI model (Nonaka, 1991, 1994; Nonaka & Takeuchi, 1995) is a contextualized model, embedded and shaped by context. Nonaka & Konno (1998) adapted the concept of *ba*, which they consider "to be a shared space that serves as a foundation for knowledge creation" (p. 40). This shared space also points to the 'cultural situatedness' of the SECI model as it suggests that contexts have to be shared with others who have a similar understanding of the situation in order to be meaningful to them – and members of a different culture often have quite different understandings of the same situation. Therefore, it is often more difficult to use a *ba* as a shared space for knowledge creation, because that shared space may be interpreted differently by members of different cultures, thus leading to problems in knowledge creation.

Glisby & Holden (2003) criticized SECI and posited that it is not universally applicable because it stems from a particular context, in this case from a Japanese context. Some researchers, for example Li & Gao (2003), claimed that the term 'tacit' is used differently from Polanyi's (1966) work. Weir & Hutchings (2005) acknowledge that the SECI model is not universally applicable, but also suggest that SECI does have some relevance to knowledge management cross-culturally. We suggest that SECI can be applied in a variety of contexts, as long as its origin and cultural situatedness are kept in mind and as long as it is adapted and modified accordingly in order to be relevant for the purpose for which it is applied.

Roy & Gupta (2007) examined the suitability of the SECI model in describing knowledge processes in product development of a small Indian company. They found that the knowledge conversion modes of SECI are not adequately represented in the manufacturing firm that they observed. Thus, they argue that the SECI model cannot be applied universally due to its embeddedness in Japanese business contexts (Roy & Gupta, 2007). They base their report on one particular case and therefore on one particular context, making it difficult to even speculate whether a) the idiosyncrasies of the reported company, b) the cultural value context or c) other factors have a decisive impact on the reported non-universality of SECI. In the case of India as a country with a large variety of ethnic groups and sub-cultures, making any predictions of why the SECI model may be less relevant in this context than in the Japanese context in which it was developed is even more difficult.

APPLYING THE SECI MODEL: THE ROLE OF CULTURE AND CONTEXT

In this section, we will discuss the impact of culture and context on knowledge creation and suggest how the SECI model can be applied to reflect on knowledge creation in a business setting and to analyze it. In order to do this, the four knowledge conversion modes will be examined separately. Afterwards, we will show how others have adapted the SECI model to either make it more suitable for a different context or apply it at an individual level rather than at the organizational level for which it was originally developed.

Knowledge Creation: The Impact of Culture and Context

Although the SECI model was originally conceived as a model of organizational knowledge creation involving the individual, teams and the organization as a whole, SECI is a useful anal-

ogy for learning at an individual level. Let us take a computer software course as an example: Employees learn how to use a new version of a software not only through reading teaching materials handed out by their trainer in a conventional software course, but they may learn far more by merely observing other colleagues who have already been using that version for quite some time. Furthermore, experimenting with the new software and learning by doing, using it in a context which is relevant for a particular employee, are also ways of learning to use the software. As we can see in this example, several SECI modes are involved in describing these learning processes.

The SECI model can also help to stress the importance of interaction in informal knowledge processes (Hoe, 2006). Whereas formal and structured knowledge processes take place in an organization, it is particularly the informal and largely unstructured knowledge processes that are essential for tacit knowledge to be shared. It is therefore important that an organization does not hamper spontaneous talks in the copier room, but create opportunities for colleagues to interact with each other without the restricting structure of formal meetings involving an agenda.

We believe that it is possible for an organization to facilitate and manage the context and climate of tacit knowledge sharing. Through a review of the literature, McAdam, Mason & McCrory (2007) identified a number of sub-types or epitomes of tacit knowledge which make the concept of tacit knowledge easier to operationalize in a business setting. They list the following epitomes of tacit knowledge: intuition, skills, insight, know-how, beliefs, mental models, and practical intelligence (McAdam, Mason & McCrory, 2007). When businesses use these epitomes as categories to explore their 'tacit knowledge inventory' it will be easier for them to grasp and detect this tacit knowledge.

As we have seen above, Tsoukas (2003) strongly recommends not to try to mechanically convert and 'translate' tacit knowledge into explicit knowledge but argues in favour of fostering social interaction as a means of 'accessing' tacit knowledge. Although Nonaka & Takeuchi (1995) argue in favour of a conversion of tacit and explicit knowledge so that knowledge creation can take place, Tsoukas's (2003) emphasis on interpersonal interaction as a facilitator of making tacit knowledge at least partly explicit is to be welcomed. To put it another way: "New knowledge comes about not when the tacit becomes explicit, but when our skilled performance is punctuated in new ways through social interaction" (Tsoukas, 2003, p. 410). Nurturing a culture and climate of knowledge sharing, discussion and informal interactions at the workplace is essential for making use of tacit knowledge. This may seem inefficient and leading nowhere to an outside observer, but it can be a powerful way of tapping into tacit knowledge.

Culture and the Four SECI Modes

The purpose of this section is to introduce some elements of culture at various levels and explore their relationship with and impact on knowledge conversion via the four SECI modes. We argue that there is no established procedure to analyze culture taking it into account in order to make knowledge creation more effective and efficient. It is essential to be aware of the impact that culture can have on the four SECI modes and to be open-minded in the analysis of the context in which knowledge is created within an organization as a whole or a team.

Different levels of culture can impact on context and thus influence knowledge creation and knowledge conversion processes of the four SECI modes. Hofstede & Hofstede (2005) suggested six levels of culture, namely national, regional/ethnic/religious/linguistic, gender, generation, social class and organizational or corporate. In this chapter, we will focus on national culture and organizational culture as these two levels may be the most important ones in knowledge creation and most of the research has been done in these two

areas. In addition to this, individual-level values (e.g. Schwartz, 1992, 1994) as the third level of culture which impacts on context and, in the end, knowledge creation, should be included.

In order to explore the impact of national and organizational culture and individual-level values on knowledge conversion within the four SECI modes, we chose elements of Hofstede's (1980, 1994) set of cultural dimensions, the KEYS: Assessing the Climate for Creativity tool (Amabile et al., 1996), and some of the individual-level values of the Schwartz Value Survey (Schwartz, 1992). On the basis of these frameworks that describe culture, we will provide some examples of how cross-cultural differences can have an impact on the SECI modes and what this means for applying SECI in a business context. It is important to note that this is not an exhaustive list, but exemplars to illustrate the cultural situatedness of the SECI model and of knowledge creation.

Hofstede (1980, 1994) developed several cultural value dimensions. His individualism-collectivism dichotomy has been widely used and applied in research to date and is arguably the most widely used dimension of Hofstede's set of values (Schwartz, 1994). Hofstede (1994) defines individualism as "[pertaining] to societies in which the ties between individuals are loose: everyone is expected to look after himself or herself and his or her immediate family" (p. 51). Collectivism, on the other hand, "pertains to societies in which people from birth onwards are integrated into strong, cohesive ingroups, which throughout people's lifetime continue to protect them in exchange for unquestioning loyalty" (Hofstede, 1994, p. 51). Prototypical examples of countries that score high on individualism are the USA and the UK, whereas several South American countries score high on collectivism (Hofstede, 1994). In addition to individualism-collectivism, we employ the power distance dimension as another important aspect of cross-cultural differences at a national level (Hofstede, 1994). Power distance is defined as "the extent to which the less powerful members of institutions and organizations within a country expect and accept that power is distributed unequally" (Hofstede, 1994, p. 28). Malaysia and some Central American countries score high on power distance, whereas Austria and Scandinavia score particularly low (Hofstede, 1994). We will now look at knowledge creation processes of the four SECI modes from the perspective of these two value dimensions.

Socialization as a knowledge conversion mode is closely connected with group processes and organizational culture (Takeuchi & Nonaka, 2004). Although scoring medium on the individualism-collectivism scale, Japan is certainly more collectivist than, say, the US (Hofstede, 1994). In the Socialization mode, the relatively strong group-think mentality in Japan favouring members of one's ingroup is likely to create difficulties in inter-organizational knowledge transfer, whereas knowledge transfer among teams of one's own organization is likely to be more effective (Hofstede, 1994). From a power distance perspective, cultures that score low on power distance are more likely to support an open and non-threatening environment for brainstorming than cultures that score high on power distance.

Externalization typically involves concept creation and is facilitated by dialogue and collective reflection (Takeuchi & Nonaka, 2004). When going back to the two value dimensions we have just introduced, there do not seem to be substantial differences in knowledge conversion from the perspective of individualism-collectivism and power distance. However, differences are more obvious in the Combination mode.

The Combination mode by definition focuses on explicit knowledge only. Japanese companies focus more on tacit knowledge, whereas organizations in Western cultures focus more on explicit knowledge (Takeuchi & Nonaka, 2004). It is important to keep in mind that cognitive processes differ across cultures (Nisbett et al., 2001). These differences may explain that American companies, for example, put a very strong emphasis on the

Combination mode and on explicit knowledge or information, whereas Japanese companies do not. In general, it is difficult to decide whether cross-cultural differences in knowledge creation are caused by differing cognitive processes, national culture or organizational culture. Presumably, all levels can potentially be involved and are likely to be interdependent and differ in salience according to context.

Finally, as the Internalization mode is closely linked to learning by doing and to actually applying knowledge and skills, it is arguably closely influenced by the local context of a specific organization rather than by national cultural values.

Let us now move on to organizational culture. There are several ways to operationalize organizational cultures (Ashkanasy, Wilderom & Peterson, 2000), but, by way of example, we have chosen the KEYS: Assessing the Climate for Creativity tool (Amabile et al., 1996) because it examines creativity within an organization and is thus closely linked to the concept of knowledge creation.

KEYS includes scales that are positively related to creativity and called stimulant scales and scales that are negatively related to creativity and called obstacle scales (Amabile et al., 1996). The conceptual categories underlying these scales stem from a review of previous research and from a critical incidents study investigating creativity (Amabile, 1988). The KEYS instrument assesses the following six practices that encourage creativity: organizational encouragement, supervisory encouragement, work group supports, sufficient resources, challenging work, and freedom. It also assesses two practices that inhibit creativity, namely organizational impediments, and workload pressure (Amabile et al., 1996).

We have chosen two of these categories as examples to illustrate how these categories can impact on knowledge creation and the SECI model. Let us first consider Sufficient Resources as a category for encouraging creativity. The category of Sufficient Resources is about "access to appropriate resources, including funds, materials, facilities, and information" (Amabile et al., 1996, p. 1166). This can have an impact on all four SECI modes, as resources can mean having an appropriate infrastructure for informal meetings which would foster and facilitate knowledge conversion in the Socialization and Externalization modes. Having sufficient access to information is a typical example of the Combination mode as it is in this mode in which information is being combined. Finally, having an adequate infrastructure and environment contributes to a more effective and efficient learning by doing in the Internalization mode.

Organization Impediments is one of the two categories of KEYS which inhibits creativity (Amabile et al., 1996). It is defined as "an organizational culture that impedes creativity through internal political problems, harsh criticism of new ideas, destructive internal competition, an avoidance of risk, and an overemphasis on the status quo" (Amabile et al., 1996, p. 1166). For example, in terms of the Socialization mode, destructive internal competition may mean that people are not willing to share their knowledge with new colleagues as they may feel they are in an overly competitive environment, not trusting other colleagues (Alavi, Kayworth & Leidner, 2006), and therefore not wanting to share their expertise. Moreover, harsh criticism of new ideas by superordinates or peers will make employees wary of sharing ideas in the Externalization mode as the context for sharing ideas is likely to be a threatening rather than an encouraging environment. In terms of the Combination mode, destructive internal competition could lead to information hoarding and employees will be reluctant to pass information on to others. Finally, in the Internalization mode, an avoidance of risk will lead to a low tolerance for mistakes in learning by doing.

The final perspective that we want to take here is the perspective of individual-level values, based on the Schwartz Value Survey (Schwartz, 1992, 1994; Schwartz & Bilsky, 1987, 1990). This value set conceives individual values as both the product of a shared culture and a product of an

individual's experience (Schwartz, 1994). It not only identifies the values as such, but specifies a circular structure of relations among – and oppositions between – them (Schwartz, 1992). As with the examples involving Hofstede's dimensions and KEYS, we will use the values of Power and Benevolence from the Schwartz Value Survey to illustrate how individual-level value differences can have an impact on the four knowledge conversion modes.

Power is about "social status and prestige, control or dominance over people and resources" (Schwartz, Melech, Lehmann, Burgess, Harris & Owens, 2001, p. 521). In the Socialization mode, the direct sharing of experiences among colleagues may be hampered by employees who score high on Power, because they may not be willing to share knowledge with others, as they believe this could lead to a loss of power within the company. In the Externalization mode, in the dialogue involved in it, employees who score high on power may use ambiguous concepts and metaphors in order to avoid having to share knowledge in a meaningful way. In the Combination mode, information hoarding may be a strategy of an employee scoring high on Power. Finally, in the Internalization mode, the individual-level value of Power does not seem to have a direct effect, as Power is about a certain power relationship with others, whereas Internalization is closely linked to an individual only (Takeuchi & Nonaka, 2004).

Benevolence is about "preservation and enhancement of the welfare of people with whom one is in frequent personal contact" (Schwartz et al., 2001, p. 521). In the Socialization mode, if the giver of knowledge scores high on Benevolence, he or she is likely to be willing to share knowledge and closely working together with the receiver of knowledge. People scoring high on Benevolence are also likely to invest considerable time and effort to make knowledge explicit in the Externalization mode and thus support their colleagues. In the Combination mode, information is not hoarded, but shared, sometimes to such an extent that there

Table 1. Examples of impact on the four SECI modes: Hofstede, organizational culture via KEYS and Schwartz Value Survey

	Hofstede	Organizational culture: KEYS	Schwartz Value Survey
Socialization	Ingroup favouritism by cultures high on collectivism, potentially creating barriers for inter-organizational knowledge transfer Freer and less threatening environment for brainstorming in cultures scoring low on power distance	Sufficient resources: Appropriate infrastructure for informal meetings which would foster and facilitate knowledge conversion Destructive internal competition: employees are not willing to share knowledge because of distrust of colleagues	Scoring high on Power: reluctant to share knowledge due to fear of losing power Scoring high on Benevolence: likely to be willing to share knowledge and closely working together with the receiver of knowledge
Externalization	Few differences expected from the perspective of individualism-collectivism and power distance	Sufficient resources: Appropriate infrastructure for informal meetings which would foster and facilitate knowledge conversion Harsh criticism of new ideas will make employees wary of sharing ideas	Scoring high on Power: employees may use ambiguous concepts and metaphors to avoid sharing knowledge in any meaningful way Scoring high on Benevolence: likely to invest considerable time and effort to make knowledge explicit and thus support their colleagues
Combination	Western cultures have a stronger focus on Combination than Eastern cultures	Sufficient resources: Having appropriate access to information Destructive internal competition could lead to information hoarding	Scoring high on Power: information hoarding Scoring high on Benevolence: information is not hoarded, but shared, sometimes leading to information overkill
Internalization	Heavily depending on a concrete context and situation, therefore less likely to be heavily influenced by national culture only	Sufficient resources: Adequate infrastructure and environment contributes to more effective and efficient learning by doing Risk avoidance will lead to a low tolerance for mistakes in learning by doing	Scoring high on Power: unlikely to have a direct effect, as Power is about a power relationship with others, not linked to an individual's mind Scoring high on Benevolence: analogous to scoring high on Power

could be an information overkill. In the Internalization mode, analogous to Power, Benevolence does not seem to have a direct effect because it is about a certain relationship with others rather than closely linked to an individual.

Table 1 summarizes how some of Hofstede's dimensions (Hofstede, 1980, 1994), elements of organizational culture via KEYS (Amabile et al., 1996), and some individual-level values of the Schwartz Value Survey (Schwartz, 1992, 1994) impact on the four SECI modes and their corresponding *ba*. The table can only begin to outline some hypothetical examples; other examples and scenarios are certainly possible. In our opinion, it is worthwhile to empirically test and explore some of them in order to better understand how certain levels of culture impact on knowledge conversion processes in the four SECI modes.

There are, however, other differences, even quite substantial ones, in how Japanese and

Western companies approach knowledge creation. Western organizations often focus on explicit knowledge which is easy to store and to transmit, whereas Japanese organizations put a higher emphasis on tacit knowledge, arguing that knowledge is primarily tacit and highly situated and contextualized (Takeuchi & Nonaka, 2004). This fundamental difference in cognitive processes (Nisbett, 2003) suggests that Japanese companies may emphasize the importance of the Socialization mode, because they see "sharing and creating tacit knowledge through direct experience" (Takeuchi & Nonaka, 2004, p. 9) as essential for successful knowledge creation. Companies from the West, however, are likely to focus primarily on the Combination mode, as this is strongly about explicit knowledge and about "systemizing and applying explicit knowledge and information" (Takeuchi & Nonaka, 2004, p. 9). However, it is important to note that Nisbett (2003) suggests that a Westerner does not necessarily focus strongly on categorizing the world around her, but can fall in the middle between a Western focus on categorizing and an Eastern focus on relationships. This depends on the personality of the individual and on the concrete situation and context. Yet, in a multicultural team, it is essential to be aware of potential differences regarding the importance that people put on the knowledge conversion modes. In order to accommodate these differences managers may want to encourage Easterners within a team to put a stronger emphasis on explicit knowledge and therefore the Combination mode. At the same time, Westerners could benefit from a more implicit and experiential approach to knowledge creation. However, depending on the characteristics of the team and its context, managers might prefer not to accommodate these differences between Westerners and Easterners as these cognitive differences can potentially lead to more creativity and innovation. Discussing openly the different foci on either explicit knowledge and Combination or on implicit knowledge and Socialization can make the team members aware of how the others tick and enable them to see aspects of a situation or problem that they had not thought about before.

Modified Versions of the SECI Model: Adapting to Context

The SECI model may need modification in order to incorporate culture more explicitly and to reflect the impact of culture on knowledge creation more fully. This section gives examples of how others have adapted the SECI model to either make it more suitable for a different domain or apply it at an individual level rather than at an organizational level for which it was originally intended.

In the context of research into scaffolding mechanisms in e-learning environments, Bryceson (2007a, 2007b) proposed a model of knowledge acquisition in e-learning environments called ESCIE,

which is based on the SECI model. The acronym represents the five stages of the model: explicitization, socialization, combination, internalization, and externalization. The e-learning cycle begins with the making explicit (Explicitization) of the lecturer's knowledge of the course contents. In the second phase, Socialization, students then discuss their ideas in an online forum, and they combine various pieces of information such as the discussion postings, texts, videos, etc. (Combination). Internalization of new knowledge is the next step, and, finally, this internalized knowledge can be made external again (Externalization) through report writing (Bryceson, 2007a).

Albeit not modified to account for cultural differences, the ESCIE model (Bryceson, 2007a) is one example of how a model is adapted and changed to make it more suitable and useful for a particular domain. Analogous to the ESCIE model which starts with the explicitization mode in which the lecturer presents the course contents, the SECI model can be modified by adding a 'culturization' mode. This 'culturization' mode would not be part of the knowledge creation spiral but would act as a framework in which companies can analyze how culture at various levels manifests itself in their organization and what impact these cultural factors could have on knowledge creation. After having done this cultural assessment in the 'culturization' mode, the four SECI modes can be applied and adapted accordingly, if necessary.

Chatti, Klamma, Jarke & Naeve (2007) reported another application of the SECI model in the context of Web 2.0. As both SECI and the concept of Web 2.0 rely on community and collaboration, they argued that Web 2.0 features can be modelled onto the four SECI modes. Thus, they proposed a convergence of learning, knowledge management and Web 2.0 features. For example, they regard communities and networks as pertaining to the Socialization mode, blogs, wikis and chat as pertaining to the Externalization mode, RSS feeds and social bookmarking as pertaining to the Combination mode, and learning by doing as pertaining to the Internalization mode (Chatti et al., 2007). This is a good example of the adaptability of SECI into related domains, away from organizational knowledge creation. It also focuses on the individual level of learning processes rather than organizational knowledge creation and learning. Yet another example of applying the SECI model in research in technology-mediated communication with a particular focus on virtual *ba* is presented by Saari, Laarni, Ravaja, Kallinen & Turpeinen (2004).

The examples of adaptations of the SECI model mentioned above illustrate the usefulness of the SECI model by either applying the complete model, adapting it, or applying some selected parts of it in other domains and for other purposes. The inconsistencies and difficulties in defining key elements of SECI – particularly tacit knowledge and *ba* – make it difficult to describe SECI conceptually and employ it in academic research projects. However, when it comes to applying SECI in business settings and contexts, these difficulties and shortcomings, may be regarded as a blessing in disguise: Practitioners who apply the SECI model for their own purposes in a business setting feel less restricted by the definitions of the concepts of the model and are therefore freer to use parts of the model in a modified way.

SUGGESTIONS FOR FURTHER RESEARCH

Throughout the chapter, we have raised a variety of issues concerning the cultural situatedness of the SECI model and the importance of context for using the model appropriately in an organization. The examples mentioned in Table 1 act as a starting point and preliminary ideas for further research. Unfortunately, there is a distinct lack of reports and case studies dealing with implementing the SECI model and using it for organizational knowledge creation. In our opinion, the merit of SECI is its

theoretical basis that it provides that can potentially be used in practice. Rice & Rice (2005) point out that empirical research involving the SECI model is made difficult by the philosophical nature of concepts such as *ba*. Another problem is the difficulty to clearly delineate between explicit and tacit knowledge, making statistical testing difficult (Rice & Rice, 2005). There is a lack of empirical research into *ba* (Rice & Rice, 2005) but this would be very worthwhile as getting an insight into how *ba* works and should be facilitated in order to maximize knowledge creation is central to a thorough understanding of the SECI model.

Therefore, comparative or multiple-case studies (Yin, 2003) into how specific organizations apply the SECI model for their own purposes would be useful. That way, comparisons of how the model is used and how useful and helpful this is for the particular context of the company can be made. If cases are chosen in the same industry and the same country, organizational or individual factors are likely to cause any observed differences. If subsidiaries in various countries are chosen, national culture arguably has a greater potential impact. These comparisons can be conducted at various levels, the most important levels arguably being national culture, organizational culture, and professional culture. If SECI was generally considered useful in a Japanese context but much less so in an American context, one could argue that SECI focuses too strongly on tacit knowledge to be useful in a culture that places a higher emphasis on codified knowledge.

Although the SECI model was originally developed for examining knowledge creation within an organization, its application should not be limited to this context. For example, researchers could explore how the SECI model can be adapted to examine *personal* knowledge development processes and the impact of culture and values in a given learning or working environment. As Web 2.0 technologies enable people to establish and maintain various forms of online communities which aim to facilitate social interaction and information and knowledge sharing, any attempt to apply the SECI model in order to study knowledge creation within an online community would help to develop a better understanding of the sustainability of online communities and their contributions to knowledge creation and sharing for a much wider community of Internet users.

CONCLUSION

We have started the chapter by discussing one of the most notoriously difficult to explain concepts: culture. It was suggested that the concept be defined in a very broad way, including several levels of culture such as national, organizational, professional and others. The SECI model and *ba*, a physical and virtual space and context for knowledge creation, was explained and we suggested that SECI as a model is culturally situated because it stems from a particular cultural context. Not only is the model itself culturally situated, but the knowledge creation processes and modes that it describes are themselves strongly influenced and shaped by culture and cultural values (Hofstede, 1994; Nisbett, 2003). We then offered some suggestions of how the SECI model can be applied in an organizational setting, before making suggestions for further research.

Various levels of culture influence and shape a particular context. In turn, context strongly influences the SECI model and its four knowledge conversion modes. This means that culture at its various levels impacts on organizational knowledge creation via context as a proxy. When examining organizational knowledge creation, the levels of culture that have the strongest impact on context and in the end on knowledge creation are arguably national culture and organizational culture. However, the importance of the impact of values at the individual level should not be underestimated. It is the dynamic interplay of these various levels, guided and determined by particular circumstances, that makes the concept of culture and its impact on organizational knowledge creation so difficult to explore and understand.

It is the varying salience and importance of cultural factors that make it difficult to map knowledge creation processes in an organization using the SECI model. However, we have shown that the SECI model can – and indeed should – be adapted in order to be successfully applied in different contexts. SECI has also been applied at an individual level rather than an organizational level and seems thus to be a useful tool to investigate both personal knowledge development and organizational knowledge creation. Adding a 'pre-mode' called 'culturization' to the four original SECI modes, which would act as a framework in which companies can analyze how culture at various levels manifests itself in their organization and what impact these cultural factors could have on knowledge creation, would make the SECI model more appropriate for use in a multicultural context. It must be said here, though, that culture is indeed a difficult to explain, difficult to grasp, and often elusive concept, which can mean a lot of things to different people in different situations. However, being aware of culture and its impact on knowledge creation and the application of the SECI model will enrich the insights of an organization into their knowledge creation and the processes involved in it.

Organizational knowledge creation is a difficult and complex process which requires effort and commitment from all employees within a company. The 'carrier of knowledge' *per se* is the individual, but it is possible to aggregate and share this knowledge with immediate colleagues and team members. However, a shared context is necessary for other members of a community of practice to make sense of this shared knowledge. That knowledge can then finally be embedded in organizational routines and processes. The SECI model or a version adapted to the needs of the organization can act as a useful starting point to explore knowledge creation.

REFERENCES

Alavi, M., Kayworth, T. R., & Leidner, D. E. (2006). An empirical examination of the influence of organizational culture on knowledge management practices. *Journal of Management Information Systems*, 22(3), 191–224. doi:10.2753/MIS0742-1222220307

Amabile, T. M. (1988). A model of creativity and innovation in organizations. In B. M. Staw & L. L. Cummings (Eds.), *Research in organizational behavior vol. 10* (pp. 123-167). Greenwich, CT: JAI Press.

Amabile, T. M., Conti, R., Coon, H., Lazenby, J., & Herron, M. (1996). Assessing the work environment for creativity. *Academy of Management Journal*, 39(5), 1154–1184. doi:10.2307/256995

Ardichvili, A., Maurer, M., Li, W., Wentling, T., & Stuedemann, R. (2006). Cultural influences on knowledge sharing through online communities of practice. *Journal of Knowledge Management*, 10(1), 94–107. doi:10.1108/13673270610650139

Argyris, C., & Schön, D. A. (1978). *Organizational learning: A theory of action perspective*. Reading, MA: Addison-Wesley.

Argyris, C., & Schön, D. A. (1996). *Organizational learning II: Theory, method, and practice*. Reading, MA: Addison-Wesley.

Ashkanasy, N. M., Wilderom, C. P. M., & Peterson, M. F. (Eds.). (2000). *The handbook of organizational culture and climate*. Thousand Oaks, CA: Sage.

Begoña Lloria, M. (2008). A review of the main approaches to knowledge management. *Knowledge Management Research & Practice*, 6, 77–89. doi:10.1057/palgrave.kmrp.8500164

Bhagat, R. S., Kedia, B. L., Harveston, P. D., & Triandis, H. C. (2002). Cultural variations in the cross-border transfer of organizational knowledge: An integrative framework. *Academy of Management Review*, 27(2), 204–221. doi:10.2307/4134352

Bryceson, K. (2007a). The online learning environment: A new model using social constructivism and the concept of 'Ba' as a theoretical framework. *Learning Environments Research*, 10(3), 189–206. doi:10.1007/s10984-007-9028-x

Bryceson, K. (2007b). SECI, BA, ESCI and VAG: Linking models of knowledge acquisition, elearning and online immersive worlds to create an innovative learning environment. In G. Richards (Ed.), *Proceedings of the World Conference on E-Learning in Corporate, Government, Healthcare, and Higher Education 2007* (pp. 2365-2372). Québec, Canada: AACE.

Carr-Chellman, A. A. (Ed.). (2005). *Global perspectives on e-learning: Rhetoric and reality*. Thousand Oaks, CA: Sage.

Chatti, M. A., Klamma, R., Jarke, M., & Naeve, A. (2007, July). *The Web 2.0 driven SECI model based learning process*. Paper presented at the 7th IEEE International Conference on Advanced Learning Technologies (ICALT 2007), Niigata, Japan.

Glisby, M., & Holden, N. J. (2003). Contextual constraints in knowledge management theory: The cultural embeddedness of Nonaka's knowledge-creating company. *Knowledge and Process Management*, 10(1), 29–36. doi:10.1002/kpm.158

Gourlay, S. (2004). *The SECI model of knowledge creation: Some empirical shortcomings*. Retrieved October 16, 2008, from http://kingston.eprints.org/2291/1/Gourlay%202004%20SECI.pdf

Hall, E. T. (1976). *Beyond culture*. New York: Doubleday.

Hildreth, P. M., & Kimble, C. (2002). The duality of knowledge. *Information Research, 8*(1). Retrieved August 15, 2008, from http://informationr.net/ir/8-1/paper142.html

Hoe, S. L. (2006). Tacit knowledge, Nonaka and Takeuchi SECI model and informal knowledge processes. *International Journal of Organization Theory and Behavior, 9*(4), 490–502.

Hofstede, G. (1980). *Culture's consequences: International differences in work-related values.* Beverly Hills, CA: Sage.

Hofstede, G. (1994). *Cultures and organizations: Software of the mind. Intercultural cooperation and its importance for survival.* London: HarperCollins.

Hofstede, G., & Hofstede, G. J. (2005). *Cultures and organizations: Software of the mind.* London: Harper Collins Business.

Johnson, B., Lorenz, E., & Lundvall, B.-Å. (2002). Why all this fuss about codified and tacit knowledge? *Industrial and Corporate Change, 11*(2), 245–262. doi:10.1093/icc/11.2.245

Kluckhohn, F. R., & Strodtbeck, F. L. (1961). *Variations in value orientations.* Evanston, IL: Row, Peterson and Company.

Lave, J., & Wenger, E. (1991). *Situated learning: Legitimate peripheral participation.* Cambridge, UK: Cambridge University Press.

Lee, C. K., Foo, S., & Goh, D. (2006). On the concept and types of knowledge. *Journal of Information & Knowledge Management, 5*(2), 151–163. doi:10.1142/S0219649206001402

Li, M., & Gao, F. (2003). Why Nonaka highlights tacit knowledge: A critical review. *Journal of Knowledge Management, 7*(4), 6–14. doi:10.1108/13673270310492903

McAdam, R., Mason, B., & McCrory, J. (2007). Exploring the dichotomies within the tacit knowledge literature: Towards a process of tacit knowing in organizations. *Journal of Knowledge Management, 11*(2), 43–59. doi:10.1108/13673270710738906

Michailova, S., & Hutchings, K. (2006). National cultural influences on knowledge sharing: A comparison of China and Russia. *Journal of Management Studies, 43*(3), 383–405. doi:10.1111/j.1467-6486.2006.00595.x

Nickols, F. W. (2000). The knowledge in knowledge management. In J. W. Cortada & J. A. Woods (Eds.), *The knowledge management yearbook 2000-2001* (pp. 12-21). Boston: Butterworth-Heinemann.

Nisbett, R. E. (2003). *The geography of thought: How Asians and Westerners think differently... and why.* New York: The Free Press.

Nisbett, R. E., Peng, K., Choi, I., & Norenzayan, A. (2001). Culture and systems of thought: Holistic vs. analytic cognition. *Psychological Review, 108*(2), 291–310. doi:10.1037/0033-295X.108.2.291

Nonaka, I. (1991). The knowledge-creating company. *Harvard Business Review, 69*(3), 96–104.

Nonaka, I. (1994). A dynamic theory of organizational knowledge creation. *Organization Science, 5*(1), 14–37. doi:10.1287/orsc.5.1.14

Nonaka, I., & Konno, I. (1998). The concept of 'Ba': Building a foundation for knowledge creation. *California Management Review, 40*(3), 40–54.

Nonaka, I., & Takeuchi, H. (1995). *The knowledge-creating company: How Japanese companies create the dynamics of innovation.* New York: Oxford University Press.

Nonaka, I., & Toyama, R. (2003). The knowledge-creating theory revisited: Knowledge creation as a synthesizing process. *Knowledge Management Research & Practice*, *1*(1), 2–10. doi:10.1057/palgrave.kmrp.8500001

Nonaka, I., Toyama, R., & Byosière, P. (2001). A theory of organizational knowledge creation: Understanding the dynamic process of creating knowledge. In M. Dierkes, A. Berthoin Antal, J. Child, & I. Nonaka (Eds.), *Handbook of organizational learning and knowledge* (pp. 491-517). Oxford, UK: Oxford University Press.

Pauleen, D. J. (Ed.). (2007). *Cross-cultural perspectives on knowledge management*. Westport, CT: Libraries Unlimited.

Polanyi, M. (1966). *The tacit dimension*. New York: Anchor Day Books.

Rice, J. L., & Rice, B. S. (2005). The applicability of the SECI model to multi-organisational endeavours: An integrative review. *International Journal of Organisational Behaviour*, *9*(8), 671–682.

Rokeach, M. (1973). *The nature of human values*. New York: Free Press.

Roy, A., & Gupta, R. K. (2007). Knowledge processes in small manufacturing: Re-examining Nonaka and Takeuchis' model in the Indian context. *Journal of Entrepreneurship*, *16*(1), 77–93. doi:10.1177/097135570601600104

Saari, T., Laarni, J., Ravaja, N., Kallinen, K., & Turpeinen, M. (2004). Virtual ba and presence in facilitating learning from technology mediated organizational information flows. In *Presence 2004, Proceedings of the Seventh Annual International Workshop* (pp. 133-140). Retrieved August 12, 2008, from http://www.temple.edu/ispr/prev_conferences/proceedings/2004/Saari,%20Laarni,%20Ravaja,%20Kallinen,%20Turpeinen.pdf

Schwartz, S. H. (1992). Universals in the content and structure of values: Theoretical advances and empirical tests in 20 countries. In M. Zanna (Ed.), *Advances in experimental social psychology* (Vol. 25, pp. 1-65). New York: Academic Press.

Schwartz, S. H. (1994). Beyond individualism/collectivism: New cultural dimensions of values. In U. Kim, H. C. Triandis, C. Kagitcibasi, S.-C. Choi, & G. Yoon (Eds.), *Individualism and collectivism: Theory, method, and applications* (pp. 85-119). Thousand Oaks, CA: Sage.

Schwartz, S. H., & Bilsky, W. (1987). Toward a psychological structure of human values. *Journal of Personality and Social Psychology*, *53*, 550–562. doi:10.1037/0022-3514.53.3.550

Schwartz, S. H., & Bilsky, W. (1990). Toward a theory of the universal content and structure of values: Extensions and cross-cultural replications. *Journal of Personality and Social Psychology*, *58*, 878–891. doi:10.1037/0022-3514.58.5.878

Schwartz, S. H., Melech, G., Lehmann, A., Burgess, S., Harris, M., & Owens, V. (2001). Extending the cross-cultural validity of the theory of basic human values with a different method of measurement. *Journal of Cross-Cultural Psychology*, *32*(5), 519–542. doi:10.1177/0022022101032005001

Senge, P. M. (2006). *The fifth discipline: The art & practice of the learning organization*. New York: Currency Doubleday.

Stenmark, D. (2001). Leveraging tacit organizational knowledge. *Journal of Management Information Systems*, *17*(3), 9–24.

Takeuchi, H., & Nonaka, I. (Eds.). (2004). *Hitotsubashi on knowledge management*. Singapore: John Wiley & Sons.

Triandis, H. C. (1995). *Individualism and collectivism*. Boulder, CO: Westview Press.

Trompenaars, F., & Hampden-Turner, C. (1997). *Riding the waves of culture: Understanding cultural diversity in business*. London: Nicholas Brealey.

Tsoukas, H. (2003). Do we really understand tacit knowledge? In M. Easterby-Smith & M. A. Lyles (Eds.), *The Blackwell handbook of organizational learning and knowledge management* (pp. 410-427). Malden, MA: Blackwell.

Viale, R., & Pozzali, A. (2007). Cognitive aspects of tacit knowledge and cultural diversity. In L. Magnani & P. Li (Eds.), *Model-based reasoning in science, technology, and medicine* (pp. 229-244). Heidelberg, Germany: Springer.

von Krogh, G., Ichijo, K., & Nonaka, I. (2000). *Enabling knowledge creation: How to unlock the mystery of tacit knowledge and release the power of innovation*. Oxford, UK: Oxford University Press.

Voronov, M., & Singer, J. (2002). The myth of individualism-collectivism: A critical review. *The Journal of Social Psychology*, *142*(4), 461–480.

Weir, D., & Hutchings, K. (2005). Cultural embeddedness and contextual constraints: Knowledge sharing in Chinese and Arab cultures. *Knowledge and Process Management*, *12*(2), 89–98. doi:10.1002/kpm.222

Wenger, E. (1998). *Communities of practice: Learning, meaning, and identity*. Cambridge, UK: Cambridge University Press.

Wenger, E. (2004). Knowledge management as a doughnut: Shaping your knowledge strategy through communities of practice. *Ivey Business Journal, 2004*(January/February). Retrieved August 12, 2008, from http://www.iveybusinessjournal.com/view_article.asp?intArticle_ID=465

Yamazaki, Y. (2005). Learning styles and typologies of cultural differences: A theoretical and empirical comparison. *International Journal of Intercultural Relations*, *29*(5), 521–548. doi:10.1016/j.ijintrel.2005.07.006

Yin, R. K. (2003). *Case study research: Design and methods*. (3rd ed.). Thousand Oaks, CA: Sage.

Zhu, Z. (2004). Knowledge management: Towards a universal concept or cross-cultural contexts? *Knowledge Management Research & Practice*, *2*, 67–79. doi:10.1057/palgrave.kmrp.8500032

FURTHER READING

Alvesson, M. (2002). *Understanding organizational culture*. London: Sage.

Ang, Z., & Massingham, P. (2007). National culture and the standardization versus adaptation of knowledge management. *Journal of Knowledge Management*, *11*(2), 5–21. doi:10.1108/13673270710738889

Baumard, P. (1999). *Tacit knowledge in organizations*. London: Sage.

Bhatt, G. D. (2000). Organizing knowledge in the knowledge development cycle. *Journal of Knowledge Management*, *4*(1), 15–26. doi:10.1108/13673270010315371

Dana, L.-P., Korot, L., & Tovstiga, G. (2005). A cross-national comparison of knowledge management practices. *International Journal of Manpower*, *26*(1), 10–22. doi:10.1108/01437720510587244

Dierkes, M., Berthoin Antal, A., Child, J., & Nonaka, I. (Eds.). (2003). *Handbook of organizational learning and knowledge*. Oxford, UK: Oxford University Press.

Easterby-Smith, M., & Lyles, M. A. (Eds.). (2003). *The Blackwell handbook of organizational learning and knowledge management*. Malden, MA: Blackwell.

Frappaolo, C. (2008). Implicit knowledge. *Knowledge Management Research & Practice, 6*, 23–25. doi:10.1057/palgrave.kmrp.8500168

Gourlay, S. (2006). Towards conceptual clarity for 'tacit knowledge': A review of empirical studies. *Knowledge Management Research & Practice, 4*, 60–69. doi:10.1057/palgrave.kmrp.8500082

Holden, N. J. (2002). *Cross-cultural management: A knowledge management perspective*. Harlow, UK: Financial Times/Prentice Hall.

Jimes, C., & Lucardie, L. (2003). Reconsidering the tacit-explicit distinction: A move toward functional (tacit) knowledge management. *Electronic Journal of Knowledge Management, 1*(1), 23–32.

Nonaka, I., Toyama, R., & Konno, N. (2000). SECI, ba and leadership: A unified model of dynamic knowledge creation. *Long Range Planning, 33*(1), 5–34. doi:10.1016/S0024-6301(99)00115-6

Smith, P. B., & Schwartz, S. H. (1997). Values. In J. W. Berry, M. H. Segall, & C. Kagitcibasi (Eds.), *Handbook of cross-cultural psychology, vol. 3: Social behavior and applications* (2nd ed.) (pp. 77-118). Needham Heights, MA: Allyn & Bacon.

Vygotsky, L. S. (1978). *Mind in society: The development of higher psychological processes*. London: Harvard University Press.

Yi, J. (2006). Externalization of tacit knowledge in online environments. *International Journal on E-Learning, 5*(4), 663–674.

Chapter 3

Knowledge, Culture, and Cultural Impact on Knowledge Management:
Some Lessons for Researchers and Practitioners

Deogratias Harorimana
Southampton Solent University, UK

ABSTRACT

This chapter offers a taste of the ingredients for further debates that continue to emerge from within knowledge management communities. The author has identified the nuts and bolts of the debate encountered by managers who find themselves faced with high costs involved in breaking cultural barriers, and offers suggestions as to how these can be overcome. From an academic perspective, the author argues that successful knowledge creation and management comes from the combination of two schools of thought – social and technological - and that any considerations that sideline either of these will be wrong or may be hard to justify, when related to the claim of best practice and/or the rationale of quality delivery of the business case. The chapter argues that current organisational practices involving a strong emphasis on team work and the ability to use technologies dominate business operations hence, it is equally important to unblock the human factors that are likely to hinder people's interaction within a team as it is to keep to the minimum physical barriers and systems that may impede this exercise.

INTRODUCTION TO KNOWLEDGE

Although the debate on 'knowledge' has existed for centuries, dating back to Plato's (427- 348/347 BC)[1], definition of knowledge as "justified true belief", knowledge has been defined differently and there exists disagreement on what constitutes knowledge.

The Collins English Dictionary (1998:857) defined knowledge as:

"...(i) expertise, and skills acquired by a person through experience or education; the theoretical or practical understanding of a subject, (ii) what is known in a particular field or in total; facts and information or (iii) awareness or familiarity gained by experience of a fact or situation."

DOI: 10.4018/978-1-60566-790-4.ch003

Existing disagreements were underlined recently by scholars during the 9th European Academic Conference on Knowledge Management (2008) where scholars summed up the debate by arguing that *"there is no solid agreement on what KM is, nor even on what constitutes knowledge"* (Rees, 2008:1). Academics further argued that:

- Knowledge management is a cross-cutting issue, not a single subject domain
- To date there remains disagreement on methodologies, definitions and processes of research and working within knowledge and its management
- There are, however, emerging trends, but no new dominant approaches and methodologies regarding knowledge and its management,
- Within the limitations of agreement, there were shared grounds and common fundamentals.

Referring to the above aspects of knowledge management research, Bolissani (2008) shows that academics are in agreement on the types and composites of knowledge – and how knowledge transfer can be achieved (both by focusing on characteristics of codified and tacit knowledge). Codified knowledge is that which can be written down, stored and transmitted through material forms, as opposed to tacit knowledge which is by and large accepted as a form of experience which can be learnt though interaction and in action learning. Tacit knowledge cannot be written down (Polyani, 1966). From the broad discussion that will follow, the reader will discover that there is a need to think beyond the meanings different authors have taken forward regarding cultural implications on knowledge management issues. The main reason is because there are possibilities that discussing culture in written forms poses challenges that the debate itself can be limited by the contextual analysis as well as perspectives of the author. In any case however, there is a general

agreement that knowledge transfer and knowledge management are understood as the sharing of ideas, knowledge or experiences between a group of people, between units of a company, or between a company and its customers and vice versa. The authors accept that knowledge can be either tangible or intangible and knowledge transfer is therefore a process responsible for gathering, analysing, storing and sharing this knowledge within an organisation with the primary purpose of managing that knowledge to improve as to improve efficiency by reducing the need to self-repeat in the search through the existing knowledge.

The Types of Knowledge: A Cultural Perspective

Research into cultural implications for knowledge creation, its transfer and management cannot underestimate types of knowledge and how they fit into a broad contextual analysis of culture. The best classification of types of knowledge and how they relate to each other was identified by Lundvall and Johnson (1994). In their argument, Lundvall and Johnson (1994) differentiated between diverse kinds of knowledge which are important in the knowledge-based economy: know-what, know-why, know-how and know-who. For example, market prospecting for a new product or recruiting labour, and training staff has to use its know-how. The same is true for the skilled worker operating complicated machine tools. Know-how is typically a kind of knowledge developed and kept within the boundaries of an individual firm. One of the most important reasons for the formation of industrial networks is the need for firms to be able to share and combine elements of know-how. This is why known-who has become increasingly important. Know-who involves information about who knows what and who knows how to do what. It involves the formation of special social relationships which make it possible to get access and utilise the knowledge of experts efficiently. It is significant in economies where skills are widely dispersed because of a highly developed division of labour among organisations and experts. For the modern manager and organisation, it is important to use this kind of knowledge in response to the acceleration in the rate of change. The know-who kind of knowledge is internal to the organisation concerned to a higher degree than any other kind of knowledge.

Within the knowledge management research community, there is a shared belief that knowledge is about context and value for benefit. Knowledge is a much broader concept than information. Information is generally regarded as the know-what and know-why. The know-why is given important consideration because it sets the scene - the context of what is being done. The contextual element has been attached to the "why" - knowing-why entails unpacking the elements of human culture and behaviour, personal experiences and the environment which influenced the decision-making process. The context constitutes essential elements that the world tends to define as organisational, or based on culture and/or behaviour. Culture and behaviour are factors of predictability that are critical to and influential over how people forge relationships between each other - and ultimately, influence whether people can engage in knowledge sharing and transfer activities. As we accept that knowledge creation and transfer represent an essential step towards achieving competitive advantage (making use of knowledge for commercial ends), we can argue that the know-how and know-why knowledge represent the types of knowledge which are near to being market commodities or economic resources, and near to becoming integral to economic production functions. The transfer of know-how for example is widely thought to be the most prestigious resource for the business world. Know-why refers to the scientific knowledge of the principles and laws of nature and it underlies recent technological development advances in most industries. The production and reproduction of know-why is often organised in specialised organisations, such as research

laboratories and universities. To gain access to know-how, firms have to interact with each other and with organisations that own the know-how in order to access the special skills and identify the capabilities required to embed the know-how - if this can be successfully acquired.

This process of acquiring know-how leads to the much more serious question of knowing why. Know-why knowledge becomes a contextual form which supports the transfer of the know-how. It is the step which makes sense of the whole. Know-why represents sense-making, the predictability of an action and reaction to an action. Knowing how and why leads not to a completeness of the process, but rather leads into the next, equally important, question of what should be the next course of action? Or, in other words, what would be the best mechanism of transfer of this know-how knowledge? This involves an exploration of ideas for example as to whether the manual, written form (codification process) would a better mechanism than the one where people would be involved in knowledge transfer-as an interactive mechanism to access experiences - Gourlay (2006) calls this the transfer of tacit knowledge.

With regards to differentiating between the above two possible forms of knowledge transfer (codification or people's interaction) will assist in decision making, and therefore in answering the question of "knowing-who" to engage in order to access know how within its entirety or within a modified context. The "know-who" is rather more a tacit form of knowledge and will be more difficult to measure. The-"why" someone judges the most appropriate person to relate to is very subjective and difficult to objectively assess. The circumstances that lead to the final decision may be dependent on several interconnected factors such as relevance, cultural background of the parties and how they relate to each other, all of which have not been commonly agreed to-and can actually be subjected to academic debates. The "know-who" is therefore context-dependent and rarely relies on facts. The reference to facts however is classified as the know-what knowledge. Know-what refers to knowledge about facts. Here, knowledge is close to what is normally called information. In some complex areas, experts must have a lot of detailed information that makes up, if taken together, 'knowledge', which enables them to undertake their jobs.

Knowledge Has Been Associated With Competitive Advantage: But How Does This Fit With Culture and Beliefs?

There is a consensus among post industrial-age scholars on knowledge and its management in that knowledge represents a primary resource of organisations (Drucker, 1992). More recently, Birkinshaw (2001) told the knowledge management community that knowledge is a company's only enduring source of advantage in an increasingly competitive world. But this was not the first reference to this debate, it merely emphasised Drucker's (1994:9) argument that:

"...How well an individual, an organization, an industry, a country, does in acquiring and applying knowledge will become the key competitive factor. The knowledge society will inevitably become far more competitive than any society we have yet known - for the simple reason that with knowledge being universally accessible, there will be no excuses for non-performance..." and an addition to the Organization for Economic Development conclusion (1999:7) that showed that "...the role of knowledge (as compared with natural resources, physical capital and low-skill labor) [was taking on] greater importance [and that] though the pace may differ, all OECD economies [were] moving towards a knowledge-based economy".

The above observations reflect the importance of knowledge in achieving a competitive advantage. That said, the above reflections demonstrate the critical need for businesses to sharpen their

employees' ability to become knowledge workers, in order to stay at the competitive edge of business performance. To achieve this however, many businesses must be able to continuously innovate and identify potential for new product development. Such an activity can be achieved by regularly responding to the changing business climate and organisational behaviours; it involves being regularly engaged in knowledge creating, transferring, and exploitation. Such a demand continues to be an increasingly critical factor driving the survival and success of corporations, and of societies.

One of the debates that have continued to challenge scholars thus far is on the nature of knowledge itself which is ambiguous, subjective and likely to change due to bias within cultures, languages and environmental landscapes. For example, knowledge of local practices and cultures is often perceived as an essential element for a business to enter new market places. Other problems and challenges companies will continue to encounter are how to identify which type(s) of knowledge can be transferred and how to transfer those identified as more important than others; for example, while deploying an employee to a new market which is opening further afield may appear to be a feasible option, the practice is costly and there are human factors such as difference in cultures, behaviours and value-systems, which may be a source of mistrust between locals and the international expatriate.

The other option which may be used is that of documenting processes and requesting that local staff practice and implement these processes following the manuals provided. This practice is probably a cheaper way of transferring knowledge than the deployment of an experienced staff. It is a mechanism that isolates cultural factors; in other words, there are no requirements to understand the contextual background of that knowledge being implemented. What we are experiencing in business practice however is a combination of these two practices, by transferring experiences with a back-up of written standards in manuals. The ability of an institution to combine knowledge from different locations around the world (and therefore the ability to operate successfully in a multicultural environment) is becoming increasingly important as a determinant of competitive success. The implications for business are that those trading on the global stage are engaged with people from different cultures which are geographically dispersed, where people believe and work differently and where priorities are set according to knowledge of and exposure to the world's affairs, as well as operating within differing local dynamics. Linking the components of knowledge and local cultures, beliefs and values is key to the success of businesses in a globalised world economy.

Knowledge in Cultural Diversity

"Cultures heavily influence what is perceived as useful, important, or valid knowledge in an organization. Culture shapes what a group defines as relevant knowledge and this will directly affect which knowledge a unit focuses on" (De Long and Fahey, 2000: 113).

Williams *et al* (1998) argue that organisations are located in countries with differing cultural backgrounds; therefore a cross-cultural business relationship is influenced by the cultural background of the organisation. This is also the case for knowledge transfer issues. According to Simonin (1999) the central aspect that facilitates transfer of knowledge is the cultural and social background of the persons transferring and/or receiving knowledge. Knowledge itself, and consequently the use of knowledge, are deeply embedded in their cultural context. Organisations may be unable to see beyond their routines and customary practices (Williams *et al*, 1998). Despite the fact that research into knowledge transfer has intensified in recent years, it is rare

that organisations themselves are considered to have a cultural background; yet their employees do. Many studies of knowledge management do not engage with cultural issues on the issues related to organisational versus employee's culture when it comes to knowledge transfer. For example Argote and Ingram (2000) studied knowledge transfer by using organisational networks; Cumming and Teng (2003) studied knowledge transfer among and between R&D organisations; Zander and Kogut's (1996) empirical analysis studied the speed of knowledge transfer between organisations, and Szulanski's (1996) study focused on impediments to knowledge transfer practices in a firm. Szulanski's study identified the factors that make it easy or difficult to transfer knowledge; among others, the relationship between the source and the recipient. Simonin's (1999) study focused on inter-alliance knowledge transfer of marketing know-how. All these studies are concerned with cultural distance as a constraint on the transfer of knowledge but they do not specify whether this cultural distance applies to the different units of organisations or to different individuals within organisations.

Williams *et al* (1998) noted that the degree of cultural distance is considered one of the major obstacles to successful performance in cross-cultural business relationships. The main argument here is that common identity as opposed to the cultural distance between different groups impacts on knowledge sharing and transfer. Cultural distance is born out of culture-based factors that impede the flow of information between the firm and its partners, and it is also the case that cultural differences of employees of an international subsidiary for example may raise barriers to understanding between members of the same organisation despite similarities and other many forms of interactions and values that may make up a relationship between a company and its subsidiaries.

According to Simonin (1999), cultural barriers can even be found in a parent company with many cross-border subsidiaries where, despite several similarities, the success of such a multinational business depends by and large on the interpretation of local dynamics, culture and language. Such interpretations of local dynamics constitute a real ingredient of what the business practice is about, and what elements of knowledge one company values and focuses on more than others.

The indications here appear to be that the success of knowledge transfer across boundaries depends on the similarities that can be identified between partners (the source of the knowledge and the receiver of the knowledge). If we considered the cultural barriers as important, there would be an absolute necessity for business managers to align their business modelling with the cultural background within which they wish to trade. Understanding of the role culture plays in employee's performance and how it relate and /or impact the business is constitute an essential step towards positive results. Understanding how culture can influence business relationships however, requires an appropriate mind-set, a mindset which is ready to identify cultural challenges and recognise how the manifest within an organisation. Such a mindset will be a driver of the business towards a developed local approach to solve global challenges. Recognising the cultural barriers has other effects other than how business modelling and delivery can be done. For example an integration of cultural values within cross boundary businesses means that the former cannot easily (or successfully) network and share knowledge with their counterparts from different cultures and business practices. The question of how to break knowledge-sharing barriers therefore becomes an important one; a common approach is to seek an intermediary, a trust builder and/or a relationship broker. Within multinationals, there are existing mechanisms that make knowledge sharing possible - this is achieved through virtual Communities of Practice (CoPs).

The Communities of Practice concept was introduced as a form of group-based learning where people of similar interests and common goals meet to share ideas, learn new things from each other and advance organisational performance as a result of a desire to advance career goals (Lave and Wenger, 1991; Wenger, 1998). Within the organisation, Wenger (1998) argues that there is a need to link the process of learning, one's behaviour and the environment to allow CoPs to prioritize and value what they focus on.

Considering the process of learning as being central to human identity, a primary focus of Wenger's work (1998) was on learning as a form of social participation, where the individual was seen as an active participant in the practices of social communities, and constructing personal identity through the community's interaction. Although Lave and Wenger's (1991) and Wenger's (1998) work constitute a significant contribution towards our understanding of the concept of CoPs, their work lacked the consideration of an important factor which characterizes people's learning and knowledge sharing processes, that of cultural dynamics. By assuming that a CoP is homogenous, Lave and Wenger (1991), Wenger (1998) forgot that, when people meet for the purpose of learning and sharing knowledge, each one values one set of knowledge over another set, depending on one's background and experience. Within the organisational practices, knowledge sharing is best facilitated if the realities of CoPs are recognised, cultural similarities and values are identified and when the change process is designed.

Typifying Culture in an Organisation

In a study conducted within 15 high tech manufacturing and R&D industries, Harorimana (2008) demonstrated that the respondents in his research have argued that it is not possible to separate their cultural behaviours, either as individuals or as members of communities of practice because they were 'units' that add up to the whole of the community. The research found that institutional culture can be linked to the employees themselves while actually referring to the organisational culture. In the thesis, respondents were unable to distinguish between what the managers see and value within the organisation; first as individuals and second as organisational managers, responsible for upholding standards and accountable to their employer. This internal self-contradiction was higher within organisations that adopted a top-down culture. This is the type of organisation where managers hold different views and priorities which do not necessarily reflect the overall priorities of the large human resource composition of the company. This type of culture is generally closed to scrutiny and questioning; it is characterized by an instructional regime which is less flexible concerning - and less responsive to - the changing environment within which organisation exist and operates.

Another significant factor for knowledge managers to consider when they are working within the organisation is the process of cultural change. If an organisation is, for example, acquired by and merged with another organisation, both of which have previously worked differently or have different values, there are associated cultural changes and values that should be foreseen by the managers. For example, the recent work into cultural influence during organisational reform and change in four financial organisations showed that an organisation's culture can play a significant role in facilitating the change process (Harorimana, 2008). Harorimana's research required employees to make a judgment on where they found themselves when they had to face changes taking place in the organisations he studied as part of his doctoral thesis. Within two of the organisations, changes consisted of change in ownership (privatisation to foreign investors), and one to which structural changes related, while two others had seen the governance of the organisations handed over a system of shared responsibility between teams of foreign gatekeepers and indigenous owners. This shift had caused operational staff to respond to changes in the form of a shift in major strategic directions of the firms in question. The research also found that the lower the education level and

the experience in relevant work of the employee, the lower the resistance to change was, and the higher the flexibility for learning new ways of working and achieving results. Those who were classed as average (these were employee who are educated to degree level with a maximum of five years experience in their current jobs) were more open to learning new things and to change than their counterparts in higher categories. The later are employees with a Masters degree, are in generally in supervisory positions and have considerable experience of five years or more. These employees have decision making responsibilities over their junior counterparts defined above. People in this position have expressed greater contempt to organisational change, they tended to resist against shifts in new practices and in general sense, they prefer to maintain old practices. To succeed in cultural change such as this one, it is imperative for senior managers to effect change within middle management ranks before pushing change further down the ranks of operational and front desk staff.

THE KNOWLEDGE GATEKEEPER: A BROKER OF CULTURAL BARRIERS

It is accepted that in many cases, business dealings require an intermediary in the form of a relationship broker. In many cases this person, or gatekeeper, can serve as a trust builder within two distant groups or business communities. The gatekeeper is someone well informed who understands the context, the culture and the business practice of each of the parties who is seeking to enter into a business relationship. This person is also involved in many innovation and knowledge transfer projects.

The concept of knowledge gatekeeper came from Allen and Cohen (1969), who argued that a "gatekeeper" refers to a key person or a group of people who facilitate information transfer by informal communication means. They argued that the strategy used is that of intermediation, when organisations or companies seeking out gatekeepers with the aim of delivering information to parties who may not otherwise deal directly with, and between, each other. When the concept was first introduced, knowledge gatekeepers were considered as solely as those who have had an international exposure. Allen and Cohen (1969) described International Gatekeepers as those engineers or scientists who have worked in other countries and returned home. Their point was that engineers and scientists visiting from other countries have a high level of contact in the foreign arenas, but they would have insufficient domestic contact to be International Gatekeepers. Due to the changing business landscape however, the nature of the knowledge gatekeeper has evolved to include small groups within organisations, individuals who broker relationships and can build trust, and organisations that are acting as innovation catalysers, knowledge brokers and channels through which knowledge transfer can be facilitated by reducing cultural differences (Harorimana, 2008).

Although gatekeepers have been described by some as mediating individuals or knowledge brokers, not everyone agrees. Persson (1981) discusses Allen's studies of gatekeepers in research and development (R&D) organisations; he argues that Allen's flow model does not indicate with whom the gatekeeper is communicating, what is being discussed, or what effect the gatekeeper has on internal informal dissemination. Using an empirical study of an R&D organisation, Persson presented an argument that gatekeepers can contribute to an elitist pattern of distribution rather than to a reduction of the information gap. However, it is apparent from studies that followed that this view was not followed up any further, and that it has since been laid to rest leaving those questions that were being asked, as unanswered.

Aloni's (1985) literature survey demonstrates that the subject of gatekeepers has been mentioned only infrequently in the management literature

and abstracts of information science in the years leading up to 1985. There is no further reference to this beyond those dates in current literature in management sciences and its associated branches such as Knowledge Management. What Aloni's (1985) literature reveals is that even management scientists viewed informal information transfer as a special type of organisational communication arrangement. Such a view however does not warrant the conclusion that the gatekeepers' role is insignificant and that it should not form a strand of management studies.

For example, there is a growing confidence among researchers that knowledge gatekeepers are actually essential for business performance and delivering results. Probably, one of the most striking issues arising from this topic is the shift from the subject domain of the research. Initially conceptualisation of the knowledge gatekeeper seemed to be led by technology transfer (see Allen and Cohen, 1969, Allen 1970, 1977; Allen, 2006). Recent studies however do suggest a significant shift from perceptions of the subject as management and technology issues towards a new perspectives based on knowledge, competitive advantage and innovation (see Pinch *et al* 2003; Morrison, 2008; Harorimana, 2008, Allen, 2006) - a reflection of the changes in the business landscape where the environment and cultural changes in business interaction have been valued within the knowledge society.

Future Research Considerations

This journey to understanding cultural implication of knowledge sharing is a complex that is can hardly be studied to the completeness. The evidence pointed towards a two levels of significant influence on knowledge sharing. These were identified as Organisational (corporate) culture and employee's (individual) culture. Within organisations, there exists a visible corporate culture in the form of a symbolic system as well some sets of accepted fundamentals of a corporate worldview. But again, not all departments or divisions within the same organisation follow the same cultures, systems and way of working. We have therefore two important questions that need to be answered:

Within the same corporate, does the element of different cultural levels and categories have positive or negative impact on organisational performance and outputs? Are these differences measurable against the way knowledge sharing can be handled collectively and individually?

Moreover the above question, there is a problem of developing indices against which measuring cultural implications on knowledge sharing and transfer within organisations. From a methodological point of view, we have to competing views—the study of culture in itself is highly qualitative. However, the studies of organisation systems have tended to be highly quantitative. To date, within KM community, we are broadly lacking a systematic method that can be credible to serve as a reference point for the study of culture with the KM context.

By introducing the notion of corporate culture, we also recognise the role systems including computers, the system of corporate standards, and the system of corporate values, which all represent a significant role of knowledge management These systems are significant factors which have not been studied and no significant contribution in that regard we have. We, for example need to know if there, exist some rituals which are typical for a culture of structured knowledge-documentation within a department or an enterprise area. We need guidance principles and behavioural commands that lead to a culture in which employees consider and value their own knowledge within wider contexts including corporate benefits without fear of loosing one's power and competitiveness.

CONCLUSION

For many years now, the work of many scholars has continued to develop sets of definitions of "knowledge". Furthermore; studies of knowledge have continued to evolve depending on the school of thought being followed, which is derived either from a sociological background or technological developments. In this chapter, the author has identified the rationale of research into cultural implications for knowledge creation, sharing and management. This chapter sets the scene for the study of cultural implications for knowledge sharing and transfer and identifies the benefits of managing cultural change to business

The author of this chapter has defined knowledge and knowledge management from a knowledge based economy perspective. The author argued that culture in an organisation can be studied from two points of view, and levels; the individual and the organisational. At the individual level, culture influences what one perceives as useful and should be focussed on. Within the organisation, culture is perceived as a way of doing things, the way of life of an organisation. The author shows however that many managers within organisations may not necessarily identify themselves with the organisation overall; to such an extent that departments may set up their own priorities. Such practices maybe good indicators of luck of a shared understanding of organisational values and goals but more importantly, they represent potential areas of conflicts within employees as it maybe a indicator of lack of good relationships and team work culture within the organisation. From the management practice perspective, it is generally it is not possible for a manager within an organisation to separate from organisational values, culture and employees' behaviours. It is believed that organisational culture is not distinct from its employees' culture, because from one by one of many employees we arrive to the 'units' that adds up to the sum of the organisational valued asset-its staff. The chapter shows that institutional culture can be linked to the employees themselves even when people are actually referring to the organisational culture.

In breaking down cultural barriers, businesses are recommended to create a conducive environment for facilitating this, including fostering a responsive workforce which is flexible, and adopting a flatter organisational structure, where every employee can relate to the rest of the organisation. Communities of practice were identified as an important mechanism for creating harmony and reducing cultural barriers inside the organisation. Outside the organisation, knowledge gatekeepers were seen as the best mechanism for breaking barriers of culture. A knowledge gatekeeper can bring parties together; act as a knowledge broker and an information trafficker. Considering inter-organisational relationships, it is necessary to employ a trust-building agent who can is independent, well informed and ready to move back and forth along the business chain.

REFERENCES

Allen, S. (2006). *Geography and economy*. Oxford, UK: Oxford University Press.

Allen, T. J. (1970). Communication networks in R&D laboratories. *R & D Management, 1*(1), 14–21. doi:10.1111/j.1467-9310.1970.tb01193.x

Allen, T. J. (1977). *Managing the flow of technology: Technology transfer and the dissemination of technological information within the research and development organization*. Cambridge, MA: MIT Press.

Allen, T. J., & Cohen, S. I. (1969). Information flow in research and development laboratories. *Administrative Science Quarterly, 14*(1), 12–19. doi:10.2307/2391357

Aloni, M. (1985). Patterns of information transfer among engineers and applied scientists in complex organizations. *Scientometrics, 8*(5/6), 279–300. doi:10.1007/BF02018054

Argote, L., & Ingram, P. (2000). Knowledge transfer a basis for competitive advantage in firms. *Organizational Behavior and Human Decision Processes, 82*(1), 150–169. doi:10.1006/obhd.2000.2893

Birkinshaw, J. (2001). Why is knowledge management so difficult? *Business Strategy Review, 12*(1), 11–18. doi:10.1111/1467-8616.00161

Bollisani, E. (Ed.). (2008). *Building the knowledge society on the Internet: Sharing and exchanging knowledge in networked environments*. Hershey, PA: Information Science Reference.

Collins English dictionary (4th ed.). (1998). Glasgow, Scotland: Harper Collins.

Cummings, J. L., & Teng, B. S. (2003). Transferring R&D knowledge: The key factors affecting knowledge transfer success. *Journal of Engineering and Technology Management, 20*(1), 30–68. doi:10.1016/S0923-4748(03)00004-3

De Long, D. W., & Fahey, L. (2000). Diagnosing cultural barriers to knowledge management. *The Academy of Management Executive, 14*(4), 113–127.

De Long, D. W., & Fahey, L. (2000). Diagnosing cultural barriers to knowledge management. *The Academy of Management Executive, 14*(4), 113–127.

Drucker, P. (1994). The age of social transformation. [from http//www.providersedge.com/docs/leadership_articles/Age_of_Social_Transformation.pdf]. *Atlantic Monthly, 274*(5), 53–80. Retrieved March 2, 2007.

Drucker, P. F. (1992). The new society of organizations. *Harvard Business Review, 70*(5), 95–104.

Gourlay, S. (2006). Towards conceptual clarity for 'tacit knowledge': A review of empirical studies. *Knowledge Management Research and Practice, 4*(1), 60–69. doi:10.1057/palgrave.kmrp.8500082

Harorimana, D. (2007). Boundary spanners and networks of knowledge: Developing a knowledge creation and transfer model. In D. Remenyi (Ed.), *Proceedings of the Academic Conferences International* (pp. 430-435).

Harorimana, D. (2008). *An investigation into the role of gatekeepers in the knowledge transfer process: A study based on manufacturing high tech industries, financial and R&D Firms.* Unpublished doctoral thesis, Nottingham Trent University and Southampton Solent University, Southampton, UK

Harorimana, D. (2008). Leading firms as knowledge gatekeepers in a networked environment. In E. Bollisani (Ed.), *Building the knowledge society on the Internet: Sharing and exchanging knowledge in networked environments* (pp. 260-281). Hershey, PA: Information Science Reference.

Harorimana, D. (2008). Understanding the role of knowledge gatekeepers in knowledge identification, translation and transfer process: Some empirical evidences. In *Proceedings of the European Conference on Knowledge Management*, Southampton Solent University.

Kogut, B., & Zander, U. (1996). What firms do? Coordination, identity, and learning. *Organization Science, 7*(5), 502–518. doi:10.1287/orsc.7.5.502

Lave, J., & Wenger, E. (1991). *Situated learning legitimate peripheral participation.* Cambridge, UK: Cambridge University Press.

Lundvall, B.-Å., & Johnson, B. (1994). The learning economy. *Journal of Industry Studies, 2*, 23–42.

Morrison, A. (2008). Gatekeepers of knowledge within industrial districts: Who they are, how they interact. *Regional Studies, 42*(6), 817–835. doi:10.1080/00343400701654178

OECD. (1999). *The knowledge-based economy a set of facts and figures.* Paris: OECD.

Persson, O. (1981). Critical comments on the gatekeeper concept in science and technology. *R & D Management, 11*(1), 37–40. doi:10.1111/j.1467-9310.1981.tb00447.x

Pinch, S., Henry, N., Jenkins, M., & Tallman, S. (2003). From industrial districts to knowledge clusters a model of knowledge dissemination and competitive advantage in industrial agglomerations. *Journal of Economic Geography, 31*, 665–682.

Polanyi, M. (1966). The tacit dimension. New York: Doubleday and Co.

Rees, J. (2008). *Notes from summary of issues raised at ECKM 08.* Reading, UK: Academic Conference Ltd.

Simonin, B. L. (1999). Ambiguity and the process of knowledge transfer in strategic alliances. *Strategic Management Journal, 20*(7), 595–623. doi:10.1002/(SICI)1097-0266(199907)20:7<595::AID-SMJ47>3.0.CO;2-5

Szulanski, G. (1996). Exploring internal stickiness impediments to the transfer of best practice within the firm. *Strategic Management Journal, 17*, 27–43.

Wenger, E. (1998). Communities of practice: Learning as a social system. *Systems thinker, 9*(5).

Williams, J. D., Han, S.-L., & Qualls, W. J. (1998). A conceptual model and study of cross-cultural business relationships. *Journal of Business Research, 42*, 135–143. doi:10.1016/S0148-2963(97)00109-4

ENDNOTE

[1] There exists also disagreement on the exact date of Plato's birth, and different authors also argue over the date of the death of this philosopher who was under the mentorship of Socrates and Aristotle.

Chapter 4
Strategising Impression Management in Corporations:
Cultural Knowledge as Capital

Caroline Kamau
Southampton Solent University, UK

ABSTRACT

Impression management is a powerful psychological phenomenon with much unexplored potential in corporate settings. Employees or corporations can deploy impression management strategies in order to manipulate others' perceptions of them. Cultural knowledge is powerful capital in impression management, yet this has not been sufficiently explored in previous literature. This chapter argues that impression-motivated employees or corporations need to perform a three-step knowledge audit: (i) knowing what their impression deficits are; (ii) knowing what impression management strategy is needed to address that deficit, based on the taxonomy of impression management strategies tabulated here; (iii) knowing what societal (e.g. collectivist culture or individualist culture) or organization-specific cultural adjustments are needed. A cultural knowledge base can thus be created through cross-cultural training of and knowledge transfer by expatriates. Multinational corporations can also benefit from utilising the knowledge presented in this chapter in their international public relations efforts.

INTRODUCTION

The success of knowledge transfer often depends on incidental or subsidiary information accompanying the knowledge itself. Communication between humans usually involves nonverbal cues such as facial expressions, gestures, body posture, tone of voice, gaze, clothing style and use of props. Nonverbal cues

therefore have an important communicative function (DePaulo, 1992), such as in terms of conveying information on emotional states (Ekman & Friesen, 1971). An individual can strategically manipulate the nonverbal signals that they transmit through a process known as impression management or self presentation (Leary & Kowalski, 1990). Impression management is the strategic attempt to control how one is perceived by others in order to fulfil a deeper aim (Rosenfeld, Giacalone & Riordan, 1995), such

DOI: 10.4018/978-1-60566-790-4.ch004

as exuding competence in a particular knowledge field or being taken seriously as an expert. There is considerable evidence in organizational settings that impression management by employees can influence supervisors' ratings of them (Wayne & Liden, 1995; Vilela et al, 2007), increase chances of promotion (Westphal & Stern, 2007) and increase others' perceptions of ones credibility (Leigh & Summers, 2002). Individuals with knowledge on impression management strategies may therefore successfully utilise this knowledge to, for example, maximise their capacity to influence their organization's policies and practices. The success of impression management strategies depends on both societal cultural norms on appropriate social behaviour (DePaulo, 1992) and on organization-specific culture (Drory & Zaidman, 2007), as well as individual characteristics (Snyder, 1974).

Impression management in corporate settings has a lot of unexplored potential. This chapter begins by discussing nonverbal communication and compiling a taxonomy of impression management strategies typically used in corporate settings. Cultural knowledge relevant to impression management is an invaluable resource to individuals in corporate settings. This chapter explores the impact of societal cultural norms on workers' choices of impression management strategies, focussing on the contrast between collectivist cultures (e.g. the Far East) and individualist cultures (e.g. Western Europe and North America). The impact of organization-specific culture on employees' impression management strategies is then discussed. This chapter therefore argues that employees need to acquire a tacit or explicit knowledge base on impression management, and to perform an audit of their impression deficits, the impression management strategies required to resolve these deficits, and the adjustment in strategy needed to accommodate society or organizational cultural norms or individual difference variables. The benefits of cross-cultural adaptation by expatriates, based on fact-finding and the accumulation of knowledge through interactions, and cross-cultural training of expatriate employees, will then be discussed. Having explored impression management from the perspective of employees as individuals, this chapter then goes on to argue that multinational corporations should utilise the kind of knowledge presented in this chapter in their international public relations efforts. Ethical considerations for employees or corporations (concerning their choice of impression management strategy) are then discussed, after which further research questions will be outlined.

Theoretical Background: What is Impression Management?

Imagine that Gary, a new systems analyst at an IT department, wants to suggest a major restructuring of a large database. However, his seniors have a reputation for being resistant to change and they are usually hostile towards ideas generated by newcomers. Gary therefore needs to find a way of making his seniors more receptive towards him as a potential agent for change. Soon after joining the corporation, Gary frequently indicates that he agrees with his seniors' policies, he laughs generously at their jokes, he frequently does favours for them, and he regularly drops hints that he really admires them. Weeks later, Gary approaches his seniors and casually asks what they think about restructuring the database. Are his seniors likely to say no? Probably not – at least much less so than if Gary had not deployed the impression management strategy of ingratiation. Impression management is therefore a strategic attempt to influence others' perceptions or reactions in order to fulfil a personal objective (Leary & Kowalski, 1990), a social objective (Baumeister and Tice, 1986) or a material objective (Leary & Kowalski, 1990).

Based on Rosenfeld, Giacalone & Riordan's (1995) wide scale literature review, table 1 presents a taxonomy of impression management strategies that are widely used in corporate settings.

Impression management begins with "impression motivation" (Leary & Kowalski, 1990, pp 35), whereby a person tries to gauge what others think of them and they develop a desire to control this. Impression management therefore begins with the gathering of information that enables an individual to determine what strategy is needed and why. Leary & Kowalski (1990) suggest that "People deliberately search for cues regarding others' impressions of them and attend selectively to information that is relevant to making the right impression." (pp 36). An individual then needs to establish what their motive is. For instance, their desire may be personal – to fulfil an ambition or to construct or maintain a public identity, which is said by Baumeister & Tice (1986) to be a major motive behind impression management. Alternatively, the motive may be purely social – e.g. wanting to be liked or respected (Baumeister & Tice, 1986). Some employee ranks may be predisposed towards such social motives. For example, Palmer, Welker, Campbell & Magner's (2001) study of 95 middle/upper-level managers suggests that managers are predisposed towards impression management tactics that are concerned with gaining approval from employees. Another possible motive behind impression management is the quest for material gains (Leary & Kowalski, 1990) such as receiving a pay increase through promotion. Strategies such as ingratiation have been shown to successfully impact on liking (Vonk, 2002) and on employees' promotional chances Westphal & Stern, 2007, 2006). For instance, Westphal & Stern (2007) surveyed managers and CEOs at some of the Forbes 500 companies, and they found that deployment of ingratiatory tactics such as opinion conformity, doing favours and flattery increased the managers/CEOs' chances of being recommended for board appointments.

After the impression motivation stage is the "impression construction" stage (Leary & Kowalski, 1990, pp 35), whereby an individual deploys an impression management strategy (see table 1). This involves the enactment of behaviours that

fulfil the motive behind wanting to control others' impressions. People often use nonverbal behaviour in their impression management strategies, since much of human communication occurs without words (DePaulo, 1992). Such behaviour may be subtle, such as the use of gait and walking style to convey information on age, power and mood (Montepare & Zebrowitz-McArthur, 1988), or it may be more overt. For instance, a data clerk who has made many mistakes with data entry one afternoon may yawn a lot and drink coffee in order to give the impression that fatigue is the reason for the errors. However, not all impression management is exclusively nonverbal. In the previous example, fictitious Gary used both nonverbal behaviour (e.g. doing favours for his seniors) and verbal impression management tactics (e.g. saying that he agrees with them).

Overarching Argument: The Need for Integrated Knowledge About Impression Management in Corporate Settings

This chapter argues that knowing what impression management strategies there are, however, is not enough. Employees and/or corporations wishing to deploy impression management strategies must gain knowledge on a number of other important factors: cultural factors and individual difference variables. This is because the success of impression management attempts depends on general cultural norms (DePaulo, 1992), the culture of an organization (Drory & Zaidman, 2007) and on interpersonal or individual characteristics (Wayne & Liden, 1995). To date, literature integrating all these concepts (impression management in corporate settings, societal culture, organizational culture, individual differences) is lacking. For instance, relevant literature published in management journals (e.g. Liden & Mitchell, 1988; Westphal & Stern, 2007) tends to focus on workplace impression management strategies per se (particularly ingratiation). Relevant literature

Table 1. Taxonomy of impression management strategies commonly used in organizational settings*

Impression management strategy			Example
Ingratiation: colloquially referred to as "sucking up to" or "buttering up" someone with the expectation that one will be liked more	Ingratiation through opinion conformity	Agreement with some disagreement	Mary tells her dissertation supervisor how fantastic his recent article was, how original his thinking is and how similar it is to her own opinion, except for one minor detail.
		Transformation of disagreement into agreement	Samson's says that he disagrees with his project manager's new marketing plan but later in the meeting he starts nodding and saying that he now sees how wonderful the plan is.
	Ingratiation through doing favours	Ordinary favours	Matt offers to walk across town daily to collect his department director's favourite takeaway lunch.
		Favours that cannot be directly repaid	Lucy offers to baby-sit her manager's pets for a week during her vacation leave.
	Ingratiation through flattery	Flattery via third-parties	During an office party, Thomas tells his supervisor's husband that she has a fantastic, remarkable leadership style.
		Timely flattery	Several weeks before a promotions review, Myra tells her office manager how much she wishes that he could run the entire organization because he does such a great job.
Self-promotion: emphasising ones strong points with the expectation that listeners will have a high opinion of oneself	Self-promotion to show competence		Patrick often talks to his workmates about what he learned during his student days at the prestigious Harvard University.
	Self-promotion with some self-criticism		Betty tells her colleagues how lousy she is at golf but how quickly she can clinch a sale with any type of buyer.
	Self-promotion to compensate for weakness		After finding a new software package difficult to use, Henry tells workmates what a whiz he usually is with most computer programmes.
Intimidation: behaving in a threatening or cold manner in the hope that doing so will instil fear in others	Intimidation for downward influence		Rachel, the head chef, shouts and uses bad language at junior chefs who make a mistake.
	Intimidation for counter-power		Peter is a union activist and he threatens to get his union to alert the press about practices at the company if his supervisor makes him work on weekends.
Exemplification: behaving like a highly conscientious person, with the intention of making onlookers think highly of oneself	Exemplification through model behaviour		Her colleagues and supervisors always find Gertrude working at her desk, no matter how early they arrive in the morning.
	Exemplification through self-sacrifice		Charlie, a hotel worker, takes the shifts that other workers dislike and he does not take any days off during high season.
Supplication: belittling or criticising oneself in the hope of evoking liking from others	Supplication to evoke compassion		Melissa, who has just joined a theatre company, criticises herself often and says that she does not feel good enough to be an actor.
	Supplication through exchange		Oscar, a university researcher, talks about how bad he is at writing reports but offers to show a colleague how to analyse the data.
Indirectness: use of third parties to help one enact an impression management tactic (e.g. ingratiation, exemplification) or to increase ones own social standing	Indirect impression management through associations with others		Drew, a new associate professor of literature, talks often about his good friend the Pulitzer Prize winner.
	Indirect impression management through 'basking in reflected glory'		The day after their firm won a coveted regional award, employees wore t-shirts with the firm's name during weekends and non-working hours.
	Indirect impression management through boosting		Estate agents working at a company that was severely fined for malpractices tell people that their company is actually one of the best estate agents in the country.

continued on following page

Table 1. continued

Impression management strategy		Example
Acclamation: making a false or exaggerated positive claim to enhance ones image	Acclamation through claiming entitlement for positive outcomes	When sales of her company's newspaper trebled, writer Martha says that her articles contributed to the increase in copies bought.
	Acclamation through enhancement	When her marketing team received a commission from a successful local company, Frieda tells colleagues that the company is one of the most successful companies in the country.
Showing group loyalty: behaving in ways that display ones group identity so as to increase other group members' liking of oneself	Showing group loyalty through slating the disloyal	Esther, who works for a supermarket chain, shows dislike for employees who do not buy groceries at that supermarket chain.
	Showing group loyalty through perpetuating norms	Morris always carefully checks with colleagues what the organization's traditional policies and practices are, before doing anything.
Other nonverbal: Use of other nonverbal strategies or the manipulation of ones nonverbal behaviour to help fulfil an impression management aim.	Use of nonverbal status symbols	On his desk, stockbroker Stuart has a photo of himself holding a sports trophy, sailing on a yacht, and he wears expensive-looking clothing.
	Use of exaggerated nonverbal behaviour	Edna shows that she likes her new workplace by grinning a lot and laughing indulgently at any joke made by a colleague.
	Use of nonverbal behaviour to conform	Workers at a creative consultancy firm have a certain unspoken fashion code, which Ian mimics when he becomes an employee.

*This taxonomy of impression management strategies is based on the comprehensive literature review by Rosenfeld, Giacalone & Riordan (1995)

published in cross-cultural management journals (e.g. Richardson & McKenna, 2006) tends to focus on the role of societal culture per se in workplace impression management. Relevant literature published in human resources journals (e.g. Drory & Zaidman, 2007) tends to focus on the impact of organizational culture on choice of impression management strategies. Relevant literature published in psychological journals (e.g. DePaulo, 1992) tends to focus on the impact of individual difference variables on impression formation and impression management. This chapter therefore integrates these facets of knowledge about impression management in corporate settings, also presenting (later on in this chapter) an impression management knowledge audit model for impression-motivated employees or corporations to use.

Knowledge about Societal Culture and Impression Management

Firstly, let us explore the role of societal culture. The cultural norms of the target audience determine the appropriateness of particular impression management tactics particularly when employees are operating in new cultural settings. This is particularly evident if we consider the impact of cultural norms on the appropriateness of different impression management strategies when used in Far Eastern cultures, compared to Western cultures. The kinds of nonverbal communication that can be acceptably utilised vary from culture to culture, according to culturally-specific norms known as 'display rules' (Ekman & Davidson, 1994). Culturally-specific display rules determine the appropriateness of particular nonverbal behaviours and people therefore needs to know what a given culture's norms and display rules are:

"To use nonverbal behaviours successfully for self presentation, people need to have some basic knowledge ... of the kinds of nonverbal behaviours that are appropriate to use at particular times and in particular situations, and of the kinds of reactions and interpretations that particular nonverbal behaviours are likely to elicit from others. ...The abstract understanding of display rules ... is important." (DePaulo, 1992, pp 214)

In Far Eastern cultures, impression management in many social situations is governed by the notion of "face" or "saving face", which can be defined as the avoidance of social embarrassment or loss of dignity (Ting-Toomey, 1994). In Chinese culture, 'saving face' is termed *mien-tzu*, which denotes having propriety/respectability, social prestige and keeping a good reputation (Chang & Holt, 1994). The central role of the notion of 'face' in impression management in Far-Eastern cultures is likely to be due to the collectivistic nature of such cultures. Collectivism involves emphasis on group identity, group norms and group harmony over personal needs/identity (Triandis, 1989; Hofstede, 1980), with Far Eastern cultures being examples of collectivistic cultures (Markus & Kitayama, 1991). The notion of 'saving face' may thus be closely linked to the desire to be seen as someone who represents the prototypical group member, who does not violate group norms and who contributes well to the wellbeing/stability of the group. For instance, Jackson et al (2006) found that collectivism is a significant predictor of group productivity.

This altogether leads us to expect that the impression management tactics of exemplification and supplication are commonplace in Far Eastern corporate settings, and that the tactics of self-promotion or acclamation are relatively rare in the Far East, compared to the West. Another characteristic of collectivism is reverence for authority figures (Triandis & Gelfand, 1998), which ties in well with the idea that ingratiation in the Far East is based on acquiescence to the group's existing structure and the desire to show that one is not challenging that structure. In corporate settings in Far Eastern countries such as China, collectivism is also likely to be prevalent because many businesses are family owned (Silverthorne, 2005).

A qualitative study of Chinese people by Chang & Holt (1994) found that placing high importance on *mien-tzu* often led to employees not wanting to own up to being wrong about something, especially to someone of lower 'status' (such as in terms of age or employment rank). In addition, they found that *mien-tzu* is often used as a social bargaining tool, such that someone with a high amount of *mien-tzu* is likely to exact strong influence over other people. For example, if two neighbours have a dispute, a third neighbour with a lot of *mien-tzu* because he/she is a respected teacher in the local school has the capability to intervene and help the neighbours resolve their dispute. Chang & Holt write that "Work on ones *mien-tzu*, therefore, involves attempts to manipulate degrees of relationship so as to augment ones social resources" (pp 122). Concurrently, a person interacting with someone of higher *mien-tzu* would therefore act deferential, self-abasing in acknowledgement of the other person's higher status. We would therefore expect that impression management in Chinese corporate settings is governed by the concept of *mien-tzu*, with high-ranking employees manipulating their own prestige to exact influence or power over their subordinates, and with subordinates playing up to senior employees' *mien-tzu* and using ingratiating tactics that signal their respect. The impression management strategy of ingratiation (see table 1) might thus be commonplace in Chinese workplaces.

Therefore, based on collectivist norms, Far Eastern cultures may deem some impression management strategies in table 1 appropriate or desirable, whereas other strategies may be deemed unacceptable. Likewise, some impression management strategies may lead to successful outcomes in Western European/ North American societies, whereas other strategies are likely to be unsuccessful because of individualist norms. Individualism involves emphasis on personal needs and personal identity over group needs/identity (Triandis, 1989). Impression management through self-promotion or acclamation is likely to be a regular feature in Western corporate settings because Western European and North American cultures are regarded as prime examples of individualistic cultures (Markus & Kitayama, 1991). Furthermore, in individualistic cultures, impression management strategies such as exemplification, supplication and ingratiation are likely to be motivated by individual ambitions, rather than concerns about the group.

Particular impression management strategies may therefore either be deemed socially inappropriate because they violate collectivist or individualist cultural norms, or they may evoke suspicion or cynicism about the actor's motives. Vonk's (1998) studies, conducted in the Netherlands, suggest that people in individualist cultures dislike and are suspicious of colleagues who behave in an ingratiatory manner towards seniors. In a study of supervisor/subordinate pairs from Spain, Vilela et al (2007) found a weak, albeit significant, correlation between ingratiation by employees and liking by supervisors. On the contrary, it is possible that employees in Far Eastern corporate settings have different attitudes to ingratiation, viewing it less cynically than Western workers would, and overt ingratiation might be more effective in collectivist cultures than in individualist cultures.

Likewise, whereas norms of 'face' in the Far East may necessitate strategies such as supplication, a study conducted in France by Chambon (2005) suggests that supplication by employees in individualist settings is not well received by supervisors and it does not produce favourable impressions. Vilela et al's (2007) Spanish findings suggest that exemplification by employees has virtually no correlation with supervisors' liking of employees, whereas the tactic of exemplification is likely to be effective in the Far East. In addition, the strategy of self-promotion is likely to be rare in the Far East and the strategy of showing group loyalty is likely to be commonplace. Granose (2007) found that Chinese managers were likely to use collectivist tactics such as contributing to the organization; Shahnawaz & Bala (2007) found that Indian workers in IT/fast food companies were more likely to use collectivist tactics than individualist ones; Chang & Lu's (2007) Taiwanese study found that organizational loyalty was a key feature of corporate culture there. Similarly, Parkes, Bochner & Schneider (2001) found that collectivism amongst workers in South East Asia led to positive outcomes such as tenure, whereas collectivism did not have such an effect in Australia. Kurman (2001) similarly found that the strategy of self-promotion was less prevalent amongst people in Singapore and China than people in Israel.

It is therefore in the interests of Western people working in Far-Eastern corporations (or vice versa) to be aware of cultural norms on impression management strategies when establishing themselves. In addition to cross-cultural variation, some impression management strategies are appropriate in some types of organizations but not others, because of the nature of an organization's culture.

Knowledge About Organizational Culture and Impression Management

When choosing impression management strategies, employees should take into account not only their surrounding culture but also the specific culture of their organization. Drory & Zaidman (2007) argue that:

"In the context of their work environment, individuals choose their impression management strategies to maximize their personal gain, [but employees] adopt the functional and appropriate impression management tactics, which will best serve their interests under the existing organi-

zational system." (Drory & Zaidman, 2007, pp 291)

Drory & Zaidman (2007) hypothesised that the types of impression management strategies used by employees in the military (as a 'mechanistic' organization) would differ from those used by civilian organizations in Israel. Mechanistic organizations are defined by Drory & Zaidman as those with a rigid hierarchy, high levels of formality, emphasis on employee obedience to seniors and minimum opportunities for innovative input by employees. On the other hand, organic organizations are defined by Drory & Zaidman as having a high level of informality, with frequent contact between seniors/juniors, many opportunities for employees to make innovative changes, and so on. Drory & Zaidman found that the Israeli army officers made more impression management attempts than employees in non-military Israeli organizations, and that army officers made more ingratiation attempts than employees in less mechanistic organizations. This supports Liden & Mitchell's (1988) argument that one of the causes of ingratiatory behaviour in organizational settings is the nature of the organization's culture, such as in terms of the level of inter-dependence within it.

The influence of organizational culture can therefore mean that there are variations in the use of impression management strategies even *within* a wider cultural setting, such as an individualistic one. Rao, Schmidt & Murray (1995) investigated whether the amount of "formalization and routinization" (pp 153) within an organization would correspond with the use of ingratiation as an impression management tactic. Rao et al surveyed 134 manager-subordinate pairs from British manufacturing firms, government bodies and educational institutions. They determined the organizations' culture using a measure with items such as: the degree of written work schedules, emphasis on written documents, standard operating procedures, defined job responsibilities, and so

on. Unlike Drory & Zaidman (whose study was conducted in Israel), Rao et al's British study found no significant correlation between the use of ingratiation by employees and the degree of formality/routine in the organizations surveyed.

Organization culture may thus create variations within one wider cultural context (individualist or collectivist), especially for some impression management strategies. Rao et al (1995) suggested that the use of ingratiation may be less typical or effective in British workplaces than in some other Western countries, such as the United States, – a difference which may be due to organization culture. Wayne & Liden (1995) surveyed pairs of US supervisors/subordinates and found a significant positive correlation between use of ingratiatory impression management tactics and liking by supervisors. Schmidt & Kipnis's (1984) and Westphal & Stern's (2007) US studies found similar results. There is therefore an interaction between national culture and organizational culture, as Parkes, Bochner & Schneider (2001) found in their study of workers from Australia and South-East Asia. The extent to which national culture takes precedence over organizational culture (or vice versa) may depend on a number of factors – such as the degree of similarity between the two or the cultural diversity of employees in an organization.

Therefore, successful impression management in corporate settings requires that an individual gains important knowledge about both societal and organization-specific culture, and that an individual then uses that knowledge to strategise their impression management.

Knowledge About Individual Differences and Impression Management

Irrespective of the culture of the actor or target(s), a person planning an impression management strategy should consider the individual characteristics of each target. Leary & Kowalski (1990)

Table 2. 3-step knowledge audit model for impression management

Knowledge audit step 1	Knowledge audit step 2	Knowledge audit step 3			
Impression deficit	Impression management strategy needed	Adjustment in strategy required?			
= desired impression minus actual impression		Adjustment required by culture?			Other adjustments required?
		Collectivist culture	Individualist culture	Organizational culture	
=Acceptance deficit	=Show group loyalty	No	Yes	Analyse	Case-by-case basis: Individual differences variables – e.g. high status of targets; self-monitoring trait in self
=Compassion deficit	=Supplication	No	Yes	Analyse	
=Competence deficit	=Exemplification	No	Yes	Analyse	
=Credibility deficit	=Indirect tactic	No	No	Analyse	
=Liking deficit	=Ingratiation	No	Yes	Analyse	
=Power deficit	=Intimidation	Yes	No	Analyse	
=Respect deficit	=Self-promotion	Yes	No	Analyse	
=Reward deficit	=Acclamation	Yes	No	Analyse	
=Status deficit	=Other nonverbal behaviour	No	No	Analyse	

show that the individual attributes of the target audience determine the nature/intensity of impression management strategies chosen. Furthermore, a person's individual characteristics may make them more competent at impression management or their individual characteristics may influence others' receptiveness to them. Let us now explore some of the individual differences variables to consider in step three of the impression management knowledge audit model in table 2.

One important individual difference variable to consider is the status or power of the targets or the actor. Generally speaking, people exert more impression management efforts if the target people possess attributes such as high status, power or attractiveness (Schlenker, 1980). Individuals/ corporations may also need to adjust their impression management strategy to accommodate their own characteristics. High status, power and/ or attractiveness are likely to make them more successful at impression management (DePaulo, 1992; Schlenker, 1980). At the same time, some characteristics, such as high status, may make some impression management strategies inappropriate or even counter-productive (e.g. ingratiation, supplication), and other strategies

may backfire, especially when made public (e.g. intimidation).

Another important individual difference variable to consider is the level of 'self-monitoring' of the actor. Synder (1974) showed that some individuals are more adept at impression management because they possess high levels of a trait called self monitoring – a trait associated with high need for approval (Paulhus, 1982). Such individuals are also more successful at monitoring the success of their impression management attempts (Gangestad & Snyder, 2000) because of their level of attentiveness to situation cues (Snyder, 1974). People who score highly on the Self Monitoring Scale were found to be able to facially/vocally act out random emotions more successfully than low self monitors, as well as being able to decode others' facial/vocal emotional expressions (Snyder, 1974).

The other important individual difference variable to consider is the gender of the actor or the target(s). Despite advances in gender equality in many countries, sex-role stereotyping still has a pervasive effect on impression formation and on the success of particular impression management strategies. For instance, in their study of 760 US directors, Westphal & Stern (2007) found that male directors who deployed the strategy of ingratiation were more likely to be promoted than female directors who deployed the same strategy. Impression management strategies such as self-promotion are more frequently used by males than females (Thornton et al, 2006), and women who engage in the strategy of self-promotion may receive hostility because they are viewed as having violated gender stereotypes. Shimanoff (1994) reviewed studies on gender differences in face-saving behaviour and concluded that women in many cultures behave in a more polite, subservient way, than men. Supplication has likewise been found to be more prevalent amongst females than males, (Thornton et al, 2006), perhaps because of gender-role stereotypes. At the same time, it is sensible for impression motivated individuals to avoid using tactics (e.g. flattery as part of ingratiation) that targets of an opposite gender could construe as sexual harassment. Timmerman & Bajema's (1999) review of numerous studies concluded that definitions of sexual harassment vary, but may include such behaviour as unwanted compliments about clothing or appearance.

Another important individual difference variable to consider in impression management is based on the concept of 'idiosyncrasy credits.' Hollander (1958) postulates that "…by conforming to group norms, people accumulate "idiosyncrasy credits" that allow them to deviate from norms in the future" (see Leary & Kowalski, 1990, pp 42). This suggests that, for example, an individual who usually engages in supplication in conformity to a societal or organizational cultural norm accumulates 'credits' that allow him/her to deviate from that supplication without jeopardising his/her acceptance by the group.

Therefore, impression-motivated individuals or corporations need to know about the role of individual difference variables, as well as knowing about the benefits of both society- and organization-specific cultural knowledge.

Integrating and Auditing Impression Management Knowledge: A 3-Step Knowledge Audit Model

The first thing that an impression-motivated individual needs to do is to acquire knowledge about other peoples existing impressions of them. An individual who wants to manage others' impressions of them will need to seek information about what these impressions are in the first place. Individuals then need to have explicit knowledge of their desired impressions, and to then find out whether there is a deficit between their desired impressions and the actual impressions that people have of them. Overall, there is often a "degree of discrepancy between the image one would like others to hold of oneself and the image one believes others already hold." (Leary & Kowalski, 1990, pp 39). An impression-motivated individual may find out that there is a deficit in the extent to which they are perceived as competent, powerful, respected, and so on.

Secondly, after identifying the nature of the impression deficit, an individual needs to identify the most appropriate strategy to rectify this deficit – something which requires the kind of knowledge that has been presented in this chapter. Table 2 pairs each type of impression deficit with the strategy most likely to rectify that deficit.

Of course, more than one impression management strategy may be deployed to attempt to correct a particular deficit. For example, a meta-analytic study by Gordon (1996) of ingratiation studies found that ingratiatory tactics have a significant effect on both performance evaluations and liking.

Thirdly, individuals need to find out what the local cultural norms are, as well as finding out about their organizational culture. This will determine the appropriateness of each potential impression management strategy. Individuals or corporations would therefore need to adjust the nature (see table 1) of their impression management strategy or its intensity, depending on the cultural context. For example, in a Western context, a liking deficit may be solved with an indirect, rather than direct, ingratiation strategy. Therefore, rather than issuing overt flattery, an individual may indicate their flattery through imitation or through a third party. In an Eastern context, rather than engaging in overt self-promotion, an individual may couple their self-promotion with self-criticism, or they may emphasise the contribution of others to their achievements. Furthermore, individuals may need to adjust the nature or intensity of their strategy to suit the specific culture of their organization, and they may also need to adjust their strategies according to their own individual characteristics or those of their target audience.

How can employees – in particular those about to embark on international assignments – acquire this knowledge? Let us now consider the knowledge-enhancing role of cross-cultural training.

Creating an Impression Management Knowledge Base through Cross-Cultural Training

Learning a language, reading a travel guide book or watching television programmes of films from a prospective host country is something that some expatriates are likely to do before commencing their jobs abroad. However, more formal cultural knowledge than this is needed. Prior familiarity with a prospective host culture is beneficial to cultural adaptation (Selmer, Chiu & Shenkar, 2007), but familiarity alone cannot sufficiently prepare expatriates for cultural adaptation. Selmer et al found that German expatriates in the USA were better culturally adjusted than American expatriates in Germany, perhaps because of the Germans' prior familiarity with American culture (through, say, American television programmes or films). Nevertheless, Selmer et al recommended formal cross-cultural training for expatriates before they begin working in new cultural settings. In particular, would-be expatriate workers need to acquire

in-depth knowledge about the host country's cultural norms on interpersonal behaviour and on behaviour in workplaces. Organizations can devise formal cross-cultural training programmes for would-be expatriates, in order to increase their cultural knowledge base.

In fact, a cultural knowledge deficit can lead to unreceptive behaviour towards people in the host culture. Richardson & McKenna (2006) conducted a qualitative study of 30 British expatriate academics in the United Arab Emirates, New Zealand, Singapore and Turkey and found that some participants discussed a "lack of local knowledge, not being able to relate to people, not having interactions with locals" (pp 13). Cross-cultural training of expatriates should therefore be useful in giving employees knowledge that they can utilise in the new cultural setting, also focussing on giving expatriates knowledge on workplace norms specific to the culture in question.

Having prior cultural knowledge would prevent misunderstandings based on a lack of awareness about impression management behaviour in the new culture. Consider Peltokorpi's (2006) qualitative study of 30 Nordic managers working in Japan from Denmark, Norway, Sweden and Finland. Peltokorpi asked the Nordic managers about their views of Japanese employees' workplace behaviour. The Nordic managers commented on the prestige associated with age in Japan, such that seniority in rank was often associated with age, rather than competence, and such that "fresh ideas presented by young employees were often shot down before they reached the expatriate managers" (Peltokorpi, 2006, pp 110) because it was considered inappropriate for those of junior rank to present ideas directly to seniors. The Nordic managers also commented on the passiveness of Japanese employees in meetings, with the expatriate managers expressing frustration that the employees did not articulate their own feelings or ideas. The Nordic managers found all these cultural differences problematic. However, prior cross-cultural training would have provided knowledge about impression management in workplaces and the impact of Japanese cultural norms on this. For example, junior Japanese employees' shyness in meetings was probably part of their impression management strategies of supplication and conformity to the concept of 'face' – whereby Japanese juniors might not have wanted to risk embarrassing a senior by contradicting his/her ideas in a meeting. The Nordic managers found it problematic that junior Japanese employees sought guidance when asked to complete a task. Again, the Nordic managers appeared to have misinterpreted that as a lack of independence when in fact the junior Japanese employees were probably deploying the impression management strategy of supplication, a strategy which was probably usually rewarded by Japanese seniors. The Nordic managers appeared to have recognised the central role of collectivist cultural norms because they pointed out that "… virtually nothing [in the Japanese workplaces] was indicated to occur as a result of individual effort… Individualist and opportunistic behaviour can lead to social sanctions, such as exclusion from the principle social unit" (Peltokorpi's, 2006, pp 112). However, despite recognising this, the expatriate Nordic managers found it problematic that the Japanese employees worked very well in teams but not so well if alone. Cross-cultural training could have enabled the expatriate managers to recognise the extent to which the impression management strategy of showing group loyalty, based on strong collectivist norms, explains the Japanese employees' focus on team work, as opposed to individual output.

Therefore, cross-cultural training should equip expatriates with knowledge about impression management strategies prevalent in the host culture. Why is this important? Cultural knowledge can make expatriates more culturally adaptive to their new work environment which, as we will now see, has positive effects on their work performance and adjustment.

The Benefits of Cultural Adaptation by Expatriates

Cross-cultural adaptation or flexibility by expatriates has many benefits. Before exploring those benefits, it is important to note that adaptation to a new culture need not be assimilation. Pires, Stanton & Ostenfeld (2006) suggest that "adjustment strategies based on immersion in a foreign culture" (pp 156) can be beneficial to expatriates, but this fits the definition of assimilation. Assimilation involves a total immersion into a new culture and the abandonment of ones old culture (Berry, 2001), whereas cultural adaptation suggests a much more temporary or context-dependent kind of cultural flexibility. Yamazaki & Kayes' (2007) study of Japanese expatriate managers in the US suggested that they devised ways of adapting to their new culture without actually assimilating in it, suggesting that expatriates do not need to change their cultural practices or beliefs. Therefore, cultural adaptation by expatriates is so called because it involves a dynamic process that ideally begins with fact-finding (such as from cross-cultural training) and continues through interactions with locals that allow further acquisition of knowledge about the impression management tactics that work in that culture.

Cultural adaptation by expatriates has been found to have a positive impact on their work performance and/ or adjustment. For example, Shaffer et al (2006) conducted a study of Japanese expatriates working in or soon to be working in the US, as well as Korean expatriates working in other parts of Asia, the Americas and Europe. They found significant, albeit moderate, correlations between cultural flexibility, interaction adjustment (e.g. socializing with locals) and work adjustment (e.g. performing well in ones role). In a separate study of Western expatriates (mainly from the US, UK and Australia) working in Hong Kong, Shaffer et al found significant correlations amongst cultural adjustment, adjustment in interactions (such as socialising with Hong Kong nationals on a daily basis) and cultural adjustment. Likewise, Selmer (2006) conducted a study of 165 expatriate managers working in China from Western countries such as the US, Germany, Britain and Australia. Selmer found that the participants' adjustment to working in a new cultural setting was positively correlated with their adjustment to interacting with the people in their host country. Similarly, Liu & Shaffer's (2005) study of expatriate managers working in Hong Kong and China found that the extent to which the expatriates had Hong Kong/ Chinese interpersonal skills was significantly correlated with both work adjustment and interaction adjustment. This altogether suggests that expatriates' work performance is related to their cultural flexibility, their adjustment to their host culture, and their interactions with local people. This is an empirically robust finding. There is also widespread evidence that adjustment to work, adjustment to social interactions, and adjustment to the environment/culture are three distinct variables (e.g. see Shimoni, Ronen & Rozimer's, 2005, factor analysis using data from expatriates working in Israel). This means that an expatriate's adjustment to a new workplace is not the same as adjusting to a new culture, and therefore he/ she needs to pay attention to both factors.

There is evidence that some expatriates are aware of the benefits cultural adjustment. Stahl & Caligiuri (2005) found that, of 116 German expatriates working in the US and Japan, 18% of the expatriates adopted the strategy of interaction adjustment (e.g. inviting locals to visit their home), and 17% adopted the strategy of behaving in ways that save others' face. However, the remaining percentage of expatriates that did not demonstrate cultural adaptation was still substantially large. Stahl & Caligiuri found that 25% of the expatriates adopted the strategy of intentionally violating local cultural norms and 21% adopted the strategy of negatively comparing the host culture with their own home culture. This suggests that a small but significant number of expatriates do the opposite of cultural adaptation – something which may

have an unfavourable impact on the impressions that they form and the failure of their impression management attempts. This is likely, in turn, to have a negative impact on their work performance and it may harm their employers' interests because the cultural adjustment process can be beneficial to business negotiations. Moore's (2006) qualitative study of German expatriates working in the London branch of a German multinational bank found that the participants deployed impression management strategies that enabled them to be effective negotiators between the London branch and the head office. These strategies included variously showing group loyalty to the London office or to the German headquarters, playing on their London identity, or assuming an Anglo-German identity.

There is also evidence suggesting that cultural adaptation enhances knowledge transfer by expatriates. Liu & Shaffer's (2005) study of expatriate managers working in Hong Kong and China found a significant correlation between knowledge transfer performance (in terms of e.g. transferring information from the host organization to the home country or vice versa) and work performance, with this being significantly correlated with interaction adjustment. The knowledge gained through cultural adjustment by an expatriate can itself be a beneficial part of the knowledge transferred. Hocking, Brown & Harzing (2007) conducted a case study of a transnational firm and found that the learning of local knowledge by expatriates could be transferred to the home headquarters and therefore increase the latter's global capabilities. Expatriates should thus be seen as useful fact-finders who can transfer their new cultural/ social knowledge to their home organization, which should in turn incorporate this knowledge into a formal cross-cultural training programme for other employees.

What about multinational corporations? Although most impression management in workplace settings occurs at the individual level (that is to say, the actor is an individual rather than a group or organization), this is not to say that corporations cannot deploy impression management strategies. In fact, it can be argued that corporations operating in other cultures *should* gain knowledge about impression management strategies and use this in their public relations efforts.

Future Trends: Utilising Impression Management Knowledge in Corporate Public Relations

Impression management by organizations is what is conventionally known as public relations. If organizational impression management is concerned with creating favourable impressions in other countries, it is known as international public relations (see Curtin & Gaither, 2007; Sriramesh & Vercic, 2001). However, corporate public relations are often concerned with that kind of organizational impression management that produces increases in, for example, product sales. In fact, as is evident with individual impression management, the goals of organizational impression management in new contexts should be more than simply marketing a product/service or increasing sales. In fact, it can be argued that – especially when a corporation is operating in a new culture – other impression management goals must *necessarily* be fulfilled before secondary goals such as increasing sales can be fulfilled.

For example, 'green' (i.e. eco-friendly) values have become very popular in British culture, to such an extent that some social commentators argue that the green movement has been appropriated by mainstream society (e.g. Giddens, 2006), with increasing demand for products such as eco-friendly property (Telegraph, 2004). Many British companies now incorporate a 'green' message in their marketing material and websites, irrespective of whether these messages are relevant to their products or services. For example, a 2008 conference entitled 'Green Marketing' targeted themes such as making marketing more eco-friendly, recognising the marketing benefits of eco-friendly

values, and so on, with scheduled speakers from mainstream organizations such as the Advertising Standards Authority (a regulatory body), Marks & Spencers, the BBC and British Telecom. Many companies in the UK now conform to eco-friendly values such as use of recycled paper, minimization of energy waste, and so on, integrating them into their corporate ethics. For example, HSBC, British Airways, British Gas, ITV, and many other major UK corporations coalesce with the Carbon Neutral Company, which runs a "carbon offset scheme" (Adam, 2006) that involves planting trees and creating eco-parks to compensate for the corporations' negative impact on the environment. Many UK companies and public institutions also promote Fairtrade-certified produce and about 300 towns across the UK refer to themselves as "Fairtrade towns" (Fairtrade Foundation, 2008). Eco-friendly values have thus become so prevalent in the UK that contrary corporate behaviour is often considered a scandal and is ostracised in the media. For example, corporate executives or major politicians/ public figures using a private jet or driving so called 'gas guzzling' cars are often strongly criticised for having a large 'carbon footprint' (see e.g. BBC, 2006; Reuters, 2007). All this would mean that a new company wishing to fulfil the goal of gaining customers in the UK might first have to fulfil the goal of being viewed as an eco-responsible company. Likewise, in other cultures, there are particular important social values that new corporations need to learn about if they wish to manage the impressions that others have of them in those cultures.

Therefore, firstly, organizations operating in other countries need to engage in a considerable amount of fact-finding in order to determine what their impression management goals are. Secondly, having determined their goals, corporations operating in foreign cultures, should – like individuals working in cross-cultural settings – perform the kind of impression management knowledge audit depicted in table 2. Organizational impression management falls into the realm of public relations, and therefore it would fall upon public relations and marketing staff to seek and utilise knowledge on the appropriateness of different impression management strategies in the new culture. Therefore, such an impression management knowledge audit should establish: what a corporation's goals are, what strategies are feasible or appropriate in a given culture, and how those strategies can be varied to accommodate successful public relations tactics used in that culture.

Adapting impression management strategies to different cultural contexts is something which Coca Cola has often attempted. With regards to the US market, Curtin & Gaither (2007) point out that: "For almost 100 years… the company [Coca Cola] had spent millions of dollars developing an image steeped in nostalgia and small town America" (pp 46), with Coke succeeding in being viewed as a product that is as American as 'baseball or hamburgers' (pp 47). At the same time, in India, Coca Cola adapted its public relations tactics, emphasising its commitment to the community: "…we are deeply involved in the life of the local communities in which we operate" (Coca Cola India; cited in Curtin & Gaither, 2007, pp 22). This resulted in many Indians – particularly those living close to Coca Cola factories – emphatically describing Coke as an Indian product (Curtin & Gaither, 2007). In Africa, the corporation created the Coca Cola Africa Foundation, an organization for "social investment" that addresses both "individual and collective needs" (Coca Cola website, 2008), perhaps in recognition of the likelihood that African cultures have both collectivist and individualist characteristics. Coca Cola's African mission statement is notably different from the corporation's Spain Foundation, which focuses on promoting fine arts amongst youths, or the corporation's Nordic Environmental Foundation, which promotes eco-friendly projects (Coca Cola website, 2008). In Japan and China, Tian (2006) similarly argues that "… Coca Cola has been integrating local traditional cultural factors into its strategies" (pp 16) and on its China website

the corporation shows its identification with Chinese culture.

It can therefore be argued that Coca Cola's public relations (or impression management) attempts involve localised cultural adaptation. Nevertheless, these attempts are sometimes undermined by other factors and Coca Cola therefore has to make a continuing effort to maintain its desired impressions. For example, Coca Cola in India has faced widespread criticisms, boycotts and demonstrations because of allegedly emitting toxic sludge (BBC News, 2003a), depleting local water sources (BBC News, 2005) and because coke drinks there allegedly contain pesticide pollutions (BBC News 2003b). In the UK, Coca Cola miscalculated the nature of the market for bottled water when it launched a brand of bottled purified tap water (called 'Dasani') that received heavy criticism for not only being 'mere' tap water but for also containing levels of bromate that contravened UK limits (BBC News, 2004). Dasani was subsequently withdrawn from the UK market. In Belgium, there was a temporary ban on Coca Cola drinks after some consumers complained of shivering, nausea and other symptoms and the corporation embarked on an 'aggressive' campaign to rebuild its image (Johnson & Peppas, 2003). Therefore, Coca Cola needs to regularly monitor and update its impression management strategies because its public image is itself not static.

Similarly, McDonalds recognises the need for cultural adaptation, such as by including meal variations based on local customs. For instance, McDonald's sells falafel burgers in Egypt and Morocco, burrito breakfasts in the US, kosher meals in countries such as Israel, halal meat in countries such as Malaysia, serving coffee in china cups in Portugal, spicy chicken burgers in Singapore and so on. McDonalds has also learned to adapt itself to suit the needs that are of high importance in a given culture – such as studious behaviour by children and youths. In China and Singapore, McDonald's has gained fame as a place where children can do their homework (Zukin & Maguire, 2004).

However, there are ways in which McDonald's can further adapt itself to suit local cultural norms. For example, Eckhardt & Houston (2002) found that Chinese participants described seating arrangements at McDonald's restaurants as "too public" (pp 72) because of their open-plan nature, compared to the cubicle-style of many Chinese restaurants. Eckhardt & Houston report that Chinese couples on dates in McDonald's restaurants felt more exposed and uncomfortable than they would have felt if seating arrangements were similar to those found in traditional Chinese restaurants or noodle bars. In addition, McDonald's was slow to adapt to the eco-friendly culture that has been gaining popularity in Britain and other Western countries, governing negative attitudes towards artificial ingredients in food, genetically modified produce and crops not grown organically. The bestselling film "Supersize Me" (Spurlock, 2004), which was a case-study of the effects of McDonald's meals on health, was arguably a product of this growing cultural phenomenon. McDonald's sales that year were affected; for example, in the UK, the companies profits fell from £83.8 million in 2003 to £23.5 million in 2004 (see Oliver, 2005). McDonald's refuted the film's claims but it then discontinued 'supersize' meal options and introduced a 'Premium' line in North America, parts of Europe and Australia/New Zealand. This meant that salads and healthy options such as deli sandwiches were introduced in these parts of the world, although they are may not be financially successful. The fact that this menu continues to be offered in the West and is not available worldwide suggests that the move by McDonald's was strategic and that it was an example of adjustment to cultural values of growing importance in the West.

Furthermore, McDonald's is often associated with the standardization of eating habits, the elimination of culinary variety and with emphasis on cheap, quick food. This has spawned regional movements such as the European/North American Slow Food Movement (see slowfood.com), which is against the notion of fast food and supports the more traditional restaurant format. In addition to being associated with the standardization of eating habits, McDonald's is also often associated with American culture, meaning that some regions of the world resist "McDonaldization" because they associate it with "Americanization" (Illouz & John, 2003, pp 202; see also Bryman, 2003). This has led to regular global protests (such as during the Worldwide Anti-McDonald's Day) as well as perceptions of conflict between other national identities and consumption at McDonald's (see e.g. Illouz & John, 2003, who discuss attitudes towards McDonald's in Israel).

Therefore, global corporations such as McDonald's often struggle to maintain the impression that they are truly global and not merely expansions of a corporation from one nation. Some corporations seem to recognise the difficulty of attaining a truly global identity, and they capitalise on their exoticism as representatives of particular cultures, viewing this as a more achievable primary impression management goal. For example, KFC (Kentucky Fried Chicken) emphasises its roots in American cuisine, giving customers in other countries the impression that they are participating in an authentic American eating experience (see Friedman, 1999). Other corporations – rather than emphasising a global identity that downplays national differences – focus on the impression management goal of appearing diverse. For example, it can be argued that the multinational bank HSBC (Hong Kong & Shanghai Banking Corporation) has recognised the benefits of possessing an image of national diversity, and its public relations attempts often revolve around the slogan "The world's local bank" (HSBC, 2008). Another example is provided by two members of HSBC, Gakovic & Yardley (2007), who discuss "global talent management" (pp 201), which emphasises national diversity of recruits, as the bank's "organizational development solution" (pp 201). Nevertheless, the impression management aim of appearing global and diverse may be difficult for

HSBC to fulfil because its business is unlikely to be equally distributed across all countries with a HSBC presence.

As we have seen, some multinational corporations have recognised the benefits of cultural adjustment and strategic international public relations. However, such corporations are arguably in the minority. For example, in terms of advertising in other countries, many corporations use the same television commercials (albeit for dubbing voices in other languages or adding subtitles), believing that the commercials' success will be replicated in new countries. In fact, what corporations should do is to regard television commercials or other publicity platforms as important opportunities for impression management, and to therefore begin by performing the knowledge audit in table 2 before creating or editing commercials to suit each cultural context. Let us consider some hypothetical examples of this in table 3. In each example, we see how the same impression management goal can be fulfilled in different, culturally-specific ways. The examples in this table illustrate the differences between collectivist and individualist cultures, and they demonstrate ways in which a primary cultural theme (e.g. individualism or collectivism) can be reinforced even whilst trying to meet secondary impression management goals such as being viewed as efficient, polite, popular, down-to-earth, and so on.

In addition, as Curtin & Gaither argue, global corporations need to recognise the potentially diverse forms that public relations could take in other countries – and to realize that these forms can be radically different from their own public relations activities at home. For example, Curtin & Gaither report that public relations in India often takes the form of dance, skits and plays; in Ghana, storytelling is often used as a public relations method; poetry is often used in Saudi Arabian public gatherings as part of public relations, and so on.

At the same time, corporations need to evaluate the ethics of their chosen impression management tactics, ensuring that their cultural adaptation is not based on harmful over-generalisation (i.e. stereotyping) of their targets' culture. The need for ethical standards also applies to impression management by individuals.

Controversies: The Ethics of Impression Management

In the example provided in table 1, if Gertrude (who turns up to work at her desk very early in the morning in order to give her supervisors the impression that she is conscientious) actually spends the extra time writing a blog, her impression management behaviour seems deceptive. If Samson actually thinks that his project manager's new marketing plan is awful, but he starts saying that it is wonderful in order to ingratiate himself, this would be deceptive. The head chef Rachel, who shouts and uses bad language at junior chefs as part of the strategy of intimidation may succeed in gaining her juniors' respect but at a considerable cost to their mental wellbeing. If Martha erroneously believes that her articles contributed to the increase in newspaper copies sold and tells people this, it might be more beneficial to her professional ambitions if she objectively evaluates the quality of her articles instead. Therefore, strategies such as ingratiation, exemplification, acclamation, self promotion, and others, might sometimes seem to involve deception of others, self-deception, an exaggeration of the truth, the omission of the truth or harm to others' wellbeing.

James Westphal, in an interview by Capos (2008), discussed the ethical costs of impression management strategies to corporations. In particular, Westphal discussed the ethics of ingratiation, which he argued is not frowned upon and very much the norm in US corporations. Westphal argued that "Ingratiation can have adverse consequences, depending upon the company's situation… Our research suggests that if directors are appointed on the basis of their ingratiatory behaviour, they are less likely to [question or

Table 3. Examples of how corporations can deploy impression management strategies

Impression management goal (multinational corporation)	Known strategy to fulfil goal	Culture-specific example (corporate)	
		Collectivist culture	**Individualist culture**
Imagine if Microsoft, a software company, wants to give the impression that it offers the most efficient software.	**Acclamation**	In a Chinese commercial, Microsoft could claim that it's anti-virus software enable people to collectively defend China's computer networks.	In an American commercial, Microsoft could claim that it's anti-virus software enable each individual subscriber to have the best defended computer.
Imagine if Phillips, an electric appliance company, wants to give the impression that its employees are conscientious.	**Exemplification**	In a Chinese version of its website, Phillips could depict its factory employees working over-time to ensure that all households are well equipped.	In an American version of its website, Phillips could depict its factory employees working over-time to ensure that hard-working individuals the best equipped homes.
Imagine if CNN, a cable/satellite television channel, wants to give the impression that prototypical local people watch it.	**Indirect tactic**	In a broadcast to China, CNN could depict a well-known Chinese family organising a gathering to watch CNN together.	In a broadcast to USA, CNN could depict a wealthy American celebrity watching CNN and benefiting materially from doing so.
Imagine if Ford, an automobile company, wants to give the impression that it its employees are immensely polite.	**Ingratiation**	In a Chinese commercial, Ford could depict employees in a Ford showroom being very polite to clients whose qualities (e.g. age) are typically accorded respect.	In an American commercial, Ford could depict employees in a Ford showroom being very polite to clients whose qualities (e.g. success) are typically accorded respect.
Imagine if HSBC, a banking company sternly wants to give the impression that it offers authoritative advice.	**Intimidation**	During a feature on a Chinese discussion programme, community leaders could warn viewers to listen to HSBC's advice or risk their financial future.	During a feature on an American discussion programme, a well-known entrepreneur could warn viewers to listen to HSBC's advice or risk financial ruin.
Imagine if Emirates, an airline, wants to give the impression that it has international experts recommend it.	**Self-promotion**	In a press release in China, Emirates could report that travel experts gave it a star rating, and suggest that this indicates that the international community is pleased with it.	In a press release in the USA, Emirates could report that renown travel experts gave it a star rating, and suggest that this is benefits the image of travellers who use it.
Imagine if Hilton, a hotel chain, wants to give the impression that it is a member or supporter of a given cultural group.	**Show group loyalty**	In brochures to be distributed in China, Hilton could depict itself as a long-standing host of Chinese cultural events and a hotel chain that upholds Chinese traditional décor and cuisine.	In brochures to be distributed in the USA, Hilton could depict itself as a hotel chain that respects the individuality of guests in the USA, varying the menu and décor of rooms to suit various tastes.
Imagine if Fedex, a courier company, wants to give the impression that it is an unpretentious company.	**Supplication**	In a documentary to be broadcast in China, Fedex could depict its courier staff as people who make humorous, self-abasing gaffs in their attempt to deliver a package to a community organization in China.	In a documentary to be broadcast in the USA, Fedex could depict a member of its courier staff as a person who makes humorous, self-abasing gaffs in his/her attempt to deliver a package to a prototypical American.

monitor the decision made at board level]." (cited in Capos, 2008). Westphal reported that managers who lack high-level management experience are most likely to engage in ingratiation, thus gaining access to positions that they otherwise would not have qualified for. Although this may seem beneficial to both the promoted managers and those doing the promoting (whose self esteem would be boosted by ingratiation from former), Westphal pointed out that it is not beneficial to the company as a whole or its shareholders. For example, a company's performance could suffer if it is led by someone without the appropriate level of competence. Westphal thus recommends that board recruitment is done by outsiders such as head-hunting firms, rather than through informal networks, because the most ingratiatory internal employee or the most ingratiatory external candidate known via social circles (rather than necessarily the most competent) is otherwise likely to be promoted.

What about ingratiation through favours (see table 1)? Westphal (cited in Capos, 2008, who interviewed him for an article) reported that favour-doing is quite common on the US Wall Street, with favours often being market-oriented, such as in terms of recommending someone for a job or as a supplier. However, Westphal argued that "favour-rendering" is not bribery or fraud. Perhaps the ethics of ingratiation through doing favours depends on whether an individual's competitors (e.g. their co-workers) have the opportunity or the capability to do similar favours. If Matt (see table 1) volunteers to collect his department director's favourite takeaway lunch, this does not seem unethical since his co-workers could volunteer to do the same. If Matt chose to give his department director a $50 gift voucher for Christmas, this might not be bribery since the sum is one which co-workers can afford and the occasion is one which all co-workers have the opportunity to give gifts. If, however, Matt decides to give his director $1000 – even if as a Christmas gift – then this might seem like bribery, especially if Matt is secretive about his gift and if the circumstance suggests that it is a bribe (say, if, the director is in the process of deciding who gets a large bonus or pay rise). In addition, Westphal pointed out that long-term shareholders could lose out if the favour-rendering affects their long-term investments.

Therefore, some instances of impression management are ethically questionable. However, does this necessarily have to be the case: do these strategies necessarily have to be deployed in an unethical manner? In the table 1 examples, Gertrude could spend the extra time actually working, and therefore deploy the strategy of exemplifica-

tion without deceiving her supervisors. Samson could deal with his situation by using a different type of ingratiation. Rather than choosing the deceptive strategy of transforming disagreement into agreement (when in fact he strongly disagrees with his project manager's plan), he can choose the strategy of ingratiation through flattery whilst sticking to his disagreement. Samson can therefore think of genuine compliments to relay to his project manager, relay them, and then thoughtfully explain why he disagrees with the marketing plan. Head chef Rachel could fulfil her impression management goal of gaining her juniors' respect without deploying the strategy of intimidation in the way that she did. Instead, Rachel could still adapt an aloof, formal demeanour, sternly criticising the food rather than criticising a junior chef's character, and therefore adapting the strategy of intimidation without putting her staff's mental wellbeing in jeopardy. Likewise, rather than deceiving herself about the impact of her articles on her newspaper's sales, Martha could solicit genuine feedback about her articles and base an impression management strategy on that feedback.

Further Research Questions

Having integrated knowledge from different disciplines (e.g. applied psychology, management, human resources), it is important for this knowledge to be utilised in generating empirical research on impression management in corporate settings. Firstly, during the process of researching this chapter, the author found that most published research articles focus on one or a few of the impression management strategies presented in table 2. A single psychometric scale measuring *all* of the strategies (and sub-strategies) presented in table 2 therefore needs to be developed. Secondly, considering that a new impression management knowledge audit model has been presented in this chapter, it is important to empirically test this model, also ensuring that cross-cultural samples and samples from different types of organizations are used. Thirdly, it is argued that individuals or corporations need to regularly re-run the three steps of the audit in table 2, based on new knowledge that they acquire, and therefore the process of impression management should be a dynamic process using the audit model as a guidance tool rather than as a prescriptive one. It is argued that employees or corporations that run this knowledge audit should be more successful at impression management than individuals or corporations who do not do so. Therefore, the third important further research question should investigate this hypothesis. For instance, it is predicted that expatriates who obtain relevant cross-cultural training should be more successful (in terms of impression management) in their host cultures than expatriates who do not obtain such training. Research should also explore the benefits of cross-cultural training in impression management processes within organizations with employees from different cultures, as well as exploring the interaction between organizational culture and national culture. Empirical investigations of these research questions will be of great value.

CONCLUSION

Having compiled a taxonomy of impression management strategies typically used in corporate settings, this chapter explored the role of cultural knowledge on impression management. Cultural knowledge was discussed as something which serves as powerful capital in impression management and as something which concerns both the specific culture of a given organization and the surrounding societal culture. For instance, would-be expatriates wishing to deploy impression management strategies can benefit from establishing a knowledge base about their prospective host culture through attending cross-cultural training. In addition to adjusting for culture, employees or corporations need to adjust their impression

management strategy to accommodate the individual characteristics of their target person(s). Therefore, an impression management knowledge audit by employees or corporations should be concerned with acquiring knowledge about not just the psychology of impression management but also cultural adaptation/ flexibility as well as individual differences. Corporations can likewise utilise the knowledge presented in this chapter to maximise their international public relations attempts. Both individual employees and corporations as a whole should consider the ethics of their chosen impression management tactics and realise that impression management strategies *can* and should be deployed ethically. One of the further research questions outlined highlighted the need for cross-cultural research testing the benefits of the presented knowledge audit model for employees or corporations using it.

REFERENCES

Adam, D. (2006). Can planting trees really give you a clear carbon conscience? *The Guardian*. Retrieved from http://www.guardian.co.uk/environment/2006/oct/07/climatechange.climatechangeenvironment

Baumeister, R. F., & Tice, D. M. (1986). Four selves, two motives, and a substitute process self-regulation model. In R. F. Baumeister (Ed.), *Public self and private self* (pp. 63-74). New York: Springer-Verlag.

BBC. (2006). *Hypocrisy claim over Cameron bike*. Retrieved from http://news.bbc.co.uk/2/hi/uk_news/politics/4953922.stm

Berry, J. W. (2001). A psychology of immigration. *The Journal of Social Issues*, *57*(3), 615–631. doi:10.1111/0022-4537.00231

Capos, C. (2008). *The currency of favours* (James Westphal interview). Retrieved from http://www.bus.umich.edu/NewsRoom/ArticleDisplay.asp?news_id=12754

Chambon, M. (2005). How to look modest in an organization: Supervisors' perceptions of subordinates' account for success. *Psychologie du Travail et des Organisations, 11*(3), 151–164. doi:10.1016/j.pto.2005.07.003

Chang, H.-C., & Holt, R. (1994). A Chinese perspective on face as inter-relational concern. In S. Ting-Toomey (Ed.), *The challenge of facework: Cross-cultural and interpersonal issues*. Albany, NY: State University of New York.

Chang, K., & Lu, L. (2007). Characteristics of organizational culture, stressors and wellbeing: The case of Taiwanese organizations. *Journal of Managerial Psychology, 22*(6), 549–598. doi:10.1108/02683940710778431

Coca Cola. (2008). *Regional and local foundations*. Retrieved from http://www.thecoca-colacompany.com/citizenship/foundation_local.html

DePaulo, B. (1992). Nonverbal behaviour and self-presentation. *Psychological Bulletin, 111*, 203–243. doi:10.1037/0033-2909.111.2.203

Drory, A., & Zaidman, N. (2007). Impression management behaviour: Effects of the organizational system. *Journal of Managerial Psychology, 22*(3), 290–308. doi:10.1108/02683940710733106

Eckhardt, G. M., & Houston, M. J. (2002). Cultural paradoxes reflected in brand meaning: McDonald's in Shanghai, China. *Journal of International Marketing, 10*(2), 68–82. doi:10.1509/jimk.10.2.68.19532

Ekman, P., & Davidson, J. (Eds.). (1994). *The nature of emotion: Fundamental questions*. New York: Oxford University Press.

Ekman, P., & Friesen, W. V. (1971). Constants across cultures in the face and emotion. *Journal of Personality and Social Psychology, 17*, 124–129. doi:10.1037/h0030377

Fairtrade Foundation. (2008). *About fairtrade towns*. Retrieved from http://www.fairtrade.org.uk/get_involved/campaigns/fairtrade_towns/about_fairtrade_towns.aspx

Friedman, T. L. (1999). *The Lexus and the olive tree*. New York: Farrar, Straus and Giroux.

Gangestad, S. W., & Snyder, M. (2000). Self-monitoring: Appraisal and reappraisal. *Psychological Bulletin, 126*, 530–555. doi:10.1037/0033-2909.126.4.530

Giddens, A. (2006). We should ditch the green movement: The climate change debate is too important to be left in the hands of those who are hostile to science and technology. *The Guardian*. Retrieved from http://www.guardian.co.uk/commentisfree/2006/nov/01/post561

Gordon, R. A. (1996). Impact of ingratiation on judgments and evaluations: A meta-analytic investigation. *Journal of Personality and Social Psychology, 71*(1), 54–70. doi:10.1037/0022-3514.71.1.54

Granose, C. S. (2007). Gender differences in career perceptions in the people's republic of China. *Career Development International, 12*(1), 9–14. doi:10.1108/13620430710724802

Green Marketing Conference. (2008). *Grange City Hotel*. Retrieved from http://www.haymarketevents.com/conferenceDetail/278

Hocking, J. B., Brown, M., & Harzing, A. (2007). Balancing global and local strategic contexts: Expatriate knowledge transfer, applications, and learning within a transnational organization. *Human Resource Management, 46*(4), 513–533. doi:10.1002/hrm.20180

Hofstede, G. (1980). *Culture's consequences: International differences in work-related values.* Beverly Hills, CA: Sage Publications.

Hollander, E. P. (1958). Conformity, status, and idiosyncrasy credit. *Psychological Review, 65,* 117–127. doi:10.1037/h0042501

HSBC. (2008). *Global website.* Retrieved from http://www.hsbc.com

Jackson, C., Colquitt, J. A., Wesson, M., & Zapata-Phelan, C. (2006). Psychological collectivism: A measurement validation and linkage to group member performance. *The Journal of Applied Psychology, 91*(4), 884–899. doi:10.1037/0021-9010.91.4.884

Johnson, V., & Peppas, S. C. (2003). Crisis management in Belgium: The case of Coca Cola. *Corporate Communications: An International Journal, 8*(1), 18–22. doi:10.1108/13563280310458885

Kurman, J. (2001). Self-enhancement: Is it restricted to individualistic cultures? *Personality and Social Psychology Bulletin, 27*(12), 1705–1716. doi:10.1177/01461672012712013

Leary, M. R., & Kowalski, R. M. (1990). Impression management: A literature review and two-component model. *Psychological Bulletin, 107*(1), 34–47. doi:10.1037/0033-2909.107.1.34

Leigh, T. W., & Summers, J. O. (2002). An initial evaluation of industrial buyers' impressions of salespersons' nonverbal cues. *Journal of Personal Selling & Sales Management, 22*(1), 41–53.

Liden, R. C., & Mitchell, T. R. (1988). Ingratiatory behaviour in organizational settings. *Academy of Management Review, 13,* 572–587. doi:10.2307/258376

Liu, X., & Shaffer, M. (2005). An investigation of expatriate adjustment and performance: a social capital perspective. *International Journal of Cross Cultural Management, 5*(3), 235–254. doi:10.1177/1470595805058411

Markus, H. R., & Kitayama, S. (1991). Culture and the self: Implications for cognition, emotion, and motivation. *Psychological Review, 98,* 224–253. doi:10.1037/0033-295X.98.2.224

Montepare, J. M., & Zebrowitz-McArthur, L. A. (1988). Impressions of people created by age-related qualities of their gaits. *Journal of Personality and Social Psychology, 55,* 547–556. doi:10.1037/0022-3514.55.4.547

Moore, F. (2006). Strategy, power and negotiation: Social control and expatriate managers in a German multinational corporation. *International Journal of Human Resource Management, 17*(3), 399–413. doi:10.1080/09585190500521359

News, B. B. C. (2003a). *India to test Coca-Cola sludge.* Retrieved from http://news.bbc.co.uk/2/hi/south_asia/3133259.stm

News, B. B. C. (2003b). *Indian colas 'not unsafe'.* Retrieved from http://news.bbc.co.uk/2/hi/south_asia/3126519.stm

News, B. B. C. (2004). *Coke recalls controversial water.* Retrieved from http://news.bbc.co.uk/1/hi/business/3550063.stm

News, B. B. C. (2005). *Indian Coca-Cola protest to go on.* Retrieved from http://news.bbc.co.uk/1/hi/world/south_asia/4603511.stm

Oliver, M. (2005). McLibel. *The Guardian.* Retrieved from http://www.guardian.co.uk/news/2005/feb/15/food.foodanddrink

Palmer, R. J., Welker, R. B., Campbell, T. L., & Magner, N. R. (2001). Examining the impression management orientation of managers. *Journal of Managerial Psychology, 16*(1), 35–49. doi:10.1108/02683940110366588

Parkes, L. P., Bochner, S., & Schneider, S. K. (2001). Person-organisation fit across cultures: An empirical investigation of individualism and collectivism. *Applied Psychology: An International Review, 50*(1), 81–108. doi:10.1111/1464-0597.00049

Paulhus, D. (1982). Individual differences, self presentation and cognitive dissonance: Their concurrent operation in forced compliance. *Journal of Personality and Social Psychology*, *43*(4), 838–852. doi:10.1037/0022-3514.43.4.838

Peltokorpi, V. (2006). Japanese organizational behaviour in Nordic subsidiaries: A Nordic expatriate perspective. *Employee Relations*, *28*(2), 103–118. doi:10.1108/01425450610639347

Pires, G., Stanton, J., & Ostenfeld, S. (2006). Improving expatriate adjustment and effectiveness in ethnically diverse countries: Marketing insights. *Cross Cultural Management*, *13*(2), 156–170. doi:10.1108/13527600610662339

Rao, A., Schmidt, S. M., & Murray, L. H. (1995). Upward impression management: Goals, influence strategies, and consequences. *Human Relations*, *48*, 147–167. doi:10.1177/001872679504800203

Reuters. (2007). *Prince Charles shows of smaller carbon footprint*. Retrieved from http://www.reuters.com/article/environmentNews/idUSL2691546320070626

Richardson, J., & McKenna, S. (2006). Exploring relationships with home and host countries: A study of self-directed expatriates. *Cross Cultural Management*, *13*(1), 6–22. doi:10.1108/13527600610643448

Rosenfeld, P., Giacalone, R. A., & Riordan, C. A. (1995). *Impression management in organizations: Theory, measurement, practice*. London: Routledge.

Schlenker, B. R. (1980). *Impression management: The self-concept, social identity, and interpersonal relations*. Monterey, CA: Brooks/Cole.

Schmidt, S. M., & Kipnis, D. (1984). Managers' pursuit of individual and organizational goals. *Human Relations*, *37*, 781–794. doi:10.1177/001872678403701001

Selmer, J. (2006). Adjustment of business expatriates in greater China: A strategic perspective. *International Journal of Human Resource Management*, *17*(12), 1994–2008.

Selmer, J., Chiu, R. K., & Shenkar, O. (2007). Cultural distance asymmetry in expatriate adjustment. *Cross Cultural Management*, *14*(2), 150–160. doi:10.1108/13527600710745750

Shaffer, M. A., Harrison, D. A., Gregersen, H., Black, J. S., & Ferzandi, L. A. (2006). You can take it with you: Individual differences and expatriate effectiveness. *The Journal of Applied Psychology*, *91*(1), 109–125. doi:10.1037/0021-9010.91.1.109

Shahnawaz, M. G., & Bala, M. (2007). Exploring individualism-collectivism in young employees of new organizations. *Journal of Indian Psychology*, *25*(1-2), 24–40.

Shimanoff, S. B. (1994). Gender perspectives on facework: Simplistic stereotypes vs. complex realities. In S. Ting-Toomey (Ed.), *The challenge of facework: Cross-cultural and interpersonal issues* (pp. 159-207). Albany, NY: State University of New York Press.

Shimoni, T., Ronen, S., & Roziner, I. (2005). Predicting expatriate adjustment: Israel as a host country. *International Journal of Cross Cultural Management*, *5*(3), 293–312. doi:10.1177/1470595805060812

Silverthorne, C. P. (2005). *Organizational psychology in cross-cultural perspective*. New York: New York University Press.

Snyder, M. (1974). Self-monitoring of expressive behaviour. *Journal of Personality and Social Psychology*, *30*(4), 526–537. doi:10.1037/h0037039

Spurlock, M. (Director). (2004). *Supersize me* [Motion picture]. USA: Samuel Goldwyn Films.

Sriramesh, K., & Vercic, D. (2001). International public relations: A framework for future research. *Journal of Communication Management*, *6*(2), 103–117. doi:10.1108/13632540210806973

Stahl, G. K., & Caligiuri, P. (2005). The effectiveness of expatriate coping strategies: The moderating role of cultural distance, position level, and time on the international assignment. *The Journal of Applied Psychology*, *90*(4), 603–615. doi:10.1037/0021-9010.90.4.603

Telegraph. (2008). *Green grows the value so when you go eco-friendly*. Retrieved from http://www.telegraph.co.uk/property/main.jhtml?xml=/property/2004/06/26/prgre26.xml

Thornton, B., Audesse, R. J., Ryckman, R. M., & Burckle, M. J. (2006). Playing dumb and knowing it all: Two sides of an impression management coin. *Individual Differences Research*, *4*(1), 37–45.

Tian, Y. (2006). Communicating with local publics: A case study of Coca Cola's Chinese website. *Corporate Communications: An International Journal*, *11*(1), 13–22. doi:10.1108/13563280610643516

Timmerman, G., & Bajema, C. (1999). Incidence and methodology in sexual harassment research in northwest Europe. *Women's Studies International Forum*, *22*(6), 673–681. doi:10.1016/S0277-5395(99)00076-X

Ting-Toomey, S. (Ed.). (1994). *The challenge of facework: Cross-cultural and interpersonal issues*. Albany, NY: State University of New York.

Triandis, H. C. (1989). The self and social behaviour in differing cultural contexts. *Psychological Review*, *96*, 506–520. doi:10.1037/0033-295X.96.3.506

Triandis, H. C., & Gelfand, M. (1998). Converging measurement of horizontal and vertical individualism and collectivism. *Journal of Personality and Social Psychology*, *74*, 118–128. doi:10.1037/0022-3514.74.1.118

Vilela, B. B., González, J. A. V., Ferrín, P. F., & del Río Araújo, M. L. (2007). Impression management tactics and affective context: Influence on sales performance appraisal. *European Journal of Marketing*, *41*(5-6), 624–639. doi:10.1108/03090560710737651

Vonk, R. (1998). The slime effect: Suspicion and dislike of likeable behaviour toward superiors. *Journal of Personality and Social Psychology*, *74*(4), 849–864. doi:10.1037/0022-3514.74.4.849

Vonk, R. (2002). Self-serving interpretations of flattery: Why ingratiation works. *Journal of Personality and Social Psychology*, *82*(4), 515–526. doi:10.1037/0022-3514.82.4.515

Wayne, S. J., & Liden, R. C. (1995). Effects of impression management on performance ratings: A longitudinal study. *Academy of Management Journal. Special Issue: Intra- and Interorganizational Cooperation*, *38*(1), 232-260.

Westphal, J. D., & Stern, I. (2006). The other pathway to the boardroom: Interpersonal influence behaviour as a substitute for elite credentials and majority status in obtaining board appointments. *Administrative Science Quarterly*, *51*(2), 169–204. doi:10.2189/asqu.51.2.169

Westphal, J. D., & Stern, I. (2007). Flattery will get you everywhere (especially if you are a male Caucasian): How ingratiation, boardroom behaviour, and demographic minority status affect additional board appointments at U.S. companies. *Academy of Management Journal*, *50*(2), 267–288.

Yamazaki, Y., & Kayes, D. C. (2007). Expatriate learning: Exploring how Japanese managers adapt in the United States. *International Journal of Human Resource Management*, *18*(8), 1373–1395.

Zukin, S., & Maguire, J. S. (2004). Consumers and consumption. *Annual Review of Sociology*, *30*, 173–197. doi:10.1146/annurev.soc.30.012703.110553

Chapter 5
Potentials for Externalizing and Measuring of Tacit Knowledge within Knowledge Nodes in the Context of Knowledge Networks

Christian-Andreas Schumann
University of Applied Sciences Zwickau, Germany

Claudia Tittmann
University of Applied Sciences Zwickau, Germany

ABSTRACT

The currently developing knowledge society needs high quality knowledge bases with wide-spreading knowledge sources. Because of the complexity of knowledge, they organize in knowledge networks. In addition, the intellectual capital of organizational units influences more and more the market value of organizations and companies. Thus, it is a challenging question to look at how intellectual capital can be developed and measured from tacit knowledge, and which factors of trust, risk, and compliance influence this. This chapter will describe the approach of knowledge nodes, the small components of knowledge networks, and their processes and their influence onto the value of knowledge networks.

INTRODUCTION

Constellation of Knowledge, Knowledge Society, and Knowledge Networks

The relevance of knowledge is referred by a long list of publications about knowledge, knowledge trans-fer, knowledge sharing, knowledge networks, etc. Thus, the definition and importance of knowledge changed significantly. In some context, knowledge changes to innovation; it changes to intellectual capital (Mertins, Alwert and Heisig 2005). Knowledge belongs to the intangible assets.

The society and the further development of the society will be influenced more and more by knowledge (Gilbert 2005). Therefore, the society changed to a knowledge society which refers to

DOI: 10.4018/978-1-60566-790-4.ch005

economic, political and social changes which are taking place as societies move from industrial to the post-industrial age. In this context intellectual capital as intangible asset represses more and more the importance of the other assets like money or land (Jennewein 2005).

The paradox of the knowledge society is the opposite of knowledge and nescience (Jischa 2008: p.280). There is knowledge and the complexities of things are not known. In decision processes of politics and economics it is important to manage knowledge on one side and handle with nescience, too (Böschen, Schneider and Lerf 2004).

There are lots of knowledge islands which have to be connected and an effective knowledge transfer needs to be implemented (von Krogh, Back and Enkel 2007: p.2). Already Castells in (Castells 2000) described the change to a network society. These networks in broad and general context developed out of the demands of the society.

The knowledge society needs to cross-link knowledge of organizational units to knowledge networks. Thus, it is possible to reach higher knowledge potentials and create new knowledge out of this. The increase of knowledge will be influenced by knowledge sharing processes between the organizational units. One of the main problems is the role of tacit knowledge, the knowledge not structured and formalized, the knowledge expressed by peoples activities.

Perspectives onto Knowledge in International and Intercultural Context

Knowledge and knowledge transformations are influenced by the cultural, political and social dimension. Additionally, globalization effected higher complexity of the knowledge structures and the knowledge interfaces. Problems, e.g. the same knowledge may have a different meaning in different cultural context; have to be solved to make intercultural knowledge useable.

Culture has various dimensions. (Joynt and Warner 1996) define culture in a broader view with the dimensions human nature, relations to nature, activity orientation, human relationships, relations to time, and space orientation. In other views, e.g. in (Triandis 1995: p.43), culture is characterized as a pattern of shared beliefs, attitudes, norms, roles and values that are organized around a theme and that can be found in certain geographic regions during a particular historic period. This second view is the better base for deriving a system of parameters. It is fundamental for an attempt to describe culture and transfer it into an appraisable system.

Knowledge is categorized in different sub-ideas. One of this is to divide knowledge into explicit and tacit knowledge. The explicit knowledge is codified or codifiable. Thus, this knowledge can be saved and transferred or transformed into other contexts like different culture, other languages, or different social preconditions. But barriers for knowledge sharing, especially between different cultures have to be respected (Möller and Svahn 2004).

Otherwise, tacit knowledge, the knowledge consisting mainly of experiences, is really hard to catch; inside cultures as well as between cultures; individualism cultures as well as collectivism cultures. To analyze and understand this, the consideration of culture as a system is necessary.

Intercultural Tacit Knowledge within Science and Business Networks

For efficiently handling and exploitation of the complexity of knowledge and the permanently increasing flood of information, companies and research units or institutes merge to networks; business networks as well as knowledge networks (Drucker 1995). As society develops to a knowledge society, networks develop to knowledge networks.

Cross-linked knowledge is needed for reaching knowledge literacy, the skill for using knowledge usefully and competently. It is fundamental for reaching business or research goals. Knowledge literacy and knowledge networking produces a higher knowledge level and new knowledge by exchanging knowledge. It can be utilized as a driver for innovations. In fact: knowledge transfer and knowledge sharing need knowledge cooperation (Lembke 2005).

The intention of the knowledge networks is the cross-linking of knowledge and information for increasing the knowledge potential and to create new knowledge. Furthermore, it is not enough to build up regional knowledge networks; the actors of knowledge tend to be intercultural.

An important part of the knowledge potential of the knowledge network is the knowledge partly codified in tacit knowledge, the knowledge inside people's minds. From this fact the growing relevance of tacit knowledge for knowledge development and further use of this knowledge in business or scientific scope is derivable. Therefore, the knowledge networks have the goal to extract this tacit knowledge.

On the one hand it is obvious that exactly this knowledge is needed for developing improvements and innovations. Otherwise, constitution of the process for extracting this knowledge is pretty difficult. Conducive for this is the motivation of the network actors to share knowledge. During the knowledge sharing process it is possible to transfer also tacit knowledge.

But there are also barriers blockading the exchange of knowledge. To them belongs the fact that knowledge networks have no static structure. They have – in most cases - a fixed kernel, but in the outer elements more fluctuating structures. Every single network actor will evaluate the chances and risks which of his knowledge he can offer in which intensity.

Following this development, a totally distinct form of organization with own regularities and social rules grows. The realization of the SECI-model by Nonaka and Takeuchi ((Nonaka and Takeuchi 1995)) seems to be a wishful thinking. This model is a pure abstract scientific approach, without respecting the influence of emotions, fears, cultural barriers.

General Perspective of this Chapter

In this chapter – basing on the functional chains of knowledge networks – the concept of a model will be introduced, which allows the measuring of knowledge potentials for knowledge nodes, knowledge-sub-networks, and complete knowledge networks basing on the key figure: knowledge node.

This is fundamental for intelligent knowledge networks which make tacit knowledge of their participants and actors useable; externalize it; finally, create their own tacit and explicit knowledge. Exploitation of tacit knowledge is fundamental for developing knowledge networks and increasing the knowledge level.

An important part of the measuring of knowledge is in this context the tacit knowledge. On the fundamental structure of intangible assets, consisting of human capital, relational capital, and structural capital, it is possible to assign the tacit knowledge mainly to the human capital.

In this constellation it is useable in two variants. On one hand there is the possibility to use the tacit knowledge unexploited, what improves the knowledge value of the owning knowledge node. Otherwise, it is possible to enclose the tacit knowledge while the knowledge sharing lifecycle. In this case, the knowledge value or potential of the whole organizational structure increases.

The rules and their effects of these two variants as well as their integration in a whole model for measuring knowledge shall be described in this chapter in detail.

The intention is to introduce the current state of development and the next steps of research.

BACKGROUND

Current Problems and Potentials of Knowledge

The structure of knowledge environment for companies or organization units is going to reach a high complexity level. The exponential increase of information and knowledge in global context creates new challenges in finding out the essential knowledge needed for the fulfilling of knowledge goals. This complexity is not longer controllable by single persons or inside companies. Furthermore, for maintaining economical or scientific competitiveness, it is not enough to be content with own internal or regional knowledge resources. It will rather be necessary to disclose new knowledge resources and develop new knowledge strategies.

Therefore, organizational structures in form of communities of practice, knowledge communities, and knowledge networks develop intensely (Bernus 2005; Schumann, Tittmann and Tittmann 2008).

Along with this structural or organizational evolution, knowledge sharing and knowledge transfer are fundamental challenges for knowledge communities and knowledge networks (Probst, Raub and Romhardt 2006: p.17). Correlating to this development concepts of interorganizational activities like interaction, communication, and cooperation become more and more relevant (Caspers, Bickhoff and Bieger 2004; Lembke 2005).

Also the latest trend report, presented at the KnowTech 2007, about knowledge management by Bitkom and a cooperating knowledge management research group (Bitkom 2007) results among other facts in the trend to knowledge networking, especially in an international context.

The scientific progress and the innovation, initiated by knowledge networking, have to be balanced against the adversities and obstacles.

To these barriers belongs the knowledge drain by careless knowledge transfer, the deliberate sharing of untrue knowledge, the fear of losing knowledge levels by sharing knowledge, and so on. But these are fundamental more economic and self-protecting blockades. Furthermore, in international networks barriers like different language, different cultural level, different confessions, and so on, will be added (Ardichvili, Maurer, Li et al. 2006). Thus, there are two dimensions of adversities in knowledge cooperations.

For that reason it is more important than ever to find new solutions in knowledge cooperation, international accommodation, and ideas for benchmarking the knowledge progress and enhancement, in order to make the knowledge transfer measureable.

Definition of Tacit Knowledge in Intercultural Context

There are a lot of different categorizations of knowledge. But all further concepts are based on the differentiation into factual knowledge and practical knowledge, which was defined by the British philosopher Gilbert Ryle (Ryle 1949). In this definition factual knowledge is the "know-that"; and practical knowledge the "know-how". Both knowledge types are developed out of learning, application and reflection of learned facts. But there is no statement about the capturing and saving of knowledge.

Especially in the economic literature about knowledge management the distinction between explicit and implicit (or tacit) knowledge was developed (Nonaka and Takeuchi 1995). These terms can be retraced to biologist, chemist, and philosopher Polanyi (Polanyi 1967).

Explicit knowledge is codeable or already codified knowledge can be expressed in diverse notations like formal language or can be saved in data or knowledge bases. Therefore, it is easy to share and transfer this knowledge (Liebowitz

2000; Caspers, Bickhoff and Bieger 2004). Knowledge actors can read and learn this knowledge.

In contrast, tacit knowledge is the knowledge and experience inside the brain of every single person. This knowledge cannot be formalized and saved in an easy way. It is a challenge to extract this knowledge and make it usable for other persons or organizations (Goranzon, Ennals and Hammeron 2005: p.189-191; Porschen 2008). For example, if an employee leaves the company and does not pass on his or her know-how and information by communication to any other employee, this knowledge, including experiences, procedures, rules, is lost for the company.

There are ideas for collecting this tacit knowledge and converting it into explicit knowledge. On one hand every expert and knowledge carrier who is involved in organizational structures can transmit this knowledge actively or passively to other relevant members of the organization, it is a kind of organizational learning. Otherwise, the knowledge carrier can try to express the knowledge and, for example, to write it down. In research organizations tacit knowledge will be published in conferences, papers, or books. This is a possible method for externalizing knowledge, projectable to companies.

But this process of extracting tacit knowledge and transferring it to other individuals has to overcome the difficulties of reflecting the intercultural aspects like described before. This means, the tacit knowledge will be externalized. Then it will be merged with the cultural dimensions of the recipients. This cultural parameterization can lead to following results:

- the recipient accesses the same knowledge as the expert
- the recipient misunderstands the knowledge and interprets it in another way
- the recipient can merge the knowledge with his or her own knowledge and improves the knowledge

The fact is, knowledge input will be evaluated and merged in most cases with own experiences and knowledge.

Additionally, as tacit knowledge influences the market value of every person, it should be carefully handled, but one must consider that it is closely coupled on a person, consequently going away with the person. Organizations need to try and keep this knowledge, because it is an important part of the market value of the company, too.

Knowledge Networks: Types and Structures

Knowledge cooperation can be realized in different organizational structures like knowledge communities and knowledge networks. For exchanging and externalizing personal implicit knowledge, knowledge cooperation is because of the social and collective activities a needful form of organization. But because of contentions in the economic markets and in the scientific fields, every activity of knowledge sharing, every creation of knowledge networks takes place in the field of tension between cooperation and competition.

There are a lot of theoretical concepts for the organizational structures *knowledge network* and the structure of these knowledge networks is already defined in literature; primarily basing on the concepts of business networks (Miroschedji 2002). Most of these ideas are too general; there are less or fragmental ideas of detailing the knowledge networks and their knowledge potentials.

Therefore, the definition of strategic business networks (Ortmann and Sydow 2001; Kuhlin and Thielmann 2005; Sydow 2006), a more detailed structure definition of knowledge networks, is possible. Distinguishing marks are the consistence of network actors, the cooperative connections between network actors, and the pursuit of knowledge goals. In the context of this paper the following definition of knowledge networks, which can be further detailed in a wider and closer range, is possible: Interorganisational knowledge networks are the interconnection of more than two network actors for reaching knowledge goals by sharing and diffusing knowledge.

Depending on the intentions of the network they can be business oriented, science oriented, or business and science oriented (mixed).

A network can be described as a construct of nodes and edges, like in the graph theory (Gross and Yellen 2006). The nodes are the actors of the networks and their relations and interactivities are the edges. In knowledge networks the components are knowledge nodes and knowledge edges. Every partner of knowledge cooperation is called a knowledge actor.

The knowledge node can be an individual person, an organizational group, or a whole organization (e.g. companies, universities, institutes, or government/administration). It depends on the investigations made (Götz 2002). Therefore, it is expedient to define roles for each knowledge node. Basing on this precondition, the knowledge node can be assigned purpose dependent (Zhuge 2006). The role-based view allows the better linking of the knowledge network with the activities and roles of the business processes.

The following framework for the nodes of knowledge networks basing on the ideas of Sydow (Sydow 2006) can be defined:

*The **size** of such networks will be determined by the number of nodes, but the optimum or maximum size is not examined yet. Knowledge networks can work in regional, national, or multinational context. They also can be specified or specialized in different branches or sciences.*

*The **diversity** of the networks is the number of different groups of actors within the network. Each network recursively consists of sub-networks, depending on the investigation background.*

Some authors also use the classification of the networks into operation divisions. But it can be said that this is similar to the role dependent view. If the idea of roles is applied to the networks there is no other functional categorization necessary.

The edges of knowledge networks are the relations between the knowledge nodes and reflect the interactions, communication and knowledge flows between the nodes. The knowledge flows define the intensity of knowledge transfer on a special subject or science. But it is also possible to transfer complex structures of cross-science knowledge. That's a fundamental problem for the further research in the valuation of the flowing knowledge energy. How to categorize and measure it?

The edges may be examined in the perspective of content (What is exchanged?) and the perspective of characteristics (How the content will be exchanged?). The content of the edges in knowledge networks is of course the knowledge. But the media are not specified. It may be conversation, but it also may be electronical files.

Important parameters of knowledge edges are the following:

The **density** defines the grade of intensity of the relations and interactions inside the network. There is no equal distribution inside the networks. Maybe there are some concentrations or centers of knowledge activities.

The **interdependence** describes the cross-dependence between the network actors. But here are differences between business networks and science or research networks. The business networks need knowledge results for their business processes. Against, research networks in most cases can set their own knowledge goals.

The **organizational skill** of the knowledge network will be determined by the two dimensions culture and structure. The specification of this component reaches a high complexity.

The development of knowledge networks can reach a level on the scale from temporary networks to permanent networks. Most networks have a fixed kernel and the surrounding knowledge nodes are dynamic. Therefore it is not easy to define a border for knowledge networks (Thorelli 1986). The definition of a border is subjective and depends on the focus of the examining situation.

There are always, sometimes latent, relations between actors of different networks. Otherwise, the same actor or sub-network may be part of more than one network. This causes the **permeability** of knowledge networks, the use of network-internal knowledge outside the network. Permeability is an indicator for knowledge outflows and knowledge inflows. It mainly influences the strength and durability of knowledge networks, because intensive outflows of highly potentiated knowledge lead to a relocation of the knowledge concentration.

MEASURING (TACIT) KNOWLEDGE WITHIN KNOWLEDGE NODES ISSUES, CONTROVERSIES, PROBLEMS

Challenges of Intercultural Knowledge Sharing

At this point it is necessary to trace two questions. The first question is about the level of regarding the measurability of (tacit) knowledge in knowledge sharing models. The second question is related to barriers to be overcome for extracting and/or measuring tacit knowledge.

Through a social or human process information will be converted into knowledge, and knowledge will be improved into new knowledge and innovation. Thus, the **knowledge lifecycle** and its management is the way from the creation of knowledge until obsolescence or its transitions into new knowledge. It is the cycle from the origin of knowledge to the reuse of knowledge and reaching a higher knowledge level (Bernard and Tichkiewitch 2008). Along this lifecycle – in each process step - knowledge has a value

There are different models for the knowledge lifecycle, and there are analogies between the knowledge lifecycle and the SECI-model (Nonaka

and Takeuchi 1995); or in other words SECI belongs to the knowledge lifecycle models.

In a more systemic view the main phases of the knowledge lifecycle can be declared as knowledge acquisition, knowledge modeling, knowledge annotation, and knowledge reuse (Millard, Tao, Doody et al. 2006). This model is correct, but not detailed enough. It handles knowledge in an abstract way and does not represent the real complexity of the knowledge lifecycle. If the fourth step – knowledge reuse – is analyzed, it also should contain the problem of the handling of obsolete knowledge; and it should include the handling of external knowledge.

Therefore, the extended models like described by (Matthews and Harris 2006) are more useable.

This model (Figure 1) shows the process from the creation of knowledge in individuals minds, the tacit knowledge; followed by storing (externalizing) this knowledge. The stored knowledge can be used and reused. Afterwards it is possible to share the knowledge. Finally knowledge will be disposed, either it is obsolete and has to be unlearned or it can be used for creating new knowledge. This model is an approach to detail the processes in knowledge networks and to parameterize every step of the process. But the lack of these models is that measuring of knowledge is not possible. It needs an extension of this view to the tacit knowledge to valuate the enormously important knowledge for the market value of an individual, an organization or company. Therefore, a model will be needed for examining both, the knowledge lifecycle and the coupled knowledge valuation.

In this context the question occurs whether knowledge is a product. On the one hand it is possible to see knowledge as information about a product or a production process; on the other hand knowledge is a product, because it is something having a value and can be sold or bought. Therefore, it may be meaningful to see knowledge as product; to compare knowledge and products.

Figure 1. Tacit knowledge in the knowledge lifecycle

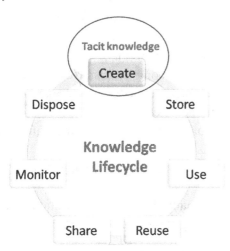

There exists for products the idea of the product lifecycle, led by the product lifecycle management (PLM). PLM is the process of managing products (of a company) along their whole lifecycle, from the ideas and concepts until their disposing or recycling (Stark 2007).

The phases of product lifecycle management are conception, design, realization, use, service, evaluate, and dispose. These steps have different perspectives in the product and the "knowledge as product" context (Table 1).

The main difference is that knowledge cannot be disposed after the lifecycle. Of course, the explicit knowledge (as text files, in databases) can be deleted if it is obsolete. The tacit knowledge inside the people's mind always develops driven by any process the people are involved. Obsolete knowledge only can be unlearned!

This fact from the knowledge lifecycle becomes an important trend in the product lifecycle, which also evolves from existing knowledge and produces new knowledge about the products and their construction, development, or service. The knowledge about the products and the customer needs becomes more and more important, especially in the global context. All the enhanced knowledge while the product lifecycle, bad experiences, mistakes as well as new developed concepts, is capital for further developments. Therefore, it should be saved and be used for further progress.

A product gets its value during the lifecycle. Exactly this is the commonness between both, product and knowledge. Thus, knowledge lifecycle is really close to the product lifecycle. In most cases both lifecycles work integrated.

As both lifecycles are usually coupled onto management systems, or special information or data management systems, it is a good way for

Table 1. Product versus "knowledge as product"

Phase	Meaning for product	Meaning for knowledge as product
Conception	Finding an idea and concept for the product	Creating a knowledge goal and finding out knowledge needs
Design	Making a construction concept for the product	Designing a model for extraction and saving the knowledge
Realization	Construct or build the product	Finding out internal and external sources for the knowledge; bring them together and combine them to reach knowledge goals
Use	Application of the product	Application of the knowledge
Service	Adapting and customizing the product	Adapting and adjusting the knowledge
Evaluation	Evaluation of the product based upon the product experiences and its practical application	Evaluation of the truth and consistence of knowledge based upon practical application and experiences
Dispose	Dispose a product	Disposing obsolete knowledge and reusing improved knowledge

grabbing tacit knowledge from the staff as well as from the systems itself.

Besides the measurement of knowledge there is a gap between the increasing number of knowledge sources and the issue of the information flood, the symptoms of information overload (Gehle 2006). The cultural differences lead also to various **barriers** or disturbances in knowledge activities. Some of these barriers are (Bendt 2000):

- Lacking willingness for sharing knowledge (fears of losing power or superiority thinking)

- Lacking willingness for absorption (refusal of new or strange ideas)
- Complicated relations (mostly in economic or political context)
- Missing common language
- Misinterpreting or distortion of information or knowledge by communication intermediates
- Cultural philosophy against knowledge transfer
- Barren organizational peripherals

Additionally there are organizational differences forcing knowledge barriers. In the western

Figure 2. Knowledge development cycle - from individual to organisational networks

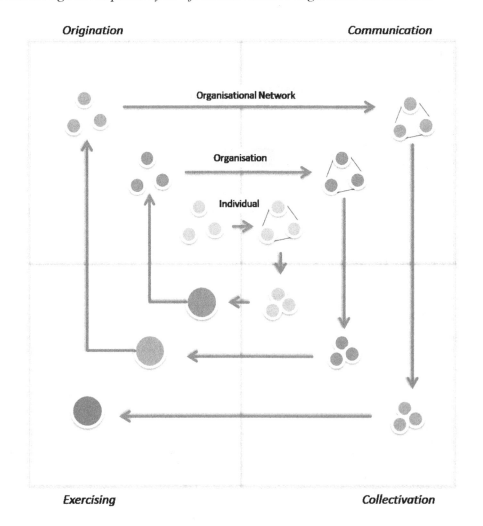

cultural area people follow up the individualism strategy, trying to control the nature; otherwise, in eastern/Asian cultures people organize themselves in whole, living organizations, harmonizing with nature (Nonaka and Takeuchi 1995).

Thus, how the measurement and the barriers can be brought together? Especially in the perspective of tacit knowledge the knowledge lifecycle is primarily a social and learning process; secondary a systemic and technical process. The origin of the knowledge is the tacit knowledge of individuals, built up by own experiences and explicit (saved) knowledge existing for the individual or the organizations where the individual is part of. The main problem the knowledge lifecycle has to solve is the extraction of tacit knowledge and to bring it successively into the knowledge flow. Therefore, the social process and the technical process for capturing tacit knowledge have to be cross-linked.

Nonaka has defined the concept of *Ba* (Nonaka and Konno 1998). *Ba* is a key place for knowledge creation. It means a common background, an emotion, conditions for sharing the own context

– including individual history – with the others. In this context *Ba* is a place for exchanging tacit knowledge, including love, trust, safety, and respect. Established *Ba* leads to an open communication culture.

In expanding the idea of *Ba* by projecting it onto knowledge networks, the concept of the knowledge development cycle results (Figure 2). In the beginning of knowledge networking there are the individuals with their tacit knowledge. When the *Ba* culture developed and along with it the knowledge, the organization will reach a level as close as it would be an individual, but on a higher level. The *Ba* brings individuals and their knowledge together. Thus, finally the knowledge networks can reach the *Ba* culture.

While this *Ba* process, the measurement of knowledge can be integrated – from the individual to the organizational network. In this context the knowledge value develops in three dimensions: from individual to collective; from face-to-face to virtual and recursively in every organizational level, because every organizational level develops its own tacit knowledge!

Figure 3. Knowledge Sharing Lifecycle (Schumann, Tittmann and Tittmann 2008)

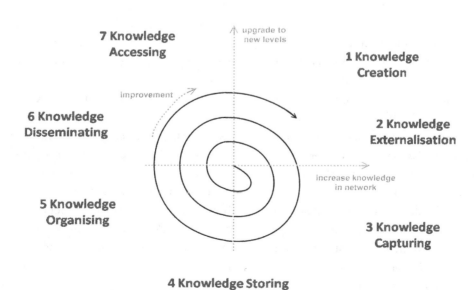

Intercultural knowledge networks have an own culture. It is a long lasting process to define and establish, or find out common values and qualities, trust for building up a kind of new culture, a special networking culture. The "Commitment to Organizational Culture" (Alas and Vadi 2006) is the attribute of changes (Harkins, Carter and Timmins 2000).

Tacit knowledge is mostly a unique selling proposition. Therefore, it is only capturable in the knowledge lifecycle and the knowledge sharing lifecycle of the knowledge networks by creating a typical knowledge networking culture. Similar problems are discussed in many sciences (Marra 2004; Newell 2005).

Knowledge Literacy within the Knowledge Sharing Lifecycle

Every business objective is based on knowledge goals. A knowledge goal can be reached by building up knowledge networks. Hence the main goal of knowledge networks is the knowledge cooperation and the knowledge sharing.

The knowledge sharing lifecycle is the process for exchanging explicit knowledge, externalizing tacit knowledge and reaching a higher knowledge level (Davies, Duke and Sure 2004). Fundamental for the knowledge sharing lifecycle is the creation of knowledge, tacit as well as explicit. This step is followed by the externalization of knowledge (e.g. by storytelling, by doing, by digital documents). Afterwards the knowledge will be captured, stored, and organized. Exactly this knowledge can be disseminated inside the knowledge network or to other networks. The knowledge can be accessed and used for creating new knowledge (Furst, Reeves, Rosen et al. 2004).

Literacy in its fundamental context means the ability to read and write in a formal language. Maybe it is similar to the term communication. Therefore, literacy is fundamental for information and knowledge transfer. Since the beginning of human beings there was only tacit knowledge.

Literacy enabled the chance to externalize this implicit knowledge.

The way from tacit knowledge to personal and organizational knowledge literacy needs the fulfillment of several sub-skills: identification of knowledge needs, localization of knowledge, organization of knowledge, goal-oriented selection of knowledge, and purpose-optimized representation of knowledge.

The main problem is, most people undervalue the importance of knowledge literacy in two directions. On the one hand knowledge literacy can be used to increase the knowledge level of the organization. Otherwise, there is the risk to become knowledge exhausted.

SOLUTIONS AND RECOMMENDATIONS

Knowledge Interdependencies

A look back to the concepts of *Ba* model and the knowledge (sharing) lifecycle model shows the needs for an integrated model of social and technical view. For realizing a better integration and valuation of tacit knowledge inside a culture or intercultural knowledge network and to enable the measurement of knowledge, it is necessary to analyze more detailed the interactions inside the knowledge networks and between the networks (Figure 4).

On one side, in the meta level, the overall processes of the knowledge networks should be examined. In the next step, the micro level, it is necessary to define the smallest possible or as small as possible unit of knowledge carriers.

There are knowledge processes, knowledge flows and interactions on the meta level of knowledge networks as well as on the micro level of knowledge nodes. The interdependencies are regulated by the knowledge and business goals, and by the knowledge energy. Therefore, processes and structures of the object classes in the framework

Figure 4. Cross-linked knowledge networks (Schumann and Tittmann 2007: p.880)

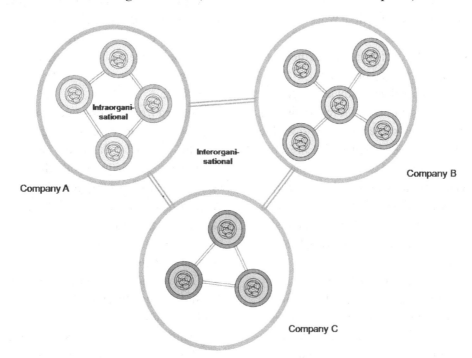

of knowledge networking and their interaction-model have to be examined closely. The result is to derive a knowledge flow and interaction model. This gives chances for a better understanding and organization of the information and knowledge flows; finally, for integrating and capturing tacit knowledge.

Abstract Model Knowledge Node and Knowledge Energy

The intentions for developing an abstract model for knowledge node and knowledge energy are concentrated on a better understanding and valuating of knowledge networks; and as basis for simulations of knowledge networks. This becomes a tool for analyzing as small as possible knowledge carriers and estimating their knowledge energy in an absolute potential as well as relatively to the knowledge network. On the basis of these elements it is possible to estimate or measure the knowledge value of the whole knowledge

network or their sub networks. Furthermore, it is possible using these knowledge nodes for examining the knowledge flows with their causes and effects. This measurement model can further be used for different cases, in scientific as well as in business scope.

A **knowledge node** is a small knowledge unit, the smallest possible knowledge carrier. It may be a single person, a group of persons, a part of an organization, a whole organization, or a company. The structure of the knowledge node is or should be defined by roles. These roles associate process steps of the workflow to the knowledge node. Thus, the business processes and the knowledge processes are cross-linked.

A knowledge node contains knowledge, or **knowledge energy**. The knowledge energy is the potential or energy existing inside a knowledge node. Similar to the physical energy definition (Yurke and Denker 1984; Halliday, Resnick and Walker 2007), knowledge energy is the ability of a system, to do knowledge work (Zhuge, Guo and Li 2006). But in physical systems as well as knowledge networks the possible work strongly depends on which changes of state or transfers the bordering system allows. It correlates to the set of rules influencing the energy processes.

Knowledge potential or knowledge energy is an important driver during the cross-linking of knowledge nodes. On the base of knowledge energy will be decided, which nodes are connecting by which rules. Additionally, there are interdependencies between knowledge energy and the caused knowledge flows. An exemplary rule is that knowledge flows from knowledge nodes with higher knowledge energy to nodes with lower knowledge energy.

There is a definition of knowledge flow by Zhuge (Zhuge 2002) as a process of knowledge passing between people or knowledge processing mechanism with three crucial attributes: direction (sender and receiver), content (sharable knowledge content), and carrier (media which passes the content). This definition is in a generalized but adaptable context the knowledge flow between knowledge nodes. But for further ideas it is important to see the knowledge flow not only in a systemic and explicit view. In some cases also tacit knowledge can flow, expressed as knowledge activities.

The problem is that knowledge energy is not a static factor or matter. It changes depending on the knowledge flows. Every input or output influences the energy. The development of knowledge energy depends on the three dimensions age, priority, and diffusion of knowledge. The dimension *age* means that knowledge loses value and meaning as older as it is, if it will not be increased and evaluated. The *priority* of knowledge means the actuality and degree of innovation of the knowledge. Therefore, new and innovative knowledge has a high priority and consequently the knowledge energy reaches a high level. Otherwise, if the new knowledge is already common knowledge, the knowledge energy is lower. The third dimension, *diffusion*, means that knowledge with a wide diffusion has only a little value. Against, knowledge with nearly no diffusion has a high value; hence a high knowledge energy. Therefore the goal of every knowledge node and knowledge actor should be to have new, innovative, and sparsely diffused knowledge.

Derived from the preconditions, the structure of knowledge nodes can be developed (Figure 5). The kernel of the node is the knowledge itself. This knowledge inside the nodes belongs to different **knowledge domains.** A knowledge domain can be categorized into different ways; scientific categories (e.g. chemistry, physics), branches (e.g. education, finance, architecture), or technologies.

The knowledge inside the domains or inter-divisional has different levels of importance. Therefore, it is set on special **knowledge priorities**. Thus, new and important knowledge is laid on a high priority level; otherwise the older and commonly known knowledge is laid on lower priority levels. Depending on the knowledge priorities it is possible to control and secure the knowledge flows. For example, to a knowledge recipient with a low knowledge level in a domain should not be transferred the high priority leveled knowledge.

A further indicator for the knowledge inside the domain is the **knowledge density**. The density describes how much knowledge is available per knowledge domain in a knowledge priority.

The density, domains, and priorities of knowledge are main indicators of the knowledge nodes (Figure 5). This all belongs to the kernel of the knowledge node.

The content of the kernel is influenced by **knowledge activities**. These are learning, searching, offering, and processing. These activities influence the knowledge in the kernel. The intention of the activities is the improvement of the inner knowledge.

Finally, there are **knowledge connectors** - the connecting interfaces. Their task is to connect the knowledge nodes of a network and to realize the

Figure 5. Structure of a knowledge node

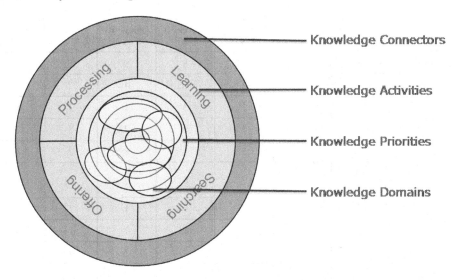

knowledge flow. The knowledge connectors also contain secure functions to transfer knowledge by predefined rules.

Use Case – Education Network Saxony

The Education Network Saxony has the intention to develop the e-learning processes amongst the universities in Saxony (Germany). For a special project five universities built up a network. In the context of this chapter every university is a knowledge node.

For the project the competences in e-learning of every university have been evaluated. These competences are the knowledge domains. Furthermore, the knowledge energy of these knowledge domains has been identified.

Result is following simplified structure (Table 2):

The table shows the knowledge levels from 1 to 9 (1-low; 9-very intensive) in four top-domains and their subdomains. With this rating it is possible to find out the knowledge competence of every university, every knowledge node. Furthermore, it is possible to evaluate the average knowledge as well as the absolute or relative knowledge.

Additionally, it is derivable if there is knowledge at all in one domain. Furthermore, it can be checked if there is a big or small difference between maximum and minimum knowledge level. The motivation for knowledge transfer depends on this. If the difference is going to zero – like "Business Process Management" – every node contains nearly the same knowledge. Whereas, when the difference is relatively high, it is an optimal constellation for knowledge transfer.

Tacit Knowledge as a Part of Knowledge Nodes in the Intercultural Focus

Tacit knowledge is a huge part of knowledge nodes, because it empowers the node to do any activities. If there would be only explicit knowledge, the complexity of knowledge networks could be reduced to an information system with permissions and rules. Furthermore, tacit knowledge is the origin of explicit knowledge.

As stated in the previous part of the paper, knowledge nodes consist of a role associated part of organizations or complete organizations. Every individual brings along explicit and tacit knowledge. But the main focus is on the special

Table 2. Knowledge prioritization in a knowledge network

		University 1	University 2	University 3	University 4	University 5	*Minimum*	*Maximum*	*Average*
Science Knowledge	Business Sciences	3	7	5	8	9	*3*	*9*	*7*
	Computer Sciences	8	2	3	6	4	*2*	*8*	*5*
	Architecture	6	8	3	3	5	*3*	*8*	*5*
Technical Knowledge	System Analysis	5	7	3	6	7	*3*	*7*	*6*
	System Development	7	2	3	8	8	*2*	*8*	*6*
	Business Process Management	6	7	7	8	7	*6*	*8*	*7*
Marketing Knowledge	Consulting	3	9	4	9	1	*1*	*9*	*5*
	Marketing	2	2	2	8	7	*2*	*8*	*4*
	Network Management	6	7	9	4	7	*4*	*9*	*7*
Production Knowledge	Content-Production	8	2	6	6	4	*2*	*8*	*5*
	Media Technology	4	4	3	8	5	*3*	*8*	*5*
	Competence Development	6	3	1	2	1	*1*	*6*	*3*

knowledge and intuitions of every individual. All this knowledge will be part of the kernel of the knowledge node. In the beginning there is more tacit than explicit knowledge in the kernel and it is very difficult to categorize it and put it into knowledge domains. It is analogical to processes in individual minds. There is a lot of explicit knowledge, many experiences, a lot of ideas and know-how to do something in a special way; but all this tacit knowledge is spanned over different scopes. Therefore, it is a challenge to pick out this knowledge and try to estimate its value.

When a knowledge node is forming up (Figure 6), it consists of one or more individuals or organizational units from different cultural background with own explicit and tacit knowledge. The knowledge inside the individuals is allocated in differing parts. Furthermore, the importance and the density of the knowledge are unequally disposed. Thus, some individuals have more tacit knowledge as others; or they have more important knowledge on a special scope. Therefore, the development from individuals

to knowledge nodes will be briefly described in more detail (Figure 6).

In the first step, the finding phase, the individuals check out, if an association brings the chance to reach a higher knowledge level. In the positive case the process of coupling will be forced. For this purpose it is necessary to define common goals. Furthermore, intercultural differences have to be reduced to a common dominator.

When the coupling is executed, the merging process can start. In this phase the individuals start to offer their knowledge from specified scopes, to exchange and to synchronize their knowledge. Furthermore, during the unifying phase, the knowledge will be consolidated until it is no longer identifiable for externals which individual of the knowledge node is the origin of it.

Therefore, as seen in the unification-step, there are two kernels, an explicit knowledge kernel and a tacit knowledge kernel. They developed from the individual kernels by merging.

In the final phase starts the process of knowledge improving by knowledge sharing (knowl-

Figure 6. Development of tacit knowledge in knowledge nodes

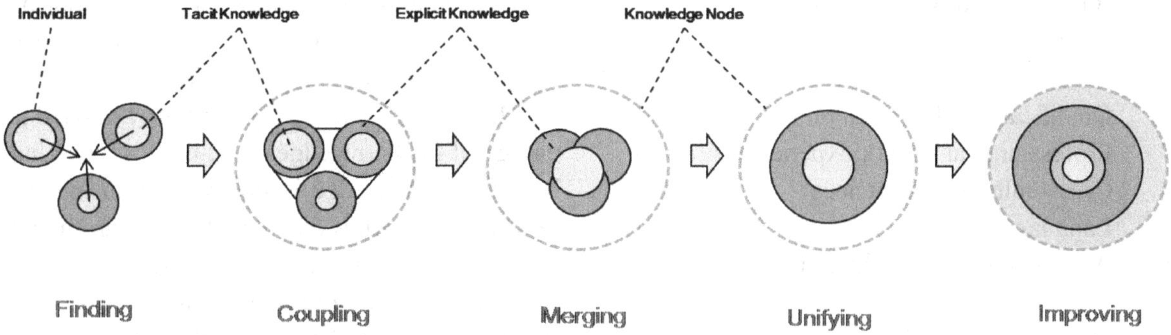

edge inputs and outputs). During this process the former tacit knowledge from the individuals becomes more and more explicit. They transfer it by communication and during the processes to the other actors of the node. Furthermore, during the knowledge activities the knowledge node enhances new tacit and explicit knowledge. This new knowledge is not coupled onto the individuals, but to the knowledge node as a whole.

It is not possible to project this process of knowledge development inside the knowledge nodes differentiated to the individuals. Every individual of the node evaluates the new developed knowledge with the own knowledge. But because of the varying knowledge absorption skills of every individual their knowledge levels and knowledge structures finally will be different.

The Value of Tacit Knowledge

In case of knowledge transfer or output as service, the measurement of both, the explicit and tacit knowledge, is necessary.

At this point, the main structure of knowledge node, the integration of tacit knowledge, and the main parameters are discussed.

The balance of knowledge, the so called intellectual capital statement, can be analyzed with various models, like Skandia navigator, Wissensbilanz Germany, Intangible Assets Monitor. Most of them identify the knowledge in the three categories

human capital, structural capital and relational capital (Bodrow and Bergmann 2003; Mertins, Alwert and Heisig 2005). The human capital is the talent base of the individuals (in companies the employees). To the human capital belong the individuals, their education, and their competencies and skills. The tacit knowledge belongs to the human capital, too (Dekkers 2005).

The structural capital is the information and knowledge base of the node; the no-human knowledge. Also the business processes belong to the structural capital. Finally, the relational capital are the networks and relations of every individual or organizational unit and the interaction of the processes (Bornemann and Sammer 2002).

To get an estimation of the intellectual capital statement of the knowledge nodes, it seems a good way to examine them into the three dimensions human capital, relational capital, and structural capital (Figure 7). Indicators for every dimension have to be defined. These indicators depend on the knowledge goals of the knowledge networks. Knowledge goals define the direction and strategy for the further development of the intellectual capital of the knowledge network and the knowledge node. Because of the specifics of the knowledge goals human capital, relational capital, and structural capital will be developed (Mertins, Alwert and Heisig 2005: p.208-209; Völker, Sauer and Simon 2007: p. 74-76). For international knowledge networks and the knowledge nodes the following indicators influence the intellectual capital and consequently the knowledge energy:

Indicators Human capital:

- Qualification of the individuals
- Professional and work experience
- Cross-cultural experiences
- Language skills
- Age of skills and qualifications

Indicators Structural capital:

- Explicit knowledge as data, information, or knowledge bases
- Value of replacement of the knowledge base
- Processes of knowledge input and knowledge output

Indicators Relational capital:

- Relations of every individual in functional context
- Relations of individuals in social and inter-cultural context
- Relations of individuals in business context

Figure 7. Model for estimating knowledge value of a knowledge node

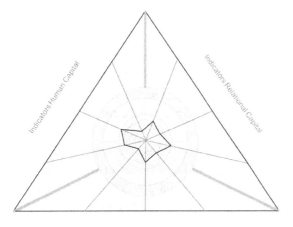

Indicators Structural Capital

From the dimensions of culture and the cultural tacit knowledge, further indicators can be derived. Thus, religion, norms, roles, or geographic regions are important aspects. They influence the tacit knowledge and consequently the knowledge energy of the knowledge node, because the kind how tacit knowledge is internalized inside the individuals depends on the cultural environment and preconditions. Otherwise, exactly these influences have to be respected and analyzed for making accessible and externalize intercultural tacit knowledge.

If there is knowledge and experiences about the way tacit knowledge is generated in different cultures, the process for externalizing knowledge out of individuals mind and intuitions can be derived.

But for deriving also intellectual capital statements special patterns have to be developed; patterns of multiple keys, more like a matrix. The task of the matrix is to project or map a special cultural view onto the inner cultural parameters of the knowledge network (Table 3).

Afterwards, it is possible to get the necessary tacit knowledge from individuals by the further knowledge processes inside the knowledge network.

Development of Intellectual Capital Statement and Tacit Knowledge by Internal and External Processes

In the foundation phase of knowledge nodes, the tacit knowledge cannot be explicitly valuated. But the tacit knowledge itself, existing in forms like skills or competencies or qualifications, can be used exactly in that individual-coupled way. Therefore, it is only possible to estimate the value of this knowledge. Usually the necessary investments to reach this level of skill can be taken as adequate value estimation. This means, which efforts are necessary to qualify an individual or organization to reach this level of knowledge.

Table 3. Sample mapping parameters

		Culture of Knowledge Node				
Culture of Individual	Portability of language	1	2	3	4	5
	Social dependencies of knowledge	1	2	3	4	5
	Cultural openness	1	2	3	4	5
	Cultural value of knowledge	1	2	3	4	5
	...	1	2	3	4	5

Through following internal and external knowledge processes and knowledge flows, parts of this tacit knowledge can be captured by other individuals as well as by information and knowledge systems (Foos, Schum and Rothenberg 2006; Wickramasinghe 2006).

The internal knowledge processes and processing focuses on the increasing of the inner knowledge level by sharing knowledge and processing new knowledge inputs. Furthermore, the inner processes try to disperse and make accessible the individuals knowledge to all individuals of the knowledge node.

The external knowledge flows send knowledge to other nodes of the network and get knowledge from other nodes. Furthermore, there are knowledge flows between nodes from external networks or other sources beyond the border (permeability).

Therefore it is useful to measure and valuate the intellectual capital statement, the knowledge energy, for every node periodically or event-driven, e.g. measure the changes after every knowledge flow or after reaching a knowledge goal. Then it is possible to compare the knowledge nodes.

Hence, the evolution of the knowledge level is influenced by every knowledge event, internal as well as external.

If the measure or value is estimated or estimable, it can further be used in a monetary or nonmonetary context, depending on the goals of the intellectual capital statement.

Rules and Restrictions in Knowledge Flows in Intercultural Context

One of the main tasks of the strategic knowledge management is the realization of knowledge goals (Back, von Krogh, Seufert et al. 2005). Therefore knowledge goals are a driver for cross-linking of knowledge nodes to knowledge networks.

The development of knowledge nodes and their cross-linking to knowledge networks forces on the one hand the realization of knowledge goals. Otherwise, there are also rules and restrictions for these connections. Knowledge networks and any knowledge activities between knowledge nodes are determined by the three perspectives risk management, knowledge improvement, and innovation increase. **Risk management** means the authorized and secured knowledge transfer inside the networks and beyond the network borders, because knowledge is the most important business good in knowledge based processes, it is resource and material. The **knowledge improvement** has the goal to improve the knowledge level inside the knowledge nodes as well as in the knowledge networks. Finally, the **innovation increase** uses existing knowledge and new knowledge by knowledge flows for creating new ideas and innovations; it is the learning results dimension.

Following these main paradigms there are rules for the knowledge flows inside the knowledge network.

First of all the definition of **initiation rules** for knowledge flows is necessary:

- Pull: A knowledge node has a knowledge demand and looks for a knowledge node, having the right knowledge.
- Push: A knowledge node offers or distributes new knowledge to the surrounding nodes.

One package of rules is defined for the **compensation of knowledge energy** between knowledge nodes by knowledge activities:

- Knowledge energy of a knowledge domain always flows from the node with the higher potential to the node with lower potential.
- Depending on the motivation, knowledge flows are bidirectional between two knowledge nodes. The transferred knowledge potential will be approximately similar, but may belong to different knowledge domains.

- Every knowledge transfer changes the energy of the knowledge domain of the participants. The energy of the sender sinks and the energy of the recipient increases.

Otherwise, a package of rules has to be defined for **secure knowledge transfer**:

- Existing knowledge (or skills and competences) will be classified into knowledge priorities. These knowledge priorities range from low level with common knowledge up to high level with specific knowledge.
- Before a knowledge flow will be initiated, a maximum security level of transferable knowledge will be determined

Furthermore, there are rules and restrictions necessary for knowledge flows between knowledge networks, rules for the permeability.

Figure 8. Consequences of knowledge flows

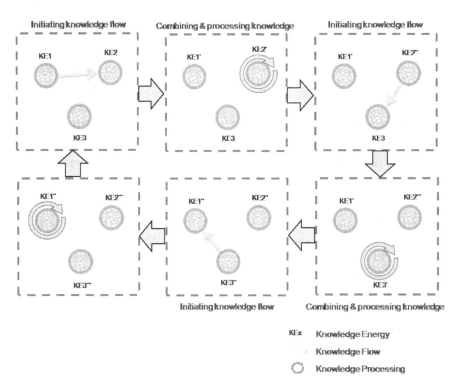

Consequences of Knowledge Flows onto Knowledge Nodes

Every knowledge flow changes and influences the knowledge potential of the knowledge nodes. It is determined by the input of human, structural, and relational capital as well as inner knowledge processing. Furthermore, it is determined by the output of the knowledge node while the knowledge flows. Therefore, knowledge activity may be the knowledge output divided by the knowledge input. The result of this defines the changing of the knowledge energy.

Every knowledge output leads to knowledge inputs in other knowledge nodes. The knowledge increase of every node depends on the difference between output and input. If a knowledge node has more output than input in a knowledge domain, it will lose energy. The more knowledge is distributed and diffused to other nodes the value of exactly this knowledge sinks. Otherwise, the transferred knowledge can be used in other nodes to increase their inner knowledge by combining it with existing knowledge and by knowledge processing.

Knowledge inputs activate the knowledge lifecycle of the knowledge node. Consequently, incoming knowledge will be compared with existing knowledge, and the knowledge processing will be started and new knowledge may be produced. This new knowledge leads to higher knowledge energy and increases the importance of the knowledge node relatively to the other nodes (Figure 8). The knowledge absorption process depends on the knowledge literacy, the skill to handle with knowledge.

But within the inner knowledge lifecycle it is also necessary to find out obsolete knowledge. The knowledge removal may also lead to new cognitions inside the knowledge node.

Regarding the knowledge network with its knowledge nodes as enclosed system, without knowledge exchange, knowledge flows are initiated for a space of time. But the intensity of the transferred knowledge becomes lesser until there are no more knowledge flows. The reason is that a knowledge balancing between the knowledge nodes takes place.

For example (Table 4), starting point is a small network with three knowledge nodes (KN), consisting of institutions with different entrance knowledge levels in the knowledge domains (KD) of content-production, media didactics, and content-marketing. The intention of the network is to extend competences in the e-learning scope.

In the assumption of a starting knowledge distribution V1; there is a knowledge flow (KN1, KN2; KD1) from KN1 to KN2 in the KD1. The result is the knowledge shifting V2. Other knowledge flows (KN1,KN2;KD3) and (KN2,KN3;KD3) with low knowledge level differences in the specified knowledge domain occurs a knowledge balancing (V3).

An exceptional case is that a knowledge node is inactive and participates in no knowledge transfers. These nodes will successively lose their knowledge energy, because knowledge reduces its importance by and by.

Table 4. Sample for results of knowledge flows

	KD1	KD2	KD3
KN1	8	1	6
KN2	3	7	5
KN3	4	7	4
V1			

	KD1	KD2	KD3
KN1	**6**	1	6
KN2	**5**	7	5
KN3	4	7	4
V2			

	KD1	KD2	KD3
KN1	6	1	**5**
KN2	5	7	**5**
KN3	4	7	**5**
V3			

Tacit Knowledge Sharing

Knowledge sharing will not be activated by itself. But which are the motivations and drivers for sharing knowledge as knowledge node in a knowledge network? A knowledge network is a technical and a social system, but the technical part is fundamental for the knowledge exchange. The more important part is the social system view, because the knowledge network and the knowledge nodes consist of individuals. In such a social system individuals provide something of value – in this context knowledge – to other individuals; and they expect to receive something with an equal or greater value in return (Palmisano 2008).

Thus, the main goal is to reach a win-win situation. No-one gives any knowledge for nothing.

An important criterion – especially inside scientific knowledge networks – is **reciprocity**. It means that there is a faith in the knowledge partners that they are ready to share important knowledge with the others. The motivation for this is not diffused where knowledge is important for business values.

Another motivation driver is **reputation**. This is the believing in the obtaining of acceptance for knowledge achievements. But the danger of ideas theft is given.

Sometimes knowledge sharing takes place because of **altruism**. It is a kind of solidarity; giving knowledge for a good cause. Altruism contains the trust that the recipients of the knowledge use it wisely and purposefully for their intentions.

Finally, there are **monetary** motivations. It is possible to make a payment for the value of knowledge. In this context knowledge providing is a service which "produces" knowledge on demand.

In a broader view the motivation can be classified into intrinsic and extrinsic (Ryan and Deci 2002). The intrinsic motivation is an inner desire to do knowledge activities. Otherwise, the extrinsic motivation is forced by external influences; e.g. if an external outcome is needed. It depends on the goals and orientations of the knowledge networks whether it is more intrinsic or extrinsic.

The knowledge transfer and the intensity of the knowledge flows will be influenced by the social exchange theory (Cook and Rice 2003). This theory means that everyone will make rational choices for any relationship and exchanging anything. It is influenced by economical, social, psychological components.

Therefore, it is necessary to respect these social parameters as motivation drivers and include them in the knowledge node cultural rules.

FUTURE TRENDS

As intellectual capital statement plays an increasing role and the intercultural structures also grow and develop to a high level of complexity, it needs more investigations into the knowledge network culture. If it is possible to declare and define the social, economical, and psychological rules and structures as detailed as possible, there are chances for better knowledge cooperation and for better knowledge sharing motivations, especially in intercultural context.

Main driver will be the development to knowledge on demand – knowledge preparation and provision as service.

For fulfilling these intentions, it is necessary to analyze more detailed the knowledge nodes as small units in the knowledge networking environment and find out their scientific regularities. Additionally, a simulation model on this rules concept is needed for exploring the behavior of the knowledge node inside the networks from merging to disposing.

Within these both further tasks, one more theoretical and one more practical, it is the goal to build up a model with fundamental rules for externalizing higher potentials on tacit knowledge and create a measurement for the knowledge energy.

CONCLUSION

Because of the increasing dynamics and the barriers in the network cooperation it is not easy to find a common model for externalizing and measuring tacit knowledge in knowledge nodes and consequently in knowledge networks. But basing on the various models for intellectual capital statements, complemented by the regularities of knowledge nodes and knowledge flows, it is possible to approach to an estimation model for knowledge energy and the value of tacit knowledge.

These parameters of this model will always be specialized to the cultural philosophy of the knowledge network origin. These differences are caused by the philosophies of the basic initiators of the network; they crucially influence the main cultural strategy of the knowledge network. For example, there is a distinction if an Asian initiator creates the network or a European initiator will do that.

Therefore every intellectual capital statement will be individual; it depends on the intentions and perspectives of the viewer. But it is an important step to realize what is the value of the individual's knowledge.

REFERENCES

Alas, R., & Vadi, M. (2006). The impact of organisational culture on organisational learning and attitudes concerning change from an institutional perspective. *International Journal of Strategic Change Management, 1*(1), 155–170. doi:10.1504/IJSCM.2006.011109

Ardichvili, A., Maurer, M., & Li, W. (2006). Cultural influences on knowledge sharing through online communities of practice. *Journal of Knowledge Management, 10*(1), 94–107. doi:10.1108/13673270610650139

Back, A., von Krogh, G., Seufert, A., et al. (2005). *Putting knowledge networks into action.* Berlin, Germany: Springer Verlag.

Bendt, A. (2000). *Wissenstransfer in multinationalen unternehmen.* Wiesbaden, Germany: Gabler Verlag.

Bernard, A., & Tichkiewitch, S. (2008). Methods and tools for effective knowledge life-cycle-management. Berlin, Germany: Springer Verlag.

Bernus, P., & Fox, M. (2005). *Knowledge sharing in the integrated enterprise.* New York: Springer Verlag.

Bitkom. (2007). *Trends im wissensmanagement 2007 bis 2011.* Frankfurt, Germany: KnowTech 2007.

Bodrow, W., & Bergmann, P. (2003). *Wissensbewertung in unternehmen.* Berlin, Germany: Erich Schmidt Verlag.

Bornemann, M., & Sammer, M. (2002). *Anwendungsorientiertes wissensmanagement.* Wiesbaden, Germany: Deutscher Universitätsverlag.

Böschen, S., Schneider, M., & Lerf, A. (2004). *Handeln trotz nichtwissen. vom umgang mit chaos und risiko in politik, industrie und wissenschaft.* Frankfurt, Germany: campus.

Caspers, R., Bickhoff, N., & Bieger, T. (2004). *Interorganisatorische wissensnetzwerke.* Berlin, Germany: Springer Verlag.

Castells, M. (2000). *The rise of the network society.* Oxford, UK: Blackwell Publishing.

Cook, K. S., & Rice, E. (2003). Social exchange theory. In *Handbook of social psychology.* New York: Springer Verlag.

Davies, J., Duke, A., & Sure, Y. (2004). OntoShare- an ontology-based knowledge sharing system for virtual communities of practice. *Journal of Universal Computer Science, 10*(3), 262–283.

Dekkers, R. (2005). *(R)Evolution*. New York: Springer Verlag.

Drucker, P. F. (1995). The network society. *International forum on information and documentation, 20*(1), 5-7.

Foos, T., Schum, G., & Rothenberg, S. (2006). Tacit knowledge transfer and the knowledge disconnect. *Journal of Knowledge Management, 10*(1), 6–18. doi:10.1108/13673270610650067

Furst, S. A., Reeves, M., & Rosen, B. (2004). Managing the life cycle of virtual teams. *The Academy of Management Executive, 18*(2), 6–20.

Gehle, M. (2006). *Internationales wissensmanagment*. Wiesbaden, Germany: Deutscher Universitätsverlag.

Gilbert, J. (2005). *Catching the knowledge wave? The knowledge society and the future of education*. Wellington, New Zealand: NZCer Press.

Goranzon, B., Ennals, R., & Hammeron, M. (2005). *Dialogue, Skill and tacit knowledge*. West Sussex, UK: Wiley & Sons.

Götz, K. (2002). *Wissensmanagement - zwischen wissen und nichtwissen*. Mering, Germany: Hampp Verlag.

Gross, J. L., & Yellen, J. (2006). *Graph theory and its applications*. Boca Raton, FL: Chapman & Hall/CRC.

Halliday, D., Resnick, R., & Walker, J. (2007). *Fundamentals of physics*. New York, Wiley & Sons.

Harkins, P., Carter, L. L., & Timmins, A. J. (2000). *Linkage Inc.'s best practices in knowledge management and organizational learning handbook: Case studies instruments models research*. Lexington, MA: Linkage Incorporated.

Jennewein, K. (2005). *Intellectual property management*. Heidelberg, Germany: Physica Verlag.

Jischa, M. F. (2008). Management trotz nichtwissen. In A. von Gleich & S. Gößling-Reisemann (Eds.), *Industrial ecology* (pp. 271-283). Wiesbaden, Germany: Vieweg+Teubner.

Joynt, P., & Warner, M. (1996). *Managing across cultures*. London: Thomson Business Press.

Kuhlin, B., & Thielmann, H. (2005). *Real-time enterprise in der praxis*. Berlin, Germany: Springer Verlag.

Lembke, G. (2005). *Wissenskooperation in wissensgemeinschaften*. Wiesbaden, Germany: LearnAct.

Liebowitz, J. (2000). *Building organizational intelligence*. Boca Raton, FL: CRC Press.

Marra, M. (2004). Knowledge partnerships for development: What challenges for evaluation? *Evaluation and Program Planning, 27*(2), 151–160. doi:10.1016/j.evalprogplan.2004.01.003

Matthews, K., & Harris, H. (2006). Maintaining knowledge assets. In J. Mathew, J. Kennedy, L. Ma, & A. Tan (Eds.), *Engineering asset management*. London, Springer Verlag.

Mertins, K., Alwert, K., & Heisig, P. (2005). Wissensbilanzen. Berlin, Germany: Springer Verlag.

Millard, D. E., Tao, F., & Doody, K. (2006). The knowledge life cycle for e-learning. *International Journal of Continuing Engineering Education and Lifelong Learning, 16*(1), 110–121. doi:10.1504/IJCEELL.2006.008921

Miroschedji, S. A. (2002). *Globale unternehmens- und wertschöpfungsnetzwerke*. Wiesbaden, Germany: Deutscher Universitäts-Verlag.

Möller, K., & Svahn, S. (2004). Crossing East-West boundaries: Knowledge sharing in intercultural business networks. *Industrial Marketing Management, 33*, 219–228. doi:10.1016/j.indmarman.2003.10.011

Newell, S. (2005). Knowledge transfer and learning: Problems of knowledge transfer associated with trying to short-circuit the learning cycle. *Journal of Information Systems and Technology Management, 2*(3).

Nonaka, I., & Konno, N. (1998). The concept of ba. *California Management Review, 40*(3), 40–54.

Nonaka, I., & Takeuchi, H. (1995). *The knowledge creating company*. New York: Oxford University Press.

Ortmann, G., & Sydow, J. (2001). *Strategie und strukturation*. Wiesbaden, Germany: Gabler Verlag.

Palmisano, J. (2008). A motivational model of knowledge sharing. In F. Burstein & C. W. Holsapple (Eds.), *Handbook on decision support systems 1*. Berlin, Germany: Springer Verlag.

Polanyi, M. (1967). *The tacit dimension*. London: Routledge & Kegan Paul PLC.

Porschen, S. (2008). *Austausch impliziten erfahrungswissens*. Wiesbaden, Germany: Verlag für Sozialwissenschaften.

Probst, G. J. B., Raub, S., & Romhardt, K. (2006). *Wissen managen*. Wiesbaden, Germany: Gabler Verlag.

Ryan, R. M., & Deci, E. L. (2002). Overview of self-determination theory: An organismic dialectical perspective. In E. L. Deci & R. M. Ryan (Eds.), *Handbook of self-determination research* (pp. 3-33). Boydell & Brewer.

Ryle, G. (1949). *The concept of mind*. Chicago, IL: University of Chicago.

Schumann, C.-A., & Tittmann, C. (2007). Multilevel cross-linking and offering of organisational knowledge. In B. Martins & D. Remenyi (Eds.), *Proceedings of the 8th European Conference on Knowledge Management, ECKM2007,* Barcelona, Spain (pp. 878-883).

Schumann, C.-A., Tittmann, C., & Tittmann, S. (2008). Merger of knowledge network and users support for lifelong learning services. In M. Kendall & B. Samways (Eds.), *Learning to live in the knowledge society*. Berlin, Germany: Springer Verlag.

Stark, J. (2007). *PLM enabling global products*. London: Springer Verlag.

Sydow, J. (2006). *Management von netzwerkorganisationen*. Wiesbaden, Germany: Gabler Verlag.

Thorelli, H. B. (1986). Networks: Between markets and hierarchies. *Strategic Management Journal, 7*(1), 37–51. doi:10.1002/smj.4250070105

Triandis, H. C. (1995). *Individualism and collectivism*. Boulder, CO: Westview.

Völker, R., Sauer, S., & Simon, M. (2007). *Wissensmanagement im innovationsprozess*. Heidelberg, Germany: Physica-Verlag.

von Krogh, G., Back, A., & Enkel, E. (2007). *Knowledge networks for business growth*. Berlin, Germany: Springer.

Wickramasinghe, N. (2006). Knowledge creation: A meta-framework. *International Journal of Innovation and Learning, 3*(5), 558–573.

Yurke, B., & Denker, J. S. (1984). Quantum network theory. *Physical Review A., 29*(3), 1419–1437. doi:10.1103/PhysRevA.29.1419

Zhuge, H. (2002). A knowledge flow model for peer-to-peer team knowledge sharing and management. *Expert Systems with Applications, 23*(1), 23–30. doi:10.1016/S0957-4174(02)00024-6

Zhuge, H. (2006). Knowledge flow network planning and simulation. *Decision Support Systems, 42*(2), 571–592. doi:10.1016/j.dss.2005.03.007

Zhuge, H., Guo, W., & Li, X. (2006). The potential energy of knowledge flow. *Concurrency and Computation, 19*(15), 2067–2090. doi:10.1002/cpe.1143

Chapter 6

Toward a Living Systems Framework for Unifying Technology and Knowledge Management, Organizational, Cultural and Economic Change

Peter L. Bond
Learning Futures Consulting, UK

ABSTRACT

This chapter raises difficult questions regarding the validity and motive for prolonging current forms of economic development and competition in the face of the much heralded global environmental crisis threatened by humankind's success as a species. In response, a living systems theoretical framework is introduced that provides many elements of a possible new paradigm of economic development one that closes the gap between the social and natural sciences. New forms of explanation for organization and culture are developed from the perspective of complexity science to produce a synthesis of knowledge management and new philosophical, sociological, anthropological, and, distinctively, biological perspectives of technology, which effectively reconciles the practices of technology, knowledge and cultural change management.

INTRODUCTION

At the start of the 21st Century a new kind of crisis is exercising the minds of politicians and economists, particularly, but not exclusively, those in post industrial economies. Politicians effectively hold the fate of the species in their hands and they are in a quandary. They need assistance. This time the

impending and much heralded crisis is not a normal and familiar economic downturn of the business cycle, it is an ecological crisis and a cultural crisis too. Politicians are slowly realising the solution is not simply one of gaining competitive edge, nor how a nation state can sustain its position in the GDP league table, but rather how our current manner of living can be sustained in the face of global climate change, imminent ecological disasters, unprecedented growth in global population, and

DOI: 10.4018/978-1-60566-790-4.ch006

severe resource depletion. Many believe it cannot. Many more believe it can.

Here is the challenge in a nutshell. The billion or so people who live in advanced industrialised nations consume 32 times the resources and produce 32 times the waste as an average citizen of a developing country. If China were to suddenly catch up, global consumption would roughly double (oil by 106%, and metals by 94%). If India did so too, the world rate would be pushed up eleven fold. If all developing countries were to catch up, this would be equivalent to increasing the world population from 6.5 to 72 billion people (from Diamond, 2008). These are startling statistics, but ultimately meaningless, because such figures are utterly unobtainable. To convince developing countries otherwise is, Diamond says, 'a cruel hoax'. Paradoxically, global economic prosperity depends on decoupling consumption from the quality of life experience, and a marked reduction in consumption in the First World.

The position taken here is that to truly understand the nature of this crisis, and have any chance of coping with it, the gap that has grown between the natural and social sciences, including economics and management and organization development theory, must be closed. Thus, the intent of this chapter is to tempt, to encourage, to persuade, and to inspire its reader to adopt a systems theory of living as the basis of a new theoretical framework for managing technology, innovation, knowledge, and cultural change, which is proffered as a potential component of a new model of economic and social development and means of delivering a globally shared vision of the future of the last hominids, *homo sapiens sapiens*.

The chapter structure divided roughly into four parts. The first will explore the sources of pressure which are likely to force the reformulation of current models of international economic development, including competitiveness strategy. The second part will begin with an attempt to define the seemingly intractable nature of the problem neatly

captured above in the words of Jared Diamond. As part of the discussion of solutions, a perspective from the complexity sciences is introduced. A family of related 'complexity' inspired concepts is discussed briefly before recommending Maturana and Varela's theory of the biology of cognition as a suitable means of integrating social and natural sciences, at the same time emphasising the need to manage knowledge. In part three, the task of weaving together the new theoretical framework begins by first considering in detail the nature of technology. Technology, it is argued, is synonymous with knowledge. The word 'technology' refers to a shared knowledge of technique and can also be equated to a paradigm, an ecology of ideas-in-practice, or an ecology of solutions. These perspectives are then drawn together to suggest technology may also be equated to culture that is generated and sustained by sharing the knowledge of practices, strategies, or solutions, which, together, contribute to the differences and similarities that arise between social groups. Differences in culture, it is suggested, are outward signs of adaptation to localised environmental conditions. This new perspective emphasises the significance of learning in the process of developing cultural spaces and therefore the value of knowledge management as a means of managing change. This understanding of technology bridges the gap between the old and a new, natural science based, paradigmatic framework. Maturana and Varela's theory of the biology of cognition (BoC), the organism-environment system theory of psychologist Timo Järvilehto, actor-network theory and Max Boisot's knowledge perspective of the development of cultural spaces, are drawn together to provide a description of the dynamics of organizational and cultural change emphasising the function of conversations. The chapter concludes with implications and opportunities for a new and cross disciplinary paradigmatic framework that incorporates an appreciation of what it is to be human and respect for the natural environment.

TECHNICISATION, CONSUMPTION AND LOOMING CULTURAL CRISIS

The Good and Bad of Capitalism and Competition

Capitalist industrial society is geared to the design, production, and diffusion of solutions in return for a profit or exceptional return on investment. Individual companies compete over resources and for their share of solution users. By such processes natural objects are transformed, destroyed, degraded, decomposed, recomposed, transposed, transferred, and transported and, thus, our natural world is dominated and controlled. The more extensively Nature is displaced the more society improves; the more complex are the artefacts a society produces the more progressive it is. Competition is good. It stimulates efficiency and higher productivity, it disciplines managers, it reinforces incentives for innovation and it speeds up the adjustment to change. Countries that promote competition and provide the appropriately liberal regulatory reforms are thought to experience higher growth rates and lower unemployment than those who don't (Gurria, 2008).

In the past twenty years or so, remedies for declining competitiveness have included improving company and country performance in the management of technology and innovation (MOTI), creating the right kind of organizational culture, and being more effective at managing knowledge assets, have each been explored. In an industrial age, competitive advantage would be gained by developing, or adopting, a new technology. In an information age, learning, the creation and application of new knowledge, is considered the key to greater competitiveness (Senge, 1990). The management of technology and innovation, and later knowledge management, became significant elements of competitiveness policy and the main mechanism through which governments aspired to deliver economic prosperity and increasing standards of living to their citizens.

It is clearly the case, that innovative solutions may bring forth benefits, but they often produce unanticipated costs, harmful side effects, or not enough of the desired effect. New techniques, new means, and new molecules all too often produce unanticipated and deleterious side effects. This process is referred to as technicisation, which philosopher of technology Jacques Ellul (1964) thought certain to destroy the society it is meant to serve. We are trapped by this viscous circle of invention and innovation in which every technical solution draws forth another to resolve the imperfections of its antecedent. This continuous substitution is the mechanism that underpins profitable growth. It is the raison *d'etre* of marketing executives to lubricate this process by creating need.

As the first decade of the 21st century comes to an end, it is becoming clearer that technicisation and high levels of consumption does not make us happy and does not add to our well being. As Oliver James (2007, 2008) has so arrestingly articulated, affluence does not necessarily bring us happiness or well-being, it gives us affluenza. Affluenza is a painful, contagious, socially transmitted condition of overload, debt, anxiety, and waste resulting from a dogged pursuit of more (DeGraaf, Wann, & Naylor, 2001). It is a condition, say Hamilton & Denniss (2005) 'in which we are confused about what it takes to live a worthwhile life.' (p.7). Although people within individual enterprises may consider that they do good by providing solutions, solution making tied to profit making is perverting the concept of what humans desire and doing a great deal of harm.

The politician's frustration with the current system of delivering prosperity in a form that really matters, in health and well-being is evident in the following extract from the UK's traditional Party of business.

[The] damaging impact of our economic growth on the environment is increasingly obvious. Most urgently, global climate change tells us that our

reliance on fossil fuels must be brought swiftly to an end. But climate change is only one symptom of the damage wrought by today's lifestyles. There are others too: on a global level, we are seeing desertification, soil erosion, the destruction of forests and the continued extinction of unique species. At a national and local level we suffer air, noise, and light pollution, thoughtless development and the destruction of valued wildlife sites. What is going wrong? Standard economic theory tells us that there is a direct link between material wealth and human happiness. The more we have, in material terms, the more content it was thought we would be. The reality, however, seems to be more complex. When a nation is already wealthy, the continued pursuit of a very narrowly defined economic growth can have the effect of degrading the quality of life even while the figures show that it is increasing the standard of living. (Gummer, & Goldsmith, 2007)

Although there are long standing and well rehearsed arguments against the unbridled competition of free market fundamentalism, that it is socially divisive, produces large scale social inequality, and is culture destroying, it remains the most successful mechanism yet to emerge for developing economies to raise standards of living (although relatively) and for encouraging innovation, which provides the most wonderful and marvellous array of labour saving, life enhancing, and life saving products and services. This analysis led Giddens (1998) to propose a Third Way. The Third Way attempts to regulate or manage competition in the interests of the whole community, to encourage sustainable economic growth and to produce a society based on social justice. Contrary to the view of Angel Gurria, OECD Secretary general (see above), competition is not the only effective stimulator of innovation, regulation is effective too. There are many examples of new products and new industrial sectors born of regulation. For example, hybrid vehicles, catalytic exhausts, and solvent free paint. Michael Porter, the business

strategy guru, has argued that state regulation should be considered a positive determinant of competitive advantage in its own right (Porter and van der Linde, 1995) which can enhance the competitiveness of a geographical region. But our dilemma remains. Whilst we cannot abandon antibiotics, computers, refrigerators, the materials used to construct them and the electricity to operate them, the cost of further technical evolution that treats technology as independent from society and Nature is much too high.

In the next section we will consider the well-being of three disciplines that were, in the past, instruments of competitiveness policy and thus economic growth. The purpose of the review will be to establish whether or not they are ripe for a paradigm shift and therefore suitable for inclusion in some future framework of guidance for solving complex economic development problems.

DEFINITIONAL DISSENSUS AS PRESSURE FOR PARADIGM SHIFT

What is a Paradigm?

This brief discussion is as relevant to shifting economic development theory, as it is to any social or natural science. Thomas Kuhn, the science historian responsible for the popular use of the term today, says a paradigm is: 'the entire constellation of beliefs, values, techniques, and so on, shared by its members' (Kuhn, 1972, p. 175). A paradigm emerges from collaborative problem solving. Those who become members undergo a professional initiation process designed to ensure they assimilate the same knowledge base and behavioural repertoires expected by established members. A paradigm is what its community of members shares, and, conversely, a scientific community consists of members who share a paradigm. A paradigm, in this original sense, can appertain to a particular science discipline (chemistry, physics, astronomy), but also to a more extensive framework within which scientists in general operate. The term scientific revolution usually refers to radical change in the overarching paradigm, as in the case of the shift from the Newtonian to the quantum mechanical basis of physics.

Usually, paradigms evolve only slowly, through a process Kuhn called normal science, which involves puzzle solving, by which process the fine tuning of theories and experimental apparatus is achieved. Alternative explanations, if they precipitate significant support, tend to undermine an existing paradigmatic framework. If support becomes widespread then a tipping point could be reached making scientific revolution a possibility. When mature and stable, a paradigmatic framework acts as a guide to problem solvers. It supplies examples of solutions (referred to as exemplars), but most essentially it also supplies many of the problems the community agrees need resolution. A paradigm will fail in this regard if it is immature (preparadigmatic) or destabilised by controversy and close to revolution. It is suggested in the following that the disciplines of technology and knowledge management, and cultural studies of human organizations, are in a preparadimatic phase of development and therefore fail to provide adequate guidance for would be problem solvers. Immaturity is indicated by the presence of definitional dissensus or lack of agreement on concepts which are widely considered to be significant in creating a coherent paradigm.

What's in a Word: Technology

The management of technology and innovation began to emerge as a discrete area of study in the mid 1980s and technical innovation was thrust to the top of government and corporate agendas as the principal for gaining competitive advantage. It is therefore the would-be adherents of the MOTI paradigm who will be leading efforts to create competitive advantage from technology. These are managers and academics who create and utilise the methods and models by which products or

manufacturing hardware are conceptualised and fabricated. It is, therefore, very significant that failure to form a coherent paradigm is widely recognised.

The problem primarily revolves around failure to reach agreement on what technology is. Although this shortcoming is recognised it remains unresolved. See, especially, Anderson (1993), and also Brown and Karagozoglu (1989.), Badawy (1996), Bond (1997, 2000, 2003); van Wyk (2002 and 2004), and Shenhar et al (2005). However, the problem of dissensus extends well beyond MOTI and is proven to be one of the most persistent of academic issues across the whole of science and technology studies, of which the sociology and philosophy of technology are parts. Even within the latter fields, debate over the nature of technology is vociferous (Rammert, 1999; Kroes, 1998; Brey, 1999; Pitt, 2000). See also: Bijker (1997) and Bijker, Pinch, & Hughes (1987), Latour (1987) for a sociological perspective. For technology-as-process see (Scarborough & Corbett, 1992).

In everyday parlance, when the word technology is used it tends to refers to gadgets, tools, devices, hardware, machines, as varied as mp3 players and car production systems to space rockets. This is a very narrow definition which does much to undermine the development of a coherent paradigm. That this situation exists is very surprising indeed, given the fact that over forty definitions have been gathered by the Indian Institute of Technology in Madras, India (http://www.techmotivator.iitm.ac.in/Definitions.htm-accessed 20/07/08). For example, Technology is defined as follows.

The use of tools, machines, materials, techniques, and sources of power to make work easier and more productive.

The use of tools, power, and materials, generally for the purposes of production.

Scientific study and use of mechanical arts and applied sciences, e.g. engineering.

The fundamental application of scientific knowledge to the practical arts, resulting in improved industrial and commercial products of greater value to people.

The study, development, and application, of devices, machines, and techniques, for manufacturing and productive processes.

The sum of a society's or culture's practical knowledge, especially with reference to its material culture.

The study and knowledge of the practical, especially. industrial, use of scientific discoveries.

Systematic knowledge and action, usually of industrial processes but applicable to any recurrent activity.

The first two are close to the popular interpretation, the remainder have in common the idea of creating knowledge through study. This is entirely consistent with the notion of what an -ology is. An -ology is a body of knowledge created by systematic study or investigation. In the case of technology, what is being studied is technique or method. This interpretation of what technology is will be expanded upon later.

What's in a Word: Knowledge

Parallels with the MOTI experience may be drawn with knowledge management. In KM, definitional dissensus centres around the meaning of knowledge. Once again, the presence of dissensus is widely recognised (e.g., see Wiig, 1999). The greatest criticism concerns the idea that knowledge can be treated as a discrete quantifiable object that can be commodified and distributed to be enjoyed like a bar of chocolate. The commodity analogy, so it is thought, is grossly misleading. For Blackler (1995) the idea of knowing, a process, was preferable to knowledge-as-object. As the controversy raged in its early days, like MOTI, KM began to be labelled a fad (e.g. Swan et al, 1999). There was an apparent failure to develop a consensus on the meaning of knowledge and, therefore, what it is that Knowledge Managers manage. The central proposition that knowledge could be managed has been openly questioned (Wilson: 2002). Critical

of the approach of Western management and business commentators to the task of managing knowledge, Takeutchi (1998) said: "[I]t would be pitiful, however, if 'knowledge management' ended up being just a buzzword or if [it] degenerated into little more than a fad....."

Despite the fact that the knowledge-as-object concept remains dominant, and has severe limitations when it comes to dealing with how people learn to create new knowledge and assimilate the ideas in such things as this paper, a corporate policy document, or an unfamiliar set of instructions, KM has been cleared of the 'fad' label by several significant commentators. Ponzi and Koenig (2002) concluded it had staying power and that it had the potential of becoming a significant part of the managerial tool box. Davenport and Prusak (2003) felt that KM is an idea of great value to managers, and is not a passing fad. This apparent success will be built upon in this chapter.

What's in a Word: Culture

The study of culture appears to have a greater incidence of definitional dissensus than either MOTI or KM. Culture has been defined in so many different ways by sociologists, ethnographers and anthropologists that it is difficult to choose representative illustrations. However, most definitions at least relate to human groups. Ten are given here <http://www.tamu.edu/classes/cosc/choudhury/culture.htm> including the following from Hofstede (1997).

Culture is the cumulative deposit of knowledge, experience, beliefs, values, attitudes, meanings, hierarchies, religion, notions of time, roles, spatial relations, concepts of the universe, and material objects and possessions acquired by a group of people in the course of generations through individual and group striving.

Culture is the systems of knowledge shared by a relatively large group of people.

Culture is communication, and communication is culture.

The first two of these bear similarity to several of the previous definitions of technology, a point that will be revisited presently.

From a Kuhnian perspective, vociferous debate about definitions is a necessary and natural process out of which a paradigm may or may not emerge. From an academic's position, definitional dissensus presents an exciting intellectual challenge and, thus, the opportunity to publish contributions to a debate. But the ambiguity of core disciplinary concepts is not just a paradigmatic issue, it also presents a problem of a more practical nature. The question one has to ask is: If a solution itself is judged to be ambiguous (e.g., to improve your performance manage your knowledge more effectively) what message does this send to the problem owner? Failure to agree on core concept definitions may be one reason why otherwise good ideas are cast down as fads.

THE PROBLEM AND THE OPPORTUNITY TO SOLVE IT

The main problem presented in this paper is the imminence of a global economic and subsequent cultural crisis as knock-on effect. Its very intractability creates uncertainty as to how it can be tackled. Previously there was a simple enough solution—grow out of it. This is no longer an option. We have seen in the words of Diamond and the UK's Conservative Party, the political party of business, and there are many besides voicing the same concerns, that we can no longer sustain the levels of consumption and waste the First World expects. If billions in developing countries move up, a billion in the West will have to move down to balance the rise in consumption. This demands radical cultural change. Economic growth, certainly as we currently measure it, is irreconcilable with environment protection. What is the way forward?

Politicians are stuck between a rock and a hard place. It is they who have to decide which policy to adopt, which solution to follow. The choices appear stark. Policy makers are pulled in what seem to be opposite directions. Either they are pro-business, and decide to facilitate growth through competition in a free and deregulated market, or pro-ecology. Green growth, the solution inherent in Giddens' Third Way, is a compromise, a solution which will leave all stakeholders dissatisfied.

In the short term it may be possible to reduce the deleterious effects humans are having on the planet by targeting legislation. Sweden is one example of where strong environment protection measures have created a strong national competitive advantage (Bråsjö and Blomqvist 2006). Replacing GDP as a measure of national competitiveness might also help. However, in the longer term, the contradictions evident within the current economic system will have to be resolved without compromise. In his theory of inventive problem solving, Genrich Altshuller (1996) suggests that all truly inventive steps derive from contradiction resolution. One approach to this kind of problem is to expand the boundaries of the system to be improved to include components that were formerly in its environment and to try to find a non-compromise solution for the wider system. This is, essentially, the rationale behind creating a living systems framework for economic and social system development. This kind of thinking is evident in the emerging science of complex systems, living and otherwise dynamic. Already there are a number of paths to explore.

Complexity science has been touted as the basis of the next managerial revolution and is gaining in prominence as more and more books are published, many aimed at the business community. Notwithstanding the definitional dissensus surrounding the concept of complexity, and the danger of it attracting 'fad' status, it *is* finding use in organisation and management development and thereby raising awareness amongst managers of the potential application of natural scientific explanations to organization behaviour. See, for example, Lissack & Roos (1999), Lewin and

Regine (1999), Stacey *et al* (2000), Shaw (2002) and Macmillan (2004). However, the natural science in these publications is sparse indeed. On the other hand, there are natural scientists actively promoting the application of 'complexity thinking' to the crisis outlined above and, clearly, the two camps need to be brought together.

Natural scientist Edward Wilson is co-developer of gene-culture coevolution theory with Charles Lumsden (Lumsden & Wilson, 1981). He believes the crisis has been brought about by a lack of understanding of Nature (Wilson 1998). He recognises that responding to the crisis in an effective way, indeed even recognising its existence, is made more difficult by the lack of a common reference point for scholars. His way forward is to create a 'unifying theory of humanity,' at the heart of which is natural science. This he calls gene-culture coevolution. Physicist Fritjof Capra (1996 and 2001) has put forward the idea of a deep ecology paradigm to encapsulate a more holistic and systemic way of understanding the world that he clearly hopes will lead to a fuller appreciation of the looming ecological crisis. A crisis, he says, that was born of a series of misperceptions, one of which is the belief that unlimited material progress could be achieved through economic and technological growth. The principal force for change is much higher levels of what he calls ecoliteracy, understanding living systems.

Capra's notion of a deep ecology provides a welcome emphasis on life and Nature whilst acting as an umbrella for the new or complexity sciences, a pillar of which is the systems theory of living devised by the biologists Humberto Maturana and Francisco Varela, usually referred to as autopoietic theory or more properly as the biology of cognition (BoC). For reasons which will become clear, the BoC is the preferred foundation for a future paradigm. Of the different concepts or systems of ideas from complexity science, the BoC is perhaps the most difficult to access, but there have been a number of attempts to apply its principles to different aspects of social system

and people development (Zeleny & Hufford, 1992; Mingers, 1990, 1991, 1996; Bilson, 1996, 2006; Brocklesby & Campbell-hunt, 2007; Brocklesby, 2007; Brocklesby & Mingers, 2004; Bond, 2000, 2002, 2003, 2004a, 2004b, 2005, 2006; Reynolds, 2004; Bopry, 2005).

Before exploring the application of the BoC and some complementary theories, we must revisit the meaning of the word technology and how what it stands for can be used as a bridge between the BoC and more the conventional paradigm.

TECHNOLOGY: A WORD REVISITED

The word technology is relatively new to the English lexicon. Political economist Karl Marx noted its use by a German engineer called Beckmann in a publication of 1772. Marx used it when referring to the 18th century men of learning who had set out to create technology: 'to achieve a precise knowledge of the handicrafts, manufactures and factories. Some made them subjects of special studies. It was only in modern times that the connection of mechanics, physics, chemistry, etc., with the handicrafts was properly recognised. Otherwise the rules and customary practices were handed down in the workshops from the masters to the journeymen and apprentices, and thus there was a conservative tradition.' (Marx: 1861 p.63). The French historian of techniques Bertrand Gille says technology should be understood as a knowledge which is distinguished from science by its subject matter and technical reality, but is nevertheless a science by its psychology and by the methodic way in which it poses problems and by the importance of expressing in a dissertation the operation of technique, the precision of its steps, the generality of the concepts to which it gives freedom and the use it makes of mathematics through the precision of its observations and measurements (Gille: 1986b p.965). Pierre Dussauge and colleagues (1992) drew on Bertrand Gille's definition when they sought to clarify the meaning of technology and management as a crucial step toward establishing MOTI as true academic discipline. Dussuage's definition of technology was never widely accepted by his peers.

Marx, Gille, and thus Dussauge et al, tend toward a formalised form of technology, an extensive and formal body of knowledge, not simply of manufacturing or engine design, but also of measuring and analytical devices that enabled further development of the scientific method itself. Similarly, Lienhard (2000) recognises *techne* as what a painter, stonemason, millwright, or glassblower might do, and -ology as the lore of something. Technology, he says, is the lore of making and doing, but is separate from the actual act of glassblowing or machining, as if it were a store or archive of techniques one may draw from. Thus Lienhard appears more inclined to the view of technology as the explicit or formal knowledge of crafting.

The concise Oxford Dictionary echoes the positions of Marx, Gille, and Liennhard, defining technology as the science of the practical or industrial arts. From the same source, 'science' refers to an organised body of knowledge, of a particular topic, that has been accumulated in a systematic manner. Thus, technology is the outcome of a systematic learning process, an organised body of knowledge that arises from study of techniques and discourses on their further development.

The educationalist Dennis Herschbach (1995, 1996, 1997a, 1997b) presents a slightly different view, one more inkeeping with the Ancient Greek concept of *techne*. The Ancient Greeks sought to explain the existence and use of tools by creating a mythology of *tekhne* (Gille:1986a). *Tekhne* designates practical activity, with and without tools, and is associated with *metis* or practical intelligence, and *sollertia* meaning manual dexterity. Metis is the mother of Athene, inferring that one must have practical intelligence before one can practice. *Tekhne* denotes everything to do with material creation including skill, dexterity, and knowledge. It was also associated with the ability to create an illusion of life by crafting realistic statues of men, women, and animals. Subsequently, such an ability became associated with artisanship and the production of beautiful and wondrous artefacts. For the Ancient Greeks at least, Art and technology appear to be, if not the same, of the same essence. Techne, therefore, is a rich concept and is not simply equatable to a formal knowledge, but what we would call today a mixture of formal (explicit) and tacit knowing about doing. In other words, knowledge of bringing forth artefacts with tools. A mixture of know-how and the imagination of the artist.

Anthropologists see technology as the body of knowledge available to a society or culture that is of use in fashioning tools and practising with them in a process of crafting, and extracting or collecting materials for a variety of uses, including the further production of implements. A more radical interpretation comes from the philosopher of technology Joseph Pitt who has suggested that technology be understood as 'humanity at work' (Pitt; 2000. p. xi.11). Pitt says that technology involves 'the deliberate design and manufacture of the means to manipulate the environment to meet humanity's changing needs and goals' (pp. 30-31). He includes in his list of 'means' all kinds of organisations, implying that companies, governments, and even schools are also tool-like in nature.

From the definitions above, MOTI might be regarded as knowledge management of a particular kind, perhaps limited to industrial practices. However, just where does one draw a line between the industrial arts and all the other techniques required to produce a result within an industrial context? Indeed, does a line need to be drawn?

Technology as Knowing about Techniques

Drawing on the above, technology, it is suggested, is the sum of the knowledge of the totality of means, practices, or techniques a community, a society, a business enterprise, or other form of organization, uses to realise its goals. The roots of its derivation suggest that 'knowing' is both explicit and tacit. Ordinarily, the word technique refers to method or performance in any art or practical skill. Extraordinarily, the term can refer to methods in general, and to broader organizational means by which purpose is achieved. In the first instance, technique is the method of achieving one's purpose, it is how we accomplish a task. Good piano technique, for instance, involves the harmonious working together of all the parts of the body in relation to the instrument, with the mind as director of what becomes 'technical action'. The mind is an intrinsic, inseparable, part of technique. It appears to direct the activities of the body in a flow of processes from the brain through the sensory-motor system, to the instrument of action and finally to the object of action. Technique is a collection of movements of the fingers, hands, arms, and, in some cases, of mouth and lips, the process or operation of directing tools or other instruments (such as the hands and teeth) toward a desired end. Technique refers to the specific practice that produces a specific kind of result. One can master the techniques of dancing, painting with water colours, shooting with a bow or gun, and carpentry. Equally, one can master the use of an industrial sewing machine, an electrically powered lathe, a steam engine, or a car. Our 'technological' manner of living began and evolved with such techniques, but more ancient and tribal societies have not succumbed to technisation and overconsumption, far from it. They subsist, but appear to be happy and well.

Turning to the extraordinary. The term 'technique', may also apply to the methods or strategies of directing people, as opposed to tools, and to more complex combinations involving autonomous human *and* nonhuman actors, such as machines or Nature itself, as in the case of wind blowing the sails of windmills. The ordinary and extraordinary can be brought together by regarding technique as the system that produces the desired result.

The term system, as it is used here, refers to a definition offered by Humberto Maturana and is: '[A] collection of elements that interact and relate with each other in such a way that the interactions that any of those elements have, and the results of those interactions, depend upon its relations with the others.' (Maturana et al, 1995.)

In the case of 'ordinary' technique, a particular person, a player, a crafter, a technician, a practitioner, is an integral component of the system. A particular person produces a particular and idiosyncratic kind of result. That is to say, if a particular person is replaced by another particular person the result will be different. This is because the precise and specific nature of the relations between the person and their instrument will be different and the precise nature of the systems will differ. In the case of broader and more extensive technical systems, the influence of the human component is less, either because their involvement in the operation of the system is peripheral, or they are expected to behave as unconscious (machinelike) actors within the system. It might be concluded, then, that technology refers to the body of knowledge accumulated by the systematic study of the operations of socio-technical systems, whether or not they involve a human being as a direct form of acting component. The scope of such a definition can be extended beyond, but still include, the analysis of the operations of engineered machines. It might also be applied to biological machines by adopting the idea of 'mechanicism', described in the Encyclopaedia Autopoietica (http://www.enolagaia.com/EA.html) as the fundamental approach taken by Maturana and Varela in addressing living systems. This is an approach to describing systems operations that asserts that the only factors operating in the organization of living systems are physical factors, and that no nonmaterial vital organising force is necessary (Maturana and Varela, 1980, p. 137). An explanatory stance from which '...[N]o forces or principles will be adduced which are not found in the physical universe.' (Varela, 1979, p.

6.) Clearly, this is already an approach accepted by engineers, chemists, physicists, and so on. The mechanicistic outlook is the intellectual bridge between biologists and the engineer-designers who, predominantly, lead the development of technical systems, both large and small.

The next several sections indicate how broad the scope of technology studies could become once the idea of technology-as-instrument is abandoned.

Technology as Culture

The concept of culture emerges from a desire to indicate that differences in behaviour occur between human groups. Different behaviours suggest different results, although these may be subtle. Studies of human groups provide the prototypical cases of cultural transmission which may then be applied to nonhuman groups of animals, such as chimpanzees. The differences in behaviour so distinguished must be a result of some form of social learning (Boyd & Richerson,1996) and not be due to environmental or genetic factors. This filters out behaviours due to differences in, for example, birth defects, accidental infection or injury to a high proportion of the group from, say, background radiation or toxins in the environment. For a behaviour to be cultural in origin it must also be a persistent characteristic, typically lasting from generation to generation. Similarly, Nishida (1987) defines cultural behaviour as that which is: i) transmitted socially rather than genetically, ii) shared by many members within a group, iii) persistent over generations, and iv) not a result of adaptation to different local conditions. The latter feature seems to rule out differences, for example, between coastal and mountain dwellers, which conclusion is, perhaps, a little surprising. If a behaviour persists, it is assumed to be useful to the group as a whole. One of the key determinants of cultural development is individual learning. This takes place in 3 steps: i) discovery and learning of a particular behaviour; ii) its testing and evaluation

by an individual; iii) rejection or incorporation into an individual behaviour repertoire (Castro and Toro, 2004). However, there is still a requirement for a mechanism to assure persistence from one generation to the next.

To summarise the brief consideration of culture, the behavioural differences between social groups, designated as cultural traits and thus as distinguishing features, are acquired through a mix of social and individual learning. Generational persistence suggests the existence of what Boesch *et al* (1994) refer to as a permanence guaranteeing mechanism, which, as we will see presently, is languaging or conversation. In evolutionary terms, cultural differences are an outward sign of successful adaptation to a particular environmental niche. In other words, the differences result from successful adaptation and are therefore associated with environmental differences. Success clearly depends on co-operation within a group, although competition is characteristic of intergroup behaviour.

Another approach to understanding cultural development, this time from a KM perspective, has been developed by Max Boisot (1994, 1995, 1998). Boisot's ambition is to show that the basis of business-to-business and country-to-country competition is fundamentally different in the information-age (i.e., the knowledge-age) compared to the energy or industrial age (see Boisot's 1995 and 19981998 publications for confirmation of this). To do better in the present we must improve our understanding of how information (or knowledge) is created and flows to form the assets from which competitive advantage is first derived and then sustained. Advantage is to be found in useful and therefore valued differences. Boisot's approach is grounded in theories of information processing and he often refers to the information-data processing capacity of human brains. The development of what he calls a cultural space begins with problem solving, a process similar to the formation of a scientific paradigm discussed earlier. Referring to Figure 1 and the idea of pro-

Figure 1. K flow in C-space. [Adapted from Boisot, M. (1994) p. 83 .]

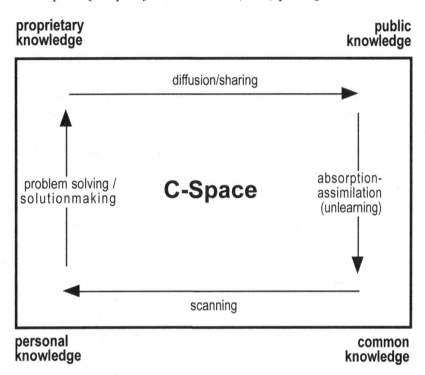

prietary knowledge. Proprietary knowledge (KP) has a value to the individual or group that creates it. KP is never 'knowledge for knowledge sake', it has value because it serves a purpose. KP is the result of problem solving, a process that involves the codification or articulation of the personal knowledge (PK) of a problem. KP can be a problem definition or a fully articulated solution concept. A solution being a system that performs better than the system it displaces. A conceptual solution, a design, is, therefore, a vision of a system that will produce a desired result. KP is diffused by sharing during problem solving, but to become Boisot's public knowledge (PK) solutions have to be even more widely shared by being put into practice by a large proportion of group members. Subsequently, such systems are assimilated or absorbed by a community to form a background of implicit, commonly held, knowledge (CK) of both solutions in practice and of extant problems. These different forms of knowledge exist simulta-

neously and are created through the concurrently operating processes bounding the cultural space. The cycle repeats as the imperfections of solutions are discovered, beginning with scanning, the process of recognising systems that do not deliver the desirable result.

As the cycle of knowledge production repeats, time after time, its impact is felt as a continuous restructuring of cultural space. Mostly, this is incremental, a fine tuning of the extant systems, sometimes it is both extensive and radical. The persistence of particular systems over time in a particular cultural space, such as machines and techniques, is indicative of their 'fit' within it. Persistence is a mark of utility, of usefulness, of functionality, and ultimately of value to society. Because many solutions are systems that incorporate some form of physical instrument (tools, machines, buildings, roads and rail ways and canal ways), the structure of Boisot's cultural space will appear to be held firmly in place by an instrumental apparatus, tools, machines, buildings, and so on, which is, mistakenly, referenced as technology. However, although artefacts are only indicative of technology, they nonetheless provide a frame of reference from which cultural characteristics can be inferred. Moreover, according to anthropologist Merlin Donald (1993), artefacts, particularly graphical artefacts such as signs and symbols, act as an extension of biological memory, providing reminders of who we are, of where we are, of what our role is in the wider human system. We live in nothing less than an ecology of memory traces that we access both consciously and unconsciously. This then relates to the idea that objects perform relations, or more specifically, objects precipitate the concept of systems, as suggested by the Actor-Network theorist John Law (see later section). In this way, artefactual results of systems as solutions, as well as enabling practices, simultaneously constrain thoughts about future practice. The archive of solutions, the artefactual environment, is a reminder of the structure of the system and acts as a brake on invention-innovation. However, what actually maintains a cultural space is the distinctive combination of practices which incorporate such artefacts in some manner or other that produce a distinctive combination of results, reminiscent of the corporate signature said to be the result of core-competency (Hamel and Prahalad (1994).

Technology, Ecology, and Complex Adaptive Systems

A cultural space is a result of problem solving and is maintained by practising solutions. The results of such practices serve to characterise the space so created. In this section it is shown that C-space can also be conceived as a seamless network of solutions that, in effect, behaves as an ecology of ideas-in-practice. Technology, therefore, may be conceived as the knowledge of a particular ecology of ideas that have been put into practice.

It is well known that particular geographical regions of the Earth are characterised by their ecosystems. Ecosystems are persistent and their capacity for regeneration is astounding (as in the case of the area around Chernobyl). Yet they are also sensitive to pressure from without and can easily be degraded or destroyed. Ecosystems are, as are all other natural systems, complex adaptive systems (CAS)[1] and adapting, or evolving, is an invariant characteristic of their operation. Human society is also a complex adaptive system (Buckley, 1968; Mitleton-Kelly, 1997). Maturana has defined a system as a collection of elements (components) that interact and relate with each other in such a way that the interactions that any of those elements have, and the results of those interactions, depend upon its relations with the others. The specific kind of components, and the specific relations between them, together constitute the structure of the system (Maturana and Varela: 1980). Maturana also allows for structural components to be dynamic in nature, and therefore practices, or technical actions, are also components. Cultural space, as an exemplary CAS, is continuously subject to internal pressures to restructure that come from new conceptualisations of both problems and solutions. There is a certain degree of plasticity in the system structure that allows some changes to take place without disintegration. For example, incremental innovations, modified as opposed to entirely new solutions, and radical innovations, are both admitted by the structure although the latter would result in a significant restructuring and to extensive destruction of some parts of the existing system, brought about by what the economist Joseph Schumpeter (1947) called 'a gale of creative destruction' (p83).

As suggested earlier, the persistence of solutions within this ecology is indicative of utility, of usefulness, of functionality. The persistence of instruments and associated practices impart to cultural spaces a particular character, a distinct identity, that emerges from the dynamic interplay of ideas-in-practice. The network of persistent practices provides the underlying characteristic structure of large scale cultural spaces such as the Ancient Egyptian and Roman cultures. Although the pace of evolution is very different, the same argument would apply to individual enterprises. It is by passing on the knowledge of such practices (fashioning tools and practising with them) from generation to generation that systems retain some characteristic structure, even whilst they are undergoing evolutionary changes.

To summarise the position thus far, three different results of treating technology as knowledge have been developed, each providing a different perspective. A complex systems or network perspective has been introduced in which technology can be interpreted as the knowledge of the operations of a human system, a complex, adaptive and socio-technical kind of system. In the following sections of the paper this concept of a human system will be extended to incorporate the processes of learning, conversing and emotioning and innovating.

KNOWING, DOING, AND EMOTIONING GROW CULTURAL SPACES

The biology of cognition is radical in many ways and so provides a very different perspective of familiar and common concepts. One of these is knowledge. Predominantly, knowledge is treated by KM practitioners as a commodity, as bits of data or stocks of documents that may be stored, shared for mutual benefit or traded for a profit. What is being unfolded here, albeit gradually, is in essence an approach to KM practice based on biologic and not computer logic. Previously it has been said that the suffix ' -ology' indicates a body of knowledge. The biology of cognition is thus the body of knowledge generated through study of the biological phenomenon named 'cognition'. In Maturanian terms, cognition is doing, it is not something that just goes on in the brain

or the nervous system. This point needs some clarification.

According to Maturana and Varela, cognition is a matter of interacting in the manner(s) in which one is capable of interacting with the environment or medium of operation, and not processing in the brain what is objectively there to be seen. 'Living systems are cognitive systems, and living as a process is a process of cognition.' The process of cognition is the actual and specific, perhaps idiosyncratic, certainly characteristic, acting or behaving in this domain (see Maturana & Varela, 1980, p. 13). The knowing-doing cycle is cognition. In an explanation of what we call knowledge, meaning to have knowledge or to know, Maturana and Varela say 'All doing is knowing and all knowing is doing.' (Maturana & Varela, 1992, p. 27). Knowing is about being able to operate effectively in the environment in which we live. Figure 2 depicts a cycle of learning by an individual who comes to know by doing. What one truly knows is only manifest in doing. Knowing how to pass an exam in business management, is not the same as knowing how to manage. The diagram shows a virtuous cycle of positive growth in stocks of personal 'knowing' and the results of 'doing'.

Figure 3 is an extension of figure 2 and is based on a systems dynamics modelling convention[2]. It represents an (ideal) growth cycle for any kind of social system. The positive signs indicate the self reinforcing nature of the cycle ideal. The elliptical areas show the rising stocks of social assets, which are the positive outcomes of the processes that precede them. The smaller circle (same as figure 2) indicates a cycle that leads to the personal growth of an individual as they come to be a valued member, an asset, of a social grouping. Individuals become social assets when what they are able to contribute to concerted practices which produce results valued by the group. An individual will seek to validate their knowledge, and confirm their value, through conversation with others [3] and it is through such conversations that knowledge is shared. The result of sharing is

Figure 2.

what Boisot has called Public Knowledge which is taken-to-be-shared by all (most) members of a group. Public Knowledge facilitates collective or concerted actions by the group, the results of which are assimilated by individual learners who confirm its utility, or otherwise, through conversation with others, a process similar to learning about cultural traits mentioned previously. Knowledge of the group grows through repeating cycles, but it does so in a direction imposed by the nature of the problems that have to be addressed in order to maintain its existence within a particular operating context. Learning, doing, and conversational practices are therefore adaptive mechanisms of the human CAS and apply equally to the survival of an individual within a group.

Regarding Boisot's c-space and figure 1. Whilst Personal Knowledge is a result solely of an individual learning-doing process, Proprietary Knowledge can be a result of either individual or of concerted (shared) problem solving activity, which will, of course, involve conversations. Such conversations, it is suggested, are of two types: conversations about extant systems (ideas already in practice), their operations and expected outcomes, and conversations about concepts of improved systems, and their operations and related outcomes. At a particular moment in time and of place in cultural space, the network of such con-

versations will be observed to have produced an 'archive of solutions' (Rammert, 1999) to which distinct groups and enterprises have contributed according to the circumstances in which their individual subcultural spaces developed. Each different kind of cultural space is integrated through collective practices, of which the most significant is conversation. Their differences are maintained through networks of conversations about the specific kind of problems they face and the value attached to specific kinds of solutions created in response. Networks of conversation lead both to the expansion and consolidation of cultural spaces, and so appear to maintain the system in a state of dynamic equilibrium in which a tension exists between staying the same and innovating to gain an improvement (usually a local improvement).

To understand the nature and source of this tension it is useful to add another dimension to learning and conversation, namely, emotioning.

Conversation, Emotioning and Innovation

A paradigm, a cultural space, an ecology of ideas-in-practice, and a social system, are four different ways of distinguishing a single phenomenon—human society, which is the concrete result of the underlying processes of learning, doing, and conversing. Conversation, according to Maturana, is a braided flow of languaging and emotions that we, as observers of conversations, perceive as taking place between people who are interacting in language. Hence, in conversation we appear to be mutually involved in an interlocking series of exchanges each of which has the effect of orienting the conversants around each other's point of view. **NB.** This, essentially, describes the activity of managing or coordinating behaviour. An observer distinguishes a pattern of transactions, of recurrent events, between the two. The effect of the one on the other, and vice versa, is to trigger structural changes within the bodyhoods of the

Figure 3.

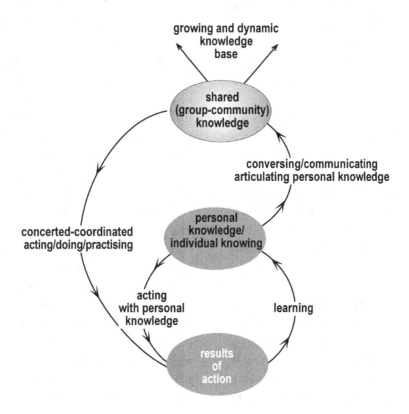

conversants. They are thus said to be structurally coupled, meaning the conduct of one is a constant source of stimuli for the other. Structural change, importantly, involves a flow of emotions and the conduct of each participant corresponds to how the stimulus has been received by the other. The varying flow of different kinds of emotions enables the particular character of a conversation to be distinguished.

The entanglement of emotions with behaviour is taken further by psychologist Timo Järvilehto (1998a,1988b,1999, 2000)[4] in his treatment of a 'result-of-action'. Again, the concept he has in mind is not a familiar one. Although the everyday meaning of result does work with the process depicted in figure 3, Järvilehto's result-of-action is a complex notion that is intimately tied to the explanation and operation of what he refers to as the organism-environment system or O-ES. Having in mind the definition of system given earlier, a result

of acting is that which is perceived by one's self (the mind aspect of technique) and is described as the reorganisation or restructuring of the relations between the self and the perceived components of the organism-environment system (O-E S). For instance, if one were shaping wood with a chisel using a particular technique, then the components of the environmental aspect of the system would be the chisel, the wood (the object of action), a workbench, and the organismic aspect would be parts of the body involved in the action (arteries and veins containing taking blood through muscles and brain), and one's mind or self, which is directing the action. The O-ES would operate within a wider environment that could also include artefacts in the work space (an array of tools, the building in which the action takes place), an overseer or master observing the crafting action. By its nature, this kind of result-of-action is impossible to articulate fully, partly because of the sheer complexity of the specific dynamic relations between a self and her environment, partly because of the dynamic nature of acting, and partly because knowing a result is felt or experienced. A result-of-action is something of which we are personally aware, involving changes both in cognitive structure and bodyhood and in the relations between one's self and other components of, for instance, a technical system. A result-of-action constitutes a change in the structure of the human-medium system that gives rise to a feeling of knowing that becomes the basis of future action, a bodily disposition to act. 'Every perceived change in the environment means a change in behaviour, and a new possibility of realising the results of behaviour.' (Järvilehto: 1998 p.351).

Furthermore, emotioning can be positive or negative and a complex mixture of the two changing moment by moment, but is most conspicuous at the moment of the result. If acting flows smoothly, then it indicates a flow of positive emotioning. Punctuated action, indicated by moments of hesitation, is indicative of negative emotioning brought about by a failure to obtain the desired or expected result, a failure to achieve a particular organisation of relations in the organism-environment system. If a bad workman always blames his tools, it is because he cannot gain the right set of relationships between himself, his tool, and the object of his action. Negative emotionings, Järvilehto says, are expressions of 'problems' in the organism-environment system, and are therefore crucial to organization development. The repression of negative emotions, such as the discontent arising from the use of a particular product or tool, means that the problematic situation will not be revealed and will therefore not be resolved. What Järvilehto calls the 'disintegrative factors' stay in the system and their real causes remain hidden. Emotion, he says, is the way to have knowledge about the presence of such disturbing factors and sharing such emotions associated with results of action, or the failure to attain an expected or desired result, are clearly important to problem recognition, and ultimately

to innovating (for detail see Järvilehto: 2000). It will be appreciated that emotioning associated with practice, with doing, including conversing, is the mechanism underlying the production of Boisot's Personal Knowledge. Negative emotioning (felt as dissatisfaction and discontent) underlies a desire for change, for a different set of dynamic relations. Positive emotioning, on the other hand, which we desire to repeat time and again, through both new and familiar practices, would appear to be both a source of continuity *and* change.

Referring once again to figure 3, one will appreciate that the depicted process is iterative and is continuous, proceding as moment by moment interactions between individual learners acting in concert and the conversations they have about their result-of-actions, both positive and negative. It is through such conversations that new result-of-actions (which are experiences of doing) become articulated and through which new and improved practices eventually emerge to be sustained by the new networks of conversations which they precipitate.

Result-of-Actions and the Creation of Cultural Spaces

Järvilehto's result-of-action is a personal event that may or may not precipitate a conversation about it. A new cultural space is stabilised, or de-stabilised, through conversations. In this section a familiar crafting practice is used to illustrate the process both from an actor-network and a systems perspective.

Crafting is foundational to our modern technological society and anyone who engages in the activity knows how emotioning it can be. Examples of crafting of any kind (or any sport involving bats, racquets, clubs, even a motor driven vehicle or bicycle) would serve to exemplify the biology of technical action, here the process of creating a clay pot using a potting wheel has been chosen (for other examples, including music making and composition see Bond, 2002).

Starting with an amorphous mass of wettish clay in the centre of a spinning wheel, the potter will push it and pull it until a pot is brought into being. The pot emerges from the organism (potter) - environment system from between her hands, moment by moment, result-of-action by result-of-action, until what she deems to be end-point is reached, the point at which she feels satisfied what has been produced is right (or wrong, if that's the way things have gone). Either way, she will experience, as most artisans seem to do, a feeling that the end point is reached and that she should do no more. Refer again to figure 3 and consider what is happening to precipitate a distinguishable cultural space. For the pot to become a socially useful artefact first it has to be dried then 'fired' and, depending upon the purpose for which it was made, maybe glazed and refired. It has to withstand transportation to a prospective user and must persist as a functional artefact during many uses. From an actor network perspective, the pot is said to perform relations.[5]

John Law contends that an object, a concrete artefact such as the wet pot, is an effect of an array of relations, the effect of a network. An object emerges at, or can be observed to be at, an intersection of relations and is maintained as such (as an object of a particular kind with particular characteristic attributes) while those relations hold together (Law, 2000). It is conceivable that as new attributes are recognised or discovered that the network of relationships will be changed and extended. For example, Apple's iMac was never just a computer it was also a style icon, and a qualitatively different network precipitated around it to maintain its existence as the unique product it was. This is consistent with the social constructionist notion that a particular product design emerges at what subsequently becomes a point of equilibrium at which a variety of forces, emanating from diverse social groups of would-be users and other stake holders, are held in balance (e.g. Bijker et al). The object is thus the fulcrum and could be conceived as a 'held

point' in a particular web of relations. This set of relations or network has to be understood as a continuous web extending from within an object and outward—beyond it. In a subtle change of position, Law suggests that objects are performing these networks, a view that unquestionably stems from the willingness of actor-network theorists to accept non-humans as actors within a network of relations. This unconventional view means that an object, by seeming to act on its observers, maintains a network of relations. Law's idea is easily extended to any type of artefact to provide unique and valuable insights into how technical systems develop. For further examples, including the performance of relations from mediaeval ships documents and text books, see Law (1987) and Law and Singleton (2000). Alternatively, it might be said that systems form around the pot.

A system has been defined as a collection of elements that interact and relate with each other in such a way that the interactions that any of those elements have, and the results of those interactions, depend upon its relations with the others. From this latter part of the definition arises one of the tenets of the biology of cognition, the principle that the behaviour of a system is determined by its structure. Structure is defined as the actual static or dynamic components plus the actual relations that take place between them (Maturana and Varela, 1980). It follows that the behaviour of any system (e.g. any natural or engineered system, or combination of) is simultaneously enabled and constrained by its structure. No change can take place in the structure that is not permitted by it, and the actions of external agencies do not determine the changes that take place. When Law refers to 'objects performing relations', from a Maturanian position, he is referring to a process of structuration or system forming. For example, immediately following production of the pot it has to become part of a pot drying system. Subsequently, other systems come into being around it: a system for firing; a system for safe storage; a system of transportation; a system of value exchange, so that it may be 'sold' and 'bought; and lastly, but certainly not least, a system of use, within which the pot is a key functional component, such as containing and pouring, or cooking. The lowly clay pot can be conceived as a focal point or catalyst for relations precipitation is it moves through physical space.

The primary mechanism by which this system forming occurs is not explicitly specified by John Law, however, from the Maturanian perspective, it is, emphatically, conversation. In the context of socio-technical systems formation, conversations about results lead toward, and initiate the establishment of, new sets of relations and hence new systems. In most approaches to explaining 'technology' the pot is the only result that matters, and is probably why an instrumentalist approach to understanding technology dominates so. However, from the perspective of the O-ES and Actor-Network Theory, the wet pot is only part of the overall experience of creation, only part of the overall experiencing of result-of-actions. Here, then, at the most fundamental level of the technical phenomenon, is the point at which a biology of technology and innovation begins to indicate a possible new direction for technology and economic studies.

ORGANISM-MEDIUM SYSTEMS THINKING-A FUTURE RESEARCH PARADIGM

The intent of this chapter was to tempt, encourage, persuade, and to inspire its reader to adopt a living systems theoretical framework for managing technology, innovation, knowledge, and cultural change as a necessary step toward developing a new system of economic and, consequently, social development. Understanding what might be called the technological phenomenon is crucial to any debate about alternative economics because technicisation, driven by that most demanding capitalist imperative—to strive to make an above

average return on financial investments, is at the heart of the problem of overconsumption which has led to the pandemic of Affluenza.

Understanding technology for what it is, the body of knowledge created by the systematic study of technique, and then extending it beyond its narrowly defined industrial applications so that it may be considered as the study of human organism-environment/medium systems, creates the possibility of bringing together three major areas of study that already make important contributions to understanding how organizations work and how they co-operate and compete depending on circumstances. The three, the constructivist school of science and technology studies, knowledge management, and cultural change management, all unstable scientific paradigms in themselves, when brought together under the umbrella of Maturana's biology of cognition, with the support of Järvilehto's Organism-Environment System theory, suddenly begin to provide radically new insights into the way the organizations of humans are created and sustained. The will undoubtedly be some readers who feel the definition of technology has been stretched much too far, but to create a new paradigm existing definitions have to be stretched to beyond their breaking point, to the point at which they cease to fit existing explanatory frameworks, but, in their revised form, fit a new network of ideas.

By emphasising the situatedness of individual learning, by referencing crafting, and to the significance of conversations about practice and the results of practice, it has been shown how individual technical actions and collective individual learning amalgamates to create a situated or contextualised culture that is naturally congruent with the environment from which it emerged. This gives weight to the idea that only by thinking local and acting local will cultural differences, and therefore competitive advantage, arise.

Although there is much more to be said about recursion and non-linear dynamics of socio-technical systems, Järvilehto's concept of result-of-action provides a useful starting point, it also indicates that focusing on the most obvious product of technical action, the artefact, will inevitably lead to an underdetermination of the factors influencing the nature and direction of cultural development, which is inevitably bound to the nature and direction of practice innovation.

The result-of-action also goes some way toward explaining the emergence of distinctive kinds of cultural space. Complexity thinking encourages pattern recognition and, just as there is an analogy to be drawn between individual and organisational learning, there is also one to be drawn between the emergence of individual style and cultural style. We readily recognise the individual ways in which actors and musicians perform and the way in which paintings, drawings, or sculptures reflect the different styles in which artists bring into being their artefacts. Culture is in effect, collective style and an explanation for differences between cultures will only emerge from a biology of interaction between individuals and the collective. But, perhaps the most underdetermined factor in cultural evolution are our emotions, and only a living system theory of technology and innovation can hope to provide a suitable development framework. Maturana has said:

[W]estern culture [..] depreciates emotions, or at least considers them a source of arbitrary actions that are unreliable because they do not arise from reason. This attitude blinds us about the participation of our emotions in all that we do as the background of bodyhood that makes possible all our actions and specifies the domain in which they take place. This blindness, I claim, limits us in our understanding of social phenomena.

And further:

Our life is guided by our emotions because our emotions define the relational domain in which we act, and hence, what we do. Each culture is defined by a particular configuration of emotion-ing that guides the actions of its members, and is conserved by those actions and the learning of the configuration of emotioning that defines it by the children of its members. If this systemic dynamics of constitution and conservation of a culture is broken, the culture comes to an end. (Maturana 1997)

The centrality of emotions in all that we do is most readily illustrated through arts and crafts and sport and it is here that we can appreciate what Maturana means when he concludes that it is not 'technology' that guides modern life, but rather it is emotions, specifically the emotions under which we use or invent it. Whether it is invented from the desires of power, riches, or fame, or whether it is out of love for our families, our communities, or humankind. We *can* choose between protecting the environment and conspicuous consumption.

REFERENCES

Altshuller, G. (1996). *And suddenly the inventor appeared: TRIZ, the theory of inventive problem solving.* Worcester, MA: ICAL Innovation Center.

Anderson, P. (1993). Toward exemplary research in the management of technology - an introductory essay. *Journal of Engineering and Technology Management, 10,* 7–22. doi:10.1016/0923-4748(93)90056-O

Badawy, M. K. (1996). A new paradigm for understanding management of technology: A research agenda for 'technocologists'. *International Journal of Technology Management, 12*(5/6), 717–732.

Bijker, W. (1995). *Bikes, bakelite, and bulbs: Steps toward a theory of socio-technical change.* Cambridge, MA: MIT Press.

Bijker, W., Pinch, T., & Hughes, T. (Eds.). (1987). *The social construction of technological systems: New directions in the sociology and history of technology*. Cambridge, MA: MIT Press.

Bilson, A. (1997). Guidelines for a constructivist approach: Steps toward the adaptation of ideas from family therapy for use in organization. *Systems Practice, 10*(2), 154–177. doi:10.1007/BF02557914

Bilson, A. (2007). Promoting compassionate concern in social work: Reflections on ethics, biology and love. *British Journal of Social Work, 37*(8), 1371–1386. doi:10.1093/bjsw/bcl060

Blackler, F. H. M. (1995). Knowledge, knowledge work and organizations: An overview and interpretation. *Organization Studies, 16*(6), 1021–1046. doi:10.1177/017084069501600605

Boisot, M. (1994). *Information and organization: The manager as anthropologist*. London: Harper and Collins.

Boisot, M. (1995). *Information space: A framework for learning in organizations*. London: Routledge.

Boisot, M. (1998). *Knowledge assets: Securing competitive advantage in the information economy*. Oxford, UK: Oxford University Press.

Bond, P. L. (2000). Knowledge and knowing as structure: A new perspective on the management of technology for the knowledge based economy. *Int. J. of Technology Management, 20*(5/6/7/8), 528-544.

Bond, P. L. (2002). *Conversations with organisations and other objects. Featuring a mujician, two bears, and two ceramic pots*. Paper presented at the Art of Management and Organisation Conference, King's College, London.

Bond, P. L. (2003). The biology of technology: An exploratory essay. *Knowledge, Technology, and Policy, 16*(3), 125–142. doi:10.1007/s12130-003-1036-2

Bond, P. L. (2004a). Maturana, technology, and art: Is a biology of technology possible? *Cybernetics & Human Knowing, 11*(2), 49–70.

Bond, P. L. (2004b). Communities of practice and complexity: Conversation and culture. *AMED's Organisations & People Journal, 11*(4).

Bond, P. L. (2005). *The emergence of complex emotioning innovating and polytechnical systems. An essay on the biology of technology*. Paper presented at Conference on Complexity and Society, University of Liverpool, Liverpool, UK.

Bond, P. L. (2006). Emotioning, foundational knowledge and enterprise creation. *Organisation and People, 13*(1), 42–49.

Bopry, J. (2005). Levels of experience: An exploration for learning design. *Educational Media International, 42*(1), 83–89. doi:10.1080/09523980500116688

Boyd, R., & Richerson, P. J. (1996). Why culture is common but cultural evolution is rare. *Proceedings of the British Academy, 88*, 77–93.

Bråsjö, E., & Blomqvist, P. (2006). *Swedish strengths in the environmental industry*. Stockholm: Kungl. Ingenjörsvetenskapsakademien (IVA).

Brey, P. (1999). Philosophy of technology meets social constructivism. *Techne, 2*(3/4).

Brown, W., & Karagozoglu, N. (1989). Systems model of technological innovation. *IEEE Transactions on Engineering Management, 36*(1). doi:10.1109/17.19977

Buckley, W. (1968). Society as a complex adaptive system. In Open System Group (Eds.), *Systems behaviour*. London: Open University/Harper and Row.

Capra, F. (1996). *The web of life*. London: Harper Collins.

Capra, F. (2001). *The hidden connections. A science for sustainable living.* London: Harper Collins.

Castro, L., & Toro, M. A. (2004). The evolution of culture: From primate social learning to human culture. *Proceedings of the National Academy of Sciences of the United States of America, 101*(27), 10235–10240. doi:10.1073/pnas.0400156101

Cohen, I. J. (1989). *Structuration theory: Anthony Giddens and the constitution of social life.* London: Macmillan.

Copenhagen, Denmark (Vol. 2, pp. 668-678).

Davenport, T., & Prusak, L. (2003). *What's the big idea?* Boston: Harvard Business School Press.

DeGraaf, J., Wann, D., & Naylor, T. H. (2001). *Affluenza: The all-consuming epidemic.* San Francisco: Berrett, Kohler Publishers Inc.

Diamond, J. (2008). *What's your consumption factor?* Retrieved August 3, 2008, from http://www.nytimes.com/2008/01/02/opinion/02diamond.html

Donald, M. (1993). Précis of origins of the modern mind: Three stages in the evolution of culture and cognition. *The Behavioral and Brain Sciences, 16*(4), 737–791.

Dussauge, P., Hart, P., & Ramanantsoa, B. (1992). *Strategic technology management.* Chichester, UK: John Wiley and Sons.

Ellul, J. (1964). *The technological society* (J. Wilkinson, Trans.). New York: A.A. Knopf.

forget people? In *Proceedings of the 7ᵗʰ European Conference on Information Systems,*

Giddens, A. (1998). *The third way. The renewal of social democracy.* Cambridge, UK: Polity Press.

Gille, B. (Ed.). (1986a). *The history of techniques - volume 1.* Montreux, Switzerland: Gordon and Breach.

Gille, B. (Ed.). (1986b). *The history of techniques - volume 2.* Montreux, Switzerland: Gordon and Breach.

Glasersfeld, E. v. (1995). *Radical consructivism: A way of knowing and learning.* London: Falmer Press.

Griffin, D., Shaw, P., & Stacey, R. (1999). Knowing and acting in conditions of uncertainty: A complexity perspective. *Systemic Practice and Action Research, 12*(3), 295–309. doi:10.1023/A:1022403802302

Gummer, J., & Goldsmith, Z. (2007). *Blueprint for a green economy. A report to the shadow cabinet.* Quality of Life Policy Group. Retrieved July 21, 2008, from www.qualityoflifechallenge.com/documents/fullreport-1.pdf

Gurria, A. (2008). *Competition brings prosperity* [Presentation to OECD Competition Committee]. Retrieved July 21, 2008, from http://www.oecd.org/document/3/0,3343

Hamel, G., & Prahalad, C. K. (1994). *Competing for the future.* Boston: Harvard Business School Press.

Hamilton, C., & Denniss, R. (2005). *Affluenza: When too much is never enough.* Crows Nest, Australia: Allen and Unwin.

Herschbach, D. R. (1995). Technology as knowledge: Implications for instruction. *Journal of Technology Education, 7*(1), 14–24.

Herschbach, D. R. (1996). Defining technology education. *The Journal of Technology Studies, 22*(2), 6–9.

Herschbach, D. R. (1997a). From industrial arts to technology education: The eclipse of purpose. *The Journal of Technology Studies, 23*(2), 20–28.

Herschbach, D. R. (1997b). From industrial arts to technology education: The search for direction. *The Journal of Technology Studies, 23*(1), 24–32.

Hofstede, G. (1997). *Cultures and organizations: Software of the mind.* New York: McGraw Hill.

James, O. (2007). *Affluenza.* London: Vermillion.

Järvilehto, T. (1998a). The theory of the organism-environment system: I. Description of the theory. [from http://wwwedu.oulu.fi/homepage/tjarvile]. *Integrative Physiological and Behavioral Science, 33,* 321–334. Retrieved March 2006. doi:10.1007/BF02688700

Järvilehto, T. (1998b). The theory of the organism-environment system: II. Significance of nervous activity in the organism-environment system. [from http://wwwedu.oulu.fi/homepage/tjarvile]. *Integrative Physiological and Behavioral Science, 33,* 335–343. Retrieved March 2006. doi:10.1007/BF02688701

Järvilehto, T. (1999). The theory of the organism-environment system: III. Role of efferent influences on receptors in the formation of knowledge. [from http://wwwedu.oulu.fi/homepage/tjarvile]. *Integrative Physiological and Behavioral Science, 34,* 90–100. Retrieved March 2006. doi:10.1007/BF02688715

Järvilehto, T. (2000). The theory of the organism-environment system: IV. The problem of mental activity and consciousness. [from http://wwwedu.oulu.fi/homepage/tjarvile]. *Integrative Physiological and Behavioral Science, 35,* 35–57. Retrieved March 2006. doi:10.1007/BF02911165

Järvilehto, T. (2000). Feeling as knowing: Emotion as reorganization of the organism-environment system. *Consciousness & Emotion, 1*(2), 53-65. Retrieved March 2006, from http://wwwedu.oulu.fi/homepage/tjarvile

Kim, D., & Lannon, C. P. (1994). *A pocket guide to using archetypes.* Waltham, MA: Pegasus Communications Inc.

Kroes, P. (1998). Technological explanations: The relation between structure and function of technological objects. *Philosophy and Technology, 3*(3).

Kuhn, T. S. (1972). *The structure of scientific revolutions.* Chicago: University of Chicago Press.

Latour, B. (1987). *Science in action.* Cambridge, MA: Harvard University Press.

Lave, J., & Wenger, E. (1991). *Situated learning: Legitimate peripheral participation.* Cambridge, MA: Cambridge University Press.

Law, J. (1987). Technology and heterogeneous engineering: The case of the Portuguese expansion. In W. Bijker, T. Pinch, & T. Hughes (Eds.), *The social construction of technological systems: New directions in the sociology and history of technology.* Cambridge, MA: MIT Press.

Law, J. (2000). *Objects, spaces, others.* Retrieved March 30, 2006, from http://www.comp.lancaster.ac.uk/sociology/soc027jl.html

Law, J., & Singleton, V. (2000). *This is not an object.* Retrieved March 30, 2006, from http://www.comp.lancs.ac.uk/sociology/soc032jl.html

Lewin, R., & Regine, B. (1999). *The soul at work: Unleashing the power of complexity science for business success.* London: Orion.

Lienhard, J. H. (2000). *The engines of our ingenuity. An engineer looks at technology and culture.* New York: Oxford University Press.

Lissack, M., & Roos, J. (1999). *The next common sense.* London: Nicholas Brealey.

Lumsden, C. J., & Wilson, E. O. (1981). *Genes, mind, and culture: The coevolutionary process.* Cambridge, MA: Harvard University Press.

Marx, K. (1861). *Economic manuscripts of 1861-63. Part 3. Relative surplus value division of labour and mechanical workshop. Tool and machinery.* Retrieved April 2005, from http://www.marxists.org

Maturana, H. (1997). *Metadesign*. Retrieved August 1, 2005, from http://www.inteco.cl

Maturana, H., Mpodozis, J., & Lettelier, J. C. (1995). Brain, language and the origin of human mental functions. *Biological Research, 28*, 15–26.

Maturana, H., & Varela, F. (1980). *Autopoiesis and cognition: The realization of the living*. Dordrecht, The Netherlands: D. Reidel.

Maturana, H., & Varela, F. (1992). *The tree of knowledge: The biological roots of human understanding*. Boston: Shambhala.

McMillan, E. (2004). *Complexity, organizations and change*. London: Routledge.

Mingers, J. (1989). An introduction to autopoiesis: Implications and applications. *Systems Practice, 2*(2), 569–584. doi:10.1007/BF01059497

Mingers, J. (1991). The cognitive theories of Maturana and Varela. *Systems Practice, 4*(4), 319–338. doi:10.1007/BF01062008

Mingers, J. (1996). A comparison of Maturana's autopoietic social theory and Giddens' theory of structuration. *Systems Research, 13*(4), 469–482. doi:10.1002/(SICI)1099-1735(199612)13:4<469::AID-SRES81>3.0.CO;2-I

Mittleton-Kelly, E. (1997). *Complex adaptive systems in an organisational context*. Paper presented at the British Academy of Management Conference, London.

Nishida, T. (1987). Local traditions and cultural transmission. In B. B. Smuts, D. L. Cheney, R. M. Seyfarth, R. W. Wrangham, & T. T. Struhsaker (Eds.), *Primate societies*. Chicago: University of Chicago Press.

Pitt, J. (1999). *Thinking about technology*. New York: Seven Bridges Press.

Ponzi, L., & Koenig, M. (2002). Knowledge management: Another management fad? *Information Research, 8*(1). Retrieved August 15, 2004, from http://informationr.net/ir/8-1/paper145.html

Porter, M. E., & van der Lind, C. (1995). Towards a new conception of the environment-competitiveness relationship. *The Journal of Economic Perspectives, 9*, 97–118.

Rammert, W. (1999). Relations that constitute technology and media that make a difference: Toward a social pragmatic theory of technicisation. *Techne, Journal of Philosophy and Technology, 4*(3). Retrieved March 1999, from http://scholar.lib.vt.edu/ejournals/SPT/v4n3/pdf/

Reynolds, M. (2004). Churchman and Maturana: Enriching the notion of self-organization for social design. *Systemic Practice and Action Research, 17*(6).

Scarborough, H., & Corbett, J. M. (1992). *Technology and organization*. London: Routledge.

Schumpeter, J. A. (1947). *Capitalism, socialism and democracy*. New York: Harper and Brothers.

Senge, P. (1990). *The fifth discipline: The art and practice of the learning organisation*. London: Random House.

Shaw, P. (2002). *Changing conversations in organizations: A complexity approach to change*. London: Routledge.

Shenhar, A. J., van Wyk, R., Steganovic, J., & Gaynor, G. (2005). *Technofact: Toward a fundamental entity of technology - a new look at technology and MOT*. Retrieved December 2005, from http://howe.stevens.edu/CTMR/WorkingPapers/WP2005/index.html

Stacey, R. D., Griffin, D., & Shaw, P. (2000). *Complexity and management: Fad or radical challenge to systems thinking?* London: Routledge.

Swan, J. A., Scarbrough, H., & Preston, J. (1999). Knowledge management – the next fad to

Takeutchi, H. (1998). *Beyond knowledge management: Lessons from Japan*. Retrieved January 15, 2005, from http://www.sveiby.com/articles/LessonsJapan.htm

Van Wyk, R. J. (2002). Technology: A fundamental structure. *Knowledge, Technology, and Policy, 15*(3).

van Wyk, R. J. (2004). *A credo for MOT*. Retrieved August 2004, from http://iamot.org/homepage/ACREDOFORMOT-2004.pdf

Varela, F. (1979). *Principles of biological autonomy*. New York: Elsevier (North-Holland).

Wenger, E. C. (1998). *Communities of practice: Learning, meaning and identity*. New York: Cambridge University Press.

Wheatley, M. J. (1992). *Leadership and the new science: Learning about organization from an orderly universe*. San Francisco: Berrett-Koehler.

Wheatley, M. J., & Kellner-Rogers, M. (1996). *A simpler way*. San Francisco: Berrett-Koehler.

Wiig, K. M. (1999). What future knowledge management users may expect. *Journal of Knowledge Management, 3*(2), 155–165. doi:10.1108/13673279910275611

Wilson, T. D. (2002). The nonsense of knowledge management. *Information Research, 8*(1). Retrieved February 6, 2003, from http://InformationR.net/ir/8-1/paper144.html

Zeleny, M., & Hufford, K. D. (1992). The application of autopoiesis in systems analysis: Are autopoietic systems also social systems? *International Journal of General Systems, 21*, 145–160. doi:10.1080/03081079208945066

ENDNOTES

[1] An introduction to the application of the CAS model to MOTI may be seen in Bond (2000).

[2] The presentation of Figure 3 is consistent with the conventions of systems dynamics modelling made more accessible in the guise of the 'Systems Thinking' methodology developed by Peter Senge, Daniel Kim and colleagues (Kim and Lanon: 1994) and explored in great depth in Senge's book The Fifth Discipline (Senge: 1990)

[3] The growth of the individual learner-actor and its link to organisational learning has also been explored more recently in the context of communities of practice and the application of activity theory to the sharing of knowledge and growth of organisational competence. Especially, Jean Lave and Etienne Wenger (1991) and Wenger (1998).

[4] Timo Järvilehto is Professor of psychology at University of Oulu, Faculty of Education and Kajaani University Consortium, Kajaani, Finland. Since 1990 he has been developing a radically different approach to understanding human behaviour under the heading 'systemic psychology', based on the theory of the organism-environment system (O-ES), which has a high degree of resonance with Maturana and Varela's biology of cognition.

[5] During the crafting process, the pot and the technique or system of production are co-created. For more on the co-creation of product and enterprise see Bond 2006.

Section 2

Chapter 7
Strengthening Knowledge Transfer between the University and Enterprise:
A Conceptual Model for Collaboration

José L. Pineda
Tecnológico de Monterrey, Mexico

Laura Esther Zapata
Tecnológico de Monterrey, Mexico

Jacobo Ramírez
Tecnológico de Monterrey, Mexico

ABSTRACT

In today's world, where uncertainty and the rapidity of technological changes predominate, companies need to generate and adopt knowledge continuously in order to build a sustainable competitive advantage. In this context, analyzing the collaborative relationships existing between the university and firms is relevant. The aim of this chapter is to explore the role of the university as a generator and disseminator of knowledge, as well as the difficulties it faces in making the results of its research available to the business world. The collaboration efforts between the academic and business worlds are assessed in order to ultimately propose the review of teaching, continuing education, and consulting as knowledge dissemination channels. This research project has been conducted in the context of a Mexican university. Besides the findings of the current and future research projects, the matter of the question is the redefinition of the university and its role in society. In business schools in particular, the pending issue is to discuss the basic aim of academic research in management.

1. INTRODUCTION

This chapter reviews the role of the university as a generator and disseminator of knowledge, as well as its difficulties in getting the results of its research to the business world. It also analyzes the characteristics of both academic institutions and business organizations that determine the dissemination and adoption of new knowledge. In addition,

DOI: 10.4018/978-1-60566-790-4.ch007

collaboration efforts between academia and firms are assessed.

The origin of a significant competitive advantage for enterprises lies in their capacity to create and integrate new knowledge into their operations. This is particularly relevant in the increasingly dynamic, volatile settings in which organizations currently work (Teece, Pisano & Shuen, 1997; Grant, 1998). Part of the new knowledge acquired by companies is not generated inside them, but comes from external sources, such as consulting organizations, independent professional services and universities.

Over the past few years, universities have been seen to participate strongly in introducing innovations into companies' administrative processes. This has been possible thanks to two major trends. On the one hand, the firms' interest in learning and continuous improvement, motivated by a climate of growing competitiveness, and on the other, the universities' efforts to further promote the dissemination of the results of their research in the business world. First of all, the findings of empirical research conducted by academic media will naturally and necessarily be considered as an important source of knowledge innovation for the company.

However, in reality, business practice has little to do with the academic world and its contributions from research (Pfeffer & Fong, 2002). It takes many years (if ever) for the knowledge innovations generated in universities to be integrated into organizational operations. There appears to be a huge gap between universities and firms that makes it difficult for businesses to adopt innovations from academia (Starkey & Tempest, 2005). As a result of this gap, cooperation projects between universities and firms have been initiated with the main goal of guiding and integrating academic research into business practice, thus forming the appropriate channels to produce a flow of innovations originating in academic research between academic institutions and the business world. Nevertheless, not all of the university-firm projects

for developing research applied to the business world are always successful (Pfeffer, 2007).

This chapter offers an exploratory investigation that identifies some of the relevant elements that facilitate or prevent the generation of knowledge in a private Mexican university and how this knowledge is disseminated and used in companies. In the next section, it presents a conceptual model in which some knowledge dissemination channels are suggested and some practical implications are exposed. This chapter aims to make a contribution to academic literature, as little research has been conducted analyzing knowledge transfer between universities and enterprises in emergent economies.

2. BACKGROUND

The relationship between universities and firms can be viewed from the perspective of knowledge generation and adoption processes. Historically, the university has been the leading institution of modernity, the place where knowledge, culture and society converge (Starkey & Tempest, 2005). The university has been conceived as an institution that produces and protects knowledge, provides society with professionals who are ready to enter into economic activities, and that also supports the cultural and industrial development of a region or nation. The changes experienced by societies in relatively recent times have represented a challenge for university institutions, which have had to find new positions and obtain new definitions. Academic institutions are now expected to be disseminators of the new knowledge that they generate through research and such knowledge must be useful and have an impact on firms. Nowadays, the university faces the challenge of reacting before a globalized world that demands that it should play a role that is more in keeping with the practical interests of the business sector in particular and of society in general. The concept of the autonomous university existing in isolation from the rest of the community is now questioned (Hagen, 2002). From this vision, the principal criticism of the university is its self-absorption, its continuous dialogue with itself and its lack of involvement with the material development of society. In addition to this, to some observers, universities are seen as a generator of frustrations. It is argued that some universities develop skills and provide knowledge that do not reflect the needs of the increasingly dynamic environment in which enterprises operate (Pfeffer, 2007).

2.1 Knowledge Generation and Dissemination

Throughout history, society has seen universities as knowledge generation centers. The dissemination of knowledge to the entities that have the capacity to assimilate it for its efficient use in the interests of society depends on the universities. There are two actors in this dissemination process: the source of the knowledge, in this case the university, and the receiver: the firm.

The source of knowledge is the most important participant in the knowledge dissemination process since it has the knowledge that needs to be transferred. The source is expected to have the capacity to transmit the message and the desire to share its knowledge (Szulanski, 1996). The university has fulfilled its historical role as a knowledge disseminator, on one level, through the academic preparation of the members of society. On another level of dissemination, and in the face of a new social exigency, the university has focused on research and the dissemination of the findings of such research.

The receiver of the knowledge has been analyzed in terms of the absorptive capacity by Cohen & Levinthal (1990). These authors argue that, at both an individual and an organizational level, the absorptive capacity depends on the ability of the recipient to add new knowledge to the exist-

ing knowledge and the efficiency with which it is transferred depends precisely on this capacity (Grant, 1996). Moreover, the efficiency of adding new knowledge to existing knowledge can increase when it is expressed in terms of a common language. Therefore, locating mechanisms that can be used to codify and transfer knowledge into an accessible language for the receiver is important (Leonard-Barton, 1988).

Knowledge transfer is a complex process that requires time, effort and internal resources, specifically on the part of the receiver, in order to assimilate it (Nonaka, Toyama & Nagata, 2000, p.7). It is difficult to evaluate, absorb and use the "imported" knowledge if a company does not have the internal capacity to do so (Cohen & Levinthal, 1990). Very often, people understand and absorb new knowledge, but do not use it. There are several reasons for this: mainly the lack of respect for or confidence in the source, but also pride, obstinacy, lack of time, lack of opportunity and the fear of running risks (Szulanski, 1996).

According to O'Dell & Grayson (1998) and Ruggles (1998), organizational culture and the senior management's support are important with regard to the components of the transfer context: an open, receptive organizational culture facilitates the transfer of an activity from one work area to another. On the other hand, the socio-economic context (Meyer, 1977; OECD, 2007), in other words, the external factors in which organizations operate, play an important role in the knowledge transfer process. However, studies conducted by Szulanski (1996), Fiddler (2000), Gupta & Govindarajan (2000), and Zapata (2004) suggest that the richness of the communication media used for transferring knowledge, the characteristics of the knowledge itself and the short physical distance between one organizational area and another are more relevant than matters related to participants' motivation in the knowledge transfer process.

2.2 The Absence of Knowledge Transfer

In the setting of business faculties and schools, the university's knowledge transfer process to firms is not that effective. A gap seems to exist between them that obstructs the flow of knowledge innovations from the university towards the firm: Unnecessarily complex, grandiloquent language; a somewhat impractical vision of the research; relative ignorance of business practice; and the perception of a low level of reliability (Pineda & Zapata, 2007).

Universities generate, by means of their research projects, new knowledge in the area of business administration. This research activity, and as a result its publications, contributes largely to the construction of the prestige and reputation of institutions of higher education (Armstrong & Sperry, 1994; Gunther, 2007). However, part of the knowledge generated by academic research projects is never adopted by firms or it takes years for it to be transferred. Still, university institutions worldwide have opened up centers for linking them with firms in order to narrow the gap between academic research and its application in businesses. Despite this, business schools' influence on business administration practices is far from significant.

Academic literature presents different research projects that theoretically and empirically assess the knowledge transfer (KT) process in different settings. For example, (Ghoshal and Bartlett, 1988; Appleyard, 1996; Szulanski, 1996; O'Dell and Grayson, 1998; Simonin, 1999; Dixon, 2000; Gupta and Govindarajan, 2000; Cummings, 2004; Zander y Kogut, 2005 KT research in KIF firms, Darr, Argote and Epple, 1995; Rolland and Chauvel, 2000; Tsai, 2001) presents a theoretical model to assess KT. However, to our knowledge, Pfeffer & Fong (2002) offers one of the most robust methods for analyzing the degree of the impact of business schools on company administrators. The first method consisted of a review of the list of the top business books compiled by the US journal Business Week to specify the books written by authors who belong to academia. They assumed that the books listed as the best in the field of business administration influence business managers significantly. By studying the lists from three different years, Pfeffer & Fong detected that about 20% of the top ten business books were written by people from the academic world. This trend is not optimistic since the percentage of the books on Business Week's list that were written by academic authors has decreased year by year.

While Business Week's list of the top business books reflects the assessment and judgment of its editors, the same journal's list of the business book bestsellers corresponds to the opinion of the market itself. On reviewing the list, Pfeffer & Fong discovered that since 1995, the first year the list was generated, no more than two of the top 15 bestsellers, in any year, were written by academics.

Another indicator of the relatively low level of influence of business administration academics on company administrators has been obtained by Rigby (2001) through the analysis of the sources of the ideas and the business management techniques incorporated by companies by hiring consulting services. In an annual survey of consultants and administrators, Rigby's findings indicate that less than a third of the ideas and techniques paid for by companies to incorporate into their administration processes come from academia. According to these data, academic research in the area of business administration only contributes modestly to the acquisition of new knowledge – ideas and techniques – on the part of company administrators.

Ankers & Brennan (2002), in their study based on interviews with company directors, point out that the interviewees do not consider academic research to be very relevant since, in their opinion, this type of research focuses little on the everyday problems of administrative practice. Companies, according to their own administrators, need practical, clearly explained, readily available solutions.

2.3 Determining Factors in the University-Firm Partnership

Various studies have focused on the elements that affect the ties between universities and companies, factors that facilitate or hinder the innovation transfer or adoption process. For example, Zapata (2004) indicates some of the factors peculiar to organizations that affect the adoption of new knowledge. The primordial factor consists of the characteristics of the organizational culture, since an open, flexible organization is usually more successful in encouraging its members to adopt and share their knowledge and also facilitates communication amongst the members of the firm.

According to Hansotia (2003), innovative organizations do not penalize employees who risk trying out new ways of doing things. Zapata (2004) describes this manifestation of organizational culture as a support mechanism for the senior management. A company that is used to adopting innovations usually has a management that rewards, or at least does not penalize, the flexibility required for creativity.

Zapata (2004) also notes another organizational aspect, which is the design of the physical space in which employees interact. Close, open workplaces facilitate communication and, therefore, the exchange of ideas. Communication within the company and towards the outside is also backed by a rich variety of communication tools made available to personnel.

It is worth noting the factors peculiar to academic institutions that determine the effective transfer of innovation to companies. From the viewpoint of company administrators, the university's weaknesses are perceived as the reasons that explain the low level of influence of academia on administrative practice. Hansotia (2003) points out that few arguments have been directed at the business world regarding the superiority of

the innovations arising from academic research. In this sense, the university is at fault by failing to clearly demonstrate the advantages of adopting an innovation for a company. Zapata (2004) believes this is a factor that affects the reliability of the source. The trust of the person who adopts new knowledge in the source of said innovation is highly important for the successful completion of the adoption (Davenport & Prusak, 2001). Trust among members of an organization is one of the outcomes of the organizational culture. However, it is important to highlight that trust is shaped by the socio-cultural factors of the organization's location.

Ankers & Brennan (2002), in their investigation with business administrators, found some elements that, from the viewpoint of businesspeople, can be attributed to university institutions. It is worth pointing out in particular that the administrators are not familiar with and, in fact, have no interest in academic research dissemination channels. According to company directors, academic research is highly idealistic and only addresses very theoretical issues, while organizations need practical solutions to their problems.

Another factor that makes university research inaccessible is the grandiloquence of the language normally used in its publication. This is a codification problem that makes knowledge dissemination unnecessarily complicated. Papers published in academic journals are incomprehensible for businesspeople owing to their highly ostentatious language.

The factors that influence the effectiveness of the ties between the university and the firm are related to the cultures of both the academic institution and the organization, and the socio-cultural factors and values (House et al., 2004) where these institutions operate. Their expectations differ. The university usually considers that pure research is necessary for the advancement of human knowledge, while the firm views it as useless, since it requires the development of knowledge that can be quickly applied to solve practical problems. People in the academic world also express themselves with a jargon viewed as presumptuous and unnecessarily complex by their business counterparts. The university and the firm also have different expectations related to intellectual property rights, the timing and rhythm of the research and the materialization of its findings, all of which hinders their collaboration experiences.

Another discrepancy lies in an equally important matter concerning the nature of the research. From the university's point of view, many academics defend the prioritization of theoretical research, i.e. research that seeks answers to fundamental questions and does not necessarily have any practical applications on the short term in business practice (Poyago-Theotoky, Beath & Siegel, 2002). Of course, this vision contrasts sharply with the expectations of business administrators, who want and expect every research project to have a quick, useful application in business management.

The determining factors in the dissemination of the university's knowledge and its adoption by the firm can be summarized and classified as 1) Characteristics of the source; 2) Characteristics of the receiver; and 3) Socio-cultural differences arising from the particular idiosyncrasy.

Characteristics of the source:

- Unnecessarily complex and grandiloquent language
- Relatively unpractical vision of the research
- Relative ignorance of business practice
- Lack of credibility

Characteristics of the receiver:

- Organizational culture
- Innovation assimilation capacity
- Ignorance of academic sources of information
- Perception of academic sources' low level of credibility

Socio-cultural differences arising from the particular idiosyncrasy:

- Discrepancies on the nature of the research
- University's and company's work styles
- Different rhythms in the development of the research
- Discrepancies on intellectual property rights
- Values

2.4 Building Bridges: University-Firm Partnership Projects

The gap between academic research and business practice has not gone unnoticed by universities or firms. In the face of the rapid transformations undergone by society over the past few decades, the role of the university has gradually been redefined worldwide. It is becoming increasingly urgent in social and economic sectors for institutions of higher education to play a more active role in the development of communities in general and of firms in particular (Hagen, 2002).

Collaboration projects have been signed around the world between universities and firms in some cases to incorporate the findings of academic research into business projects that represent economic benefits. Poyago-Theotoky, Beath & Siegel (2002) identify three basic cooperation schemes between universities and firms. A frequent form of collaboration is when the firm hires the services of an academic or a university to conduct research on the company's behalf. In reality, this is a form of consulting rather then basic research. A second form of cooperation is presented when the university develops a plan for applying the outcome of its research commercially and seeks the help of a firm related to the discipline in question. In this type of relationship, the academic institution conserves the intellectual property rights. A third, very common, type of university-firm collaboration is a midpoint between the two aforementioned

Figure 1. Charts the aforementioned characteristics that determine the process of innovation dissemination from the university to the firm

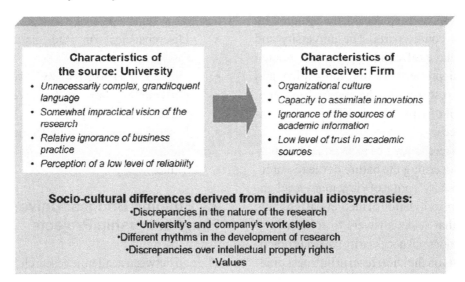

schemes. In this type of projects, the university and the firm develop a set of ideas and concepts that are at the basic or embryonic phase in order to generate practical commercial applications.

Pessacq, Iglesias & Willis (2004) present a cooperative-associative system between firms and the university based on the concept of shared-risk development. In this model, the firm contributes the idea, economic structure and management of potential customers and suppliers, while the university contributes the knowledge and capacity to accompany the development, starting with a technical-financial feasibility analysis. The university's capacities and resources are fully applicable to improving the firm's production processes. The members of the academic council can contribute their knowledge and their capacity for analysis in product or service innovation, the selection or design of production technology and in establishing guidelines for the effective exportation of products.

This type of collaboration projects usually focuses more on areas of engineering, as well as on the application of manufacturing patents or processes. Universities set up technology transfer

departments or offices whose main objective is to foment and coordinate collaboration projects with industry by facilitating technology dissemination, registering patents and marketing technology (Horng & Hsueh, 2005; Pfeffer, 2007). Finding points for cooperation in the area of administration and business is a bit more complicated. The innovations adopted by company administrators concentrate on administrative models and techniques that quickly help to make management processes more efficient and generate an advantage over competitors. Said innovation adoption normally comes far more from consulting companies than from academic research.

3. THE CASE: KNOWLEDGE DISSEMINATION THROUGH THE TRADITIONAL CHANNELS IN A MEXICAN UNIVERSITY

In order to have a better understanding of the phenomenon in which academic research in administrative science influences the adoption process of an innovation in the business world, the following sections present exploratory research aimed at observing the degree to which teaching, continuing education and consulting disseminate the knowledge developed through university-based research. Given the fact that the phenomenon under research is located in a relatively emerging phase of development (Hernández, Fernández & Baptista, 2003, p. 115), an exploratory methodology has been selected.

First of all, semi-structured interviews were conducted with faculty members from a private Mexican university using the critical incident technique: we asked the interviewees about the sources of knowledge they use to carry out their teaching, continuing education and consulting activities. We also asked them about their most recent research in such a way that we would be able to identify in which situations they had applied their findings. The profile of the faculty members selected have several characteristics in common: 1) Teaching-oriented faculty members whose main activity is teaching ; 2) Faculty members with a solid career in teaching combined with one or two of the following activities: consulting, continuing education and research; 3) Years of experience; and 4) age. This profile helped us to build a heterogeneous sample, as we were looking for subjects with different perspectives of the theoretical background presented.

Next, we complemented our data collection by interviewing middle- and upper-level managers from four companies with international presence operating in Mexico. It is important to mention that the companies were not randomly selected, but because of their innovative profile. This is a relevant remark because the companies selected are locally and nationally recognized by their products and services, which are developed based on continuing innovations in technologies and management.

Our study's sample consisted of 20 university professors who work at the business school of a private Mexican university. Twelve of the professors teach at undergraduate level and the other eight

have been assigned to the postgraduate area.. It is important to underscore that their main activity is teaching and that they also participate in continuing education and consulting activities.

The data were collected from 2006 to 2007. Diverse sources of information were used in order to obtain construct validity: semi-structured, in-depth interviews with upper and middle level managers and review of the companies' websites, internal documents that were provided by the companies, pamphlets and other secondary data.

It is now necessary to verify whether the channels traditionally used by universities – particularly business schools – to disseminate knowledge to society are incorporating the findings of academic research in the field of business administration. Historically, universities have influenced society through the preparation and training of individuals who at a given moment will enter corporations. Formalized educational systems are, in fact, theories of socialization institutionalized as rules at the collective level (Calori, Lubatkin & Veiga, 1997). Here education is seen as an allocating institution –operating under societal rules which allow the schools to directly confer success and failure in society quite apart from any socializing effects. The educational institutions, in particular their respective school systems, represent the vehicle by which the historical conjunctures from their past influence the administrative routines adopted by modern institutions (Calori, et al., 1997). Therefore, it is important to analyze whether undergraduate and graduate education incorporates the findings of the business administration research conducted by the university itself. If the university incorporates the innovations obtained from research into its academic programs, this would be a direct way of ensuring its impact on the business world. In order to understand the context of the education system in Mexico, the following section presents its most salient characteristics.

3.1 Mexico –Education Systems

The Mexican education system has some original features: it has an important private sector, from elementary school to higher education. Public and private sectors provide pre-elementary schooling with a view to promoting equality of opportunity. Nonetheless, Mexican public universities have a surprisingly low status in the eyes of prospective students and employers. Neither the civil service nor top management recruits regularly from these universities. Those who aspire to top management and commercial jobs bypass the public university and turn to the competitive-entry private universities and business schools which are exceedingly numerous in Mexico. According to official data (ANUIES, 2004 in Valera, 2006),Mexican higher education (public and private) comprises about 20% of the population between the ages of 20 and 24. In 2005, approximately 2.4 million students were enrolled in higher education. Of the higher education students, 83.4% were registered in undergraduate studies in universities and technological institutions; 7.4% in teacher's training colleges, 3.0% in Technological Universities, and 6.2% in graduate studies.

In Mexico, for historical reasons the basic role assigned to schools has been to educate and integrate citizens into society as well as to train the labour force. The aim of the Mexican education system has been to bring all the members of a given age group up to at least the level of the vocational education certificate, technical certificate or higher education. On the other hand, Mexican education has traditionally been a politically charged issue, perhaps more so than in other countries. Given the fact that *"the Mexican educational system comes from a phase of expansion during the post-war, when the economy grew based on industry, with its effects on social policy, welfare institutions and access to education"* (Valera, 2006, p. 55). However, Mexico's Ministry of Education *(Secretaria de Educación Pública, SEP)* is centralized at the national level and has maintained a tight control over most aspects of its primary and secondary school systems. The SEP oversees the hiring and evaluation of most of the nation's teachers. Additionally, the SEP retains an impressive formal power over funding, curricula and pedagogical methods, and even publishes the textbooks to be used in all public schools.

The field of higher Education in Mexico consists of 334 public universities, and 411 private universities (Neu et al., 2007). However, universities are only one sub-group of institutions in that there are also research, technical, vocational and teacher training *(escuelas normales)* institutes. Including all types of higher education institutions, the system has a total of 989 public and 1,430 private institutions of higher education (ibid).

3.2 An Empirical View in Mexico

The professors interviewed in the study indicated that their practical professional experience is the principal source of knowledge used in teaching their subject. Secondly, they use the textbooks indicated in the curricular programs and popular administration and business books. The third source of knowledge used in teaching consists of journals on administration and business topics; prestigious non-blind review journals, such as The Economist and Harvard Business Review. Articles from academic journals are rarely used as a source for teaching. Only professors with a doctoral degree normally use academic journals, although not as a first choice. The interviewees consider that the content of these journals is too complex and often too obscure for the average undergraduate student. Another reason given for not using this material in teaching is that it is too theoretical and not practical enough.

Continuing education constitutes a second means of knowledge dissemination for university institutions and also represents a significant source of income. The programs are designed for professionals who want to update their knowledge or training in a particular area of knowledge in which they have no university preparation. Continuing education is a good source of training for companies' managerial and operative personnel. Given the relevance of this dissemination channel for the university and for the firm, it is worth finding out which sources of knowledge are required when designing their content.

According to the professors who participate in continuing education programs, their own professional experience as practitioners constitutes the main source of knowledge used for designing the programs. Popular books and journals on business administration topics are the second and third sources of information. The professors base these decisions on the fact that students participating in extension courses are normally looking for new knowledge that can be quickly applied in their working context. The content most appreciated by participants is new, practical business management tools, as well as innovation in administrative approaches, together with the perception that too much theory is not much use in business management.

The third dissemination channel used by the university to transfer knowledge to firms consists of consulting activities. By nature, consulting is a direct form of intervention and influence on the daily organization of company management. For firms, consulting is one of the main sources for acquiring new knowledge. Firms normally hire consulting services in order to solve concrete administration problems as fast as possible. They also seek these services for support in making strategic planning decisions. The interviewed professors who also work as consultants coincide in that their own professional experience, as directors and as consultants, is the main source of knowledge used in this activity. It is not easy to apply new knowledge produced by theoretical research in each of the consulting cases.

For the majority of the company directors who participated in the study, time is one of the most important factors to be considered in the new knowledge adoption process. The managers interviewed mentioned that this is a critical aspect when evaluating the knowledge supplier. The current business environment forces firms to solve problems in increasingly shorter time periods. The most valuable help in these cases comes from consultants, either companies or independent individuals. In general, company directors are not familiar with the academic sources of knowledge. In fact, they are not interested at all in finding out about the academic information vehicles.

For companies, the determining factors that have the greatest influence on the effectiveness of the adoption include contextual, organizational, human and socio-cultural factors. Firms with more horizontal structures are more likely to be successful in adopting new knowledge in their administrative processes. Organizations with very vertical structures have a long decision-making chain, thus minimizing individuals' freedom and initiative in innovation. Firms with a less hierarchized organizational structure, with a short span of control and a participative management style offer the conditions that provide flexibility for individuals and foment personal and group initiative for innovation.

4. HOW CAN ACADEMIA REACH THE PRACTITIONERS?

4.1 Reward System and Performance Evaluation

So far, evidence has shown that the high and medium managerial levels in companies – the people responsible in the last instance for finding and incorporating new business management knowledge in their organizations – do not know about, nor are they interested in knowing about, the media in which academic research findings are published. In the few cases in which a director has had contact with an academic journal, the content of the same has been seen as too complex and unnecessarily obscure.

Company directors do not read academic journals. However, they are familiar with and do read popular administration and business journals. There is an abundance of famous titles in both English and Spanish. Although they might not necessarily be the only or the best journals, Harvard Business Review, The Economist and Business Week are some of the most well known titles in the business practice milieu worldwide. On a regional level, there are well reputed journals with an acceptable readership level among people in the world of business.

As discussed previously in this chapter, academics from business schools have very little influence on administrative practice. This can be concluded by observing the lists of the best-seller, and, therefore, most read and, perhaps, most influential administration and business books. A similar conclusion on this influence might be reached by observing the collaborators in the popular business journals.

A proposal for business schools to become more relevant – and influential – in administrative practice consists of slightly modifying the system of incentives and acknowledgements for professors' and researchers' performance. The university usually encourages its faculty to conduct research and publish the results of studies in the most prestigious academic journals. The classification systems that order academic journals according to their impact, expressed by the number of quotations and references made to the articles published in the same, are known throughout the teaching world. The better the classification of the journal in which the professor has published research papers, the better his or her evaluation will be. The number of times that a professor's article is cited by other research colleagues in their own work is also important. The popular journals read by the people who practice business administration do not appear in any of these publications, academic journal classifications or levels of impact.

Ten or fifteen of the articles published in The Economist or in The Wall Street Journal have not even remotely been acknowledged in the academic world in a single article published in an academic journal positioned at the top of the various rankings. However, The Economist or The Wall Street Journal evidently has a far greater impact on people who manage firms than the most prestigious academic journal in the world.

In view of this, if the university wants its research to have a greater impact on business practice, we have proposed a system of incentives and evaluation for professors that recognizes and values publications in the mass dissemination media in the area of administration and business. We are not trying to discourage publications in academic journals, but to incorporate the recognition of articles published in the media that have a real influence on administrators. Some professors will continue to publish in academic journals, but, undoubtedly, others will publish in the mass media. In fact, some people will find the idea of writing for this type of publications very attractive.

This proposal by no means seeks to lower the level of research work and publications, but to adapt it to a wider audience who has no contact with the academic media for disseminating new knowledge. Ultimately, the idea is to disseminate the knowledge generated by academic research so that it will be available to and influence the business world.

A reward system for academics should also consider the research projects where professors collaborate with companies and other organizations. It is important to point out that when academics work on applied research projects with businesses, they are not writing articles than can be published in the most prominent journals.

4.2 Education with Applied Research Orientation

Business schools have been dedicated to the education of managers and practitioners of the future. However, graduate and undergraduate programs usually do not have an orientation toward applied research. With luck, students learn specific concepts, constructs and techniques, and develop certain competencies related to management and business. Graduate and undergraduate programs with an applied research orientation could provide the students with the scientific background that could help to understand the role of research in the practice of management. Teaching in Business Schools must find a balance between scientific rigor and applied knowledge.

Some specific courses could be designed to engage students in a real and practical business situation. This could be a problem or a situation that requires a scientific approach in order to find the optimal solution. These kinds of projects would be a good link between companies and the Business School and represent a good opportunity to reinforce the flow of communication and understanding between them. In this way, the future managers will recognize the value and usefulness of the academic research in the practice of business.

On the other hand, Business Schools can develop executive doctoral programs focused on the education of people that will be part of the practice of management in companies. From the manager's perspective, a common criticism related to the university is that academics live in an unreal world –in a bubble- and that Business Schools are isolated. This point of view can be modified by building bridges to allow people from business practice to cross to the academic world without leaving the everyday business operation.

In an executive program, doctoral students would not leave their companies to enter the academic world as full time doctoral students. In this case, the doctoral student is always a practitioner and he or she could bring practical problems from his or her organization to the classroom in the form of academic research projects. Similarly, the doctoral student could apply the academic training and methodologies to the business world. The aim of an executive doctoral program is not necessarily the education of a purely academic

researcher, but the development of a researcher with one foot in academia and the other in business practice.

4.3 The Role of the Advisory Board

How can we reduce the existing gap between the university, Business Schools, and enterprises? The answer is not so simple. As we can see, there are some mechanisms that could impact the reduction of this gap. We also believe that the inclusion of a neutral 'entity' could support it. This entity must be integrated by members from the academic world, practitioners and entrepreneurs, but also by community leaders who believe in the relevance of applied research.

The starting point for this entity might be dialogue, to communicate their needs and expectations, and, thus, the solutions. Dialogue among members provides the opportunity to eliminate the mystifying features of the university and its grandiloquent language and for the firm, its ignorance of academic sources of information. Besides that, community leaders would play the role of the transmitter of society's needs and its perceptions about what actions universities and firms must take.

The aim of an advisory board is to constitute a space where universities, managers and entrepreneurs, and members of the community can meet and share their needs and concerns about knowledge and education. We cannot forget the role of the university in modern society, as a knowledge generator and disseminator. Business Schools must meet the requirements of the productive sector and, at the same time, they should preserve their independence of thought. A council of this kind is a channel that opens the university to society. It is also an instrument for gathering the suggestions of the business community regarding the curriculum of the graduate and undergraduate programs.

As shown in Figure 2, a model for collaboration between the university and the business world includes two main strategies –channels, because

Figure 2.

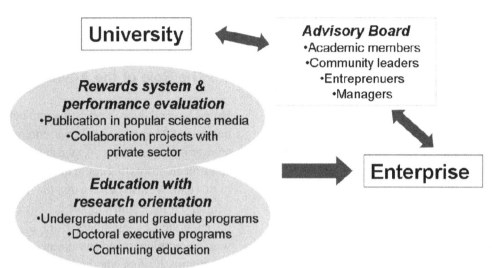

they facilitate the dissemination of knowledge that can be controlled by the university. This is a matter of willingness to redefine the ways used by the academic world to recognize the merits of its members.

5. PRACTICAL IMPLICATIONS AND FUTURE LINES OF RESEARCH

In the current business setting, where constant technological change and uncertainty prevail, firms need to generate and adopt knowledge continuously in order to be able to create a sustainable competitive advantage. This is the context faced by the university and in which it must modify its role as an institution that creates and preserves knowledge to a more active role as a disseminator of this valuable resource. However, reality shows that, at least in the case of administrative science, for companies, the university's influence on the new knowledge adoption process is minimal.

Academic research findings are discussed almost exclusively in academia and they rarely reach company administrators. A variety of factors that can be attributed to both the university and the firm determine the transfer and adoption of

academic knowledge in businesses. In academia, the use of an extremely grandiloquent and unnecessarily complex language that is practically incomprehensible for company directors can be seen as a determining factor in knowledge transfer. The academic world is also known for its lack of vision in research and its ignorance of business practices. On the other hand, the determining factors for knowledge adoption in companies include the nature of the organizational culture, their capacity to generate and assimilate innovations and their ignorance of academic sources of knowledge, together with their lack of confidence in universities as a source of relevant, applicable innovations.

Each party's own particular idiosyncrasy is a determining factor in knowledge transfer and adoption. There are discrepancies between the university and the firm that are related to expectations regarding research. While some people in the world of academia favor pure research, the environment of business practice is looking for applied research with development times that are much shorter than those normally proposed by the university institution.

On the other side of the spectrum, the sociocultural context found in Mexico challenges the mutual understanding, knowledge transfer and collaboration between universities and enterprise. The challenge is to develop a change in the students' and professors' mentality and in the educational system that prevails in Mexico. According to researchers, teaching in Mexican universities has traditionally focused on preparing professionals who use knowledge, rather than researchers who produce it (Fortes & Adler Lomnitz, 1994). In fact, the socialization of scientists in Mexico and Latin American countries occurs under adverse conditions compared to the conditions that prevail in the USA and European countries, for example. The challenge remains in Mexico where scientists and researchers still lack recognition within their society. However, Mexico has made fundamental changes to redirect this trend. In 1985, Mexico established the National Research System (SNI), in order to increase the salaries of researchers in Mexico and thus prevent "brain drain" (CONACYT).

University-firm collaboration projects are common and boast several success stories. In these cases, sometimes with the backing of government agencies, it has been possible to combine the research resources of the academic world with the company's efforts in order to develop practical industrial applications. Nevertheless, this situation generates other issues that are worth analyzing, such as the nature and ultimate aims of university research and this institution's raison d'être itself. Whether the university should conduct research on what the market requires or, on the contrary, it should continue with its own research interests regardless of its influence on companies is a topic worth discussing.

Apart from the aforementioned collaboration projects, the impact of the university on society in general and on companies in particular resulting from academia's traditional knowledge dissemination channels should be addressed. These means of dissemination include teaching, continuing education and consulting. The historical impact of the university on society through teaching is undeniable. Through teaching-learning activities, the university contributes to preparing human resources who will enrich the labor market. Continuing education and consulting are resources designed to provide firms with new knowledge by means of professional training and consulting for decision-making.

The evidence shown by this study, limited to a merely Mexican context, suggests that the new knowledge generated in academic research is not included in the dissemination channels used by the university mentioned in the previous paragraph. In the field of business administration, practical professional experience, mass dissemination media such as journals and books, and textbooks represent the main sources of knowledge.

6. CONCLUSIONS

The increasingly dynamic environment in which businesses perform forces them to acquire new knowledge, often turning to external sources. In this context, analyzing the collaborative relationships existing between the university – seen as a source of new knowledge – and firms as a receiver of it, is relevant. A fluid, positive exchange partnership between institutions of higher education and businesses would give organizations access to the new knowledge obtained through academic research, continuing education and consulting, while allowing the university to broaden its influence on business practices. Nevertheless, the reality, at least with regard to administrative sciences, is that the university has little influence over firms' adoption of administrative processes.

For firms' managers it is difficult, if not impossible, to know what academic researchers are investigating. The results of academic research are mainly exposed in academia and published in scientific journals. Besides that, the determining factors of the university's characteristics include the use of overly pompous, grandiloquent language, a somewhat impractical vision of the research conducted, ignorance of business practice, and their perception as an unreliable source of knowledge. On the other hand, the determining characteristics of the receiver of knowledge, firms, include the nature of their organizational culture, their absorptive capacity for innovations, unawareness of the channels used to disseminate academic publication, and also distrust of such channels.

Additionally, the discrepancy in the nature and expectations of the research, the different work styles, the different rhythms in the development of research projects versus the organization's requirements, and the discrepancies over intellectual property rights are other significant elements in the transfer and adoption of new knowledge between these entities.

In order to close the gap in the university-firm relationship, the study of the effectiveness of traditional and obvious knowledge diffusion mechanisms is pertinent. These dissemination channels are teaching, continuing education, and consulting. The social impact of teaching, at both undergraduate and postgraduate levels, is more than contrasting. Likewise, continuing education and consulting are channels that often are the last resort of firms' managers for acquiring new knowledge.

The empirical study exposed in the present chapter explores the diffusion mechanisms of academic research to society, specifically to firms. It has been also the goal of the current research to determine the variables involved in the phenomena, in order to develop a more comprehensive investigation. Evidence suggests that the knowledge derived from academic research is not transferred by the university's traditional channels. Professional experience as a practitioner, textbooks, popular management books and magazines are among the most valued sources of knowledge to be transferred in teaching, continuous education and consulting activities.

Similarly, this chapter proposes a specific dissemination channel model that can be used by the university to open its doors to society and contribute in better ways in the knowledge assimilated by organizations. The aim of the proposal is to gain relevance for Business Schools in the world of businesses, in a way where organizations can also enter the academic sphere. It is a strategy to build prestige and practical relevance for the research conducted in the university. In other words, the proposed model for knowledge dissemination from universities to enterprises illustrates a common ground where academia and enterprise speak –literally- the same language.

Besides the findings of the current and future research projects, the matter of the question is the redefinition of the university and its role in society. In business schools in particular, the pending issue is to discuss the basic aim of academic research in management. As mentioned at the beginning of this chapter, a deeper question lies beneath this research line that has to do with the redefinition of the role of the university in today's society and of the aims of research. These topics have yet to be studied and discussed from a perspective that is more closely linked to the philosophy of science. In short, the challenges for Mexico rest on investment in education, basic research and cooperation / training programs in order to co-finance collaborative research projects.

ACKNOWLEDGMENT

This project has been funded by the Endowed Research Chair for European Studies within the School of Government, Social Sciences and Humanities at the Tecnológico de Monterrey, Mexico.

REFERENCES

Ankers, P., & Brennan, R. (2002). Managerial relevance in academic research: An exploratory study. *Marketing Intelligence & Planning, 20*(1), 15–21. doi:10.1108/02634500210414729

Appleyard, M. M. (1996). How does knowledge flow? Interfirm patterns in the semiconductor industry. *Strategic Management Journal, 17,* 137–154.

Armstrong, J. S., & Sperry, T. (1994). Business school prestige- research versus teaching. *Interfaces, 24,* 13–43. doi:10.1287/inte.24.2.13

Calori, R., Lubatkin, M., Very, P., & Veiga, J. F. (1997). Modelling the origins of national-bound administrative heritages: A historical institutional analysis of French and British firms. *Organization Science, 8*(6), 681–696. doi:10.1287/orsc.8.6.681

Cohen, W. M., & Levinthal, D. (1990). Absorptive capacity: A new perspective on learning and innovation. *Administrative Science Quarterly, 35,* 128–152. doi:10.2307/2393553

Cummings, J. N. (2004). Work groups, structural diversity, and knowledge sharing in a global organization. *Management Science, 50*(3), 352–264. doi:10.1287/mnsc.1030.0134

Darr, E. D., Argote, L., & Epple, D. (1995). The acquisition, transfer, and depreciation of knowledge in service organizations: Productivity in franchises. *Management Science, 41*(11), 1750–1762. doi:10.1287/mnsc.41.11.1750

Davenport, T. H., & Prusak, L. (2001). *Conocimiento en acción, cómo las organizaciones manejan lo que saben.* Buenos Aires, Argentina: Editorial Prentice Hall.

Dixon, N. (2000). *Common knowledge. How companies thrive by sharing what they know.* Cambridge, MA: Harvard Business School Press.

Fiddler, L. (2000). *Facilitators and impediments to the internal transfer of team-embodied competences in firms operating in dynamic environments.* Unpublished doctoral dissertation, Boston University, Boston.

Fortes, J., & Adler, L. (1994). *Becoming a scientist in Mexico: The challenges of creating a scientific community in an underdeveloped country.* University Park, PA: The Pennsylvania State University Press.

Ghoshal, S., & Bartlett, C. A. (1988). Creation, adaptation and diffusion of innovations by subsidiaries of multinational corporations. *Journal of International Business Studies,* (Fall): 365–388. doi:10.1057/palgrave.jibs.8490388

Grant, R. M. (1996). Toward a knowledge-based theory of the firm. *Strategic Management Journal, 17,* 109–122. doi:10.1002/(SICI)1097-0266(199602)17:2<109::AID-SMJ796>3.0.CO;2-P

Grant, R. M. (1998). *Dirección estratégica.* Madrid, Spain: Civitas.

Gunther, R. (2007). No longer a stepchild: How the management field can come into its own. *Academy of Management Journal, 50*(6), 1365–1378.

Gupta, A. K., & Govindarajan, V. (2000). Knowledge flows within multinational corporations. *Strategic Management Journal, 21,* 473–496. doi:10.1002/(SICI)1097-0266(200004)21:4<473::AID-SMJ84>3.0.CO;2-I

Hagen, R. (2002). Globalization, university transformation and economic regeneration. A UK case study of public/private sector partnership. *International Journal of Public Sector Management, 15*(2), 204–218. doi:10.1108/09513550210423370

Hansotia, B. J. (2003). Bridging the research gap between marketing academics and practitioners. *Journal of Database Marketing & Consumer Strategy Management, 11*(2), 114–120. doi:10.1057/palgrave.dbm.3240212

Hernández, R., Fernández, C., & Baptista, P. (2003). *Metodología de la investigación.* Mexico City, Mexico: McGraw-Hill Interamericana.

Horng, D., & Hsueh, C. (2005). How to improve efficiency in transfer of scientific knowledge from university to firms: The case of universities in Taiwan. *Journal of American Academy of Business, Cambridge, 7*(2), 187–190.

House, R. J., Hanges, P. J., Javidan, M., Dorfman, P. W., & Gupta, V. (2004). *Culture, leadership, and organizations: The GLOBE study of 62 societies.* London: Sage.

Leonard-Barton, D. (1988). Implementation as mutual adaptation of technology organisation. *Research Policy, 17*, 251–267. doi:10.1016/0048-7333(88)90006-6

Meyer, J. W. (1977). The effect of education as an institution. *American Journal of Sociology, 83*(1), 55–77. doi:10.1086/226506

Neu, D., Silva, L., & Ocampo-Gomez, E. (2007). Diffusing financial practices in Latin America higher education understanding the intersection between global and influence and local context. *Accounting, Auditing & Accountability Journal, 21*(1), 49–77. doi:10.1108/09513570810842322

Nonaka, I., Toyama, R., & Nagata, A. (2000). A firm as a knowledge-creating entity: A new perspective on the theory of the firm. *Industrial and Corporate Change, 9*(1), 1–20. doi:10.1093/icc/9.1.1

O'Dell, C., & Grayson, C. J. (1998). If only we knew what we know: Identification and transfer of internal best practices. *California Management Review, 40*(3), 154–170.

OECD. (2007). *Education and training policy: No more failures ten steps to equity in Education.* Paris: OECD.

Pessacq, R. A., Iglesias, O., & Willis, E. (2004). *Hacia un nuevo paradigma en la relación Universidad-Empresa.* Buenos Aires, Argentina: IV CAEDI: Cuarto Congreso Argentino de Enseñanza de la Ingeniería.

Pfeffer, J. (2007). A modest proposal: How we might change the process and product of managerial research. *Academy of Management Journal, 50*(6), 1334–1345.

Pfeffer, J., & Fong, C. T. (2002). The end of business school? Less success that meets the eye. *Academy of Management Learning & Education, 1*, 78–95.

Pineda, J. L., & Zapata, L. E. (2007). From universities to corporations: Determining factors in the diffusion and adoption of knowledge. In *Proceedings of the 8th European Conference on Knowledge: Vol. 2.* (pp. 788-793). England: Academic Conferences International.

Poyago-Theotoky, J., Beath, J., & Siegel, D. S. (2002). Universities and fundamental research: Reflections on the growth of university-industry partnerships. *Oxford Review of Economic Policy, 18*(1), 10. doi:10.1093/oxrep/18.1.10

Rigby, D. (2001). Management tools and techniques: A survey. *California Management Review, 43*(2), 139–160.

Rolland, N., & Chauvel, D. (2000). Knowledge transfer in strategic alliances. In Ch. Depres & D. Chauvel (Eds.), *Knowledge horizons, the present and the promise of knowledge management.* MA: Butterworth-Heinemann.

Ruggles, R. (1998). The state of the notion: Knowledge management in practice. *California Management Review, 40*(3), 80–89.

Simonin, B. L. (1999). Ambiguity and the process of knowledge transfer in strategic alliances. *Strategic Management Journal, 20*, 595–623. doi:10.1002/(SICI)1097-0266(199907)20:7<595::AID-SMJ47>3.0.CO;2-5

Starkey, K., & Tempest, S. (2005). The future of the business school: Knowledge challenges and opportunities. *Human Relations, 58*(1), 61–82. doi:10.1177/0018726705050935

Szulanski, G. (1996). Exploring internal stickiness: Impediments to the transfer of best practices within the firm. *Strategic Management Journal, 17,* 27–43.

Teece, D. J., Pisano, G., & Shuen, A. (1997). Dynamic capabilities and strategic management. *Strategic Management Journal, 18*(7), 509–533. doi:10.1002/(SICI)1097-0266(199708)18:7<509::AID-SMJ882>3.0.CO;2-Z

Tsai, W. (2001). Knowledge transfer in intraorganizational networks: Effects of network position and absorptive capacity on business unit innovation and performance. *Academy of Management Journal, 44*(5), 996–1004. doi:10.2307/3069443

Valera, G. (2006). The higher educational system in Mexico at the threshold of change. *International Journal of Educational Development, 26,* 52–66. doi:10.1016/j.ijedudev.2005.07.012

Zander, U., & Kogut, B. (1995). Knowledge and the speed of transfer and imitation of organizational capabilities: An empirical test. *Organization Science, 6*(1), 76–92. doi:10.1287/orsc.6.1.76

Zapata, L. E. (2004). *Los determinantes de la generación y la transferencia del conocimiento en pequeñas empresas de tecnologías de la información en Barcelona.* Unpublished doctoral dissertation, Universidad Autónoma de Barcelona, Barcelona.

Chapter 8
Impact of Organizational Culture on Knowledge Management in Higher Education

Roberto Biloslavo
University of Primorska, Slovenia

Mojca Prevodnik
University of Primorska, Slovenia

ABSTRACT

Knowledge management is a set of purposeful activities led by management in order to enable and support generation, storage, transfer and application of knowledge within an organization so as to create value and improve the organization's effectiveness. The effectiveness of these activities is in a large part dependent on organizational culture, which can support or impede the two-way social process of learning and knowledge sharing between individuals, groups, organizations, and artifacts. This chapter discusses the fundamentals of organizational culture and knowledge management, their definitions, components, and processes. Specifically, the study presented is focused on how different types of organizational culture, as defined by the competing values framework, might be related to the iterative processes of knowledge generation, storage, transfer, and application in higher education.

INTRODUCTION

In the knowledge society, also known as the post-industrial, post-capitalistic and information society, knowledge is its most important production factor, rather than capital, land or labor (Drucker, 1993). In modern economy successful organizations are organizations which create, store, share and embody new knowledge in the form of new or improved products and services. Therefore, it is not surprising that in the last decade and a half, a new field of research in management has been developed, known as 'knowledge management' (KM). Knowledge management is a complex multi-faced and multi-layered concept which we can define as a coherent system of activities oriented to "find, select, organize, disseminate, and transfer important

DOI: 10.4018/978-1-60566-790-4.ch008

information and expertise necessary for activities such as problem solving, dynamic learning, strategic planning and decision making" (Gupta et al., 2000, p. 17).

Knowledge management is especially important for organizations that are comprised of experts (Dawson, 2000) where success depends upon the generation, utilization, and uniqueness of their knowledge base (Donaldson, 2001). Such institutions are characterized as having knowledge as both their main production factor and their final product (Goddard, 1998). It would seem appropriate to consider higher educational institutions as organizations comprised of experts.

Higher educational institutions (HEIs), just as any other organization that operates in a dynamic environment, have to respond rapidly to changing environments in order to survive. They also need to anticipate further changes that will require yet more redesign in organizational structure and practice. A number of different external drivers of change regarding HE have been cited in the literature (Bates, 1997; Levine, 2000; Middlehurst & Woodfield, 2006), these are the radical shift from an industrial to a knowledge society, government's demand for usable knowledge and cost efficiency, demographic changes, market pressures from industry, internationalization of higher education, lifelong learning, the paradigm shift from teaching to learning, new technologies, and globalization. All these drivers bring new challenges to HEIs, which, it has been argued, can be partly solved by adopting forms and practices used in private and corporate management, especially regarding forms of educational governance (Meyer, 2002), but in the largest part only effective KM seems to be the appropriate solution.

Ward (Zappia, 2000) wrote, that education "is an enterprise so wholly dissimilar from those of ordinary business life that an entirely different set of principles must be applied to it throughout." The nature of HEIs is that they are at the same time educational and research institutions where knowledge processes (should) occur on a daily

basis. It is perhaps because of this specific nature that most KM research has been done in the commercial sector while comparatively little has been done to investigate KM processes within HEIs, as Sharimllah Devi et al. (2007) write (see also Kidwell et al., 2000; Park et al., 2004).

On the other hand, we cannot properly discuss about KM if we do not consider its relation to organization culture. Organization culture develops during the process of external adaptation and internal integration and consists of underlying assumptions, collective memories, and core values which most people share (Schein, 1984). Most scholars agree that organizational culture has a large impact on the processes within organizations, starting with Schein (1996, p. 231) who claimed that culture is "one of the most powerful and stable forces operating in organizations" (see also Bollinger & Smith, 2001). This view is also shared by managers as the benchmarking company survey ranked culture as the most critical success factor (Mertins et al., 2001). Based on that we can conclude that people within HEIs have to accept some common rules and ways of doing, which are part of the organizational culture, if they want to effectively work together, learn, and share knowledge.

The aim of this chapter then is to develop a better understanding of the relationship between organizational culture and KM processes in HEIs. The Competing Values Framework devised by Robert E. Quinn and John Rohrbaugh was used to analyze the differences in organizational culture profiles and how the might be related to the various KM processes. Such an understanding would enable practitioners to be aware of the impact different cultural types might have on KM processes in HEIs and based on that prepare possible future activities for better managing scholarly knowledge in a certain cultural setting or changing organizational culture through appropriate initiatives.

The results of our research reveal that there are significant relationships between some organizational cultural types and KM processes within HEIs. These results are mostly in line with similar studies conducted by other researchers on the topics of organizational culture and knowledge management. However, others deviate and give us an intriguing starting-point for further discussion. Yet, we need to be careful in the interpretation of our results because of the limited sample size.

BACKGROUND

Organizational Culture

Throughout human evolution many different types of cultures at different levels of human society have emerged and they impact each other through language, symbols, rules, gestures, and ways of thinking, feeling, and acting. Tylor (1871) was the first scholar who defined culture. He claimed that culture is "that complex whole which includes knowledge, belief, art, moral, law, custom, and any other capabilities and habits acquired by man as a member of society" (id.: 1). An extended form of this definition more than a century later is offered by Schein (1992, p. 12) who described culture as "[a] pattern of shared basic assumptions that the group learned as it solved its problems of external adaptation and internal integration, that had worked well enough to be considered valid, and therefore, to be taught to new members as the correct way to perceive, think and feel in relation to those problems". Schein (1985) argued that culture is composed of three dimensions – assumptions, values and artifacts. Sharimllah Devi et al. (2007, p. 61) define assumptions as "widely held, ingrained subconscious view of human nature and social relationships that are taken for granted". Values represent preferences for alternative outcomes and ways to achieve them, and just like physiological and psychosocial needs, are part of man's essence. Artifacts embrace the more visible, tangible and audible manifestations of culture that include rituals, slogans, traditions and myths.

As mentioned before, different levels of culture exist. Hofstede (1997), who stressed that we do not inherit the culture, but we learn it, enumerated six different layers of culture or, as he wrote, of "mental programming". The sixth is that of organizational culture. According to Hofstede (1997, p. 18) "corporate culture is a soft, holistic concept with, however, presumed hard consequences". Cameron and Quinn (1999, p. 15) went deeper into the concept and defined organizational culture as a reflection of "what is valued, the dominant leadership style, the language and symbols, the procedures and routines, and the definitions of success that make an organization unique". Tavčar and Biloslavo describe organizational culture as "a set of all artifacts of employees' behavior, including values and basic underlying assumptions which coordinate this behavior" (Biloslavo, 2006, p. 122). For Hatch and Schultz (1997, p. 363) organizational culture "forms the context within which identity is established, maintained and changed and corporate attempts to manipulate and use it are interpreted, assessed and ultimately accepted, altered or rejected". Referring to these definitions, we can conclude that organizational culture is a set of explicit and implicit rules of what is and is not acceptable behavior in an organization, influenced by core values, norms and underlying assumptions.

Kotter and Heskett (1992) wrote that organizational culture has two levels, which differ in terms of their visibility and their resistance to change. The first level is almost invisible and consists of values shared by the people, which are hard to change. People are usually unaware of values they share and this is the reason they prefer the current state. The second level is more visible and easier to change, because it represents behavior patterns that exist in the organization and which employees – old and new – follow. The two levels are strongly connected and influence each other.

In respect to the fact that "values are both more accessible than assumptions and more reliable than artifacts" (Howard, 1998, p. 233), organizational values are seen as the most suitable manifestation of organizational culture from the point of view of culture research. Lamond (2003, p. 47) came to the conclusion that organizational values differ from wider cultural values and "should be seen as more specific conceptions of the desirable by which organizational members, individually and collectively, judge the organization's end states, and methods of reaching them, as desirable or not".

Handy (1976) was the first scholar who went deeper into exploring the nature of different organizational culture, referring to the work of Roger Harrison. According to them both, four main types of organizational culture exist and these are: power culture, role culture, task culture, and person culture (Handy, 1993). Their work was continued by Deal and Kennedy (1982), who also defined four types of culture based on two criteria – speed of feedback and level of risk. The work-hard play-hard culture, tough-guy macho culture, process culture, and bet-the-company culture were formulated. In the meantime, other scholars have tried developing new models, also deriving knowledge from psychology. Starting with the Jungian framework for identifying personality types in 1923 and continuing with the work of different psychologists (Myers, Briggs and others), it is now known that most of us form similar categories for organizing information in our minds, and this is called the psychological archetype (Cameron & Quinn, 1999). Referring to the latter, such underlying archetypes influence interpretations of cultural information in organizations, and also the way of experiencing and transmitting culture (Cameron & Freeman, 1991). This was the basis for Quinn and Rohrbaugh's competitive values model of organizational effectiveness presented in 1981, later renamed Competing Values Framework (CVF).

With statistical analysis two major dimensions were found that divided indicators into four main groups (so called core dimensions). The first dimension divides effectiveness criteria into two groups – one emphasizes flexibility, individuality, and spontaneity (a more organic view), the other, stability, order, and control (a more mechanistic view). The second dimension has effectiveness criteria which stress an internal orientation, smoothing activities, and integration on one side, and external orientation, competition and differentiation on the other. These two dimensions form four quadrants that represent a distinct set of organizational effectiveness criteria of what is valued in a certain type of organization or more explicitly - culture.

That is why, Quinn and Rohrbaugh named these quadrants hierarchy, market, clan, and adhocracy. The hierarchy culture type represents a well-structured and formalized organization, where formal procedures, rules, policies and clear expectations bind the organization together. The main strategic tasks are maintaining the stability and smooth-running of the organization which will ensure the organization's efficiency. This culture type is very similar to the bureaucratic organization which Max Weber created. The market culture type represents an organization as a market. This means it is open to the external environment and there are numerous transactions which enable the organization to gain competitive advantage and market leadership. Such an organization is strictly goal oriented and operates by market rules. The main values are competitiveness and productivity. The clan culture type is like an extended family where everyone takes care of each other, and it is a nice place to work. Such an organization is therefore tightly connected and teamwork prevails. The main strategic objectives are building the commitment through mentorship which enables personal growth and a positive working climate. The adhocracy culture type is a very dynamic and creative place to be. Therefore the organization is very flexible, which enables innovations, growth and the gaining of new resources (id. 33-40).

However, we need to emphasize that each cultural type has its own weaknesses and strengths, and one is not better than another. For that reason, some authors as Grey and Densten (2005) have come to the conclusion that effective organizations present all four organizational culture types in a "balanced" measure. It is important to mention that CVF is also used as a guide for change and therefore another dimension is significant – the dimension of dynamics which separates quadrants on the basis of speed (how quickly?) and scope (how much?) of needed action for change from one to another. Therefore, changes from the lower left quadrant to the upper right quadrant can be incremental to transformational (i.e. a question of magnitude), and from the lower right corner to the upper left corner fast to long-term (i.e. a question of velocity) (Quinn et al., 2006). To be able to measure and to define organizational cultures, Cameron developed a CVF culture questionnaire with a six-item ipsative measure (Quinn, 1988, pp. 142-143). Each item has four descriptions of organization and respondents are asked to distribute 100 points among them. This distribution shows the respondent's view of the organization.

Different empirical research studies have found that CVF has both face and empirical validity, and helps incorporate many of the dimensions of organizational culture proposed by various researchers (see Goodman et al., 2001; Kwan & Walker, 2004; Lamond, 2003; Zammuto et al., 1999). Howard (1998) in his study concludes that the CVF perspective provides a valid metric for understanding organizational cultures. It is based upon these arguments that we adopted the CVF to measure the organizational culture of the HEIs under study.

Knowledge

Knowledge may be defined as contextualised information, experience, perspectives and insights that provide a framework from which to evaluate the events of the world and act upon them (Davenport & Prusak, 1998). Steyn (2004, p. 617) furthers

this definition by stating that knowledge is "the personal ability to interpret information through a process of giving meaning to the information and an attitude of wanting to do so". It originates and is applied in the minds of people, is essentially related to human action and is context specific and relational. It is dynamic in nature due to its constant changes. We consider that knowledge provides an individual or group with the capacity to act, and it is developed through formal learning, practical hands-on experience and socialization. Knowledge is anchored in the beliefs of its holder. Core of individual's knowledge is therefore hard to capture in words or in any other unequivocal explicit symbols. For this reason corporate databases and ICT infrastructure that support information exchange and storage cannot be the sole element of KM. KM needs to encompass broader issues that include people, process, technology and culture (Kakabadse et al., 2001).

Drucker (2001, p. 287) wrote that "knowledge is not impersonal, like money. It does not reside in a book, a databank, a software program; they contain only information. It is always embodied in a person, carried by a person; created, augmented, or improved by a person; applied by a person; taught and passed on by a person; used or misused by a person." Drucker implicitly described two types of knowledge in this definition – tacit and explicit. The first scholar, who argued that there is a clear distinction between explicit knowledge and tacit knowledge, was Michael Polanyi, who established that we know much more than we can say (Gamble & Blackwell, 2001). The 'explicit' dimension of knowledge is easily codified, communicable and transferable as it can be expressed in words, drawings and numbers. It is absorbed by organizations by abstracting it from the individuals who possess it and embedded into the written strategies, structures, policies and norms of organizations (Krome-Hamilton, 2005/2006). The 'tacit' dimension of an individual's knowledge is "sticky knowledge" (Szulanski, 1996) embedded in individual action (i.e., skills, habits and experience) and cognition (i.e., values, perspectives and insights) that is context-specific, difficult to communicate and even more difficult to transfer. It is important to recognize that explicit knowledge represents only the tip of the iceberg of an entire body of knowledge (Roth, 2003) and cannot be of practical use if individuals do not simultaneously apply relevant tacit knowledge represented by their own experience and contextual understanding.

Besides individual knowledge we can also define organizational knowledge. Tsoukas (2001, p. 983) defines organizational knowledge as "the capability members of an organization have developed to draw distinctions in the process of carrying out their work, in a particular concrete context, by enacting sets of generalizations (propositional statements) whose application depends on historically evolved collective understandings and experiences". Starbuck (1992) sees it as "stocks of expertise", which an organization has, uses, sells or elevates. Knowledge becomes organizational knowledge when there are processes in place to transform tacit knowledge to explicit knowledge, allowing others in the organization to use it for decision making (Broadbent, 1998). Basically knowledge creation in organizations is the process of mobilizing tacit knowledge possessed by individuals in the form of cognition (Kolb, 1984) and practical skills (Brown & Duguid, 1991), and transferring it to the knowledge stock embedded in computer supported knowledge repositories, organizational practices and organizational culture (Krome-Hamilton, 2005/2006). It can also be concluded that organizational knowledge is a strategic asset of an organization and properly managed can represent a source of competitive advantage for any type of organization.

Knowledge Management Processes

Leading on from the above discussion, we can say that knowledge management enables and supports knowledge creation and its application in organizations. Knowledge management starts and finishes with the individual, and through it members of an organization develop new job-related technical, normative or procedural knowledge, or new interpersonal skills, while at the organizational level they collectively develop new, or update existing, organizational products, practices, and/ or organizational values. KM is thus composed of different processes.

Several scholars have defined KM processes, starting with the SECI model by Nonaka and Takeuchi (1995). They described how to convert different forms of knowledge with four modes, which they named socialization (from tacit to tacit), externalization (from tacit to explicit), combination (from explicit to explicit), and internalization (from explicit to tacit). Because knowledge creation is an ongoing process, a constant interaction between tacit and explicit through the four modes, a spiral of knowledge is formed.

Another model is that of Demerest, as one of the so-called socially constructed models, it "views knowledge as being intrinsically linked to the social and learning processes within the organization" (McAdam & McCreedy, 1999, p. 102). The model emphasises social interaction and describes four processes – knowledge construction, embodiment, dissemination, and use.

We also propose a model based on four processes: knowledge generation, storage, transfer, and application. While we present the four processes in successive manner for convenience of discussion, we emphasize that there exists considerable interdependency among them. First, new knowledge can be created or acquired within the *knowledge generation* process. Knowledge is, in the first place, always created at the individual level by combining existing knowledge, which is comprised partly of knowledge that the individual already possesses, partly of knowledge available to the individual from others in hard copy, electronic format or different other forms of artifacts and partly of knowledge available to the individual from his/her interactions with others. It is, for various reasons, sometimes easier and cheaper for an organization to go and search for external knowledge. External knowledge is available in different forms from experts, consultants, business partners (i.e., suppliers, customers and even competitors), and can be bought or leased. Internally or externally generated knowledge can then be linked, combined and integrated as to add more value to organization's stakeholders.

New knowledge that is created in the knowledge generation process needs to be stored for later use as an organizational memory. The process of *knowledge storage* involves finding ways of converting documents, models, human insights and other artifacts into forms that make retrieval and transfer easy without losing the 'true meaning' of the knowledge. This can be done with the use of information technology such as, for example, with the development of repositories or maps of an organization's knowledge about its customers, projects, processes, suppliers, competitors, technology and the organization's knowledge itself. Having said this, we need to bear in mind that information technology can effectively deal with only a small part of the entire body of organizational knowledge (i.e., only that knowledge which is explicit), the bulk of organizational knowledge is stored in the form of organizational routines, operating paradigms, power structures and organizational culture (i.e. implicit collective knowledge).

Unfortunately, "the mere possession of potentially valuable knowledge somewhere within an organization does not necessarily mean that other parts of the organization benefit from this knowledge" (Szulanski, 2000, p. 10). To overcome this problem, an organization needs to find a way to make barriers to *knowledge transfer* more permeable. We can identify two generic knowledge transfer strategies: 'push' and 'pull' (Davenport & Prusak, 1997). The 'push strategy' is characterized by a central provider who decides which knowledge is to be distributed to whom, while in the 'pull strategy' it is the user who judges what knowledge he/she needs. One key finding of recent research in KM is that for effective knowledge transfer a high level of interpersonal trust is needed (Andrews & Delahaye, 2000; Davenport & Prusak, 1998; Hislop, 2005; Maznevski & Chudoba, 2000; Newell & Swan, 2000; Roberts, 2000). Without trust, no organization's policy or system (i.e., its control and reward system or information system) can successfully mitigate barriers that exist between individuals, groups, departments or projects.

Ultimately, without *knowledge application*, all the aforementioned processes are of little value. Only through the application of knowledge can an organization ensure that its knowledge amounts to a viable source of sustainable competitive advantage. To be of value to the organization's stakeholders, organizational knowledge needs to be transformed into more effective and efficient organizational processes, better products or both.

We can conclude that "KM processes are heavily influenced by the social settings in which they are embedded and are subject to various interpretations based upon organizational norms and social interactions among individuals" (Alavi et al., 2006, p. 193).

Organizational Culture and KM Processes

Bell DeTienne et al. (2004) wrote that organizational culture impacts not only on actions and relationships of everyone in an organization, but also on the management of knowledge. Alvesson and Kärreman (2001) and McDermott (1999) came to the conclusion based on their own research that managing knowledge partly becomes a matter of managing organizational culture. A similar opinion is held by Gayle et al. (2003, p. 41) who argue that "culture may be viewed as both the framework that influences, and is influenced by decision making and by the behavior of people making these decisions".

Ribiere and Sitar (2003, p. 41) similarly claimed that "organizational culture is the main barrier to success or an important precondition [of KM initiative failure]" and confirmed their claim with results from Pauleen and Mason's research from New Zealand, where 45% of respondents indicated organizational culture as the main impediment to knowledge sharing (see also Berman Brown & Woodland, 1999; Gold et al., 2001, p. 189). Gupta et al. (2000, p. 18) argued, that "[o]ften, organizational culture itself prevents people from sharing and disseminating their know-how in an effort to hold onto their individual powerbase and validity. Determining who knows what in an organization itself could be a time consuming and daunting task". The results from the Jarvenpaa and Staples's study (2001) showed that organizational culture had a very direct impact on how individuals perceived the ownership of organizational knowledge. In a similar vein O'Dell and Grayson see organizational culture as "a key driver and inhibitor of knowledge sharing" (in Rollett, 2003, p. 24), and Geng et al. (2004, p. 1031) wrote that "cultural expectations may suggest priorities and needs for using knowledge". However, Alavi et al. (2005/06) conducted research that showed that the relationship between organizational culture and KM is even more complex than we thought, because it impacts not only on knowledge sharing and seeking but also on everything related to KM (i.e. technology selection, the role of KM leaders and the expected outcome of KM use.

In their paper, De Long and Fahey (2000) argued that culture shapes assumptions about which knowledge is important. They even stress that not only culture, but particularly subcultures heavily influence which knowledge will be focused on and managed. Because culture is a set of explicit and implicit rules, we can suppose that it also influences the distribution of knowledge throughout the organization that is between the organization and individuals. Regarding the latter, it is obvious that culture has a great impact on social interactions in organizations. If employees can freely socialize and communicate and do not feel pressured by the rules, we can assume that this

has a positive effect on knowledge processes and consequently on organizational success. Lastly, culture dictates who will be the source of new knowledge – internal or external environment. The organization can adopt it from external sources (often structured knowledge) or can create it internally with the information from the external environment and then interpret it "in the context of the firm's existing knowledge to create new knowledge that becomes a basis for action" (De Long & Fahey, 2000, p. 123).

In a similar way we can understand Chin-Loy's (2003) argument that since organizational culture influences decision making, management style, employee relations and behavior pattern in the organizations, any KM initiatives must match the organizational culture. Lawson (2003) summarized findings of several researches and found out that "for the effective implementation of knowledge management a certain culture type must be present in an organization" (id. 28) or as she wrote "cultural dimensions" like sharing, flexibility, collaboration, trust, learning and innovation (id. 43; see also Manville & Foote, 1996; Park et al., 2004). This implies that a strong relationship between organizational culture and knowledge management processes exists.

ISSUES, CONTROVERSIES, PROBLEMS

Higher Education in State of Flux

Higher educational institutions are complex political systems where the varying interests of stakeholders are in constant flux (Mintzberg, 1983) because of the changes in global and also local environment (i.e. funding, accountability, conditions of academic work, open boarders and higher/smaller numbers of students) (see also Deem, 2003). While, as one might expect, there are different and contradictory emphases in priorities depending on different stakeholders' interests and local culture, the actual sense of unease within HE is not limited to one or few countries but is a global phenomenon as explained by Sir Christopher Ball (1990, p.190) almost two decades ago: "Many nations, rich or poor, in each of the three worlds and all of the five continents, exemplify the interesting modern paradox of dissatisfaction with their systems of education and desire to increase educational opportunities. They seek both "more" and "different" … This creative dissatisfaction is the result of social, political and economical pressures. The most important of these are the issues of wealth creation, equity and cost." At the same time we cannot change HEIs overnight if we want to preserve their role as the storehouse of past erudition and the creator of new knowledge.

Traditionally, universities have been considered to be 'bureaucratic' institutions (Mintzberg, 1983) and, more specifically, professional bureaucracies. Chubb and Moe (1990), for example, have described schools and educational systems as being the most rigid, unresponsive and bureaucratic of institutions. Organization that can be defined as professional bureaucracies have a clear division of labor tasks (e.g. in HEIs we can find a clear division between different departments and research areas), clearly defined authority and responsibility (i.e. in a HEI a tenured professor has considerable autonomy whereas a young research assistant needs to be very careful what he or she says or does), and a strong emphasis on formal expertise (i.e. in HEI there is a clear differentiation between an assistant professor, an associate professor and a full professor in terms of their status, their assumed range and grasp of specific knowledge domains and their power within the organization). On the one hand, the procedures are standard, but also complex, but on the other, there are high levels of professionalism and professional autonomy and expertise has authority (Martin & Marion, 2005).

Weick (1976) claims that HEIs are a good example of loosely coupled systems which means that there is a kind of connection between the parts but at the same time each part has its own orientation and identity (i.e. departments, programs, teaching, research, courses as well as professors are largely independent from each other). Therefore there is a common idea or strategy that holds HEI together but at the same time different actors start many different actions, projects etc., which can be more or less in line with the main orientation of the HEI. As to preserve the common orientation HEIs developed a kind of formal collective process where new ideas receive support or are dampened based on their fitness with the system (Mintzberg, 2007). Unfortunately this process is almost entirely subjective and some good ideas and initiatives will not pass because misunderstood, novel or politically threatening. Basically the same thing happens also with the new knowledge development and application.

Giroux (2003), referring to Hoftstadter, pointed out three interesting points about HE:

- HE, for many educators, represents the central site for keeping alive the tension between market values and those values representative of civil society (more tacit).
- The growing importance of corporate culture has, at least in USA, begun to uproot the legacy of democracy, and the rights that have historically defined the purpose of HE.
- HE is becoming more and more profit-oriented and corporations are more willing to provide resources.

Serban and Luan (2002, p. 1) claim that "colleges and universities exist to create and share knowledge". HEIs are about the creation, transformation and transmission of knowledge (Laudon & Laudon, 1999) or as Clark (1984, p.107) would say "clusters of professionals tending various bundles of knowledge". Therefore the greatest challenge to modern HEIs is to meet the needs of the academic staff who are simultaneously developers, users, and carriers of high level knowledge, and generators and learners of new knowledge. Under the relentless pressure of different forms of e-learning and virtual universities on one side and budget constraints on the other, HEIs are in the process of transforming themselves from 'bricks and mortar' to 'bricks and click' cost-sensitive organizations. Given these circumstances we believe effective knowledge management is of vital importance for increasing the quality and efficiency of education and research, for retaining the best professors and researchers, for developing new curricula, for improving cost efficiency and for exceeding the limits of time and space allowing for the fulfillment of student expectations anywhere and at anytime.

Organizational Culture, KM Processes and HEIs

The main purpose of KM, according to Wiig (1997), is maximization of the organization's knowledge-related effectiveness and returns from its knowledge assets and their constant renewal. In the era of globalization, information and communication technology, and constant environmental change, knowledge and especially the ability to manage knowledge has become the most important component of organizational success for all types of organizations. Sallis and Jones (2002) argue that in the 21st century the most successful organizations will be those that are to use information and manage it wisely in order to create sustained additional value for their stakeholders. This also refers to HEIs. Geng et al. (2005, p. 1032) share a similar opinion as they see knowledge management in HE "as the art of increasing value from selected knowledge assets", which could improve its effectiveness.

Joseph (2001) defines KM from the perspective of HEIs as a process where organizations formulate ways in the attempt to recognize and archive assets within the institutions that are derived from the employees/academics of various departments of faculties, and in some cases, even from other organizations that share similar areas of interest. Knowledge in HE can be found in many forms or, as Geng et al. (2005, p. 1032) argue, two types – scholarly and operational. Scholarly knowledge is expressed through teaching, research documentation, publications, conferences, patents, and service activities. Operational knowledge becomes explicit through employees who also provide support functions and services.

HEIs are specific, because knowledge is their input and also output. Wiig (1997, p. 7) claims that "faculties within universities and other learning institutions have been concerned about knowledge transfer processes and the creation and application of knowledge for several millennia". Similarly, Rowley (2000) writes that the educational sector has always been recognized as the focal point for various knowledge processes, namely, knowledge creation, dissemination and learning.

Tippins (2003) stressed that managing knowledge in HE is often very difficult because of several bureaucratic and cultural factors which present obstacles. Referring to several scholars he explained:

- Knowledge is considered as private property and not as an asset with a value.
- Knowledge is considered as a possible source of differentiation or power, but usually this has the opposite effect.
- There is a lack of interest because of complacency and disengagement from the learning process. This usually influences the promotion process.
- HE members possess different levels of knowledge stores and capabilities. Although willingness to give an explanation exists, the explanation would not be sufficient because of the lack of knowledge.
- There is a lack of social interaction which influences effectiveness of the communication process and the creation of social networks.

- Unawareness of where to look or what to seek (i.e. seminars are offered, but not well attended).
- Time and resource constraints (i.e. everything is available apart from time).

It is our contention that the main obstacle to effective implementation of knowledge management in HEIs is the basic nature of these organizations. Although it is generally accepted that knowledge is an asset that increases in value when shared by individuals it is interesting to observe that many faculty members consider knowledge to be their private property (Wind & Main, 1999). Knowledge is considered a possible source of individual differentiation (Wiig, 1993) that gives power to whomever possesses it. Srikanthan and Dalrymple (2002) claim that "typical current culture in higher education is bureaucratic in nature, more prone to conflict than collaboration". Some negative implications of such a view are:

- knowledge is not shared freely between faculty members and in some cases knowledge may even be lost,
- knowledge is not enriched by different perspectives from different fields of study and in this way educational standards may be compromised or, at least, opportunities to generate new knowledge are foregone.

White and Weathersby (2005) state that, in HEIs, persistent obstacles exist that hinder the development of learning communities. In practice, these obstacles include a high need for individual autonomy, varying conceptions and understanding of knowledge, internal competition, negative aspects of expert status and posturing, and the significant use of electronic, relatively impersonal modes of communication (Tippins, 2003).

We can conclude that although HEIs are educational and research institutions at the same time, and therefore knowledge is their main input and also output, the impact of organizational culture on KM processes is still very strong. This does not differentiate HE institutions from other organizations on the contrary it reinforces the notion that HE institutions are the ideal place for considering and researching KM processes.

Empirical Research

Sampling Approach

Regarding the institutions selected we employed two criteria. The first criterion was a track record of student enrolment in the last decade. The second criterion was an extension of use of ICT to support learning and teaching processes within a HEI. The former criterion was chosen based on the supposition that HEIs with a good track record of student enrolment are more willing to undertake such a research than HEIs with a bad track record of student enrolment, which are more focused on solving their day-to-day funds related difficulties. The later criterion was chosen based on the proposition that ICT has an important impact on effectiveness of KM processes (Syed-Ikhsan & Rowland, 2004). ICT can give an important support to explicit knowledge storage and transfer. Yet at the same time, with the intensive use of ICT, faculty can work from home and commute to work only when necessary. Therefore, social networks are harder to develop and as a result, so too are the conditions for effective knowledge creation (i.e. especially is difficult to build trust between co-workers). Based on the above stated criteria, we selected three business faculties (each one is part of different university), a faculty of organizational sciences, a faculty of social sciences, and a faculty of sport.

Before sending a questionnaire to the selected HEIs we asked their deans for their permission to conduct our study. Sadly, only two of them gave us permission to proceed - a faculty of business (HEI1), and a faculty of sport (HEI2). However, the explanations of other four deans for rejecting our request were very interesting and show the current atmosphere in Slovenian HE:

- *"If we allow you to do your study in our institution it will reveal too much about ourselves and based on that we can lose our competitive advantage or other HE institutions can use your data to gain an advantage over us."* (Dean of the business faculty 1)

- *"Data within your study are so important and sensitive, and therefore crucial for our institution, that I cannot allow your study to be done. We do not trust you because some members of your team could take advantage of it."* (Dean of the business faculty 2)

- *"We had a similar study which was done in several stages – as a real project - and there is no need to bother my employees with another one. And also, this is not the right time for doing such research because my colleagues have better things to do."* (Dean of the faculty of social sciences)

- *"Your research will burden my colleagues even more. We have a lot of problems right now even without your research. It would be hard to answer these questions. I am sorry, but you will have to collect data in another way."* (Dean of the faculty of organizational sciences)

As can be seen from the statements above, these deans believe that the data collected during this kind of research are strategically sensitive and it is implied that they also believe organizational culture and KM processes can represent a source of competitive advantage, whether is or is not this to be true in their case. These statements again confirm that organizational culture and KM processes are seen as critical for an HE institution's success in the globalized higher education market.

At the time the study was conducted, the business faculty (HEI1) had 37 full- and 53 part time members of academic staff. The faculty of sport (HEI2) had 78 full- and 34 part-time members of academic staff. All of these individuals

were involved in the study. However, we did not include the administrative staff in our study since it is our contention that the members of the academic staff are those most actively involved in issues pertaining to KM processes (Chaudhry & Higgins, 2003; Luby, 1999). The academic staff is responsible for generating knowledge via research, and for disseminating knowledge via lecturing and consulting.

We sent the questionnaire to the academic staff of both institutions by email in May 2007. We asked them if they preferred to get a printed version of it. If answer was positive we sent a printed version of the questionnaire by regular mail the second day after we got the email reply.

The Questionnaire

The research was grounded in two stages. Firstly, the questionnaire was piloted on a sample of faculty from our own higher education institution in order to test its appropriateness, readability and comprehensiveness. The second stage comprised the design and implementation of the study.

The research instrument was based on work by Wilkens et al. (2004), translated into Slovene and elaborated to reflect current conditions in the Slovenian higher educational sector. Initially, we tested the questionnaire on a small sample of academics, refined it and conducted a pilot survey in our own institution. The initial questionnaire was structured around four basic KM processes and consisted of 37 statements designed to elicit responses on a six-point Likert-type scale ranging from 1 (very strongly disagree) to 6 (very strongly agree). After piloting the questionnaire we adjusted some statements as to improve its readability.

The final questionnaire consisted of three sections, the details of which are explained below:

1. Section 1 contains Organizational Culture Assessment Instrument (OCAI) developed and validated by Cameron and Quinn (1999) based on the theoretical model of CVF.

The OCAI consists of six questions. Each question has four alternatives. By dividing 100 points among these four alternatives we can assess which type of organizational culture according to CVF is present in the organization. The list of six content dimensions is not comprehensive, but different studies have proven it to provide an accurate picture of the type of culture that exists in an organization.

2. Section 2 contains questions concerning the nature and characteristics of knowledge management processes as perceived by the academic staff. This part of the questionnaire was divided into four themes relating to four knowledge management processes, namely the generation, storage, transfer and application of knowledge.

3. The last section contains a limited number of questions designed to collect some general data about the individual characteristics of the respondent (i.e., gender, academic position, etc.)

Of the 202 questionnaires distributed, 79 were returned (55 from HEI1, 24 from HEI2), constituting a 39% response rate. After checking all the questionnaires returned, we eliminated 1 questionnaire from organizational culture assessment as some data were missing in the first part. We consider the response rate to be low in the HEI2. Due to their interest as knowledge creators and users, we had incorrectly assumed respondents would be eager to collaborate in the research.

The limited sample size does not allow us to generalize our results. Despite this limitation, data could be compared with results in similar studies (Kwan & Walker, 2004; Sharimllah Devi et al., 2007). However, we would like to emphasize that even if limited sample size is a clear limitation from a quantitative point of research our results are still interesting because they could give us some new information that could be lost by averaging within the big sample. As such they could open

some new directions for further research and hypothesis testing.

Data were analyzed with SPSS 13.0 for descriptive statistics and reliability analysis.

Sample Characteristics

Table 1 presents the respondents' characteristics. Of the respondents in the sample, 24% had been employed in HE1 and 92% in the HEI2 for 5 years or more. The years of work experience in this particular organization is relevant because in an expert organization such as a HEI, knowledge management processes are complex and we assume that respondents with longer work experience can better recognize some of the soft, 'fuzzy' elements of these processes hidden behind people's formal and informal relationships and modes of communication.

There is a significant discrepancy between the sample and the population regarding job status. In the sample, 60% of respondents in the HEI1 and 96% in the HEI2 were employed in either a full-time capacity or had appointments that were in excess of 50% full-time status, while in the whole employee population only 41% of staff in the HEI1 and 70% in the HEI2 were in either of these categories. It could be assumed that respondents with full time or more than 50% full time positions form a more cohesive group with more commonly shared goals and values compared to those who are employed for less than 50% full-time positions or on a contractual basis. These full-time academic staff members have more personal interest in and commitment to the long-term success of the organization than others and are therefore more likely to be interested in knowledge management processes and hence in the results of our study as well.

The most important difference between the two samples can be found in the number of days that employees spend at each institution. In the case of HEI1 we can see that we have more or less equal distribution of employees who spend

Table 1. Demographic information of the two HEIs

	HEI 1		HEI 2	
	Sample of respondents (n =55)		Sample of respondents (n =24)	
	f	%	f	%
Gender				
male	33	60	20	83
female	22	40	4	17
Academic title				
teaching assistant	18	33	9	37,5
lecturer	15	27	0	0
senior lecturer	8	15	0	0
assistant professor	9	16	3	12,5
associate professor	5	9	10	42
professor	0	0	2	8
Employment era at HEI				
less than 5 years	42	76	2	8
5 years or more	13	24	22	92
Type of employment:				
full time	33	60	23	96
half-time	5	9	0	0
contract	5	9	1	4
I weekly spend at HEI (*in average*)				
less than a day	15	27	0	0
1 – 2 days	12	22	0	0
2 – 3 days	14	25,5	0	0
more than 3 days	14	25,5	24	100

less than 1 day at the institution, 1 to 2 days, 2 to 3 days, and more than 3 days. Such a limited presence of these employees at the institution is likely to limit trust building and also inhibit knowledge sharing at least when we talk about knowledge, particularly the sharing of knowledge through face-to-face communication. In contrast to HEI1, in the HEI2 all respondents spend more than 3 days at the institution, which we believe can positively influence trust building among them if the proper cultural values are in place and this is not just a result of the organization's policy requirement.

Results

The results of our study are interesting, but should be considered in light of the inherent limitations that have been mentioned above.

Tables 2 to 5 provide descriptive statistics and also validity tests. Cronbach's alpha was used to assess the reliability of the instrument. All constructs had an alpha value of greater that 0.7, ranging from 0.828 to 0.872. For convergent validity, items having item-to-total correlation scores lower than 0.4 were dropped from further analysis. Ten items relating to different KM processes had an item-to-total correlation of less than 0.4 and thus were eliminated from further analysis. A study was then performed on the 27 items that measured the four KM processes. (Table 2, Table 3, Table 4, Table 5)

The average means of the four KM processes in the HEI1 vary quite significantly as it goes from the highest value of 4.22 for knowledge generation to the lowest value of 2.1 for the knowledge storage, with the other two values for knowledge transfer and application both above 3. On the other hand, values of the four KM processes in the HEI2 do not vary significantly. All means are between 3.04 and 3.6. The data reveal that the HEI2 is effective in knowledge generation, and application but it is not so in knowledge transfer. In consideration of the scale employed, we can define all results above 3 as good and results below 3 as poor. Based on that we can see that both institutions have good knowledge generation, application, and transfer. However, between all four processes only knowledge generation in HEI1 could be considered to

be very good. On the other hand the HEI1 has a poor knowledge storage.

Table 6 shows the average scores for all the cultural types as obtained from the OCAI. These scores are presented in Figure 1 for easier comparison between the two institutions. Regarding organizational culture, we can see that the HEI1 is characterized by the dominant market culture with the presence of all three other cultural types. The least present is the clan culture. However, the differences between the adhocracy, hierarchy and clan culture are quite small. On the other hand, the HEI2 is characterized by a hierarchy culture with the difference between the dominant cultural type and the clan and adhocracy cultural types, notably the least present.

HEI1 has a strong market culture which is in line with being a newer institution. It had and still has to generate new knowledge (new products and services) if it wants to be successful and gain competitive advantage. The main aim is to differentiate itself from others and to

Table 2. Statistics for knowledge generation

Cronbach's Alpha = 0,835		HEI 1		HEI 2	
StatementMy HE institution (HEI) actively supports cooperation with other HEIs on joint projects.	Item-to-total correlation0,500	Mean4,2000	Std. Deviation1,63752	Mean3,5833	Std. Deviation1,63964
My HEI constantly benchmarks itself with the best HEI from its field.	0,487	4,2545	1,56605	3,2500	1,42188
My HEI regularly includes well-known practitioners in its educational process.	0,478	3,9636	1,69928	4,0000	1,47442
My HEI has well developed research activities.	0,668	4,0727	1,41231	3,6667	1,30773
My HEI encourages student involvement in its research activities.	0,511	4,2182	1,28655	3,4583	1,35066
My HEI invites world-known academics to give guest lectures.	0,640	4,2182	1,43618	3,8750	1,36135
My HEI actively supports publishing of (short) research reports.	0,594	4,0364	1,76345	3,5417	1,69344
My HEI encourages its employees to publish their work (i.e. monograph, books, text book, …)	0,658	4,8182	1,61120	3,5000	1,50362
Knowledge generation		**4,2227**	**0,26200**	**3,6094**	**0,23773**

* Agree is the sum of very strongly agree, strongly agree and agree

** Disagree is the sum of very strongly disagree, strongly disagree and disagree

Table 3. Statistics for knowledge storage

Cronbach's Alpha = 0,843		HEI 1		HEI 2	
StatementMy HEI regularly stores knowledge (has an archive) on the content and implementation of educational process.	Item-to-total correlation 0,773	Mean 2,4545	Std. Deviation 2,22626	Mean 3,7917	Std. Deviation 1,53167
My HEI regularly stores knowledge (has an archive) on the content and implementation of research projects.	0,736	2,3636	2,32828	3,7917	1,55980
My HEI has a well-structured documentation of employees' competencies and achievements.	0,662	2,2182	2,07891	2,8333	1,60615
My HEI has an archive of most important lectures and researches as examples of best practices.	0,549	1,4000	1,71702	2,7917	1,91059
Knowledge storage		**2,1091**	**0,48265**	**3,3021**	**0,56558**

* Agree is the sum of very strongly agree, strongly agree and agree
** Disagree is the sum of very strongly disagree, strongly disagree and disagree

Table 4. Statistics for knowledge transfer

Cronbach's Alpha = 0,828		HEI 1		HEI 2	
StatementMy HEI has an efficient system of coaching and mentoring young academics.	Item-to-total correlation 0,512	Mean 3,1818	Std. Deviation 1,59966	Mean 3,4583	Std. Deviation 1,38247
My HEI enables young academics to become aware of different research topics.	0,571	3,7455	1,62410	3,6250	1,43898
My HEI actively supports participation in multi-disciplinary research teams.	0,474	3,6727	1,62224	3,5833	1,21285
My HEI encourages the debate on main concepts and terminology from research and educational fields (i.e. Wikipedia style).	0,634	3,6545	1,55418	2,9583	1,54580
My HEI regularly organizes presentations and debates on research achievements of employees.	0,617	3,9091	1,55483	2,9583	1,42887
My HEI regularly organizes internal educational workshops on educational methods and approaches.	0,589	3,6000	1,60555	2,6250	1,55515
My HEI has an effective computer based system for accessing and searching in its own knowledge bases.	0,452	3,3636	1,77809	3,3750	1,66322
My HEI has an efficient computer based system to support collaboration between employees.	0,453	2,5455	1,87398	2,6250	1,78916
My HEI has a lot of space where employees can informally meet and talk.	0,513	3,2727	1,55700	2,1667	2,01444
Knowledge transfer		**3,4384**	**0,40924**	**3,0417**	**0,50561**

* Agree is the sum of very strongly agree, strongly agree and agree
** Disagree is the sum of very strongly disagree, strongly disagree and disagree

'beat them in their own game' without mercy. Organizational change within the institution was not incremental but rather over night. Namely, it has transformed from a small business college to state-known faculty with strong international relationships. The dominant market culture is, on the other hand, well balanced with adhocracy culture. Creative and crazy ideas are needed if the organization wants to be innovative and break new ground. For organizations like HEI1 there is

Table 5. Statistics for knowledge application

Cronbach's Alpha = 0,872		HEI 1		HEI 2	
StatementMy HEI successfully applies best practices in educational process.	Item-to-total correlation 0,693	Mean 3,7818	Std. Deviation 1,41016	Mean 4,2083	Std. Deviation 1,06237
My HEI successfully applies best practices in research projects.	0,708	3,9273	1,46382	3,9583	0,95458
My HEI successfully applies disposable knowledge for development of new curricula.	0,668	4,0182	1,54549	3,4583	1,10253
My HEI successfully applies disposable knowledge for development of new research projects.	0,687	4,0545	1,35289	3,6250	0,87539
My HEI successfully makes use of disposable intellectual potential.	0,736	3,4909	1,51380	2,9583	1,36666
My HEI successfully applies disposable knowledge for promotion of its research and educational potential.	0,565	4,0727	1,56175	3,4167	1,34864
Knowledge application		**3,8909**	**0,22327**	**3,6042**	**0,43918**

* Agree is the sum of very strongly agree, strongly agree and agree

** Disagree is the sum of very strongly disagree, strongly disagree and disagree

little time at their disposal and if they want to create value, they have to be fast or proactive. This shows HEI1's extensive use of ICT in support of educational process. It was the first in the state to include e-learning in its educational process (e.g. the e-classroom) and is constantly developing and improving it. We could say that it is on the way to another transformation to become a 'bricks-and-click' organization.

Striving for the first position in the market, however, is not without casualties. The organization is not a very friendly place to work. There is a huge employee turnover and people do not really know each other because the growth has been so fast. The workforce is hired mostly as the need arises. This must be changed in the future, otherwise there will be harmful consequences. Also the results of the KM processes show that the organization is very good in knowledge generation, which shows that it is capable of competing on the market and selling its services. Low value of knowledge storage process could be the consequence of its fast growth. This could mean that organization has lack of employees appointed to take care of knowledge storage or lack of proper ICT support or simply lack of time because ev-

erything develops too fast. We can conclude that higher education sector from this point is no different than the business sector.

In contrast to HEI1, there is HEI2 with its dominant hierarchy culture. This was not surprising because it is a member of a very rigid system of our oldest university. Everything has to be in order, procedures are well-known and a lot of time is needed to change them. Study programs have not changed a lot since it was established or, to put it in another way, they changed only when there was a clear demand (reactive style). Employees have to be present at the faculty every day. This is in line with Cameron et al. (2006) findings. If any changes happen, they happen only when they are absolutely necessary and then in a step-

Table 6. Organizational cultural types scores based on the CVF

	HEI1	HEI2
The Clan Culture	20	19
The Adhocracy Culture	26	18
The Market Culture	32	27
The Hierarchy Culture	22	36

Figure 1. Organizational cultural types in the two HEIs

Types of organizational culture in two Slovenian HE institutions

by-step manner. As new knowledge is created slowly organization has time to store it, which is also supported by many organization's formal policies. However even the most rigid systems have to adapt if the environment is changing. The HEI2 has realized that it needs to change in the near future if it wants to attract students and the revenue they bring. HEI2 is trying to adapt its programs to the Bologna process and is looking for partners to help it to create new and attractive study programs. These changes must be made quickly to match the pace of emerging competition. In Slovenia, as in some other former socialist countries in Europe, new faculties and new programs spring up almost over night.

The Pearson correlation analysis presented in Table 7 shows that a strong correlation exists between some cultural types as well as between different KM processes. Meanwhile, only clan and market culture types have significant correlation with KM processes.

It is important to point out that findings of Kwan and Walker's study (2004) in Hong Kong's nine HE institutions confirm that market culture is not unusual for new HE institutions just as hierarchy culture is not unusual for older HE institutions.

Sharimllah et al. (2007) conclude from their study in a public university in Malaysia that there is a strong correlation between adhocracy and market culture and KM processes. Hierarchical culture had the lowest positive correlations with KM processes.

Solutions and Recommendations

From the point of view of KM processes, we can see that a significant correlation between knowledge generation, transfer and application exists. This result can be explained if we understand KM processes as interlinked parts of a continuous knowledge generation process (i.e. knowledge spiral) similar to one proposed by Nonaka and Takeuchi (1995). As more knowledge is generated within an organization, more knowledge can be transferred and in the final stage applied, which again creates even more fertile ground for new knowledge generation.

On the other hand, we can conclude based on the results that no direct correlation exists between knowledge generation and knowledge storage, which in our opinion demands careful reflection. We speculate that a few possible explanations

Table 7. Correlation between organizational culture and KM processes

Correlations		Clan	Adhocracy	Market	Hierarchy	K_ generat	K_ storage	K_ transfer	K_ appl
Clan	Pearson Correlation	1	-0,127	-,649(**)	-,438(**)	,250(*)	,229(*)	,335(**)	,318(**)
	Sig. (2-tailed)		0,269	0,000	0,000	0,028	0,044	0,003	0,005
	N	78	78	78	78	78	78	78	78
Adhocracy	Pearson Correlation	-0,127	1	-0,080	-,530(**)	0,195	-0,222	0,134	-0,019
	Sig. (2-tailed)	0,269		0,484	0,000	0,087	0,051	0,242	0,872
	N	78	78	78	78	78	78	78	78
Market	Pearson Correlation	-,649(**)	-0,080	1	-0,121	-0,201	-,309(**)	-,358(**)	-,286(*)
	Sig. (2-tailed)	0,000	0,484		0,290	0,078	0,006	0,001	0,011
	N	78	78	78	78	78	78	78	78
Hierarchy	Pearson Correlation	-,438(**)	-,530(**)	-0,121	1	-,243(*)	0,184	-0,149	-0,076
	Sig. (2-tailed)	0,000	0,000	0,290		0,032	0,107	0,192	0,509
	N	78	78	78	78	78	78	78	78
K_generat	Pearson Correlation	,250(*)	0,195	-0,201	-,243(*)	1	0,197	,497(**)	,722(**)
	Sig. (2-tailed)	0,028	0,087	0,078	0,032		0,083	0,000	0,000
	N	78	78	78	78	78	78	78	78
K_storage	Pearson Correlation	,229(*)	-0,222	-,309(**)	0,184	0,197	1	,378(**)	,342(**)
	Sig. (2-tailed)	0,044	0,051	0,006	0,107	0,083		0,001	0,002
	N	78	78	78	78	78	78	78	78
K_transfer	Pearson Correlation	,335(**)	0,134	-,358(**)	-0,149	,497(**)	,378(**)	1	,552(**)
	Sig. (2-tailed)	0,003	0,242	0,001	0,192	0,000	0,001		0,000
	N	78	78	78	78	78	78	78	78
K_appl	Pearson Correlation	,318(**)	-0,019	-,286(*)	-0,076	,722(**)	,342(**)	,552(**)	1
	Sig. (2-tailed)	0,005	0,872	0,011	0,509	0,000	0,002	0,000	
	N	78	78	78	78	78	78	78	78
**. Correlation is significant at the 0.01 level (2-tailed).									
*. Correlation is significant at the 0.05 level (2-tailed).									

exist for such a result. The one that seems the most likely to us is that the majority of people perceive knowledge storage as a specifically designed activity that organizations perform so as to transform human capital (i.e. knowledge in employees' heads) into structural capital. From that point of view, knowledge storage seems to be the most "artificial" among all KM processes in the sense that other processes more or less "emerge" from individuals in social relationships, while knowledge storage is a more "planned" or intended process performed by somebody outside the subjects indirectly involved in the knowledge spiral. Also, it is quite probable that in the respondents' minds knowledge storage is primarily linked to explicit knowledge, which is going to be digitalized or stored in some tangible form. Because of this, respondents unintentionally skip the possibility that implicit knowledge is stored in form of organizational anecdotes or stories, for example.

Based on our results, however, we can conclude that knowledge storage is indirectly linked to the process of knowledge generation in a similar way as we find in Nonaka and Takeuchi's (1995) process of knowledge combination. Knowledge stored in different forms within an organization is linked together during the execution of tasks at hand. Such a conclusion is confirmed by the significant correlation that exists among knowledge storage, transfer, and application.

Other results regarding KM processes confirm findings from other similar studies. The study's results show that significant correlation either among knowledge storage, transfer, and application and between knowledge transfer and application exists. The amount of knowledge application is then indirectly linked to the effectiveness of knowledge storage as well as transfer.

The most important difference between our study and others is the "missing" link between some organizational cultural types and KM processes. Different empirical research confirms that a positive correlation exist between cultural types

according to CVF and KM (Lawson, 2003; Sharimllah Devi et al., 2007). In our study we found that a significant correlation at the 0.01 level exists between the clan culture and knowledge transfer, and application, and between the market culture and knowledge storage, and transfer. Further, we found a significant correlation at the 0.05 level between the clan culture and knowledge generation, and storage, between the market culture and knowledge application, and between the hierarchy culture and knowledge generation. As we can also see, with the exception of the clan culture, all other correlations are negative. Reasons for such results are as follows:

1. The study's results confirm that organizational culture is a very important organizational characteristic in relation to KM processes; however, it is not the only one. Gupta and Govindarajan (2000) conclude based on their research that KM processes are influenced by six organizational factors: information systems, organizational structure, reward systems, processes, people, and leadership. Even if we regard some of these factors to be cultural artifacts (e.g. structure, reward system, processes, leadership), we need to consider that organizational characteristics can change for various reasons without changes happening in cultural values or assumptions, and still these changes affect employees' behavior and therefore directly influence KM processes. We can then conclude that organizational culture influences KM processes not only directly but also indirectly through cultural artifacts. At the same time there are other organizational factors that impact KM processes.

2. In our study adhocracy does not correlate to any one of the KM processes. This is again a deviation from other research where this cultural type was determined to be the best cultural type for new knowledge creation. In our opinion this result can be explained

by the difference in basic values of adhocracy and the basic idea behind KM, which assumes that KM processes are purposeful and continuous activities performed by the organization. Within adhocracy, people have a lot of freedom for improvisation and experimentation for developing 'break-through' knowledge, while knowledge generated within KM processes is more incremental even if is new for the organization, perhaps even for other organizations. Because of the continuity and purposefulness of the activities that we asked about, we also assume they cannot be improvised. We still believe that the adhocracy cultural type has an important influence on developing the rule-breaking knowledge but this particular knowledge and related psychological processes are not part of the KM model, which takes a more macro view of knowledge-related processes within an organization.

3. Market culture with its highly demanding goals and hard-driving competitiveness is not an appropriate place for effective KM processes. As the study's results show, market culture is negatively correlated to all KM processes, with the exception of knowledge generation (i.e. there does not exist statistically significant correlation). This result can be explained by a willingness of employees inside such a culture to compete and win, as possession of knowledge can give them a kind of competitive advantage when they hoard it from their co-workers (i.e. reward system is based on other goals and not on the amount and quality of shared knowledge). On the other hand, the same employees do not want to apply new knowledge if they are uncertain if by applying it they will achieve their demanding goals.

4. Clan culture with its values of care for each other and teamwork is based on our study the most important cultural type for KM processes. Our results show this type

of organizational culture positively influences all KM processes. However, even if we found that in both HEIs a certain level of clan culture exist, from our study as well as from other studies, we can come to the conclusion that this type of organizational culture is not prevalent in HEIs. This could therefore form the direction for possible future changes in HEIs.

Future Research Directions

Future research could be directed at collecting and analyzing responses about KM processes and organizational culture across a greater number of departments and faculties in order to build up a 'true picture' of the knowledge spiral within HEIs and the impact of organizational culture upon it. In the future cultural and behavioral issues which have a profound effect on successful KM implementation can be addressed in more detail especially regarding tacit knowledge transfer, new knowledge creation and breakthrough innovation. Also the relationship between KM processes and culture change within HEIs can be addressed, maybe by use of the dimension of culture dynamics as proposed by Quinn et al. (2006).

The second stream of research can be more oriented to the question of distinction between teaching oriented knowledge and research oriented knowledge (Lueddeke, 1998) as well as between scholarly and administrative knowledge. In the HE we can find either predominantly research or teaching oriented universities as well as universities that try to excel in both. However the last ones are often stuck-in-the-middle. Yet could be interesting to explore if organizational culture as well as KM related processes are different based on HEI's strategic orientation to mostly promote research, teaching or both of them equally.

CONCLUSION

The research instrument presented in this study enables one to assess the effectiveness of KM processes in HEIs and additionally to better recognize how organizational culture impacts these processes. The questionnaire can help HEIs that are eager to develop further their KM processes in different ways. Firstly, managers of HEIs might use the questionnaire developed in the study to determine if there is a gap between the optimum and the institution's actual KM effectiveness. HEI managers would then be in a position to clearly communicate to the academic staff what it is they are trying to achieve. Secondly, the questionnaire might be used to determine if there are any significant discrepancies between the managers' and the academic staff's perceptions of KM effectiveness. If serious gaps do exist, the detailed nature of the questionnaire would direct managers on how to close the gaps. Thirdly, a proposed approach of assessing organizational culture and KM processes at the same time may also have a strategic application. HEI managers might take the results of similar studies into account and determine whether or not any proposed strategy would improve KM processes, and if the proposed strategy is feasible with regard to the dominant cultural profile.

Given the importance of KM for any expert organization, the management of KM processes should not be left to chance. Pan and Scarbrough (1999) also write that the real challenge for HEIs is to develop and continuously maintain a knowledge-enterprising culture whereby employees trust each other and therefore feel comfortable and motivated to share knowledge. This enables them to create new ideas (entrepreneurs) and gain appropriate rewards. In a similar vein, Steyn (2004, p. 629) writes that if HEIs want to become global organizations they will have "to move from predominantly collegially networked institutions with a limited international learner base and/or knowledge base towards the creation of a shared, extensive, global knowledge base".

REFERENCES

Alavi, M., Kayworth, T. R., & Leidner, D. E. (2006). An empirical examination of the influence of organizational culture on knowledge management practices. *Journal of Management Information Systems*, *22*(3), 191–224. doi:10.2753/MIS0742-1222220307

Alvesson, M., & Kärreman, D. (2001). Odd couple: Making sense of the curious concept of knowledge management. *Journal of Management Studies*, *38*(7), 995–1008. doi:10.1111/1467-6486.00269

Andrews, K. M., & Delahaye, B. L. (2000). AT influences on knowledge processes in organizational learning: The psychosocial filter. *Journal of Management Studies*, *37*(6), 797–810. doi:10.1111/1467-6486.00204

Ball, C. (1990). *More means different: Widening access to higher education*. London: RSA.

Bates, T. (1997, June). *Restructuring the university for technological change*. Paper presented at The Carnegie Foundation for the Advancement of Teaching, What Kind of University, London, GB.

Bell DeTienne, K., Dyer, G., Hoopes, C., & Harris, S. (2004). Toward a Model of effective knowledge management and directions for future research: Culture, leadership, and CKOs. *Journal of Leadership & Organizational Studies*, *10*(4), 26–43. doi:10.1177/107179190401000403

Berman Brown, R., & Woodland, M. J. (1999). Managing knowledge wisely: A case study in organisational behaviour. *Journal of Applied Management Studies*, *8*(2), 175–198.

Biloslavo, R. (2006). *Strateški management in management spreminjanja*. Koper, Slovenia: Fakulteta za management.

Biloslavo, R., & Trnavčevič, A. (2007). Knowledge management audit in a higher educational institution: A case study. *Knowledge and Process Management, 14*(4), 275–286. doi:10.1002/kpm.293

Bollinger, A. S., & Smith, R. D. (2001). Managing organizational knowledge as a strategic asset. *Journal of Knowledge Management, 5*(1), 8–18. doi:10.1108/13673270110384365

Broadbent, M. (1998). The phenomenon of knowledge management: What does it mean to the information profession? *Information Outlook, 2*(5), 23–36.

Brown, J. S., & Duguid, P. (1991). AT organizational learning and communities of practice: Toward a unified view of working, learning, and innovation. *Organization Science, 2*(1), 40–57. doi:10.1287/orsc.2.1.40

Cameron, K. S., & Freeman, S. J. (1991). Cultural congruence, strength, and type: Relationships to effectiveness. *Research in Organizational Change and Development, 5*, 23–58.

Cameron, K. S., & Quinn, R. E. (1999). *Diagnosing and changing organizational culture*. Reading, MA: Addison-Wesley, Inc.

Chaudhry, A. S., & Higgins, S. (2003). On the need for a multi disciplinary approach to education for knowledge management. *Library Review, 52*(1-2), 65–69. doi:10.1108/00242530310462134

Chin-Loy, C. (2003). *Assessing the influence of organizational culture on knowledge management success*. Unpublished doctoral dissertation, The Wayne Huizeng School of Business and Entrepreneurship, Nova Southeastern University, Florida.

Chubb, J. E., & Moe, T. M. (1990). *Politics, markets and America's schools*. Washington: The Brookings Institution.

Clark, B. R. (Ed.). (1984). *Perspectives on higher education: Eight disciplinary and comparative views*. Berkeley, CA: University of California Press.

Davenport, T. H., & Prusak, L. (1997). *Information ecology: Mastering the information and knowledge environment*. New York: Oxford University Press.

Davenport, T. H., & Prusak, L. (1998). *Working knowledge: How organizations manage what they know*. Boston: Harvard Business School Press.

Dawson, R. (2000). *Developing knowledge-based client relationship: The future of professional services*. Boston: Butterworth-Heinemann.

De Long, D. W., & Fahey, L. (2000). Diagnosing cultural barriers to knowledge management. *The Academy of Management Executive, 14*(4), 113–127.

Deal, T. E., & Kennedy, A. A. (1982). *Corporate cultures*. Reading, MA: Addison-Wesley.

Deem, R. (2003). Gender, organizational cultures and the practices of manager-academic in UK universities. *Gender, Work and Organization, 10*(2), 239–259. doi:10.1111/1468-0432.t01-1-00013

Donaldson, L. (2001). Reflections on knowledge and knowledge-intensive firms. *Human Relations, 54*(7), 955–963. doi:10.1177/0018726701547008

Drucker, P. F. (1993). *Post capitalist society*. New York: Harper-Business.

Drucker, P. F. (2001). *The essential Drucker*. New York: HarperCollins Publishers Inc.

Gamble, P. R., & Blackwell, J. (2001). *Knowledge management: A state of the art guide*. London: Kogan Page Lim.

Gayle, D. J., Tewarie, B., & White, A. Q. (2003). *Governance in the twenty-first-century university: Approaches to effective leadership and strategic management: ASHE-ERIC higher education report*. San Francisco: Jossey-Bass.

Geng, Q., Townley, C., Huang, K., & Zhang, J. (2005). Comparative knowledge management: A pilot study of Chinese and American universities. *Journal of the American Society for Information Science and Technology, 56*(10), 1031–1044. doi:10.1002/asi.20194

Giroux, H. A. (2003). The corporate university and the politics of education. *Revista Praxis, 2*, 22-31. Retrieved June 15, 2007, from http://www.revistapraxis.cl/ediciones/numero2/giroux_praxis_2.htm

Goddard, A. (1998). Facing up to market forces. *Times Higher Education Supplement, 13*, 6–7.

Gold, A. H., Malhotra, A., & Segars, A. H. (2001). Knowledge management: An organizational capabilities perspective. *Journal of Management Information Systems, 18*(1), 185–214.

Goodman, E. A., Zammuto, R. F., & Gifford, B. D. (2001). The competing values framework: Understanding the impact of organizational culture on the quality of work life. *Organization Development Journal, 19*(3), 58–67.

Grey, J. H., & Densten, I. L. (2005). Towards an integrative model of organizational culture and knowledge management. *International Journal of Organisational Behaviour, 9*(2), 594–603.

Gupta, A. K., & Govindarajan, V. (2000). Knowledge management's social dimension: Lessons from Nucor Steel. *Sloan Management Review, 42*(1), 71–81.

Gupta, B., Iyer, L. S., & Aronson, J. E. (2000). Knowledge management: Practices and challenges. *Industrial Management & Data Systems, 100*(1), 17–21. doi:10.1108/02635570010273018

Handy, C. (1993). *Understanding organizations* (4th ed.). London: Penguin Books.

Hatch, M., & Schultz, M. (1997). Relations between culture, identity and image. *European Journal of Marketing, 31*(5/6), 356–365. doi:10.1108/eb060636

Hislop, D. (2005). *Knowledge management in organizations*. Oxford, UK: Oxford University Press.

Hofstede, G. H. (1997). *Cultures and organizations*. New York: McGraw-Hill.

Howard, L. W. (1998). Validating the competing values model as a representation of organizational cultures. *The International Journal of Organizational Analysis, 6*(3), 231–250. doi:10.1108/eb028886

Jarvenpaa, S. L., & Staples, S. D. (2001). Exploring perceptions of organizational ownership and expertise. *Journal of Management Information Systems, 18*(1), 151–184.

Joseph, M. F. (2001). Key issues in knowledge management. *Knowledge and Innovation: Journal of the Knowledge Management Consortium International, 1*(3), 231–250.

Kakabadse, N. K., Kouzmin, A., & Kakabadse, A. (2001). From tacit knowledge to knowledge management: Leveraging invisible assets. *Knowledge and Process Management, 8*(3), 137–154. doi:10.1002/kpm.120

Kidwell, J. J., Vander Linde, K. M., & Johnson, S. L. (2000). Applying corporate knowledge management practices in higher education. *EDUCAUSE Quarterly, 23*(4), 28–33.

Kolb, D. A. (1984). *Experiental learning: Experience as the source of learning*. Englewood Cliffs, NJ: Prentice Hall.

Kotter, J. P., & Heskett, J. L. (1992). *Corporate culture and performance*. New York: The Free Press.

Krome-Hamilton, M. (2005/2006). The transformation of heterogenous individual learning into organizational knowledge: A cognitive perspective. *International Journal of Knowledge. Culture and Change Management, 5,* 59–68.

Kwan, P., & Walker, A. (2004). Validating the competing values model as a representation of organizational culture through inter-institutional comparisons. *Organizational Analysis, 12*(1), 21–37. doi:10.1108/eb028984

Lamond, D. (2003). The value of Quinn's competing values model in an Australian context. *Journal of Managerial Psychology, 18*(1), 46–59. doi:10.1108/02683940310459583

Laudon, K., & Laudon, J. (1999). *Management information systems-organization and technology in the networked enterprise*. Englewood Cliffs, NJ: Prentice Hall.

Lawson, S. (2003). *Examing the relationship between organizational culture and knowledge management*. Unpublished doctoral dissertation, The Wayne Huizenga School of Business and Entrepreneurship, Nova Southeastern University, Florida.

Levine, A. E. (2000, October 7). The future of colleges: 9 inevitable changes. *Chronicle of Higher Education*.

Luby, A. (1999). Accrediting teaching in higher education – voices crying in the wilderness. *Quality Assurance in Higher Education, 7*(4), 216–223. doi:10.1108/09684889910297721

Lueddeke, G. (1998). UK higher education at a crossroads: Reflections on issues and practice in teaching and learning. *Innovations in Education and Training International, 35*(2), 108–116.

Manville, B., & Foote, N. (1996). Strategy as if knowledge mattered. *FastCompany, 2,* 66-68. Retrieved February 1, 2008, from http://www.fastcompany.com/magazine/02/stratsec.html

Martin, J. S., & Marion, R. (2005). Higher education leadership roles in knowledge processing. *The Learning Organization, 12*(5), 140–151. doi:10.1108/09696470510583520

Maznevski, M., & Chudoba, K. (2000). Bridging space over time global virtual team dynamics and effectiveness. *Organization Science, 11*(5), 473–492. doi:10.1287/orsc.11.5.473.15200

McAdam, R., & McCreedy, S. (1999). The process of knowledge management within organizations: A critical assessment of both theory and practice. *Knowledge and Process Management, 6*(2), 101–113. doi:10.1002/(SICI)1099-1441(199906)6:2<101::AID-KPM53>3.0.CO;2-P

McDermott, R. (1999). Why information technology inspired cannot deliver knowledge management? *California Management Review, 41*(4), 103–117.

Mertins, K., Heisig, P., & Vorbeck, J. (2001). *Knowledge management. Best practices in Europe*. Berlin, Germany: Springer.

Meyer, H. D. (2002). The new managerialism in education management: Corporatization or organizational learning? *Journal of Educational Administration, 40*(6), 534–551. doi:10.1108/09578230210446027

Middlehurst, R., & Woodfield, S. (2006). Quality review in distance learning: Policy and practice in five countries. *Tertiary Education and Management, 12*(4), 37–58. doi:10.1007/s11233-005-4072-5

Mintzberg, H. (1983). *Structure in fives: Designing effective organizations*. Englewood Cliffs, NJ: Prentice-Hall.

Mintzberg, H. (2007). *Tracking strategies... toward a general theory*. New York: Oxford University Press.

Newell, S., & Swan, J. (2000). Trust and inter-organizational networking. *Human Relations, 53*(10), 287–328.

Nonaka, I., & Takeuchi, H. (1995). *The knowledge-creating company: How Japanese companies create the dynamics of innovation*. New York: Oxford University Press.

Pan, S. L., & Scarbough, H. (1999). Knowledge management in practice: An exploratory case study. *Technology Analysis and Strategic Management, 11*(3), 359–374. doi:10.1080/095373299107401

Park, H., Ribiere, V., & Schulte, W. D. (2004). Critical attributes of organizational culture that promote knowledge management technology implementation success. *Journal of Knowledge Management, 8*(3), 106–117. doi:10.1108/13673270410541079

Quinn, R. E. (1988). *Beyond rational management: Mastering the paradoxes and competing demands of high performance*. San Francisco: Jossey-Bass.

Quinn, R. E., Cameron, K. S., DeGraff, J., & Thakor, A. V. (2006). *Competing values leadership: Creating value in organizations*. Cheltenham, UK: Edward Elgar Publishing, Inc.

Ribière, V., & Sitar, S. A. (2003). Critical role of leadership in nurturing a knowledge-supporting culture. *Knowledge Management Research & Practice, 1*, 39–48. doi:10.1057/palgrave. kmrp.8500004

Roberts, J. (2000). From know-how to show-how? Questioning the role of information and communication technologies in knowledge transfer. *Technology Analysis and Strategic Management, 12*(4), 429–443. doi:10.1080/713698499

Rollett, H. (2003). *Knowledge management: Processes and technologies*. Boston: Kluwer Academic Publishers.

Roth, J. (2003). Enabling knowledge creation: Learning from an R&D organization. *Journal of Knowledge Management, 7*(1), 32–48. doi:10.1108/13673270310463608

Rowley, J. (2000). Is higher education ready for knowledge management? *International Journal of Educational Management, 14*(7), 325–333. doi:10.1108/09513540010378978

Sallis, E., & Jones, G. (2002). *Knowledge management in education: Enhancing learning & education*. London: Kogan Page.

Schein, E. H. (1984). Coming to a new awareness of organizational culture. *Sloan Management Review, 25*(2), 3–16.

Schein, E. H. (1985). How culture forms, develops, and changes. In R. Kilman, M. J. Saxton, et al. (Eds.), *Gaining control of the corporate culture* (pp. 17-43). San Francisco: Jossey-Bass.

Schein, E. H. (1992). *Organizational culture and leadership*. San Francisco: The Jossey-Bass Inc.

Schein, E. H. (1996). Culture: The missing concept in organization studies. *Administrative Science Quarterly, 41*(2), 229–240. doi:10.2307/2393715

Serban, A. M., & Luan, J. (Eds.). (2002). *Knowledge management: Building a competitive advantage in higher education* (New Directions for Institutional Research, No. 113). San Francisco: Jossey-Bass.

Sharimllah Devi, R., Chong, S. C., & Lin, B. (2007). Organizational culture and KM processes from the perspective of an institution of higher learning. *Int. Journal of Management Education, 1*(1/2), 57–79.

Srikanthan, G., & Dalrymple, J. F. (2002). Developing a holistic model for quality in higher education. *Quality in Higher Education, 8*(2), 215–224. doi:10.1080/1353832022000031656

Starbuck, W. H. (1992). Learning by knowledge intensive firms. *Journal of Management Studies, 29*(6), 713–740. doi:10.1111/j.1467-6486.1992.tb00686.x

Steyn, G. M. (2004). Harnessing the power of knowledge in higher education. *Education, 124*(4), 615–631.

Syed-Ikhsan, S. O. S., & Rowland, F. (2004). Knowledge management in a public organization: A study on the relationship between organizational elements and the performance of knowledge transfer. *Journal of Knowledge Management, 8*(2), 95–111. doi:10.1108/13673270410529145

Szulanski, G. (1996). Exploring internal stickiness: Impediments to the transfer of best practice within the firm. *Strategic Management Journal, 17*, 23–43.

Tippins, M. (2003). Implementing knowledge management in academia: Teaching the teachers. *International Journal of Educational Management, 17*(7), 339–345. doi:10.1108/09513540310501021

Tsoukas, H., & Vladimirou, E. (2003). What is organizational knowledge? *Journal of Management Studies, 38*(7), 973–993. doi:10.1111/1467-6486.00268

Tylor, E. B. (1871). *Primitive culture: Researches into the development of mythology, philosophy, religion, art and custom, vol. 1.* London: John Murray.

Weick, K. E. (1976). Educational organizations as loosely coupled systems. *Administrative Science Quarterly, 21*, 1–19. doi:10.2307/2391875

White, J., & Weathersby, R. (2005). Can universities become true learning organizations? *The Learning Organization, 12*(3), 292–298. doi:10.1108/09696470510592539

Wiig, K. M. (1993). *Knowledge management foundations.* TX: Schema Press.

Wiig, K. M. (1997). Knowledge management: An introduction and perspective. *The Journal of Knowledge Management*, September, *1*(1), 6-14.

Wilkens, U., Menzel, D., & Pawlowsky, P. (2004). Inside the black-box: Analysing the generation of core competencies and dynamic capabilities by exploring collective minds. *An Organisational Learning Perspective. Management Review, 15*(1), 8–26.

Wind, J., & Main, J. (1999). *Driving change.* New York: The Free Press.

Zammuto, R. F., Gifford, G., & Goodman, E. A. (1999). Managerial ideologies, organisation culture and the outcomes of innovation: a competing values prospective. In N. Ashkanasy, C. Wilderon, & M. Peterson (Eds.), *The handbook of organisational culture and climate* (pp. 263-280). Thousand Oaks, CA: Sage Publications.

Zappia, C. A. (2000). The private sector and public higher education. *Perspectives, 38*(5). Retrieved June 15, 2007, from http://www.historians.org/perspectives/issues/2000/0005/0005spl5.cfm

ADDITIONAL READING

Agasisti, T., & Catalano, G. (2006). Governance models of university systems—towards quasi-markets? Tendencies and perspectives: A European comparison. *Journal of Higher Education Policy and Management, 28*(3), 245–262. doi:10.1080/13600800600980056

Augier, M., & Thanning VendeIø, M. (1999). Networks, cognition and management of tacit knowledge. *Journal of Knowledge Management, 3*(4), 252–261. doi:10.1108/13673279910304005

Birnbaum, R. (1991). *How colleges work: The cybernetics of academic organization and leadership*. San Francisco: Jossey-Bass.

Bleiklie, I., & Henkel, M. (2005). *Governing knowledge: A study of continuity and change in higher education – a festschrift in honour of Maurice Kogan*. Dordrecht, The Netherlands: Springer.

Bolman, L. G., & Deal, T. E. (2008). *Reframing organizations: Artistry, choice and leadership*. San Francisco: John Wiley & Sons.

Busch, P. (2008). *Tacit knowledge in organizational learning*. Hershey, PA: IGI Publishing.

Dalkir, K. (2005). *Knowledge management in theory and practice*. Burlington, MA: Elsevier Butterworth-Heinemann.

Harris, P. (2005). *Managing the knowledge culture*. Amherst, MA: HRD Press.

He Aronowitz, S. (2001). *The knowledge factory: Dismantling the corporate university and creating true higher learning*. Boston: Beacon Press.

Ibarra, H., & Hunter, M. (2007). How leaders create and use networks. *Harvard Business Review, 2007*(January), 40–47.

Ichijo, K., & Nonaka, I. (2006). *Knowledge creation and management: New challenges for managers*. New York: Oxford University Press.

Kikoski, C. K., & Kikoski, J. F. (2004). *The inquiring organization: Tacit knowledge, conversation, and knowledge creation: skills for 21st-century organizations*. Westport, CT: Praeger Publishers.

Lytras, M., Russ, M., Meier, R., & Naeve, A. (Eds.). (2008). *Knowledge management strategies: A handbook of applied technologies*. Hershey, PA: IGI Publishing.

Marginson, S. (2006). Dynamics of national and global competition in higher education. *Higher Education, 52*, 1–39. doi:10.1007/s10734-004-7649-x

O'Dell, C., & Grayson, C. J. (1998). *If only we knew what we know: The transfer of internal knowledge and best practice*. New York: The Free Press.

O'Dell, C., & Leavit, P. (2004). *The executive's role in knowledge management*. Houston, TX: American Productivity & Quality Center.

Seufert, A., Von Krogh, G., & Bach, A. (1999). Towards knowledge networking. *Journal of Knowledge Management, 3*(3), 180–190. doi:10.1108/13673279910288608

Trnavčevič, A., & Logaj, V. (2008). From quality to audit culture: Who dares to say NO? In *Proceedings of the TEPE Conference 2008*. Retrieved October 10, 2008, from http://www.pef.uni-lj.si/tepe2008/papers/Trnavcevic_Logaj.pdf

Von Krogh, G., Ichijo, K., & Nonaka, I. (2000). *Enabling knowledge creation: How to unlock the mystery of the tacit knowledge and release the power of innovation*. New York: Oxford University Press.

Chapter 9
Best Practices of Knowledge Strategy in Hospitals:
A Contextual Perspective Based on the Implementation of Medical Protocols

Cláudio Reis Gonçalo
Universidade do Vale do Rio dos Sinos, UNISINOS, Brazil

Jacques Edison Jacques
Universidade do Vale do Rio dos Sinos, UNISINOS, Brazil

ABSTRACT

This study analyses best practices of knowledge strategies in hospitals considering the implementation of medical protocols. Protocols are research products originated from the based-on-evidence medicine. Knowledge strategy depends on specific organizational context that can be expressed by its barriers and enablers. Eight hospitals were studied in the state of Rio Grande do Sul, Brazil, involving multidisciplinary teams of the cardiology services which are acknowledged as the area of expertise with more implemented protocols. The same protocols are available in all investigated hospitals and are implemented by different practices in daily activities. A formal structure for the promotion of the organizational context is proposed in relation to the protocol implementation. The following factors were found as critical for the promotion of knowledge strategies' best practices in hospitals: a common language for sharing information among different professionals; the knowledge gap as a corporate vision, and the particular hole of information technology.

INTRODUCTION

The purpose of this study was to better understand how to explore best practices of knowledge strategies in the hospital organizations. Knowledge strategy depends on a favorable organizational context

(Berwick, 1996; Blackler, 1995; Snoweden, 2002). From a socio-cultural perspective, the creation of an adequate context is the crucial factor for the promotion of knowledge strategy, in accordance with the structure of the organization. In this perspective, the foundations for the knowledge management are the feasibility factors that are necessary to the creation and transferring of knowledge in the organizations

DOI: 10.4018/978-1-60566-790-4.ch009

(Ichijo at al., 1998; Hansen et al., 1999; Von Krogh et al., 2000; Nonaka et al., 2006).

This research explored barriers and enablers to the creation and transferring of knowledge by the implementation of medical protocols. It was investigated hospitals which work with clinical guidelines searching services standards of diagnosis and treatment according to scientific recommendations and medical bodies. In particular, it was studied the context for enabling knowledge through the identification of the critical elements that could promote original practices of knowledge strategy in hospitals by the issuing of the role of medical protocols' implementation. The investigation also was concerned to the consideration of knowledge as a strategic asset in the strategic formulation of the hospital, expressed in the whole process of conception, creation, and implementation of protocols.

Medical protocols are a product of Based-Evidence-Medicine (BEM). Based-Evidence-Medicine is the integration of the best evidence gathered from scientifically oriented research with the clinical ability of the doctor in charge of the decision and the patient's preference (Sacket, 2003). Eight hospitals were studied in the state of Rio Grande do Sul, Brazil, involving multidisciplinary teams organized around cardiology services. This area of expertise is acknowledged as the one with more implemented protocols.

In this way it is first presented conceptual topics about knowledge strategy in relation to hospitals, making it clear that the meaning of the protocols is a deployment of clinical guidelines. Next, a socio-cultural perspective proposed for the analysis of the hospital context aiming at promoting knowledge strategies is described. In the ensuing sections methodological procedures are shown and a brief analysis of the study in the "organizational field"- cardiology through multiple cases studies. A general analysis for the promotion of the required organizational context is offered and it is suggested a managerial framework. Finally, is presented the concluding considerations

on the research, highlighting as critical factors for promoting practices of knowledge strategy: a uniform language validated by the professionals; the lack of a strategic conception in the treatment of information and knowledge, and the lack of adequate support from the IT systems.

ORGANIZATIONAL KNOWLEDGE AND COGNITIVE BARRIERS

Knowledge has been claimed as one of the most important sources of competitive advantage and sustained performance based on worker's intelligence, as well as an important source of superior performance in turbulent environments (Prahalad & Hamell, 1990; Spender & Grant 1996; Nonaka et al., 2006).

Organizations are social 'organisms' and it is well known that organizational actions happen as the results of dynamic interactions between social and formal systems. The concept of organizational knowledge involving facts and values can, therefore, be explored in both logical constructions (formal and structured systems) and cognitive constructions (informal and unstructured systems).

The analytical life cycle of the organizational knowledge, shown in the Figure 1, involves two dimensions of knowledge: one based on formal systems and another based on cognitive systems. Knowledge based on formal systems includes all the required explicit knowledge for the implementation of any organizational process, such as: strategic planning, managerial model or information system. Knowledge based on cognitive systems mostly depends on people's understanding on the application of the formal systems including for instance learning process, decision-making process or leadership characteristics. The cycle starts over again as soon as any experience creates new knowledge which will be incorporated in the formal structure.

The structured knowledge from the current protocols is easily accessible by hospitals. The implementation of protocols will be supported by

Figure 1. Life cycle of the organizational knowledge

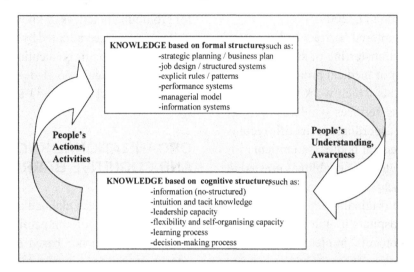

a learning process which will occur with the application of the available protocols to the particular context of the hospital. This is an opportunity to the creation of knowledge based on hospital's cognitive structures that it will promote how to apply the acknowledged protocol's structured knowledge in day-by-day activities.

Cognitive perspective on organizational culture focuses on ideas, concepts, beliefs, values or norms, while anthropology and sociology also describe it as 'organized knowledge' (Sackman, 1991). This "organized knowledge" is constituted by:

- the existing knowledge stored in people's minds,
- the mental modes used to explore it and
- the ideas or theories employed collectively to support their interpretations about what organization represents (Spender, 1998).

In this study, we are concerned with the ideas or theories employed collectively in order to enable knowledge in organizations. In particular, supported by a cognitive perspective the collective meanings and actions which consciously create organizational strategic choices which result in the creation and transfer of knowledge.

A practical manner for promoting knowledge strategies can start searching for the organization's cognitive barriers which are embedded in the organizational culture. The fewer the organizational cognitive barriers, the greater the use of the organizational intelligence. When managers realize where the cognitive barriers are, they can better make decisions to reduce or eliminate them. In this way, they will be able to promote successful knowledge strategies for developing strategic capabilities.

Epistemology provides fundamental assumptions on which to structure the knowledge-based view of the firm before researching the concept of knowledge itself. Distinct epistemologies may be conducive to the practice and research of knowledge management including the cognitive theory, the autopoietic theory and connectionistic theory (Venzin et al., 1998). Cognitive theory, the epistemological assumption underpinning this research, seeks to explain knowledge anchored in philosophy, psychology, linguistic, anthropology, neuroscience and artificial intelligence.

Organizational intelligence is a complex concept which has different meanings. The meaning which is used in this research is *the potential to create and transfer knowledge*, generating a particular way of using this knowledge to discover creative and innovative solutions in the decision making process (Pór, 1995; March, 1999). An organization acts in an intelligent way when, using their skills, it is able to overcome cognitive barriers and find specific solutions to existing problems in each context. In this way, the required knowledge strategy will be directly related to the intelligence context, and will be defined and recognized in a particular cognitive perspective of an organization.

An organisational capability can be defined as "…a high-level routine (or collection of routines) that, together with its implementing input flows, confers upon an organisation's management a set of decision options for producing significant outputs of a particular type" (Winter, 2000, p.982). The strategic capabilities assumed to support the specified cognitive skills in the implementation of protocols are learning and problem-solving, strategic decision-making, knowledge strategies and self-organising as semi-autonomous systems (Eisenhardt, 1999; Nonaka et al., 2000; Spender, 1996). Strategic capability consideration will only be built into the activity and put into action, if cognitive skills were promoted to make a difference in the working methods within an organization.

Strategy and knowledge have been studied in a research field, *the knowledge-based view of the firm* that is a confluence of a number of studies on resource-based theory of the firm and epistemology. The knowledge-based view of the firm considers as a general hypothesis (Grant, 1997) that: (1) knowledge is a differential productive resource; (2) different types of knowledge vary in their transferability; (3) individuals are the main agents of knowledge; and, (4) most knowledge is subject to economies of scale and scope.

KNOWLEDGE STRATEGIES

The concept of strategy as referred to in this chapter is a perspective shared by the members of an organization, through their intention and by their actions, and supported as a portfolio by a self-sustaining critical mass of sense-making opinion in the organization (Weick, 1995; Mintzberg, 1987; Eden & Ackermann, 1998). In this way, strategy can be expressed by the "character" of an organization as in the metaphor proposed by Selznick (1957), also called by Mintzberg (1987) the "personality" of the organization.

Organizations do not operate randomly without any intention, acting even by unconscious decision or by deliberate decision in relation to strategy matters. Strategic plans can be very useful to animate and orient people, but however malleable a plan might be, it cannot anticipate the rapid change of environments. Considering knowledge as strategic content, an organizational strategy can only be recognized in the personnel's day-to-day actions, in particular when personnel use the required knowledge for the performance of a specific activity. The success of a deliberate decision to acquire new knowledge which is expressed in a strategic plan will depend entirely on the understanding of strategy as a perspective shared by the members of an organization.

Studies about organizational performance in relation to strategy have been done to include the relation of context to content and to process (Pettigrew & Whipp, 1994; Ketchen, D.; Thomas, J., & Mcdaniel, R., 1996; Wit, B., & Meyer, R., 1998). The research structure about knowledge strategy in this respect can be based on these three dimensions: content, process and context, which are:

a) *content*, the organizational knowledge which is the knowledge as the strategic focus, explained by "the what" and its meanings in different categories;

Table 1. The Content: the conceptual knowledge

Perspectives	Meaning of knowledge	Implications for knowledge management
Systemic	Knowledge is represented by the acquired experience in the process	Focus is on the flow of knowledge and in the process of creating, storing, sharing and distributing knowledge.
Capability	Knowledge has the potential to motivate action.	Focus is on the strategic building of core competencies and know-how within the organization.
Professional Practice	Knowledge is in the performance of the activity	Focus is to promote an environment of individual / organizational learning

b) *process*, the knowledge strategic process which is how knowledge is promoted within the organization, and

c) *context*, the cognitive context which is inside the organization which enhance knowledge.

This study is focused on the analyses of cognitive barriers paying special attention to knowledge in the conceptual dimension. The objective is not to analyze the currently available knowledge but to discover how personnel can acquire the knowledge required to perform activities (the process), what this knowledge means to activities (the content) and why this knowledge is been developed in this manner (the context).

The *content dimension* of the knowledge strategy involves the conceptual knowledge which in this research means the three perspectives: systemic, capability and professional practice (see Table 1 based on Alavi(2001), Wigg(1993) and Zack (1999))

In the *systemic perspective*, knowledge is in the process itself. For example, people have knowledge of work through projects, sharing information through Internet, networking or building equipment on demand. Hence, knowledge is in the systems or in the applied methodologies.

In the *capability perspective*, knowledge has the potential to influence action. It is the knowledge which generates the potential that later becomes a differential for the organization in the performance in certain types of processes. In other words, it is the applied knowledge that is built up over time

in the organizational activity and its recognition by the client / society.

In a *practical professional perspective*, knowledge is in the experience an, also in the performance of an activity. It is the automatic knowledge, the one which becomes routine through the exercise of everyday work. The necessary data and information are accessed as part of the activity in the construction of specific knowledge. It also embodies the knowledge of the facts and decisions through interaction between tacit and implicit knowledge for the performance of the activity.

Considering the *process dimension*, knowledge strategies can be analyzed in two dimensions: the tactical and the strategic formulation (Buckowitz & Wiliams, 2000). The tactical formulation is the day-to-day use of knowledge to respond to demands or opportunities from the marketplace. The strategic formulation is the more long-range process of matching intellectual capital to build strategic capability. In this research the focus is to analyze both: the tactical and the strategic formulation of knowledge strategy.

The tactical process of knowledge management is related to the operations of the activities, including tasks as: gathering the required information for daily work; using knowledge to create value, learning with the experiences and storing knowledge into the systems for others to access as they face similar problems ("avoiding the recreation of the wheel") (Buckowitz & Williams, 2000).

The *tactical strategy* for the implementation of knowledge, also known as the knowledge management process, is usual divided as defined by Alavi & Leidner (2001) in the following dimensions:

a) *Knowledge creation/acquisition* which involves the sources of knowledge and the conditions to enable personnel actions;
b) *Knowledge storage* which involves finding the explicit knowledge from the individuals and the organizational processes, to codify and store it;
c) *Knowledge application* which involves the use of knowledge to improve organizational performance and increase of learning-by-doing systems;
d) *Knowledge distribution* which involves the knowledge sharing through the mutual exchange of ideas, with or without technical strategies to make it easier for any person in the organization to access useful information for his job.

These four strategic dimensions of knowledge promotion in the organizations can be distinguished in two basic set of processes: the creation of knowledge and the transfer of knowledge. In which the strategic problem is the creation of knowledge including the dimensions *knowledge creation/acquisition* and *knowledge storage*; and, the strategic problem is the transfer of knowledge including *knowledge application* and *knowledge distribution*. These processes of enabling knowledge will depend on the incremental development of a strategy, insofar as knowledge is an intangible and complex asset.

The *strategic formulation* of knowledge management requires the alignment of the organization's business strategy with the intended knowledge strategy. This strategic process demands a continual assessment of existing skills, attitudes and knowledge of the organization's personnel and a comparison with future needs (Buckowitz & Williams, 2000). The role of the organizational leadership in the formulation of knowledge strategy must be performed as a partner

with the middle management and the front line. The organizational context will be critical point to promote a sharing environment which is the most important characteristic of a knowledge creation culture.

The incremental development of a strategy occurs in a spiral movement that requires the team to change constantly between formulation and implementation until they find a committed direction (Gladstein & Quinn, 1985). When the strategic objective is concerned with organizational knowledge, we propose to apply the same spiral movement representing a team that will move back and forth between general knowledge and specific knowledge. During a knowledge development period, personnel will inevitably cross a blurred line representing a cognitive boundary between strategic knowledge formulation and strategic knowledge implementation.

In addition, Nonaka & Takeuchi (1995) proposed the well-known spiral of knowledge creation with four widely acknowledged stages: socialization, combination, externalization and internalization. Nonaka & Takeuchi's spiral represents the process of transferring individual knowledge creation to the pool of collective knowledge representing everyone's efforts in both the specific and general knowledge domains. The application of these concepts related to knowledge creation theory is a new paradigm in health institutions. New knowledge transformed into information with more clinical effect should be inserted in a known organizational context (Zack, 1999a; Guptill, 2005; Nonaka et al., 2006).

In sum, knowledge strategy refers to the employment of knowledge processes in an existing or new knowledge domain in order to achieve strategic goals, in a knowledge-based view of the firm (Zack, 1999a; Hansen et al., 1999; Nonaka & Takeuchi, 1995; Nonaka et al., 2006). Basically organizations attempt to derive the best business value from their existing knowledge-based assets or try to create new competitive knowledge-related assets where required (Wiig, 1997; Hansen et al., 1999; Bukowitz & Williams, 2000; Whittington 2006). Existing knowledge promotes the development of the organizational experience in day-to-day activities, and new knowledge will be created from an organizational vision which intends to achieve this in the long-term mostly through developing intellectual capital.

This study investigated the hospital's context to promote knowledge strategies in relation to the implementation process of medical protocols which is briefly presented in the following section.

Medical Protocols

Medical protocols, also called clinic or institutional, are product of Based-on-Evidence Medicine (BEM). Based on Evidence Medicine is the integration of the best evidence gathered from scientifically oriented research with the clinical ability of the doctor who is in charge of the decision involving the patient's preference (Sacket, 2003). It is a method of medical work which aims at various objectives through the qualification of the decision process.

"Best scientific evidence" is understood as the research process which is clinically relevant based on preferably random, double-blind and multi-centered studies, which are accurate and precise, about diagnosis methods, the power of prognostic indicators and the efficiency and safety of therapeutical, preventive and rehabilitation regimes. According to Drummond et al. (2002), the word evidence is used in BEM as a criterion of higher accuracy in certain findings and opinions based on data and information whose analysis is done within previously stipulated standards.

"Clinical ability" is the union of knowledge and medical experience to evaluate all the aspects of the problems that afflict the health of a patient, be it organic or emotional. The "values of the patients" are the beliefs and experiences that give shape to the patients' expectation and behavior elements that need to be considered and shared at the time

of making a decision. Highlighting the integration of these three aspects (evidences, clinical ability and patients' values), Sacket (2003) comments that doctors and patients form a diagnostic and therapeutic alliance which optimizes clinical results and life quality.

As a result, this management model is based on the construction of instruments called clinical guidelines, that is, documents systematically developed by competent medical bodies. The medical protocols represent that more specific part, being therefore deployment of the clinical guidelines applicable to certain characteristic groups of patients.

Therefore, it could be highlighted that the guidelines assume the responsibility for the hospital organization and that the protocols are related to the responsibility of the care team which decides to use them. In any case, the creation of clinical guidelines and their deployment in medical protocols, as well as their implementation and application, are processes based on concepts belonging to the management of knowledge. Coffey, Richards, Remmert, Leroy, Schoville & Baldwin (2005) observe that the challenge to reduce the time spent in hospitals and consequently, the costs, is the key motivation for the development of medical protocols.

Medical protocols are tools that result from the express agreement between the two parts: the doctors (or care teams) and patients (and their families). Because of this, as important as the content (or possibly even more important than the content itself) are the elements involved in the construction of such protocols following the clinical guidelines. It is of vital importance that both parts feel totally committed, creating a favorable environment, which is an important challenge for clinical managers.

KNOWLEDGE STRATEGY IN HOSPITAL ORGANIZATIONS

The application of knowledge management theory in hospital organizations seemed originally to be a new concept; nevertheless, this is one of the most oriented organizations for the specific use of knowledge in daily activities. In the management of the health processes it is usual to focus on the transference of knowledge, although in knowledge creation this focus may be lacking in the managerial process. In particular, knowledge management theory is a new opportunity for hospital organizations if knowledge is considered as one of the critical assets for the business strategy of health institutions.

The quality of the medical services takes center stage in any improvement program in health organizations. Provonost; Nolan; Zegwe; Miller & Rubin (2004) observe that the big opportunity to improve the results of health care performance of hospitals will be based not only on the discovery of new treatments but also on the knowledge of how to administer already existing therapies. In order to improve, therapists need to know what to do and how to do it, and be able to develop the care process. This is why it is concluded that programs of how enabling knowledge can be a strategic alternative for hospitals (Laverde, 2003).

Knowledge management in health organizations can be understood as the alignment of people, processes, data and technologies to optimize information, cooperation, expertise and experience to guide the organizational performance and growth (Guptill, 2005). Based on this conception it is observed that the management of knowledge can offer elements for everyone, especially doctors, to see the health organization under a holistic perspective joining revolutionary technologies and care processes (Sewell, 1997).

The learning and the exercise of knowledge creation in the organizations depend on a favourable structural context which favors the sharing of knowing "how-to-do" (Berwick, 1996; Blacker,

1995; Snoweden, 2002). This study investigates a context which promotes the differentiation of the health organization to implement the medical protocols. The step of knowledge acquisition through protocols is available to all health organizations. The difference may occur in the knowledge creation from the particular manner in which they are implemented in each organization.

Applying the three dimensions for analyzing the promotion of knowledge strategies, the meanings for promoting knowledge in hospitals, based on the implementation of protocols, are:

- dimension content, the conceptual knowledge is derived from the way of implementation of protocols;
- dimension context, it is represented by the cardiology services, and
- dimension process, it is represented by the creation and transference of knowledge.

From a socio-cultural perspective, the promotion of an adequate context in accordance with the structure of an organization is the crucial factor for the creation of knowledge. In this perspective it is assumed that the foundations of knowledge management are the feasibility factors (enabling) which are necessary for people to create and share the acquired knowledge (Von Kroght et al., 2000; Ichijo et al., 1998). The identification of barriers and enablers can help the managers to better identify the organizational level to implement changes. Table 2 below shows the barriers and enabling factors of the organizational context to the promotion of knowledge strategy in the investigation of this study (Von Krogh et al., 2000; Alavi, 2001 & Crossan et al.,1999).

RESEARCH METHODOLOGICAL PROCEDURES

The qualitative research was applied to explore how medical chiefs enable knowledge in the

Table 2. Perspective for the Analysis of the Organizational Context

Dimensions of Organizational Context	Critical Categories
Knowledge Enablers (EN)	EN1- Managerial actions promoting the awareness of a knowledge gap as an organizational challenge EN2- The management of conversations for either: confirming the existence knowledge, or aiming the creation of new knowledge EN3- Building process with the use of Information Technology as a support tool to promote knowledge management
Knowledge Barriers (BA)	BA1- Difficulty to alter paradigms (objectives, rules, indicators and goals) and to create a new performance language in relation to promoting knowledge strategy BA2- Difficulty to create a knowledge sharing context BA3- Difficulty to promote interactions in a knowledge spiral

health organizations by the implementation of protocols. The chosen method was the multiple-cases studies that searched for the personnel's interpretations of knowledge strategies use in relation to their experience (Whittington, 2006). The health professionals were motivated to give examples and remember stories of how they created and transferred knowledge in the specific protocol implementation mentioned during the interviews. The cases studies were conducted as exploratory studies (Yin, 1994; Parker, 2000; Bosi, 2004). The investigation of eight hospitals allowed searching for evidence from different organizational contexts. The whole research process can be summarized in the following topics:

- *Analysis Units:* There were two analysis units:
- *Health teams organized in cardiology services,* including leader's teams and associated personnel (nurses and physiotherapists) with multi-disciplinary teams who are responsible for creating medical protocols. Cardiology was chosen because this medical service is acknowledged as the one with the most protocols implemented. In this analysis unit, the main research focus was the organizational context highlighting the barriers and the enablers to promote knowledge strategies. In sum, 30 health professionals were investigated in this group.

- *Group of hospital directors and medical chiefs,* including clinical directors, executive directors and nursing directors. In this analysis unit, the investigation explored if there was any evidence in the corporate strategy that could support any knowledge strategy from the application of medical protocols. In sum, 22 health professionals were investigated in this group.
- *Focus Group:* A focus group was investigated. Three meetings were happen, with a total duration about of six hours. The group was composed of three cardiologists (one of them was the leader) and three nurses (the hospital leader and two nurses of the cardiology service). From that, it was possible to define the main and understandable research questions for applying in the interviews.
- *Interviews:* Interviews were the basis for the research, providing the data for open coding and leads for further investigation. Forty-four individual interviews were conducted, following a semi-structured procedure with different professionals. Each of interviews took about of fifty minutes' duration, in the months of October, November and December 2006. In sum, it took about sixty hours of recorded interviews that were listened and transcribed.
- *Direct and Participant Observations:* To control potential bias and distortions in

Table 3. Characteristics of the investigated hospitals

Hosp.	Characteristics					
	Clinical Focus	**Public or Private**	**The Majority of the patients**	**Number of beds**	**Research& Teaching**	**Cardiologists/ Implemented Protocols**
A	General	Only Private	Private health plan	350	No	25 cardiol. 10 protocols
B	General	Mixed	Federal health plan (SUS)	600	Yes -	40 cardiol. 15 protocols
C	Emergency	Mixed	Federal health plan (SUS)	100	Yes	14 cardiol. No protocols
D	General	Only Private	Private health plan	180	No	20 cardiol. 10 protocols
E	General	Only Private	Private health plan	300	Yes	30 cardiol. 15 protocols
F	Emergency	Mixed	Federal health plan (SUS)	100	No (initial program)	8 cardiol. 15 protocols
G	General	Only Private	Private health plan	200	Yes	12 cardiol. No protocols
H	General	Mixed	Private health plan	300	No	25 cardiol., 15 protocols

the narratives of the participants it was possible *directly to observe* people on-the-job as suggested by Yin (1994), during the visits happened in the exploratory research. In addition to that, it was also use *participant observations* in three hospitals investigated. As one of the authors was a medical leader in other clinical specialization, he could better observe the cardiology services and better explore the meaning of different conversations among the health professionals.

• *Documental Analysis:* It was analyzed information from results of meetings in relation to protocol implementation, algorithms from medical protocols and performance results of health care processes.

THE CASE STUDIES

To investigate knowledge strategy was required evidence gleaned from close observation in day-by-day actions and mainly semi-structured interviews. For that, in these case studies it was addressed the following principal research question:

How can the hospital context enable knowledge from the implementation and formulation of medical protocols?

This study investigated the same research field represented by the cardiology services from the different hospitals. It is noted that the same protocols are available in any hospitals certainly including the eight researched ones. To be available them is not enough. To implement them is the challenge that requires solving managerial and technical problems on which there are the opportunities to promote organizational knowledge strategies. The table 3 shows some characteristics of these hospitals that took part of the research.

SUS means Health Unique System that is the Federal Govern's Health Program in Brazil that is mostly attended by Public Hospitals and, also, by Philanthropic Hospitals which include Private Hospital.Considering the whole set of researched

Table 4. General Characteristics of the whole set of hospitals

Characteristics of the whole Set of hospitals	Quantity of Hospitals
General Treatment	6
Specific (Emergency)	2
Private Only	4
Public (just SUS)	3
Mixed	4
Researching &Teaching	4
Medicine Students	4
Unable to implement Card. Protocols	2
Up to 10 cardiology protocols	2
More than 10 cardiology protocols	4

hospitals, six of them are located in Porto Alegre – the capital of Rio Grande do Sul, one in its metropolitan area and, other, in the mountains region of the State. The total of 44 interviewers include: 14 directors, 8 medical leaders, 10 medics who are members of the cardiology service, 12 other professionals who are part of the service (nurses and physiotherapists). Other characteristics of the whole set of hospitals are presented in the Table 4.

The Case Studies Analysis: Highlighting Topics

Following are presented some important topics based on found evidence in the categories investigated. It was analyzed the enablers and the barriers organizing the information in two perspectives:

- from the viewpoint of the health teams organized in the cardiology services on which practices of knowledge strategy is represented by its *implementation dimension*, and
- from the viewpoint of the hospital directors and medical leaders on which practices of knowledge strategy is represented by its *formulation dimension*.

Practices of knowledge strategy x implementation dimension from the perspective of the medical teams organized in cardiology services –

Four hospitals with Research & Teaching (R&T) activities and other four without these activities in their operation were chosen to the research. Selecting this whole set of hospitals, it was possible to organize them in these two dimensions. The first information, observed in this classification, is that the set of hospitals with R&T has less implemented protocols (see table 5), even though the hospitals have more cardiologists and beds.

The implementation of protocols created a common language that had supported a sharing environment. It is recognized as a particular form to break learning barriers and create knowledge.

I think that for the creation of protocols the most important enabling factor in a context is the need that we, teachers, have to equalize language with the residents. Protocol language is one (...) it makes the group, in which people come from different backgrounds, become homogeneous in favor of an environment focused on teaching. (Source: a cardiologist from an R&T hospital)

Table 5. Hospital's characteristics expressed with or without Research & Teaching Activities

Dimensions of Analysis		Set of Hosp.	Total Beds	Implem. Protocols	Total of Cardiol.	Cardiol. Interv.	Other Interv.
R & T	With R&T	B – C E – G	1200	30	96	8	15
	Without R&T	A – D F – H	930	50	78	6	15
	Total	Whole Set	2130	80	174	14	30

To work in the creation of protocols together with the doctors is a great opportunity to establish a unique language (...) which enhances our relationship with them (...) making communication easier. (...) we feel part of the process. The same language, when used by all nurses, "reaches" even the assistant nurses thus making the task easier to be controlled. (Source: a chief nurse and a physiotherapist from an R&T hospital)

The interviewees were concerned to the way and to the tools used to disseminate the knowledge creation from the implementation of medical protocols. The most important disapproval was about how the information systems were used to support them, including:

- the difficulty of communication with IT professionals;
- lack of training programs regarding IT;
- difficulty to access diagrams and algorithms on the computer terminals;
- no protocols in the computerized means;
- lack of updated protocols;
- no meetings notes were received on which protocols were discussed.

It is possible to assume that there are many difficulties to transfer knowledge using information systems in the hospitals studied. Just in two of them (Research & Teaching hospital) there was a positive reference to IT as a supportive element for the communication of the medical protocols, after designed, throughout the organization.

The higher the knowledge barriers, the more difficulties will be the implementation of medical protocols. The Hospital C, even having R&T activities, has only protocols in nurse services. In this hospital the cardiology group does not have his implementation of protocols. Also, the cardiologist group of hospital G has a higher barrier to the implementation of his protocols than the construction of them (see table 6).

Medical protocols get us closer to the other professionals and consultation gains more quality and ease. When I am not in the hospital and something happens to one of my patients I know the teams will make decisions agreed during the protocol creation. I work in institutions where there are no protocols and I feel very insecure. I keep on phoning until I can go to the place

(Source: a cardiologist)

During the interviews with cardiologists and other professionals it was evident that the implementation of medical protocols was a big chance for everybody to level concepts, processes and objectives, what means to create a common language. So, even when the barrier of different professional backgrounds existed it had to be overcome.

Practices of knowledge strategy x formulation dimension from the perspective of the hospital directors and medical chiefs –

This exploratory phase of the research inves-

Table 6. Enablers and Barriers in the investigated hospitals

Research Dimensions		Set of Hosp.	Specific Evidence	
			Knowledge Enablers (EN)	Knowledge Barriers (BA)
Research & Teaching	With R&T	B – C E – G	•EN1 (Hosp. B, E) The use of BSC (Balanced Scorecard) clarify the organizational knowledge to decrease the knowledge gap. •EN2 (Hosp. B, E) The common language is very used enhanced by the R&T environment. Although, the conversations are not managed as a knowledge enabler. •EN3 (Hosp. B, E) Information Technology (IT) is perceived as one of the major knowledge enabler. There are some experiences on the promotion of knowledge strategies with the IT support.	•BA1 (Hosp. C) The lack of a managerial model applied for the whole hospital. •BA2 (Hosp. C, G) The weak commitment of persons to the construction and to the application of a new medical protocol. Both hospitals criticize their information systems. •BA3 (Hosp. C) Meetings are very rare what makes very difficult to discuss new ideas.
	Without R&T	A – D F – H	•EN1 (Hosp. A, F) The strategic planning is implemented and recognized by the personnel. Although, there is not declared a new knowledge vision in all hospitals. •EN2 - The common language is very used. The conversations are not managed as a knowledge enabler. •EN3 – IT is considered crucial factor to promote knowledge management, although there is a lack of application on this matter.	•BA1 (Hosp. H) The managerial model is only applied to the administrative activities. •BA2 (Hosp. H) IT has not been applied to share information, as they recognized that it should had. •BA3 (Hosp. H) There is no priority to share clinical problems and the organization culture do not facilitate knowledge strategies.

tigated the medical leaders from the cardiology services and, also, the hospital directors who were responsible for the strategic formulation. In particular, the investigation was concerned to the consideration of knowledge as a strategic asset in the strategic formulation of the hospital, expressed in the whole process of conception, creation, and implementation of protocols. The revealed evidence allows summarizing in the following topics:

• Formal projects of knowledge management in the researched hospitals

None of the hospitals has developed any formal projects of knowledge management in spite of the implementation of protocols were an opportunity for promoting the creation and transference of knowledge.

The medical leaders presented the control instruments of the implementation of protocols as diagrams, graphics or analytic maps which show how hospitals are concerned to this practice. Having these control indicators is a chance of learning about the process which will be specific for each hospital, although this know-how is still not recognized as a knowledge creation process.

The knowledge management theory is considered a challenge to the hospital organizations as a possibility to develop the formal and informal structure for taking into consideration what the hospitals know and need to know.

• Formal processes of choosing leaderships responsible for the building of protocols

In all hospitals investigated, the responsibility of building protocols is assumed by the medical leaders of the cardiology services. All leaders were doctors and, so, nurses or administrators were not found in a leadership position for the implementation of new protocols.

Only two of the hospitals investigated had leaders specialized in epidemiological diseases which is the discipline that is more involved with the methodological procedures in the construction of protocols.

- The knowledge value gained from the implementation process of protocols

About 75% of the interviewees evaluated the conversation for the implementation of protocols as very important to team learning, which mostly depends on:

- the team's wish to implement protocols for producing standards in the health services;
- the promotion of new knowledge during the debate of specific issues that must be considered in the planning of the implementation;
- the commitment of the team with varied activities which will demand efforts to overcome individual and organization barriers;
- the debate concerning the divergences between what was planned and what really happened, involving issues such as the variability of using resources and the expectation of results based on quality performance;
- the common language used among the professionals which is supported by medicine based-on-evidence, and
- information technology supporting the implementation and the analysis of the results.

Two problems occurred more frequently which were the commitment of the team and problems with the information technology as mentioned by one medical leader:

Our information technology definitely doesn't help. We made the service process and we try to access the Intranet, for instance, on how many patients were affected by the use of protocols... what was the level of adhesion of the doctors...

what results were achieved, etc. And it takes a long time to implement our demands... So, we are getting less motivation... Then, I start thinking that it should be more important...After all, I am always hearing from the Directors that this is strategic to the hospital. (Source: Medical chief from a private hospital)

- The right context for promoting knowledge

Creating the right context had the most impact on how the concept of implementation of protocols could be best exploited. As the medical protocols are processes which frequently incorporate new technologies, this concept must be developed as soon as new knowledge is acquired.

The chiefs of the cardiology services agreed that there is a common practice of sharing experiences in their scientific field among partners. The implementation of protocols depends on the right context which, first of all, had promoted the sharing of explicit knowledge concerning cardiologic diseases.

Technical knowledge used in different treatments makes it difficult to create a pattern, because it depends on the tacit knowledge of each medical doctor. The right context which will promote a knowledge creation process is that where a common language is used among the different professionals. The success of clinical protocols depend on its comprehension by doctors, nurses, nutritionists and all professionals who are responsible for taking care of the patient.

After the commitment of the colleagues to the building of medical protocols and the adhesion of their applications, the rest flows in a natural way... (Source: Medical chief from a public hospital)

• Strategy and knowledge creation based on the implementation the protocols

The potential of knowledge creation from the implementation process of medical protocols promotes both basic strategies in hospital organizations: survival and advancement strategies. The promotion of survival strategy, in which the hospitals focus on knowledge to sustain their present level of market position and organizational performance (Von Krogh et al., 2000) is expressed on the lower operation costs and on higher consistent results. The promotion of advancement strategy, in which the hospitals focus on knowledge to acquire future success opportunities and improved performance (Von Krogh et al., 2000), is expressed on the use of the most modern techniques and update knowledge.

A few days ago, I was working in other hospital and I had to assist a patient in a critical condition. At that moment, I was in doubt about which exams would be necessary right away. I remembered, then, of the protocol we had implemented here in this Institution. I called a colleague, we discuss the case and I made up my mind based on the protocol built here. (Source: a medical chief)

Doctors working in different hospitals can evaluate different strategies in their daily routines. Having experience in hospitals with or without implemented protocols, for following a same clinical procedure, doctors can see how performance is improved. The required knowledge is always acquired during the process of protocol implementation in which the health professional can discuss problems in different contexts.

• Integration and combination of hospitals' resources

The integration and combination of all hospitals' resources will be necessary to put medical protocol into operation. The most important

characteristics of the services offered in hospitals are that the client (patient) participates and observes the whole services process and, therefore, it is he who evaluates the services during the process. Being aware of the client's evaluation of resource integration, hospital organizations can better use the client's perception for managing their resources based on a systemic view and on efficient activities.

An example is a special role performed by some doctors who are responsible for all kinds of intensive care problems and are called as consultants. These professionals are in all hospitals solving problems that demand critical diagnosis and emergent solutions. They work as a mobile team which needs to know different protocols implemented in diversely specialized knowledge fields. This organizational structure promotes a dynamic capability for problem solving in a fast and integrated form whose performance depends on the organizational culture.

A dynamic capability needs to be recognized from the client and from the understanding which enables the organization to perform their activities (Teece et al., 1997; Dosi et. al, 2000). In a hospital organization, the more integrated the activities, the more the clients will recognized its organizational capability. On one side, good experiences are rapidly recognized by the clients who are participants for the whole hospital process; on the other side, difficult integration and bad use of resources are also quickly recognized.

• Knowledge as a strategic content

The most valued strategic content is the *know-how* which is encouraged by the process of protocol implementation. Having resources is not enough; but extremely necessary. It goes beyond that: the study of the use of different resources will develop the required knowledge to face specialized problems. Having modern equipments is not enough to guarantee quality service. If health professional are up-to-date, the organization can promote the right context to develop new knowledge using the implementation of protocols.

I work in a hospital where I face services procedures that could be improved to use of the resources better. But, in this hospital, there are no implemented protocols. The resources are there, but, there is a lack of management of the services "embedded" in knowledge. (Source: a medical chief)

Hospitals are not recognized for using this *know-how* as a competitive advantage for having specific strategic capabilities. The organizational culture in a hospital separates the strategic problems from operational problems, since operation is all running and the care can not stop for "rethinking the way of doing things". From the other side, when knowledge is the content, the strategic decision also should comprehend strategy as the way of performing the activities.

As the organizational culture is supported by a bureaucratic managerial system, the responsibility for creating market strategies is taken by the directors. Medical chiefs and other health professionals must take care of tactical and operational strategies, in daily activities. One exception is the integration and combination of the resources which is the responsibility of managerial leaders.

Strategies in relation to knowledge content stimulate an organization to create different types of knowledge, recognize the knowledge created and transfer experiences among personnel. This motivation will be gradually integrated into the organizational culture characterizing the knowledge sharing environment as "the way of doing things".

• The differentiation is on the implementation process

Medical protocols can and should be accessed by all hospitals since the improvement of the health sector is a social responsibility. If the

implementation process is only considered as an operational decision, it will be possible to imitate it and, therefore, will not provide a competitive advantage.

Otherwise, if the implementation is planned as a strategic activity, the process will be complex and will build managerial competence. This makes imitation difficult as it requires the transfer of managerial competence which takes a long period to create and be adapted to each organization.

Here, where I am responsible for building medical protocols, there is an environment and resources to work with (....).There are hospitals where I would never assume this task. They are hospitals where the clinic's staff is not committed, even with difficulty to share experiences and discuss cases studies. (Source: a managerial chief)

Therefore, the creation of a strategic content from the building of medical protocols will depend on an organizational attitude which is an expression of the organizational culture. To sum up, the differentiation process will include:

• organizational learning, through experience sharing changing concepts, processes, indicators, and, even, business strategies;
• organizational innovation process, through the creation of new knowledge;
• focus on client, since protocols are approaches of giving to the patients exact what they need with more security;
• social responsibility, since protocols promote an ethical way of taking care in the healthy services;
• results orientation, by organizing the commitment to reach outcomes with an integrated and systemic way of evolving all interested elements.

Table 7. Promoting Organizational Context from Strategic Process

		Organizational Context	
		Providing Context	**Sharing Context**
Strategic Process	Managerial capacity	(A) Managing conversations	(B) Knowledge content
	Strategic content of knowledge	(C) Resources integration	(D) Dynamic capability

THE ORGANIZATIONAL CONTEXT TO PROMOTE KNOWLEDGE

Organizational Context and Strategic Managerial Process

The relation between the organizational context and the strategic managerial process is shown in a Matrix in Table 7 which is obtained from the results of the research. The strategic managerial process is more influenced by the managerial capacity and the strategic content of knowledge. The organizational context is represented by the enabling and sharing dimensions.

The managerial performance is analyzed in quadrant A in order to provide the right context which is necessary for the implementation of medical protocols (see the above Matrix). The managerial capacity has been used to manage conversations to promote a unique and codified language among the personnel.

In quadrant B, the managerial capacity is focused on the promotion of context sharing. There is a very strong sharing process in the hospitals when the content is technical knowledge and it is shared with the personnel (inside the hospital). When the content is related to strategic topics to implement advancement strategies, there is a lack of sharing which could be improved with the commitment of the personnel. Also, there is a lack of knowledge sharing among hospitals that could be improved to increase the performance of the health sector.

In quadrant C, the strategic content of knowl-edge means how knowledge creation from the protocols implementation can be managed as a strategic opportunity for providing the right context. There is very little strategic use of the knowledge acquired during the process of protocol implementation. Although the knowledge integration, from the combination of different resources, is expressed merely in the organization operations, but it is still not used as a strategic advantage.

In quadrant D, the strategic content of knowl-edge can be managed to promote a sharing context which could access new strategic opportunities. There is no evidence on the use of this opportu-nity shared with different suppliers, for instance. The sharing context can create a specific dynamic capability which will be recognized by patients, suppliers, and other stakeholders.

There is a challenge to face in hospitals that is the cultural change from practical experiences to new scientific experiences. It was observed that some doctors were skeptical about the new knowledge created when they started to participate in the meet-ings to discuss and create medical protocols. Up to that moment they practiced empirical medicine based on their personal experiences and not neces-sarily in accordance with scientific recommenda-tions. They argued that many patients had done well through this practice so, just a few things needed to be changed. There were success stories until then (failure stories were not talked about it).

Even thus, it was not found evidence of knowl-edge strategy in the hospitals' strategic planning. A hospital's strategy for knowledge management should reflect its competitive strategy.

None of the hospital directors or medical leaders acknowledged a specific program articulated from higher administration planning that could encourage the development of knowledge through of the implementation of medical protocols. The encouragement, in most of the cases, was restricted to an informal invitation issued by a medical leader to join the team which was creating the protocols. This is very revealing information which indicates that none of the investigated hospitals implemented a knowledge strategy project promoted from the implementation of protocols. It is observed that structured projects on knowledge management could ease the constitution of teams, the justification of concepts and the enabling of knowledge.

The management leaders of private hospitals were most worried, not only by the fact that the knowledge provided by the protocols needs always being updated, but also by the communication of this knowledge to the doctors.

Promoting the Required Organizational Context: A Framework

Regarding the strategic opportunity for knowledge creation from the implementation process of medical protocols, we suggest the following managerial framework with seven activities to provide the required organizational context:

1. *to organize the strategic planning of health care,* including institutional projects responsible for creating and transferring knowledge obtained from the experiences of protocol implementation, supported by medicine based-on-evidence.

2. *to bring together systematically the medical chiefs and other health professionals of specialized services* to analyze the trends of the epidemiological data, research of new resources and technologies and new models of health care. This activity is based on research in addition of encouraging the commitment of the all health professionals; this will provide information to decide on the strategic choices. This will be focused in the period of strategic health care planning.

3. *to establish a knowledge advancement strategy,* expressed in a common language, for all hospital personnel promoting understanding and realizing the importance of each individual for the success of the institutional project. To instill the "knowledge vision", in accordance with the deliberate strategy, will be the main organizational goal which will facilitate the promotion of the organizational context of valuing new experiences and initiatives.

4. *to transfer the acquired new knowledge* to the all clinical professionals, asking for suggestions and analyzing the level of adhesion in the use of protocols. This activity also has the important function of lowering the organizational barriers that may emerge, promoting the right context to the sharing beliefs and ideas. The more participation, the more clinical professional will be committed.

5. *to organize and stimulate the creation of specialized groups* that will be able to share technical experiences and create new knowledge during the protocol implementation process. These specialized groups should involve health professionals including medical doctors, nurses, nutritionists and physiotherapists.

6. *to promote the required information technology* that will be necessary to access, codify, transfer and store the acquired knowledge before, during and after the implementation process of clinical protocols.

7. *to manage the knowledge creation as a strategic content* that will be an opportunity to create dynamic capabilities recognized by patients in the clinical treatment of specialized medical services.

FUTURE OPPORTUNITIES

This study investigates the knowledge management theory in the hospital organizations from the perspective of the organizational context assuming that the best managers can do is to provide conditions to promote the creation and transference of knowledge (Krogh et. al., 2000; Nonaka et al., 2006). In particular, we were concerned to knowledge strategies that refer to the employment of knowledge creation processes in the clinical protocols implementation, in an existing or new knowledge domain in order to achieve strategic goals, in a knowledge-based view of the firm (Zack, 1999b; Hansen et al., 1999; Nonaka & Takeuchi, 1995; Nonaka et al., 2006).

Regarding theoretical contributions, we study a specific research field which is knowledge creation and transfer in the implementation process of clinical protocols in the cardiology services. We propose to analyze knowledge strategy in two dimensions represented by its implementation process and by its formulation process.

In the implementation process, we investigated from a perspective of the analysis of the organizational context. This perspective consists of searching for organizational barriers and enablers. Organizational barriers may emerge and, in these circumstances, managers will need to face them. Organizational enablers will be the promoters for the required context.

In the formulation process, we analyze knowledge creation and transfer as a strategic opportunity. We propose to develop the strategic process based on the managerial capacity and the real value of strategic content of knowledge. This will provide the specific and sharing organizational context. There is very little strategic use of the knowledge acquired during the process of protocol implementation.

The knowledge management theory applied in the health system offers a spectrum for many future studies. In particular, focusing clinical protocols, this study could be pursued in studies following on from this investigation, such as:

- how health insurance (suppliers) can apply knowledge management concepts regarding knowledge from the protocol implementation as a strategic asset;
- how the organizational culture can be encouraged to understand and to value the process of knowledge creation and transfer in the clinical operations;
- how the medical culture can be enabled into a knowledge sharing context;
- how a corporative university can be responsible for knowledge strategies;
- how a hospital can learn with the patient's experiences;
- how information systems can enable a knowledge sharing context;
- how different areas of expertise can share knowledge content;
- how hospital services can store knowledge experiences;
- how to evaluate the strategic content of knowledge as an intangible asset, developing assessment systems for clinical services that could be used to improve their performances and create new opportunities.

CONCLUSION

The purpose of this study was to better understand how to explore some practices of knowledge strategy in the hospital organizations. It was chosen to research the cardiology services from the perspective of knowledge barriers and knowledge enablers investigating the medical protocol implementation. Considering that the best a leader can do is to enable knowledge, this study proposed to recognize specific conditions in the hospital context that were required to create and transfer knowledge.

Eight hospitals were studied in the "cardiology field", which is recognized in the health environment as the one with access to the same medical protocols and which uses them in accordance with the different characteristics of the organizations. This study was characterized by the interdisciplinary conceptual exercise, establishing a connection between the science of administration and health science, founded on knowledge management strategy in relation to Based-Evidence Medicine (BEM).

Different barriers and enablers were found in the hospital context, such as:

a) The difficulty of the hospital directors and medical leaders to translate the medical services and to strategically align with them. This barrier is detected by the absence of communication of the strategic intentions of the hospitals regarding the use of protocols and which have an impact on the sharing of new knowledge.

b) The hole of information technology in relation to hospitals' knowledge strategy is perceived as a knowledge enabler. Even though, it is merely understood as an administrative tool that supports the use of medical protocols on the day-by-day activities.

c) In all hospitals the common language is mentioned as an advantage to share information, but the conversations among different professionals are not managed as a knowledge enabler.

The organizational context required to promote practices of knowledge strategies in hospitals was analyzed in four critical dimensions: managing conversations, resources integration, knowledge content and dynamic capability. The managerial capacity has been used to manage conversations to promote codified language among the personnel. When the content is related to strategic topics to implement advancement strategies, there is a lack of sharing which could be improved with the commitment of the personnel. The strategic content of knowledge can be managed to encourage a sharing context which could access new strategic opportunities.

Regarding managerial contributions, there is a new opportunity for hospital organizations to manage knowledge as a strategic asset, which is well-known as the business core of clinical services. We proposed a framework for the promotion of the required organizational context regarding the creation and transference of knowledge during the protocol implementation in the cardiology services.

The main contribution of this study is directed to the health system in as much as it tried to characterize how the use of medical protocols can be developed to promote best practices of knowledge strategy. The approach of this study is not one of competition among hospitals. The more knowledge can be acquired and transferred, the more health problems will be solved in the society. The health management, applying knowledge strategy concepts, can be a particular managerial alternative for creating and transferring innovative solutions to complex problems.

REFERENCES

Alavi, M., & Leidner, D. (2001). Review: Knowledge management and knowledge management systems: Conceptual foundations and research issues. *MIS Quarterly, 25*(1), 107–136. doi:10.2307/3250961

Berwick, D. (1996). A primer on leading the improvement of systems. *BMJ (Clinical Research Ed.), 132*, 619–622.

Blackler, F. (1995). Knowledge, knowledge work and organizations: An overview and interpretation. *Organization Studies, 16*, 1021–1046. doi:10.1177/017084069501600605

Bosi, M., & Mercado-Martinez, F. (2004). *Pesquisa qualitativa de serviços de saúde.* Rio de Janeiro, Brazil: Vozes.

Bukowitz, W. R., & Williams, R. L. (2000). *The knowledge management fieldbook*. London: Pearson Education Limited.

Coffey, R., Richards, J., Remmert, C., Leroy, S., Schoville, R., & Baldwin, P. (2005). An introduction to critical paths'. *Quality Management in Health Care*, *1*, 46–55.

Crossan, M., Lane, H., & White, R. (1999). An organizational learning framework: From intuition to institution. *Academy of Management Review*, *24*(3), 522–537. doi:10.2307/259140

Dosi, G., Nelson, R. R., & Winter, S. G. (2000). *The nature and dynamics of organizational capabilities*. New York: Oxford University Press.

Drummond, J., Silva, E., & Coutinho, M. (2002). *Medicina baseada em evidências: Novo paradigma assistencial e pedagógico*. São Paulo, Brazil: Atheneu.

Eden, C., & Ackermann, F. (1998). *Making strategy: The journey of strategic management*. London: Sage Publications.

Eisenhardt, K. M. (1999). Strategy as strategic decision making. *Sloan Management Review*, *40*(3), 65–73.

Gladstein, D., & Quinn, J. (1985). Making decisions and producing action: The two faces of strategy. In J. M. Pennings et al. (Eds.), *Organizational strategy and change*. San Francisco: Jossey-Bass Inc.

Grant, R. M. (1997). The knowledge-based view of the firm: Implications for management practice. *Long Range Planning*, *30*(3), 450–454. doi:10.1016/S0024-6301(97)00025-3

Guptill, J. (2005). Knowledge management in health care. *Journal of Health Care Finance*, *31*, 10–14.

Hansen, M., Nohria, N., & Tierney, T. (1999). What's your strategy for managing knowledge? *Harvard Business Review*, (March-April): 106–116.

Ichijo, K., Krogh, G., & Nonaka, I. (1998). Knowledge enablers. In G. Von Krogh, J. Roos, & D. Kleine (Eds.), *Knowing in firms*. London: SAGE Publications.

Ketchen, D., Thomas, J., & Mcdaniel, R. (1996). Process, content and context: Synergistic effects on organizational performance. *Journal of Management*, *22*, 231–257. doi:10.1016/S0149-2063(96)90048-3

Laverde, G. P. (2003). *Administração hospitalar*. Rio de Janeiro, Brazil: Guanabara Koogan.

March, J. G. (1999). The pursuit of organizational intelligence. MA: Blackwell Publishers Inc.

Mintzberg, H. (1987). The strategy concept I: Five ps for strategy. *California Management Review*, (Fall).

Nonaka, I., Krogh, G. V., & Aben, M. (2001). Making the most of your company's knowledge: A strategic framework. *Long Range Planning*, *34*, 421–439. doi:10.1016/S0024-6301(01)00059-0

Nonaka, I., & Takeuchi, H. (1995). *The knowledge creating company*. New York: Oxford University Press.

Nonaka, I., Von Krogh, G., & Voepel, S. (2006). Organizational knowledge creation theory: Evolutionary paths and future advances. *Organization Studies*, *27*, ll79–ll1208. doi:10.1177/0170840606066312

Parker, R., & Rea, L. (2000). *Metodologia de pesquisa: Do planejamento à execução*. São Paulo, Brazil: Pioneira.

Pettigrew, A., & Whipp, R. (1994). Managing the twin processes of competition and change – the role of intangible assets. In P. Lorange, B. Chakravarthy, J. Roos, & A. Van de Ven (Eds.), *Implementing strategic processes: Change, learning and cooperation*. Cambridge, MA: Blackewell Business.

Pór, G. (1995). The quest for collective intelligence. In K. Gozdz (Ed.), *Community building – renewing spirit & learning in business*. San Francisco: Sterling & Stone.

Prahalad, C. K., & Hamel, G. O. (1990). The core competence of the corporation. *Harvard Business Review, 68*, 79–91.

Provonost, P., Nolan, T., Zegwe, S., Miller, M., & Rubin, H. (2004). How can clinicians measure safety and quality in acute care. *Lancet, 363*, 1061–1067. doi:10.1016/S0140-6736(04)15843-1

Sackett, D. (2003). *Medicina baseada em evidências: Prática e ensino*. São Paulo, Brazil: Artmed.

Sackman, S. A. (1991). *Cultural knowledge in organisations –exploring the collective mind*. London: SAGE Publications.

Selznick, P. (1957). *Leadership in administration: A sociological interpretation*. New York: Harper and Row.

Sewell, N. (1997). Continuous quality improvement in acute health care, creating a holistic and integrated approach. *International Journal of Health Care Quality Assurance, 10*, 20–26. doi:10.1108/09526869710159598

Snowden, D. (2002). Complex acts of knowing: Paradox and descriptive self-awareness. *Journal of Knowledge Management, 6*(2), 100–111. doi:10.1108/13673270210424639

Spender, J.-C. (1996). Making knowledge the basis of a dynamic theory of the firm. *Strategic Management Journal, 17*, 45–62.

Spender, J.-C. (1998). The dynamics of individual and organizational knowledge. In C. Eden & J.-C. Spender (Eds.), *Managerial and organizational cognition theory, methods and research*. London: SAGE Publications.

Spender, J.-C., & Grant, R. (1996). Knowledge and the firm: Overview. *Strategic Management Journal, 17*, 5–9.

Teece, D. J., Pisano, G., & Shuen, A. (1997). Dynamic capabilities and strategic management. *Strategic Management Journal, 18*, 509–533. doi:10.1002/(SICI)1097-0266(199708)18:7<509::AID-SMJ882>3.0.CO;2-Z

Venzin, M., Krogh, G. v., & Roos, J. (1998). Future research into knowledge management. In G. v. Krogh, J. Roos, & D. Kleine (Eds.), *Knowing in firms, understanding, managing and measuring knowledge*. London: SAGE Publications.

Von Krogh, G., Ichijo, K., & Nonaka, I. (2000). *Enabling knowledge creation: How to unlock the mystery of tacit knowledge and release the power of innovation*. Oxford, UK: Oxford University Press.

Weick, K. E. (1995). *Sensemaking in organizations*. London: SAGE Publications.

Whittington, R. (2006). Completing the practice turn in strategy research. *Organization Studies, 27*, 613–634. doi:10.1177/0170840606064101

Wiig, K. M. (1993). *Knowledge management foundations: - Thinking about thinking – how people and organizations create, represent and use knowledge*. Arlington, TX: Schema Press.

Winter, S. G. (2000). The satisfying principle in capability learning. *Strategic Management Journal, 21*, 981–996. doi:10.1002/1097-0266(200010/11)21:10/11<981::AID-SMJ125>3.0.CO;2-4

Wit, B., & Meyer, R. (1998). *Strategy: Process, content, context*. London: International Thomson Business Press.

Yin, R. (1994). *Case study research: Design and methods*. Thousand Oaks, CA: SAGE Publications.

Zack, M. H. (1999a). Managing codified knowledge. *Sloan Management Review, 40*, 45–58.

Zack, M. H. (1999b). Developing a knowledge strategy. *California Management Review, 41*(3).

Chapter 10
Knowledge Cultures, Competitive Advantage and Staff Turnover in Hospitality in Australia's Northern Territory

Kalotina Chalkiti
Charles Darwin University, Australia

Dean Carson
Charles Darwin University, Australia

ABSTRACT

This chapter investigates the strategies used by hospitality businesses in the Northern Territory (NT) of Australia to remain competitive in the face of high rates of staff turnover. The authors suggest it could be beneficial to foster a symbiotic relationship between staff and knowledge retention with an explicit focus on the social aspects of managing knowledge in a hospitality environment. The authors propose a knowledge mobilization or flow strategy to complement staff and knowledge retention strategies. Creating and sustaining a competitive advantage through knowledge management (KM) practices that recognize the industry's specific context and allow it to compete for customers and staff in the global marketplace is imperative for the NT hospitality sector. The proposed strategy could make hospitality businesses more adaptable in the face of staff turnover and more flexible by fostering a context that nurtures the mobilization or flow of disparate and person specific knowledge. This chapter describes and critically reviews what is known about staff turnover in hospitality, the case study destination and its hospitality sector. Semi-structured interviews with 13 managers of hospitality businesses and representatives of industry organizations and the destination marketing organization (DMO) in the NT revealed current and desired strategies for managing turnover as well as how turnover affects relationships, knowledge management and idea generation.

DOI: 10.4018/978-1-60566-790-4.ch010

INTRODUCTION

Competition in the tourism marketplace becomes more intense as the destination matures (Butler, 1998). This is the case for tourism in Australia, which is exposed to increasing pressures from rising fuel prices, the preference of Australians to travel overseas rather than within their own country, declines in traditionally important markets in Europe and Asia, and the emergence of nearby countries (China, Viet Nam, etc) as competing destinations. Maintaining a competitive advantage, both as an individual business within a destination and as a destination-based collection of businesses within the global tourism marketplace, is likely to be dependent on the ability to manage knowledge and support innovative strategies (Poon, 1993; Carson & Macbeth, 2005).

Accommodation businesses are at the heart of tourism systems. It is the presence of overnight accommodation as part of a trip away from home that distinguishes tourism from other travel. The capacity of accommodation businesses to manage knowledge is influenced by the characteristics of their workforce, and particularly by the high levels of staff turnover that have been attributed to high levels of casual staffing, relatively low salaries, and poor pathways for career development (Akrivos et al., 2007). The strategies to deal with staff turnover have in the past mainly focused on increasing retention and improving recruitment practices (Zhang & Wu, 2004). However, the literature has more recently suggested alternative or additional strategies that recognize the inevitability of continuing high turnover rates. These strategies seek to embrace the regular influx of new ideas that come with new people (Johannessen et al., 2001) and attempt to retain context and person specific knowledge that will enable businesses to compete in an environment of constant change.

This chapter investigates the strategies used by hospitality businesses in the NT of Australia to remain competitive in the face of inevitable staff turnover. The Territory's hospitality industry is made up of mostly small and medium sized enterprises (ABS, 2007), while tourists are attracted by the destinations experiential feel, remoteness, tropical and desert surroundings. The Territory is an interesting case because its small size, remoteness, and subsequent exposure to greater internal and external competition exaggerate the need to build effective knowledge cultures within the industry. The NT has a seasonal tourism trade, with the summers (November – April) being hot and dry in the south and hot and wet in the north, and the winters (May – October) more mild in climate and attractive for visitors.

We propose a management strategy that accepts the inevitability of staff turnover, the difficulties in externalising knowledge as a way to manage staff turnover and the need for hospitality employees to act proficiently from the very first minute they enter the business. It could be beneficial to foster a symbiotic relationship between staff and knowledge retention by focusing on the social aspects of managing knowledge in a hospitality environment. This can be achieved through a knowledge mobilization or flow strategy to complement staff and knowledge retention strategies. As observed by Seufert et al (1999) *"what is of prime importance is that [knowledge] creation and sharing processes are encouraged not just the accumulation of data"* (p. 183). Following on from Seufert et al's work, this strategy pinpoints the importance of sharing knowledge in labour dynamic industries. Creating and sustaining a competitive advantage through knowledge management (KM) practices that recognize the industry's specific context and allow it to compete for customers and staff in the global marketplace is imperative for the NT hospitality sector. The proposed strategy could make hospitality businesses more flexible and adaptable to change by fostering a context that nurtures the mobilization or flow of disparate and person specific knowledge to enable businesses to compete. Therefore, even though this chapter investigates staff turnover, a pure human resource management (HRM) topic, it explicitly looks at how hospitality businesses can ensure their KM processes are not impeded by HRM issues that create labour dynamic environments.

This chapter describes and critically reviews what is known about staff turnover in hospitality, the case study destination and its hospitality sector. Semi-structured interviews with 13 managers of hospitality businesses and representatives of industry organizations and the destination marketing organization (DMO) in the NT revealed current and desired strategies for managing staff turnover. In addition, the findings provide evidence on how staff turnover impacted peer relationships, knowledge management and idea generation, thus offering a fresh and potentially value adding research focus. These findings were critiqued against the literature to assess the extent to which NT hospitality businesses are able to remain locally and globally competitive while working with the inevitability of staff turnover. A knowledge mobilization/flow strategy is proposed. If used with staff and knowledge retention strategies it could make hospitality businesses flexible, responsive and competitive in the face of certain, predictable and inevitable staff turnover. Finally, directions for future research are suggested.

The NT is a special case study combining a number of interesting features. Tremblay (2005) summarised the supply and demand features the NT offers. It is geographically isolated which suggests more manageable spatial boundaries, has reasonable tourism resources that develop tourism offerings and attracts a mixture of market segments. As a tourism destination, the NT offers well known attractions that are highly accessible and unique in nature. A combination of small and medium sized enterprises under independent or international conglomerate governance offers memorable guest experiences. Additionally the NT is known for its transient character primarily because of its sheer geographical remoteness. From a tourist perspective, visitors tend to use

the NT as a hub while passing through from Asia to Australia; similarly tourism labour use the NT as a short term career or life experience stop. Combining, the aforementioned, the NT is a case-location where turnover patterns and consequences manifest in more extreme forms than other destinations.

Methods

Primary data were collected from hospitality businesses located in the NT of Australia through semi-structured interviews over a period of three months (May, June, and July, 2008). Initial contact with the businesses was made through telephone calls. We asked to speak to the general managers or the human resource managers; after introductions and information about the study, interviews were booked.

Our sample comprised of 13 respondents; two key industry bodies and 11 businesses. The businesses represented various hospitality sectors (e.g. accommodation, restaurants) and were located in three NT areas, namely Darwin, Kakadu and Alice Springs. Respondents held managerial positions (e.g. general manager, human resource manager); the majority of them had undergraduate and postgraduate qualifications, had been employed in the sector for more than five years and for less than two with the business they represented. The hospitality businesses targeted their sales and marketing efforts towards the luxury tourism market and operated all year round. Businesses were independently managed and owned, some of the accommodation businesses were part of international corporate chains.

The interviews lasted for approximately 20 minutes. Respondents' perceptions were sought on 5 staff turnover related questions:

1) magnitude of staff turnover in their business;

2) main reasons causing staff turnover;

3) main consequences of staff turnover;

4) ways to manage the occurrence and consequences of staff turnover;
5) other important human resource
challenges.

We were particularly interested in the consequences of staff turnover in the areas of peer
relationships/interactions and knowledge management. Although respondents were not directly
asked about these areas, the majority of respondents referred to them throughout the interview.
However, there were respondents who did not refer
to them at all. In these cases the chief investigator
prompted them to comment on the importance of
both peer relationships and knowledge management in their work environment and how they
were affected in the presence of staff turnover.
Interviews were audio recorded, giving the chief
investigator the opportunity to review the interviews as often as needed. Each interview was
reviewed at least twice to ensure data reliability
and minimize potential interviewer bias effects.

Staff Turnover in Hospitality

Increasing high rates of staff turnover have become
a feature of most industries particularly in developed nations (Saxenian, 1994; Cooper, 2001). The
global causes include increasing labour mobility
stimulated by high rates of post-secondary attainment and low rates of unemployment. Tourism
is a typical example; turnover contributes to the
industry's labour and service volatility (Hjalager
& Andersen, 2001; Birdir, 2002; Zhang & Wu,
2004; Marhuenda et al., 2004; Akrivos et al., 2007;
Zopiatis & Constanti, 2007). The same applies in
the Australian and NT hospitality sector. The 2006
Labour Mobility Survey in Australia (ABS, 2006)
reported that nearly 40% of all people employed in
the accommodation sector stayed in their jobs for
less than one year. People entering employment
were as likely to come from some other sector as
to have been previously employed in hospitality.
The rest of this section provides a critical literature

review of the causes, consequences and ways to
manage staff turnover in the hospitality sector and
in particular the NT.

Causes

The reasons contributing to the heightening and
ultimately the inevitability of staff turnover can
vary depending on the type of turnover, the context
of the industry sector and location of the business.
Documented causes of staff turnover generally
conform to the major theories of migration (Lee,
1966). Push factors operate to reduce dissatisfaction with existing circumstances, and pull factors
operate to suggest increased satisfaction arising
from a change of circumstances. Factors may be,
among other things, economic or social. Economic
drivers include the guarantee of improved conditions and the perception that the opportunity for
improved conditions will exist (Ranis & Stewart,
2006). Social causes of staff turnover have been
documented as including a desire to move closer to
family and friends, the desire for lifestyle changes
throughout an individual's life cycle, and the
desire to avoid risk or unpleasant circumstances
(Vaugeois & Rollins, 2007). Social and economic
causes of staff turnover may manifest themselves
in different ways in different work places.

In hospitality, commonly cited causes of staff
turnover include the low specialisation of skills
and limited opportunities for career progression
(Hartman & Yrle 1996; Deery & Shaw, 1997;
Ladkin & Juwaheer, 2000; McCabe & Savery,
2007), seasonal changes in work availability, and
the use of tourism jobs (which are often part-time
or casual as well as seasonal) as a source of income
while actively pursuing alternatives (through
education) or taking a '*career break*' (Vaugeois
& Rollins, 2007). Other causes are related to an
enterprise's social context (e.g. peer relationships,
family relationships or labour) (Krackhardt &
Porter, 1986; Birdir, 2002; Carbery & Garavan,
2003), labour motivations (Milman, 2003; Martin,
2004) and an overall dissatisfaction with tourism

employment (e.g. financial rewards).

NT DMO and industry organisations related staff turnover in the NT to the tendency of tourism labour to pursue travel, work and living experiences. The desire of a working holiday where people travel to places, experience the lifestyle and meet new people through work suggests the recruitment of tourism labour may continue to be relatively easy (Mohsin, 2003a). What will continue to challenge businesses though is the capacity to sustain a desirable number of employees to enable the continuous operations of businesses– how long before employees decide to pack up, travel to a new place and experience a different lifestyle? The location of the business may offer some guidance as to how frequently or under which circumstances tourism workers may come and go both from the business but also the region. The NT offers a combination of remote (rural) and city (urban) hospitality businesses where turnover in the former occurs more frequently than the latter. Additionally, the financial attractiveness of other industries the region has to offer (e.g. mining) compared to the low pay and other peculiar employment characteristics of the tourism industry can further amplify voluntary exits from the industry as a whole.

A better in-depth feel of the factors contributing to the inevitability of staff turnover in the NT were provided by the hospitality businesses. The causes of voluntary staff turnover could be summarized in four categories: a) personal, b) hotel, c) industry, and d) destination specific. With regards to the personal reasons, employees were attracted to and left the Territory for career progression opportunities. Considering the intense competition in hospitality businesses in bigger Australian cities and the less frequent promotional opportunities within businesses, employees with career prospects in hospitality considered moving to the Territory for a short while (up to 24 months) to gain work experience and move up a couple of hierarchical ranks before moving to bigger cities. Others left to move closer to friends, family, and

pursue travel-work-lifestyle experiences, while others referred to conflicts between peers (e.g. management and owners; supervisor and employees or amongst employees). The inherent limitations of the hospitality industry (e.g. low financial rewards, emotional burnout, and unsociable hours) triggered exits from the industry and in some cases the region too. Finally the Territory's remoteness and isolation caused accessibility difficulties but most importantly contributed to the blurring of work and play in highly remote tourism destinations (e.g. Kakadu, Jabiru). The sheer remoteness amplified the emotional burnout of peers who interact 24/7 with guests and colleagues. Similar findings were reported by city based businesses too. The majority of the employees came from southern Australian states and had no pre-existing social support networks (e.g. family, friends). Therefore, employees would tend to interact with each other, both professionally and socially; suggesting the blurring of work and play even in lesser remote locations (e.g. Darwin).

CONSEQUENCES

Businesses

The financial implications of staff turnover have been summarized in the literature as separation, replacement, training and lost productivity costs (Hinkin & Tracey, 2000). The impact of such costs is felt more in businesses operating seasonally, just like the NT. Seasonal businesses have comparatively less time (usually 6 months) to operate, which makes it essential to proficiently train new employees in a timely fashion to commence their responsibilities and minimize the possibilities of compromising the delivery of experiences. Interestingly, our interview findings confirmed that financial implications were important but businesses had not assessed the magnitude of the financial loss. Similarities have been identified in the literature too; for example, Pizam and

Thornburg (2000) confirmed that the *"majority... never computed the average costs of employees or managers turnover"* (p. 216).

Remaining Employees

A different angle to interpret staff turnover consequences was suggested in the 1980s. Mowday (1981), Mowday, Steers and Porter (1982), Dalton and Krackhardt (1983) and Krackhardt and Porter (1985; 1986) suggested that staff turnover affects the people remaining within the hospitality and service businesses. Mowday (1981) argued that remaining employees' perception to work affected the way they interpreted their colleague's exit thus influencing the way they themselves were affected by turnover. This demonstrated that although staff turnover removed an employee from the work environment; employee exits influenced the perceptions and employment orientations of those who stayed. Similarly Dalton and Krackhardt (1983) argued that staff turnover caused some form of disruption and urged research attention towards a qualitative evaluation; looking at *"who"* has left as opposed to *"how many"* actually left. His work suggested that depending on who leaves the businesses, the impact of staff turnover on remaining employees varied. Lastly, significant contributions came from Krackhardt and Porter's work (1985; 1986) on the topology of staff turnover consequences. They demonstrated that turnover affected a group of related employees, a *"social network"* because *"a person leaving creates a hole in the network, no matter what the reason"* (p. 52). These findings strengthened the idea that *"turnover is concentrated in patterns that can be delineated in a network...as opposed to randomly throughout a work group"* (p. 54). The importance of this work is that it suggests and enables us to strategically act upon staff turnover. Krackhardt and Porter (1985; 1986) contribute by enlightening us with the topological feel of staff turnover. As opposed to trying to win the staff turnover battle as a whole, now turnover can be monitored and studied in concentration...exactly where it occurs and knowing who or where it is most likely to affect.

With the turn of the century, Rowley and Purcell (2001) confirmed Krackhardt and Porters (1985; 1986) findings on the topological occurrence (employee networks) and consequences of staff turnover (morale, idea generation), while Cho et al. (2006) suggested that staff turnover contributed to an employee's emotional instability in a hospitality business. Work in this stream has shown that staff turnover affects employees who remain with businesses; while the way they are affected depends on how they relate to an exiting peer (e.g. friends) and how they interpret their exit (e.g. dissatisfaction with the business). Unfortunately, hospitality research has paid little attention to the applicability and further investigation of these findings. In other words, research investigating the topological consequences of staff turnover in hospitality businesses is limited.

NT Hospitality Sector

Taking into consideration the aforementioned literature, we sought the NT hospitality businesses perspective. NT hospitality businesses explained that staff turnover affected peer networks at two levels, namely: a) peer to peer relationships; b) business to customer relationships. At a hierarchical or department level, respondents referred to friendship relationships to explain how staff turnover affected group behaviour. When peers are friends or relate in ways other than professional, an unexpected absence or turnover of one tends to influence similar behaviours. For example, *"if someone goes, they all go"..."one wants to finish earlier, they all want to finish the same time"* (Business A). Absenteeism or turnover occurring in groups or networks of peers relating in similar ways (e.g. communication) has been discussed in Krackhardt and Porter (1985; 1986). They studied staff turnover in a communication network and found that *"staff turnover snowballs... turnover* does not occur randomly throughout a work group....it is concentrated in patterns that can be delineated by role similarities" (Krackhardt & Porter, 1986; p. 54). In other cases, turnover made peer collaboration difficult because group dynamics changed. Staff turnover changed peer to peer relationships which in turn introduced changes to the way peers collaborated. Similar findings have been reported; for example *"the loss of workmates can lower morale further amongst those who stay behind...and can impair the effectiveness of the team"* and overall can be *"disruptive for continuing staff"* (Rowley & Purcell, 2001; p. 164; p. 172). In the case of business and customer relationships, loyal guests may witness a constant change in the employees they interact with. For example, guests might be required to deal with someone who does not remember their name or other guest specific information that contribute to memorable guest experiences. For some guests this might suggest a compromise in the flawless personalized service they have experienced up to now, resulting in less loyal clientele; this is known as the subliminal effect (Manley, 1996).

A Network Perspective

Fundamental to the interpretation of staff turnover as having inherently positive or negative impacts on the KM processes is an understanding of how social networks contribute to managing knowledge and what impacts staff turnover might create. Given the popularity of team based organisational structures (Lee & Moreo, 2007, p. 58) employees form and participate in networks for reasons such as their common participation in *"production processes"* (e.g. production and delivery of experiences) or due to common perceptions or beliefs. As networks foster processes such as information sharing, knowledge creation, idea generation and so on; they are considered to be *'transactive knowledge systems'* (Wegner, 1987 in Cross et al., 2001, p.216). Unfortunately networks are not fully depicted in formal organi-

sational structures, and it is often those outside the organisational structures which significantly influence work processes and outputs (Cross et al., 2001). For example, the exit of an employee who is a popular source of advice may disrupt the network by affecting its performance (Staw, 1980). Formal organisational structures present only the professional relationships of peers, but peers relate in a multitude of interdependent ways in a work environment (e.g. professional, social). This gives employee networks both a social and a professional facet which cannot be ignored. Peers can trust one another, socialise, share information and so on; these associations are not necessarily depicted in formal organizational structures. The existence and interdependency of these relationships can positively or negatively influence business performance (Robins & Pattison, 2006).

From a negative aspect, some consider knowledge to be embedded in a network of employees, and it is claimed that disrupting the network fundamentally degrades facets of knowledge; such as loss of *"corporate memory"* (Adams, 1995). NT DMO and industry organizations argued that the constant movement of employees and the lack of formalized knowledge management practices contributed to knowledge attrition. However, the negative effect of knowledge attrition varied, depending on the hierarchical level of the employees. Should management staff exit the business, knowledge attrition might create more of an impact compared to operational staff. Similar findings have been extensively documented (e.g. Cotton & Tuttle, 1986; Carbery & Garavan, 2003). Such knowledge attrition consequences had been felt by NT hospitality businesses too. However, respondents also commented on the detrimental loss of other types of knowledge; for example, the loss of *"people and/or collaboration knowledge"*. Knowing with who to collaborate and how to collaborate with peers had a positive influence in the work environment. Knowing who to contact, knowing what knowledge/expertise they have, knowing how and when to approach them are further examples. Given that hospitality businesses heavily rely on peer collaboration to deliver experiences, the loss of *"people and/or collaboration knowledge"* can be detrimental. Another type of knowledge respondents frequently referred to was the loss of *"place or local"* knowledge; for example, sightseeing suggestions, history of the region, bus stops and so on. The recruitment of non-Territorians and the frequent turnover of employees meant that new employees required time to familiarize themselves with the area and acquire local knowledge; something that in turn impacted guest experiences. When asked to comment on the importance of both *"people and/or collaboration"* and *"place/local knowledge"* types compared to the standard product knowledge of businesses, respondents believed that product and place/local knowledge were required. However, *"people and/or collaboration knowledge"* was more important as it gave employees the opportunity to operate as proficiently as possible in a short space of time.

It's not all that bad though. On a positive note, there is literature suggesting that knowledge, skills and experience across the organisation can actually be enhanced by a certain level of staff turnover (Johannessen et al, 2001). New people bring with them experiential knowledge, relationships, networks and other social capital that can add to the businesses knowledge base and help build competitive advantage. Competitive advantage can be enhanced by importing knowledge from elsewhere into the business, from other regions, from competitor businesses, and from outside the sector completely (Mu et al., 2008). Even by displacing people from the existing work group, either because of their poor performance or because they move to a new position (inside or outside the business) businesses can connect disparate employees who hold distinct and value adding skills or can give access to other networks (Burt, 2001). Some countries promoting out-migration of skilled workers rely on such strategies to receive direct and indirect remittances (Mendola, 2006). NT

hospitality businesses reported similar benefits. When asked to compare between the innovative capabilities of high turnover teams, respondents confirmed that despite formally encouraging idea generation through corporate programs, most ideas originated from new employees. Thus turnover may have a positive effect. A number of reasons explained this. New employees tend to be more innovative or creative due to their need to prove their capabilities. Others bring in a wealth of work and life experience, attitude and so on. Similar characteristics were reported by Mohsin (2003b). Apart from turnover, the idea generation potential of businesses and employees can be enhanced through other, less obvious causes of change: for example, flexible labour strategies that aim to provide labour support in a Just-In-Time (JIT) fashion (Lai & Baum, 2005). Such staffing changes positively contributed by introducing *"different skills and experience"*, thus giving teams and businesses the ability to be more creative and have more ideas (Lai & Baum, 2005). This suggests that NT hospitality businesses that made extensive use of casual staff but also a rotating roster with compositionally different shifts - both daily and weekly - facilitated the combination of *"different skills and experience"* which led on to new ideas. These findings could perhaps reveal the innovative potential NT hospitality businesses have because of staff turnover, the mode of operation (e.g. shiftwork) as well as the characteristics of tourism labour. The NT is known to attract a labour force that has embarked on a travel, lifestyle and work experience journey (Mohsin, 2003). For some, this is not temporary; moving from one place to another for the sake of experiencing the way of life, interacting with new people and engaging in new or alternative employment is a way of life. Therefore, in the case of the NT, the reported creativity of new employees and the ability of businesses to generate new ideas due to frequent staff turnover could be explained by labour force characteristics (Mohsin, 2003; Carson, 2008). However, even in the absence of turnover, other, more subtle and less visible forms of change (shifts, casual staff) bearing the aforementioned experiential labour characteristics positively contributed to the NT hospitality idea generation.

MANAGEMENT

The literature proposes three ways to manage staff turnover, namely through: a) retaining staff, b) retaining knowledge, and c) enterprises social context.

Staff Retention

This section summarises the key literature in favour of retaining staff as a way to control turnover. However, the published literature fails to recognize and consider the inherent dynamic nature of the hospitality industry labour force. Labour force factors like turnover, casual staff or shiftwork increase the volatility of businesses. The case deteriorates in the NT, an Australian region known for its transient labour force. Therefore, for NT hospitality businesses, researchers who aim to minimize turnover solely from an HR perspective (staff retention) fail to accept the transitivity of the NT tourism labour and the other factors (shifts) creating similar labour volatility. Should they do so, they will be able to progress discourse and help businesses "*exploit*" the limited tenure of employees from a KM perspective. Knowing employees will leave the business and the NT, finding ways for them to contribute to the KM processes of a business holds more potential than trying to retain them.

Businesses have been trying to manage turnover by retaining staff through personal development programs; financial rewards, training, and improved recruitment processes (Deery & Shaw, 1997; MacHatton & Dyke, 1997; Woods et al., 1998; Rowley & Purcell, 2001; Lynn, 2002; Joliffe & Farnsworth, 2003; Lai & Baum, 2005; Cho et al., 2006; McCabe & Savery, 2007 and Wildes, 2007).

In Australia, Deery and Shaw (1997) explored the concept of turnover culture from the perspective of the employees in Australian hotels; arguing that employees leave for career progression reasons or industry/job dissatisfaction. They suggested training and career progression opportunities as a way of retaining employees. Davies et al (2001) explored the effect of appraisal, remuneration and training on reducing hotel turnover; showing that only product related training reduced turnover. In 2006, the Tourism and Transport Forum of Australia released a report on staff turnover in the hotel sector, arguing that the low specialisation of skills, the seasonality of the sector, and the limited opportunities for career progression often drove employees to consider hotels as a stepping stone when in need of a career break. The report argued that what is needed is a long term strategic approach to structure a labour supply strategy for the industry as a whole. McCabe and Savery (2007) investigated labour mobility of managers in the convention and exhibition industry. They found that managers "*flutter*" from business to business or department to department for career progression reasons, suggesting it might be viable to offer career progression opportunities to employees. Poulston (2008) examined common hospitality problems (e.g. staff turnover) with the aim of identifying relationships between them and concluded that training can reduce staff turnover. Dickson and Huyton (2008) investigated the extent to which welfare and human resource management impacts on customer service in an Australian ski resort. However, they addressed only the blurring of work and play between employees and customers as opposed to peer to peer. They suggested that staff retention for seasonal employees can be ensured through company and regional factors (e.g. living conditions, pay, management skills and employment conditions). Overall, focus in this literature is primarily on retaining staff through personal development opportunities.

NT DMO and industry organizations reported that investing in professional development opportunities may effectively control or minimize staff turnover. For example, both businesses and industry bodies can look at a) creating a highly skilled workforce; b) accessing quality employment; c) better workforce planning; d) expanding the traditional workforce; and e) offering accreditation programs and industry awards to promote excellence through knowledge management practices (i.e. adoption of best practices). The literature makes similar suggestions (Birdir, 2002), especially for a region like the NT. The NT reportedly is a workforce training and development career stop. As referred to previously, the majority of the respondents were from southern Australian cities. They were attracted to the NT on "*a short term pain but long term gain*" mission. They recognized the transiency of hospitality labour and acted upon it strategically. Their short term stay in the NT (short term pain) would give them a career boost that could be quantified in two to three hierarchical promotions. This would give them the opportunity to pursue better employment opportunities at their preferred locations (e.g. Asia, southern Australian cities), therefore giving them a long term gain. However, given the heightening occurrence of voluntary staff turnover, strategies promoting career progression opportunities might encourage employees to stay longer but not forever; suggesting that resources in this respect could be wasted (Dalton & Krackhardt, 1983).

NT hospitality businesses frequently resorted to staff retention strategies due to the labour shortage the region is already experiencing. Certain businesses paid particular attention to their recruitment strategies. Some recruited internally or from social and professional networks. Sourcing staff internally was frequently used because employees recognized that not everyone is suitable for certain jobs. Businesses offered intra-departmental transfers to employees who were underperforming or wanted to leave. This strategy aimed to exhaust all possibilities of retaining staff considering the difficulty of sourcing staff from a labour market experiencing substantial shortages. They specifi-

cally looked for ambitious employees with a long term focus in hospitality, living in the NT and attributes/qualities such as leadership, mannerism and so on. Given the transient nature of the NT, for most businesses, the willingness to live in Darwin and the NT was highly valued. Others paid particular attention to training programs. As the majority of the respondents were members of larger, international corporations with standardized training programmes, the content of training programmes was delivered in-house. Other businesses adopted a rather direct or aggressive approach to minimizing staff turnover. Some customize their employment contracts to include "*lock in*" clauses; for example fixed employment tenure (e.g. 18 months, 3 years). The contractual agreements were used by businesses which had sourced labour from neighbouring countries (e.g. the Philippines). Finally, some businesses engaged in flexible labour strategies (casual staff) to balance irregular demand and staff turnover. The use of casual staff is not a novelty for Australia as the extensive use of casual staff in the Australian hotel industry was reported by Timo (2001). Hiring casual staff was acknowledged as a well-suited and cost effective solution, especially for NT businesses experiencing radical demand fluctuations and seasonality. Cost effectiveness was the main benefit respondents referred to and is congruent with literature findings (Lai & Baum, 2005; Lee & Moreo, 2007). Our findings reported similar benefits deriving from casual staff employment, such as Lai and Baum (2005) who considered "*Just-in-Time labour*" as a way to increase "*the capacity for innovation*" in a hospitality enterprise because casual staff "*can bring different skills and experience to the work situation*" (p. 98). Although our respondents who made extensive use of the services of casual staff referred to innovation or idea generation benefits, these benefits were inferior when they considered the large scale negative implications of flexible labour strategies. Respondents explained that casual staff have a short term focus on hospitality and their current job. Casual work for them is just a way to supplement their income. They are not familiar with the business culture, missions, values or clientele, and less interested in commenting on current practices and offering new, fresh ideas. Casual staff can jeopardize service and experience quality as they do not relate to a business culture or values and lack *"people and/or collaboration"* and *"product knowledge"*. Given that *"people and/or collaboration knowledge"* act in a catalytic way towards connecting and enabling the function of peer networks, but require time to develop, casual staff could perhaps impede a businesses operations.

What was encouraging though was that NT businesses are recognizing the importance of peer relationships as a facilitator of new employee adaptation. For example, acknowledging how daunting it could be for young individuals to move to another, remote area just like the NT, many businesses provided support networks to new employees. When they recruited through corporate programs (e.g. gap year or university career placements), the businesses raised familiarity between new recruits by sending them group emails. In these cases businesses had the mediatory role of relationship building between new employees who would have to live in a new place away from home and their social and family support networks and work with other employees. Such efforts enabled the adaptation of new employees to the NT and the new work environment. Similarly, few businesses that acknowledged the impact of staff turnover on collaboration knowledge ensured they enlightened employees on this aspect during their orientation or socialization programs. These activities aimed to radically help peers establish temporal support networks with other peers, in the hope of helping them adapt and extend their stay with the business and the NT.

Knowledge Retention

Very little of the published literature reports the effectiveness of staff retention strategies. The limited reported success of staff retention strategies (Woods et al., 1998) have made businesses look for other methods to manage staff turnover. Retaining staff knowledge (Rowley & Purcell, 2001; Hjalager & Andersen, 2001) has been a popular strategy representing an advancement to minimizing staff turnover through staff retention (Bonn & Forbringer, 1992; Chapman & Lovell, 2006). Focus on retaining knowledge has evolved from researchers who argued that businesses wanting to remain competitive ought to differentiate, lock in customers and streamline processes through knowledge. As products, services and processes in a hospitality environment are standard yet volatile, knowledge can help businesses differentiate and become competitive. For example, services can become more personalized through their transformation to experiences and increase guest loyalty. Advocates of this view such as Hjalager and Andersen (2001) suggested that, as staff cannot be retained, there is a *"need for a better understanding...to create and maintain repositories of knowledge and competence, strategies that are possibly less dependent on the availability of human resources with tourism specific qualifications...it is what management can do to hold on to non trivial and enterprise specific knowledge"* (p. 116; 126).

Implications of knowledge loss depend on its content or substance that varies between hierarchical levels (Carbery & Garavan, 2003). Hjalager and Andersen (2001) referred to *"non trivial and enterprise specific knowledge"* but failed to elaborate on the actual content of knowledge. With their reference to *"non trivial and enterprise specific"* knowledge we assume they referred to knowledge specifically concerning the product and enterprise as an employer (e.g. long or short term focus). They proposed the use of *"semi manufactured items, components, software packages and capital equipment"* that embed knowledge so that *"even under conditions of rapid staff turnover and somewhat persisting low skills, crucial knowledge can be preserved in the enterprise - employees cannot easily take embedded knowledge with them when they leave"* (p. 126). This line of work supports the extensive work on the technological aspect of knowledge management (Adamides & Karacapalidis, 2006) which argues that knowledge can be managed through software programs and so on. Knowledge management research in tourism though still remains understudied and we do not have substantial literature on the effectiveness of such technological solutions (Scarbrough, 2001; Lundvall & Nielsen, 2007). Considering that Australian tourism businesses have been considered as slow adopters of knowledge management processes (Cooper, 2006,; this begs for more work on the knowledge management processes of Australian hospitality businesses.

NT hospitality businesses deploy knowledge retention strategies too. However, they suggested that externalising and recording an employee's knowledge has proven to be ineffective. Many respondents mentioned that they purposively kept the contact details of employees who left because, even though they recorded the content and process of their work /role in a detailed manner, remaining employees that had taken over the new role had difficulty following the recorded work instructions. In such cases, businesses contacted the ex-employees to obtain clarifications or tips. That was because externalized knowledge lacked what they referred to as the *"human factor"*. When asked to elaborate, the respondents explained that the *"human factor"* is made up from an employee's life, work and travel experiences; these attributes are what make an employee and their knowledge distinct and value adding to the workplace and team yet difficult to externalize and record. In this vein, respondents suggested that a sole focus on recording work instructions, especially in a hospitality business which relies more on people and/or collaboration, is ineffective.

As the hospitality industry delivers experiences, time is of utmost importance. Speed and responsiveness enhanced with product/work knowledge enable peers to deliver memorable experiences. In hospitality the seamless and time efficient delivery of an experience is just as important as the knowledge substance or content of the experience. The latter is partially provided by recording work instructions. Partially provided because the *"human factor"* is what adds the finishing touch to a guest experience. The former though is indifferent to recorded product knowledge; it relies on what respondents referred to as *"people and/ or collaboration knowledge":* knowing who to contact, how to collaborate, when and so on. Of course these types of knowledge are difficult to record primarily because of their dynamic character. These have been referred to as relational characteristics (Borgatti & Cross, 2003) that are dynamically co-constructed from peer interaction (Carley & Krackhardt, 2001). Therefore, they are fluid and subject to peer interaction which makes them almost impossible to record.

Our findings validate published literature suggesting that knowledge retention strategies are problematic. For example, there is work suggesting the detrimental effect towards a sole focus on managing tourism knowledge through Information and Communication Technologies (ICT). ICTs ignore the human, social and personalised aspect of tourism enterprises. Of course turning towards knowledge retention is an advancement considering the inevitability of staff retention, but to what extent can knowledge be effectively retained? There is a significant amount of literature (Peroune, 2007) explaining how externalised and recorded knowledge is of lesser value compared to context and person specific knowledge. Research work in favour of knowledge retention disregards the importance of peer interaction in the work environment; which makes us wonder; *What happens to group or relational knowledge? What happens when employees leave, employees who know how to work with their peers...how is that knowledge preserved?...can employees store their personal and relational knowledge in ICTs... can this knowledge ever be recorded and if it was how quickly could employees pick it up to operate?* The element of time and speed becomes critical in hospitality environments in a state of constant flux. In this case, it could be that *"people and/ or collaboration knowledge"* can facilitate the timely and seamless operation of highly dynamic hospitality environments.

Change of Focus

Encouragingly, in light of the ineffectiveness of knowledge retention strategies, NT hospitality businesses referred to the importance of peer relationships in the work environment. In particular, the participants argued in favour of managing or monitoring peer relationships as a way of minimising the consequences of and working with staff turnover.

The diversity of hospitality employees made peer relationships critical for the creation and delivery of experiences because experiences are the product of formal and informal, visible and invisible, diverse and interdependent relationships. Relationships created a friendly and cooperative atmosphere which in turn created a relational bond between peers. This relational bonding facilitated effective and efficient collaboration and coordination because of the familiarity and comfort employees would feel. They knew how to work with each other, knew *"what ticks them off"* and so on. For example, this bonding enabled cross departmental cooperation, information sharing and created synergies from the combination of diverse employment backgrounds and skills. These findings are in accordance with work from Borgatti and Cross (2003) who argued that *"less attention has been paid to learned characteristics of relationships that affect the decision to seek information from other people"* (p. 432). Their work highlighted the role of three relational characteristics that predict the behaviour of seeking

or sharing information, namely: a) knowing what another person knows, b) valuing what that other person knows in relation to one's work and c) being able to gain timely access to that person's thinking. These are relational characteristics that are learnt from the social interaction of peers. However, Borgatti and Cross (2003) suggest that these relational characteristics predict the behaviour of information seeking or sharing. Whether peers will seek or share information is not solely dependent on addressing these relational characteristics as there might be other motivations beyond the availability of relational characteristics and not of interest in this book chapter. Nonetheless, this line of work lays the foundation that, in dynamic environments like hospitality where staff turnover is one cause of change and fluidity (others being casual or shift work etc), these relational characteristics could play a facilitating role in sharing knowledge. Therefore, in highly mobile or turnover environments finding ways to foster the co-construction of relational characteristics or knowledge could help businesses implement a knowledge flow or mobilization strategy.

On another note, relationships also helped monitor staff turnover. Knowing the types and interdependencies of relationships among peers, businesses could hypothesize when turnover would occur or where turnover would impact. Similar patterns of behaviour (e.g. absenteeism, low productivity) emerged within groups of related employees. These findings are in accordance with other work that suggested the topological occurrence and consequences of staff turnover in groups of related employees (Krackhardt & Porter, 1985; 1986).

Given the importance businesses attributed to peer relationships, we asked businesses how they managed relationships in the work environment. Respondents explained that their approach to fostering and managing peer relationships varied in two ways: a) by hierarchical level and b) by the duration of peer interaction. From a hierarchical perspective, peer relationships were encouraged and nurtured within departments but not so much across hierarchical levels. The reason was that it was necessary to sustain boundaries of authority such as between supervisors and staff. Depending on the duration of peer interaction in the work environment, peer relationships required to be "*refreshed*" or "*built*". For example, in remotely located resorts (e.g. Kakadu), peers interact both throughout their work day but also during personal time (blurring work and play). In these cases, relationships need to be "*refreshed, rejuvenated*" as peers tend to "*get bored with each other*" or "*need a change*" (Business B). Similarly, in less remote areas where peers were not limited to social interaction with other peers, relationships had to be "*built*" or initiated to foster a collaborative environment but also to act as a support network to employees who were away from home. Respondents cited some specific strategies used to manage peer relationships. Various social events (e.g. Christmas parties) gave peers the opportunity to interact on a social level. These events raised peer familiarity which contributed to the welcoming of new employees in a group of existing peers while relationally aligning and ironing out relational barriers between existing peers (e.g. putting faces to names etc). A more formalized approach to relationship building or relational alignment was facilitated through shift work. Many businesses had a number of different shifts during the day and changed the composition of shift teams on a daily basis. This provided the opportunity for employees to work for different time lengths throughout the week with different peers. Although shift work served convenient purposes for some businesses, others purposively used shift work in two ways: a) for peer to peer relationship building; and b) to enable the cooperation of diverse personalities and expertise to enhance group learning and idea generation.

In summary, the published literature focuses on the causes, consequences and management of staff turnover. Firstly, turnover has been mostly voluntary triggered by career progression op-

portunities (Deery & Shaw, 1997; Ladkin & Juwaheer, 2000; McCabe & Savery, 2007) and social context (Pizam & Thornburg, 2000; Birdir, 2002; Milman, 2003; Martin, 2004; Karatepe & Uludag, 2008). Secondly, it has been argued that turnover affects the people remaining with the business. Mowday (1981) argued that the orientation to work of remaining employees affects the way they interpret their colleagues' exit. Dalton and Krackhardt (1983) argued that staff turnover caused some form of disruption and urged research attention towards *who* is leaving and not *how many* are leaving. Krackhardt and Porter's work (1985; 1986) suggested that turnover affected employees related in many ways (e.g. friends). These findings have been confirmed in recent research (Rowley and Purcell, 2001; Cho et al., 2006). Thirdly, the occurrence and consequences of staff turnover have been managed in three ways: a) retaining staff, b) retaining knowledge and c) managing employees' social context. Staff are retained through personal development programs; financial rewards, training and so on (Deery & Shaw, 1997; MacHatton & Dyke, 1997; Woods et al., 1998; Rowley & Purcell, 2001; Lynn, 2002; Joliffe & Farnsworth, 2003; Lai & Baum, 2005; Cho et al., 2006; McCabe & Savery, 2007). Other businesses retain knowledge (Rowley & Purcell, 2001; Hjalager & Andersen, 2001) but fail to offer a definitive solution (Polanyi, 1966). Findings from our interviews with NT hospitality businesses suggest there is a need to study the way employees relate in a work environment. It may be that understanding how peers relate and collaborate in a dynamic work environment could offer some direction as to how to organise and manage hospitality businesses in light of certain, predictable and inevitable staff turnover. Our focus is not to minimize or eradicate staff turnover but to find ways for businesses and peers to continue being operational throughout inevitable staffing changes. The findings accentuate the importance of peer relationships in light of inevitable turnover and socially motivated tourism labour. Such findings become more evident and require urgent attention in tourism destinations like the NT. The region's location, the remoteness of social and family support coupled with the social motivations of its tourism labour suggest that peer relationships in NT hospitality businesses play a catalytic role in the sector's performance.

COMPETING IN THE FACE OF HIGH STAFF TURNOVER: THE SYMBIOSIS OF KNOWLEDGE RETENTION AND MOBILIZATION/FLOW STRATEGIES

Even though studies on staff turnover in the NT hotel sector are limited, it is likely that the general patterns observed in other destinations are even more extreme in the Territory. This is because of the remoteness and isolation of the NT. Many peculiarities of the NT accentuate the special attention it requires which can be attributed to its peripheral tourist destination characteristics (Lee-Ross, 1998). In remote and peripheral destinations, *"obtaining and long term retaining of trained and experienced staff may be very difficult"* (Hohl & Tisdell, 1995; p. 519). In this respect, high levels of turnover in the NT become inevitable, explained by its *"degree of geographical isolation"* as it is situated at some distance from places of economic isolation (Kvist & Klefsjo, 2006; p521). Employees who are used to working and living in larger cities tend to find their adaptation to a considerably smaller place more difficult for a number of reasons (e.g. cost of living). Overall, the NT hospitality sector is likely to be more susceptible to staff turnover consequences because of the region's remoteness, and high influx of employees seeking work, travel and living experience, and transfers due to better career opportunities (high wages, working hours), emotional labour, training pressures and social life (Mohsin, 2003c).

Our research in the NT emphasizes what has been reported in the staff turnover literature. Staff turnover is seen as a major challenge, and its consequences are related directly to knowledge management and the ability for hospitality businesses to remain operational and deliver memorable experiences. It is important to stress that under the pressures of change through turnover; hospitality businesses must not only struggle to sustain competitiveness, but most importantly should strive to remain operational. For a business to continue functioning, disparate knowledge stocks must interact to fulfill tasks; in other words – to make things happen. Capitalizing on these stocks, to create new and more value adding knowledge will make them innovative and competitive. Therefore, remaining operational is a prerequisite to becoming innovative and competitive. In this respect, there appears to be a reluctance to accept high rates of staff turnover as a normal part of doing business in the sector and in the NT. Most strategies are still aimed at improving retention of staff, even though managers admit that these strategies have limited impact. Many of the reasons why people leave the sector are beyond the control of the employers themselves – hospitality businesses offer round the clock employment, casual employment and low skilled employment which is ideal for students working part-time, and for people (particularly young people) in career transition or taking a '*gap year*' and the like. The hospitality sector is labour intensive but with relatively low yields meaning that jobs are low paid and labour conditions change according to seasons. Apart from turnover being inevitable, it is also predictable to an extent. Depending on the season, their social relationships or the location; staff will always come and go. The international literature shows consistent patterns of turnover and lengths of employment, which makes it easy to identify exit points for individual staff (when they finish their university degree or their gap year, for example). Therefore, contrary to Hinkin and Tracey (2000) who suggested that hospitality businesses *"have an opportunity to gain competitive advantage by [staff] retention and develop-*

ment" (p. 20), the ineffectiveness of staff retention strategies and the inevitability of staff turnover in the NT urge us to revisit the knowledge attrition repercussions of staff turnover. This will allow us to find ways to give guidance to businesses that rely on employees to successfully delivery KM processes to remain operational and, in turn, to help hospitality businesses. Attention must be drawn to the ways knowledge is managed, to ensure it a) never stagnates and retains its value adding qualities, and b) it is mobilized in time to benefit businesses. In a state of constant labour change and intensified competition, hospitality businesses must mobilize or make knowledge flow to remain operational while capitalizing on it to remain competitive.

So how do NT hospitality businesses manage knowledge in a labour dynamic environment? Hospitality businesses in the NT recognize that knowledge management processes are among the key impacts of staff turnover. Considering the limited attention paid to such strategies in the management and academic literature (Hinkin & Tracey, 2000), the reported lack of formal or proactive knowledge retention strategies in the NT hospitality sector came as no surprise. Knowledge was managed through reactive and ad-hoc approaches. For example, respondents worked closely with the employee scheduled to leave to externalize and record their knowledge. Frequently though, the recorded knowledge was not of much help to the remaining employees. This was because the externalized knowledge covered facets of processes which could be externalized but lacked the value adding and competitive qualities an employee's expertise and experience attributes to the knowledge. This validates Polanyi's (1966) renowned phrase *"we know more than we can tell"*. The knowledge we hold enables us to fulfill our tasks to the desirable standards set by our employer; however, trying to explain and record the *"secrets"* or *"tips"* to our success is not feasible. On the contrary, when externalizing and recording our knowledge we

usually disclose or are only able to disclose a small percentage of what we know. Therefore, considering this difficulty to externalize person or context specific knowledge which in itself is what adds value to a business and contributes to its competitiveness, continuing to solely focus on externalizing and recording product knowledge may not be advisable. Although product knowledge may create the hospitality experience, it is *"people and/or collaboration knowledge"* that creates the experience. In this vein, *"people and/or collaboration knowledge"* can make businesses operating in labour dynamic environments more flexible and adaptable.

Dalton and Krackhardt (1983) argued that flexibility is imperative for businesses that want to manage staff turnover. In this vein, the tourism and hospitality literature on flexibility and adaptability can be summarized in two schools of thought. The first one denotes flexibility as deriving from the social interaction of peers (Woods et al., 1998; Rowley & Purcell, 2001) while the other suggests flexible staffing strategies (Jolliffe & Farnsworth, 2003; Lai & Baum, 2005). The latter is a derivative of tried and tested staff retention strategies, while the former suggests an alternative focus, that of focusing on peer relationships to find ways to achieve *"flexibility"* that will enable hospitality businesses to continue functioning irrespective of staff turnover.

Peer relationship or *"relational flexibility"* plays a catalytic role in hospitality businesses and complements product knowledge retention. Although product knowledge may offer the content of the hospitality experience, it is peer relationship or relational flexibility that enables employees to put product knowledge into play and deliver experiences. The question though is: *What are the components or facilitators of peer relationship or "relational flexibility?*

A number of researchers addressed the need for flexibility in hospitality businesses and proposed ways to do so. Woods et al (1998) suggested businesses could respond through *"socialisa-*

tion programs" to help new employees get accustomed to their new working environment. They addressed the need to raise awareness and familiarity between the new employee and the new work environment but did not elaborate on the agenda of the *"socialisation program"*. In this vein, Rowley and Purcell (2001) referred to the *"social benefit"* of training and development as they strengthen social ties between peers which in turn facilitate a better understanding of the businesses goals. Social ties benefit peers by enabling them to collectively understand how to function as a team while adhering to the goals of the business. Jolliffe and Farnsworth (2003) proposed a continuum of HRM strategies to deal with the peculiarities of seasonal employment. Businesses challenging seasonality have more of a long-term focus on staff retention, recruitment and so on. On the contrary, businesses embracing seasonality resort to casual employment, multi-tasking and so on. Lai and Baum (2005) suggested the importance of flexible labour strategies as a solution to the inability to retain staff by arguing that the *"challenge for management is how to maintain flexibility in relation to both scheduling and reaction to demand fluctuations in hotel operations"* (p.87). In anticipation of irregular demand, businesses have to adapt their *"production system"* and their labour force through *"multi tasking, cross training and flexible work hours"* or externally through Just-In-Time hiring. Given the centrality of peer interaction in hospitality businesses, how do these strategies address the need to work together, interact and collaborate? Flexibility is more than just becoming proficient in a colleague's tasks; it is about knowing how to work together. Similarly, targeting labour flexibility on a JIT basis through external sources (casual staff) creates similar concerns. Although casual staff are hired as and when needed, giving businesses the opportunity to manage costs, such external labour sources might equally strain the hotel's operational flexibility. This is because casual staff, apart from lacking similar relational,

collaboration or interaction flexibility, also lack an understanding of the enterprise's mission, culture and so on. Lai and Baum (2005) and Jolliffe and Farnsworth, (2003) focus on *"labour"* flexibility as a way to fill in or take up new employees as and when the situation arises. However, is this an effective or viable way to manage seasonality? It might be worth shifting the focus from flexible staffing solutions towards flexibility in peer relationships. Therefore, in labour-dynamic environments where businesses compete through their ability to manage knowledge, flexible peer relationships can help support the knowledge management processes of the NT hospitality sector. The social interaction of peers positively contributes to the creation and updating of relational characteristics (e.g. know how) that in turn support peer relationships and promote their flexibility. As networks are dynamic (Seufert et al., 1999), changes in social interaction will consequently change those relational characteristics that facilitate the mobilization or flow of knowledge. This suggests that, apart from networks being dynamic, the factors (relational characteristics) contributing to the flexibility and adaptability of a business are dependent on peer interaction. However, this line of research begs for further empirical investigation.

In the meantime, how can hospitality businesses continue to manage knowledge in labour-dynamic environments? We embrace the idea that staff turnover is inevitable and that businesses have to find ways to work with it. Irrespective of short or long tenure, hospitality employees come and go. Therefore, in anticipation of certain and predictable turnover, we are interested in exploring the facilitating role of flexibility in such a dynamic industry to foster knowledge management processes such as sharing knowledge. Businesses need to find ways to a) *"exploit"* employees' skills, diversity or relationships during their short tenure, and b) ensure their operations remain unaffected (in negative ways) by staff turnover. Doing so will help businesses with knowledge management processes such as knowledge creation. Central to this is the need to explore, describe and understand how we can "*exploit*" the tenure of employees to ensure that even during their brief stay and employment in the NT, they positively contribute to knowledge management processes. This can strengthen the competitive advantage of hospitality businesses as they will foster some form of flexibility within their teams or team based operations that will enable them to counter-balance knowledge related staff turnover consequences. Our data suggests that peer relationships and the "*social benefits*" they create could be the key towards achieving flexibility that will continue to support knowledge management processes. Given the difficulty in retaining staff, we suggest businesses should tap into other strategies to become dynamic and competitive. "*Social benefits*" can help build dynamic and flexible work environments while promoting relational characteristics that seem to facilitate KM processes such as knowledge sharing. The creation and strengthening of social ties between peers will increase their "*people and/or collaboration knowledge*" and enable them to interact and collaborate with peers in a shorter timeframe. Indeed, the need to focus on peer relationships as the facilitator of knowledge sharing in the hospitality sector is accentuated in the literature. Given that tourism labour purposively seeks social interactions, potential lies in the ways peers relate as a way to "*exploit*" their capabilities during their tenure with the business. The idea of focussing on peer relationships and interaction as a way to build people/collaboration knowledge and enable the seamless cooperation of peers, even when staff turnover is a reality, is strengthened by literature that describes tourism staff as highly individualistic personas. Employees matching this profile are in need of satisfying their social and lifestyle aspirations through their employment. Therefore, they are more than likely to purposively strike up a multitude of relationships, as work for them has a different meaning; it's a lifestyle choice...an outlet to fulfil their ego-social

motivations. Chapman and Lovell (2006) accept the inevitability of staff turnover and in light of sustaining operational business and service levels; they suggest the idea of an attitudinally and behaviourally flexible hospitality workforce as a way to remain competitive. For Chapman and Lovell (2006), flexibility has a different meaning; they consider flexibility through the attitudinal and behavioural qualities of hospitality employees as the key towards the "*social awareness and flexibility of trainees in preparing for careers in this complex industry*" (p.80). This book chapter and proposed KM strategy extends this proposition by suggesting that attitudinally and behaviourally flexible peers can positively support KM practices in highly dynamic environments. For example, Wildes' (2007) research in US hospitality found that younger age groups found the presence of "*fun*" an important aspect in their work life. Unfortunately the authors do not provide any further information or explanation for the substance of "*fun*". We assume fun depends on the composition of work teams so is highly dependent on the individuals as personalities and the ways they relate to each other. Fun denotes more of a social substance in peer relationships. Although not clearly stated, the reference to "*fun*" could suggest a different or an additional form of peer relationships (e.g. friends, romantic) and the presence and importance of such relationships in the workplace. The authors refer to the "*fun*" environment as a staff turnover moderator but, in light of certain turnover, how is the "*fun*" environment affected and/or how is an employee's performance impeded? Similar ideas have been proposed by Lee and Moreo (2007) who addressed the need to understand the diverse nature of seasonal hospitality employees. They suggest that seasonal workers perceive different social and moral values. This group of workers is in search of pleasure experiences while having diverse characteristics (e.g. work experience, place of origin). In this vein, enterprises should work on socialisation processes to satisfy the social interaction aspirations of workers but also to bridge interaction and collaboration among peers.

From the above, we can distinguish two different strategies towards business flexibility. The first one denotes flexibility deriving from the social interaction of peers (Woods et al., 1998; Rowley & Purcell, 2001) while the other suggests flexible staffing strategies (Jolliffe & Farnsworth, 2003; Lai & Baum, 2005). We believe the latter is a derivative of the tried and tested staff retention strategies, while the former suggests an alternative focus, that of focusing on peer relationships to find ways to achieve "*flexibility*" that will enable the KM processes of hospitality businesses to continue functioning irrespective of staff turnover. Similar suggestions have been made by Seufert et al. (1999) who provided a conceptualization of a knowledge network and suggested that attitudinal or behavioural factors such as "care" enable KM processes such as knowledge sharing.

The findings from the NT provide a unique perspective. Attention must be given to ways to mobilize or facilitate the flow of product knowledge which can be supported by people and/ or collaboration knowledge. While most of the literature looked at staff and knowledge retention and development strategies towards managing the KM implications of turnover, the balance is now shifting towards the consideration of knowledge mobilization strategies. In practice, businesses should pursue a mix of strategies. Apart from being concerned about their staff's well being, the direct costs of turnover (recruitment and training) and that some level of staff turnover is inevitable and beneficial (Dalton & Krackhardt, 1983; Saxenian, 1994), they also recognize that knowledge management processes such as knowledge sharing cannot be separated from peers. On the contrary, knowledge is context and person specific; therefore, sharing knowledge that occurs in certain hospitality contexts also depends on peers but not on peers in isolation, rather on peer interaction. Peer interaction produces peer relationship or relational knowledge. Relational knowledge can have the capacity of connecting

knowledge and making it interact. Therefore, finding ways to mobilize and share these person specific knowledge stocks irrespective of the time peers will spend in a business or the NT is imperative and seems to be related to relational characteristics produced by peer interaction. In this vein, we propose a knowledge mobilization or flow strategy to manage the KM consequences of staff turnover. What is critical in an environment of constant and predictable turnover, where employees and the groups they participate in are diverse in nature and central to the operation of a hospitality business, is to find ways to mobilize the diverse and disparate stocks of knowledge of individuals. Seufert et al. (1999) suggested that "*the key to obtaining long term competitive advantage is not to be found in the administration of existing knowledge but in the ability to constantly generate new knowledge...*" (p. 183); this argument has been supported in the work of Von Krogh (1998) and Von Krogh et al., (2001). Our proposed KM strategy acknowledges their work but suggests taking a step back. In sectors experiencing various forms of labour changes (e.g. turnover, casual staff, shifts etc), creating new knowledge to become competitive is desirable but, prior to striving for competitiveness, businesses ought to remain operational. The symbiosis of knowledge retention and mobilization/flow strategies is not necessarily stabilising – its purpose is to work with inevitable levels of staff turnover and enable hospitality businesses to continue functioning and competing irrespective of labour changes. The symbiosis aims to make the KM processes of hospitality businesses flexible and adaptable in relation to how hospitality businesses can support KM processes in mature and labour dynamic environments. Mobilising the knowledge and making it flow between peers, throughout the group and the business will allow hospitality businesses to achieve collective outcomes and create a sustainable competitive advantage (Cross et al., 2001; Robins & Pattison, 2006).

CONCLUSION

It is imperative for researchers and businesses to accept the inevitability of staff turnover. We have enough evidence to argue that staff turnover cannot be eradicated. In this vein, businesses have two options….live with it or perish. From the scant evidence on the effects of staff turnover on KM and peer relationships and the unique perspective offered by the NT hospitality sector, it would be extremely narrow minded to disregard their potential and continue wasting resources to eradicate it. Businesses must find a way to continue competing irrespective of the presence of staff turnover, and academics through their research ought to suggest ways of doing so. Future work should take on more of a qualitative and longitudinal approach to the KM consequences of staff turnover. Unfortunately we know a lot about the financial, time and service quality implications of staff turnover but very little when it comes to how remaining employees are affected and how these changes affect the way businesses manage knowledge.

In this vein, given the socially driven motivations of hospitality employees, we assume they relate both professionally and socially in the work environment and the content and interdependencies of these relationships play a part in their performance (Robins & Pattison, 2006). Seufert et al (1999) concluded that *"connectivity to a network and competence of managing networks have become key drivers"* (p. 184). Therefore, in businesses where employees hold a central role, their performance depends on the way they interact and share knowledge with their peers and they purposively initiate and foster social relationships… we ask…how does staff turnover affect the way peers relate?…the way they share knowledge… and most importantly how do we manage these implications and ensure KM processes of hospitality are minimally disrupted?

This aspect has attracted little attention but nonetheless the value adding potential of this approach has been indirectly denoted in a few research papers. For example, Carbery and Garavan (2003) found that cognitive and psychological dimensions trigger managerial turnover in hotels by looking at how the individual's views and perceptions towards employment or their employer triggered turnover. However, they did not consider the influence of peers on an individual's cognitive and psychological cognitions. This cannot be ignored in hospitality, where employees participate and interact in dynamic teams to deliver experiences; cognitive and psychological cognitions are formed and reformed at a group level. In this case, *"how would staff turnover affect an individual's or a team's cognitive and psychological dimensions and therefore performance?"*. Similarly, Watson (1994) referred to the socially created orientations to work through interaction both within and outside the work environment, something Martin (2004) has partially explored by having investigated an employee's orientation to hospitality employment, demonstrating how orientations underpin attitudes to stay and behaviour in the work environment. Employees are drawn to a hospitality business by the social context it provides. The social context of a business is formed both internally (peer relationships) or externally (friendship, relatives). For example, Martin (2004) referred to how orientations to work might change depending on circumstances within work a possible *"circumstance"* could be the exit of staff and the introduction of new. In this case, staff turnover might alter an individual's orientation to work (like vs. dislike) or peer relationships (exit of friends). Finally, Karatepe and Kilic (2007) and Karatepe and Uludag (2008) work can equally apply to tourism employees who live, work and socialize together. Their research from hotels in Jordan, Turkey and Cyprus found that work-family conflict increased the turnover intention of staff. We hypothesize that conflict arising between peers who share a house or work together could possibly have similar implications and trigger turnover. This is common in remote tourism locations where employees live and work together. Karatepe and Kilic (2007) and Karatepe and Uludag (2008) stressed the need for family friendly work practices and an overall attention to the personal and family needs of employees; we suggest similar action should be taken in the case of peers who live and work together. Their work indirectly connects personal relationships to professional behaviour (e.g. sharing knowledge), performance and turnover consequences, which is of course worthwhile to study. However, we suggest reversing the argument and ask *"how does staff turnover affect employees' personal or professional relationships"*, and *"how do these relationship changes affect their contribution to the KM processes of a business such as sharing knowledge and competitiveness?"*

FUTURE RESEARCH DIRECTIONS

Future research should study a hospitality department or a group of employees to advance our knowledge on the presence, importance and ways to manage *people or collaboration knowledge*. This is because *"social networks are powerful forces in organisations, forces that influence micro level motives as well as more aggregated phenomena"* (Krackhardt & Porter, 1985; p. 260). Due to the complexity of such a research project, a longitudinal study with frequent data collection phases would be the preferred approach while semi-structured interviews and observation are the desired data collection techniques. Given the inevitability of staff turnover and other *indirect* causes of disruption (e.g. shiftwork, casual staff), it would be interesting to study the adaptation mechanisms or strategies of employees. Understanding how employees adapt to constant change could inform business processes and strategies. Such findings can enable hospitality businesses to become flexible with regards to how people work together, exploring, describing and analysing the ways remaining employees adapt to radical or less radical changes.

Finally, we will continue researching this area to identify desirable implementation factors for the proposed knowledge flow or mobilization strategy.

REFERENCES

Adamides, E., & Karacapalidis, N. (2006). Information technology support for the knowledge and social processes of innovation management. *Technovation, 26*, 50–59. doi:10.1016/j.technovation.2004.07.019

Adams, S. (1995). The corporate memory concept. *The Electronic Library, 13*(4), 309–312. doi:10.1108/eb045380

Akrivos, C., Ladkin, A., & Reklitis, P. (2007). Hotel managers' career strategies for success. *International Journal of Contemporary Hospitality Management, 19*(2), 107–119. doi:10.1108/09596110710729229

Australian Bureau of Statistics. (2007). *NT at a glance*. Retrieved August 10, 2008, from http://www.abs.gov.au

Birdir, K. (2002). General manager turnover and root causes. *International Journal of Contemporary Hospitality Management, 14*(1), 43–47. doi:10.1108/09596110210415123

Bonn, M. A., & Forbringer, L. R. (1992). Reducing turnover in the hospitality industry: An overview of recruitment, selection and retention. *International Journal of Hospitality Management, 11*(1), 47–63. doi:10.1016/0278-4319(92)90035-T

Borgatti, S. P., & Cross, R. (2003). A relational view of information seeking and learning in social networks. *Management Science, 49*(4), 432–445. doi:10.1287/mnsc.49.4.432.14428

Burt, R. S., & Schott, T. (1985). Relation contents in multiple networks. *Social Science Research, 14*, 287–308. doi:10.1016/0049-089X(85)90014-6

Butler, R. (1998). Seasonality in tourism: Issues and implications. *Tourism Review, 53*(3), 18–24. doi:10.1108/eb058278

Carbery, R., & Garavan, T. N. (2003). Predicting hotel managers' turnover cognitions. *Journal of Managerial Psychology, 18*(7), 649–679. doi:10.1108/02683940310502377

Carley, K., & Krackhardt, D. (2001). *A typology for network measures for organizations.* Retrieved August 10, 2008, from http://www.casos.cs.cmu.edu/bios/carley/working_papers.php

Carson, D. (2008). The 'blogosphere' as a market research tool for tourism destinations: A case study of Australia's NT. *Journal of Vacation Marketing, 14*(2), 111–119. doi:10.1177/1356766707087518

Carson, D., Boyle, A., & Hoedlmaier, A. (2007, March). *Plan or no plan? The flexibility of backpacker travel in Australia.* Paper presented at CAUTHE 2007, Australia.

Carson, D., & Macbeth, J. (Eds.). (2005). *Regional tourism cases: Innovation in regional tourism.* Altona, Australia: Common Ground Publishing.

Chapman, J. A., & Lovell, G. (2006). The competency model of hospitality service: Why it doesn't deliver. *International Journal of Contemporary Hospitality Management, 18*(1), 78–88. doi:10.1108/09596110610642000

Cho, S., & Woods, R. H., SooCheong, J., & Mehmet, E. (2006). Measuring the impact of human resource management practices on hospitality firms' performances. *International Journal of Hospitality Management, 25*(2), 262–277. doi:10.1016/j.ijhm.2005.04.001

Cooper, C. (2006). Knowledge management and tourism. *Annals of Tourism Research, 33*(1), 47–64. doi:10.1016/j.annals.2005.04.005

Cooper, D. (2001). Innovation and reciprocal externalities: Information transmission via job mobility. *Journal of Economic Behavior & Organization, 45*, 403–425. doi:10.1016/S0167-2681(01)00154-8

Cotton, J. L., & Turtle, J. M. (1986). Employee turnover: A meta analysis and review of implications for research. *Academy of Management Review, 11*, 55–70. doi:10.2307/258331

Cross, R., Borgatti, S., & Parker, A. (2001). Beyond answers: Dimensions of the advice network. *Social Networks, 23*, 215–235. doi:10.1016/S0378-8733(01)00041-7

Dalton, D. R., & Krackhardt, D. M. (1983). The impact of teller turnover in banking: First appearances are deceiving. *Journal of Bank Research, 14*(3), 184–192.

Davies, D., Taylor, R., & Savery, L. (2001). The role of appraisal, remuneration and training in improving staff relations in the Western Australian accommodation industry: A comparative study. *Journal of European Industrial Training, 25*(7), 366–373. doi:10.1108/EUM0000000005837

Deery, M. A., & Shaw, R. N. (1997). An exploratory analysis of turnover culture in the hotel industry in Australia. *International Journal of Hospitality Management, 16*(4), 375–392. doi:10.1016/S0278-4319(97)00031-5

Dickson, T. J., & Huyton, J. (2008). Customer service, employee welfare and snowsports tourism in Australia. *International Journal of Contemporary Hospitality Management, 20*(2), 199–214. doi:10.1108/09596110810852177

Hartman, S. J., & Yrle, A. C. (1996). Can the hobo phenomenon help explain voluntary turnover? *International Journal of Contemporary Hospitality Management, 8*(4), 11–16. doi:10.1108/09596119610119930

Hinkin, T. R., & Tracey, J. B. (2000). The cost of turnover. *The Cornell Hotel and Restaurant Administration Quarterly*, *41*(3), 14–21.

Hjalager, A. M., & Andersen, S. (2001). Tourism employment: Contingent work or professional career? *Employee Relations*, *23*(2), 115–129. doi:10.1108/01425450110384165

Hohl, A., & Tisdell, C. (1995). Peripheral tourism: Development and management. *Annals of Tourism Research*, *22*(3), 517–534. doi:10.1016/0160-7383(95)00005-Q

Johannessen, J., Olaisen, J., & Olsen, B. (2001). Mismanagement of tacit knowledge: The importance of tacit knowledge, the danger of information technology and what to do about it. *International Journal of Information Management*, *21*, 3–20. doi:10.1016/S0268-4012(00)00047-5

Johannessen, J. A., Olsen, B., & Lumpkin, G. T. (2001). Innovation as newness: What is new, how new, and new to whom? *European Journal of Innovation Management*, *4*(1), 20–31. doi:10.1108/14601060110365547

Jolliffe, L., & Farnsworth, R. (2003). Seasonality in tourism employment: Human resource challenges. *International Journal of Contemporary Hospitality Management*, *15*(6), 312–316. doi:10.1108/09596110310488140

Karatepe, O. M., & Kilic, H. (2007). Relationships of supervisor support and conflicts in the work-family interface with the selected job outcomes of frontline employees. *Tourism Management*, *28*(1), 238–252. doi:10.1016/j.tourman.2005.12.019

Karatepe, O. M., & Uludag, O. (2008). Affectivity, conflicts in the work-family interface, and hotel employee outcomes. *International Journal of Hospitality Management*, *27*(1), 30–41. doi:10.1016/j.ijhm.2007.07.001

Krackhardt, D., & Porter, W. E. (1985). When friends leave: A structural analysis of the relationship between turnover and stayers attitudes. *Administrative Science Quarterly*, *30*, 242–261. doi:10.2307/2393107

Krackhart, D., & Porter, W. E. (1986). The snowball effect: Turnover embedded in communication networks. *The Journal of Applied Psychology*, *71*(1), 50–55. doi:10.1037/0021-9010.71.1.50

Kvist, A., & Klefsjo, B. (2006). Which service quality dimensions are important in inbound tourism?: A case study in a peripheral location. *Managing Service Quality*, *16*(5), 520–537. doi:10.1108/09604520610686151

Ladkin, A., & Juwaheer, T. D. (2000). The career paths of hotel general managers in Mauritius. *International Journal of Contemporary Hospitality Management*, *12*(2), 119–125. doi:10.1108/09596110010309925

Lai, P. C., & Baum, T. (2005). Just-in-time labour supply in the hotel sector: The role of agencies. *Employee Relations*, *27*(1), 86–102. doi:10.1108/01425450510569328

Lee, C., & Moreo, P. J. (2007). What do seasonal lodging operators need to know about seasonal workers? *International Journal of Hospitality Management*, *26*(1), 148–160. doi:10.1016/j.ijhm.2005.11.001

Lee, E. (1966). A theory of migration. *Demography*, *3*, 47–57. doi:10.2307/2060063

Lee-Ross, D. (1998). Comment: Australia and the small to medium-sized hotel sector. *International Journal of Contemporary Hospitality Management*, *10*(5), 177–179. doi:10.1108/09596119810227703

Lundvall, B., & Nielsen, P. (2007). Knowledge management and innovation performance. *International Journal of Manpower*, *28*(3/4), 207–223. doi:10.1108/01437720710755218

Lynn, M. (2002). Turnover's relationships with sales, tips and service across restaurants in a chain. *International Journal of Hospitality Management, 21*(4), 443–447. doi:10.1016/S0278-4319(02)00026-9

MacHatton, M. T., & Dyke, T. V. (1997). Selection and retention of managers in the US restaurant sector. *International Journal of Contemporary Hospitality Management, 9*(4), 155–160. doi:10.1108/09596119710185837

Manley, H. (1996). Hospitality head hunting. *Australian Hotelier*, 8-11.

Marhuenda, F., Martinez, I., & Navas, A. (2004). Conflicting vocational identities and careers in the sector of tourism. *Career Development International, 9*(3), 222–244. doi:10.1108/13620430410535832

Martin, E. (2004). Who's kicking whom? Employees' orientations to work. *International Journal of Contemporary Hospitality Management, 16*(3), 182–188. doi:10.1108/09596110410531177

McCabe, V. S., & Savery, L. K. (2007). "Butterflying" a new career pattern for Australia? Empirical evidence. *Journal of Management Development, 26*(2), 103–116. doi:10.1108/02621710710726026

Mendola, M. (2006). *Rural out-migration and economic development at origin. What do we know?* (Sussex Migration Working Paper N.40). Retrieved August 10, 2008, from http://dipeco. economia.unimib.it/persone/mendola/CV-07BI-COC.pdf

Milman, A. (2003). Hourly employee retention in small and medium attractions: The central Florida example. *International Journal of Hospitality Management, 22*, 17–35. doi:10.1016/S0278-4319(02)00033-6

Mohsin, A. (2003a). Backpackers in the NT of Australia - motives, behaviours and satisfactions. *International Journal of Tourism Research, 5*(2), 113–131. doi:10.1002/jtr.421

Mohsin, A. (2003b). Service quality assessment of restaurants in Darwin, NT, Australia. *Journal of Hospitality and Tourism Management, 10*(1), 12–23.

Mohsin, A. (2005c). Service quality assessment of 4-star hotels in Darwin, NT, Australia. *Journal of Hospitality and Tourism Management, 12*(1), 25–36.

Mowday, R., Steers, R., & Porter, L. (1982). *Employee-organization linkages*. New York: Academic Press.

Mowday, R. T. (1981). Viewing turnover from the perspective of those who remain: The relationship of job attitudes to attributions of the causes of turnover. *The Journal of Applied Psychology, 66*(1), 120–123. doi:10.1037/0021-9010.66.1.120

Mu, J., Peng, G., & Love, E. (2008). Interfirm networks, social capital, and knowledge flow. *Journal of Knowledge Management, 12*(4), 86–100. doi:10.1108/13673270810884273

Peroune, D. (2007). Tacit knowledge in the workplace: The facilitating role of peer relationships. *Journal of European Industrial Training, 31*(4), 244–258. doi:10.1108/03090590710746414

Pizam, A., & Thornburg, S. W. (2000). Absenteeism and voluntary turnover in Central Florida hotels: A pilot study. *International Journal of Hospitality Management, 19*, 211–217. doi:10.1016/S0278-4319(00)00011-6

Polanyi, M. (1966). *The tacit dimension*. Garden City, NY: Doubleday.

Poon, A. (1993). *Tourism, technology and competitive strategies*. UK: C.A.B International.

Poulston, J. (2008). Hospitality workplace problems and poor training: A close relationship. *International Journal of Contemporary Hospitality Management, 20*(4), 412–427. doi:10.1108/09596110810873525

Robins, G., & Pattison, P. (2006). *Multiple networks in organizations. Australian Defence Science and Technology Organisation (DSTO)*. Retrieved August 10, 2008, from http://www.sna.unimelb.edu.au/publications/publications.html

Rowley, G., & Purcell, K. (2001). "As cooks go, she went": Is labour churn inevitable? *International Journal of Hospitality Management, 20*(2), 163–185. doi:10.1016/S0278-4319(00)00050-5

Saxenian, A. L. (1994). *Regional advantage: Culture and competition in Silicon Valley and Route 128*. Cambridge, MA: Harvard University Press.

Scarbrough, H. (2001). Knowledge management, HRM and the innovation process. *International Journal of Manpower, 24*(5), 501–516. doi:10.1108/01437720310491053

Seufert, A., Von Krogh, G., & Bach, A. (1999). Towards knowledge networking. *Journal of Knowledge Management, 3*(3), 180–190. doi:10.1108/13673279910288608

Staw, B. M. (1980). Rationality and justification in organizational life. In B. M. Staw & L. L. Cummings (Eds.), *Research in organizational behavior* (Vol. 2, pp. 45-80). Greenwich, CT: JAI.

Stewart, F., & Samman, E. (2006). Human development: Beyond the human development index. *Journal of Human Development, 7*(3), 323–358. doi:10.1080/14649880600815917

Timo, N. (2001). Lean or just mean? The flexibilisation of labour in the Australian hotel industry. *Research in the Sociology of Work, 10*, 287–309. doi:10.1016/S0277-2833(01)80030-3

Tremblay, P. (2005). Learning networks and tourism innovation in the top end. In D. Carson & J. Macbeth (Eds.), *Regional tourism cases: Innovation in regional tourism* (pp. 53-59). Australia: Common Ground Publishing Pty Ltd.

Vaugeois, N., & Rollins, R. (2007). Mobility into tourism: Refuge employer? *Annals of Tourism Research, 34*(3), 630–648. doi:10.1016/j.annals.2007.02.001

Von Krogh, G. (1998). Care in knowledge creation. *California Management Review, 40*, 133–153.

Von Krogh, G., Nonaka, I., & Aben, M. (2001). Making the most of your company's knowledge: A strategic framework. *Long Range Planning, 34*(4), 421–439. doi:10.1016/S0024-6301(01)00059-0

Watson, T. (1994). *In search of management: Culture, chaos and control in managerial work*. London: International Thomson Business Press.

Wegner, D. (1987). Transactive memory: A contemporary analysis of group mind. In B. Mullen & G. Goethals (Eds.), *Theories of group behavior* (pp. 185-208). New York: Springer.

Wildes, V. J. (2007). Attracting and retaining food servers: How internal service quality moderates occupational stigma. *International Journal of Hospitality Management, 26*(1), 4–19. doi:10.1016/j.ijhm.2005.08.003

Woods, R., Heck, W., & Sciarini, M. (1998). *Turnover and diversity in the lodging industry*. American Hotel Foundation.

Zhang, H. Q., & Wu, E. (2004). Human resources issues facing the hotel and travel industry in China. *International Journal of Contemporary Hospitality Management, 16*(7), 424–428. doi:10.1108/09596110410559122

Zopiatis, A., & Constanti, P. (2007). Human resource challenges confronting the Cyprus hospitality industry. *EuroMed Journal of Business, 2*(2), 135–153. doi:10.1108/14502190710826022

ADDITIONAL READING

Anckar, B., & Walde, P. (2001). Introducing Web technology in a small peripheral hospitality organization. *International journal of contemporary hospitality management, 13*(5), 241-250.

Australian Bureau of Statistics. (2006). Labour force survey and labour mobility. Retrieved August 10, 2008, from http://www.abs.gov.au

Burt, R. S. (2001). Structural holes versus network closure as social capital. In N. Lin, K. Cook, & R. S. Burt (Eds.), *Social capital: Theory and research* (pp. 31-56). New York: Aldine de Gruyter.

Carson, D., & Taylor, A. (2008). Sustaining four wheel drive tourism in desert Australia: Exploring the evidence from a demand perspective. *The Rangeland Journal, 30*(1), 77–83. doi:10.1071/RJ07036

Castells, M. (1996). *The rise of the network society. The information age: Economy, society and culture vol. I.* Oxford, UK: Blackwell.

Chalkiti, K., & Sigala, M. (2008). Information sharing and idea generation in peer to peer online communities: The case of 'DIALOGOI'. *Journal of Vacation Marketing, 14*(2), 121–132. doi:10.1177/1356766707087520

Cross, R., Parker, A., Prusak, L., & Borgatti, S. (2001). Knowing what we know: Supporting knowledge creation and sharing in social networks. *Organizational Dynamics, 30*(2), 100–120. doi:10.1016/S0090-2616(01)00046-8

Gustafson, C. M. (2002). Employee turnover: A study of private clubs in the USA. *International Journal of Contemporary Hospitality Management, 14*(3), 106–113. doi:10.1108/09596110210424385

Karatepe, O. M., & Baddar, L. (2006). An empirical study of the selected consequences of frontline employees' work-family conflict and family-work conflict. *Tourism Management, 27*(5), 1017–1028. doi:10.1016/j.tourman.2005.10.024

Krackhardt, D., McKenna, J., Porter, L. W., & Steers, R. M. (1981). Supervisory behaviour and employee turnover: a field experiment. *Academy of Management Journal, 24*(2), 249–259. doi:10.2307/255839

Lee, T. W., & Maurer, S. D. (1997). The retention of knowledge workers with the unfolding model of voluntary turnover. *Human Resource Management Review, 7*(3), 247–275. doi:10.1016/S1053-4822(97)90008-5

Mertins, K., Heisig, P., & Vorbeck, J. (2000). *KM best practices in Europe.* Berlin, Germany: Springer Verlag.

Olsen, M. D., & Connolly, D. J. (2000). Experience-based travel. How technology is changing the hospitality industry. *The Cornell Hotel and Restaurant Administration Quarterly, 40*(1), 30–40.

Price, J. L. (1977). *The study of turnover.* Ames, IA: Iowa State University Press.

Robinson, R. N. S., & Barron, P. E. (2007). Developing a framework for understanding the impact of deskilling and standardisation on the turnover and attrition of chefs. *International Journal of Hospitality Management, 26*(4), 913–926. doi:10.1016/j.ijhm.2006.10.002

Ross, G. (1997). Career stress responses among hospitality employees. *Annals of Tourism, 21,* 41–49. doi:10.1016/S0160-7383(96)00032-1

Ross, L. E., & Boles, J. S. (1994). Exploring the influence of workplace relationships on work-related attitudes and behaviors in the hospitality work environment. *International Journal of Hospitality Management, 13*(2), 155–171. doi:10.1016/0278-4319(94)90036-1

Ryan, C. (1995). Tourism courses: A new concern for new times? *Tourism Management, 16*(2), 97–100. doi:10.1016/0261-5177(94)00017-5

Sigala, M., & Chalkiti, K. (2007). Improving performance through tacit knowledge externalisation and utilisation: Preliminary findings from Greek hotels. *International Journal of Productivity and Performance Management, 56*(5-6), 456–483. doi:10.1108/17410400710757141

Sigala, M., & Chalkiti, K. (2007). New service development: Preliminary findings on process development and assessment from the Greek hotels. *Advances in Hospitality Leisure, 3,* 129–149. doi:10.1016/S1745-3542(06)03008-6

Szivas, E., & Riley, M. (1999). Tourism employment during economic transition. *Annals of Tourism Research, 26*(4), 747–771. doi:10.1016/S0160-7383(99)00035-3

Weiermaier, K. (1999). *Partnerships in tourism as a tool for competitive advantage in tourist SMEs.* Paper presented at the CISET Conference, Venice.

Chapter 11

Creating Competitive Advantage in Scottish Family Businesses:
Managing, Sharing and Transferring the Knowledge

Claire Seaman
Queen Margaret University, UK

Stuart Graham
Queen Margaret University, UK

ABSTRACT

This chapter seeks to consider both the role that knowledge transfer may have in family businesses and the different manners in which knowledge transfer may take place within this diverse environment. The economic, social and community importance of family businesses within Scotland is considered, alongside the different manner in which family businesses commonly operate and the implications for knowledge transfer. The importance of knowledge transfer in the creation of competitive advantage within a family business environment and the relatively limited nature of research in this area are explored, highlighting the need for further research both to support the on-going development of a strategy for family businesses in Scotland and to facilitate future development of high quality knowledge transfer. Key to all of this, however, is an increased understanding of what is meant by knowledge transfer and the breadth of ways in which it happens.

INTRODUCTION

The importance of knowledge – its acquisition, transfer and management – in the development of competitive advantage is well established and acknowledged (Davenport and Prusack, 1998, pxi). Knowledge has been defined in a variety of ways, within which some consistent themes emerge: an initial definition, from Zander and Kogut (1995) would be 'what you know and how you know it', although other authors have highlighted the importance of contextualisation (Randeree, 2006) and the distinction that knowledge as a concept is both broader and deeper than data or information, but often encompasses both. Knowledge forms a highly fluid mix which includes experience, values, contextual information which serves as a lens through

DOI: 10.4018/978-1-60566-790-4.ch011

which new information and suggestions can be viewed (Davenport and Prusack, 1998, p5). Within business, knowledge is perceived as being both vital and complex; a challenging mixture which merits considerable discussion and debate. Similarly, the importance of the economic and social contributions of family businesses is well established worldwide and, despite somewhat sparse research within Scotland itself, within the UK. Far less research, however, has been conducted which looks at knowledge transfer within family businesses *per se*, still less where a business is part of Scotland's thriving SME sector.

Family businesses may be defined in a number of ways - and indeed represent an area of academic activity where no one, single definition may be agreed upon - but three factors tend to remain constant throughout the literature: the economic importance of family businesses, their disproportionate representation within the SME sector and the blending of family and business culture to create a unique and often highly fluid environment for active knowledge transfer. The combination of these three factors creates an area where research is currently sparse but where, given the acknowledged importance of family businesses and the role of knowledge transfer in the creation of competitive advantage, future research is vital to facilitate optimal business development in diverse communities and is likely to focus around current work in the area of knowledge integration and dynamic organisational adaptation within family firms (Chirico and Salvato, 2008).

Within the current academic literature relating to family business, a number of themes emerge which are likely to impact upon knowledge transfer and business learning. One such theme is the relatively private nature of family businesses, which in turn tends to mean that accurate information about them is not readily available (Astrachan and Shanker, 2006). A second constant theme is the importance of the contribution that family businesses make to economic, social, cultural and community development, whether that

be in the UK (Reid and Harris, 2004), the USA (Astrachan and Shanker 2006), in the Chinese economy (Chung and Yuen, 2003; Poutzioris et al, 2006) or amongst distinct and relatively discrete minority communities (Dhaliwal and Kangis, 2008). The combination of a sector of clear and, to some extent, measurable, importance where robust data are nonetheless difficult to establish, illustrates both the dilemma of family business research and its importance

The impact of family business culture on knowledge transfer and the implications of the relatively informal working practices often identified within family-based SMEs offer a parallel area for research where the development of effective strategies for engagement is of critical importance. Links between current KT policy and the specific needs of family businesses will be explored as part of both local and national strategies for engagement, both as they occur at present and as they might develop in the light of current research. Notable, however, are indications that knowledge transfer is primarily a social activity (Lucas and Ogilvie, 2006) and one that may be more easily facilitated within flatter management structures (Drucker, 1998): the impact of such factors within a family context remains to be explored.

In considering the topic of family businesses, it is worth noting at the outset one major paradox that underpins much of the current body of research and has tended to influence perceptions of the dominant theme within the subject. Much of the early and continued research within the family business environment focuses upon the transfer of knowledge, or lack of it, that occurs in relation to succession planning and the handing over of a business from one generation to the next. Whilst this remains a critical and totally legitimate area of enquiry, a central thesis of this chapter is that the importance of knowledge transfer in the development of competitive advantage within a family business environment is far broader than this and the manner in which knowledge transfer takes place varies widely. Specifically, the transfer of knowledge between and within organisations is an important dimension but the twin factors of the family and the socially constructed nature of knowledge (Pittaway et al, 2005) will influence knowledge acquisition, management and transfer in a much broader sense. With implications for areas as diverse as the development of public policy for business support, new business development and the facilitation of an enterprising culture, Chapter 12 sets out to focus on the strategic importance of knowledge transfer within family businesses and its role in the development of competitive advantage. Such consideration will also take account of how family businesses, with their own special cultural characteristics and identities, might contribute towards the economic development of a nation, Scotland, seeking to build its comparative advantage stimulated by a new political era within the country and aspirations for its future position within Europe.

BACKGROUND

Family Businesses – A Special Case

Research into family enterprises continues to evolve and gather momentum, but an underlying seminal conclusion that has been reached is that 'family firms are more complicated in many respects compared with their non-family counterparts', a factor which may account for them having been largely ignored by mainstream researchers (Zahra et al 2006 p614). The interaction of family culture with the various levels of organisational culture (Getz et al, 2004) being a primary difference attributed as a significant complicating factor within the family enterprise. Similarly, the SME sector is often more complicated to engage in challenging academic research and the concentration of family firms within the SME sector may have lead to their being doubly under-represented in current research. One result of the distinguishing features and characteristics

which set these forms of businesses apart from others, is the proposition that, irrespective of their size, the 'family business should be regarded as a special case' (Reid and Adams 2001).

Warranting special case status or not, twenty years ago, Ward (1987) suggested that the toughest job on earth was keeping a family business alive (Seaman et al, 2007). What is also clear from the literature, however, is that the management challenges associated with the family business sector have not diminished over the past two decades (Seaman et al, 2007, 2009). On the contrary, in today's environment of global change, family businesses are faced with immense pressure necessitating their adaptation if they are to seize the emerging opportunities at home and abroad. Whilst needing to maintain their often highly distinctive identifies, failure to adapt could signal a decline in current competitiveness and their ultimate demise (Zahra et al 2006). The development of competitive advantage – of which knowledge acquisition, transfer and management are key factors – remains an area of substantial interest.

The Worldwide Contribution of Family Businesses

Family businesses are a major source of economic activity and wealth-creation Worldwide, existing and flourishing across geo-political frontiers, markets, areas and legal forms of business (Poutzioris et al, 2006, Harding 2006, IFB 2008). Similarly, viewed on a worldwide basis, family businesses are the most numerous type of business and despite much academic debate about the precise definition of a family business, estimates of the proportion of family businesses within the economies of developed countries remain remarkably constant at around two thirds of business operations (Poutzioris et al, 2006, Harding 2006, IFB, 2008). In parallel, current estimates indicate that around half of GDP economic activity and private employment occurs within family firms (Shanker and Astrachan, 1996, Harding, 2006), highlighting that they are numerous but also concentrated within the SME sector.

In terms of economic growth and development worldwide there is currently considerable debate, the general consensus being, that whilst family businesses provide an important contribution to economic and social development, defining and quantifying that contribution poses substantial challenges (Allio, 2004). Whilst a number of different methodologies have been proposed, the variety of different business models and the different manner in which business information is collected worldwide make direct assessment of growth potential and comparison between different countries and cultures difficult (Astrachan and Shanker, 2006). Part of this difficulty lies in the distinction between the assessment of potential growth within an individual business and the potential for the start-up and initial development of successful new family businesses. Predicting business start-up rates depends largely on past trends, whilst within the individual business, family businesses may or may not see growth as a key goal; a factor associated with the cultural values held within the business and the family associated with its development. Regardless of their strategic objectives, family businesses represent 'the engine that drives socio-economic development and wealth creation around the world' (Pistrui et al, 2006 p 460).

Pursuing a Universal Definition of a 'Family Business'

Whilst it is safe to make the assumption that the family business predates the records of history (Colli, 2003), what it actually represents remains an unresolved issue for ongoing deliberation. As is the case in many areas of business related research, endeavouring to define family business with clarity and universal agreement, is a largely unattainable goal (Seaman et al, 2007, 2009).

The majority of definitions focus their efforts upon distinguishing family firms from non-family firms in some interpretive manner. However, West-head and Cowling (1997) identify three key issues frequently used by researchers in past attempts to define family businesses. The first relates to a 'single dominant family owning' more than half the shares of the business. Second is where an 'emotional kinship group' perceive their enterprise as actually representing a family business. The third issue is based upon whether the business is 'managed by members' from a single dominant family. Defining in such a manner reflects the basic stages of development through which successful family enterprises tend to travel from the family-run business on a continuum which leads to the successive development of the business as family-managed, family-governed and potentially to the development of a shareholding family where family involvement in day-to-day operations is minimal. Whilst no single articulation has achieved outright acceptance or recognition, most definitions of what constitutes a family business centre upon the significant role of the family in the determination of vision, use of control mechanisms and the formation of unique resources and capabilities (Sharma 2006), whilst overall self-perception and self-definition of the business as a 'family business' remains key to the ongoing debate.

Like the businesses themselves, the families who might own/manage them also vary widely. There are, however, three patterns of family development and behaviour that are especially common and tend to impact disproportionately upon the family business. Nicholson (2005) puts forward a characterisation of these as, the *enmeshed family*, the *fragmented family* and the *schismatic family*. Within the so called 'enmeshed family', parental control may be oppressive and accompanied by a stifling level of parental/emotional control. In such situations the family and associated business dramas are all too often played out behind closed doors, where outside help is not welcome and/or where the second or subsequent generation had to break free on a very radical basis to achieve independence. In contrast, the 'fragmented family' tends to operate with very little glue to bind the generations together and may, indeed, assume that the last thing the next generation would want is be to be 'roped into' the business. This is a complex area, however, as this type of assumption may be primarily a result of a lack of bonding between different generations, or it may be primarily a cultural ideal of the life the next generation should aim for. Indeed, the assumption that a subsequent generation will not want to be 'roped into' the business does not necessarily imply that the family ties are not strong. Finally, the 'schismatic family' is characterised by conflict, although the patterns vary widely; conflict may be generated between different generations, between different branches or 'clans' or the family may 'gang up' against one individual family member (Nicholson, 2005). Whilst each of these situations may carry a variety of positive and negative attributes for the business, the central tenet of 'emotion first' carries inherent risks. Such characterisation of the holistic 'family' element, reveals the potential influence that individual members and/or sub-grouping might have upon the business. This in turn infers critical organisational dimensions of a cultural nature, with associated implications for the manner in which knowledge is shared, managed and transferred within the 'family' context, impacting upon the ongoing competitiveness of the business itself. The relationship between family and non-family members represents another cultural dimension of significance. Dyer (1988) put forward four types of family business culture which provide a basis for such analysis: paternalistic, laissez-faire, participative and professional cultures. The classification is based upon varying assumptions about human nature, relationships, and the environment, each representing influential determinants for the effective transfer of knowledge and sustained competitiveness of an enterprise which is family based. Just as there are various ways of defining the family business, there are also many influences which can affect the performance of the family business, its culture being a dominant one.

Family, Knowledge, Strategy and Business Performance

In small enterprises, the origins of most family businesses, competitive advantage is more likely to emanate via 'accidental circumstances' as owner-managers are less capable than large enterprises of influencing the environment in which they compete (Jones, 2003, p22). However, a key competitive feature within such family businesses is the 'family' element, or orientation, which often influences the manner in which the enterprise may function, one example being the family values which can predicate its culture. The close integration between family and business, frequently associated with such enterprise, along with ownership and leadership stability, facilitates the spread and translation of values within family businesses creating unique characteristics, both in their internal workings and outward appearance. Such cultural dimensions can in themselves be a basis for the creation of distinctiveness, via for example their identity as a 'family run business' portraying a particular image, and so a prime source of competitive advantage. In such circumstances knowledge is transferred from a social based system or network, the family, into a business context. This close inter-relationship between the family and business, linked with the long term ownership-leadership of such ventures, results in values being translated in the business forming a basis for 'strategizing, through interpretations, interactions, and decisions' (Hall et al, 2006, p257). The issue of this dual inter-connected relationship, between family and business, is of central importance within family enterprises and reveals the complexity of knowledge transfer within the strategy processes adopted by many family businesses impacting upon their accomplishments and continuity.

Habberston et al (2006, p67) make the point that, 'The heart of the strategic management process is to achieve the performance outcomes that allow firms, including family-influenced firms, to be competitive over time.' They contend that, to-date, literature relating to family firms has tended to place more emphasis upon the improvement of family relationships (for example succession planning) whilst lacking a strong focus on strategic management aspects relating to the firm's performance. As a result, there is a tendency to 'discount, ignore, or isolate the family factors from the business' (p67) resorting to the adoption of traditional strategy models in consideration of such enterprises. As a consequence, it is suggested that leaders of family businesses do not take sufficient account of the significant 'systematic influences' contributing to and impacting upon the performance outcomes of their businesses. This issue reveals the apparent failing of some family business based research to take account of the knowledge related influences which the family component makes upon the strategic developments of the business; supporting the 'special case' claim for such businesses.

It is suggested that the unique 'systematic influences' associated with a family business can be captured via the organisation's idiosyncratic resources and capabilities. It is reasonable to conclude that this will incorporate the current knowledge base of the firm, its transfer and capacity to create new knowledge over time in order to remain competitive. The interactions of such a system have been termed, the 'familiness' of the business (Habberston & Williams, 1999), and the 'F-factor' (Habberston & Pistrui, 2004; Habberston et al., 2003; Uhlaner & Habberston, 2005). Various dimensions within such a system have the potential to impact upon specific aspects of the family and influence the performance of the business. Such aspects include, family leadership, vision, governance, relationships, performance objectives and strategy (Habberston & Pistrui, 2004), all having implications for the transfer of knowledge within and outside the business as part of its strategic interactions. What is important to note is that such dimensions apply to the influence of the family on the business, as opposed to

attributes necessarily of the actual family itself; they represent characteristics of the 'business family', not necessarily the entire family.

Taking this 'systematic influences' perspective, in conjunction with preceding discussions, it is reasonable to conclude that irrespective of their size, longevity, sector, economic contribution, geographic location, community origins, and the like, that the ultimate and unique defining characteristic of this type of business is the 'family' element of their organisational composition and the strategic influence this exerts upon the firm's competitive destiny (Seaman et al 2007, 2009). Along with this contention is the need to recognise the impact that drawing upon knowledge from a social system, the family, can have upon the performance of a business. As Carlock and Ward (2001) point out, there is potential to draw upon various advantages associated with 'family' orientated firms to create competitive advantage based upon their perceived, or actual, strengths including: being in business for the long term where patience can be uppermost in strategic developments; having a shared future vision and a capacity to react to changing conditions; having pride in their offering, it is their 'name on the door'; being eminently suited to position themselves in niche markets and capitalise on such opportunities; benefit from the strong commitment of people within the business and their performance levels; a strong organisational culture based upon camaraderie, etc. However, as Carlock and Ward (2001, p196) also identify, 'Good strategy rests on minimizing weaknesses as well as exploiting strengths', and there are disadvantages associated with family businesses, including: personal interests can obscure the real financial/opportunity costs in investment decisions; disharmony in personal life affecting business relations; a closed culture resistant to outside interventions; a narrow focus upon products/markets; difficulties in organisation ownership transition; etc. Clearly the role of knowledge and its effective transfer and management is crucial in utilising the potential strengths and guarding against the inherent weaknesses of the family business as it develops strategies to build its competitive advantage upon. Further, the prevention of potential knowledge loss and the associated damage to competitive advantage is a key priority for many organisations (Parise et al, 2006) of especial importance in the SME category into which many family businesses fall. In acknowledging both that SME businesses may be especially vulnerable to knowledge loss and less equipped to make best use of formalised systems (Blackmore, 2004) the challenges and importance for family businesses become clear.

Knowledge Transfer within the Family Business

Derived from the work of Davenport and Prusack (1998), Lynch (2006) defines knowledge as being:

'A fluid mix of framed experience, values, contextual information and expert insight. It accumulates over time and shapes the organisation's ability to survive and compete in markets' (p809).

For any family business the accumulation over a period of time and the transfer of such 'a fluid mix' represents a critical issue in terms of continuity, and thus survival. It represents the challenge of succession planning and the effective transfer of knowledge from one generation to the next.

Resulting from the typical long tenures, leaders of family businesses acquire significant levels of tacit knowledge relating to the enterprise (Lee et al., 2003). This 'know-how' and ingrained taken for granted knowledge, impacting upon images of reality and visions of the future (Nonaka & Takeuchi, 1995, p8), can represent the true competitiveness of the family business in terms of both the technical dimensions and beliefs/perceptions upon which the business depends. How effectively such knowledge, and social networks, are transferred across generations can be influential in

the successive generation's level of performance impacting upon the business itself as it moves through its next period of development (Cabrera-Suarez et al., 2001; Steier, 2001).

In its simplest interpretation:

'Knowledge transfer involves moving pieces of knowledge from one party to another', with boundaries separating the parties acting as 'a barrier or facilitator to the transfer' (Easterby-Smith et al., 2008).

Within the family businesses context, the 'parties' are represented by members of a family, or families, and so have particular relationships associated with them. Such relationships are in effect 'family boundaries' which have to be successfully negotiated if knowledge is to be transferred in an effective manner. Irrespective of the actual context, it should be appreciated that as Hamel (1991) identified, a key determinant regarding the extent of knowledge which is transferred is the recipient's intent to learn. Likewise, the motivations of the donor to teach are of equal importance in the process (Ko et al., 2005). Such reality is of no less importance within the family business context, as it cannot be assumed that there is a natural desire, or willingness, to engage in the process of knowledge transfer. The absorptive capacity of a recipient and the nature of the relationship with the donor are critical determinants in the effective transfer between the two parties (Cohen & Levinthal, 1990; Szulanski, 1995). The need for a supportive relationship, based upon mutual respect, best facilitates the transfer of knowledge, networks and social capital across generations (Steier, 2001). The kinship links within a family business represent a significant strength over non-family enterprises in terms of both individual and organisational relationships. Even in circumstances where family relationships might be strained due to personal or business differences, the overriding supportive based relationship which predominates is the common source of income, but also a continuity objective of maintaining the heritage of the business itself. Such circumstances can create more conducive organisational conditions than in many non-family businesses to share knowledge and enhance a mutual willingness between generations to impart and receive such knowledge. The process of knowledge transfer often starts at a very early age as, in many instances, family members are informally brought into the business when they are young, for example to help-out or due to domestic circumstances. Such experiences expose next generation members to the traditions, values, language, etc., of the business, laying the foundation to facilitate the ongoing transfer of knowledge between generations and understanding of what the business represents and respect for what has been attained by previous generations. This gradual absorption of family and business integrated knowledge and cultural awareness is a critical feature in respect to identity within a family business. In this sense identity is closely associated with the linkage between business and family reputations (Trevinyo-Rodriguez & Tapies, 2006) and the need to transfer commitment to protect their value through knowledge transfer to ensure sustained competitiveness and continuity of the enterprise.

Balancing Family Ownership/ Management Transfer of Power and Knowledge

As suggested above, the performance of a family business is influenced by the actual family members associated with the business, the effectiveness of tacit knowledge transfer between them and the resultant dominant culture which this creates. Of equal importance is the 'ownership' associated with such members and the corresponding degree of control/power they are able to exert upon the business. This in turn has implications regarding the extent to which members of the family are involved in the actual 'management' of the business, reflecting their operational engagement within it and the corresponding degree and nature of 'family' input to strategy formulation as additional siblings/generations enter the business. The inference here is that the more 'boundaries' knowledge has to negotiate the more demanding the transfer process involved (Easterby-Smith et al, 2008).

Despite the significant role that family businesses fulfil in today's world economies, it is still claimed that in reality little is known about what affect family ownership or management have on the behaviour and performance of such firms (Kets de Vries et al, 2007). This lack of insight, coupled with the potential performance implications of the balance of power between 'ownership and management', is a further complicating factor in attempting to understanding the significance of knowledge transfer within family businesses as they grow and develop over an extended period. As ownership expands through the incorporation of multiple generations into the business, so the likelihood of the 'separation of management and ownership roles' increases (Carlock & Ward, 2001, p125). This has change implications associated with levels of information sharing, percentage of family members employed, the family's level of business experience, connections among family members, the relationship between family members and business founder, degree of wealth concentration (Carlock & Ward, 2001, p125). These can all be influential factors in maintaining balance within the enterprise and effective ongoing processes of knowledge transfer within the family business in attempts to sustained competitive advantage and general performance.

By focussing on knowledge transfer within the family business, however, we address only one critical aspect of knowledge transfer; the influence of outside knowledge partners, either formal or informal, forms a second major part of this equation.

DEVELOPING SCOTLAND'S FAMILY BUSINESS SECTOR VIA EXTERNAL KNOWLEDGE TRANSFER

Europe's 'Arc of Prosperity' and Scottish Economic Development

The importance of family businesses worldwide has already been stressed, but to what extent are they being supported at a macro level? In considering this issue, the discussion moves into the realms of recognising and facilitating knowledge transfer within a family business to a national level. In respect to this perspective, Pistrui et al (2006) identify a critically important factor in regarding to the macro contribution of family businesses and their competitiveness:

'Family businesses are the engine that drives socio-economic development and wealth creation around the world, and entrepreneurship is a key driver of family businesses.' (p460)

'Entrepreneurship' and entrepreneurial behaviour is of major strategic importance within all levels of competitive activity and has significant connections with knowledge transfer interventions which might support its facilitation. Entrepreneurship has been cited as a priority in terms of further development in advancing economic performance at government levels. The European Commission (2003) emphasised the need for increased effort in this regard within their Green Paper 'Entrepreneurship in Europe':

'Europe needs to foster entrepreneurial drive more effectively. It needs more new and thriving firms willing to reap the benefits of market openings and to embark on creative or innovative ventures for commercial exploitation on a larger scale.' (p4)

The EU Green Paper makes the point that family businesses have a significant role to play in developing an entrepreneurial culture:

'Entrepreneurship is relevant for firms in all sectors, technological or traditional, for small and large firms and for different ownership structures, such as family businesses...........(p6)

In terms of the number of family businesses within the European Union it has been estimated that 85% of enterprises are family controlled (Burns & Whitehouse, 1996). Despite their current significance and future potential, however, the family business sector still lacks recognition of the opportunities it can offer to national economic development and, as a consequence, failings to exploit knowledge transfer across the sector. An example of this was illustrated during the Scottish 2007 Parliamentary election and within the manifestos of the main political parties (Conservative, Labour, Liberal Democratic and Scottish National). Whilst due attention was paid to business related issues by all parties, including the need to increase the support for Scottish based SMEs, there was an absence by all of any reference to family business *per se*.

The outcome of the May 2007 election was the dawn of a new era for Scottish politics, and the government of the economy, with the ascendance to office of a minority Scottish National Party administration. The Scottish Government (2007) set out proposals for the country's economic strategy, with the First Minister indicating key aspirations for the future:

'The purpose of the Government I lead is to create a more successful country...... through increasing sustainable economic growth.........

.... Scotland has real strength in the most vital factor for modern economies – the human capital ......Scotland's people....We need to build on this strength and, importantly, make more of it in broadening Scotland's comparative advantage in the global economy........

.....we also believe that we can achieve much more with the levers that we have.

.... by making better use of these levers, Scotland can discover much more of a competitive edge............' (pV)

The references to Scotland's 'comparative advantage' and 'competitive edge' are important from our focus upon family businesses as they have clear linkages to knowledge; be that existing knowledge with implications for greater sharing/transfer, or the creation of new knowledge within the economy. In defining 'comparative advantage' Lynch (2006, p690) states that it, 'consists of the resources possessed by a country that give it a competitive advantage over other nations.' This builds on Porter's (1990) seminal work 'The Competitive Advantage of Nations' emphasising that ultimately competitive advantage results from the effective combination of two factors, national circumstances and company strategy. Therefore, if we accept this juxtaposition, the development of Scotland's family businesses will be partly reliant upon the support of Scottish Government interventions in the economy (or as they suggest, achieving 'more with the 'levers'), if they are to further increase their competitive position and contribution to Scotland's 'sustainable economic growth'.

In respect to such economic development aspirations, the Scottish Government (2007) identifies Norway, Finland, Iceland, Ireland and Denmark, northern Europe's 'Arc of Prosperity countries – which are similar to Scotland in scale and geographically close' (p2), as being small independent economies from which it can draw lessons and approaches in pursuing its own distinctive economic strategy for Scotland. The 'Arc of Prosperity' here represents high wealth economies in terms of their world rankings. For those interested in the Scottish family business sector, the searching question to pose is:

'Does this distinctive economic strategy make any specific reference to family business?'

The answer is no it does not; an issue which will be given further consideration later in the chapter. Despite the lack of attention by political parties, evidence exists to highlight the importance of family businesses within Scotland as an individual country and as part of the United Kingdom.

Family Business in Scotland and the UK

Evidence offering insight into the role and relative importance of family businesses within Scotland is somewhat sparse, although within the UK as a whole it is suggested that family firms account for over two thirds of all enterprises (Institute of Family Business, 2007). The Scottish Executive Annual Survey of Small Businesses in Scotland contains some information on family businesses and indicates one or two key trends which appear to be emerging.

Two sets of survey results are currently available, published in 2003 and 2005 by the then Scottish Executive, which offer some consensus and interesting insights into the on-going development of family business as an area of interest For example, across both surveys, more than 50% of all small businesses surveyed were family owned and run (2003: 61%; 2005: 68%). Interestingly, too, far more data were collected in the 2005 survey, highlighting that similar proportions of businesses were family owned in Highlands and Islands compared to other geographic areas. This highlights some substantial implications for regional economic development, but there is very little detail in the figures available and scope for future research to be carried out which was not addressed within the follow-on study developed by the Scottish Government in 2008.

Of the businesses in Scotland that were surveyed, most family businesses were controlled by the first generation – 72% in 2003; 71% in

2005. The trends in terms of generational control and the factors that affect this seem very stable of the time period. Generally, the bigger and/or older the business, the less likely the first generation was to still be in direct control. Younger businesses, micro-businesses and businesses without formal employees are more likely to be in first generation control. Businesses controlled by the first generation were also slightly more likely to be proposing growth but the difference is small. The importance of definition of a family business and the distinction between a family business and a first-generation self-employment opportunity, however, remain critical albeit largely unexplored.

In addition, family businesses have been highlighted in two key areas within work carried out by the Scottish Government and the wider academic literature:

Scotland's Minority Ethnic Communities and Family Businesses

The ownership of family businesses amongst different minority ethnic communities is a much discussed area where the data collected merit some critical review. On first examination, the businesses owned and run by members of Scotland's minority ethnic communities were not significantly different from the general population. Two key factors should be highlighted here.

Firstly, the definition of minority ethnic group used for the data collection focussed heavily upon the 'traditional' well-established communities and reflects migration patterns estimated to be from before 1980. In addition, amongst minority ethnic groups, 97% of businesses were controlled by the first generation, compared to 72% of the general population. The reasons for this finding remain unclear:, although the age of the business, family attitudes to succession planning or family educational aspiration for the second and subsequent generations may all play a part and further research would be required to clarify this. Similarly, the

impact of new migrant communities on family business development (Silva et al, 2007) and the impact of rural and urban locations on the development of family businesses in minority ethnic communities (Deakins et al, 2008) are areas where research is currently being undertaken.

Available data indicate that this picture is similar across the UK; surveys conducted amongst small businesses across the UK are conducted by the DTi Small Business Service (2006), indicating that in 2006 around 67% of small businesses self-defined as a family business. Amongst these, 57% were controlled by the first generation whilst 20% were controlled by the second generation. Data remain sparse, however, and there remains little focus on those larger businesses where there is a family component. The nature, distribution and relative importance of family businesses in different and developing minority communities merits further exploration.

Family Businesses in Rural Scotland

The current vision for rural Scotland sits alongside an economic profile where family businesses provide a key part of the structure for economic activity but often operate in a distinct manner which impacts upon their interaction with formal businesses support networks. Notably, current evidence from the Scottish Government (Scottish Executive, 2005) indicates that family businesses are relatively evenly distributed across the geographic landscape; given the relative reluctance of many family businesses to undertake major geographic re-location and their relative propensity towards community involvement, the importance of family businesses within rural communities is indicated within current literature but would merit further investigation.

Rural business development in its broadest context, encompassing the role which the development of individual businesses play in economic growth, in regional development and in the development of businesses that are sustainable in social, environmental and economic terms is a key part of the current vision for Scotland (Scottish Executive, 2004). The role that family businesses play in the development of this vision – and the success that might be achieved here given the propensity of major businesses re-locating to Scotland to congregate around urban areas – has not been sufficiently highlighted.

Whether rural or urban based and irrespective of the ethnic origin of the family itself, however, the importance of family business within the literature remains clear. Similarly, the importance of knowledge development, management and transfer is broadly acknowledged: facilitating knowledge transfer at a National level becomes, therefore, a matter of some urgency.

Supporting Knowledge Transfer at a National Level within Scottish Family Businesses

The family business sector within Scotland is a vibrant one, and needs to be acknowledged as such in terms of its capacity to contribute towards the attainment of the Scottish Government's economic development strategy. The issue is how can the potential of the sector be realised and the knowledge within it harnessed and shared to facilitate this if specific Government supportive interventions are not forthcoming. This is a dilemma which has been apparent to a number of family business stakeholders for some time which led to the formation of the Scottish Family Business Association (SFBA) in 2006. The SFBA is a non-profit organisation with a mission to facilitate knowledge transfer and business learning processes in their broadest sense, via the development of structures that allow relatively easy access to specialist support, skills and help for family businesses in Scotland. This represents in effect an attempt to facilitate the development of 'critical knowledge' within Scottish family businesses. Cohen & Levinthal (1990) contend that such knowledge is not merely substantive technical based knowledge needed to

operate a business, but also an awareness of 'where useful complementary expertise resides' external to the business. This represents the broadening of an organisation's external network, having the potential to increase leverage of an individual's absorptive capabilities and strengthen overall absorptive capacity of the business in respect to both existing and new knowledge.

The adoption of this 'self-help' mindset to supporting the development of Scottish family businesses, coupled with the strategic objective of raising their profile and collective identity, is an approach which has significant merits in terms of knowledge sharing, management and transfer within a sector which is fragmented by cultural, regional, enterprise size and interest diversities. The SFBA has set itself the vision of making Scotland a world leader in supporting, educating and celebrating its family businesses. The routes by which this may be achieved and the management of the process are a subject of much current discussion, both in terms of the most effective routes by which this goal may be achieved, but also concerning the background knowledge of businesses required to facilitate a tailored approach in different geographic areas. Knowledge transfer is also a two-way process – for better of worse. Businesses may learn from others, but they also learn about others and the impact of getting it 'wrong' within a small and relatively 'closed' community may be a factor, for example, within either a rural context or a specific business sector. Understanding the profile both of business communities within a geographic area – and the internal profiles of those individual businesses forms an important starting point for knowledge transfer and learning on a national scale.

Set within this challenging environment, the SFBA has formulated a general strategy in pursuit of its vision based upon engagement with six sectors in Scotland: family businesses; political leaders; academics; professional advisers; business support organisations; and the media. Key aspects forming the basis of this strategy as they relate to each sector will be identified and indicative knowledge transfer in practice issues highlighted in respect to such strategic initiatives.

1. *Family Businesses*: The SFBA aim to raise awareness of key issues which relate to all of Scotland's business families and ensure they have access to support which will allow them to flourish. This is based upon developing a new culture amongst these family businesses so the next generation are educated and trained to professionally lead their families and companies.

For any form of knowledge transfer to occur, linkages have to be established. This is probably the greatest challenge for the SFBA, forging meaningful relationships with the vast array of family businesses that exist throughout Scotland. If this can be achieved to some meaningful degree, the creation of a national focal point can have enormous potential for supporting the competitive development, through knowledge, of the family business sector, to the benefit of individual business families, communities and overall economic progress.

2. *Political leaders*: In meeting with Scotland's policy makers, the SFBA seeks to ensure that they are aware of the importance of family business; that they consider the sector regarding all new policy and legislation and see the international and nation potential of the strategy.

Having a representative 'voice' to inform government policy on issues affecting such an important sector as family businesses will make a strategic contribution to advancing competitive performance generally within Scotland. For example, developing the business focus within Scottish heritage *via* family businesses and the business of family could be developed alongside government initiatives to increase international

trade both in terms of tourism and export sales by certain sectors of the economy if information was shared more extensively.

3. *Academics*: Working with Scotland's academic sector, the SFBA will assist universities undertake research relating to family businesses within Scotland, ensuring that the Association has relevant data. It also wants to ensure that family business specific courses are offered in Scotland's universities/colleges and create a reputation within the global academic market for excellence in family business research/education.

There is still significant potential to further the scope and volume of research within Scotland's family business sector so having the support of the SFBA in these endeavours is of significant assistance. By taking a regional focus, university studies can generate profiles of family businesses mapping their activities and characteristics and in so doing building a base which would benefit local economic development efforts. In this manner universities have the potential to become 'knowledge hubs' across Scotland creating a national network for collaborative projects. In terms of developing knowledge of family business within the curricula, entrepreneurship, for example, has increasingly become an important focus within business programmes so the family perspective could easily be incorporated as part of this subject and more generally across all areas of study.

4. *Professional Advisors*: The SFBA wish to ensure that advisors are equipped to provide support that is specific to family businesses. Also, professional courses (banking, law and accountancy) should include compulsory modules on skills related to advising family businesses.

Like most SMEs, family businesses normally rely on professional advice from external sources.

Whilst technical guidance can be given in good faith, for many advisers it a lack of knowledge and understanding of the family dimension that inhibits the processes and engagement with business family clients. Thus, knowledge development of the family motives, or lifestyle objectives, which influence business decision-making warrants increased attention by the advising community to make knowledge interventions of greater mutual benefit.

5. *Business Support Organisations*: In partnership with all related organisations, SFBA aims to ensure that best practice gets into the minds of all Scotland's family businesses.

Support organisations come in many forms and guises, from government funded to self financing, with varying objectives. They represent an extremely important part of the overall configuration of networks that business families often engage with, thus making them invaluable conduits for knowledge dissemination at national, regional and local levels. Family businesses frequently cite their personal networks, both business and social, as a key source of information and knowledge, informing their business developments and competitive posturing.

6. *Media*: The SFBA will work with Scotland's media to raise awareness of issues faced by family businesses and celebrate the success of these businesses.

Family businesses tend to be quite secretive by nature and so are cautious in terms of their openness in communicating with the external environment. However, exposure of the issues they face and increased general public awareness of their contribution is a vital knowledge sharing task which needs to be an ongoing process. Whilst the national business press is an obvious means of reporting challenges and successes within the sector as a whole, it can also profile

family businesses of varying sizes to demonstrate their depth and breath. Of equal importance for knowledge diffusion is local, trade and professional publications, all of which can add different dimensions of specific interests in line with their target audiences.

In conclusion, the SFBA strategy could be a key contributor to the development of Scotland's future economic performance. The impact of family business culture on knowledge transfer and the implications of the relatively informal working practices often identified within family-based SMEs represent an under recognised and researched area which may prove vital in the development of successful interactions between various stakeholders. If family businesses operate differently – and all the available research evidence suggests they do – their engagement with knowledge transfer activities is also likely to be different, warranting appropriately formulated processes and interventions. Understanding the nature of these differences and the variety of patterns within family businesses forms a key early goal in the development of effective strategies for engagement.

Effective strategies for engagement remain a key long-term aim of the economic regeneration agenda and building links between family businesses and the key stakeholders in this diverse market will be vital for the successful strategic development of Scotland's national and regional economies. Accommodating the 'family-factor' will remain key to the development of effective policy and the role of a dedicated organisation such as the SFBA remains a major part of that accommodation.

DEVELOPING FUTURE APPROACHES

Whilst the need for effective strategies for engagement is vital, a key and often overlooked part of this approach is the need to integrate practical knowledge transfer challenges into current and future theoretical and applied research *and vice versa*. It is here that the approach taken by the SFBA – working with the full spectrum of those who are involved with and interested in Scottish family businesses – offers both a valuable approach for Scotland and an opportunity to study the development of and engagement of individuals with the knowledge transfer process.

The final part of Chapter 12, therefore, is concerned with those diverse parts of the academic knowledge base, which will integrate with political and SFBA developments including business learning and knowledge transfer and the cultural dimension within business. The role that formalised knowledge transfer systems may play is considered, alongside key aspects within the academic literature and the development of on-going strategies for development.

Concepts, Theories and Perspectives of Business learning and Knowledge Transfer

A variety of concepts, theories and perspectives of business learning have been applied within the SME sector in Scotland, notably distinguishing between internal learning and interaction outside partners and sources of expertise, but part of the unique aspect of family business is the difficulty in delineating between the two. Within family businesses, access to the wider pool of family expertise not formally associated with the business is common and, with care, forms a key part of business learning. Within family businesses, too, the existence and perceived important of network-based learning and the development of International networks to facilitate this is an area of some interest (FBN, 2008).

A separate area of research has focussed upon the organisational context of business knowledge, linking directly to the effectiveness of Government policy in knowledge transfer and its impact on regeneration policies (Pittway et al, 2005).

The relatively informal management structures commonly associated with family businesses in their early stages of growth commonly facilitates internal knowledge transfer initially and one associated with both increased flexibility and increased profitability. This relatively informal approach to management and knowledge transfer may, however, be a key factor that limits both business growth and the ability of a business to interact with the formalised systems for knowledge transfer and external knowledge-base partners in the longer term.

Formalised models of knowledge transfer within a family business environment provide some structures for the consideration of knowledge, learning and its relationship to entrepreneurship in a family business context, but much of the work in this area has considered knowledge transfer primarily in the context of succession planning and the one-way transfer of knowledge from an older to a younger generation (Trevinyo-Rodriguez and Tapies, 2006). Succession planning remains an important focus, however, and work by Trevinyo-Rodriguez and Tapies (2006) has focussed upon classic theories of learning and applied them in the context of family business, providing a useful model linking the multiple strands and factors that contribute to knowledge transfer and business learning, but incorporating within the model factors such as culture and the family values (Trevinyo-Rodriguez and Tapies, 2006).

The applicability of KTFF (Knowledge Transfer Model in Family Firms) in a more general sense would merit further research and it is considered likely that where knowledge transfer is considered in a more general sense an extra dimension would be found representing the 'chance' element of learning. This random or 'chance' element occurs where businesses engage with knowledge transfer almost accidentally, often through the social networks within which a family business operates. Research which considers the KTFF model at different stages of business and family development would also be welcome.

Much of the debate surrounding the transfer of knowledge as a factor in business development occurs due to the sheer multiplicity of routes, mechanisms and possible channels involved. Certainly, knowledge transfer can include both internal and external learning. Learning within the business, learning within the broader family/ community context and especial importance of community in a rural context may all be relevant. Alongside this sits the work of the external agencies and the role they play in the transfer of knowledge – be they business support networks, educational establishments, professions working with businesses or any of the myriad others who interact with the business community.

Implications of Knowledge Transfer and Business Learning

Allowing knowledge transfer and business learning to be viewed as a top-down process, important only in the limited context of succession planning, risks limiting understanding of a more fluid, on-going process key to the development of individual businesses but vital also in the wider context of business families and regional economic development.

Indeed, a key thesis of current research in Scotland is that the scope of knowledge transfer is both under-researched and researched in a relatively limited sense which does not take into full account the myriad ways in which businesses learn and the diversity of explicit and tacit knowledge which is passed on.

Within knowledge transfer research, for example, some consideration is usually given to the distinction between internal knowledge transfer and interactions between a business and external knowledge partners, who may be based within the professional, business support or University sectors. One of the unique aspects of family businesses, however, lies in the difficulty in delineating between these two approaches.

Where non-family businesses are studied, the staff on the payroll of the business are usually – and rightly - considered to be the pool of internal knowledge expertise on which the business may draw. Within family businesses, however, access to the wider pool of family expertise not formally associated with the business is common and, with care, can form a natural bridge between internal and external knowledge transfer.

Similarly, all businesses tend to learn from others within their community and from the social networks with which they engage, but within the family business there is an additional tier to the knowledge pool. In considering the family business, the concept of 'one family, one business' is in itself simplistic: patterns of serial entrepreneurship within business families, where the business ethic is strong and where businesses are often developed by different family members, in different generations and sometimes in different sectors are relatively common. The key distinction in terms of knowledge transfer is that within a business family environment, the family can call upon a common experience of the merits and mechanics of being in business and a common pool of operational and strategic expertise.

This blurring of the distinction between internal and external knowledge transfer within a family business setting creates a situation where more research would be useful, but where the paradigms and approaches more commonly associated with social networking research might provide a useful perspective for knowledge transfer.

Knowledge transfer within the family business and business family environments, however, depends heavily upon family culture, is often informal and is often dependent on chance, circumstance and the individual interests and expertise of the family in its broader sense. Combined with the relatively informal management style within many family businesses, a situation is thereby created where the interaction of individual family members with business learning can potentially act as a catalyst for dynamic change within the business and offers an alternative and less well researched approach to knowledge transfer.

Family Businesses Interacting with the Knowledge Base: Universities and Formalised Systems for Knowledge Transfer

Business interaction with the external knowledge base partners, such as Universities, forms an important part of National and Global strategies for effective knowledge transfer and remains a key goal of most UK Universities. A number of different structures have been developed nationally to facilitate knowledge transfer work between industry and the knowledge base, notably Knowledge Transfer Partnerships and the core funding allocation allowance for University knowledge transfer work. In addition, a number of other sources of funding are available for knowledge transfer work, creating a variety of sources of funding for different types of projects and businesses at different stages of development.

The interaction of family businesses with formalised knowledge transfer schemes is an under-researched area which perhaps reflects the tendency within the UK to consider the family business as a business like any other and to largely ignore the family element. Similarly, this may be partly a feature of the – admittedly lessening – tendency to view knowledge transfer as distinct from and possibly inferior to – academic research. Evidence in this area is sparse, but amongst knowledge transfer professionals the challenges and opportunities provided by the family environment are widely acknowledged as an influence on the development of individual projects and the management of schemes which aim to place graduates within the family business. Indeed, the role of non-family members within a family business environment represents a substantial area of research which influences many areas of the business operation but the placing of new and often relatively in-experienced graduates

within the family business environment provides unique professional challenges.

Promoting, setting up and managing knowledge transfer projects between Universities and family businesses is a highly specialised skill which draws heavily on facilitation techniques and on an understanding of the interaction between knowledge of the business, knowledge of the family and knowledge of the interaction of the wider business environment. Managing the expectations of family, of business and of university is a major challenge, much assisted by the use of project management techniques inherent within the model for knowledge transfer partnerships. Using formalised project management techniques within the often less formal environment of a family business provides its own unique challenges, however and anecdotal evidence suggests that such techniques tend either to work extremely well or to be of very limited use. The outcomes, as with many knowledge transfer projects, depend largely upon factors such as the degree of buy-in within the company to the individual project, to the clarity and professionalism of the management and decision making structures within the company itself and to the degree to which the project 'team' becomes a functioning team.

Similarly, while diverse business cultures have an impact upon knowledge transfer so do diverse social cultures and the development of knowledge transfer projects within Scotland's minority ethnic communities is an area where future research would be useful. Knowledge transfer where the business is owned or managed by a family provide certain challenges but so does a situation where knowledge transfer is being carried out within a business where much of the workplace does not share a common first language with the ownership/management. Whilst a myriad of languages within a workforce perhaps represents an extreme, that extreme illustrates the impact of business culture.

FUTURE RESEARCH DIRECTIONS: FIRST STEPS

Integrated research to explore current understanding and develop enhanced knowledge transfer remains the key to future development, in a Scottish context and Worldwide. The importance of culture in the societal sense and internally within individual industries and businesses is well established within current research: the role of culture in facilitating proactive environments for active, on-going knowledge transfer and business learning is key and merits further research.

In addition, further research directions require to be integrated in a number of ways: closer links between knowledge transfer research *per se* and family business research are required and whilst this can be somewhat facilitated by the SFBA the importance of the family aspect merits greater acknowledgement at an academic level within Universities. Similarly, broadening current understanding of what is meant by knowledge transfer would be useful; integrating the family component within succession planning, for example, is relatively well established within current thinking. Integrating the family component within strategic business development, product development and a host of other areas is less well developed and forms a fruitful area for potential research.

In parallel lies the potential for increasing current understanding of the manner in which knowledge transfer adapts – or fails to adapt – as a family business develops. The continuum of development of a family business, from a family-operated business through the development of a managing family to potentially a shareholding family – is relatively well established, but the manner in which knowledge transfer changes during this process is less fully explored. Similarly, the role that knowledge transfer plays in the development of the family along that continuum is unclear and would merit further exploration.

Finally, the multiplicity of research potential merits a mention in its own right: knowledge transfer is partly a practical process and partly concerned with the effective transmission of appropriate academic theory. There is – and will remain – the potential for theoretical development, for observational research of the knowledge transfer process and for action-research within a business environment.

CONCLUSION

The importance of family business, in economic, social and community terms has been well established by a worldwide body of research but remains a relatively under-researched area within Scotland. The growing acknowledgement of the importance of family business, within political debate, within business support networks and within the University sector creates a situation where further research is required to underpin future developmental strategies and to form a robust platform for growth.

Similarly, the impact of knowledge transfer on strategic business development and hence on the development of competitive advantage is well established but the manner in which these processes happen in family business and in the wider environment of business families is a key area for future research which influences future economic growth and the development of competitive Nations with sustainable communities.

Scotland remains a geographically diverse country, with a variety of urban and rural areas where businesses operate. The relatively high numbers of family businesses within rural areas and their relative resistance to geographic relocation, however, create a situation where the development of sustainable competitive advantage within the family business is likely to be a vital component of Regional strategies for economic development on National and Global level.

Identifying and implementing strategies for successful knowledge transfer in diverse family environments – and learning lessons from an International perspective – is and will remain key.

FURTHER READING

Davenport, T. H., & Prusack, L. (1998). Working knowledge: How organizations manage what they know. Boston: Harvard Business School Press.

Dyer, W. G. Jr. (1998). Culture and continuity in family firms. *Family Business Review*, *1*(1), 37–50. doi:10.1111/j.1741-6248.1988.00037.x

Fletcher, D. (2002). *Understanding the small family business. Routledge studies in small business*. London: Routledge.

Getz, D., Carlsen, J., & Morrison, A. (2004). The family business in hospitality and tourism. Cambridge, MA: CABI Publishing.

Pittaway, L., Thorpe, R., Holte, R., & Macpherson, A. (2005). *Knowledge within small and medium sized firms: A systematic review of the evidence* (Lancaster University Management School Working Paper 2005/020).

Poutziouris, Z. P., Smyrnios, K. X., & Klein, B. S. (Eds.). (2006). *Handbook of research on family business*. Cheltenham, UK: Edward Elgar.

REFERENCES

Allio, M. K. (2004). Family businesses: Their virtues, vices and strategic paths. *Strategy and Leadership*, *32*(4), 24–33. doi:10.1108/10878570410576704

Astrachan, J. H., Keyt, A., Lane, S., & McMillan, K. (2006). Generic models for family business boards of directors. In P. Z. Poutzioris, K. X. Smyrnios, & S. B. Klein (Eds.), *Handbook of research on family businesses*. Cheltenham, UK: Edward Elgar.

Astrachan, J. H., & Shanker, M. C. (2006). Family businesses' contribution to the US economy: A closer look. In P. Z. Poutziouris, K. X. Smyrnios, & S. B. Klein (Eds.), *Handbook of research on family businesses*. Cheltenham, UK: Edward Elgar.

Blackmore, A. (2004). Improving the use of know-how in organisations by recognising enablers and contributors. *Journal of Knowledge Management*, *8*(2), 112–113. doi:10.1108/13673270410529154

Cabrera-Suarez, K., De Saa-Perez, P., & Garcia-Almeida, D. (2001). The succession process from a resource- and knowledge-based view of the family firm. *Family Business Review*, *14*(1), 37–46. doi:10.1111/j.1741-6248.2001.00037.x

Davenport, T. H., & Prusack, L. (1998). *Working knowledge: How organizations manage what they know*. Boston: Harvard Business School Press.

Deakins, D., Ishaq, M., Whittam, G., & Wyper, J. (2008). Diversity in ethnic minority businesses in rural and urban localities. *International Journal of Entrepreneurship and Small Business*, *7*(3).

Dhaliwal, S., & Kangis, P. (2006). Asians in the UK: Gender, generations and enterprise. *Equal Opportunities International*, *25*(2), 92–108. doi:10.1108/02610150610679529

Druker, P. F. (1998). The coming of the new organisation. *Harvard Business Review*, ▪▪▪, 1–21.

DTi Small Business Service. (2006). *Annual small business survey*. London: DTi.

Dyer, W. G. Jr. (1998). Culture and continuity in family firms. *Family Business Review*, *1*(1), 37–50. doi:10.1111/j.1741-6248.1988.00037.x

Easterby-Smith, M., Lyles, M. A., & Tsang, E. W. K. (2008). Inter-organizational knowledge transfer: Current themes and future perspectives. *Journal of Management Studies*, *45*(4), 677–690. doi:10.1111/j.1467-6486.2008.00773.x

European Commission. (2003). *Green paper entrepreneurship in Europe*. Brussels, Belgium: Commission of the European Communities.

Family Business Network International. (2008). Retrieved from http://www.fbn-1.com

Getz, D., Carlson, J., & Morrison, A. (2004). *The family business in tourism and hospitality*. Wallingford, UK: CABI Publishing.

Habberston, T. G., & Pistrui, J. (2004). *A model for strategic dialogue, establishing congruency in your mindset and methods*. Paper Presented at FBN-IFERA (International Family Enterprise Research Academy) Conference, Jonkoping, Sweden.

Habberston, T. G., Williams, M., & MacMillan, I. C. (2006). A unified systems perspective of family firm performance. In P. Z. Poutziouris, K. X. Smyrnios, & S. B. Klein (Eds.), *Handbook of research on family businesses*. Cheltenham, UK: Edward Elgar.

Habberston, T. G., & Williams, M. L. (1999). A resourced-based framework for assessing the strategic advantages of family firms. *Family Business Review, 12*(1), 1–22. doi:10.1111/j.1741-6248.1999.00001.x

Habberston, T. G., Williams, M. L., & MacMillan, I. (2003). Familieness: A unified systems theory of family business performance. *Journal of Business Venturing, 18*(4), 451. doi:10.1016/S0883-9026(03)00053-3

Hall, A., Melin, L., & Nordqvist, M. (2006). Understanding strategizing in the family business context. In P. Z. Poutziouris, K. X. Smyrnios, & S. B. Klein (Eds.), *Handbook of research on family businesses*. Cheltenham, UK: Edward Elgar.

Hamel, G. (1991). Competition for competence and inter-partner learning within international strategic alliances. *Strategic Management Journal, 12*, 83–103. doi:10.1002/smj.4250120908

Harding, R. (2006). *Family business specialist summary*. GEM Consulting for the Institute of Family Business

Institute for Family Business. (2008). *The UK family business sector: An Institute for Family Business report*. Capital Economics Institute for Family Business. (2007). *Key facts on the UK family business economy, fact sheet*. London:The Institute for Family Business.

Jones, O. (2003). Competitive advantage in SMEs: Towards a conceptual framework. In O. Jones & F. Tilley (Eds.), *Competitive advantage in SMEs*. Chicester, UK: Wiley.

Kets de Vries, M. F. R., & Carlock, R. S. with Florent-Treacy, E. (2007). *Family business on the couch*. Chichester, UK: Wiley.

Ko, D. G., Kirsch, L. J., & King, W. R. (2005). Antecedents for knowledge transfer from consultants to clients in enterprising system implementations. *MIS Quarterly, 29*, 59–85.

Lee, D. S., Lim, G. H., & Lim, W. S. (2003). Family business succession: Appropriation risk and choice of successor. *Academy of Management Review, 28*(4), 657–666.

Lynch, R. (2006). *Corporate strategy*. Harlow, UK: Pearson Education Ltd.

Nicholson, N. (2005). Family ties – binding, bonding or breaking? *Families in Business*, (March-April): 80.

Nonaka, I., & Takeuchi, H. (1995). The knowledge creating company. Oxford, UK: Oxford University Press.

Parise, S., Cross, R., & Davenport, T. H. (2006). Strategies for preventing a knowledge loss crisis. *Sloan Management Review, 47*(4).

Pistrui, D., Huang, W. V., Welsh, H. P., & Jing, Z. (2006). Family and cultural forces: Shaping entrepreneurship and SME development in China. In P. Z. Poutziouris, K. X. Smyrnios, & S. B. Klein (Eds.), *Handbook of research on family businesses*. Cheltenham, UK: Edward Elgar.

Pittaway, L., Thorpe, R., Holte, R., & Macpherson, A. (2005). *Knowledge within small and medium sized firms: A systematic review of the evidence* (Lancaster University Management School Working Paper 2005/020).

Porter, M. E. (1990). *The competitive advantage of nations*. London: Macmillan.

Poutzioris, Z. P. (2006). The structure and performance of the UK family business PLC Economy. In P. Z. Poutziouris, K. X. Smyrnios, & S. B. Klein (Eds.), *Handbook of research on family businesses*. Cheltenham, UK: Edward Elgar.

Poutziouris, Z. P., Smyrnios, K. X., & Klein, B. S. (Eds.). (2006). *Handbook of research on family business*. Cheltenham, UK: Edward Elgar.

Randeree, E. (2006). Knowledge management: Securing the future. *Journal of Knowledge Management, 10*(4), 145–156. doi:10.1108/13673270610679435

Reid, R., & Harris, R. I. D. (2004). *Family-owned SME growth in Scotland: A comparison with the UK* (Report to Scotecon).

Reid, R. S., & Adams, J. S. (2001). Human resource management – a survey of practices within family and non-family firms. *Journal of European Industrial Training, 25*(6), 310–320. doi:10.1108/03090590110401782

Scottish Executive. (2004). *The framework for economic development in Scotland*. Scottish Executive.

Scottish Executive Annual Survey of Small Businesses. (2003). *Final report enterprise and lifelong learning.*

Scottish Executive Annual Survey of Small Businesses. (2005). *Final report enterprise and lifelong learning.*

Scottish Government. (2007). *The government economic strategy*. The Scottish Government, Edinburgh, Scotland.

Scottish Government. (2008). *Annual survey of small business opinions 2006*. Scottish Government.

Seaman, C., Graham, S., & Falconer, P. (2007). *Family businesses in Scotland: In pursuit of a national strategy for local solutions*. Paper Presented at "Bridging Cultures' Confronting Theory and Practice in Family Business,' Lancaster University Management School.

Seaman, C., Graham, S., & Falconer, P. (2009). Exploring Scottish family businesses: Economy, geography and community. *International Journal of Entrepreneurship and Small Business, 7*(3).

Shanker, M. C., & Astrachan, J. H. (1996). Myths and realities: Family businesses contribution to the U.S. economy. A framework for assessing business statistics. *Family Business Review, 9*(2), 107–119. doi:10.1111/j.1741-6248.1996.00107.x

Sharma, P. (2006). An overview of the field of family business studies: Current status and directions for the future. In P. Z. Poutziouris, K. X. Smyrnios, & S. B. Klein (Eds.), *Handbook of research on family businesses*. Cheltenham, UK: Edward Elgar.

Steier, L. (2001). Variants of agency contracts in family financed ventures as a continuum of familial altruistic and market rationalities. *Journal of Business Venturing, 18*(5), 597–618. doi:10.1016/S0883-9026(03)00012-0

Steier, L. (2001). Variants of agency contracts in family financed ventures as a continuum of familial altruistic and market rationalities. *Journal of Business Venturing, 18*(5), 597–618. doi:10.1016/S0883-9026(03)00012-0

Stepek, M., & Laird, M. (2007). *SFBA strategy: A discussion document*. Scottish Family Business Association.

Szulanski, G. (1995). Unpacking stickiness: An empirical investigation of the barriers to transfer best practice inside the firm. *Academy of Management Journal, 38,* 437–441.

Trevinyo-Rodriguez, R. N., & Tapies, J. (2006). Effective knowledge transfer in family firms. In P. Z. Poutziouris, K. X. Smyrnios, & S. B. Klein (Eds.), *Handbook of research on family business*. Cheltenham, UK: Edward Elgar.

Uhlander, L. M., & Habberson, T. (2005). *Family influence, strategy, and innovation in family firms: Application of the DSP-"f" model in an exploratory four country investigation*. Paper Presented at FBN-IFERA (International Family Enterprise Research Academy) Conference, Barcelona, Spain.

Ward, J. L. (1987). *Keeping the family business healthy*. San Francisco: Jossey-Bass.

Westhead, P., & Cowling, M. (1997). Performance contrasts between family and non-family unquoted companies in the UK. *International Journal of Entrepreneurial Behaviour & Research, 3*(1), 30–52. doi:10.1108/13552559710170892

Zahra, S. A., Klein, S. B., & Astrachan, J. H. (2006). Epilogue: Theory building and the survival of family firms – three promising research directions. In P. Z. Poutziouris, K. X. Smyrnios, & S. B. Klein (Eds.), *Handbook of research on family businesses*. Cheltenham, UK: Edward Elgar.

Zander, U., & Kogut, B. (1995). Knowledge and the speed of transfer and imitation of organisational capabilities: An empirical test. *Organization Science, 6,* 76–92. doi:10.1287/orsc.6.1.76

Chapter 12
Mentoring and the Transfer of Organizational Memory Within the Context of an Aging Workforce:
Cultural Implications for Competitive Advantage

Annette H. Dunham
University of Canterbury, New Zealand

Christopher D.B. Burt
University of Canterbury, New Zealand

ABSTRACT

Organizational memory, the knowledge gained from organizational experience, has significant potential for competitive advantage. Many authors in the knowledge management and human resource management literatures consider mentoring to be a particularly effective method of transferring organizational memory. In addition, older workers are often considered ideal mentors in organizations because of their experience and alleged willingness to pass on their knowledge to less experienced employees. There is an associated assumption that these workers also anticipate and experience positive outcomes when mentoring others. This chapter considers whether these assumptions hold up in the workplaces of the 21st century, particularly within Western countries. Individualistic cultural norms and some discriminatory practices towards older workers, along with a changing career contract that no longer guarantees employment in one organization for life, may discourage knowledge sharing in organizations. This chapter discusses the constraints and motivations that may operate when older experienced workers consider mentoring others. It considers relevant global and organizational cultural characteristics that may influence mentoring to transfer knowledge, and accordingly suggests strategies for those eager to capitalise on the knowledge experienced employees possess.

DOI: 10.4018/978-1-60566-790-4.ch012

INTRODUCTION

"A survey of human resources directors by IBM last year concluded: "When the baby-boomer generation retires, many companies will find out too late that a career's worth of experience has walked out the door, leaving insufficient talent to fill the void..."

Special Report: The Ageing Workforce, Economist, February 18th-24th, 2006 (p.61)

In many countries, people are retiring earlier than ever before and the retirement of the baby boom generation (born 1946-1964) over the next two decades signals a decline in the working populations of many developed countries. Accompanying this trend is the potential loss of organizational memory, and the subsequent loss of competitive advantage. When employees retire from an organization, it may be straightforward to replace their job-related knowledge, skills and abilities; but it is much more difficult to replace the organization and industry related knowledge gained from experience.

The aging workforce phenomenon has generated a number of publications in the human resource management literature. These are aimed at helping organizations encourage older employees to work for as long as possible, together with suggestions on how to effectively harness the knowledge, skills and abilities of the older worker (e.g. Critchley, 2004; DeLong, 2004; Hankin, 2005; Hedge, Borman & Lammlein, 2006; Lahaie, 2005). Some specifically address the threatened knowledge management crisis that may accompany the loss of experienced workers (e.g. DeLong, 2004). These writers also tend to consider mentoring in organizations as a way of both ensuring vital knowledge transfer while also accomplishing the continued engagement of older workers who will feel valued for their expertise

and knowledge. It is seemingly a win-win approach for all concerned.

Underlying this perspective are several assumptions:

1) The ability to create, identify, capture and transfer organizational memory equates to competitive advantage for companies.
2) Older workers have valued knowledge and experience, and are significant repositories of organizational memory.
3) Older workers are particularly amenable to passing on their knowledge to others in the organization.
4) Older workers anticipate, and are more likely to experience, positive outcomes from mentoring others.

The knowledge management literature has given substantial focus to the contribution that the creation, identification, capture and transference of knowledge makes to an organization's competitive advantage (e.g. Cross & Baird, 2000; Kransdorff & Williams, 2000; Nonaka & Takeuchi, 1995; Stein, 1995, Zack, 1999). However, as Argote and Ingram (2000) point out, "more effort has gone into identifying knowledge as the basis for competitive advantage than into explaining how organizations can develop, retain, and transfer that knowledge"(p.156). This may be one reason why the above assumptions have escaped closer examination.

The purpose of this chapter is to critically examine these assumptions, and discuss if they are still relevant for the workplaces of the 21st Century. Workplace cultures have changed considerably. The massive organizational downsizing and restructurings of the late 1980s and 1990s have affected the psychological contract between employee and employer. In particular, organizations can seldom guarantee life-long employment for workers and this may negatively influence the loyalty and commitment that experienced employees have for their organization (Barth, McNaught & Rizzi, 1993).

Along with changes to the psychological contract, experienced workers are often (but not exclusively) in their mid to late career when considered suitable for mentoring others, and as such may be subject to less than ideal working conditions that may constrain their desire to mentor. In some organizations and cultures, they can be the target of both positive stereotypes (e.g., they have experience and are loyal to the organization), and negative stereotypes (e.g., they have outdated skills and are not so eager to learn), (Barth et al., 1993; Hummert, Garstka, Ryan & Bonneson, 2004; Sterns & Miklos, 1995). Their careers may have stagnated resulting in reduced access to and motivation for training and development activities, some workplaces may value formal credentials over the knowledge and skills gained "on the job", and they face continuing time demands at work that often preclude them from offering "extra-role" behaviours like mentoring (Davey, 2003; Davey & Cornwall, 2003; OECD, 2006). These may contribute to quite a different scenario concerning the experienced workers motivation to mentor others, and points to several costs and benefits that these workers might perceive in passing on their knowledge. Furthermore, western cultures may be particularly at risk as the presence of individualistic norms has the potential to undermine the relational infrastructure that may enhance knowledge sharing (Bright, 2005).

The chapter contributes to the discussion among knowledge management and human resource management researchers and practitioners regarding the transfer of organizational memory for competitive advantage within the context of an aging workforce. It will consider characteristics of both global and organizational cultures that may affect the transfer of organizational memory, and employee motivations to mentor. Our hope is to go beyond the prescription of "mentoring" as the general panacea for transferring organizational memory and the means to engage experienced employees, by suggesting other motivations that may be operating when experienced employees are called upon to share their knowledge.

AN AGING WORKFORCE AND RISKS TO KNOWLEDGE MANAGEMENT

Over the next 25 years, the working-age population of Europe is projected to fall by almost 50 million due to the retirement of members of the baby-boom generation born between 1945 and 1964 (New Zealand Department of Labour, 2002). All OECD countries are expecting the numbers of elderly within their populations to grow and their working population to decrease. Falling fertility rates mean that fewer new workers will be coming through to replace retiring workers, and the number of people retiring will soon exceed those entering the workforce (OECD, 2006). Within the United States, the number of workers in the over 55 group is expected to grow at four times the rate of the overall workforce (Alley & Crimmins, 2007). While not every company reflects this demographic trend (Capelli, 2003), some industries are more at risk than others are. One third of the workforce engaged in the United States energy industry for example, are aged over 50, and this age group is expected to increase by 25 percent by 2020 (Strack, Baier & Fahlender, 2008). Organizations are slowly waking up to the implications of this trend, but there is a fear that this frequently occurs only after experienced workers have "walked out the door" (The Economist, February 18th, 2006). When an age cohort representing a large proportion of the working population are exiting around the same time, as is the case of the anticipated retirement of the 'Baby Boom' generation, there is even greater impact.

ORGANIZATIONAL MEMORY

Organizational memory, the knowledge gained from "experience" within a particular work context, consists of "stored information from an organization's history that can be brought to bear on present decisions," (Walsh & Ungson, 1991, p.61). Employees, individually and collectively, represent knowledge "repositories" (Walsh & Ungson, 1991) or knowledge "reservoirs" (Argote & Ingram, 2000). The content of organizational memory broadly encompasses "organizational beliefs, knowledge, frames of reference, models, values and norms; as well as organizational myths, legends and stories" to the more explicit "formal and informal behavioural routines, procedures and scripts," within companies (Moorman & Miner, 1997, p. 92). DeLong (2004) referring to the threat to knowledge management that an aging population poses, refers to this organizational memory as (potentially) "lost knowledge" for organizations. He categorises the content areas of this knowledge as "human knowledge" or technical expertise, "social knowledge" (knowledge of relevant social networks), "cultural knowledge" (or organizational expertise) as well as the more explicit knowledge or "structured information" within organizational rules, regulations and routines.

Organizational Memory and Competitive Advantage

Through their knowledge base, organizations can differentiate themselves from their competitors (Argote & Ingram, 2000). Organizational memory represents the potential for competitive advantage, by providing a store of knowledge gained from experience that current organizational members can draw on in their practice (Cross & Baird, 2000; Stein, 1995). In this way, it is a resource, for solving problems (e.g. Cross & Baird, 2000), the development of best practices (e.g. Rulke, Zaheer, & Anderson, 2000; Szulanski, 1996),

decision-making and company strategy, (e.g. Neustadt & May, 1986; Zack, 1999), and for product and service innovation (e.g. Moorman & Miner, 1997). According to Johnson and Paper (1998) mechanisms for organizational memory have the potential to enhance learning from history (e.g. Neustadt & May, 1986), to help the organization to avoid repeating past mistakes, as well as to remember what contributed to success, and as such are a significant means of sustaining competitive advantage.

While organizational memory offers much for competitive advantage, there are several acknowledged potential drawbacks of which to be mindful. These include concerns about selective memory, denial of lessons learned, tunnel vision (or inflexibility in decision-making), and maintenance of the status quo when change may lead to more effective methods (Johnson & Paper, 1998; Kransdorff & Williams, 2000; Stein, 1995).

Organizational memory consists of both explicit and tacit knowledge (Bryant, 2005; Kransdorff & Williams, 2000). Nonaka and Takeuchi (1995) consider explicit knowledge largely impersonal, easily articulated and generally independent of context (e.g. operating instructions and procedures); compared to tacit knowledge, which is "subconsciously understood and applied, difficult to articulate, and developed from direct experience" (Zack, 1999, p.46). Tacit knowledge has both a cognitive dimension concerned with beliefs, traditions and other shared mental models; and a technical dimension incorporating skill and know-how which is largely context dependent (Stephens, Bird & Mendenhall, 2002). Tacit knowledge, is sometimes referred to as procedural knowledge and/or implicit memory which is most simply, "how to" knowledge, and is difficult to articulate and yet which is evident in improved performance (Anderson, 2000).

Some suggest that, while not exclusively so, tacit knowledge is more pertinent than explicit knowledge to the concept of organizational memory and its potential for competitive advantage (e.g. Kransdorff & Williams, 2000). In general, tacit or implicit knowledge as Nonaka and Takeuchi (1995) define it, is hard to articulate and is dependent on context and face-to-face communication in the telling. This makes it resistant to imitation and movement across organizational boundaries, and explains why tacit knowledge resources within an organization specifically equate to competitive edge.

The term "tacit knowledge" is sometimes also applied (if erroneously) to information that is not written down for other reasons. Zack (1999) suggests that in some cases knowledge is labelled "tacit" only because it has not *yet* been articulated or simply because it is potentially sensitive and considered threatening to the social and cultural status quo of the organization. Social knowledge of who actually holds relevant knowledge or influence may differ in reality to who has the authority 'on paper'. However this too has relevance for competitiveness, as knowledge considered too sensitive within the culture of one organization may be legitimised by another, resulting in the latter's gain in competitive advantage over the former (Zack, 1999). There are those who argue that any split between explicit and tacit knowledge is artificial, recognising that all knowledge has its tacit dimensions (Leonard-Barton & Sensiper, 1998; Polanyi, 1966; Rulke et al., 2000).

All knowledge resulting from the lessons the organization and its members have learned in the past is significant for competitive edge. According to Cross and Baird (2000) the explicit and tacit knowledge held by individual and groups of employees is crucial to organizations' capacity to solve problems and innovate, contributing to competitive edge. They argue that while organizational memory can be stored in non-human repositories like computer databases, and policy and procedure manuals, as well as work processes, employees often turn to trusted and capable colleagues first for information. A study by Rulke et al., (2000) supported this emphasis on the importance of relational sources of information within organizations.

Mentoring to Transfer Organizational Memory

While aspects of organizational memory can be resistant to transfer beyond organizational walls, so can it prove challenging *within* the organization's walls. According to Zack (1999), the transfer of tacit knowledge is mostly achieved through face to face interaction with the use of conversation, stories and the sharing of personal experiences, a view shared by many, (e.g. DeLong 2004; Droege & Hoobler, 2003; Lahaie, 2005; Leonard & Swap, 2005; Linde, 2001; Swap, Leonard, Shields & Abrams, 2001). Storytelling in particular is a tool mentioned frequently when transferring experiential knowledge. Linde (2001) suggests for example, that "stories provide a bridge between the tacit and the explicit, allowing knowledge to be demonstrated and learned," (p. 163). The consensus that interpersonally intensive methods point the way to effective knowledge transfer emphasises the importance of relevant talent management strategies, which can comprise one of the most enduring sources of competitive advantage for companies (Heinen & O'Neill, 2004).

Mentoring is an interpersonal relationship mentioned frequently when discussing appropriate modes of transferring organizational memory. According to DeLong (2004), mentoring and coaching are "probably the most effective ways of directly transferring critical implicit knowledge from one individual to another" (p.107). Mentoring relationships represent the ideal context for building strong ties (e.g. Granovetter, 1973) that facilitate the transfer of complex information (Hansen, 1999). In accordance with this, Swap et al. (2001) suggested mentoring offers an opportunity to pass on technical skills, and information about organizational practices, and to convey knowledge and understanding of organizational norms, values and traditions, and the power structure undergirding organizational practice. Dytchwald, Erickson and Morison (2006) acknowledge the place of mentoring to both harness the knowledge and experience of older workers while also developing the organizational capabilities of less-experienced workers. Surprisingly the mentoring literature itself has been slow to focus on the knowledge transfer purpose and value of mentoring for organizations (Bryant, 2005).

OLDER WORKERS, ORGANIZATIONAL MEMORY AND MENTORING: ASSUMPTIONS

Older Workers and Organizational Memory

There is an expectation that older workers as a group have the appropriate characteristics to be ideal mentors. This assumption appears repeatedly throughout the theoretical literature on mentoring (e.g. Kram, 1985) and in the literature regarding the management of older workers (e.g. Beehr & Bowling, 2002; Critchely, 2004; Hedge et al., 2006). Kram's (1985) early work on mentoring stated that the "older worker" was able to provide wisdom to both teach other workers and to help shape organizational policy. Beehr and Bowling (2002, p.236) also write of older workers that "their experience, contacts, and knowledge" means they are resourceful mentors for the less experienced in the organization and provide further value to the organization through advisory roles to the organization's decision-makers. Hedge et al. (2006) suggest that the mentoring role publicly values the experience of older workers. Critchley (2004) argues that the skills and qualifications of new workers cannot compete with the knowledge gained from experience that older workers typically hold.

Employers also readily value the experience that older workers offer, although there is some ambivalence here (Barth et al., 1993). O'Donohue (2000) found that employers generally believed that older workers have valuable expertise that may be lost to the organization on their retirement,

with "useful experience" the most commonly cited attribute of older workers (83% of respondents) followed by a "strong work ethic" (62%) and "client knowledge" (56%). This assumption is so strong in general that Hummert, et al., (2004) suggest that older workers can help themselves at work by leveraging off this "positive age stereotype". They are encouraged to emphasise their age group's (and by association, their own) experience and maturity, particularly when it comes to working in political positions in their organizations.

Who is an older worker? Chronological definitions focus on a particular age (Sterns & Doverspike, 1989). For example in the United States the Job Training Partnership Act and the Older Americans Act define older workers as those aged 55 years and over, although the Age Discrimination in Employment Act regard age discrimination as applying to anyone over the age of 40 (Rothwell, Sterns, Spokus & Reaser, 2008). Some chronological definitions of the older worker relate to proximity to retirement age (e.g. Fraccaroli & Depolo, 2008) but this is problematic in times when governments are abolishing mandatory retirement ages. Chronological age is a poor predictor of aging-related behaviours, and definitions and meanings assigned to the aging process vary culturally (Pecchioni, Ota & Sparks, 2004). Functional aspects of aging physical, cognitive and social also vary according to chronological age (Baltes & Baltes, 1990; Nussbaum & Baringer, 2000).

In terms of organizational memory, experience resulting from tenure in a particular occupation and/or organization (Walsh & Ungson, 1991), as well as level of responsibility within an organization (Walsh, 1995) becomes salient. Older workers, due to their greater job and organizational tenure, tend to gravitate to upper level positions in their organization (Barnes-Farrell & Matthews, 2007). Their tendency for long tenure is well documented, and has both positive (e.g. they find a greater fit over time with their job and organization, and are more loyal than younger workers) and negative (e.g. they are afraid of leaving their positions as they age as they fear their chances on a competitive job market) explanations (CROW, 2004).

However, this generalisation is open to challenge. As Pecchioni et al., (2004) point out, "the assumption that senior-level individuals in an organization are older, and junior-level individuals are younger is quickly becoming a blurred line," (p.186). Employers acknowledge not all older workers have the experience required to be effective mentors (whether this is an evaluation of quality or quantity was not specified), and recruit mentors based on relevant experience rather than age (McPherson, 2008). For our purposes however, while we do not doubt that younger workers have areas of expertise and knowledge, the focus of this chapter are experienced workers of the Baby-Boom generation (born 1946 – 1964) and those born prior to this period.

Older Workers and Willingness to Mentor

Alongside the recognition given to older workers (in general) for their experience there seems to be an assumption that they are particularly motivated to pass on their knowledge to less experienced employees (e.g. Levinson, Darrow, Levinson, Klein, & McKee, 1978; Kram, 1985). Career development theories have come to acknowledge the mentor role as being a predictable occurrence at mid-career onwards, possibly acknowledging the tenure and positions of responsibility that contribute to the acquisition of organizational memory. In Dalton, Thompson and Price's (1977) four-stage model of professional career development, for example, acting as a mentor is a key role in stage three. This is congruent with Erikson's (1963) work on "generativity" and echoed by Levinson, et al., (1978). Through the concept of "generativity", Erikson (1963) proposed that mature adults take a role of leading, teaching and nurturing the generations after them.

Generativity is a force believed to emerge around mid-life, expressed in a variety of activities and settings including work and professional contexts. In the workplace, Levinson et al. (1978) outlined the value older and more experienced employees had as mentors to less experienced workers. Employees in mid-to late career are thought to be less tied to extrinsic rewards (e.g. pay, promotion) and more influenced by intrinsic motivations, including the drive to leave a legacy for following generations (Erikson, 1963; Kram, 1985). While, generativity seems to suggest a unique motivation for mentoring others in the workplace at mid-career and beyond, pragmatically, Kauffman (1982) suggests that an employee's financial preparedness for retirement may in fact be the overriding influence on the significance they attach to intrinsic and extrinsic rewards. This may be particularly so in times when economic dependence ratios are putting pressure on pension and superannuation schemes.

Furthermore, it does not necessarily follow that generativity, as a mentoring motivation will result in the transference of work related knowledge. Kram (1983, 1985) suggested two broad mentoring functions, 'career related' and 'psychosocial' mentoring. Career related mentoring consists of the mentor offering the protégé advantageous exposure, protection, coaching, challenging assignments and sponsorship in their relationship. Psychosocial mentoring includes functions such as counselling, friendship, role modelling and acceptance.

Subsequent research has identified that these two main functions (career-related and psychosocial mentoring) are not always present in equal quantities, and that there are individual differences in the mentoring functions offered in each relationship. Allen and Eby (2004) for example, found that male mentors reported providing more "career" mentoring to their protégés while female mentors provided more "psychosocial" mentoring. Darwin (2004) proposes that individuals high in 'nurturance', 'authenticity' and 'approachability' (as evaluated as pertinent to mentoring by proté-gés) are more likely to be altruistic and relational, and therefore more likely to offer psychosocial mentoring. Alternatively, Darwin suggests, mentors high in 'competence' (characterised by skill, experience and knowledge; informative teaching and the giving of sound advice) are likely to be task-focused and contribute more to job-related and career mentoring. While workers at mid-career and beyond may have the altruistic motivation of generativity to mentor, this may not necessarily include the types of mentoring that ensure the transfer of organizational memory.

Older Workers and Mentoring Outcomes

The human resource management literature suggests that not only are experienced workers more amenable to mentoring others, they are also most likely to experience positive outcomes from doing so. Kram (1985) suggests that mentoring enables the mentor at mid-career onwards to get in touch with aspects of their past youth, and may facilitate their transition to retirement by giving opportunity for them to reflect on their career as they pass on their knowledge to others. More recently Dytch-wald et al. (2006) also point out that mentoring others should rejuvenate those in mid-career. Offering older workers the opportunity to mentor is considered a way of valuing them and encouraging employment longevity (e.g. Barnes-Farrell and Mathews, 2007; Beehr & Bowling, 2002; Hedge, et al., 2006). As such, the opportunity to mentor seems a general 'cure-all' for keeping workers at mid-career and beyond engaged in their work. There is little consideration of possible negative outcomes and possible constraints to mentoring for this group.

WILLINGNESS TO MENTOR: RESEARCH

Mentoring research bears out the influence prosocial variables like altruism and empathy have in the motivation to mentor others (Allen, 2003; Allen, Poteet & Burroughs, 1997; Aryee, Chay & Chew, 1996; Ragins & Cotton, 1993; Ragins & Scandura, 1999). Whether older workers tend to favour these altruistic tendencies compared to younger employees appears difficult to call. Indeed, Allen et al. (1997) suggest that those more interested in personal growth and development will be more likely to mentor others, and do not claim an association for these personal characteristics with age.

While it has been suggested that there is likely to be a curvilinear relationship between age and the willingness to mentor others, with a peak at mid-career e.g. Kram, 1985), a study by Ragins and Cotton (1993) found a negative linear relationship between these variables. They found tenure to have a similar negative relationship, while conversely organizational rank had a positive relationship with willingness to mentor. Participants with higher organization rank and participants with less organizational tenure were more likely to signal an intention to mentor, and anticipated fewer difficulties with doing so. Ragins and Cotton speculated that workers with less tenure may be more idealistic towards mentoring, and/or as a group, it is more likely that they would have recent experience of mentoring which consequently may have inspired their own mentoring goals. Alternatively, those with less organizational tenure may also be more ambitious to advance in the organization, and see mentoring as one way of achieving this end. Ragins and Cotton saw the relationship between rank and willingness to mentor as support for the idea that mentoring tends to be a mid-career activity through the positive relationship between age and advancement.

The negative relationship between tenure and willingness to mentor would seem to be surprising considering the assumptions about experienced workers and mentoring. Ragins and Cotton (1993) suggested this effect might be a symptom of the career plateau that can occur with the greater tenure that also equates to "experience". Allen, Poteet and Russell (1998) too found support for a relationship between hierarchical career plateau in an organization, and age and tenure, probably a result of finding fewer promotions available. Cross and Baird (2000) suggest that ironically, sometimes knowledgeable employees begin to stagnate in their career as their organizations continually exploit their known expertise at the cost of developing their skills in other areas. The employee "stalled" in their career may consequently have negative feelings toward the organization, and be reluctant to contribute beyond the requirements of their role. Older employees who themselves have never been a mentor or protégé may also be resistant to these initiatives (Ragins & Cotton, 1993). They concluded that their study suggests, "Prior experience in mentoring relationships, position and rank may be better predictors of willingness to mentor than simply age or tenure" (Ragins & Cotton, 1993, p108).

Research has identified individual differences when it comes to the costs and benefits of mentoring from the mentors' perspective (Ragins & Cotton, 1993; Ragins & Scandura, 1994, 1999). While Ragins and Cotton (1993) found both males and females shared similar intentions to mentor, females perceived more drawbacks and to mentoring than males (e.g. greater visibility with potential for negative exposure), reported less time availability to mentor; and regarded themselves as not sufficiently qualified to mentor. However, a later study of male and female executives (Ragins & Scandura, 1999) found both groups to have similar perceptions of expected costs and benefits

in mentoring, indicating the role of organizational rank (and possibly the recognised organizational memory those with rank may have (c.f. Walsh, 1995) in the willingness to mentor others). It may also suggest that those without higher position in the hierarchy may fear their knowledge and experience is somehow inadequate to pass on to others. The costs and benefits identified provide a useful framework for future research to identify the specific outcomes that older workers anticipate in mentoring others.

ORGANISATIONAL MEMORY TRANSFER AND CONTEXTUAL ISSUES

The findings discussed above should signal an alert to human resource management researchers and professionals. They raise the possibility that experienced workers may not be so enthralled with the idea of mentoring others and passing on their knowledge as is often assumed. The costs and benefits of mentoring also allow for a more realistic appraisal of the specific constraints and motivations around mentoring than just the positive outcomes promoted. Consideration of the changing nature of work, and careers, as well as aspects related to the context of an aging workforce, suggest other reasons to revisit past assumptions, as do cultural considerations – both global and organizational.

The New Career Contract

The nature of the workplace and career has changed substantially since the early work on mentoring in the workplace (e.g. Erikson 1963, Levinson et al., 1978; Kram, 1985). This has resulted in a significantly altered psychological contract (Rousseau, 1995) that could influence the older workers' willingness to mentor. In many cases older experienced employees entered the workplace when 'one career for life' and even 'one organization or job for life,' were norms (Barth et al, 1993). These both ensured continuous organizational tenure (and therefore organizational memory and the accompanying resources to pass on to others); as well as contributing to the employees' sense of loyalty to the company, that may have resulted in a willingness to mentor. Large-scale organizational restructuring and downsizing, typical of the late twentieth century, may have eroded these expectations. Companies once able to make the promise to employees that 'the company will take care of you,' and provide life-long job security, retreated to offering merely employment security (employment, but not necessarily in the same job), to withdrawing guarantees of either (Harrington & Hall, 2007).

In times when job markets are highly competitive, or in organizations that have a highly competitive culture, workers are encouraged to have a different approach to their knowledge or "human capital" and the competitive advantage it can mean for them individually (McInerney & Mohr, 2007). This has direct implications for the future of mentoring, as Geisler (2008) points out, "managers and professionals are weary of divulging their 'tricks of the trade' and their knowledge of the political and social processes that helped to elevate them to their position and keep them there" (p.241). Many countries are now relaxing or have relaxed compulsory retirement age regulations, meaning that the older experienced worker, especially in cases where they have not prepared sufficiently well financially for their retirement, may need to protect their niche and reap the financial benefits of working longer.

The Context of an Aging Workforce

In addition to the changing nature of work, certain workplace attitudes and treatments of older experienced workers may also constrain their willingness to mentor others. In the human resource management and related policy literature, several themes consistently arise that negatively impact on older

workers and may discourage work longevity, and these too may potentially discourage willingness to mentor others.

Ageism and Poor Access to Training

At the policy level, the OECD (2006) report "Live Longer, Work Longer" identifies as troubling the "negative perceptions about the capabilities of older workers to adapt to technological and organizational change"(p.10). It suggests that this may result in the depreciation of the older workers' human capital by others in the organization, as well as in the mind of the worker concerned. In many countries, employers hold negative expectations about older workers and their ability and willingness to keep up with technological change and to continue learning (Davey & Cornwall, 2003; McGregor & Gray, 2002; OECD, 2006) and as suggested, older employees themselves often share this belief (McGregor & Gray, 2002). For example, older and younger workers have exhibited differences in learning rates (Czaja & Sharit, 1993; Kubeck, Delp, Haslett & McDaniel, 1996). However, Kubeck et al. (1996) note that there was greater variability in performance with age which justifies the need to evaluate older workers as individuals rather than members of their age cohort.

While employers and older workers may share some of these stereotypes about learning performance, there are differences between the groups in regards to how *willing* older workers are to engage in training and development. While employers seem to doubt that older workers are willing to up-skill, there is some evidence that older workers themselves lament their lack of development opportunities (McGregor & Gray, 2002). As a result, there is a widening gap between job demands and the opportunities to learn new skills to meet these demands for older workers.

Consequently, age related stereotypes about the ability to train and to master technology reputedly have a significant role in limiting the older workers' access to training. According to Maurer, (2007) stereotypes can result in the older worker being denied entrance to training and development opportunities, and secondly (and less overtly) that they may receive little support or even be discouraged from participating in the training events that are open to them. Perceived discomfort with technology may particularly prevent their inclusion in some training programmes (Brooke & Taylor, 2005). Older workers themselves may start to question their own ability to learn, or the appropriateness of learning to their age and stage of life, a version of the self-fulfilling prophecy (Maurer, Weiss & Barbeite, 2003). Finkelstein, Allen and Rhoton (2003) suggest that older workers may internalise this, feeling that because they are "experienced" they should not need the guidance and support or development including being mentored themselves, when this kind of developmental support may be justified in some cases, (e.g. working in a new job context or learning new skills).

Lack of access to training and development has definite implications for potential mentors. Experience as a mentor and/or protégé relates positively to the willingness to mentor others (Allen et al., 1997), so the lack of involvement in developmental relationships even as a protégé may restrict the pool of willing mentors. Secondly, poor access to training and development may result in the conclusion that the organization does not support the experienced worker and may dampen any enthusiasm they have to reciprocate in a mentoring role (Ragins & Cotton, 1993). Finally, poor access to training for some can send a message about these workers to others in the organization. Some protégés may not be willing to have a mentor who appears stalled in their career, even if they do have considerable experience.

The lack of access to training can become a vicious cycle for experienced workers of any age, and their organizations. According to Higgins and Kram (2001), seniority no longer instantly equates to organizational value. Life-long learning is the currency of the new career (Harrington & Hall, 2007). If employees, for any reason, are not included in training events, this is both limiting for the individual's capacity to prepare for current and future career demands, and their companies' ability to adapt to change.

Credentialism

Older experienced employees may experience a further depreciation of their knowledge and skills due to the value placed on formal educational qualifications in labour markets. The validation given in the workplace to formal qualifications is not always extended to the knowledge and skills gained through experience (Davey, 2003; Davey &Cornwall, 2003). Livingstone and Sawchuk (2004), for example, while documenting the learning practices of working-class people across several industries, found that interviewees valued formal education not only for the credentialing it gives in the labour market, but for the comparatively higher self-esteem it gives in the workplace.

In many cases, older workers will have received their skills training "on-the-job" and thus lack the formal qualifications that younger workers have (Davey, 2003). The experience-based nature of organizational memory may predispose older workers to discount their knowledge compared to formal qualifications (Davey & Cornwall, 2003). Depending on their own comfort level with new technologies, these workers may fear that their knowledge is mostly obsolete in the face of new technological advances. This perceived depreciation of their knowledge resources may result in a reluctance to mentor others. Ironically, the lower than average educational qualifications held by older workers has been cited as a reason why some employers invest little in their continued training (OECD, 2006), creating a vicious cycle.

Time Demands

Perceived lack of time to mentor may also restrict experienced workers and again older workers in particular, from mentoring others. Cranwell-Ward, Bossons and Gover (2004) note that the time commitment involved is the most frequently acknowledged mentoring constraint. Some groups may signal this more than others, for example, Ragins and Cotton (1993) found women reported they had little time available to mentor. Older workers tend to seek opportunities to work less rather than more (e.g. Barth et al., 1993), and may be more resistant to involvement in mentoring initiatives unless time is allocated in some way for the purpose. While older workers may be more inclined to seek ways of achieving generativity in their lifestyle, demands from contexts external to work (e.g. family and community responsibilities) may mean that this motivation is acted out largely in those domains, to the cost of available time and energy for mentoring others in the workplace.

MENTORING AND CULTURAL IMPLICATIONS

A culture can be defined as the shared characteristics of a group (e.g. norms, values, beliefs, symbols and traditions) that make them unique (Gudykunst & Ting-Toomey, 1988). These characteristics in turn guide our interactions with each other, including the way we value older people (or not) in our groups (Ting-Toomey, 1999). Culture can be discussed at both the organizational and global level.

Global Cultures

Not all countries faced with an aging workforce also face the issues outlined above that may discourage older workers from sharing their knowledge. Cultural differences may mean that the identified threats are not as applicable to all.

Japan for example is (along with Finland, Sweden, Switzerland and Luxembourg), one of the oldest workforces in the world (Pecchioni, et al., 2004). Japan leads the world for the proportion of older people which make up its population (Rothwell et al., 2008), and is influenced by collectivist norms and values (House, Javidian, Dorfman, & Gupta, 2004).

The cultural differences between East and West are often summed as the difference between collectivism (East) and individualism (West) (Pecchioni et al, 2004). Eastern cultures are characterised by action towards group goals whether organizational, family or societal, (House et al., 2004; Kim & Yamaguchi, 1995, Triandis, 1995). There are basic power inequalities based on status and age demonstrated in social interaction (Hofstede, 1991; Pecchioni, et al., 2004), including the expectation that younger people show obedience and respect to older people (Kim & Yamaguchi, 1995). Western cultures on the other hand stress personal rights (as opposed to group obligations) and along with individualism (Kim & Yamaguchi, 1995; Pecchioni et al., 2004), value egalitarianism rather than unquestioned respect toward people of senior status. This has definite implications for the transfer of organizational memory and competitive advantage. Eastern cultural norms and values with their support of collective goals and their respect for older workers may give those organizations an advantage over Western cultures when it comes to establishing networks with knowledge "reservoirs" that enable knowledge flow.

While many aspects of mentoring appear to be universal, there seems to be cultural differences in the purpose behind mentoring relationships (Kochan & Pascarelli, 2003). Parsloe and Wray (2002) describe an "American style" which focuses on career-type mentoring or sponsorship; while a "European style" takes a developmental approach to the protégé, helping them to meet their learning goals. Bright (2005) summarised the view of mentoring in the East (Japan specifically) as "relationship based", with mentoring in the West viewed more as "strategic". Darling, Hamilton, Tokoyawa and Matuda (2002) studied mentoring processes among youth in both Japan and America and found many similarities. The major difference they found was that Japanese youth identified the presence of more mentors in their lives than the American youth did.

Few studies have focused on the mentor's willingness to mentor (Ragins & Cotton, 1993), and there is even less considering cultural differences in this area. However, Aryee et al., (1996) in a study involving a Singaporean managerial sample found that the motivation to mentor was predicted by the individual characteristics of altruism and positive affectivity, the situational characteristics of an employee development-linked reward system and opportunities to interact on the job, and the interaction of both altruism and opportunities for interaction on the job. They questioned if such results could be generalised to Western cultures due to differences between collectivism and individualism. The question is valid as Moorman and Blakely (1995) found that when operationalised as an individual difference variable, collectivist values and norms predicted organizational citizenship behaviours in the form of interpersonal helping.

Of particular interest to knowledge management initiatives across cultures is Bright's (2005) comparison of mentoring from two worldviews representing East (Japan) and West (the United States and European countries). Bright considered Japan represented the ideal comparison to Western approaches because of its own existing versions of mentoring. The senpai (senior)-kohai (junior) relationship resembles mentoring in western countries for socialising and developing the junior employee in the customs, behaviours and competencies required in their role; while the oyabun (leader)-kobun (subordinate) relationship is similar to a western apprenticeship model, where the oyabun provides guidance and protection for the kobun, and assists them to find employment.

Bright (2005) suggests that Japan has several cultural characteristics that result in the long-term emotional bonding between individuals to facilitate effective mentoring including:

1) the high value placed on continuity, 2) the high value placed on obligation and duty between individuals, 3) the notion of respect for elders, 4) the concept of seniors protecting juniors from failure, 5) the predominance of working relationships based on personal, and not contractual bonds, and, 6) the high degree of racial and gender congruence in Japanese mentoring ... which facilitates "strong tie" relationships between mentor and mentee. (p.334)

In contrast, Bright (2005) observed that Western cultures encourage strategic mentoring initiatives that emphasise contractual bonds. Bright sees Western attempts at mentoring severely hampered by individualism which can result in competition rather than cooperation between mentor and protégé, short-termism in tenure resulting in the depletion of mentoring resources and trust, with the consequences of failure often borne by employees rather than their managers, engendering mistrust and suspicion. While both cultures face knowledge management risks brought on by the aging of their workforces, collectivist cultures may have the interpersonal infrastructure to offset potential knowledge threats by facilitating the transfer of organizational memory through mentoring, and thereby gain competitive advantage.

There are caveats. Moorman and Blakely (1995) suggest, "even though overall trends may exist within cultures towards one dimension or the other, there still may be variance within a culture...." (p.129). Therefore, not all members of collectivist cultures may share the same high degree of collectivism, and not all members of Western cultures necessarily share the trait of individualism to the same degree. As noted, Western mentoring research has also shown altruism to predict mentoring (e.g. Allen, 2003; Allen, et al., 1997; Ragins & Cotton, 1993; Ragins & Scandura, 1999).

There is also some suggestion that organizational cultures may not always reflect their wider culture in terms of norms and values. McCann and Giles (2006) in what they describe as the first cross-cultural (Thailand and the United States) research looking at intergenerational communication in the workplace found little difference in the (negative) views held by younger bankers towards older bankers between these countries in spite of norms of respect for older people particularly characteristic of one of those countries. Unexpectedly, Thai bankers considered others to be less accommodating in general (e.g. supportive and helpful) than did American bankers. McCann and Giles (2006) suggest that organizations differ from non-organizational intergenerational contexts (like family) and this may explain their results. One explanation they see is cultural convergence resulting in "environmental changes, and their subsequent impact on societal norms and values," that "could potentially hasten the blurring of certain cultural boundaries" and result in both countries seemingly alike in their "Westernization" (McCann & Giles, 2006, p. 98).

There is also some awareness in Eastern countries that the filial notions of respect for older adults may be changing to consist of politeness rather than obedience (Ingersoll-Dayton & Saengtienchai, 1999) possibly indicating a drift toward Western values. Therefore, while Eastern cultural norms in general may afford some advantage to organizations in relational knowledge-sharing initiatives, this should not be generalised to all organizations within those cultures, for all time.

Organizational Cultures

Organizational cultures too are thought to influence the transfer of organizational memory through mentoring (Bright, 2005; Bryant, 2005; Cross & Baird, 2000; McInerny and Mohr, 2007;

Nahapiet, Gratton, & Rocha, 2005). Bright (2005) questions if Western organizations can maximise knowledge sharing roles when they take such a contractual approach to mentoring rather than establishing the relational structures that may guide a more natural flow of knowledge sharing.

Building a relational culture is a common theme in literature that seeks to encourage the transfer of knowledge via mentoring. Bryant (2005) for example, found that higher perceived levels of peer mentoring were associated with perceptions of higher levels of knowledge creation and sharing. Cross and Baird (2000) suggest relationships that facilitate knowledge sharing often develop after individuals have participated in groups and/or on projects with one another. They consider this achieves two purposes: time working together builds the reciprocity and trust required to share knowledge, and secondly informs all participants as to the specific knowledge each holds.

Other cultural values also have impact. McInerny and Mohr (2007) suggest that in organizations where there is "an active interest in learning, innovation and continuous change," that, "knowledge sharing in order to achieve the organization's mission becomes routine," (p.65). They echo Cross and Baird (2000) in emphasising an underlining trust in supporting knowledge management activities within organizations. Bright (2005) too suggests that a culture where senior management are willing to take responsibility for failures by protecting junior employees engenders more trust than those where company failure may lead to a pay-out for senior managers, in contrast to redundancy for their employees.

When intellectual property concerns arise, trust can provide reassurance for knowledge sharing activities. Traditionally, McInerny and Mohr (2007) claim, rather than viewing knowledge sharing as an intrusion, knowledgeable employees willingly shared what they knew through conversation, mentoring, apprenticeships and formal teaching methods. They acknowledge, like Bright (2005), that short-termism works against trust, whereas (like Cross & Baird, 2000) a longer shared history between employees can build this vital component.

In competitive environments, McInerny and Mohr (2007) suggest that there are other mentoring benefits like recognition and status for the mentor that could be emphasised to employees. They accept that when organizations have competitive rather than collaborative cultures, knowledge sharing will always seem risky. They suggest that specific benefits for mentors like recognition and status within the organization could be further emphasised along with the encouragement that sharing knowledge increases organizational power, and the power of those within it.

Nahapiet et al., (2005) agree that many organizations see people as being motivated primarily by self-interest, and that this belief runs counter to the cooperation norms needed to facilitate information sharing. They offer an alternative approach modelled on Aristotelian ethics that emphasise a striving for excellence, an integration of self with others, the habits of cooperation and the importance of relationships, to facilitate cooperation in organizational contexts. The inclusion of project groups and communities of practice meet these aims (Nahapiet et al., 2005); and these are also characterised by many of the same features that are promoted for effective mentoring: knowledge is grounded in everyday events, acquired situationally, based on social processes and within complex social environments (Clutterbuck & Megginson, 2005),

TACKLING POTENTIAL MENTORING CONSTRAINTS FOR OLDER WORKERS

In a bid to address the challenges of an aging workforce, the OECD (2006) calls for work to be more attractive for older workers, with financial incentives to encourage their work longevity, employment practices aimed at hiring and retaining older workers, help and encouragement to remain employable, and a shift in attitudes towards individuals working at an older age. The latter two remedies in particular also offer possible solutions for encouraging experienced workers to pass on their organizational memory through mentoring relationships.

Combating Ageism and Ensuring Access to Training and Development

Ageism can be pervasive within some organizational contexts. Barth et al (1993) suggest that ageism and the stereotypes and discrimination involved is more significant than reported. There is an urgent need to both expose and address any myths and stereotypes, making way for changes that can better utilise the potential of these employees (Brooke & Taylor, 2005). Human resource management strategies need to focus on individual attributes rather than assumptions made about age.

To reinforce access to training, there needs to be some accountability among human resources professionals for the development of all employees regardless of age. Training all employees, but particularly managers, in the adverse effects of stereotypes, along with a zero-tolerance of age discrimination is important (Maurer, 2007). The older workers that does lack comfort with new technologies require training in these skills, not exclusion from these training events. At the same time, younger workers considered more at ease with new technologies need opportunities to develop diverse skills beyond that domain (Brooke & Taylor, 2005).

If access to training is open to all, there is also a need to incorporate styles of training that are particularly conducive to learning for older workers (Barth et al, 1993; Dychtwald et al., 2006; Maurer, 2007; Strack et al., 2008). Strack et al. (2008) in particular advise against using a "one size fits all" approach with older workers that may ignore their particular strengths as well as their particular training needs. A "continuous learning" approach acknowledges the central tenets of the new career contract and offers a useful framework (Hall & Mirvis, 1995). In this approach, employees take responsibility for their own change and development, learning occurs "on the job", and as required, to meet real job demands (Hall & Mirvis, 1995). A life span approach to career development is central to providing resilience in an era of rapid change (Sterns & Dorsett, 1994). Maintaining professional competence while warding off skill obsolescence means that career development cannot be just for the young, new and/or inexperienced employee.

Training and development practices will likely play a crucial role in contributing to a mentoring culture where the experienced employee can confidently pass on their knowledge to others. Barth, et al. (1993) report a systematic bias against investment in training for older workers, but believe that addressing this issue will result in older workers having the greatest potential for increased productivity.

Flexible Work Arrangements

Providing older workers with access to flexible work arrangements may free them up to realistically consider the mentoring role. Many of the arrangements devised by companies to help working parents also have relevance for older workers including job-sharing, part-time work and work at home (Barth et al., 1995; Davey & Cornwall, 2003). Barth et al. (1993) suggest interventions such as phased retirement and making opportunities for workers over the age of 55 to transfer to jobs with reduced pay and responsibilities. Allowing older workers to pursue relationships and activities outside of work that will grow in importance as retirement approaches may result in willingness to assist the organization in turn with its own policies, including knowledge management initiatives. In summary, as Strack et al. (2008) advise, by "Actively addressing demographic

risk to retain the skills and know-how needed to ensure future viability can give companies a competitive advantage over rivals" (p.128). They add that competitive edge will be gained by those companies who adopt these strategies sooner rather than later.

BUILDING A MENTORING CULTURE

Organizations wanting to capitalise on mentoring to transfer organizational memory may also need to address other aspects of their culture that may be inhibitive. Examining cultural norms that undermine relational efforts at transferring knowledge and adopting more group focused norms and values (Bright, 2005; Nahapiet et al., 2005) may be the starting point. Furthermore, there will be a need to raise awareness of the positive outcomes of mentoring and to address employees' perceived mentoring constraints. Providing mentor-training opportunities for employees to enable them to engage competently and confidently as mentors can facilitate both goals (Megginson & Clutterbuck, 2006). Giving employees at all stages of their careers mentors of their own may encourage them to reciprocate in mentoring others, and send the message to the organization that they are still learning (Allen et al, 1997; Finkelstein, Allen & Rhoton, 2003).

It is also important to promote particular benefits of mentoring for late career employees. For example, Kram (1985) suggested that mentoring others could facilitate healthy adjustment to the end of a career. In a life-span approach to career development the role of mentor may take on significance in ensuring overall satisfaction with one's career, and the accompanying acceptance of its eventual closure.

While adoption of the strategies outlined should maximise the pool of willing mentors, not all experienced workers will necessarily want to participate, regardless of how well an organization supports mentoring initiatives. Mentoring schemes have the most potential to succeed when mentors and protégés have some control of the process and have a say in their own participation (Cranwell-Ward et al., 2004). Removing choice will only serve to weaken mentoring efforts, when alternatively focusing on and promoting effective existing mentoring relationships that do exist, may eventually help to address the concerns reluctant employees may have about the process.

ORGANIZATIONAL MEMORY AND MENTORING IN THE CONTEXT OF AN AGING WORKFORCE: AN AGENDA FOR FUTURE RESEARCH

A number of possible constraints exist within the context of the new career contract and an aging workforce that might discourage experienced workers from mentoring others. Global and organizational cultures also have specific values and norms that have potential impact. This makes research into the area timely. In cultures (global and/or organizational) where ageism exists, its pervasive affect particularly upon limiting training opportunities, along with the depreciation of experience gained on the job as opposed to that gained through educational qualifications may lead older employees to underestimate the knowledge and skills they have, or to doubt the value of their experience. Similarly, for all workers, regardless of their age, the degree to which they perceive their organization supports them may erode their willingness to accept further responsibility and contribute more to the organization by mentoring. For many older experienced workers, at a time in their lives when they may want to ease back on some of their work commitments, the addition of further demands may prove to be a deciding factor and a "push" in their plans for retirement. Identifying which costs are particularly salient for older, experienced workers and their willingness to mentor is a research priority.

While it is important that research considers relevant constraints to mentoring for these workers, it should be careful not to ignore individual characteristics that may still uniquely motivate these employees to mentor regardless of the costs. Experienced workers at mid to late career are reportedly more inclined to want to develop workers due to intrinsic motivations like generativity, and the personal satisfaction that helping others can bring (e.g. Erikson, 1963, Levinson et al., 1978, Kram, 1985). Further research is required to examine the relationship between generativity and the willingness to mentor at work, taking into account the type(s) of mentoring functions that result. It needs to take into consideration the specific outcomes experienced workers perceive in acting as a mentor. These research initiatives can result in better-targeted and improved human resource management practices.

The work by McCann and Giles (2006) also opens up an agenda to examine cross-culturally, intergenerational communication within organizations. Others may want to build empirically on Bright's (2005) suggestion that Eastern cultures have an edge over the West in establishing effective mentoring systems to transfer knowledge, due to the collectivist norms of these cultures, and to evaluate its impact on competitive advantage.

Effective knowledge management in companies will also depend on the degree to which younger and older, novice and experienced workers are able to learn from each other. Co-learning as opposed to the more "one-sided" nature of conventional mentoring is an important feature of "continuous learning" (Hall & Mirvis, 1995). Generation Y, the latest generation to enter the workforce, are by the broadest definition those born between 1977 and 2002. This age group are comfortable with mentoring relationships, and have often experienced these in school-based programmes (Zemke, Raines & Filipczak, 2000). There will be a need for age groups to see past value conflicts based on generational and cohort differences in attitudes to work, and for human resource practices that integrate these perspectives.

As Brooke and Taylor (2005) conclude, "policy makers need to consider inter-age relations… rather than just the interests and utilisation of so-called 'older workers'" (p.426). Research that examines willingness to mentor as well as willingness to *be mentored* within all age and experience groups in organizations shows some potential. The co-learning approach will be crucial in all human resource management initiatives, including mentoring to transfer organizational memory.

CONCLUSION

Organizations that stress continuous learning will find that their older workers will continue to provide competitive advantage for many years.

(Harrington & Hall, 2007, p.193).

Work in the 21st century has changed from the mid nineteen-eighties when theory and research on mentoring in the workplace were first influential. Careers and organizational structures have changed. Research needs to give focus to how these changes may have altered the motivations that experienced workers have toward sharing knowledge as much as it continues to investigate how effective knowledge management contributes to competitive edge. There is a need to examine more closely the assumptions that older workers in particular have valued organizational memory, are particularly amenable to mentoring others, and anticipate and experience largely positive outcomes for doing so. Contextual factors including the new career contract and concerns about poor management practices and their consequences for older workers may mean that these beliefs may no longer hold as they once did.

There is also a need to consider the impact of both global and organizational culture on knowledge management initiatives and in particular, the transfer of organizational memory through interpersonal means, with a view to building organizational cultures conducive to knowledge sharing.

When all is considered, experienced older workers still represent a potential competitive edge for organizations. Knowledge and expertise accrue over time, and these workers have more tenure than most in their organizations and industries. The outcomes of their time investment will rest largely on the extent to which they have pursued continuous learning and been given access to opportunities for development throughout their careers. These two characteristics will be pivotal in maximising the number of individuals who remain up-to-date in their skills and knowledge, and will likely determine the level of engagement they retain in their careers. This will in turn ensure that these knowledge 'repositories' or 'reservoirs' have both the means, and the inclination, to pass on their prized knowledge to others and contribute to the competitive advantage of their organizations.

REFERENCES

Allen, T. D. (2003). Mentoring others: A dispositional approach. *Journal of Vocational Behavior*, *62*(1), 134–154. doi:10.1016/S0001-8791(02)00046-5

Allen, T. D., & Eby, L. T. (2004). Factors related to mentor reports of mentoring functions provided: Gender and relational characteristics. *Sex Roles*, *50*(1-2), 129–139. doi:10.1023/B:SERS.0000011078.48570.25

Allen, T. D., Poteet, M. L., & Burroughs, S. M. (1997). The mentor's perspective: A qualitative inquiry and future research agenda. *Journal of Vocational Behavior*, *51*(1), 70–89. doi:10.1006/jvbe.1997.1596

Allen, T. D., Poteet, M. L., & Russell, J. E. A. (1998). Attitudes of managers who are more or less career plateaued. *The Career Development Quarterly, 47*(2), 159–172.

Alley, D., & Crimmins, E. (2007). The demography of aging and work. In K. S. Shultz & G. A. Adams (Eds.), *Aging and work in the 21st century* (pp. 7-23). Mahwah NJ: Lawrence Erlbaum Associates.

Anderson, J. R. (2000). *Cognitive psychology and its implications* (5th ed.). New York: Worth.

Argote, L., & Ingram, P. (2000). Knowledge transfer: A basis for competitive advantage in firms. *Organizational Behavior and Human Decision Processes, 82*(1), 150–169. doi:10.1006/obhd.2000.2893

Aryee, S., Chay, Y. W., & Chew, J. (1996). The motivation to mentor among managerial employees. *Group & Organization Management, 21*(3), 261–277. doi:10.1177/1059601196213002

Baltes, P. B., & Baltes, M. M. (1990). Psychological perspectives on successful aging: The model of selective optimization with compensation. In P. B. Baltes & M. M. Baltes (Eds.), *Successful aging: Perspectives from the behavioral sciences* (pp. 1-34). New York: Cambridge University Press.

Barnes-Farrell, J. L., & Mathews, R. A. (2007). Age and work attitudes. In K. S. Shultz & G. A. Adams (Eds.), *Aging and work in the 21st century* (pp. 139-162). Mahwah NJ: Lawrence Erlbaum Associates.

Barth, M. C., McNaught, W., & Rizzi, P. (1993). Corporations and the aging workforce. In P. H. Mirvis (Ed.), *Building the competitive workforce: Investing in capital for corporate success* (pp. 156-200). New York: John Wiley & Sons.

Beehr, T. A., & Bowling, N. A. (2002). Career issues facing older workers. In D. C. Feldman (Ed.), *Work careers: A developmental perspective* (pp. 214-241). San Francisco: Jossey-Bass.

Bright, M. I. (2005). Can Japanese mentoring enhance understanding of Western mentoring? *Employee Relations, 27*(4/5), 325–339. doi:10.1108/01425450510605679

Brooke, L., & Taylor, P. (2005). Older workers and employment: Managing age relations. *Ageing and Society, 25*, 415–429. doi:10.1017/S0144686X05003466

Bryant, S. (2005). The impact of peer mentoring on organizational knowledge creation and sharing: An empirical study in a software firm. *Group & Organization Management, 30*(3), 319–338. doi:10.1177/1059601103258439

Capelli, P. (2003). Will there really be a labor shortage? *Organizational Dynamics, 32*(3), 221–233. doi:10.1016/S0090-2616(03)00034-2

Center for Research into the Older Worker (CROW). (2004). *Job transitions* (Briefing Paper 3). Centre for Research into the Older Workforce: University of Surrey.

Clutterbuck, D., & Megginson, D. (2005). *Making coaching work: Creating a coaching culture*. London: Chartered Institute of Personnel and Development.

Cranwell-Ward, J., Bossons, P., & Gover, S. (2004). *Mentoring: A Henley review of best practice*. Basingstoke, UK: Palgrave Macmillan.

Critchley, R. K. (2004). *Doing nothing is not an option: Facing the imminent labor crisis*. Mason, OH: Thomson South-Western.

Cross, R., & Baird, L. (2000). Technology is not enough: Improving performance by building organizational memory. *Sloan Management Review, 41*(3), 69.

Czaja, S., & Sharit, J. (1993). Age differences in the performance of computer-based work. *Psychology and Aging*, *8*(1), 59–67. doi:10.1037/0882-7974.8.1.59

Dalton, G. W., Thompson, P. H., & Price, R. L. (1977). The four stages of professional careers: A new look at performance by professionals. *Organizational Dynamics*, *6*(1), 19–42. doi:10.1016/0090-2616(77)90033-X

Darling, N., Hamilton, S., Tokoyama, T., & Matuda, S. (2002). Naturally occurring mentoring in Japan and the United States: Social roles and correlates. *American Journal of Community Psychology*, *30*(2), 245–271. doi:10.1023/A:1014684928461

Darwin, A. (2004). Characteristics ascribed to mentors by their protégés. In D. Clutterbuck & G. Lane (Eds.), *The situational mentor: An international review of competencies and capabilities in mentoring* (pp. 29-41). Aldershot, UK: Gower.

Davey, J. (2003). Opportunity or outrage? Redundancy and educational involvement in mid-life. *Journal of Education and Work*, *16*(1), 87–102. doi:10.1080/1363908022000032902

Davey, J., & Cornwall, J. (2003). *Maximising the potential of older workers* (NZiRA Future Proofing New Zealand Series). Wellington, New Zealand: New Zealand Institute for Research on Ageing.

DeLong, D. W. (2004). *Lost knowledge: Confronting the threat of an aging workforce.* New York: Oxford University Press.

Droege, S. B., & Hoobler, J. M. (2003). Employee turnover and tacit knowledge diffusion: A network perspective. *Journal of Managerial Issues*, *15*(1), 50.

Dychtwald, K., Erickson, T. J., & Morison, R. (2006) *Workforce crisis: How to beat the coming shortage of skills and talent.* Boston: Harvard Business School Press.

Erikson, E. H. (1963). *Childhood and society* (2nd ed.). New York: Norton.

Feldman, D. C. (1999). Toxic mentors or toxic protégés? A critical re-examination of dysfunctional mentoring. *Human Resource Management Review*, *9*(3), 247–278. doi:10.1016/S1053-4822(99)00021-2

Finkelstein, L. M., Allen, T. D., & Rhoton, L. A. (2003). An examination of the role of age in mentoring relationships. *Group & Organization Management*, *28*(2), 249–281. doi:10.1177/1059601103028002004

Fraccaroli, F., & Depolo, M. (2008). Careers and aging at work. In N. Chmiel (Ed.) *An introduction to work and organizational psychology: A European perspective* (pp. 97-118). Malden, MA: Blackwell.

Geisler, E. (2008). *Knowledge and knowledge systems: Learning from the wonders of the mind.* Hershey, PA: IGI Publishing.

Granovetter, M. S. (1973). The strength of weak ties. *American Journal of Sociology*, *78*(6), 1360–1380. doi:10.1086/225469

Gudykunst, W. B., & Ting-Toomey, S. (1988). *Culture and interpersonal communication.* Newbury Park, CA: Sage.

Hall, D. T., & Mirvis, P. H. (1995). The new career contract: Developing the whole person at midlife and beyond. *Journal of Vocational Behavior*, *47*(3), 269–289. doi:10.1006/jvbe.1995.0004

Hankin, H. (2005). *The new workforce: Five sweeping trends that will shape your company's future.* New York: AMACOM.

Hansen, M. T. (1999). The search-transfer problem: The role of weak ties in sharing knowledge across organization subunits. *Administrative Science Quarterly*, *44*(1), 82. doi:10.2307/2667032

Harrington, B., & Hall, D. T. (2007). *Career management & work-life integration: Using self-assessment to navigate contemporary careers.* Thousand Oaks, CA: Sage.

Hedge, J. W., Borman, W. C., & Lammlein, S. E. (2006). *The aging workforce: Realities, myths, and implications for organizations.* Washington, DC: American Psychological Association.

Heinen, S. J., & O'Neill, C. (2000). Managing talent to maximise performance. *Employment Relations Today, 31*(2), 67–82. doi:10.1002/ert.20018

Higgins, M. C., & Kram, K. E. (2001). Reconceptualizing mentoring at work: A developmental network perspective. *Academy of Management Review, 26*(2), 264–289. doi:10.2307/259122

Hofstede, G. (1991). *Culture and organizations: Software of the mind.* New York: McGraw-Hill.

House, R. J., Hanges, P. J., Javidan, M., Dorfman, P. W., & Gupta, V. (2004). *Culture, leadership, and organizations: The GLOBE study of 62 societies.* Thousand Oaks, CA: Sage.

Hummert, M. L., Garstka, T. A., Ryan, E. B., & Bonneson, J. L. (2004). The role of age stereotypes in interpersonal communication. In J. F. Nussbaum &. J. Coupland (Eds.), *Handbook of communication and aging research* (pp. 91-114). Mahwah, NJ: Lawrence Erlbaum Associates.

Ingersoll-Dayton, B., & Saengtienchai, C. (1999). Respect for the elderly in Asia: Stability and change. *International Journal of Aging & Human Development, 48*(2), 113–130.

Johnson, J., & Paper, D. J. (1998). An exploration of empowerment and organizational memory. *Journal of Managerial Issues, 10*(4), 503.

Kauffman, N. (1987). Motivating the older worker. *SAM Advanced Management Journal, 52*(2), 43–48.

Kim, U., & Yamaguchi, S. (1995). Cross-cultural research methodology and approach: Implications for the advancement of Japanese social psychology. *Research in Social Psychology, 10,* 168–179.

Kochan, F. K., & Pescarelli, P. T. (2003). Culture, context, and issues of change related to mentoring programs and relationships. In F. K. Kochan & P. T. Pescarelli (Eds.) *Global perspectives on mentoring: Transforming contexts, communities, and cultures* (pp. 417-428). Greenwich, London: Information Age.

Kram, K. E. (1985). *Mentoring process at work: Developmental relationships in organizational life,* Glenview, IL: Scott, Foresman.

Kransdorff, A., & Williams, R. (2000). Managing organizational memory (OM): The new competitive imperative. *Organization Development Journal, 18*(1), 107.

Kubeck, J. E., Delp, N. D., Haslett, T. K., & McDaniel, M. A. (1996). Does job-related training performance decline with age? *Psychology and Aging, 11*(1), 92–107. doi:10.1037/0882-7974.11.1.92

Lahaie, D. (2005). The impact of corporate memory loss: What happens when a senior executive leaves? *Leadership in Health Services, 18*(3), 35–48. doi:10.1108/13660750510611198

Leonard, D., & Swap, W. (2005). *Deep smarts: How to cultivate and transfer enduring business wisdom.* Boston: Harvard Business School Press.

Leonard-Barton, D., & Sensiper, S. (1998). The role of tacit knowledge in group innovation. *California Management Review, 40*(3), 112–134.

Levinson, D. J., Darrow, C. N., Klein, E. B., Levinson, M. H., & McKee, B. (1978), *The seasons of a man's life.* New York: Alfred A. Knopf.

Linde, C. (2001). Narrative and social tacit knowledge. *Journal of Knowledge Management, 5*(2), 160–171. doi:10.1108/13673270110393202

Livingstone, D. W., & Sawchuck, P. H. (2004). *Hidden knowledge*. Aurora, Ontario: Garamond.

Maurer, T. J. (2007). Employee development and training issues related to the aging workforce. In K. S. Shultz & G. A. Adams (Eds.), Aging and work in the 21st century (pp. 163-178). Mahwah, NJ: Lawrence Erlbaum Associates.

Maurer, T. J., Weiss, E. M., & Barbeite, F. G. (2003). A model of involvement in work-related learning and development activity: The effects of individual, situational, motivational, and age variables. *The Journal of Applied Psychology, 88*(4), 707–724. doi:10.1037/0021-9010.88.4.707

McCann, R. M., & Giles, H. (2006). Communication with people of different ages in the workplace: Thai and American data. *Human Communication Research, 32*(1), 74. doi:10.1111/j.1468-2958.2006.00004.x

McGregor, J., & Gray, L. (2002). Stereotypes and older workers: The New Zealand experience. *Social Policy Journal of New Zealand, 18*, 163–177.

McInerney, C. R., & Mohr, S. (2007). Trust and knowledge sharing in organizations: Theory and practice. In C. R. McInerney & R. E. Day (Eds.), *Rethinking knowledge management: From knowledge objects to knowledge processes* (pp. 65-86). New York: Springer.

McPherson, M. (2008). *Older workers: Employers speak out*. Auckland, New Zealand: Equal Employment Opportunities Trust (EEO).

Megginson, D., & Clutterbuck, D. (2006). Creating a coaching culture. *Industrial and Commercial Training, 38*(5), 232–237. doi:10.1108/00197850610677670

Moorman, C., & Miner, A. S. (1997). The impact of organizational memory on new product performance and creativity. *JMR, Journal of Marketing Research, 34*(1), 91. doi:10.2307/3152067

Moorman, R. H., & Blakely, G. L. (1995). Individualism collectivism as an individual difference predictor of organizational citizenship behavior. *Journal of Organizational Behavior (1986-1998), 16*(2), 127.

Nahapiet, J., Gratton, L., & Rocha, H. O. (2005). Knowledge and relationships: When cooperation is the norm. *European Management Review, 2*(1), 3. doi:10.1057/palgrave.emr.1500023

Neustadt, R. E., & May, E. R. (1986). *Thinking in time: The uses of history for decision-making*. New York: The Free Press.

New Zealand Department of Labour. (2004). *Future of work*. Retrieved April 1, 2006, from http://www.dol.govt.nz/futureofwork/workforce-ageing.asp

Nonaka, I., & Takeuchi, H. (1995). *The knowledge-creating company: How Japanese companies create the dynamics of innovation*. New York: Oxford University Press.

Nussbaum, J. F., & Baringer, D. K. (2000). Message production across the lifespan: Communication and aging. *Communication Theory, 8*, 1–26.

O'Donohue, S. J. (2000). *A Canterbury employers' perspective on the aging workforce and the use of flexible work options for older workers*. Palmerston North, New Zealand: Master of Business Studies, Massey University.

OECD. (2006). *Live longer, work longer: Executive summary*. Paris: OECD.

Parsloe, E., & Wray, M. (2002). *Training mentors is not enough: Everything else schools and districts need to do*. Thousand Oaks, CA: Corwin Press.

Pecchioni, L. L., Ota, H., & Sparks, L. (2004). Cultural issues in communication and aging. In J. F. Nussbaum &. J. Coupland (Eds.), *Handbook of communication and aging research* (pp. 91-114). Mahwah, NJ: Lawrence Erlbaum Associates.

Polanyi, M. (1966). *The tacit dimension.* London: Routledge and Kegan Paul.

Ragins, B. R., & Cotton, J. L. (1993). Gender and willingness to mentor in Organizations. *Journal of Management, 19*(1), 97–111. doi:10.1177/014920639301900107

Ragins, B. R., & Scandura, T. A. (1994). Gender differences in expected outcomes of mentoring relationships. *Academy of Management Journal, 37*(4), 957–971. doi:10.2307/256606

Ragins, B. R., & Scandura, T. A. (1999). Burden or blessing? Expected costs and benefits of being a mentor. *Journal of Organizational Behavior, 20*(4), 493–509. doi:10.1002/(SICI)1099-1379(199907)20:4<493::AID-JOB894>3.0.CO;2-T

Rothwell, W. J., Sterns, H. L., Spokus, D., & Reaser, J. M. (2008). *Working longer: New strategies for managing, training, and retaining older employees.* New York: AMACOM.

Rousseau, D. (1995). *Psychological contracts in organizations: Understanding written and unwritten agreements.* Thousand Oaks, CA: Sage.

Rulke, D. L., Zaheer, S., & Anderson, M. H. (2000). Sources of managers' knowledge of organizational capabilities. *Organizational Behavior and Human Decision Processes, 82*(1), 134–149. doi:10.1006/obhd.2000.2892

Stein, E. W. (1995). Organizational memory: Review of concepts and recommendations for management. *International Journal of Information Management, 15*(1), 17. doi:10.1016/0268-4012(94)00003-C

Stephens, G. K., Bird, A., & Mendenhall, M. E. (2002). International careers as repositories of knowledge: A new look at expatriation. In D. C. Feldman (Ed.), *Work careers: A developmental perspective* (pp. 257-320). San Francisco: Jossey-Bass.

Sterns, H. L., & Dorsett, J. G. (1994). Career development: A lifespan issue. *Experimental Aging Research, 20*(4), 257–264. doi:10.1080/03610739408253975

Sterns, H. L., & Doverspike, D. (1989). Aging and the training and learning process in organizations. In I. L. Goldstein & R. Katzell (Eds.), *Training and development in work organizations.* (pp. 299-332). San Francisco: Jossey-Bass.

Sterns, H. L., & Miklos, S. M. (1995). Aging worker in a changing environment: Organizational and individual issues. *Journal of Vocational Behavior, 47*, 248–268. doi:10.1006/jvbe.1995.0003

Strack, R., Baier, J., & Fahlender, A. (2008). Managing demographic risk. *Harvard Business Review*, (February): 119–128.

Swap, W., Leonard, D., Shields, M., & Abrams, L. (2001). Using mentoring and storytelling to transfer knowledge in the workplace. *Journal of Management Information Systems, 18*(1), 95–114.

Szulanski, G. (2000). The process of knowledge transfer: A diachronic analysis of stickiness. *Organizational Behavior and Human Decision Processes, 82*(1), 9–27. doi:10.1006/obhd.2000.2884

Ting-Toomey, S. (1999). *Communicating across cultures.* New York: Guilford.

Triandis, H. C. (1995). *Individualism and collectivism.* Boulder, CO: Westview.

Walsh, J. P. (1995). Managerial and organizational cognition: Notes from a trip down memory lane. *Organization Science, 6*(3), 280–321. doi:10.1287/orsc.6.3.280

Walsh, J. P., & Ungson, G. R. (1991). Organizational memory. *Academy of Management Review, 16*(1), 57–91. doi:10.2307/258607

Zack, M. N. (1999). Managing codified knowledge. *Sloan Management Review, 40*(4), 45–48.

Zemke, R., Raines, C., & Filipczak, B. (2000). *Generations at work: Managing the clash of veterans, boomers, xers, and nexters in your workplace*. New York: AMACOM.

ADDITIONAL READING

DeLong, D. W. (2004). *Lost knowledge: Confronting the threat of an aging workforce*. NewYork: Oxford University Press.

Hedge, J. W., Borman, W. C., & Lammlein, S. E. (2006). *The aging workforce: Realities, myths, and implications for organizations*. Washington, DC: American Psychological Association.

Leonard, D., & Swap, W. (2005). *Deep smarts: How to cultivate and transfer enduring business wisdom*, Boston: Harvard Business School Press.

Nussbaum, J. F., & Coupland, J. (2004). *Handbook of communication and aging research* (2nd ed.). Mahwah, NJ: Lawrence Erlbaum Associates.

Section 3

Chapter 13

Learning before Doing:
A Theoretical Perspective and Practical Lessons from a Failed Cross–Border Knowledge Transfer Initiative

Helen N. Rothberg
Marist College, USA

Beate Klingenberg
Marist College, USA

ABSTRACT

Responding to increasingly competitive environments, it has become commonplace for multinationals to enter into cross-border partnerships, ventures and alliances to gain know-how, manage costs and grow revenue. The results from these activities however, have not always delivered on their promise. Part of the reason lies in the challenges of transferring knowledge compounded by an international setting. The degree of difficulty in knowledge transfer increases for multinational managers and their counterparts because cultural differences influence information processing, management styles and sense making. In addition, most knowledge transfer projects do not take the time to allow partners to develop the rapport and trust pivotal for project commitment and successful learning to occur. This chapter explores a failed knowledge transfer project between two distinct cultures and, using literature on cross-cultural knowledge transfer and communication theory as well as anecdotes from the actual process, offers a process for creating and engaging a more successful design.

INTRODUCTION

Increasingly, sustainable competitive advantage is thought to be driven by knowledge, from employees (Drucker 1991) and other firm assets (Edvinsson and Sullivan 1996) that combine to create critical core competencies (Stewart 1997; Grant 1996; Quinn

1992). This train of thought is central to the notion that knowledge should drive the firm's positioning in the marketplace. Organizations have thus made it a prerogative to try and harness the knowledge resident in their walls. Whether capturing knowledge or transferring it, academics (Barney, 1991; Grant 1996; Quinn 1992, Rothberg and Erickson, 2005), reporters (Stewart 1997) and practitioners (Davenport and Prusak, 1998; Sveiby, 1997, Saint-

DOI: 10.4018/978-1-60566-790-4.ch013

Onge, 1996) have all acknowledged the importance of strategically managing knowledge to help create and sustain ever elusive forms of competitive advantage.

A second driver of sustainable advantage is globalization, where hypercompetitive markets challenge firms to quickly create products that are better (differentiated) and cheaper (cost leadership). This dynamic demands that firms extend their value chains across country boundaries to source high value supply, manufacturing capability, and know-how from wherever it exists on the globe. These extended networks of partners, enabled through information technologies and connectivity can become a key factor in achieving success (Erickson and Rothberg, 2002). Navigation requires not only the deliberate management and deployment of knowledge, but doing so in firms whose business models and boundaries are ever changing. (Anon, 2000).

Regardless of its intent, knowledge transfer is the dissemination of know-how between partners to achieve a business outcome. This managerial imperative is challenged by the nature of knowledge and the nature of people. When knowledge transfer moves across cultures, the hurdles become even higher, hence creating an environment where sharing and learning can take place is no small task.

Early studies took a managerial view seeking advantage through best practice and discovered knowledge transfer difficulty within firms across shifts (Epple et al. 1991), and facilities (Argote et al. 1990). Later studies offer a host of processes and tactics for engaging the organization's knowledge community in sharing what they know and using what they have (Cohen and Prusak, 2004; Pfeffer and Sutton, 2003; Davenport and Prusak, 1998). Within their multinational structures, firms are currently trying to leverage the knowledge base inherent in their subsidiaries to improve their learning processes and innovative performance (Kotabe et al. 2007).

In the strategic view, studies focus on the role of knowledge sharing to create a market advantage. In an emerging industry, especially in the pre-commercial phase, innovation performance is improved when firms share knowledge, especially when they step outside the bounds of national innovative systems into global innovative systems (Spencer (2003). Such knowledge-sharing behaviour is thought to influence the institutional environment to favour a firm's technology as the industry standard (Boisot, 1995), or by attracting the influence of researcher opinion, producers of complementary products, and new entrants into the firm's technology path. If a firm perceives itself as the quicker innovator or superior learner in its industry, then it may even deliberately consider transferring knowledge outside of its walls to competitors (Zander, et al. 1995).

Whether transferring knowledge between partners within a firm's configuration across subsidiaries or to external partners, managers are challenged with crafting processes for sharing know-how. This challenge has two components; one stemming from the nature and source of knowledge and another from the inherent differences between national cultures.

Challenges in Knowledge Transfer

The first challenge for transferring knowledge stems from the dimensional nature of knowledge - simple vs. complex, tacit vs. explicit, independent vs. systemic (Garud and Nayyar, 1994), and its source - human, social, structural knowledge (De Long and Fahey, 2000), and competitive (Rothberg and Erickson, 2002). Table 1 provides working definitions of these terms.

Dimensionality of knowledge infers that knowledge is created through a combination of characteristics that render it either more or less accessible to distribute and understand. If knowledge can be considered the outcome of giving meaning to information, then it stands to reason that the more information needed to create knowledge, the more complex the knowledge is and thus the harder

Table 1. Definitions of Some Knowledge Management Terms[1]

Knowledge	"…is that which we come to believe and value on the basis of the meaningfully organized accumulation of information (messages) through experience, communication, or inference" (Zack 1999). Zack further suggests that knowledge is both a thing or object that can be stored as well as a process of application.
Simple	Knowledge that can be captured with little information and is easy to transfer (Bhagat et.al. 2002).
Complex	Knowledge that has casual uncertainties thus requires more information and is harder to transfer (Bhagat et.al. 2002).
Tacit	Knowledge that "resides in the human mind, behaviour, and perception, and thus, difficult to be formalized and communicated" (Nonaka and Takeuchi, 1995). Tacit knowledge can be highly individualized, difficult if not impossible to explain to someone else, and potentially even subconscious and can be considered incommunicable (Polanyi, 1967). It is embedded in cognitive processes and often is ingrained in culture and values (Daft and Lengel, 1986).
Explicit	Knowledge that can be codified (Davenport & Prusak, 1998) and thus is portable because it is easy to pass along and easy for organizations to capture from individuals and shared through information technology (Choi and Lee, 2003).
Independent	Knowledge that is readily described because it is not embedded in an organization (Bhagat et.al. 2002).
Systemic	Knowledge that is tied to a body of existing know-how in the transferring organization. Complex knowledge is difficult to transfer and to absorb (Bhagat et.al. 2002).
Absorptive Capacity	An organization competence, absorptive capacity is the ability to recognize, assimilate and use new knowledge and is impacted by an organization's prior related knowledge (Cohen & Levinthal, 1990).
Causal Ambiguity	Knowledge can be context-specific, so without the associations found within the originating firm, knowledge may not be understandable (Reed and DeFillippi, 1990; Lippman and Rumelt, 1982).
Sticky	Knowledge involving the application of know-how that has a tacit quality and is complex regarding situation or context is "sticky" in that it sticks to its original application and is less useful to those removing it (or it is protected by legal instruments). The dimensions of stickiness are determined by both its transmission-source and context as well as reception- recipient and its context (Von Hippel, 1994; Szulanski, 1996; Teece, 1998).
Replication	When knowledge is distinct, firms often transfer through replication so that an effort is extended to create identical activities with each partner (Williams 2007)
Adaptation	When the receiving firm understands the knowledge being transferred they adapt (Williams, 2007) or modify or combine practices from the partner.
Intellectual Capital	Intangible materials and assets of the firm that create wealth (Stewart, 1997). Bontis (1996) and Edvinson and Sullivan (1996) suggest the first three dimensions. Rothberg and Erickson (2002) suggest the fourth.
Human	Tacit knowledge embedded in the minds of employees.
Structural	Tacit and explicit knowledge embedded in organizational routines, practices, culture and systems that support human capital.
Relational	Embedded knowledge from relationships outside the organization
Competitive	Competitive knowledge resulting from market-driven analysis of information internal and external to the firm

to transfer. Transferability is also compounded by its source - is knowledge objective, codifiable and thus readily shared (explicit) or is it part of what people know instinctively or what the firm has evolved in its culture as 'how we do things around here' (tacit). If knowledge is embedded in firm systems (a form of structural capital) –or has evolved from experiences essential to its use (causal ambiguity), or is meaningful because of the culture and actions that gave birth to it (stickiness), then such knowledge will be difficult to transfer

even within firms and across subsidiaries. In these scenarios, knowledge is not only complex but also part of the fabric of the organization.

Untangling what actually is content from 'other stuff' becomes an art form.

The water gets muddier when one considers the source of knowledge. A decade of writing on intellectual capital indicates that what the firm knows creates intangible assets (tacit knowledge) that can be the source of competitive advantage. Knowing then resides in employees, organizational practices, in the firm's relationships with external stakeholders and in how it uses intelligence to strategically guide its actions. Any of these assets derive from and confound knowledge by adding the human and cultural component to the mix. Firms can suffer when key employees leave, not only because of what they know professionally (human capital), but also because of how they were socially able to manage clients or suppliers (relational capital). Employees can leave and take with them firm processes and practices, but cannot replicate them elsewhere (structural capital). Many firms can be working with the same objective data to guide their planning, but some firms achieve insights that push them to market leadership (competitive capital). All of these forms of intellectual capital combine the nature of knowledge with what is divinely human and generate tacit knowledge that is systemic and complex and thus hard to transfer.

Now take this already difficult task of transferring knowledge between partners, which really means between people and systems, and add to it the challenges that arise when one works across national cultures. Inherently, the firm will face multiple hurdles arising from 'cultural distance', and a lack of personal relationships and trust that is essential for creating understanding and cooperation (Holden, 2001). In the cross-border exchange, complex tacit systemic knowledge will be most difficult to transfer (Bhagat et al. 2002) because the causal ambiguity surrounding tacit and systemic knowledge render it difficult to codify. This contextual nature of systemic knowledge (Reed and DeFillippi, 1990) makes it 'sticky' (Szulanski, 1996; Von Hippel, 1994; Teece, 1998) requiring both replication - duplicating provided systems - and adaptation - the modification of provided systems to partner processes (Williams, 2007). . Szualnski (2004) further argues that adaptation increases the stickiness of cross-boarder knowledge transfer and reports (Szulanski, 2006) two conflicting approaches to adaptation – presumptive and conservative; and that the former

may turn out to be detrimental to performance. In other words, cross-border knowledge transfer can suffer from the 'arduous relationship' (Szulanski, 1996) between partners that is compounded by the often embedded and confounded nature of the knowledge to be transferred. What matters then is not just the creation of processes to ensure knowledge transfer, but also a consideration of both the source of the knowledge and those receiving it. Other research suggests that knowledge transfer between firms only works for explicit, and not for tacit knowledge (Grant and Baden-Fuller, 1995). However, Lane et al. (2001) suggest that tacit knowledge and its exchange is critical for international joint ventures (IJVs).

In this chapter, we approach these challenges through exploratory inquiry. The subject is the case of an actual knowledge transfer initiative between a Taiwanese and American/European firm where the first author worked in the venture as a boundary spanner and project manager. We ask the question - How could this exchange have gone better? And hence: what do managers of multinational teams need to know to have a successful knowledge transfer experience? Using lessons stemming from a literature review of cross-cultural models of engagement, knowledge management and communication we conclude with actionable suggestions for managers in creating a knowledge transfer plan.

When Knowledge Doesn't Transfer in a Multi-Cultural Context: A Brief Story[2]

This story begins with a technology transfer project between the U.S. and Taiwan. The objective of the transfer is moving newly developed manufacturing technology from the transferring company in the US (called the Firm) to a partner firm in Taiwan (called the Partner), with the purpose of enabling them to perform contract manufacturing for the multinational firm. The Taiwanese Partner is experienced and also performs in-house technology

Table 2. Knowledge Categories provided by the Firm (transferring side).

Description of Knowledge	Process specification Process flow Equipment operating instructions Testing procedures Metrics	Experience with equipment Experience with materials Experience in the interpretation of test results and metrics
Dimension of Knowledge (Garud and Nayyar, 1994)	Complex Explicit Mostly systemic	Complex Tacit Independent
Types of Knowledge (De Long and Fahey, 2000)	Structural	Human

development. However, there are certain features in the Firm's new technology that are believed to be currently unavailable at the Partner. The motivation for the transfer is therefore for the Partner to gain access to advanced knowledge, and for the Firm to find an economic manufacturing source.

The transfer project is fairly complex, due to the nature of the knowledge that comprises a "manufacturing technology". The manufacturing process requires a team of engineers and scientists of various fields (e.g. physics, materials science, electrical engineering) as well as process engineers and equipment operators to develop and implement it for manufacturing. In other words, this transfer project involves knowledge that is simultaneously tacit and explicit, complex, systemic and thus potentially sticky. Successful implementation of the manufacturing process requires two components of knowledge: detailed process specifications, process flow etc., and the experience with equipment and procedures that are used. It is a set of rules (structural knowledge) combined with experience (human knowledge) that is needed. Transferring only one component, e.g. the structural knowledge, could result in success; however, it would require the receiving firm to go through steep learning curves to substitute the lack of experience.

The transfer project hence faces three different, but interrelated challenges: the cross-cultural component of moving knowledge between cul-turally different regions; the inter-firm cultural component of possibly working with different organizational cultures; and the challenge of sharing sticky knowledge. Table 2, employing the definitions of knowledge as given in Table 1 summarizes the knowledge that needed to be transferred.

Table 3 summarizes the tools used, and lists the acceptance and success at the transferring as well as receiving side. While individuals in each the Firm or the Partner team might have had different perceptions, this table expresses the overall observation.

In the following we provide examples of tools and their failures:

The Firm engaged in knowledge transfers before, however, not with this specific firm in Taiwan, and has a business process for such projects, that includes a set of milestones requiring a well-defined list of supporting documentation. Management expects this business process to be used exactly as is regardless of the receiving site of the transfer. Following the business process, the Firm's transfer managers needed to negotiate a project plan with the Partner. These attempts were generally unsuccessful because the Partner never assigned time for this purpose during meetings. Only the individual effort of one of the transfer managers to build a personal relationship with the respective counterpart resulted in the agreement on a project plan. However, during milestone review meetings, the Partner generally presented

Table 3.

Knowledge or project management tool	Perception at Firm (transferring side)	Perception at Partner (receiving side)
Systematic project management approach: - transfer business process requiring project plan, milestones, deadlines of knowledge transfer	Viewed as essential tool for successful project management	Accepted as something the Firm does, largely ignored
Structured documents (process specifications, descriptions etc.)	Implemented in structured approach, largely used by engineers and scientists across the organization	Implemented, but used different systematic; general distribution to engineers and scientists not deemed necessary
Knowledge Management Database	Viewed as essential tool to manage knowledge exchange; low acceptance from engineers and scientists	Not deemed necessary
Communication Database	Viewed as essential tool; used only by small part of team	Preferred unstructured use of shared drives
Workshops and Face-to-Face meetings of specialists	Viewed as essential tool, success highly dependent on individual	Viewed as essential tool, but only if correct counterparts were chosen (same hierarchical position)
Firm transfer team integrated into Partner Team	Expensive solution, success dependent on individual	Viewed more as intrusion

reports that the Firm considered too shallow and which hence showed that the controlling purpose of the plan was not understood or regarded as inappropriate interference in the Partner's internal management processes.

The documentation procedures in both firms were largely different. The Firm operated in an environment of relative openness regarding distribution of official documents and access to databases. As long as a person was involved in some way in the project, access was granted. Only a few core documents were controlled strictly and were handed out on a "need-to-know" basis. The Partner, on the other hand, appeared to restrict documents entirely on a "need-to-know" basis; hence engineers had access solely to documents directly related to their area of work. In one particular instance, the Partner's management had received the entire process documentation in hardcopy, with the intent for its distribution to his engineering team. For months, meetings were extremely unproductive because the Partner's engineers did not know specific process details. It turned out that the manager had put the box with the documents under his desk – he never

distributed them in the first place – an almost bizarre example of misunderstanding of company cultures, and in this case perhaps also individual power plays or a combination of both – it was not possible to distinguish which factor might have been prevalent. Over all, this situation stoked communication difficulties between the engineers of both sides, as the knowledge level was different. The Partner management also felt that a communication database was not needed. As a consequence, the sharing of explicit knowledge between the engineers was hampered greatly.

Face-to-face meetings were often not successful as the Firm sent inappropriate people to meetings – for example, the Partner expected high-level managers, the Firm showed up with engineers. Hence, the Partner felt that their negotiation and communication culture was ignored. A very small detail, but highly important was also the seating order during meetings– from the Partner's side, the top of the table down to the last seat clearly determined the employees rank. The Firm's employees generally just sat somewhere – which caused great confusion, as the Partner never understood who is responsible for what at the Firm's side.

In an advanced stage of the project, the companies agreed to have a team of around twenty engineers from the Firm move to Taiwan and work with on site with Partner's engineers. Typically, this would foster an ideal environment for the exchange of tacit and sticky knowledge. However, the presence of the Firm's team created more aversion from Partner management. It manifested in the practice of conducting engineering meetings in Chinese[3] (the Firm's team was recruited from the U.S. and Europe and did not include anybody with sufficient Chinese language skills), restricting access to work areas, not allowing admission to the actual manufacturing flow, and limitations in intranet access. Similar to the experience with the project plan, only the development of personal relationships between some of the engineers of both firms resulted in a constructive environment. The workability then of the transfer depended not on the technical skills of a particular engineer, but on his or her ability to adapt to the different culture and reach out to build rapport and trust. Faulconbridge, 2006, and Edwards and Kidd, 2003 report a similar discovery, that successful knowledge sharing was fostered by social and cognitive practices necessary for evolving the "trust-based relationships vital for learning" (Faulconbridge, 2006 p. 20). Building trust, as is true for knowledge transfer, is a process that is dependent on both the quality of information being shared and the perceived compatibility in mental maps between parties. The quality of this exchange is influenced by the trust each player has in each other as individuals, organizations and national cultures (Edwards and Kidd, 2003). Other than in a few individual instances, the Firm and Partner seem to have approached KT more as a product than as a trust-building process that takes time.

These examples and Table 3 clearly demonstrate that the Firm and Partner did not agree on the relevance or necessity of any tool slated to be used during the transfer. It appears that these tools have different levels of relevance for each culture. For instance: for the Partner, face-to-face meet-

ings are viewed as important if the 'right' people of power are attending. The Partner's hierarchical firm culture here is reflective of Hofstede's (1980) cultural dimension of power distance. According to Hofstede, South East Asian countries, such as Taiwan, are higher in power distance then the U.S. A more hierarchical company structure, where politically people of certain rank need to be included in meetings, is therefore not a surprise and should have been anticipated by the Firm's management.

Recognition of the importance of hierarchical differences is also supported by Bhagat et al.'s (2002) integrative cross-border knowledge transfer framework where they identify distinct transacting cultural patterns. This partnership is attempting to transfer knowledge across two of these cultural patterns. In the United States, the dominant cultural pattern is "vertical individualism" whereby preferred knowledge is codifiable or explicit and independent of context. It is a matter of course to transfer. Many Asian countries are defined as having "vertical collectivist" cultures and are more in tune with paternalistic cues and knowledge about the hierarchy, demanding representation from positional authority. This sizeable gap between cultural patterns creates a cultural distance that renders this a difficult knowledge transfer process (Bhagat et al. 2002; Simonin, 1999) – exemplified in the anecdotal discussion of document and sharing processes in both firms.

The language barrier hampered communication and relationship building in many ways. The Firm assumed that the Chinese engineers would speak English. Even when Chinese engineers did speak English many of the Firm's employees complained that they could not understand their accents with some showing impatience when a Taiwanese engineer struggled to express him/herself in English. This insensitivity is particularly striking when considering that some of the European team members where also using English as a second language. Besides the actual communication barrier, this situation also resulted in tension and prevented trust building.

Other challenges may have stemmed from the newness of the Firm and Partner's relationship and the lack of a common language (in the sense of using common terms and expressions for technical facts) and 'familiarity' that develops with time. Engineering "jargon" (e.g. acronyms) between both firms differed greatly at the beginning of the project. Kotabe et al (2003), while investigating performance improvements between Japanese suppliers and American buyers in the automotive industry, discovered that high-level technology transfer improves with the duration of the partner relationship. They also indicate that pushing technology transfer too quickly can be detrimental to its success. Ford and Chan (2003) in their case study of a Japanese manufacturing subsidiary in the western U.S. discovered that Hofstede's national cultural dimensions were less significant than were the organization's culture. Holden and von Kortzfleisch (2004) took a linguistic view where knowledge transfer is a sense making activity. For knowledge to be communicated and shared, knowledge managers need to create meaning as they facilitate the shift of tacit to explicit knowledge.

These studies make one wonder whether the design of the knowledge transfer process by the Firm took into account the notion that cultural differences require individuals to not only translate but to also make sense of what is being deciphered. The Firm and Partner approach the relationship with different perspectives in what work was to be done, how it was to be done and why it was to be done in a particular way. Braganza and Mollenkramer (2002), in diagnosing a failed knowledge management initiative in "PharmaCorp" indicate that the need for sharing knowledge must be clearly linked to a job to be considered relevant. Relevance is further associated with how knowledge capture and sharing is reflective of the natural work group and its activities in project fulfilment. This is a contextual issue suggesting that for knowledge transfer to occur successfully, inclusion of those involved in the total work process will influence

the convertibility of the transfer. In short, if those who are on the receiving side (Partner) do not believe that the group is inclusive and that what is asked is relevant to what they will be doing, then what is being transferred is not likely to be successfully received.

Management Due Diligence: Investing in a Successful Knowledge Transfer Process

This project didn't work for a variety of reasons, all of which are rooted in the core decision by the Firm to design the knowledge transfer process in a unilateral and rational way. This may not have been an unlikely approach for manufacturing engineers who perceive their processes to be rather explicit and while complex readily learned by the Partner's engineers. However, the Firm's directed model created Partner resistance even before the process began. If the Partner was being relied upon for their manufacturing prowess in creating efficiency, why couldn't they then be part of the process to create the knowledge transfer that they would then implement? While the Firm chose the Partner because they were perceived as capable of managing the complexity of the process, the Partner may have perceived that the Firm thought them less than capable, in need of basic training or wouldn't they have designed the transfer process together? At the heart of this transfer block is a communication issue where perception becomes reality and here the reality of this misperception threw the project a wrench before it even began.

At the core of the challenges and solutions that we will present below is the very real notion that both parties need to be engaged, from the beginning, in creating the knowledge transfer process. Our approach takes time and commitment from all involved to build rapport and trust as much as to design how each firm can work together. What we offer is an approach that takes into account the social nature of the KT process its major transfer blocks, and what designers of KT processes in cross-cultural contexts can do to ensure successful learning and fruitful relationships.

Step 1: Get to Know Each Other

A preliminary small knowledge transfer team (KTT) of individuals representing the Firm and Partner should convene to commence due-diligence on the process. A model for why a KTT should be convened and how it works can be found in the competitive intelligence literature. Here there are many examples of how organizations build successful intelligence generating structures, rooted in the external information and internal knowledge gathering, sharing and processing practices across the organization. Core to these architectures are methods for identifying knowledge experts, for gathering their insights and then generating intelligence around strategic issues for decision makers (e.g. Gilad and Gilad, 1998; Rothberg and Erickson, 2005). The structure is based on a series of 'rings' or layers for gathering knowledge from organization members (ring one) and then generating expert commentary (ring two). Working across rings is a team of cross-functional and cross-level experts or a 'shadow team' charged with engaging decision makers, noted experts and other organization members in the discovery, integration and analytical phases of generating intelligence (Rothberg, 1997). Along with support from senior management, they help cultivate the desire to share information, knowledge, and trust in the content, applied context and importance of what is gathered, disseminated and analysed. In their charge to foster knowledge sharing and learning environments they face similar issues that a KTT would, i.e., cultural differences in systems, language, power distance and attitudes across the firm. In essence then, a shadow team and a KTT are both engaged with creating processes to facilitate competitiveness. We therefore adapt a competitive intelligence structure here as our model for creating and employing a KTT and 'two ring' model.

One of the KTT's first priorities is to define the cultural preferences of engagement for each party. Using either Hofstede's (1980) works on cultural dimensions or the more focused transactional frameworks developed by Bhagat et.al. (2002), the team needs to understand the differences in how the Partner and Firm engage their political process, manage knowledge and their cognitive patterns in employing both.

In their framework, Bhagat, et. al (2002) identify basic dimensions - individualism (a focus on self) vs. collectivism (a focus on the whole) and verticalness (creating individual power distinctions) vs. horizontalness (conformity to the in-group) that intersect and provide insight into cultural social behaviour and information processing.

Challenge: According to Bhagat's framework, the Firm is an individualistic-vertical culture, the Partner a collective-horizontal culture. The Firm is most comfortable transferring and receiving knowledge that is codifiable, and independent of organizational context. The Partner prefers knowledge that is more relational in nature and wants to know how the knowledge is embedded in the Firm. The Firm wants to organize and articulate, whereas the Partner wants to understand the context and history. While the Firm was engaging in this exchange relationship based on economic sourcing (and know-how), the Partner assumed that the Firm was engaging with them because of their know-how and cost structure to manufacture better and cheaper than the Firm. So, when the Firm approached the Partner with what it considered a superior manufacturing technology, this may have come across as very threatening to the Partner. Further, with the Firm dictating what will be done and how, the Partner may have experienced a sense of loosing control over its domain. Collective cultures look for contextual cues in their social environments and respond to information from a contextual lens (Kagitcibasi, 1987). There may have been a sense that the collective knowledge of the group was not respected and may have thus created an emotional block to the exchange process.

Even though there were in-person meetings between the Firm transfer team and Partner specialists and some integration of the Firm team into the Partner team, the processes used and formats for knowledge requirements were reflective of the vertical individualistic culture of the Firm and not the vertical collective culture of the Partner. If the Partner perceived that the wrong people were being interviewed or included in the team, communication and knowledge transfer would be stilted by the impression that those participating were not from the "in-group". Perceived level of Firm participants may also have been inappropriate as cultures that are vertical will be more responsive to people who are higher in the hierarchy than those who are lateral.

Solution: Engage the Partner in the creation of the knowledge transfer process. The goal for engaging the Partner in process development is to assist the Partner in maintaining a sense of control and credibility and thus limit the impact of emotional blocks. Once there is some understanding of the work culture, both Firm and Partner can adjust the KTT composition to include members of the appropriate rank and functional competencies to create credibility.

Engaging the Partner in the creation of the knowledge transfer process also assists with the development of processes and tools that will have relevance and that are convertible. While it is unrealistic to think that complete agreement on these issues will exist, there is a greater likelihood that each side in the exchange relationship will get what they need. There also may be the added benefit here of good will. The willingness of the Firm to take into account the working culture of the Partner may entice them to learn and use some of the tools that they may already deem irrelevant or unnecessary.

Step 2: Get to Know the Knowledge for Transfer

The dimensionality of knowledge influences the types of processes created for its transfer. Simple knowledge can require much less procedural specificity than complex systems. Explicit knowledge is readily captured and codified while tacit knowledge proves more elusive requiring multiple modalities. The cultural variable accentuates all the above.

Challenge: The Firm is an individualistic-vertical culture, the Partner a collective-horizontal culture. These cultures differ in how they process information - if the goal is to improve the absorptive capacity of the Partner, then the Partner will need more information that addresses the circumstance and chronicle of the knowledge (collectivism). The Firm may be geared to only share the end product of systems not wanting to take the time to engage in historical and contextual discussions (individualistic). However, if the goal is to make complex knowledge less sticky, then this can be viewed as an investment of time in the learning process. The dimensionality and source of knowledge needs to be addressed. The design of transfer systems needs to take into account the 'cross-cultural knowledge absorption competencies' (Kayes et al. 2005) that produce successful transfer.

Solution: Create a knowledge orientation program. The KTT, in its continuous efforts to understand the differences in cultural patterns, would create an orientation program where the types of knowledge to be conveyed are identified and diagnosed. While it takes time to develop deep sensitivity to cultural differences, starting with the type of knowledge enables reference to archetypical patterns identified earlier (e.g. Bhagat et al. 2002; Hostede, 1980). While not a remedy, these archetypes help to identify some of the key differences and potential stumbling blocks and offer a good starting point. The KTT then again considers the team's composition with regard to the dimensionality and source of the knowledge to be transferred. Based on this information the team can adjust their composition.

The solutions offered above - engaging the Partner in designing the knowledge transfer process and in creating tools for transfer - both suggest adjusting KTT composition based on cultural and learning needs. Creating large teams that satisfy both parties can yield a group of unruly proportions. Another approach to structuring a KTT is to use the double ring structure briefly identified earlier. The first ring, the inner ring, includes representative core KTT people who will actually be engaged in implementing and managing the knowledge transfer process. The second ring, or outer ring identifies experts who are enlisted for their human and structural capital and organizational positioning. These experts are brought together for initial design and progress meetings and can be accessed at any time by members of the core team. This double ring KTT can operate more adroitly than a larger inclusive group. Also, the core team, working together and across both organizations has the opportunity to develop the rapport and trust needed to work through sticky issues. In addition, this structure may enable the evolution of 'triangles of trust' (Edwards and Kidd, 2003) where information is perceived as credible and compatibility of intention between Firm and Partner strong enough to generate rich exchanges among both parties. It is also possible that this structure can facilitate the social production of new knowledge when both the Firm and Partner share ideas (Faulconbridge, 2006).

The enhanced KTT would work together to create Tables 2 and 3: the types of knowledge to be transferred, and the procedure for transfer and reporting. Creating the processes and tools for transfer and learning together with clear pathways and feedback loops can help foster relevancy that is crucial in creating acceptance

(Inkpen, 2008; Braganza and Mollenkramer, 2002). Success is also fortified when companies create tools and mechanisms that promote both replication (creating activities that are identical across locations), and adaptation (effort toward modifying and combining practices) (Williams, 2007). Focusing on the knowledge transfer relationship in cross-cultural settings, Williams reports that when knowledge is ambiguous and discrete, companies tend to replicate, and adapt when the receiving company comprehends the interactions between areas of knowledge. Both actions are necessary for successful knowledge transfer to be accomplished. The KTT identifies employees who will be impacted by the knowledge transfer, across level and function, and interviews them before the completed version of processes and tools are implemented. During the knowledge transfer process, the KTT remains engaged and continue to monitor how the tools and processes are working (feedback loop) and make adjustments as the need arises.

Throughout this solution we emphasize the need to create, monitor and adjust processes and tools as two distinct parts of the transfer procedure. The processes clearly define the knowledge transfer system, and within, knowledge and work flows. The tools are the enablers for the processes. Both are not relevant without the cultural context driving their design and use, hence the processes cannot come unilaterally from one of the transfer partners, as was the case here. Furthermore, tools cannot be mistaken as a process. A shared database, for example, is a tool – if there is no agreement on the process to use this tool, it cannot serve as a functional piece in the knowledge transfer.

Additionally, the use of electronic knowledge sharing tools can create potential obstacles, as it is likely that different companies work in different hard- and software environments. Klingenberg and Watson (2003) demonstrated that adverse Information Technology (IT) policies can be resolved when managers involve employees from the respective departments of each firm to solve actual or perceived incompatibilities. Managers should also understand that electronic knowledge sharing tools influence the character of the knowledge by forcing it into an explicit and structural framework. In other words, such tools are most likely not able to capture all nuances of the transfer of sticky knowledge that are necessary. The expert ring can be very helpful with this circumstance as well.

Most transfer tools used by the Firm are to a large extent "one-way" – information flows from the Firm to the Partner. However, and as stated earlier, although the Partner is lacking specific technological knowledge for this particular manufacturing process, it is experienced in the field. Implementing transfer procedures that allow bilateral knowledge exchange most likely raises the acceptance by the Partner. The possibility of 'reciprocity' in sharing know-how can improve the knowledge transfer process (Kachra and White, 2008). The expert ring, populated with members from both Partner and Firm creates a supportive structure for this exchange to take place.

Step 3: Develop a Common Language

The Firm and Partner are from different continents with different customs and languages. Little time was set aside for them to get to know each other and develop a common understanding of the knowledge being conveyed. The dimensionality of the knowledge required this effort by both parties because of its stickiness. Real (the fact that different languages are spoken and that these are very differently structured) as well as perceived (the "I cannot understand their English"-effect) language barriers add to a lack of common engineering terms, as was discussed above.

Challenge: While the Partner engaged translators to assist in the dissemination process, this did not guarantee that translators had the ability to decode knowledge accurately. It is probable that the newness of this relationship did not create opportunity for a common language (technical

and other) or cultural vocabulary to evolve - both necessary for successful transfer (Kotabe et al. 2003; Ford and Chan, 2003; Holden and von Kortzfleisch, 2004; Kagiticibasi, 1997). If any emotional blocks were triggered, then translators may have decided to not pass on certain bits of information perceiving them to be irrelevant.

Characteristically, individuals from collective cultures make sense of information contextually and tacitly and often do not give credence to information expressed explicitly. Add to this the challenge that much of the knowledge to be transferred was sticky; it would be incumbent upon the Firm to find convertible contexts within which to demonstrate the transfer of such knowledge.

Solution: The KTT furthers the orientation process to include contextual experience. Participants from the Partner travel to the Firm's facility to witness the manufacturing process and to engage with its engineers regarding its developmental history. Then, participants from the Firm travel to the Partner's facility and do the same. This sharing of contextual knowledge has two advantages. It fulfils the partner's need to understand the etiology of the knowledge to be transferred and perhaps renders it a bit less sticky, and works toward generating familiarity of terminology and players as well as trust building rapport.

New partners lack the 'familiarity' that develops with time. Kotabe et al (2003) discovered in an Asian-American cross-cultural knowledge exchange that technology transfer requiring higher-level capabilities improves with the duration of the partner relationship. Ford and Chan (2003) in their case study of an Asian manufacturing subsidiary in the western U.S.A. revealed that managers who shared a common language were more apt to share knowledge with each other than with their multi-cultural counterparts. Even those managers who were bi-lingual were suspect as they were seen as powerbrokers who determined which knowledge they thought was important and thus worthy of interpretation.

The design of the knowledge transfer process by the Firm did not take into account the notion that cultural differences not only include the need for translators, but also for those who can help convert what is being shared into relevant knowledge that will be meaningful to Partners. This new relationship had not yet had the time to develop a common language or set of goals and expectations to structure workflow. The Firm and Partner approached the relationship with different perspectives in what work was to be done, how it was to be done and why it was to be done in a particular way. In other words, the perceived relevance necessary for knowledge to transfer (Braganza and Mollenkramer, 2002) was not created.

Relevance is further associated with how knowledge capture and sharing is reflective of the natural work group and its activities in project fulfilment. This is a contextual issue suggesting that for knowledge transfer to occur successfully, inclusion of those involved in the total work process will influence the convertibility of the transfer. In short, if those who are on the receiving side (Partner) do not believe that the group is inclusive and that what is asked is relevant to what they are doing, then what is transferred is not likely to be successfully received. Creating a KTT with a two-ring structure can help mollify many of these concerns. A variety of players can be included in the process on an as-need basis, demonstrating to both parties a respect for human and structural capital. During these encounters, the KTT is likely to discover those individuals who have the position power and the understanding to assist in creating a common language and in developing credibility. In this case, structured the right way, more is more. This takes on even greater importance linguistically as the sooner a shared language evolves the quicker and better the transfer process can progress. In other words, members of the KTT ring system can participate in sense making (Holden and von Kortzfleisch, 2004) for both Partner and Firm. For knowledge

to be convertible, a common equivalent language needs to evolve.

Words need to be: translatable in the face of ambiguities that arise from having more than one interpretation ('convertible'), clear in their intended meaning because similar words can have different meanings (interference), and have clear counterparts in the other language (equivalence). In this view, knowledge managers need to be able to create meaning as they facilitate the shift of tacit to explicit knowledge. The KTT double-ring structure can readily support this difficult task. And again the KTT in creating joint meaning may also facilitate the evolution of 'triangles of trust' to drive successful outcomes.

When knowledge is complex and sticky, it takes more than a transliteration of tools and manuals to create meaning that rises above the noise created by translating without context. It requires that time be spent in context, not just learning about both companies' systems, but also again, in developing the rapport and trust that will be needed when translators create meaning for both parties. There is some support for the notion that technology transfer is more likely to have some success when there's relevant learning by doing (Epple et.al. 1991). Time spent experiencing each other's manufacturing processes before the transfer program is created may have served to begin to create familiarity as well as credibility by demonstrating contextually the need for the knowledge transfer to take place. Having a representative KTT would facilitate this process of translation and relevancy during both due-diligence and implementation.

To summarize: Designing and implementing a successful cross-cultural knowledge management process takes time: to understand the cultural difference between Firm and Partner that influence their organizational view, to understand the dimensionality of the knowledge and how to best transmit it, and to define a common language, based on experience, relevance and trust that will facilitate the buy-in and effort needed to decode and disseminate the tacit and explicit know-how inherent in organizational systems. Time is needed to configure the right KTT, both the internal ring of implementers and the external ring of experts, to ensure inclusiveness of both skill and influence. Time is needed to travel to both facilities and begin to unravel 'stickiness'. And time is needed to build the rapport between partners that will make the challenges arising from the above activities manageable hurdles. In short, senior management needs to approach cross-cultural knowledge transfer projects as a change management initiative. The investment in human and structural resources will have a greater opportunity to yield dividends with a strong commitment to evolve a culture among the KTT that supports camaraderie and learning. With these ingredients, there will be a higher probability that the knowledge transfer process will succeed.

FUTURE TRENDS

Future work will explore the utility of the KTT model across different cooperative strategic partnerships (such as international joint ventures and strategic alliances) and across different cultural settings in order to determine its universal applicability. The idea here is that these business models turn on the success of knowledge transfer. Ideally, future research will also provide the opportunity to apply this model in a cross-cultural knowledge transfer consultation.

CONCLUSION

This chapter presents a case of knowledge transfer between a Taiwanese and an American/European company. The character of the knowledge is "sticky", adding to the complexity of a cross-cultural transfer. Most of the used tools did not

have the anticipated success – primarily because the cultural dimensions of the two countries were ignored and not integrated in a commonly understood transfer process. Knowledge transfer frameworks for the literature are used to help explain why this occurred. Recommendations for improvements of transfer processes are offered where the core idea is including the Partner in the knowledge transfer design process and devoting time to learn about the culture and process of knowledge creation for both firms. The goal here is to create convertibility and silence the noise that results when information is presented in ways that create ambiguity or is perceived to lack equivalence. Another goal is to discover the natural work group – the KTT - as opposed to the functional work group, and identify how processes are created and whom within the Partner groups are involved in their creation. This will provide an understanding of the relationship between explicit and tacit information and the importance or lack there of - of context and its role in creating meaning. It can help identify the Partner's sense-makers. Overall, invest both human and structural capital in the knowledge transfer process by building rapport and communication skills and a commitment to succeed.

REFERENCES

Anon. (2000). How to be an e-manager? *The Economist, E-Management Survey*, 50-52.

Argote, L., Beckman, S. L., & Epple, D. (1990). The persistence and transfer of learning in industrial settings. *Management Science, 36*, 140–154. doi:10.1287/mnsc.36.2.140

Barney, J. B. (1991). Looking inside for competitive advantage. *Academy of Management Executive, 9*(4), 49–61.

Bhagat, R. S., Kedia, B. L., Haverston, P. D., & Triandis, H. C. (2002). Cultural variations in the cross-border transfer of organizational knowledge: An integrative framework. *Academy of Management Review, 27*(2), 204–221. doi:10.2307/4134352

Boisot, M. (1995). Is your firm a creative destroyer? Competitive learning and knowledge flows in the technological strategies of firms. *Research Policy, 24,* 489–506. doi:10.1016/S0048-7333(94)00779-9

Bontis, N. (1996). There's a price on your head: Managing intellectual capital strategically. *Business Quarterly,* (Summer).

Braganza, A., & Mollenkramer, G. J. (2002). Anatomy of a failed knowledge management initiative: Lessons from PharmaCorp's experiences. *Knowledge and Process Management, 9*(1), 23–33. doi:10.1002/kpm.130

Choi, B., & Lee, H. (2003). An empirical investigation of KM styles and their effect on corporate management. *Information & Management, 40*(5), 179. doi:10.1016/S0378-7206(02)00060-5

Cohen, D., & Prusak, L. (2004). *In good company: How social capital makes organizations work.* Boston, MA: Harvard Business School Press.

Cohen, W. M., & Levinthal, D. A. (1990). Absorptive capacity: A new perspective on learning and innovation. *Administrative Science Quarterly, 35,* 128–152. doi:10.2307/2393553

Daft, R. L., & Lengel, R. H. (1986). Organizational information requirements, media richness and structural design. *Management Science, 3,* 554–571. doi:10.1287/mnsc.32.5.554

Davenport, T. H., & Prusak, L. (1998). *Working knowledge.* Boston, MA: Harvard Business School Press.

De Long, D. W., & Fahey, L. (2000). Diagnosing cultural barriers to knowledge management. *The Academy of Management Executive, 14*(4), 113–128.

Drucker, P. F. (1991). The new productivity challenge. *Harvard Business Review, 69,* 69–76.

Edvinsson, L., & Sullivan, P. (1996). Developing a model for managing intellectual capital. *European Management Journal, 14*(4), 356–364. doi:10.1016/0263-2373(96)00022-9

Edwards, J. S., & Kidd, J. B. (2003). Knowledge management sans frontiers. *The Journal of the Operational Research Society, 54*(2), 130–139. doi:10.1057/palgrave.jors.2601419

Epple, D., Argote, L., & Devadas, R. (1991). Organizational learning curves: A method for investigating intra-plant transfer of knowledge acquired through learning by doing. *Organization Science, 2*(1), 58–70. doi:10.1287/orsc.2.1.58

Erickson, G. S., & Rothberg, H. N. (2002). B2B Internet applications: Strategic considerations. *Competitiveness Review, 12*(2), 57–63.

Faulconbridge, J. (2006). Stretching tacit knowledge beyond a local fix? Global spaces of learning in advertising professional service firms. *Journal of Economic Geography, 6*(4), 517–540. doi:10.1093/jeg/lbi023

Ford, D. P., & Chan, Y. E. (2003). Knowledge sharing in a multicultural setting: A case study. *Knowledge Management Research and Practice, 1,* 11–27. doi:10.1057/palgrave.kmrp.8499999

Garud, R., & Nayyar, P. R. (1994). Transformative capacity: Continual structuring by intertemporal technology transfer. *Strategic Management Journal, 15,* 365–385. doi:10.1002/smj.4250150504

Gilad, B., & Gilad, T. (1998). *Business intelligence systems: A new tool for competitive advantage.* Chicago, IL: AMACOM.

Grant, R. M. (1996). Prospering in dynamically-competitive environments: Organizational capability as knowledge integration. *Organization Science, 7*(4), 375–387. doi:10.1287/orsc.7.4.375

Grant, R. M., & Baden-Fuller, C. (1995). A knowledge-based theory of inter-firm collaboration. In *Academy of Management Best Papers Proceedings* (pp. 17-21).

Hofstede, G. (1980). *Culture's consequences: International differences in work-related values.* Beverly Hills, CA: Sage.

Holden, N. (2001). Knowledge management: Raising the spectre of the cross-cultural dimension. *Knowledge and Process Management, 8*(30), 155. doi:10.1002/kpm.117

Holden, N., & Von Kortzfleisch, H. F. O. (2004). Why cross-cultural knowledge transfer is a form of translation in more ways than you think. *Knowledge and Process Management, 11*(2), 127–136. doi:10.1002/kpm.198

Inkpen, A. (2008). Knowledge transfer and international joint ventures: The case of Nummi and General Motors. *Strategic Management Journal, 29,* 447–453. doi:10.1002/smj.663

Kachra, A., & White, R. (2008). Know-how transfer: The role of social, economic/competitive and firm boundary factors. *Strategic Management Journal, 29,* 425–445. doi:10.1002/smj.668

Kagiticibasi, C. (1997). Individualism and collectivism. In J. W. Berry, M. H. Segall, & C. Kagiticibasi (Eds.), *Handbook of cross-cultural psychology* (pp. 1-50). Needham Heights, MA: Allyn & Bacon.

Kayes, D. C., Kayes, A., & Yamazaki, Y. (2005). Essential competencies for cross-cultural knowledge. *Journal of Managerial Psychology, 20*(7), 578–589. doi:10.1108/02683940510623399

Klingenberg, B., & Watson, K. (2003). Problem analysis: Intellectual property exchange between two partner companies - an application of the theory of constraints thinking processes. In E. Omojokun (Ed.), *Proceedings of the 33rd Annual Meeting of the Southeast Decision Sciences Institute,* Williamsburg, VA (pp. 112-114).

Kotabe, M., Dunlap-Hinckle, D., & Mishra, H. (2007). Determinants of cross national knowledge transfer and its effect on firm performance. *Journal of International Business Studies, 38,* 259–282. doi:10.1057/palgrave.jibs.8400261

Kotabe, M., Martin, X., & Domoto, H. (2003). Gaining knowledge from vertical partnerships: Knowledge transfer, relationship duration and supplier performance improvement in the U.S. and Japanese automotive industries. *Strategic Management Journal, 42,* 293–316. doi:10.1002/smj.297

Lippman, S. A., & Rumelt, R. P. (1982). Uncertain imitability: An analysis of interfirm differences in efficiency under competition. *The Bell Journal of Economics, 13*(2), 418–439. doi:10.2307/3003464

Nonaka, I., & Takeuchi, H. (1995). *The knowledge-creating company: How Japanese companies create the dynamics of innovation.* New York: Oxford University Press.

Pfeffer, J., & Sutton, R. I. (2003). *The knowing-doing gap.* Boston: Harvard Business School Press.

Polanyi, M. (1967). *The tacit dimension.* New York: Doubleday.

Quinn, J. B. (1992). *Intelligent enterprise.* New York: Free Press, New York.

Reed, R., & DeFillippi, R. J. (1990). Causal ambiguity, barriers to imitation, and sustainable competitive advantage. *Academy of Management Review, 15*(1), 88–102. doi:10.2307/258107

Rothberg, H. N. (1997). Fortifying competitive intelligence systems with shadow teams. *Competitive Intelligence Review, 8*(2), 3–11. doi:10.1002/cir.3880080204

Rothberg, H. N., & Erickson, G. S. (2002). Competitive capital: A fourth pillar of intellectual capital? In N. Bonits (Ed.), *Proceedings of the World Congress on Intellectual Capital Readings* (pp. 94-113). Woburn, MA: Elsevier Butterworth-Heinemann.

Rothberg, H. N., & Erickson, G. S. (2005). From knowledge to intelligence: Creating competitive advantage in the next economy. Woburn, MA: Elsevier Butterworth-Heinemann.

Saint-Onge, H. (1996). Tacit knowledge: The key to the strategic alignment of intellectual capital. *Strategy and Leadership,* (March/April): 10–14. doi:10.1108/eb054547

Simonin, B. (1999). Transfer of marketing know-how in international strategic alliances: An empirical investigation of the role and antecedents of knowledge ambiguity. *Journal of International Business Studies, 30*(3), 463–490. doi:10.1057/palgrave.jibs.8490079

Spencer, J. W. (2003). Firm's knowledge-sharing strategies in the global innovation system: Empirical evidence from the flat panel display industry. *Strategic Management Journal, 24,* 217–233. doi:10.1002/smj.290

Stewart, T. A. (1997). *Intellectual capital: The new wealth of organizations*. New York: Doubleday.

Sveiby, K. E. (1997). *The new organizational wealth: Managing and measuring knowledge-based assets*. New York: Berrett-Kohler.

Szulanski, G. (1996). Exploring internal stickiness: Impediments to the transfer of best practice within the firm. *Strategic Management Journal, 19,* 27–44.

Szulanski, G., & Jensen, R. (2004). Stickiness and the adaptation of organizational practices in cross-boarder knowledge transfers . *Journal of International Business Studies, 34*(6), 508–523.

Szulanski, G., & Jensen, R. J. (2006). Presumptive adaptation and the effectiveness of knowledge transfer. *Strategic Management Journal, 27*(10), 10. doi:10.1002/smj.551

Teece, D. J. (1998). Capturing value from knowledge assets: The new economy, markets for know-how, and intangible assets. *California Management Review, 40*(3), 55–79.

Von Hippel, E. (1994). 'Sticky information' and the locus of problem solving: Implications for innovation. *Management Science, 40*(4), 429–439. doi:10.1287/mnsc.40.4.429

Williams, C. (2007). Transfer in context: Replication and adaptation in knowledge transfer relationships. *Strategic Management Journal, 28,* 867–889. doi:10.1002/smj.614

Zack, M. H. (1999). Developing a knowledge strategy. *California Management Review, 41*(3), 125–146.

Zack, M. H. (1999). Managing codified knowledge. *Sloan Management Review, 40*(4), 45–59.

Zander, U., & Bruce, K. (1995). Knowledge and the speed of transfer and imitation of organizational capabilities: An empirical test. *Organization Science, 6*(1), 76–92. doi:10.1287/orsc.6.1.76

ENDNOTES

[1] The authors offer the definitions most commonly used in the literature, the table does not represent an exhaustive list

[2] This case was previously introduced by the authors in "Management Challenges of Cross-Border Knowledge Transfer – A Comparison between Empirical Evidence

and A Theoretical Framework", delivered at the European Community Knowledge Management Conference, Barcelona Spain, September 2008.

[3] What is generally referred to as "Chinese" in this chapter is Mandarin.

Chapter 14
The Impact of Culture on University–Industry Knowledge Interaction in the Chinese MNC Context

Jianzhong Hong
Lappeenranta University of Technology, Finland

Johanna Heikkinen
Lappeenranta University of Technology, Finland

Mia Salila
Lappeenranta University of Technology, Finland

ABSTRACT

Recent studies on university–industry collaboration have paid a growing attention to complementary knowledge interaction, which is of crucial importance for networked learning and knowledge co-creation needed in today's rapidly changing markets and for gaining global competitiveness. The existent studies concentrate on the transfer of knowledge from the university to the company, and the impact of culture is examined with a focus on fundamentally different cultures between two types of organizations (i.e., between universities and firms). The studies, however, remain highly fragmented in cultural exploration on one level, and are primarily concerned with one-way technology and knowledge transfer. Research on more interactive knowledge interaction (e.g., collaborative knowledge creation) and especially in the Chinese context is seriously lacking. This chapter explores university–industry knowledge interaction in a broad sense, focusing on the development of a conceptual view on the understanding and analysis of the cultural impact in the Chinese MNC context. The chapter is an early work in process and it is theoretical in nature. It clarifies and elaborates key concepts and perspectives, and suggests implications for future research and practice regarding effective knowledge co-creation involving dissimilar cultures.

DOI: 10.4018/978-1-60566-790-4.ch014

INTRODUCTION

As tasks, work and projects are increasingly conducted in globally distributed contexts, seeking for and integrating complementary knowledge and building networks across geographic and cultural borders are increasingly becoming the firm's key strategy and part of operations for going international and gaining global competitiveness (Awazu, 2007; Buckley & Carter, 1999; Buckley et al., 2006; Kodama, 2003; 2005; Lindqvist et al., 2007). Due to the changing competitive landscape, external links and networking directed at the transfer and creation of knowledge, are of crucial importance for the innovative performance of firms and the advancement of new technologies (Johnston & Paladino, 2007; Santoro & Gopalakrishnan, 2000; Schartinger et al, 2002). Undoubtedly, universities play an important role in such networked innovation systems, and complementary knowledge interaction increasingly becomes a key driver for university–industry (U–I) collaboration (Lin, 2005; Santoro & Gopalakrishnan, 2000; Wang & Lu, 2007). However, many cross-border knowledge interactions including knowledge transfer projects have failed because of cultural barriers (Almeida et al., 2002; Bröchner et al., 2004; Holden, 2002; Lam, 1997; Moitra & Kumar, 2007; Siegel et al., 2003; Simonin, 1999).

Culture may enable or coerce good knowledge interaction depending on how well we know it. Previous studies have identified the following cultural barriers to or influences on effective knowledge interaction: cultural variation across nations in terms of the dimensions of individualism–collectivism and verticalness–horizontalness (Bhagat et al., 2002), cross-cultural differences in language, conception and prioritization (Kohlbacher & Krähe, 2007), differences in Hofstede's cultural dimensions of individualism/ collectivism, power distance, uncertainty avoidance, masculinity/femininity (Lucas, 2006), national or societal settings in terms of knowledge structure

and work system (Lam, 1997), language and social knowledge in the form of understanding others' behavior (Buckley et al, 2005), cultural awareness of Chinese *guanxi* (personal connection) and *mianzi* (face) in cross-border knowledge transfer (Buckley et al, 2006), Chinese *guanxi* in terms of trust, relationship commitment, and communication (Ramasamy et al., 2006), cultural distance in the transfer of marketing know-how in international strategic alliances (Simonin, 1999), and the alignment of different professional or functional cultures of executives, engineers and operators (Schein, 1996). In the specific context of U–I knowledge interaction, the impact of culture and related factors are examined and acknowledged with a focus on fundamentally different cultures between two types of organizations particularly in goal formation, time orientation, language and assumptions (Cyert & Goodman, 1997; Elmuti et al., 2005), agreeing on priorities and timescales, publishing in the public domain, and academic laissez-faire approach vs industrial lack of flexibility (Barnes et al, 2002), and cultural traits in the institutionalization of U–I knowledge transfer activates (Santoro & Gopalakrishnan, 2000). Nevertheless, the existent studies remain much fragmented in cultural exploration, and are primarily concerned with technology and knowledge transfer. Knowledge transfer is one form of knowledge interaction. Research on other types of more interactive knowledge integration such as collaborative knowledge creation, and especially in the Chinese context is seriously lacking.

Emerging markets are now seen as a major source of global innovation and knowledge management (Fu et al., 2006; Pillania, 2005). The development of new knowledge and capabilities is particularly relevant and salient in emerging and changing markets like in China (Hong et al., 2008; Khavul et al., 2007; Li & Scullion, 2006). A recent study of Huggins et al. (2007) found that North America has been the source of one half of all R&D foreign direct investments (FDI) between 2002 and 2005. Asia-Pacific, especially China and

India, has been the overwhelming destination for most of the R&D FDI, accounting for more than one half of all investments and almost three quarters of the jobs created. In China, especially R&D collaboration between multinational corporations (MNCs) and local partners has grown strikingly. In 2002, the number of MNC R&D institutes in China was 400 (Li, 2005), whereas by 2005 the number was already 750 (von Zedtwitz, 2007). Since the first establishment of a joint R&D institute by an MNC with a Chinese university in 1994, R&D collaboration between MNC subsidiaries and local universities has been growing rapidly. MNCs have become attractive research partners to Chinese universities and research institutes compared to local enterprises (Heikkinen et al., 2007; Li 2005). Several motivations for MNCs to conduct R&D activities in China have been identified, among which creating and utilizing the local talent pool has been emphasized as a key attraction to MNCs. Thus, the power of best known universities has been increasing and the passive role local universities used to play is changing. More interactive and deeper U–I relationships and collaboration are emerging (Gassmann & Han, 2004; Hong et al., 2007; Li, 2005; Li & Zhong, 2003; von Zedtwitz, 2007; Wang & Lu, 2007). On the other hand, little is known about the MNC subsidiaries' R&D collaboration with Chinese universities and research on these fast emerging U–I knowledge interaction activities is called for. U–I studies are generally conducted in a local context within the same country. U-I collaboration across nations, however, addresses more explicitly cultural issues on both organizational and national levels. The advantage in focusing on MNC subsidiaries is evident in such a research context (Almeida & Phene, 2004).

This chapter aims to develop a conceptual framework on the understanding and analysis of the cultural impact on U–I knowledge interaction in the Chinese MNC context and to suggest theoretical and practical implications for future research. We ask how and when the culture matters in U–I collaboration and knowledge interaction, and how to cope with cultural challenges when an MNC subsidiary starts collaborating with local universities. We take the R&D collaboration of Finnish MNC subsidiaries with Chinese universities as an illustration, discussing the role of the culture, trust and social networking in collaborative knowledge creation and innovation involving dissimilar cultural contexts.

In this chapter, we start a review on the study of culture, emphasizing its multi-layered, multi-level and dynamic nature. The study thus also calls our attention to examine carefully the moderating influences. Next, we deal with the concept of knowledge interaction in several research areas. After bringing in the U–I collaboration context, we specifically define what we mean by U–I knowledge interaction, identifying three modes of knowledge interaction and related U–I knowledge interaction activities. In the section "U–I Knowledge Interaction across Cultural Boundaries" we concentrate on key cultural issues, mainly including literature on U–I studies and cultural relevance in the Chinese MNC context. In the following, implications for future research are suggested and discussed. We conclude the chapter with a conceptual framework on studying the impact of culture on a MNC subsidiary's collaboration with Chinese universities and research institutes. Related managerial implications are suggested.

THE STUDY OF CULTURE

The impact of culture on organizational behaviour and interaction has been well acknowledged, whereas the study of culture is challenging due to its pervasive and complex nature and the increase of *multiculturalism* in today's globalizing businesses, organizations and societies (Craig & Douglas, 2006). The first challenge is to define what culture is, namely, its conceptualization and operationalization in research. There are numerous definitions in cultural studies. Some have defined culture in terms of *shared values, beliefs,* and *assumptions* (e.g., Sackmann, 1991; Schein 1985), whereas others emphasize more the *material culture and artifacts* and the role of *language and communication* that shape and guide social systems, group relations and collaborative activities and processes (Craig & Douglas, 2006; Sojka & Tansuhaj, 1995; Wartofsky, 1979). This seems to form two major lines in cultural studies. The first line presents the most prevalent way to perceive culture, and thus the ideal aspect of culture is accentuated. Within the second line of research on cultural artifacts and the language, scholars from social sciences and the like focus more on the mediating role in knowing and doing, whereas researchers from business and management studies pay much more attention to their practical aspects and functioning in relation to specific business governance and operations.

The new cross-cultural research considers culture not only as a multi-layered but also a multi-level construct, which consists of various levels nested within each other from the most macro-level of a global culture, through national cultures, organizational cultures, group cultures, and cultural values that are represented in the self at the individual level (Leung et al., 2005). This view places a special emphasis on the intersection of these aggregate levels and the factors, which facilitate cultural change (see Craig & Douglas, 2006). Multi-level cultural influences become more and more evident in organizations and societies. Most of the research addresses culture primarily at the levels of national or societal culture and organizational culture. In order to take an in-depth look at the culture, the study of culture at functional aspects or subunits/groups is necessary.

A national culture, also known as a national character, has been referred to as "the pattern of enduring personality characteristics found among the populations of nations" (Clark, 1990: 66). People are believed to acquire such patterns

of thinking, feeling, and acting, starting in early childhood and continuing throughout their life (King, 2007). Geert Hofstede (1980; 1997) has done pioneering work in the 1980s by developing a model to describe the national culture. For Hofstede, the most distinctive dimension between cultures is *individualism* versus *collectivism.* This emphasizes what kind of relation an individual has with the society's collectivity he/she is living in. In addition to this, other cultural dimensions developed by Hofstede include power distance, uncertainty avoidance and masculinity. An emerging cultural dimension of Confucianism reflects a dynamic, future-oriented mentality which the authors believe is more associated with the East Asian economic growth (Hofstede & Bond 1988). Subsequent works after Hofstede include, for instance, new cultural dimensions of values (Schwartz, 1994) and GLOBE's nine cultural dimensions (GLOBE is the acronym for "Global Leadership and Organizational Behavior Effectiveness", House et al., 2004). Schwartz's values may have the potential to explain greater cultural variation than Hofstede's values (Ng et al., 2006) and the GLOBE project adds two novel dimensions to Hofstede: performance orientation and humane orientation which seem to be meaningful (Leung et al., 2005). The dimension of national culture reviewed here is often associated with MNC studies.

Meyerson and Martin (1987) draw a distinction in their discussion between the *integration* and *differentiation* perspectives of the organizational culture. *Integrationist* views of the organizational culture propose that a single unified culture exists in an organization. It is characterized by consistency across individuals and units in terms of the elements of the culture including assumptions, values, and artifacts as reviewed (King, 2007; Schein, 1985). The *integrationist* view directs our attention to see an organization when making a distinction between different types of organizations like a university or a company.

The proponents of the *differentiation* perspective on culture view the organizational culture as a mix of local cultures, each with their own assumptions, values and artifacts. This is a further and more detailed analysis of the organizational culture. These organizational subcultures may reflect the organizational structure, professional occupations, task assignments, ethnic values, rank in the hierarchy, or technologies used (Bloor & Dawson, 1994). Shared assumptions typically form around the functional units of the organization, and could therefore be termed as *functional cultures*. They are often based on members' similar educational backgrounds or similar organizational experiences (Schein, 1996). Rose (1988) notes that the differentiation perspective on the organizational culture may be more realistic particularly in large complex organizations where changes are evident.

The significance of the culture to an organization has increasingly been understood as dynamic processes rather than static imposing structures (Pettigrew, 1979; Sackmann, 1991; Hong & Engeström, 2004; Hasu et al., 2005; Hong et al, 2008). Furthermore, the accelerating process of globalization, radical social and economic transformation and the increasing interconnections between cultures involve an unprecedented challenge to academic mainstream conceptions which continue to work in a tradition of cultural dichotomies (Craig & Douglas, 2006; Hermans & Kempen, 1998). Some illuminating studies shed light on a number of interesting areas of research such as the rise of the creative class in the U.S. resulting from an underlying culture that is open-minded and diverse (Florida, 2002), the construction of a new mode of thought relying on and thriving with collaboration (John-Steiner, 2000), the positive values of cultural diversity for constructing the knowledge base and learning (Boyle, 1999), and mutual adjustment and learning in joint ventures operating in China (Child, 1994). This has put learning and knowledge creation in a situation in which learning is not aimed at adapting a mainstream culture, but it is rather learning from each other or even from the culture with opposing values so that a third and new culture could possibly be generated. The above studies on moving cultures and cultural interaction indicate that cultural diversity is not something negative but rather a powerful source for creating new knowledge and cultures.

Due to multi-layered, multi-level and dynamic nature of culture, the study thus also calls our attention to examine carefully the moderating influences. This is particularly the case when studding the impact of national cultural influences, in which the moderating influences of individual, group and situational characteristics are approached (Leung et al., 2005). For instance, individual or self identity may amplify the impact of culture on beliefs. In every culture, there are people who hold beliefs different from those typical.

When a person views him or herself as a member of the national culture, and the culture is a large component of his or her self-concept, culture will have a strong and pervasive impact on his or her belief ... instead, other sources of self identity such as education or professional affiliation may play a much stronger role in defining who they are, and what motivate them personally, and which values they hold (p.369).

Other individual characteristics discussed in Leung et al.'s research include self-esteem (Van Dyne et al., 2000), self-construals (Markus & Kitayama, 1991), levels of cooperativeness and agreeableness (Chatman & Barsade, 1995), sensitivity to the 'other' cultural situation (Adair et al., 2001), etc.. They are worth noting when we make a research design in examining the impact of national culture on both individual and organizational outcomes. Additionally, moderating influence may relate also to group characteristics (e.g., early vs late stages of group development) or situational characteristics (e.g., intra vs intercultural negotiation among managers from different nations, predictable vs uncertain technological task situations).

KNOWLEDGE INTERACTION

Inter-organizational knowledge interaction is often a term freely used in the literature without any definitions or discussion. Mostly in such cases, it has just been taken or used, implying somehow a kind of knowledge exchange between two or more teams, organizations or communities that host different bodies of knowledge. The knowledge collaboration partners may often be complementary (e.g., Bukh & Johanson, 2003; John-Steiner, 2000; Santoro & Gopalakrishnan, 2000). Complementarity is one alternative that enables organizations to acquire and exploit new knowledge and it refers to the extent to which two organizations have distinct but mutually synergistic resources necessary for advancing new knowledge (Teece, 1987 / Santoro & Gopalakrishnan, 2000).

In a more serious sense, knowledge interaction has been used in several research areas. It can be seen, for instance, in U–I collaboration studies (Fukugava, 2005; Santoro & Gopalakrishnan, 2000; Schartinger, 2002), the design of a new communication medium (Nishida, 2000, 2002) and the study on channel policy (Kubota & Nishida, 2003). In the design of a new communication medium, Nishida (2000, 2002) defines dynamic knowledge interaction as interaction that brings about mutual understanding and evolution in a community. In similar vein, Kubota and Nishida (2003) adopt the term of strategic knowledge interaction for designing the knowledge channel model and discussing channel policy that represents the user intention of interacting with streaming contents.

More studies come from U–I research literature. In the study by Schartinger et al. (2002), the term *knowledge interaction* is used to describe all types of direct and indirect, personal and non-personal interaction between organizations and/or individuals from the firm side and the university side, directed at the exchange of knowledge within innovation processes. This is perhaps the best effort so far in seeing knowledge interaction as a research concept. Drawing from their U–I study in Austria, Schartinger et al. identify sixteen types of knowledge interaction, which can be classified into four major knowledge interaction models. The models can also be seen from an elaboration by Perkmann and Walsh (2006). They are i) joint research (including joint publishing), ii) contract research (including consulting, financing of public research organization research assistants by firms), iii) mobility (staff movement between universities and firms, joint supervision of students) and iv) training (co-operation in education, training of firm staff at universities, lecturing by industry staff). Some types of knowledge interaction are highly active or interactions are more intensified than others. Fukugawa (2005) studies the characteristics of knowledge interaction in terms of the firm size and concludes that university-based scientists with high research potential are linked with large firms in broad areas through highly interactive spillover channels such as joint research, whereas university-based scientists with low research potential are linked with small firms, through less interactive spillover channels such as technical consultation.

U–I COLLABORATION AND KNOWLEDGE INTERACTION

U–I collaboration may take various forms and its driving forces may also vary highly from case to case. In this section, we briefly review why there is U–I collaboration, considering complementary knowledge interaction for innovation as a primary but emerging concern. Then we clarify from the previous literature and our research experience the major forms of the collaboration. We close with an analysis on the nature of knowledge interaction in terms of U–I collaboration by identifying three distinctive U–I knowledge interaction strategies and approaches.

Why U–I Collaboration?

We argue that the primary reason for U–I collaboration is the need to gain complementary knowledge or expertise for applying it to commercial ends. After all, universities hold the access to intellectual resources and can offer a competent basic research infrastructure and conduct high-quality research, whereas companies possess practical knowledge and up-to-date technology information, contact interface with the international market, financial resources, and employment opportunities for new graduates. When discussing such U–I partnership and collaboration, Gustavs and Clegg (2005) refer to it, for instance, as the interaction between two modes of knowledge production originally proposed by Gibbons and his colleagues: mode one knowledge is defined as being "institutionalized primarily within university structures" and is discipline-based, whereas mode two knowledge is characterized as operating "within a context of application" (e.g., workplace knowledge). The TCL Corporation is one of the biggest consumer electronic groups in China. During the early stage of negotiation and actual acquisition between TCL and the French Thomson (2003–2004), TCL faced a challenge in the lack of knowledge in internationalization and its management. A related training program for TCL top management was started, and soon after a long-term agreement on "strategic knowledge alliance" between the *Guanhua* Management School of the Beijing University and TCL Group was signed. Through this collaboration, the Beijing University offers TCL management knowledge, while the university learns and updates its knowledge base in the latest technologies (see Lin, 2005).

U–I collaboration may be initiated by both economic and non-economic motivators. The economic motivators include the willingness to share R&D costs and risks, to gain new technologies and suitable equipment, to obtain access to human resources and to achieve intangible resources in the form of patents and know-how. Non-economic motivators are related to the desire to gain recognition in the scientific community and to burnish their image through studies aimed for the welfare of the society – the responsibility towards regional economic development and university policy (see also Fukukawa, 2005). In some cases, even if the economic and non-economic motivators are not obvious at the beginning, partners (should) gradually develop a coherent covenant with complementary objectives and ways of behaving (Hermans & Castiaux, 2007). It could also be understood in a more simple way by sticking out the different needs and benefits from each side of the collaboration: the major advantages *for the academic communities* – research funding and practical learning opportunities for students – and *for industry* – lower research and development costs and technology transfer opportunities that affect competitiveness (Elmuti et al., 2005).

Major Forms of Collaboration

The forms of U–I collaboration vary greatly due to various contextual factors. The major forms below we identified are mainly based on our literature study and research experience concerning MNCs' R&D collaboration with Chinese universities (see also Li, 2005; Lin, 2005). They include: 1) *Authorized or contract-based research projects* – normally companies provide research funds and equipment, and the authorized universities return research outcomes back to the companies according to agreed requirements. In this case, the research topic is given. 2) *Joint research projects* – in most cases they are partially "joint" in the early stage of the project establishment. The research topic is jointly discussed and established according to a common interest. The collaboration of MS Corporation with Chinese famous universities is a good example of this. The corporation selects every year its senior supervisors and experienced experts to form a special committee to identify and choose from the university projects which are meaningful for its own business and further develop them with universities. 3) *Collaborative training enterprises or programs* – commonly planned and developed by both partners. 4) *Joint R&D institutes* or *laboratories* – focusing on specialized areas in collaboration and creating local talent pools more and more become the true motivation of MNCs' collaboration with Chinese universities. 5) *Science and technology parks close to university campuses* – this provides a geographically convenient and common ground for U–I interaction. 6) *Technical and management consultation* is a one-way rather than interactive form since firms exclusively act as the user of knowledge instead of the co-creator of knowledge. 7) *Licensing* refers to the interest and potential of the firm in applying the inventions of university-based scientists. 8) *Donation* is the firm's long-term strategy to connect with universities for hiring competent new graduates, although this is the least interactive form of U–I collaboration. Both company-sponsored post doctoral research centres in universities and thematic joint workshops are emerging as new forms under this category.

U–I Knowledge Interaction

Typical U–I knowledge interaction is revealed, for instance, in knowledge networks (e.g., direct personal networks such as talks at academic conferences/workshops and indirect linkages intermediated by third parties such as liaison offices) (Fukugawa, 2005), strategic knowledge alliances focusing on the knowledge-based value in innovation (Lin, 2005), joint R&D projects and institutes and their evolving activities (Hermans & Castiaux, 2007; Johnson & Johnson, 2004; Li, 2005; Li & Zhong, 2003), co-operation in education and training (Ryan, 2007), science-based industrial innovation (Gu & Lundvall, 2006; Guan

et al., 2005), university-run enterprises (Eun et al., 2006) and science parks as knowledge organizations (Hansson, 2007).

In this chapter we define U-I knowledge interaction as interactive knowledge strategies, relationships, processes, activities and outcomes. Focusing on the nature of inter-organizational knowledge interaction, we have identified three approaches to U–I knowledge interaction, among which *the intensity of knowledge interaction* substantially increases from 1) technology and knowledge transfer, to 2) knowledge integration and to 3) collaborative knowledge creation (Hong et al., 2007). In simple terms, *technology and knowledge transfer (TKT)* is the communication of technology and knowledge from one agent to another (Hedlund & Nonaka, 1993). The one that provides the needed knowledge is the knowledge supplier, and the one that gets the knowledge is the knowledge recipient. Not equal to technology transfer, knowledge transfer implies a broader, more inclusive construct that is directed more toward understanding the "whys" for change. Technology transfer is a narrower and more targeted construct that usually embodies certain tools for changing the environment (Gopalakrishnan & Santoro, 2004). Davenport and Prusak (1998) argued that the knowledge transfer process consists of transformation absorption, culminating in a behavioral change by the recipient firm. Typical TKT practices include the transfer of techniques and technologies from one location to another, the commercialization of an innovation (e.g. licensing), or hiring new graduate and young talents from the collaboration universities. In this line of research, it would be interesting, for instance, to study the recruiting of graduate students in addition to the conventional focus on patent and paper studies (Agrawal, 2001).

Previous U–I knowledge interaction research focuses primarily on knowledge transfer. In a comprehensive literature review of university-to-industry knowledge transfer, Agrawal (2001) identifies four research streams. Research in the *firm characteristics* category focuses directly on company issues, such as the internal organization, resource allocation, and partnerships. In contrast, research in the *university characteristics* stream pays special attention to issues relating to the university, such as licensing strategies, incentives for professors to patent, and policies such as taking equity in return for intellectual property. The *geography in terms of localized spillovers* stream of research considers the spatial relationship between firms and universities relative to performance in terms of knowledge transfer success. The *channels of knowledge transfer* literature examines the relative importance of various transfer pathways such as publications, patents, and consulting. More specifically, a number of topics on U–I knowledge transfer appear interesting, which deal with the enabling function of trust and networking (Koschatzky, 2002; Lambooy, 2004; Santoro, 2006), the interplay between the characters of U–I relationship and the transfer of sticky knowledge (Wang & Lu, 2007), and the potentially moderating role of technical and organizational uncertainties (Daghfous et al., 2003).

Knowledge integration (KI) emphasizes the process of integrating and transforming the acquired knowledge for the firm's specific use of that knowledge according to situations and needs in a quite tailored way. Comparatively, integrating knowledge takes less time in the learning process than transferring knowledge. Grant (1996) argues that transferring knowledge is not an efficient approach to integrating knowledge. He claims that "if production requires the integration of many people's special knowledge, the key to efficiency is to achieve effective integration while minimizing knowledge transfer through cross-learning by organizational members" (114). Given the assumption about the characteristics of knowledge and the knowledge requirements of production, Grant conceptualizes the firm as an institution for integrating knowledge. One example of KI could be that firms request technical and management consultation from university-based scientists.

These consultants provide solutions, but seldom know what afterwards happens in the firm. Knowledge interaction may take very different shapes at early versus later stages. At an early stage, there are much more face-to-face contacts and personal interactions involved, which is not the case at a later stage when everything happens internally only within the recipient organization.

It seems that the concept of knowledge integration emphasizes the knowledge fit between the source and the recipient and the dominant role, and the knowledge structure exists prior to the process of knowledge integration. Comparatively, knowledge transfer emphasizes the knowledge and the wholeness of it from the source organization, and the key process is that this knowledge will be acquired or learned and used in the same way as it should be in the source organization. Thus, knowledge transfer is to make knowledge clear to others and let them be able to learn from you, whereas knowledge integration is to make your knowledge available to others and let them be able to use it directly.

Collaborative knowledge creation (CKC) refers to a situation when two or more partners come and work together to create new information and knowledge, which can be used for the benefit of both sides, and potential for their future innovation and development. The focus of CKC is on creating and developing new knowledge. In CKC, we consider a common understanding for the shared vision essential through discussion. One common practice in U–I collaboration is related to joint research projects or collaborative educational or training programs in which experts from both universities and firms are actively involved in the whole process of projects and programs. Collaborative knowledge creation is the key concept underlying collaborative innovation (Hermans & Castiaux, 2007; Hong et al., 2007; Nonaka & Takeuchi, 1995; Nonaka, 2007; Popadiuk & Choo, 2006).

The studies on knowledge creation in U–I collaborative research projects seem to present an

Figure 1. U–I Knowledge Interaction in Joint Innovation Activities

U-I Knowledge Interaction	Technology and Knowledge Transfer (TKT)	Knowledge Integration (KI)	Collaborative Knowledge Creation (CKC)
Collaboration Activities in Joint Research, Education & Innovation	licensing authorized research projects partially joint research projects Donation	technical & management consultation from research organization(s) university science & technology parks	fully joint research projects collaborative training institutes and/or programs joint R & D institutes or labs Thematic joint workshops

The intensity of knowledge interaction increases from TKT to CKC

emerging line of research (Hermans & Castiaux, 2007; Johnson & Johnson, 2004) which expands the Nonaka and Takeuchi's (1995) theorizing context from within an organization into a wider U–I context. As Nonaka et al. (2000: 30) themselves note: "For the immediate future, it will be important to examine how companies, governments and universities can work together to make knowledge creation possible." Nonaka et al.'s knowledge creation theory and concepts are also applied and discussed in a number of other U–I studies (Gustavs & Clegg, 2005; Hansson, 2007; Heikkinen et al., 2007). In this line of research, the identified knowledge interaction strategies and approaches are often mixed. Some can be clarified into knowledge transfer, and others into collaborative knowledge creation. In practice and in many cases, the boundary of the three knowledge interaction approaches is not clear and the division is made just in a relative sense and more for analytic purposes.

Different forms of U–I collaboration and knowledge interaction are intertwined as shown in Figure 1. The forms of knowledge interaction identified and presented in the figure are relative and analytic and there is much overlapping among them.

Some early findings indicate that political culture has a significant impact on the firm's choice of *exploitation-exploration* internationalization strategy (Armagan & Ferreira, 2005). Other study relates national culture to the firm's developing path on types of research laboratory meant to be capability exploiting versus capability augmenting (Ambos & Schlegelmilch, 2008). In light of this and similar theorizing regarding exploitation-exploration knowledge strategy and paradox (Grant & Baden-Fuller, 2004; Gupta et al., 2006; March, 1991; Spender, 1992), it would be interesting to examine empirically whether the primary advantage of strategic research alliances is in accessing or acquiring knowledge, and how multi-level cultures may influence on the firm's choice and resolution of balancing different knowledge interaction approaches as knowledge transfer, knowledge integration, and collaborative knowledge creation.

U–I KNOWLEDGE INTERACTION ACROSS CULTURAL BOUNDARIES

As shown by the new cross-cultural research, culture is a multi-level construct and the main stream of cultural research addresses culture primarily at the levels of national and organizational cultures. In the U–I studies with a focus on knowledge interaction, the influence of culture is mainly discussed at an organizational level, in which fundamental cultural differences between universities and companies are identified and examined. Since our research focus is on an MNC subsidiary's collaboration with Chinese universities and research institutes, in this section, we discuss, however, the cultural implications of U–I collaboration and knowledge interaction at both organizational and national levels. We first review cultural studies available in the U–I collaboration context, and then discuss U–I studies and cultural relevance in the Chinese MNC context. At the end of the section, we summarize what we draw from and reflect on our literature studies and pilot research experience in terms of organizational and national cultural influences.

Cultural Gap in U–I Organizational Type

Research on U–I knowledge interaction conducted so far is primarily related to the studies on cultural influences across organizational boundaries. Universities and companies are different in nature. Their objectives and activities are different and so are the ways of thinking and doing things. From the point of view of the organizational culture, one major difference lies in the value they hold for research and its outcomes. Universities appreciate more basic research, and companies focus on applied research; universities emphasize research value itself and companies see most often the practical side of research and profit maximization that might be derived from research. Some researchers regard the impact of such differences negatively as a collaboration barrier (Declercq, 1981), and others consider it the very reason for collaboration (Lee, 1996; Lopez-Martinez et al., 1994).

The U–I studies that deal with the fundamental differences between two types of organizations

are particularly about *goal formation, time orientation, language* and *assumption* (Cyert & Goodman, 1997; Elmuti et al., 2005), *agreeing on priorities and timescales, publishing in the public domain*, and *academic laissez-faire approach vs industrial lack of flexibility* (Barnes et al, 2002). In U–I interaction studies, this is where the impact of culture and related factors have been focused and examined. Cyert and Goodman (1997) believe that the differences between university and company partners manifest themselves in divergent goals (to create and disseminate knowledge vs to produce products and services), time orientations (longer time period and less well-defined vs quarterly goals), common language, and assumptions (reputation outside of university vs supervisors within the company). Searching for an overview of strategic alliances between universities and corporations, Elmuti et al. (2005) highlight the partners' different working cultures and values that may have negative effects on effective alliance collaboration and interaction, which must be supported by continuous learning and restructuring processes to overcome the differences. Similar to Cyert and Goodman, essential differences identified in their study include different goals (creating and spreading knowledge vs producing products and services), time approaches (long vs short term), and languages and assumptions (related to communication efficiency). In studying collaborative R&D projects, Barnes et al. (2002) conclude from their U–I collaboration cases that the main cultural issues to emerge are the needs to agree on priorities and timescales; also, prominent is the need to manage perceptions and issues on both sides regarding the academic right to publish, and the student agenda. This latter factor is related to the perceptions of the role of student researchers on such projects. Along with others, Barnes et al. (2002: 282) consider fundamental differences in the relative priorities, perspectives and time horizons of academia and industry "a major obstacle to successful university-industry collaborations." Managing the cultural gap as one of the key elements for a good practice model of collaboration management, they refer to the bridging of differing priorities/timescales, publishing in the public domain, the academic laissez-faire approach, industry's lack of flexibility, and IPR & confidentiality.

The study of Santoro and Gopalakrishnan (2000) examines the institutionalization of knowledge transfer activities between industrial firms and university research centers. This is one of few direct studies on the impact of culture on U–I knowledge interaction. Their empirical results show that knowledge transfer activities are facilitated when industrial firms have more mechanistic structures, cultures that are more stable and direction-oriented, and when the firm is more trusting on its university research center partner. Thus, they propose that the more stable and direction-oriented an organization's culture, the greater the institutionalization of knowledge transfer activities; in other words, the more flexible and change-oriented an organization's culture, the less the institutionalization of knowledge transfer activities. The key feature of stable and direction-oriented culture is thus risk-avoiding, preferring stability and status-quo rather than the uncertainty of change. In contrast, flexible and change-oriented cultures encourage risk-taking and always search for new knowledge streams. In their research the institutionalization of knowledge transfer activities include high factor loading activities like the firm's involvement in curriculum development to relatively low factor loading activities such as the number of personnel exchanges with the university research center. As we can see from the above review, U–I research and investigation on the culture is apparently within a local context, and research in cross-cultural settings remains an interesting gap. The national or societal culture, for instance, may influence U–I knowledge interaction significantly.

Cultural Relevance in the Chinese MNC Context

China is quite different from the rest of the world, and in this section we take the R&D collaboration of Finnish MNC subsidiaries with Chinese universities as an illustration, discussing the most relevant literature and our research experience regarding the role of trust and *guanxi* (informal social networking) and cultural challenges in U–I knowledge interaction in the Chinese context.

The Role of Trust and *Guanxi* In global markets it is crucial to understand the norms and conditions a company faces on foreign ground. As Doney et al. (1998: 601) wrote: "The importance and benefits of trust, and the emerging global and multicultural workplace, highlight the need for us to understand how trust develops and the ways national culture impacts the trust building process." Trust is especially fragile in cross-cultural trading relationships, because the divergent national cultures affect one's behaviour in the background. The importance of trust and trust-building processes emerge especially when a company has business units in separate countries, which have their own national and various local cultures like the case in China. Building trust is one precondition for starting collaboration, and in order to collaborate effectively in China one needs to have personal connections.

In China personal ties are nurtured and people show high loyalty to their personal networks known as *guanxi*, which are commonly used to get things done in Chinese everyday life. Plugging into the heart of economic and political life, *guanxi* grows from the power asymmetry between markets and officials, because in China (and in other emerging markets as well) the officials tend to interfere in the markets, and therefore the institutional elements cannot be trusted – law is perceived differently from cultures like the one in

Finland. Therefore it is important who you know, and who can help you sell or buy your products, and more importantly who you can trust to do so. It is also relevant if the person you know knows a person who can help you.

In some studies trust is considered as a component of *guanxi*, whereas others see that trust is an outcome of successful *guanxi*. It has been found that in collectivist cultures people tend to trust quite easily, and their motives are benevolent – *but for in-group members only* (Doney et al., 1998; Huff & Kelly, 2003). Getting into the in-group takes time and a lot of effort and nurturing. Building a relationship where there is trust between partners can be difficult and very time-consuming. Park and Luo (2001) put it felicitously in a nutshell – in China transactions often follow successful *guanxi*, while in the Western countries a relationship follows successful transactions.

The significance of trust and *guanxi* has recently been studied in connection with cross-border knowledge transfer (Buckley et al., 2006; Miesing et al., 2007; Ramasamy et al., 2006). Drawing from the case of Chinese foreign invested enterprises, Miesing et al. (2007) propose that trust-based collaboration in geographically dispersed transitional organizations is one of the key factors for successful inter-organizational knowledge transfer within transnationals. Buckley et al. (2006) examine the cultural awareness of *guanxi* and *mianzi* (face) in knowledge transfer to China. Their findings of case studies suggested that foreign investors must be aware of *guanxi* and *mianzi* in the institutions they deal with and establish institutional connections based on personal connections with local partners and government. The research findings imply that cultural awareness can affect cross-border knowledge transfer and firm performance. They argue that "given the diversity and complexity of the Chinese business environment, even for explicit knowledge to be transferred and absorbed, cultural barriers have to be removed and good inter-partner relationships have to be established." (p. 278). Also in the Chinese context, Ramasamy et al. (2006) raise an interesting question whether *guanxi* can serve as a bridge to inter-organizational knowledge transfer. In their research, *guanxi* consists of three components: trust, relationship commitment, and communication. Their results of an interview-based survey with Chinese enterprise general managers show that trust and communication are the two main channels of knowledge transfer. The authors suggest that inter-partner activities tend to be informal in China and so using informal channels (like *guanxi*) to transfer knowledge would be more desirable and practical. In the Chinese society where informality is central, *guanxi* could also improve the quality of knowledge since information passed from a *guanxi* partner to the receiver could be assured of reliability, richness and trust worthiness, thereby reducing the receiver's search cost, and allowing for more informed decisions (Luo, 1997). All these findings suggest that trust and *guanxi* may play an important role in U–I knowledge interaction in the multinational context in China.

Major Cultural Challenges Cultural challenges have much to do with the fact that we are used to thinking in our own way and tend to ignore others' mind. Taking Finland as an example, enormous cultural variations between Finland and China may lead to many difficulties and conflicts in communication and collaboration particularly because 1) it is hard to become an insider or hard to accept and collaborate with "strangers" in the Chinese culture; 2) foreigners are automatically considered "outsiders"; and 3) there are enormous misunderstandings about others' intentions and behaviour due to huge cultural variations.

In Finland personal achievements are appreciated, whereas in China the benefit of an in-group is emphasized, and an individual is motivated by the collective values and attitudes. Many foreign managers have complained that Chinese employees are lacking self-initiative and sense of responsibility in terms of task execution and innovations. This might be due to that in the Chinese culture group harmony is especially emphasized and sticking out from the group is not encouraged. Finland enjoys a rule-based culture, whereas in China personal relations or *guanxi* often override rules and regulations. Consequently, foreign partners encounter many problems in sticking to the contracts and documented procedures, whereas Chinese tend to emphasize long-term relationships and trust, and expect much flexibility from their collaborators in updating the contracts and procedures whenever necessary. In this sense, it is contracting rather than contracts that are more important in their daily business life. Even laws work differently; in Finland and other Nordic countries, they are obeyed, whereas in China they are avoided if possible. Contracts can be important in binding people to work together in Finland, whereas in China, social networking plays a far more important role in collaboration. Moreover, the importance of informality in the Chinese culture is obvious. An official group is often different from a social group. The former represents hierarchic and vertical communication on the one side, and the latter one the informal and horizontal dimension of collaboration that most likely makes things happen. The latter and informal part is more like a hidden rule which is rarely understood by Westerners. In our view, to be aware of the above cultural variations helps to understand others' views, and therefore greatly furthers cross-cultural communication and collaboration. Common language and the shared social knowledge, as believed by Buckley et al. (2005), are particularly important for the transfer of knowledge across national borders within multinational enterprises.

Our Interviews and Discussion An interview round was conducted when one of the authors attended *the Academia Summit* 2006 *Beijing* organized by a Finnish MNC. Five Chinese professors with experience in collaborating with MNCs were interviewed. They were from three Chinese universities in the field of ICT. In June 2007, two of the authors conducted another round

of interviews in five universities of the forest and printing industries in China. Nineteen professors and researchers were interviewed, most of whom quite experienced with collaborating with MNCs. The two rounds of interviewing in China worked as a pilot study for our future project on U–I collaborative knowledge creation and innovation. Each interview took approximately one hour. Based on the interviews of our pilot study, it can be said that *guanxi* and knowing the right people play an influential role at the beginning of U–I collaboration. It seems that the negotiations for joint projects are normally initiated by people who are acquainted from before and share some personal history or background.

There are various challenges in U–I collaboration between MNCs and Chinese universities. According to the interviewees the biggest challenges are related to the differences of the organizations in culture and knowledge. Universities differ from companies as institutions. Where companies aim to gain financial benefit with their operations, universities are non-profit making organizations. Yet, companies aim to carry out applied research, whereas universities are interested in basic and explorative research. Some professors also felt that the differences in management styles were very frustrating. University professors are used to flexible and long-term research with freedom, whereas companies demand reports of the achieved results on a constant basis; the rhythm is different. One example of a favourable company partner was mentioned, namely Intel. This is simply because the company strongly invests in basic research and gives freedom to the university to manage their research in their own style. One very problematic challenge was mentioned and that is the issue of IPRs. This issue is on the lips of both the company and university representatives. Chinese professors felt that the dilemma with IPRs is related to the publication of the results. Companies want to wait for the patents to be approved before publishing any critical information, whereas for researchers such waiting might be harmful, since the PhD degrees and promotions are dependent on the number of publications.

In the future the main motivation factors for U–I collaboration in Chinese universities may remain the same. However, the forms of collaboration may take a more intensive course. The interviewed professors could see the universities and the MNCs working closer both physically and mentally, and sharing working forces and knowledge to a larger extent than before. Since both partners in U–I collaboration pursue to create new knowledge out of the collaboration, the best result can be achieved when the partners have a shared understanding and a common goal throughout the whole project.

Summary and a Way Forward

As reviewed, Santoro and Goplalakrishnan (2000) examined the relationship between cultural traits and the institutionalization of U–I knowledge transfer activities. On the organizational level of cultural impact, some other studies have introduced different cultural dimensions which we think might have much to do with our study context. They include, for instance, the close relation between organizational innovation and the competing values model of organizational culture (the four orientations of support, rules, innovation and goal) (Quinn, 1988 / Ahteela et al., in press) and the time perspective between long and short term (Kilmann & Saxton, 1983). All these cultural models are largely interrelated. Studies on the impact of culture on U–I knowledge interaction, however, have so far been conducted at the organizational level of culture.

As we discussed, there are some specific characteristics related to the Chinese culture like *guanxi*. We can assume that the national culture may have a significant role in U–I collaboration as well and it would be necessary to take it into account in our study context. In broader literature on inter-cultural organizational collaboration and knowledge interaction, we found that various cultural influences are, actually, mostly discussed at the level of national cultures. Among them, national cultural influences refer to, for instance, the national cultural patterns in terms of the dimensions of individualism–collectivism and verticalness–horizontalness (Bhagat et al., 2002), national cultural characteristics in terms of Chinese *guanxi* (personal connections) and *mianzi* (face) (Buckley et al., 2006; Ramasamy et al., 2006), and national cultural dimensions originally introduced by Hofstede including individualism/ collectivism, power distance, uncertainty avoidance, and masculinity/femininity (Lucas, 2006). In other studies, cross-cultural differences and their influences in multinational contexts are differentiated as those in language barriers, conceptions of quality and prioritization of cost reduction (Kohlbacher & Krähe, 2007), common language and shared social knowledge (Buckley et al., 2005), and Japanese *organizational* versus the British *professional* societal settings (Lam, 1997). Recent studies particularly discuss the impact of political culture and national culture on the firm's choice of exploration-exploitation knowledge strategy and the paradox in capability development in international contexts (Ambos & Schlegelmilch, 2008; Armagan & Ferreira, 2005).

Drawing also from inter-cultural collaboration literature, we found that the discussion on cultural influence is often related to some aspects of knowledge that moderate cultural influences. They are, for instance, discussions on the nature of knowledge (Bhagat et al., 2002; Simonin, 1999; Szulanski, 2003), knowledge type (Bhagat et al., 2002; Buckley et al., 2005), knowledge gap (Wang & Lu, 2007) and knowledge structure (Lam, 1997). However, our study focuses on different modes of knowledge interaction as reviewed, in which knowledge transfer is only one type. We argue that in addition to those aspects of knowledge, different modes and intensity of knowledge interaction along with corresponding strategies should be taken into account and thus carefully examined. We propose that in the context of MNCs' collaboration with Chinese research organizations, the relative importance of multi-level cultural influences on cross-border knowledge interaction may differ due to the intensity of knowledge interaction: *the more interactive knowledge interaction is, the more significant the impact of culture is.* Particularly in the form of collaborative knowledge creation, knowledge is not something given but constantly modified, integrated and constructed in collaboration between the parties, and thus it requires the strongest involvement and commitment from both or more collaborative parties. In this regard, we believe the role of culture is the most significant of all.

IMPLICATIONS FOR FUTURE RESEARCH

Several implications could be drawn from our review and analysis in the chapter. First of all, U–I studies are likely to be conducted in a local context, and research in multinational and cross-cultural settings remain an interesting gap. Particularly in examining multi-level cultural influences, the study on MNC subsidiaries' R&D collaboration with local universities may provide an ideal case. Secondly, in early studies, technology and knowledge transfer is obviously the most examined topic. Other forms we identified as interactive knowledge integration and collaborative knowledge creation seem neglected to a large extent although they differ substantially from the knowledge transfer type in organizational partnership. This is especially in the case of collaborative knowledge creation, where strong involvement and commitment from both or more collaborative parties are required. In this regard, we believe the role of culture to be the most evident. We suggest that much more attention need to be paid to collaborative knowledge creation and its deep underlying cultural mechanisms. And thirdly, the previous studies on inter-cultural collaboration and knowledge interaction also draw our attention to knowledge-

specific variables themselves (the nature and type of knowledge, knowledge structure and knowledge gap as discussed in the paper). We propose that the significance of the cultural impact may differ due to the intensity of knowledge interaction, and it may accumulate with the increasing intensity of knowledge interaction from technology and knowledge transfer, to knowledge integration and collaborative knowledge creation. In future studies, it would be interesting to test the proposition empirically.

Moreover, some related methodological issues and empirical cross-cultural research deserve particular attention: 1) when studying the impact of the national culture we need to consider moderating influences. They can be, for instance, individual, group and situational characteristics, dynamic aspects of culture as moving cultures and cultural interactions, and remote and contrast institutional contexts (MNC subsidiaries vs local universities). 2) The study of the national culture should not remain at a level of addressing whether or not the national culture makes a difference, but should focus on *how* and *when* it makes a difference (Leung et al., 2005). The study of U–I knowledge interaction involving dissimilar cultural contexts may provide a work-related situation in which detailed information in terms of the efficiency of knowledge development could be explored and utilized in practice. 3) Cultural factors cannot be seen as an isolated influence. They are often mixed with other contextual factors and conditions such as cohort, gender, race as well as institutional, political, historical, or economic influences which must be cautiously treated.

CONCLUSION

The existing literature in cross-border knowledge interaction is nearly all about knowledge transfer. We argue in this book chapter that knowledge management research should pay ample attention to more interactive types of knowledge interaction, which seem to be the emerging forms of collaboration and networking particularly in today's rapidly changing markets like China. The interactive knowledge-based collaboration is particularly evident in R&D collaboration between MNC subsidiaries and Chinese universities/research institutes. In the rapidly changing business and technology environment in China, things are hard to predict in the long term and there are no ready answers ahead. In this context, a two-way interactive and collaborative knowledge creation mode increasingly becomes a necessity as well as a challenge for MNCs to gain competitive advantage in innovation. The knowledge created in such a context is often tentative and the meaning of it is constantly negotiated based on long-term trust, creative dialogue and open discussions. Under such circumstances, the examination of cultural influences also needs to be given attention and approached in these new international contexts.

Furthermore, we found that the impact of culture on U–I knowledge interaction is examined only at one level of organizational culture. We suggest that particularly in multinational organizational contexts, the impact of the national culture should be taken into account. This is not something new as it has been shown in new cross-cultural research and suggested from a broader research context of inter-cultural organizational collaboration and knowledge interaction, as we reviewed in the paper. What is new is that we note that U–I studies have so far concentrated on the collaboration issues and knowledge interaction only in a local context within the same regional or national systems, and research in multinational and cross-cultural settings remain an interesting gap. Cultural issues have therefore not received enough attention in present U–I knowledge interaction studies.

Based on the above-mentioned argumentation and as a result of our own theorizing, we would propose a tentative conceptual framework in which both multi-level cultural influences and different modes of knowledge interaction are considered for

studying the impact of culture on U–I knowledge interaction in the Chinese MNC context (Figure 2). In the framework, the case study strategy of a single MNC subsidiary operating in China is employed due to the exploratory nature of the study, focusing on R&D collaboration with Chinese universities and research institutes. The impact of culture is examined at three levels: local Chinese culture in contrast to foreign or Western cultures (collectivism vs individualism; verticalness vs horizontalness; *guanxi*-based Chinese culture vs task-oriented foreign or Western cultures), organizational cultures between universities and companies (long-term vs short-term planning; flexible & change-oriented vs stable & direction oriented) and organizational sub-unit cultures (management vs technical personnel). Moderating influences are related to three types of variables: 1) individual, group & situational characteristics (e.g., individual or self identity may amplify the impact of culture on beliefs – in every culture, there are people who hold beliefs different from those typical; intra vs intercultural negotiation among managers from different nations), 2) moving cultures & cultural interactions (e.g., the increasing interconnections between cultures), and 3) knowledge-specific variables (nature & type of knowledge, knowledge structure, knowledge gap, intensity of knowledge interaction). The focus of proposed research is on both the perceived knowledge theories and strategies (exploitation-exploration) and the modes of knowledge interaction (technology & knowledge transfer, knowledge integration, and collaborative knowledge creation).

To apply and develop such a conceptual framework should be sensitive to the alignment and tensions between collaboration parties and between organizational level efforts and external socio-cultural, economic & political enabling or coercing forces. We believe the proposed framework and research could help researchers and the like examine and identify cultural differences and barriers in building effective MNC U–I knowledge-based collaboration with local

Figure 2. A Tentative Conceptual Framework for Studying the Impact of Culture on U–I Knowledge Interaction in the Chinese MNC Context.

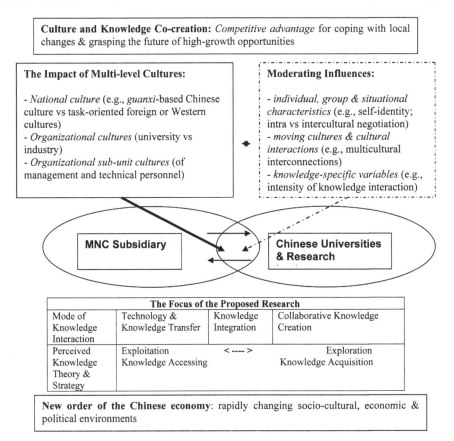

universities and research institutes for gaining competitive advantage in coping with changes and grasping the future of high-growth opportunities in the emerging markets like China.

Thus, the most important managerial implication we could suggest is related to one of the MNCs' pressing research needs and challenges in coping with changes and throbbing with the pulse of future markets. For MNCs operating in dissimilar cultures and rapidly changing markets like in China, one of the biggest challenges is to understand and model future customer needs in high velocity markets (with rapid and discontinuous changes, see Schreyögg & Kliesch, 2005) and to act accordingly. Here we refer to MNCs whose time perspectives are associated with long-term visioning – time horizons 2-3, for instance, as

called by Mehredad Baghai from the Mckensey: Horizon 2 to onboarding the next generation of high-growth opportunities in the pipeline, and Horizon 3 to incubating the germs of new businesses that will sustain the franchise far into the future. Drawing from our theorizing and research experience, we believe that the key to cope with such a challenge is first to build up *knowledge-based collaboration* with local research communities who actively interact with local marketing environments and customers of all types in order to transfer, integrate and co-create knowledge with the company. Clearly, there seems no shortcut or the best method that could be used for direct prediction or modelling purposes in hectic and turbulent business environments, but to build relatively stable and long-term knowledge-based collaboration and relationship with local research organizations. In this regard, building *guanxi* and trust encourages collaboration; especially in China it initiates, facilitates and intensifies collaboration and knowledge interaction when there are personal connections and various channels of informal social networking. China's huge talent pool increasingly attracts MNCs to look for new forms of long-term and deeper collaboration with Chinese universities and research institutes. This apparently provides a rare opportunity and new landscape for both researchers and practitioners in which knowledge and competence co-creation might be reinforced.

ACKNOWLEDGEMENT

An early version of this chapter is based on a conference paper "Collaborative knowledge creation and innovation between MNCs and Chinese universities" presented at *the 8ᵗʰ European Conference on Knowledge Management,* Barcelona September 6–7, 2007. The study is supported in part by Liikesivistysrahasto (Finnish Foundation for Economic Education). The authors are grateful for friendly and constructive comments from Julie Hermans from the University of Namur, Belgium.

REFERENCES

Adair, W. L., Okumura, T., & Brett, J. M. (2001). Negotiation behavior when culture collide: The Unites States and Japan. *The Journal of Applied Psychology, 86*(3), 371–385. doi:10.1037/0021-9010.86.3.371

Agrawal, A. (2001). University-to-industry knowledge transfer: Literature review and unanswered questions. *International Journal of Management Reviews, 3*(4), 285–302. doi:10.1111/1468-2370.00069

Ahteela, R., Blomqvist, K., & Puumalainen, K. (in press). Linking organizational culture and trust to organizational innovativeness. *Creativity and Innovation Management.*

Almeida, P., & Phene, A. (2004). Subsidiaries and knowledge creation: The influence of the MNC and host country on innovation. *Strategic Management Journal, 25,* 847–864. doi:10.1002/smj.388

Almeida, P., Song, J. Y., & Grant, R. M. (2002). Are firms superior to alliances and markets? An empirical test of cross-border knowledge building. *Organization Science, 13*(2), 147–161. doi:10.1287/orsc.13.2.147.534

Ambos, B., & Schlegelmilch, B. B. (2008). Innovation in multinational firms: Does cultural fit enhance performance? *Management International Review, 48*(2), 189–206. doi:10.1007/s11575-008-0011-2

Armagan, S., & Ferreira, M. P. (2005). The impact of political culture on firms' choice of exploitation-exploration internationalization strategy. *International Journal of Cross Cultural Management, 5*(3), 275–291. doi:10.1177/1470595805058791

Awazu, Y. (2007). Managing knowledge within and across geographic borders: The role of culture. *Knowledge and Process Management, 14*(3), 145–147. doi:10.1002/kpm.288

Barnes, T., Pashby, I., & Gibbons, A. (2002). Effective university-industry interaction: A multicase evaluation of collaborative R&D projects. *European Management Journal, 20*(3), 272–285. doi:10.1016/S0263-2373(02)00044-0

Bhagat, R. S., Kedia, B. L., Harveston, P. D., & Triandis, H. C. (2002). Cultural variation in the cross-border transfer of organizational knowledge: An integrative framework. *Academy of Management Review, 27*(2), 204–221. doi:10.2307/4134352

Bloor, G., & Dawson, P. (1994). Understanding professional culture in organizational context. *Organization Studies*, *15*(2), 275–295. doi:10.1177/017084069401500205

Boyle, D. P. (1999). The road less traveled: Cross-cultural, international experiential learning. *International Social Work*, *42*(2), 201–214. doi:10.1177/002087289904200208

Bröchner, J., Rosander, S., & Waara, F. (2004). Cross-border post-acquisition knowledge transfer among construction consultants. *Construction Management and Economics*, *22*, 421–427. doi:10.1080/0144619042000240003

Buckley, P. J., & Carter, M. J. (1999). Managing cross-border complementary knowledge: Conceptual development in business process approach to knowledge management in multinational firms. *Int. Studies of Mgt. & Org.*, *29*(1), 80–104.

Buckley, P. J., Carter, M. J., Clegg, J., & Tan, H. (2005). Language and social knowledge in foreign-knowledge transfer to China. *International Studies of Management & Organization*, *35*(1), 47–65.

Buckley, P. J., Clegg, J., & Tan, H. (2006). Cultural awareness in knowledge transfer to China – The role of *guanxi* and *mianzi*. *Journal of World Business*, *41*, 275–288. doi:10.1016/j.jwb.2006.01.008

Bukh, P. N., & Johanson, U. (2003). Research and knowledge interaction: Guidelines for intellectual capital reporting. *Journal of Intellectual Capital*, *4*(4), 576–587. doi:10.1108/14691930310504572

Chatman, J. A., & Barsade, S. G. (1995). Personality, organizational culture, and cooperation: Evidence from a business simulation. *Administrative Science Quarterly*, *40*(3), 423–443. doi:10.2307/2393792

Child, J. (994). *Management in China during the age of reform*. Cambridge, UK: Cambridge University Press.

Clark, T. (1990). International marketing and national character: A review and proposal for an integrative theory. *Journal of Marketing*, 66–79. doi:10.2307/1251760

Craig, C. S., & Douglas, S. P. (2006). Beyond national culture: Implications of cultural dynamics for consumer research. *International Marketing Review*, *23*(3), 322–342. doi:10.1108/02651330610670479

Cyert, R. M., & Goodman, P. S. (1997). Creating effective university-industry alliances: An organizational learning perspective. *Organizational Dynamics*, *25*(4), 45–57. doi:10.1016/S0090-2616(97)90036-X

Daghfous, A. (2003). Uncertainty and learning in university-industry knowledge transfer projects. *Journal of American Academy of Business*, *3*(1/2), 145–151.

Davenport, T. H., & Prusak, L. (1998). *Working knowledge: How organizations manage what they know*. Boston, MA: Harvard Business School Press.

Declercq, G. V. (1981). A third look at the two cultures: The new economic responsibility of the university. *International Journal of institutional Management in Higher Education, 5*(2), 117-122.

Doney, P. M., Cannon, J. P., & Mullen, M. R. (1998). Understanding the influence of national culture on the development of trust. *Academy of Management Review*, *23*(3), 601–620. doi:10.2307/259297

Elmuti, D., Abebe, M., & Nicolosi, M. (2005). An overview of strategic alliances between universities and corporations. *Journal of Workplace Learning, 17*(1/2), 115–129. doi:10.1108/13665620510574504

Eun, J. H., Lee, K., & Wu, G. (2006). Explaining the *university-run enterprises* in China: A theoretical framework for university-industry relationship in developing countries and its application to China. *Research Policy, 35,* 1329–1346. doi:10.1016/j.respol.2006.05.008

Florida, R. (2002). *The rise of the creative class.* New York: Basic Books.

Fu, P. P., Tsui, A. S., & Dess, G. G. (2006). The dynamics of *guanxi* in Chinese high-tech firms: Implications for knowledge management and decision making. *Management International Review, 46*(3), 277–305. doi:10.1007/s11575-006-0048-z

Fukugawa, N. (2005). Characteristics of knowledge interactions between universities and small firms in Japan. *International Small Business Journal, 23*(4), 379–401. doi:10.1177/0266242605054052

Gassmann, O., & Han, Z. (2004). Motivations and barriers of foreign R&D activities in China. *R&D Management, 34*(4), 423–437. doi:10.1111/j.1467-9310.2004.00350.x

Gopalakrishnan, S., & Santoro, M. D. (2004). Distinguishing between knowledge transfer and technology transfer activities: The role of key organizational factors. *IEEE Transactions on Engineering Management, 51*(1), 57–69. doi:10.1109/TEM.2003.822461

Grant, R. M. (1996). Toward a knowledge-based theory of the firm. *Strategic Management Journal, 17,* 109–122. doi:10.1002/(SICI)1097-0266(199602)17:2<109::AID-SMJ796>3.0.CO;2-P

Grant, R. M., & Baden-Fuller, C. (2004). A knowledge accessing theory of strategic alliances. *Journal of Management Studies, 41*(1), 62–84. doi:10.1111/j.1467-6486.2004.00421.x

Gu, S.-L., & Lundvall, B.-Å. (2006). Policy learning as a key processes in the transformation of the Chinese innovation systems. In B.-Å. Lundvall, et al. (Eds.), *Asia's innovation systems in transition.* Cheltenham, UK: Edward Elgar.

Guan, J. C. (2005). Collaboration between industry and research institutes/universities on industrial innovation in Beijing, China. *Technology Analysis and Strategic Management, 17*(3), 339–353. doi:10.1080/09537320500211466

Gupta, A. K., Smith, K. G., & Shalley, C. E. (2006). The interplay between exploration and exploitation . *Academy of Management Journal, 49*(4), 693–706.

Gustavs, J., & Clegg, S. (2005). Working the knowledge games? Universities and corporate organizations in partnership. *Management Learning, 36*(1), 9–30. doi:10.1177/1350507605049900

Hansson, F. (2007). Science parks as knowledge organizations – the "ba" in action? *European Journal of Innovation Management, 10*(3), 348–366. doi:10.1108/14601060710776752

Hasu, M., Helle, M., & Kerosuo, H. (2005). *Ethnography in expansion – emergent trends and future challenges.* Paper presented at the First ISCA Congress, Seville.

Hedlund, G., & Nonaka, I. (1993). Models of knowledge management in the West and Japan. In P. Lorange, B. Chakravarthy, J. Roos, & A. van Der Ven (Eds.), *Implementing strategic processes: Change, learning and co-operation.* Oxford, UK: Blackwell Business.

Heikkinen, J., Blomqvist, K., & Hong, J. Z. (2007). *Ba for knowledge creation in Sino-Western university-industry collaboration.* Paper presented in the Conference of EBRF 2007 - Research Forum to Understand Business in Knowledge Society, Agora - Jyväskylä, Finland.

Hermans, H. J. M., & Kempen, H. J. G. (1998). Moving cultures: The perilous problems of cultural dichotomies in a globalizing society. *The American Psychologist, 53*(10), 1111–1120. doi:10.1037/0003-066X.53.10.1111

Hermans, J., & Castiaux, A. (2007). Knowledge creation though university/industry collaborative research projects. [Retrieved from http://www.ejkm.com]. *Electronic Journal of Knowledge Management, 5*(1), 43–54.

Hofstede, G. (1980). *Culture's consequences: International differences in work-related values.* Newbury Park, CA: Sage Publications.

Hofstede, G. (1997). *Cultures and organizations: Software of the mind: Intercultural cooperation and its importance for survival.* New York: McGraw-Hill.

Hofstede, G., & Bond, M. (1988). The Confucian connection: From cultural roots to economic growth. *Organizational Dynamics, 16*(4), 4–21. doi:10.1016/0090-2616(88)90009-5

Holden, N. J. (2002). *Cross-cultural management: A knowledge management perspective.* Harlow, UK: Pearson Education.

Hong, J., Heikkinen, J., & Niemi, M. (2007). Collaborative knowledge creation and innovation between MNCs and Chinese universities, In B. Martins & D. Remenyi (Eds.), *Proceedings of the 8th European Conference on Knowledge Management, 1* (pp. 486-449). Barcelona, Spain: Consorci Escola Industrial de Barcelona.

Hong, J. Z., & Engeström, Y. (2004). Changing communication principles between Chinese managers and workers: Confucian authority chains and *guanxi* as social networking. *Management Communication Quarterly, 17,* 552–585. doi:10.1177/0893318903262266

Hong, J. Z., Kianto, A., & Kyläheiko, K. (2008). Moving culture and the creation of new knowledge and dynamic capabilities in emerging markets. *Knowledge and Process Management, 15*(3), 196–202. doi:10.1002/kpm.310

House, R. J., et al. (2004). *Culture, leadership, and organizations: The GLOBE study of 62 societies.* Beverly Hills, CA: Sage.

Huff, L., & Kelley, L. (2003). Levels of organizational trust in individualist versus collectivist societies: A seven-nation study. *Organization Science, 14*(1), 81–90. doi:10.1287/orsc.14.1.81.12807

Huggins, R., Demirag, M., & Ratcheva, V. I. (2007). Global knowledge and R&D foreign direct investment flows: Recent patterns in Asia Pacific, Europe, and North America. *International Review of Applied Economics, 21*(3), 437–451. doi:10.1080/02692170701390437

John-Steiner, V. (2000). *Creative collaboration.* New York: Oxford University Press.

Johnson, W. H. A., & Johnson, D. A. (2004). Organisational knowledge creating processes and the performance of university-industry collaborative projects. *International Journal of Technology Management, 27*(1), 93–114. doi:10.1504/IJTM.2004.003883

Johnston, S., & Paladino, A. (2007). Knowledge management and involvement in innovations in MNC subsidiaries. *Management International Review, 47*(2), 281–302. doi:10.1007/s11575-007-0016-2

Khavul, S., Bruton, G. D., Zheng, C. C., & Wood, E. (2007). Learning during and after internationalization by entrepreneurial firms from emerging economies. *Academy of Management Proceedings*, 1-6.

Kilmann, R. H., & Saxton, M. J. (1983). *Kilmann-Saxton cultural gap survey*. Pittsburgh, PA: Organization Design Consultants.

King, W. R. (2007). A research agenda for the relationships between culture and knowledge management. *Knowledge and Process Management, 14*(3), 226–236. doi:10.1002/kpm.281

Kodama, M. (2003). Knowledge creation through the synthesizing capability of networked strategic communities: Case study on new product development in Japan. *Knowledge Management Research & Practice, 1*, 77–85. doi:10.1057/palgrave.kmrp.8500012

Kodama, M. (2005). New knowledge creation through dialectical leadership: A case of IT and multimedia business in Japan. *European Journal of Innovation Management, 8*(1), 31–55. doi:10.1108/14601060510578565

Kohlbacher, F., & Krähe, M. O. B. (2007). Knowledge creation and transfer in a cross-cultural context – empirical evidence from Tyco Flow Control. *Knowledge and Process Management, 14*(3), 169–181. doi:10.1002/kpm.282

Koschatzky, K. (2002). Networking and knowledge transfer between research and industry in transition countries: Empirical evidence from Slovenian innovation system. *The Journal of Technology Transfer, 27*(1), 27–38. doi:10.1023/A:1013192402977

Kubota, H., & Nishida, T. (2003). Channel design for strategic knowledge interaction. In . *Proceedings of the KES, 2003*, 1037–1043.

Lam, A. (1997). Embedded firms, embedded knowledge: Problems of collaboration and knowledge transfer in global cooperative ventures. *Organization Studies, 18*(6), 973–996. doi:10.1177/017084069701800604

Lambooy, J. G. (2004). The transmission of knowledge, emerging networks, and the role of university: An evolutionary approach. *European Planning Studies, 12*(5), 643–657. doi:10.1080/0965431042000219996

Lee, Y. S. (1996). Technology transfer and the research university: A search for the boundaries of university-industry collaboration. *Research Policy, 25*, 843–863. doi:10.1016/0048-7333(95)00857-8

Leung, K., Bhagat, R. S., Buchan, N. R., Erez, M., & Gibson, C. B. (2005). Culture and international business: Recent advances and their implications for future research. *Journal of International Business Studies, 36*, 357–378. doi:10.1057/palgrave.jibs.8400150

Li, J., & Zhong, J. (2003). Explaining the growth of international R&D alliances in China. *Managerial and Decision Economics, 24*, 101–115. doi:10.1002/mde.1079

Li, J. D. (2005). *A study on R&D collaboration between MNCs and Chinese universities* (in Chinese). Unpublished master's thesis, Tsinghua University, China.

Li, S., & Scullion, H. (2006). Bridging the distance: Managing cross-border knowledge holders. *Asia Pacific Journal of Management, 23*, 71–92. doi:10.1007/s10490-006-6116-x

Lin, L. (2005). *Study on the university-enterprise knowledge alliance based on the theory of knowledge activity system* (in Chinese). Unpublished doctoral dissertation, Dalian University of Technology: Dalian.

Lindqvist, J., Blomqvist, K., & Saarenketo, S. (2007). The role of sales subsidiary in MNC innovativeness - Explorative study and emerging issues on knowledge transfer. In R.R. Sinkovics and M. Yamin (Eds), *Anxieties and Management Responses in International Business*. Houndmills, Basingstoke, UK: Palgrave MacMillan.

Lopez -Martinez, E. et al. (1994). Motivations and obstacles to university-industry coop eration (UIC): A Mexican case. *R & D Management, 24*(2), 17.

Lucas, L. (2006). The role of culture on knowledge transfer: The case of the multinational corporation. *The Learning Organization, 13*(3), 257–275. doi:10.1108/09696470610661117

Luo, Y. D. (1997). *Guanxi*: Principles, philosophies, and implications. *Human Systems Management, 16*(1), 43–51.

March, J. G. (1991). Exploration and exploitation in organizational learning. *Organization Science, 2*(1), 71–86. doi:10.1287/orsc.2.1.71

Markus, H., & Kitayama, S. (1991). Culture and self: Implications for cognition, emotion, and motivation. *Psychological Review, 98*, 224–253. doi:10.1037/0033-295X.98.2.224

Meyerson, D., & Martin, J. (1987). Cultural change: An integration of three different views. *Journal of Management Studies, 24*(6), 623–647. doi:10.1111/j.1467-6486.1987.tb00466.x

Miesing, P., Kriger, M. P., & Slough, N. (2007). Towards a model of effective knowledge transfer within transnational: The case of Chinese foreign invested enterprises. *The Journal of Technology Transfer, 32*, 109–122. doi:10.1007/s10961-006-9006-y

Moitra, D., & Kumar, K. (2007). Managed socialization: How smart companies leverage global knowledge. *Knowledge and Process Management, 14*(3), 148–157. doi:10.1002/kpm.278

Ng, S. I., Lee, J. A., & Soutar, G. N. (2006). Are Hofstede's and Schwartz's value frameworks congruent? *International Marketing Review, 24*(2), 164–180. doi:10.1108/02651330710741802

Nishida, T. (Ed.). (2000). *Dynamic knowledge interaction.* Boca Ranton, FL: CRC Press.

Nishida, T. (2002). A traveling conversation model for dynamic knowledge interaction. *Journal of Knowledge Management, 6*(2), 124–134. doi:10.1108/13673270210424657

Nonaka, I. (2007). The knowledge-creating company. *Harvard Business Review, 85*(7/8), 162–171.

Nonaka, I., & Takeuchi, H. (1995). *The knowledge-creating company: How Japanese companies create the dynamics of innovation.* Oxford, UK: Oxford University Press.

Nonaka, I., Toyama, R., & Konno, N. (2000). SECI, ba and leadership: A unified model of dynamic knowledge creation. *Long Range Planning, 33*, 5–34. doi:10.1016/S0024-6301(99)00115-6

Park, S. H., & Luo, Y. (2001). *Guanxi* and organizational dynamics: Organizational networking in Chinese firms. *Strategic Management Journal, 22*, 455–477. doi:10.1002/smj.167

Perkmann, M., & Walsh, K. (2006). *Relationship-based university-industry links and open innovation: Towards a research agenda* (AIM Research Working Paper Series, 041-July-2006). Loughborough University.

Pettigrew, A. (1979). On studying organizational cultures. *Administrative Science Quarterly, 24*, 570–581. doi:10.2307/2392363

Pillania, R. K. (2005). New knowledge creation scenario in India industry. *Global Journal of Flexible Systems Management, 6*(3&4), 49–57.

Popadiuk, S., & Choo, C. W. (2006). Innovation and knowledge creation: How are these concepts related? *International Journal of Information Management, 26*(4), 302–312. doi:10.1016/j.ijinfomgt.2006.03.011

Ramasamy, B., Goh, K. W., & Yeung, M. C. H. (2006). Is *guanxi* (relationship) a bridge to knowledge transfer? *Journal of Business Research, 59*, 130–139. doi:10.1016/j.jbusres.2005.04.001

Rose, R. A. (1988). Organizations as multiple cultures: A rules theory analysis. *Human Relations, 41*(2), 139–170. doi:10.1177/001872678804100204

Ryan, L. (2007). Developing a qualitative understanding of university-corporate education partnerships. *Management Decision, 45*(2), 153–160. doi:10.1108/00251740710727214

Sackmann, S. A. (1991). *Cultural knowledge in organizations: Exploring the collective mind.* Newbury Park, CA: Sage.

Santoro, M. (2006). Self-interest assumption and relational trust in university-industry knowledge transfer. *IEEE Transactions on Engineering Management, 53*(3), 335–347. doi:10.1109/TEM.2006.878103

Santoro, M. D., & Gopalakrishnan, S. (2000). The institutionalization of knowledge transfer activities within industry-university collaborative ventures. *Journal of Engineering and Technology Management, 17*, 299–319. doi:10.1016/S0923-4748(00)00027-8

Schartinger, D. (2002). Knowledge interactions between universities and industry in Austria: Sectoral patterns and determinants. *Research Policy, 31*, 303–328. doi:10.1016/S0048-7333(01)00111-1

Schein, E. H. (1985). *Organizational culture and leadership: A dynamic view.* San Francisco, CA: Jossey-Bass.

Schein, E. H. (1996). Three cultures of management: The key to organizational learning. *Sloan Management Review, 38*(1), 9–20.

Schreyögg, G., & Kliesch, M. (2005). *Dynamic capabilities and the development of organizational competencies* (Discussion Papers No. 25/05). Berlin: Freie Universität Berlin.

Schwartz, S. H. (1994). Beyond individualism/collectivism: New cultural dimensions of values. In U. Kim, H. C. Triandis, C. Kagitcibasi, S. C. Choi, & G. Yoon (Eds.), *Individualism and collectivism: Theory, method, and applications* (pp. 85-119). Thousand Oaks, CA: Sage.

Seigel, D. S., Waldman, D. A., Atwater, L. E., & Link, A. N. (2003). Commercial knowledge transfers from universities to firm: Improving the effectiveness of university-industry collaboration. *Journal of High Technology Research, 14*, 111–133. doi:10.1016/S1047-8310(03)00007-5

Simonin, B. (1999). Transfer of marketing know-how in international strategic alliances: An empirical investigation of the role and antecedents of knowledge ambiguity. *Journal of International Business Studies, 30*(3), 463–490. doi:10.1057/palgrave.jibs.8490079

Sojka, J. Z., & Tansuhaj, P. (1995). Cross-cultural research: A twenty-year review. *Advances in Consumer Research. Association for Consumer Research (U. S.)*, 461–474.

Spender, J.-C. (1992). Limits to learning from the West . *The International Executive, 34*, 389–410.

Szulanski, G. (2003). *Sticky knowledge: Barriers to knowing in the firm.* London: SAGE.

Van Dyne, L., Vandewalle, D., Kostova, T., Latham, M. E., & Cummings, L. L. (2000). Collectivism, propensity to trust and self-esteem as predictors of organizational citicenship in a non-work setting. *Journal of Organizational Behavior, 21*, 3–23. doi:10.1002/(SICI)1099-1379(200002)21:1<3::AID-JOB47>3.0.CO;2-6

von Zedtwitz, M. (2007). *Innovation in China – from an R&D perspective*. Presentation in Lotus Flower Day, VTT Espoo.

Wang, Y., & Lu, L. (2007). Knowledge transfer through effective university-industry interactions: Empirical experiences from China. *Journal of Technology Management in China, 2*(2), 119–133. doi:10.1108/17468770710756068

Wartofsky, M. (1979). *Models: Representation and scientific understanding*. Dordrecht, The Netherlands: Reidel.

Chapter 15

Exploring the Links between Structural Capital, Knowledge Sharing, Innovation Capability and Business Competitiveness:
An Empirical Study

Josune Sáenz
University of Deusto, Spain

Nekane Aramburu
University of Deusto, Spain

Olga Rivera
University of Deusto, Spain

ABSTRACT

The aim of this chapter is to analyze the degree of influence of different organizational enablers (i.e., "structural capital") on knowledge sharing, as well as the influence of the latter and other structural capital components on innovation capability, both from a theoretical and empirical perspective. Additionally, the relevance of different innovation capability dimensions (i.e., ideation, project management, and timeliness and cost efficiency) on business competitiveness will be examined. For these relationships to be tested, an empirical study has been carried out among Spanish manufacturing firms with more than 50 employees and with R&D activities. To this end, a questionnaire has been designed and submitted to the CEOs of the companies making up the target population of the research. Structural equation modelling (SEM) based on partial least squares (PLS) has then been applied in order to test the main hypotheses of the research.

DOI: 10.4018/978-1-60566-790-4.ch015

INTRODUCTION

In today's economy, innovation is considered to be one of the main drivers of business competitiveness, if not the most relevant one (Drucker, 1988; Shapiro & Varian, 1998; Sveiby, 1997). Superior innovation provides companies with the opportunity to grow faster, better and smarter than their competitors and, ultimately, to influence the direction taken by their industry (Davila, Epstein & Shelton, 2006). Therefore, understanding the sources of successful innovation has become a major challenge in academic research.

Since the seminal works by Nonaka in 1991, and Nonaka & Takeuchi in 1995, the concept of innovation has been closely related to that of "knowledge creation". Along these lines, it is generally assumed that the process of innovation consists of an ongoing pursuit of harnessing new and unique knowledge (Nonaka & Takeuchi, 1995; Subramaniam & Youndt, 2005).

According to Nonaka, von Krogh & Voelpel (2006), knowledge creation involves a continuous process through which one overcomes the individual boundaries and constraints imposed by information and past learning by acquiring a new context, a new view of the world and new knowledge. By interacting and sharing tacit and explicit knowledge with others, the individual enhances the capacity to define a situation or problem, and apply his or her knowledge so as to act and specifically solve the problem. Therefore, an organizational context intended to foster knowledge creation and innovation should promote the exchange of ideas and experiences among people.

In the case of this paper, this organizational context is going to be analyzed through the lenses of "intellectual capital" (IC) and, through the lenses of "structural capital" in particular. The latter refers to what remains within the company when the employees have left home (Edvinsson & Richtner, 1999; European Commission, 2006). It could be embedded both in the organization (internal structure) and in the relationships that the company has with its external stakeholders (external structure). Organizational design, organizational culture, policies and guidelines, strategy, technological infrastructure (i.e. technological capital) and external alliances are all structural capital components which shape the company's organizational context and which could affect knowledge sharing and innovation. The human dimension of IC (people knowledge, skills and abilities), although a relevant one, will not be considered in this research.

With this in mind, this chapter pursues a twofold objective:

- On the one hand, it aims to clarify theoretical relationships between intellectual capital (and structural capital in particular), knowledge sharing, knowledge creation, innovation capability and business competitiveness.
- On the other hand, it aspires to provide empirical evidence about the influence of: (1) several structural capital components on knowledge sharing; (2) knowledge sharing mechanisms and other structural capital components on innovation capability; and (3) different innovation capability dimensions on business competitiveness. Additionally, the role of technology intensity as a moderator variable (i.e. as a variable that could affect the nature – positive or negative – and the strength of the aforementioned relationships) will be examined.

Actually, technology intensity represents an indirect way of measuring the degree of complexity of the knowledge being dealt with in an organization. In the case of a high-tech company (for instance, in the case of an electronic device manufacturer or in the case of a firm in the aerospace industry), the nature of the knowledge involved in technological innovation (i.e. the development of new products and processes) is much more sophisticated that the one involved in a low-tech company (consider for instance the case of a paper manufacturer or of a furniture producer). The higher degree of knowledge complexity that can be found in high-tech firms could affect both the degree of relevance of structural capital components in the promotion of knowledge sharing and the type of knowledge sharing mechanism which is more effective in order to facilitate innovation. Additionally, knowledge complexity could influence the degree of relevance of each innovation capability dimension (i.e. ideation, innovation project management, and timeliness and cost efficiency) in the final success of innovation projects.

As a result of the analysis carried out, companies will obtain a set of basic guidelines in order to shape their knowledge sharing strategies and enhance their innovation capability and performance.

THEORETICAL FOUNDATIONS

Innovation as an Essential Driving Force Behind Competitiveness in the Knowledge Economy

According to Cantwell (2005), the term "competitiveness" is related to superior growth and performance, and it could be applied to firms, industries, regions and even whole nations. While classical economists were aware of the role of technology and knowledge in economic growth, Joseph Schumpeter (1934) was the one who brought innovation to the fore (Augier & Teece, 2005). In his view, economic development had to be seen as a process of qualitative change, driven by innovation, taking place in historical time (Fagerberg, 2005).

Considerable impetus for this idea came when Solow (1957) provided the important calculation that 87.5% of the growth in output in the United States between the years of 1909 and 1949 could

be ascribed to technological improvement – a specific type of innovation – alone (Augier & Teece, 2005). Indeed, nowadays, "few could object that the pursuit of competitiveness through innovation is a laudable objective of national policy, and indeed an increasingly important objective, as the role of innovation has risen in the modern knowledge-driven economy" (Cantwell, 2005, p. 544).

Therefore, innovation is not an exclusive characteristic of the current economic environment. Actually, what is new today is the urgency for innovation. According to professor Lev (2001), two main reasons explain this urgency: on the one hand, the draining of production-based scale economies as a means for achieving sustainable competitive advantages and, on the other hand, superior competitive pressure due to increasing globalisation and deregulation of key economic sectors.

Several empirical studies have analyzed the impact of innovation on business competitiveness. Most of them, however, have done so by calculating the statistical correlation between R&D investment and some measure of business growth or profitability (Griliches, 1995; Hall, 1993). As an example, Aboody and Lev (2001) analyzed R&D productivity in the chemical sector in the USA and found that, on average, each dollar invested in R&D increased present and future operating results by two dollars.

Nevertheless, R&D is just one type of innovation activity (Oslo Manual, 2005). As Teece (2007) says, "not only must the innovating enterprise spend heavily on R&D and assiduously develop and protect its intellectual property; it must also generate and implement the complementary organizational and managerial innovations needed to achieve and sustain competitiveness" (p. 1321).

In any case, as Fagerberg (2005) has pointed out, "we know much less about why and how innovation occurs than what it leads to" (p. 20). In other words, "our understanding of how knowledge – and innovation – operate at the organizational level remains fragmentary and further conceptual and applied research is needed". This chapter is intended to shed some light on this issue.

Understanding the Concept of Innovation and its Linkage with Knowledge Creation

A unique and commonly accepted definition of innovation does not exist, but most of the existing ones agree that innovation implies conceiving and implementing something new. In line with this, Thompson (1965) defined innovation as the generation, acceptance and implementation of new ideas, processes, products or services; Van de Ven (1986) pointed out that innovation is intrinsically about identifying and using opportunities to create new products, services or work practices; and Martins (2000) stated that innovation is about the implementation of a new and possibly problem-solving idea, practice or material artefact (e.g. a product) which is regarded as new by the relevant unit of adoption and through which change is brought about.

Of course, the conception of something new implies the creation of new knowledge. In other words, innovation requires new knowledge and new combinations of knowledge (Eisenhardt & Martin, 2000). As a consequence, it could be said that the capacity of an organization to innovate lies in its capacity to generate new knowledge (Nonaka & Takeuchi, 1995; Nonaka, Toyama & Byosière, 2003). This is the point of view of authors such as Fischer (2001) – who assumes that innovation depends on the accumulation and development of relevant knowledge of a wide variety; Leiponen (2006) – who understands innovation as the generation of novel combinations from existing knowledge; Plessis (2007) – who identifies innovation with the creation of new knowledge and ideas to facilitate new business outcomes, aimed at improving internal business processes and

structures and to create market driven products and services; and Lundvall & Nielsen (2007) – who state that "innovation represents – by definition – something new and therefore adds to existing knowledge" (p. 214).

Moreover, it should be noted that the generation of new knowledge is the result of an organizational learning process (Nonaka & Takeuchi, 1995; Lundvall & Nielsen, 2007). "This points to knowledge production as a process of joint production, in which innovation is one kind of output, and the learning and skill enhancement that takes place in the process is another" (Lundvall & Nielsen, 2007, p. 214). This idea of learning as the underlying process of knowledge creation and, hence, of innovation, leads us to another dimension of innovation: that related to its dynamic nature.

Actually, innovation is a "dynamic capability". This concept refers to the "the capacity of an organization to purposefully create, extend, or modify its resource base" (Helfalt *et al.*, 2007, p. 4). In particular, innovation allows the resource base of an organization to be expanded by the addition of new knowledge embedded in new products, services, processes, technologies or business methods.

The above-mentioned capability involves different steps. The first one is that of ideation (Christiansen, 2000; Davila, Epstein & Shelton, 2006), which encompasses new idea generation and selection. Selected new ideas should then be put into practice (Van de Ven & Angle, 2000). This brings us to the execution or development phase (Crhistiansen, 2000), where new products, new processes, new technologies or new business models (i.e. innovation process outputs) are brought into reality. In this phase, effective project management should be combined with the ability to fit them into budgeted costs and deadlines (i.e. timeliness and cost efficiency). Finally, all the aforementioned dimensions should lead to value creation.

Knowledge Sharing as an Essential Condition for Knowledge Creation and Subsequent Innovation

According to Nonaka, the creation of new knowledge is closely related to the continuous interaction between tacit and explicit knowledge. *Tacit knowledge* is the type of knowledge which is personal, context-specific and, therefore, hard to formalize and communicate, whereas *explicit or codified knowledge* refers to knowledge that is transmittable in formal, systematic language (Nonaka & Takeuchi, 1995).

In Nonaka's view, tacit and explicit knowledge are not totally separate, but mutually complementary entities. This means that human knowledge is created and expanded through social interaction between tacit and explicit knowledge. This interaction is called "knowledge conversion" and there are four types of it: from tacit to tacit (socialization); from tacit to explicit (externalization); from explicit to explicit (combination); and from explicit to tacit (internalization).

This tacit/explicit interaction is continuous and dynamic and is shaped by shifts between the different modes of knowledge conversion. This gives rise to a "knowledge creation spiral". As previously mentioned, *socialization* involves the conversion of tacit knowledge into a tacit one. This only can be achieved by a process of experience sharing. As a result, a set of shared mental models and technical skills will be obtained. In *externalization*, tacit knowledge is articulated into explicit concepts, using metaphors, analogies, hypotheses or models. This is triggered by dialogue or collective reflection. On the other hand, *combination* involves systemizing concepts into a knowledge system, which implies using different bodies of explicit knowledge. Documents, meetings, conversations or computerized communication networks could be used to this end. Finally, *internalization* is closely related to the idea of "learning by doing", and it means embodying explicit knowledge into a tacit one. "For explicit knowledge to become tacit, it helps if the knowledge is verbalized or diagrammed into documents, manuals or oral stories" (Nonaka & Takeuchi, 1995, p. 69).

As can be seen, in all the previously-mentioned processes knowledge sharing is involved, which means this is a critical aspect in enlarging organizational knowledge. In other words, the knowledge that the organization possesses cannot be amplified if the knowledge possessed by individuals is not shared.

In order to make knowledge sharing happen within and among organizations, several researchers have focused on the study of different mechanisms and initiatives which could act as facilitators. Many of these mechanisms take advantage of information and communication technologies (i.e. they are "ICT-based" – Dalkir, 2005; Davenport, 2007) whereas, in other cases, personal interaction between individuals is the key (i.e. "people-focused" or "people-based" knowledge management; Wiig, 2004). On-line discussion forums, intranets, extranets and knowledge repositories are examples of ICT-based knowledge sharing, while communities of practice, coaching, mentoring and employee functional rotation are examples of people-focused or people-based initiatives.

Although specific initiatives for knowledge sharing could be very helpful in order to enhance knowledge creation, knowledge sharing should not be understood as something set apart from day-to-day business management. On the contrary, knowledge sharing should pervade everyday work and be embedded in the heart of the firm's basic management processes (strategy formulation, organization and control). Otherwise, the credibility of any other specific initiatives for knowledge sharing that the company would like to implement could be seriously damaged and many opportunities for new knowledge creation could be missed.

Intellectual Capital (and Structural Capital in Particular) as a Catalyst for Knowledge Sharing and Innovation

According to Kianto (2007), IC research should address organizational capabilities for producing and mastering change through perpetual learning and innovation. In the fast-paced market environment of today and the future, it is not enough for organizations merely to leverage their existing IC.

Throughout recent years, IC has been defined in multiple ways. However, most of the definitions provided can be grouped into two categories. The first one equates the concept of IC with that of "knowledge capital". Within this category, IC is considered to be the sum of all knowledge firms utilize for competitive advantage. This is the point of view of authors such as Stewart (1997), Nahapiet & Ghoshal (1998), Sullivan (1998), and Youndt, Subramaniam, & Snell (2004).

Other authors, however, take a broader perspective and consider IC to encompass other intangible resources (not only knowledge) and activities as well. As an example, the European Commission (2006) states that:

Intellectual capital is the combination of the human, organizational and relational resources and activities of an organization. It includes the knowledge, skills, experiences and abilities of the employees; the R&D activities, the organizational routines, procedures, systems, databases and intellectual property rights of the company; and all resources linked to the external relationships of the firm with customers, suppliers, R&D partners, etc. (p. 126).

Authors such as Roos *et alter* (1997) and Bontis (1999) are closer to this second perspective.

It should be noticed that the inclusion of "activities" within the concept of IC brings us to its dynamic dimension, as opposed to the static one (Kianto, 2007). The static view of IC is closer to the resource-based view of the firm, where the main interest lies in possessing valuable, rare, inimitable and non-substitutable resources (Barney, 1991; Wernefelt, 1984). However, research has shown that the main value creation factor is how resources are exploited and explored, rather than what they are *per se* (Kianto, 2007). Therefore, activities aimed at acquiring or internally producing intangible resources, as well as at sustaining and improving the existing ones, should be analyzed.

Regardless of the perspective adopted (limited to knowledge and static, or holistic and dynamic), IC tends to be split up into different categories. Although the specific labels employed may vary, a first distinction is generally made between human and structural capital. A second distinction is then made within the latter between organizational and social capital – in the case of the knowledge perspective – and between internal and external structure – in the case of the holistic one. Both perspectives (limited to knowledge and holistic) view human capital in a similar way (the knowledge, skills and abilities residing with and utilized by individuals – Schultz, 1961), but differences arise regarding the conceptualization of structural capital and its two sub-components.

In the case of the "knowledge perspective", the type of knowledge considered lies at the basis of the distinction made between organizational and social capital (i.e. the two sub-components of structural capital). The former refers to the institutionalized knowledge and codified experience (i.e. "explicit knowledge") residing within and utilized through databases, patents, manuals, structures, systems and processes (Youndt, Subramaniam & Snell, 2004), whereas social capital is the knowledge embedded within, available through and utilized by interactions among individuals and their networks of interrelationships (Nahapiet & Ghoshal, 1998). Of course, this second definition refers to "tacit knowledge" and it is important to note that the networks and interrelationships mentioned could be both internal and external to the firm.

In the case of the "holistic" perspective of IC, the "location" of knowledge and other intangible resources and activities lies at the basis of the distinction made between internal and external structure. In accordance with this, internal structure refers to the knowledge and other intangible resources that stay within the company when the employees have left and that derive from the organization's action processes (CIC, 2003), whereas external structure refers to all resources and activities linked to the external relationships of the firm with customers, suppliers or R&D partners (Meritum Project, 2002). Those resources could be related to knowledge, but they could refer to other intangible assets as well, such as brand image, customer satisfaction, customer loyalty, negotiating power, etc.

As previously mentioned, our focus is on the organizational context that fosters knowledge sharing and creation, and subsequent innovation (therefore, on structural capital). With this in mind, the holistic perspective of IC will be adopted, as it is assumed that intangible resources and activities that favour knowledge sharing and innovation capability go beyond previously accumulated knowledge in different forms (i.e. databases, manuals, procedures, etc.) and encompass other intangible factors too, such as organizational design.

On the other hand, setting out from Sveiby's classical distinction as regards structural capital between internal and external structure (Sveiby, 1997), an additional division will be proposed for internal structure (CIC, 2003) between organizational capital (i.e. organizational design, organizational culture, organizational policies and guidelines, and strategy) and technological capital (i.e. ICT infrastructure). Figure 1 summarizes the "structural capital architecture" proposed.

DEVELOPING A RESEARCH MODEL FOR EXPLORING THE LINKS BETWEEN STRUCTURAL CAPITAL, KNOWLEDGE SHARING, INNOVATION CAPABILITY AND BUSINESS COMPETITIVENESS

Once the theoretical relationships between structural capital, knowledge sharing, innovation capability and business competitiveness have been clarified, a research model will be proposed for empirically testing the aforementioned relationships. Three layers of analysis will be considered:

- In the first one, the relationship between specific elements of structural capital and different types of knowledge sharing will be analyzed. In particular, the catalytic role of organizational design, organizational culture and technological capital will be under scrutiny.
- In the second one, the degree of influence of different types of knowledge sharing (i.e. knowledge sharing through day-to-day management processes, through specific people-focused initiatives and through ICT-based initiatives) and additional elements of structural capital (i.e. hiring and professional development policies, innovation strategy and external structure) on different innovation capability dimensions will be examined.
- Finally, the degree of relevance of each innovation capability dimension (i.e. ideation, project management, and timeliness and cost efficiency) in terms of business competitiveness will be studied.

The above-mentioned model will allow us to answer the following questions:

- Are all structural factors considered equally important in order to enhance different types of knowledge sharing? Do factors

Figure 1. Structural capital architecture

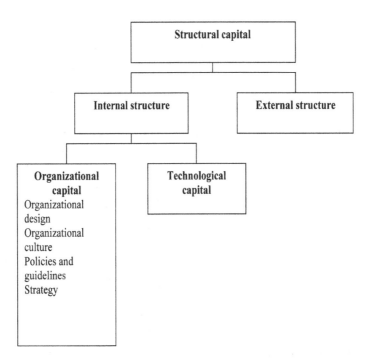

such as knowledge complexity (measured in terms of the technology intensity of the firm) affect the degree of relevance that structural conditions may have in facilitating knowledge sharing?

- Do specific innovation capability dimensions need to be reinforced by means of different knowledge sharing initiatives? What is the role of other structural conditions in the development of each dimension? Again, does knowledge complexity matter in this domain?
- Finally, are all innovation capability dimensions equally relevant when it comes to improving business competitiveness? Do company characteristics (such as technology intensity) have any influence on this issue?

The answers to these questions will provide companies with important clues as to how to shape their knowledge sharing and innovation

supporting strategies. Nevertheless, it should be noted that the model proposed is by no means absolutely comprehensive: there are additional structural factors (for instance, the company reward system) that could have an impact on the endogenous variables under study in this research. The reasons why structural factors considered have been limited have to do with the possibilities of accessing enough companies and with the length of the questionnaire to be filled in: the larger the model, the more companies are needed and the more complex the questionnaire should be. This would seriously limit the possibilities of getting enough answers.

In the following sections the research model will be outlined in more detail.

Knowledge Sharing-Related Hypotheses

The first knowledge sharing catalyst considered within structural capital is organizational design.

This refers to the type of organizational structure in place within the company, to the communication channels (both vertical and horizontal) that link different organizational units and teams, and to the physical design of the workplace.

As regards organizational structure, Nonaka & Takeuchi (1995), and Nonaka, Toyama & Byosière (2003) advocate the fact that certain types of structure facilitate knowledge sharing and knowledge creation processes more than others. In particular, they defend the hypertext type of organization (a combination of hierarchy and adhocracy) as the most suitable one in order to foster knowledge sharing and creation.

Likewise, communication channels could play a substantial role in fostering knowledge sharing and subsequent knowledge creation. As Kalla (2005) points out, knowledge sharing is a function of integrated internal communications. Although in the past knowledge flows used to be mainly vertical, from supervisor to supervisee, organizations today need to foster the flow of knowledge horizontally as well (Dalkir, 2005). Hence, it is assumed that vertical and horizontal communication channels act as catalysts of knowledge sharing.

Finally, physical design of the workplace is the last element making up organizational design that could promote or, on the contrary, hinder knowledge sharing processes. According to Nonaka, Schamer & Toyama (2001), "the single most important factor shaping the quality of knowledge is the quality of place" (p. 233). This idea is related to the concept of "ba": that is, a physical or virtual space where knowledge sharing and knowledge creation takes place (Nonaka, Reinmoeller & Senoo, 1998). Therefore, buildings and the space they embrace (the "physical ba") play a vital role in the intangible area of knowledge management (Nenonen, 2004).

In accordance with the prominent role that, from a theoretical point of view, organizational design could play in knowledge sharing, the following hypothesis has been formulated:

H1: Organizational design (i.e. the type of organizational structure in place within the company, the agility and fluidity of vertical and horizontal communication channels and the physical design of the workplace) catalyzes knowledge sharing that takes place through:

H1a: Day-to-day management processes (strategy formulation, organization and control).

H1b: Specific people-focused initiatives.

H1c: Specific ICT-based mechanisms.

Organizational culture is the second structural factor considered that, according to literature, could have a significant influence on knowledge sharing. As Dalkir (2005) points out, "corporate culture is a key component in ensuring that critical knowledge and information flow within an organization" (p. 185). Authors such as Allee (2003), Friedman, Lipshitz & Overmeer (2003) and Wiig (2004) describe the values that shape such a culture: trust, transparency, open mentality, mistakes considered as learning opportunities and cooperation and mutual help. All this gives rise to the second research hypothesis:

H2: Organizational culture acts as a catalyst of knowledge sharing that takes place through:

H2a: Day-to-day management processes (strategy formulation, organization and control).

H2b: Specific people-focused initiatives.

H2c: Specific ICT-based mechanisms.

Finally, information and communication technologies can also contribute to a great extent to knowledge sharing. According to Allee (2003), "there must be a technology infrastructure in place that really supports the right kind of conversations and connections" (p.89). In particular, the existence of specific technological tools that foster the capture and storing of knowledge, as well as the connection between individuals and groups may be very helpful (Dalkir, 2005). Therefore, the following hypothesis has been formulated:

H3: Technological capital facilitates knowledge sharing that takes place through:

H3a: Day-to-day management processes (strategy formulation, organization and control).

H3b: Specific people-focused initiatives.

H3c: Specific ICT-based mechanisms.

Innovation Capability-Related Hypotheses

As has been previously mentioned, according to theory, knowledge sharing is a necessary condition for knowledge creation and subsequent innovation to take place. Considering the existence of different types of knowledge sharing mechanisms and different innovation capability dimensions, the following set of hypotheses has been formulated:

H4: Knowledge sharing which takes place through day-to-day management processes (strategy formulation, organization and control) has a positive impact on:

H4a: The generation of new ideas.

H4b: Innovation project management.

H4c: Timeliness and cost efficiency.

H5: Knowledge sharing which takes place by means of specific people-focused initiatives positively affects:

H5a: The generation of new ideas.

H5b: Innovation project management.

H5c: Timeliness and cost efficiency.

H6: Knowledge sharing which takes place by means of specific ICT-based initiatives has a positive impact on:

H6a: The generation of new ideas.

H6b: Innovation project management.

H6c: Timeliness and cost efficiency.

On the other hand, there are other structural factors that, in addition to knowledge sharing, could also strengthen the innovation capability of firms. Organizational policies and guidelines, and more precisely, hiring and professional development policies, represent the first type of such a factor. Innovation is a human activity and, therefore, purposefully enhancing people competences related to this domain (such as creativity, entrepreneurship and leadership) could be crucial in order to facilitate successful innovation. Thus, the following hypothesis has been formulated:

H7: Hiring and professional development policies which try to foster innovation-related competences positively affect:

H7a: The generation of new ideas.

H7b: Innovation project management.

H7c: Timeliness and cost efficiency.

Strategy, and more specifically, innovation strategy, is another structural factor that could play a key role in guaranteeing the effectiveness of the innovation process. This refers to the guideline principles that indicate to an organization's members in which area knowledge creation or innovation should be pursued (Ichijo, 2007). Having a clearly established and shared innovation strategy should provide better results. This gives rise to the eighth research hypothesis:

H8: Having an explicit and organization-wide shared innovation strategy positively affects:

H8a: The generation of new ideas.

H8b: Innovation project management.

H8c: Timeliness and cost efficiency.

Finally, the mobilization of external knowledge held by outside stakeholders could be an essential aspect in order to promote knowledge creation and innovation (Nonaka & Takeuchi, 1995). In other words, the exchange of knowledge with external agents is a key element for creating new knowledge. This idea is also supported by other authors who state that "the scope and breadth of knowledge available from outside sources is generally much greater than that available from inside sources" (Maznevski and Athanassiou, 2007, p. 69). In accordance with this, the following hypothesis has been formulated:

H9: The extent to which the company has an external innovation network (i.e. a group of external collaborators in the domain of innovation) positively affects:

H9a: The generation of new ideas.

H9b: Innovation project management.

H9c: Timeliness and cost efficiency.

Business Competitiveness-Related Hypotheses

The last layer of our research connects each innovation capability dimension with business competitiveness. Although previous studies have already demonstrated the relevance of innovation as a source of superior growth and performance, they have usually done so by calculating the statistical correlation between R&D investment and some specific measure of business growth or profitability (Aboody & Lev, 2001; Griliches, 1995; Hall, 1993).

In this case, the aim is slightly different: the analysis carried out is intended to estimate the specific contribution of each innovation capability dimension to business competitiveness. This will provide companies with a useful insight in order to assess what to focus on in order to improve their innovation results.

For this to be checked, the following hypotheses have been formulated:

H10: Effective ideation management has a positive impact on business competitiveness.

H11: Effective innovation project management positively affects business competitiveness.

H12: Timeliness and cost efficiency have a positive impact on business competitiveness.

Moderator Variable

Finally, the moderator role of knowledge complexity or knowledge sophistication (measured in terms of the technology intensity of the firm) will be examined. As previously explained, in the case of high-tech firms, the knowledge dealt with is supposed to be more complex and "sophisticated" than in low-tech companies. Therefore, it would be interesting to see whether this has any influence on the relationships to be tested through the research.

Figure 2 summarizes the proposed model.

Each of the lines entering a dotted box gives rise to a set of three arrows.

It should be noticed that some of the structural capital components considered in this research have been connected to knowledge sharing (i.e. they are supposed to have a direct impact on knowledge sharing), whereas in other cases, the connection has been established between structural capital components and innovation capability. In particular, organizational design, organizational culture and technological capital have been linked to knowledge sharing, while hiring and professional policies, innovation strategy and external structure (i.e. having an external innovation network) have been connected to innovation capability. This is due to the specific nature of the elements considered within each construct.

In the case of organizational design, all the items considered (i.e. the type of organizational structure in place, vertical and horizontal communication channels, and physical design of the workplace) constitute elements that, according to literature, could facilitate or inhibit knowledge sharing. In the same way, the specific values included within organizational culture shape an organizational environment that favours knowledge sharing, although it could have been possible to consider a set of values directly connected to an innovation promoting environment (such as risk propensity or ambition). Likewise, the elements included within ICT infrastructure (i.e.

Figure 2. Research model

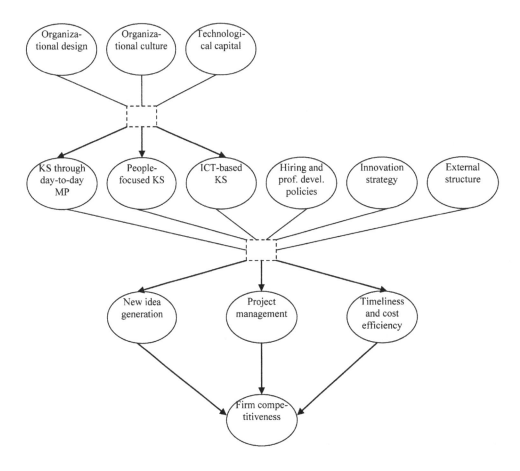

technological capital) are all knowledge sharing facilitators.

However, hiring and professional development policies considered within this research refer to the enhancement of a set of innovation-related competences (such as creativity, entrepreneurship and leadership) and not to a set of knowledge sharing-related competences (although this option could also have been possible). This is why the connection has been made between this construct and innovation capability. The same happens with the strategy-related construct: the focus is on innovation strategy and not on knowledge management strategy. Hence, the link has been established between strategy and innovation capability. Finally, external structure refers to

the existence of an external innovation network and, therefore, this should be related to innovation capability.

TESTING THE RESEARCH MODEL

Research Method

The research model previously outlined has been tested in a sample of Spanish companies.

The population subject to study was made up of Spanish manufacturing firms (energy, water and construction companies included) with over 50 employees and with R&D activities. The companies making up the target population were identified thanks to the use of the SABI data base ("Sistema de Análisis de Balances Ibéricos" / System of Iberian Balance Sheet Analysis), which contains the registered annual accounts of over 190,000 Spanish companies, selecting only those firms which had included their expenses on R&D in their balance sheet.

Although R&D refers to a specific type of innovation activity (and not necessarily the most relevant one), and although not all R&D investments are reflected on the balance sheet, this was the only way that could be used from the outside to guarantee that the companies under study were carrying out some type of innovation activity, a necessary condition to apply the research model previously described.

In order to gather information about the relevant variables of the research, a questionnaire was designed and submitted to the CEOs of the companies making up the target population by the end of the year 2006 and the beginning of the year 2007. 142 answers out of 1,239 were obtained, which means an average response rate of 11%. 75 questionnaires corresponded to medium-high and high technology companies and 67 to medium-low and low technology firms. The classification of companies as medium-high and high technology firms or as medium-low and low technology companies was made according to EUROSTAT criteria.

The sample sizes obtained are large enough to carry out a statistical study based on structural equation modelling (partial least squares approach) by means of PLS-Graph software (Chin & Frye, 2003). According to the complexity level of the model to be tested, the minimum sample size required was calculated, and this was made up of 70 firms. Thus, in the particular case of medium-low and low technology firms, the sample size is just on the border line.

Structural equation modelling (SEM) constitutes a second generation of multivariate analysis which combines multiple regression concerns (by examining dependency relationships) and factor analysis (by representing unobserved variables by means of multiple observed measures), in order to estimate a set of dependency relationships which are all simultaneously interrelated.

When applying SEM, two approaches can be used: the covariance-based approach and the partial least squares (PLS) approach. In the first case, the aim is to minimize the difference between the covariances of the sample and those predicted by the model. This approach is mainly used for confirmatory analysis. In the second case, however, the aim is to obtain determinate values of the latent variables for predictive purposes. This approach is very useful for exploratory research in which the problems explored are complex and theoretical knowledge is scarce, as is the case in this paper (Wold, 1985).

A PLS model is analyzed and interpreted in two stages: first, the assessment of the reliability and validity of the measurement model and second, the assessment of the structural model. This sequence ensures that the constructs' measures are valid and reliable before attempting to draw conclusions regarding relationships among constructs (Barclay *et al.*, 1995).

In the next section, the measurement model is presented in more detail.

Constructs and Measures

Organizational Capital

The exogenous constructs of the research are those related to the different categories making up structural capital. In particular, *organizational design* is the first one within what we have called "organizational capital".

The above-mentioned construct is made up of four formative indicators which lead to the existence of an organizational design which favours knowledge sharing. The first indicator refers to the type of organizational structure in place. For the purposes of this research, organizational structures have been classified into three different categories: level 1 knowledge sharing facilitating (i.e. the least knowledge sharing facilitating) organizational structures (that is, functional, divisional or matrix-type structures with no process- or project-based axis); level 2 knowledge sharing facilitating organizational structures (that is, process-based structures or matrix-type structures with a process-based axis); and level 3 knowledge sharing facilitating (i.e. the most knowledge sharing facilitating) organizational structures (that is, project-based structures or matrix-type structures with a project-based axis). The second and third indicators refer to the extent to which vertical and horizontal communication channels permit the flow of ideas, initiatives and points of view in an agile and fluid way, whereas the last one measures the extent to which the physical design of the work environment favours communication and dialogue among all company members. These last three indicators have been measured by means of 1 to 7 Likert scales.

Organizational culture is the second exogenous construct making up organizational capital. As already explained in the theoretical framework, this is linked to the degree of presence within the company of different values and attitudes which are related to a culture of knowledge sharing. The degree of presence of the aforementioned values and attitudes (trust, transparency, open mentality, mistakes viewed as learning opportunities, and cooperation and mutual help) has been measured by means of 1 to 7 Likert scales. All the indicators considered are reflective in nature, as they show the type of organizational culture in place within the company.

Hiring and professional development policies constitute the third exogenous construct making up organizational capital. The indicators considered within this construct measure the extent to which these policies and guidelines try to foster a set of innovation-related competences among people (i.e. creativity, entrepreneurship and leadership). These indicators have been measured by means of 1 to 7 Likert scales and are reflective in nature: that is, they show the extent to which

hiring and professional development policies are innovation-supportive.

Finally, *innovation strategy* is the last exogenous construct which shapes organizational capital. This is made up of three formative indicators which lead to the existence of an explicit and organization-wide shared innovation strategy: (1) the degree of visibility of top management's commitment to innovation (which has been measured by means of a 1 to 7 Likert scale); (2) the extent to which the company has a group of qualified people specifically devoted to facilitating the generation and implementation of new ideas (which has also been measured by means of a 1 to 7 Likert scale); and (3) the existence of different policies and guidelines related to different domains of innovation (products and/or services, production and/or service delivering methods, logistics, marketing and management methods), together with the degree of recognition of the aforementioned policies and/or guidelines by the members of the company. In the case of this indicator, managers were asked first to tell whether policies and/or guidelines existed for the different domains under consideration, and then, for those elements with specific policies and/or guidelines, the managers were asked to assess the percentage of the head count that was aware of them.

Technological Capital

In the case of *technological capital*, this is made up of three reflective indicators which show the extent to which the company is equipped with ICT systems which facilitate knowledge sharing and permanent connection with different agents. In particular, these indicators refer to the extent to which ICT systems in place facilitate the storage of organizational knowledge and its easy accessibility by the members of the company; to the extent to which they allow permanent connection among all members of the organization; and to the extent to which they facilitate continued action and joint work with external agents. All of these indicators have been measured by means of 1 to 7 Likert scales.

External Structure

As regards *external structure*, the indicators making up this construct measure the extent to which the company possesses an external innovation network. In this case, managers were asked to assess on a 1 to 7 Likert scale the degree of relevance of different external agents (i.e. customers, suppliers, firms from the same industry, firms from different industries, and universities or research centres) when it comes to developing the company's innovation strategy. These indicators are formative in nature, as they give rise to the existence of an innovation network.

Knowledge Sharing

On the other hand, the different types of knowledge sharing considered constitute the first set of endogenous constructs of the research. In the case of the *knowledge sharing which takes place through day-to-day management processes*, the following items have been measured: whether the strategy formulation process allows a wide set of contributions and viewpoint exchange to occur among the members of the company (Aramburu, Sáenz & Rivera, 2006); whether middle managers contribute effectively to the exchange of knowledge and information among upper and lower hierarchical levels (Nonaka & Takeuchi, 1995); whether strategy follow-up meetings based on the use of the balanced scorecard are an important point for reflection, viewpoint exchange and subsequent adoption of action (Simons, 1995, 2000); and the degree of incorporation of external agents' thoughts and viewpoints in management processes (Almeida, Anupama & Grant, 2003).

In the case of the *knowledge sharing which takes place through specific people-focused initiatives*, the degree of use of different mechanisms in order to promote social interaction among individuals has been measured (Wiig, 2004): communities of practice and/or meetings by fields of interest; forums; storytelling and/or lessons learned and/or best practice collection and diffusion; coaching and/or mentoring; employee functional rotation; employee external mobility; and meeting events and/or workshops in order to promote reflection as well as knowledge and experience sharing with external agents.

Finally, in the case of the *knowledge sharing which takes place through specific ICT-based initiatives*, the degree of use of different ICT-based instruments as a means for knowledge sharing has been studied (Dalkir, 2005; Davenport & Prusak, 2000): email, on-line discussion forums and/or blogs, intranet, extranet, groupware tools and on-line knowledge repositories.

All the indicators referring to this set of constructs have been measured by means of 1 to 7 Likert scales and are formative in nature: that is, the use of the different initiatives mentioned gives rise to the existence of knowledge sharing (i.e. the latent variable being studied).

Innovation Capability

The next set of constructs of the research is the one corresponding to each innovation capability dimension. The first one within this group is that related to the *new idea generation process*. In this case, the following items have been checked, all of them referring to the last 5 years: whether the company has been able to identify numerous opportunities for incremental/radical improvement; whether the firm has been able to identify many alternative or new uses for already-existing technologies; whether the new idea generation process has been managed in a conscious and effective way; and whether the company has been able to clearly distinguish which of the new opportunities identified had a greater potential for development.

As far as *innovation project management* is concerned, this encompasses the following indicators, all of them being related to the last 5 years:

whether the method used by the company for innovation project management has made things really easy; whether the company has been able to reuse knowledge generated through innovation projects carried out in the past; whether the different innovation projects carried out have been suitably coordinated; and whether role distribution in innovation projects carried out in cooperation has been the best it could be.

Finally, the *timeliness and cost efficiency* dimension is made up of the following measures (once again, all of them referring to the last 5 years): whether incremental/radical innovation projects carried out have been finished on time; and whether incremental/radical innovation projects carried out have met budgeted costs.

All the indicators corresponding to the different constructs making up the innovation capability of firms have been measured by means of 1 to 7 Likert scales and are reflective in nature: that is, they reflect the effectiveness of each innovation capability dimension.

Business Competitiveness

To bring the presentation of the measurement model to a close, only the *business competitiveness* construct remains to be explained. With a 5 year scope and using again 1 to 7 Likert scales, the following reflective measures have been chosen: whether incremental/radical innovation projects carried out have shown expected results; whether innovation results have had a very positive impact on the company's income statement; whether innovation results have had a very positive impact on the company's competitive position; and whether innovation results have allowed the company to grow and improve its market share.

MEASUREMENT MODEL EVALUATION

Following the sequence previously described in the method section, the analysis of the results obtained should begin with the evaluation of the measurement model. The aforementioned assessment differs depending on the nature of the construct under scrutiny. In the case of constructs made up of reflective indicators (i.e. when the measures observed are the consequence of the latent variable and, therefore, should be highly correlated), individual item reliability, construct reliability, convergent validity and discriminant validity should be checked. However, in the case of constructs made up of formative indicators (i.e. when the measures observed give rise to the existence of the latent variable), multi-colinearity problems should be explored.

As regards the reflective constructs of the model (the ones related to organizational culture, hiring and professional development policies, technological capital, innovation capability dimensions and business competitiveness) all the tests carried out have shown satisfactory results. Indicator loadings (individual item reliability) are greater than 0.7, with three exceptions that indeed are very close to the aforementioned limit. Thus, all the indicators have been retained in the model. On the other hand, composite reliability (which measures construct reliability) is higher than 0.8 in all cases; average variance extracted (which measures convergent validity) is greater than 0.5 in all constructs; and discriminant validity is excellent too. As regards formative constructs (i.e. the rest of the constructs of the model), multi-colinearity problems have not been identified.

Once the quality of the measurement model has been guaranteed by means of the aforementioned tests, the quality of the structural model should then be assessed. This refers to the strength of the research hypotheses and to the amount of variance explained (R^2) in the case of endogenous constructs, as well as to an analysis of the predictive power achieved. In our case, this is going to be complemented with a multi-group analysis (Chin, 2003), in order to assess whether technology intensity moderates the relationships under study.

STRUCTURAL MODEL EVALUATION

Structural Capital and Knowledge Sharing

General Overview

In order to assess the research hypotheses, path coefficient levels should be examined, as well as their degree of significance, by means of bootstrapping techniques. Tables 1, 2 and 3 summarize the results obtained in the case of knowledge sharing. In these tables, we can also see the contribution of each exogenous construct to the amount of variance explained (which has been obtained by multiplying correlation and path coefficients), as well as the predictive power achieved. The latter has been confirmed by means of a Stone Geiser test, where cross-validated redundancy (Q^2) must be higher than 0 in order to consider that the model

has predictive power for that specific construct.

According to the figures contained in the above tables, and as far as the general sample of companies analyzed is concerned, we can conclude that the three categories of structural capital considered within this layer of the research (organizational design, organizational culture and technological capital) contribute to a great extent to the knowledge sharing which takes place through day-to-day management processes (amount of variance explained: 60%). In the case of the knowledge sharing which takes place through specific people-focused and ICT-based initiatives, the explanatory power achieved is lower (41% and 36%, respectively), but still important. In any case, the three categories of structural capital analyzed exert a significant influence on each type of knowledge sharing, at least as far as the general sample of companies studied is concerned.

In the following sections, the explanatory factors behind each type of knowledge sharing will be further examined.

Table 1. Structural model evaluation – Impact of structural capital components on the knowledge sharing which takes place through day-to-day management processes

		Organizational design	Organizational culture	Technological capital	Total amount of variance explained	Predictive power Q^2
General sample	**Path**	0.334***	0.401***	0.233***		
	Correlation	0.631	0.661	0.535		
	Contribution to R²	**21.08%**	**26.51%**	**12.47%**	**60.05%**	**0.3516**
Medium-high and high-tech companies	**Path**	0.413***	0.337***	0.275***		
	Correlation	0.700	0.644	0.540		
	Contribution to R²	**28.91%**	**21.70%**	**14.85%**	**65.46%**	**0.3587**
Medium-low and low-tech companies	**Path**	0.283***	0.476***	0.146		
	Correlation	0.586	0.691	0.526		
	Contribution to R²	**16.58%**	**32.89%**	**7.68%**	**57.16%**	**0.3494**

Notes

***p<0.001, **p<0.01, *p<0.05, †p<0.1 (based on t_{499}, one-tailed test).

Table 2. Structural model evaluation – Impact of structural capital components on the knowledge sharing which takes place through specific people-focused initiatives

		Organiza-tional design	Organiza-tional culture	Technolo-gical capital	Total amount of variance explained	Predictive power Q^2
General sample	Path	0.250**	0.308***	0.251***		
	Correlation	0.509	0.533	0.480		
	Contribution to R^2	12.73%	16.42%	12.05%	41.19%	0.0850
Medium-high and high-tech companies	Path	0.233*	0.324**	0.300**		
	Correlation	0.522	0.543	0.491		
	Contribution to R^2	12.16%	17.59%	14.73%	44.49%	0.1146
Medium-low and low-tech companies	Path	0.315*	0.310*	0.204†		
	Correlation	0.564	0.572	0.513		
	Contribution to R^2	17.77%	17.73%	10.47%	45.96%	0.0727

Notes
***$p<0.001$, **$p<0.01$, *$p<0.05$, †$p<0.1$ (based on t_{499}, one-tailed test).

Table 3. Structural model evaluation – Impact of structural capital components on the knowledge sharing which takes place through specific ICT-based initiatives

		Organiza-tional design	Organiza-tional culture	Technolo-gical capital	Total amount of variance explained	Predictive power Q^2
General sample	Path	0.140†	0.179*	0.423***		
	Correlation	0.407	0.419	0.554		
	Contribution to R^2	5.70%	7.50%	23.43%	36.63%	0.0741
Medium-high and high-tech companies	Path	0.012	0.269**	0.523***		
	Correlation	0.358	0.438	0.611		
	Contribution to R^2	0.43%	11.78%	31.96%	44.17%	0.0941
Medium-low and low-tech companies	Path	0.199	0.287*	0.308†		
	Correlation	0.484	0.546	0.551		
	Contribution to R^2	9.63%	15.67%	16.97%	42.27%	0.0712

Notes
***$p<0.001$, **$p<0.01$, *$p<0.05$, †$p<0.1$ (based on t_{499}, one-tailed test).

Knowledge Sharing Through Day-To-Day Management Processes

In the case of the knowledge sharing which takes place through day-to-day management processes, organizational culture and organizational design are the two categories of structural capital that exert the greatest influence on this type of knowledge sharing, followed at a considerable distance by technological capital.

With regard to technology intensity, the following can be observed:

In the case of medium-high or high-tech companies, the most relevant explanatory factor of the knowledge sharing which takes place through day-to-day management processes is organizational design (contribution to the amount of variance explained: 29%), followed quite closely by organizational culture (22%). However, in the case of medium-low or low-tech companies, the opposite happens: organizational culture appears to be the most relevant factor within this group (contribution to the amount of variance explained: 33%), whereas organizational design is the second one (17%). In both cases, technological capital is the least relevant factor, its role being statistically significant only for medium-high or high-tech companies, where the contribution to the amount of variance explained is twice as important as it is in the case of medium-low or low-tech firms (15% against 8%). Perhaps, this is due to the greater relevance that, in general terms, technology has in high-tech companies. However, none of the differences mentioned are statistically significant.

Knowledge Sharing Through Specific People-Focused Initiatives

In the case of the knowledge sharing which takes place by means of specific people-focused initiatives, and as far as the whole sample of companies analyzed is concerned, the degree of relevance of each structural factor is very similar.

Additionally, technological intensity does not give rise to any significant difference between the different types of company considered. Indeed, the differences observed in terms of the degree of influence of each structural factor within each category (medium-high or high-tech firms *versus* medium-low or low-tech companies) are much lower than in the first case (knowledge sharing through day-to-day management processes).

Knowledge Sharing Through Specific ICT-Based Initiatives

As regards the knowledge sharing which takes place by means of different ICT-based initiatives, and taking the whole sample of companies analyzed into consideration, as expected, technological capital appears to be the most relevant structural factor in order to explain this type of knowledge sharing. Nevertheless, although organizational culture and organizational design lie far behind technological capital, their influence is still statistically significant.

With regard to technological intensity, although the difference observed does not happen to be statistically significant, the degree of influence of technological capital is noticeably higher in the case of medium-high or high-tech firms (in particular, a 15 point difference can be observed between both groups of companies). Conversely, although the difference observed is not statistically relevant either, the influence of organizational design is much stronger in medium-low or low-tech firms (contribution to the amount of variance explained: 10%), than in medium-high or high-tech companies (contribution to the variance explained: 0.43%).

By way of a conclusion, with the exception of the knowledge sharing which takes place through day-to-day management processes (where in the case of medium-high or high-tech firms the most relevant factor is organizational design, and in medium-low or low-tech firms, organizational culture), the structural factor ranking in both groups is always the same, and no significant difference exists regarding the degree of influence each structural factor exerts on knowledge sharing. Hence, the degree of "complexity" or "sophistication" of the knowledge dealt with does not affect organizational characteristics which could support the exchange of knowledge among the members of the company.

Structural Capital, Knowledge Sharing and Innovation Capability

General Overview

Tables 4, 5 and 6 summarize the results obtained in this second layer of the research. As can be seen in the aforementioned tables (and as regards the whole sample of companies analyzed), the three types of knowledge sharing considered (knowledge sharing through day-to-day management processes and through different people-focused and ICT-based initiatives), together with the remaining categories of structural capital (hiring and professional development policies, innovation strategy and external structure) have a greater impact on the first innovation capability dimension (that is, on the effectiveness of the new idea generation process). In this case, the aforementioned factors account for 46% of the amount of variance explained, whereas in the case of innovation project management and timeliness and cost efficiency, the amount of variance explained is 38% and 20%, respectively.

According to technological intensity, the ranking referring to the amount of variance explained of each innovation capability dimension is just the same for both types of company considered (medium-high or high-tech companies *versus* medium-low or low-tech firms) and identical to the one commented for the general sample. However, in general terms, the explanatory power achieved is slightly higher in high-tech companies than in the low-tech ones. In particular, the greatest difference corresponds to the third innovation capability dimension (i.e. timeliness and cost efficiency).

In the following sections, the explanatory factors behind each innovation capability dimension will be further examined.

New Idea Generation Process

In the case of the ideation stage, and as far as the whole sample of companies analyzed is concerned, the information gathered in Table 4 shows us that the three categories of structural capital considered within this layer of the research (hiring and professional development policies, innovation strategy and external structure) have a greater impact on this innovation capability dimension

Table 4. Structural model evaluation: Impact of structural capital components and knowledge sharing on the ideation stage

		KS through day-to-day MP	People-focused KS initiatives	ICT-based KS initiatives	Hiring and prof. devel. policies	Innovation strategy	External structure	Total amount of variance explained	Predictive power Q²
General sample	Path	0.091	0.064	0.200*	0.178*	0.246**	0.179**		
	Correlation	0.479	0.497	0.466	0.470	0.542	0.424		
	Contribution to R²	4.36%	3.18%	9.32%	8.37%	13.33%	7.59%	46.15%	0.1895
Medium-high and high-tech companies	Path	0.142†	0.265**	0.032	0.314**	0.159†	0.097		
	Correlation	0.553	0.625	0.459	0.584	0.593	0.376		
	Contribution to R²	7.85%	16.56%	1.47%	18.34%	9.43%	3.65%	57.30%	0.2579
Medium-low and low-tech companies	Path	0.097	-0.074	0.298*	0.088	0.180	0.352**		
	Correlation	0.416	0.421	0.551	0.392	0.511	0.565		
	Contribution to R²	4.04%	-3.12%	16.42%	3.45%	9.20%	19.89%	49.88%	0.2015

Notes
***p<0.001, **p<0.01, *p<0.05, †p<0.1 (based on t_{499}, one-tailed test).

Table 5. Structural model evaluation: Impact of structural capital components and knowledge sharing on innovation project management

		KS through day-to-day MP	People-focused KS initiatives	ICT-based KS initiatives	Hiring and prof. devel. policies	Innovation strategy	External structure	Total amount of variance explained	Predictive power Q²
General sample	Path	0.219*	0.175*	0.150*	0.094	0.073	0.124†		
	Correlation	0.518	0.525	0.435	0.369	0.419	0.341		
	Contribution to R²	11.34%	9.19%	6.53%	3.47%	3.06%	4.23%	37.81%	0.1187
Medium-high and high-tech companies	Path	0.221†	0.266*	0.189†	0.067	0.072	-0.002		
	Correlation	0.561	0.597	0.517	0.345	0.438	0.246		
	Contribution to R²	12.40%	15.88%	9.77%	2.31%	3.15%	-0.05%	43.47%	0.1464
Medium-low and low-tech companies	Path	0.237†	0.059	0.150	0.139	0.049	0.200*		
	Correlation	0.497	0.474	0.429	0.423	0.408	0.418		
	Contribution to R²	11.78%	2.80%	6.44%	5.88%	2.00%	8.36%	37.25%	0.1047

Notes

***p<0.001, **p<0.01, *p<0.05, †p<0.1 (based on t$_{4992}$, one-tailed test).

Table 6. Structural model evaluation: Impact of structural capital components and knowledge sharing on timeliness and cost efficiency

		KS through day-to-day MP	People-focused KS initiatives	ICT-based KS initiatives	Hiring and prof. devel. policies	Innovation strategy	External structure	Total amount of variance explained	Predictive power Q²
General sample	Path	0.252*	0.038	0.064	0.214**	-0.014	0.007		
	Correlation	0.385	0.329	0.267	0.344	0.264	0.164		
	Contribution to R²	9.70%	1.25%	1.71%	7.36%	-0.37%	0.11%	19.77%	-0.0971
Medium-high and high-tech companies	Path	0.291*	0.099	0.201†	0.255*	-0.064	-0.168		
	Correlation	0.457	0.437	0.432	0.379	0.289	0.038		
	Contribution to R²	13.30%	4.33%	8.68%	9.66%	-1.85%	-0.64%	33.48%	0.0296
Medium-low and low-tech companies	Path	0.170	0.076	-0.074	0.096	0.065	0.250*		
	Correlation	0.342	0.338	0.197	0.313	0.294	0.361		
	Contribution to R²	5.81%	2.57%	-1.46%	3.00%	1.91%	9.03%	20.87%	-0.1505

Notes

***p<0.001, **p<0.01, *p<0.05, †p<0.1 (based on t$_{4992}$, one-tailed test).

than knowledge sharing. As regards the latter, only the knowledge sharing which takes place through different ICT-based initiatives proves to be really significant, although important differences exist depending on company type.

In this innovation capability dimension, technological intensity becomes an important source of differences between the companies analyzed. Along these lines, the types of knowledge sharing that prove to be relevant in medium-high or high-tech firms are the ones which are simply irrelevant for medium-low or low-tech companies. Specifically, the knowledge sharing which takes place by means of different people-focused initiatives has a paramount relevance in fostering ideation in medium-high or high-tech firms, whereas in medium-low or low-tech companies its contribution is almost non-existent or slightly negative (in this case, the difference observed is statistically significant). Conversely, knowledge sharing through different ICT-based initiatives is very important for medium-low or low-tech firms, but its relevance almost disappears when it comes to the group of medium-high or high-tech companies (once more, the difference observed is statistically significant). On the other hand, although the difference found is not very great (only 3 points separate both types of company), knowledge sharing through day-to-day management processes does exert a significant influence on fostering the generation of new ideas in medium-high or high-tech companies, but it does not in the case of medium-low or low-tech firms.

These findings suggest that the degree of complexity and sophistication of the knowledge being dealt with exerts an important role in this innovation capability dimension. In the case of medium-high or high-tech companies, this complexity makes it more difficult to articulate it, a necessary condition for ICT-based knowledge sharing. Thus, personal interaction becomes more relevant. On the contrary, in the case of medium-low and low-tech firms, the lower de-gree of complexity of the knowledge being dealt with makes it easier to articulate it and to share it by means of ICT-based initiatives, this being extremely effective.

As regards the additional structural factors considered within the research, with the exception of innovation strategy (whose relevance is very similar in medium-high or high-tech companies and in medium-low or low-tech firms), again, significant differences arise depending on technology intensity. In particular, hiring and professional development policies which are aimed at fostering innovation-related abilities have a very strong influence on medium-high or high-tech firms, but a very low one on medium-low or low-tech companies. On the contrary, having an external innovation network is an extremely important factor for medium-low or low-tech firms and a quite unimportant one for medium-high or high-tech companies.

According to these results, it seems that, in medium-high or high-tech companies, enhancing internal capabilities in order to succeed in the ideation stage is a critical factor, whereas in medium-low or low-tech firms having an external innovation network is a fundamental issue (actually, the same is going to happen in the remaining dimensions of the innovation capability). The explanation for this may be related to the specific nature of each type of company: whereas in the case of medium-high or high-tech companies innovation (and, especially, technological innovation) is part of their DNA, in medium-low or low-tech firms it is not (at least, not to such a great extent). Therefore, due to this lower technology base, medium-low or low-tech firms need to have greater recourse to external agents, whereas for medium-high or high-tech firms the key issue is to enhance the capabilities of their own people.

Innovation Project Management

According to the results shown in Table 5, and as far as the whole sample of companies analyzed is concerned, knowledge sharing appears to be a much more relevant issue in reinforcing this innovation capability dimension than it was in the case of the first one. In the case of the rest of structural capital components under analysis, only the one corresponding to external structure plays a significant role in this domain, albeit a quite limited one.

On the other hand, technological intensity does not give rise to any statistically significant difference between groups of companies within this dimension. However, some specific issues need to be emphasized. The first one is that, once again, people-focused knowledge sharing has a noticeably higher relevance in the case of medium-high or high-tech firms, than in medium-low or low-tech companies. The second one refers to the relevance that external agents have in the case of medium-low or low-tech firms. In those companies, the contribution of external structure to the amount of variance explained is statistically significant and reaches the score of 8%, whereas in the case of medium-high and high-tech firms its relevance is very close to 0. In both cases, the potential reasons for these results have already been explained in the previous section.

Timeliness and Cost Efficiency

Timeliness and cost efficiency is the innovation capability dimension where the lowest explanatory power has been achieved by the research model. According to the information gathered in Table 6, and as far as the general sample of companies analyzed is concerned, there are only two elements that exert a significant influence on this issue: the knowledge sharing which takes place through day-to-day management processes, and hiring and professional development policies. As timeliness and cost efficiency are highly dependent on the performance of management processes, it is quite logical that the knowledge sharing which takes place through these processes is found to be the most relevant.

As regards technological intensity, the first thing to be noticed with regard to this contingency factor is that the amount of variance explained is much higher in medium-high or high-tech companies, than in medium-low or low-tech firms. On the other hand, the specific elements which exert a significant influence on each type of company vary: whereas in the case of medium-high or high-tech firms the most influential factor is that related to the knowledge sharing which takes place through day-to-day management processes, followed by hiring and professional development policies and by the knowledge sharing which takes place by means of different ICT-based initiatives; in the case of medium-low or low-tech firms, the only factor which exerts a significant influence on this innovation capability dimension is that related to external structure.

The fact that hiring and professional development policies constitute the most important structural component in medium-high or high-tech firms, whereas external structure is the most relevant one in medium-low or low-tech companies, could be related, once again, to the greater dependence the latter have on external agents in terms of improving their innovation capability, and mainly their technological innovation capability. In any case, the differences found in this domain are not statistically significant.

Differences are statistically significant, however, in the case of ICT-based knowledge sharing. Whereas in the case of medium-high or high tech firms its contribution to the amount of variance explained is 9%, in the case of medium-low or low-tech firms its contribution is very close to 0 (actually, it is slightly negative). As has been already mentioned, this could be due to the greater relevance that, in general terms, technology has in medium-high or high-tech firms.

Innovation Capability and Business Competitiveness

The aim of this section is to analyze the degree of influence of each innovation capability dimension on the enhancement of firm competitiveness. As can be seen in Table 7, and as far as the general sample of companies analyzed is concerned, the three dimensions considered exert a significant influence on business competitiveness and account for 46% of the amount of variance explained.

As regards the degree of influence of each specific dimension on final results, considerable differences arise depending on technological intensity. In the case of medium-high or high-tech firms, a perfect balance exists between ideation and project management, as both of them account for 21% of the amount of variance explained (timeliness and cost efficiency play a more secondary role, albeit a relevant one). However, in the case of medium-low or low-tech firms, ideation is by far the most relevant innovation capability dimension for business competitiveness, its contribution being 39%. Indeed, the differences between the two types of company examined are statistically significant, both for ideation and project management.

What could explain this situation? Considering that technological innovation (product/process) is the prevalent one among the companies analyzed, complexity and sophistication could again be behind the results obtained. In the case of a high-tech company, once the ideation phase is completed, making the new idea a reality may involve a very complicated process (consider for instance a pharmaceutical firm) and, therefore, a great part of the final success will depend on the effectiveness of the execution phase. On the contrary, in the case of a low-tech company (let us take a clothes manufacturer), once the new idea has emerged, making the new concept a reality will not be so complicated (talking in relative terms, of course) and, therefore, the main part of the success will depend on the brightness of the new idea.

CONCLUSION

The research carried out shows that structural capital components (i.e. organizational design, organizational culture and technological capital) are extremely important catalysts when it comes

Table 7. Structural model evaluation: Impact of innovation capability dimensions on firm competitiveness

		New idea generation process	Innovation project management	Timeliness and cost efficiency	Total amount of variance explained	Predictive power Q^2
General sample	Path	0.456***	0.158*	0.186**		
	Correlation	0.634	0.528	0.460		
	Contribution to R^2	**28.91%**	**8.34%**	**8.56%**	**45.81%**	**0.1921**
Medium-high and high-tech companies	Path	0.341***	0.331***	0.219*		
	Correlation	0.625	0.632	0.530		
	Contribution to R^2	**21.31%**	**20.92%**	**11.61%**	**53.84%**	**0.2617**
Medium-low and low-tech companies	Path	0.603***	-0.033	0.152		
	Correlation	0.649	0.440	0.402		
	Contribution to R^2	**39.13%**	**-1.45%**	**6.11%**	**43.79%**	**0.1596**

Notes

***$p<0.001$, **$p<0.01$, *$p<0.05$, †$p<0.1$ (based on t_{499}, one-tailed test).

to enhancing organizational knowledge sharing. In this respect, the complexity or sophistication of the knowledge being dealt with (measured in terms of technology intensity) does not significantly affect the role played by the aforementioned enablers.

On the other hand, the results obtained show that knowledge sharing and the additional structural factors studied (i.e. hiring and professional development policies, innovation strategy and external structure) contribute to a great extent to the enhancement of each innovation capability dimension (especially, when it comes to ideation and innovation project management). Nevertheless, depending on the innovation capability dimension being considered and on the technological intensity of the firm, the specific factors that appear to be more fruitful vary.

In general terms, knowledge sharing through different people-focused initiatives proves to be more useful in medium-high or high-tech firms, where the knowledge being dealt with is more complicated or sophisticated and, therefore, more difficult to articulate. Conversely, ICT-based knowledge sharing initiatives are extremely effective in medium-low and low-tech companies (where the knowledge being dealt with is less sophisticated) and when it comes to reinforcing the ideation stage of the aforementioned firms. Moreover, nurturing the abilities of their own human capital is a much more critical factor in medium-high or high-tech companies than it is in the medium-low or low-tech ones. In the case of the latter, having an external innovation network appears to be an essential aspect in order to reinforce their internal capabilities.

Technological intensity also moderates the relationship between innovation capability and business competitiveness. Whereas in the case of medium-high or high-tech firms the influence of different innovation capability dimensions is quite balanced, in the case of medium-low or low-tech firms, ideation is by far the most relevant dimension.

PRACTICAL IMPLICATIONS

From a practical point of view, the results obtained provide companies with useful insight into how to prioritise their knowledge management and innovation supporting efforts.

On the one hand, the results obtained show how relevant having a formal innovation strategy is to enhance the effectiveness of the new idea generation process. This could persuade companies without such a formal strategy to define it. For this to be done, the research shows which are the key points to bear in mind, both as far as the promotion of different knowledge sharing mechanisms are concerned, and as regards the structural capital components that should be reinforced.

In particular, the existing link between knowledge management (and, especially, knowledge sharing practices) and innovation should be highlighted. Companies should define their knowledge management strategy and their innovation strategy in a coherent and intertwined manner. As the results obtained point out, depending on the specific innovation capability dimension to be enhanced and on the degree of complexity and sophistication of the knowledge to be dealt with, different knowledge sharing mechanisms apply. Therefore, companies cannot view their knowledge management efforts independently from their innovation strategy.

Along these lines, depending on the specific weaknesses a company detects in its innovation capability, the results obtained in the research offer important clues as to how to improve the situation. For instance, let us consider a low-tech firm with serious flaws in its ideation process, but with quite a good project management system. In this case, the research carried out would suggest reinforcing the company's ICT-based knowledge sharing mechanisms, as well as intensifying its relationships with external agents. However, in the case of a high-tech company with the same problem, intensifying people-focused knowledge sharing and knowledge sharing through day-to-day management processes would be more appropriate, with the reinforcement of hiring and professional development policies and strategy communication also being a good point.

FUTURE RESEARCH DIRECTIONS

The research carried out has shed some light on the links between intellectual capital, knowledge sharing, innovation capability and business competitiveness. Nevertheless, different aspects still remain uncovered, paving the way for future research.

For instance, as regards intellectual capital, the focus of the research has been exclusively on structural capital. Future research should also include human capital, and analyze its interaction with organizational conditions in order to enhance knowledge sharing and knowledge creation. Structural capital itself (and especially, external structure) could be further developed, although this would lead to a more complicated research model and, therefore, to a substantial increase in the amount of companies that would need to be analyzed.

On the other hand, additional contingent variables could be considered, such as company size and industry type. In this research, only manufacturing firms have been studied, leaving aside service companies. It would be interesting to see whether service firms ask for different innovation facilitating conditions compared to manufacturing companies.

Finally, it should be verified whether the results obtained can be generalized in other geographical settings, or whether substantial differences exist according to geographical location.

REFERENCES

Aboody, D., & Lev, B. (2001). *The productivity of chemical research & development* (Working paper). New York: New York Stern University, Stern School of Business.

Allee, V. (2003). *The future of knowledge: Increasing prosperity through value networks*. Burlington, MA: Elsevier Science.

Almeida, P., Anupama, P., & Grant, R. M. (2003). Innovation and knowledge management: Scanning, sourcing and integration. In M. Easterby-Smith & M. A. Lyles (Eds.), *Blackwell handbook of organizational learning and knowledge management* (pp. 356-371). Malden, MA: Blackwell Publishing.

Aramburu, N., Sáenz, J., & Rivera, O. (2006). Fostering innovation and knowledge creation: The role of management context. *Journal of Knowledge Management*, *10*(3), 157–168. doi:10.1108/13673270610670920

Augier, M., & Teece, D. J. (2005). An economics perspective on intellectual capital. In B. Marr (Ed.), *Perspectives on intellectual capital* (pp. 3-27). Burlington, MA: Elsevier Butterworth Heinemann.

Barclay, D., Higgins, C., & Thompson, R. (1995). The partial least squares (PLS) approach to causal modeling: Personal computer adoption and use as an illustration. *Technological Studies*, *2*(2), 285–309.

Barney, J. (1991). Firm resources and sustained competitive advantage. *Strategic Management Journal*, *17*(1), 99–120.

Bontis, N. (1999). Managing organizational knowledge by diagnosing intellectual capital: Framing and advancing the state of the field. *International Journal of Technology Management*, *18*(5-8), 433–462. doi:10.1504/IJTM.1999.002780

Cantwell, J. (2005). Innovation and competitiveness. In J. Fagerberg, D. C. Mowery, & R. R. Nelson, (Eds.), *The Oxford handbook on innovation* (pp. 543-567). New York: Oxford University Press.

Chin, W. W. (2003). A permutation procedure for multi-group comparison on PLS models. In M. Vilares, M. Tenenhaus, P. Coelho, V. Exposito, & A. Morineau (Eds.), *PLS and related methods: Proceedings of the PLS'03 International Symposium.*

Chin, W. W., & Frye, T. (2003). *PLS-graph version 3.00.* Houston, TX: University of Houston.

Christiansen, J. A. (2000). *Building the innovative organization: Management systems that encourage innovation.* New York: St. Martin's Press.

CIC. (2003). *Intellectus model: Measurement and management of intellectual capital* (Intellectus Document No. 5). Madrid, Spain.

Dalkir, K. (2005). *Knowledge management in theory and practice.* Oxford, UK: Elsevier Inc.

Davenport, T. H. (2007). Information technologies for knowledge management. In K. Ichijo & I. Nonaka (Eds.), *Knowledge creation and management: New challenges for managers* (pp. 97-117). New York: Oxford University Press.

Davenport, T. H., & Prusak, L. (2000). *Working knowledge: How organizations manage what they know.* Cambridge, MA: Harvard Business School Press.

Davila, T., Epstein, M. J., & Shelton, R. (2006). *Making innovation work: How to manage it, measure it, and profit from it.* Upper Saddle River, NJ: Pearson Education.

Drucker, P. (1988). The coming of the new organization. *Harvard Business Review*, (January-February): 45–53.

Edvinsson, L., & Richtner, A. (1999). *Words of value – giving words to IC.* Skandia.

Eisenhardt, K. M., & Martin, J. A. (2000). Dynamic capabilities: What are they? *Strategic Management Journal, 21*(10-11), 1105–1121. doi:10.1002/1097-0266(200010/11)21:10/11<1105::AID-SMJ133>3.0.CO;2-E

European Commission. (2006). *RICARDIS: Reporting intellectual capital to augment research, development and innovation in SMEs.* Brussels, Belgium.

Fagerberg, J. (2005). Innovation: A guide to the literature. In J. Fagerberg, D. C. Mowery, & R. R. elson (Eds.), *The Oxford handbook on innovation* (pp. 1-26). New York: Oxford University Press.

Fischer, M. M. (2001). Innovation, knowledge creation and systems of innovation. *The Annals of Regional Science, 35*(2), 199–216. doi:10.1007/s001680000034

Friedman, V. J., Lipshitz, R., & Overmeer, W. (2003). Creating conditions for organizational learning. In M. Dierkes, A. Berthoin, J. Child, & I. Nonaka (Eds.), *Handbook of organizational learning & knowledge* (pp. 757-774). New York: Oxford University Press.

Griliches, Z. (1995). R&D and productivity: Econometric results and econometric and measurement issues. In P. Stoneman (Ed.), *Handbook of the economics of innovation and technological change.* Malden, MA: Blackwell Publishing.

Hall, R. E. (1993). Macro theory and the recession of 1990-1991. *The American Economic Review, 83*(2), 275–279.

Helfat, E., Finkelstein, S., Mitchell, W., Peteraf, M. A., Singh, H., Teece, D. J., & Winter, S. G. (2007). *Dynamic capabilities: Understanding strategic change in organizations.* Malden, MA: Blackwell Publishing.

Ichijo, K. (2007). Enabling knowledge-based competence of a corporation. In K. Ichijo & I. Nonaka (Eds.), *Knowledge creation and management: New challenges for managers* (pp. 83-96). New York: Oxford University Press.

Kalla, H. K. (2005). Integrated internal communications: A multidisciplinary perspective. *Corporate Communications: An International Journal, 10*(4), 302–314. doi:10.1108/13563280510630106

Kianto, A. (2007). What do we really mean by the dynamic dimension of intellectual capital? *International Journal of Learning and Intellectual Capital, 4*(4), 342–356. doi:10.1504/IJLIC.2007.016332

Leiponen, A. (2006). Managing knowledge for innovation: The case of business-to-business services. *Journal of Product Innovation Management, 23*(3), 238–258. doi:10.1111/j.1540-5885.2006.00196.x

Lev, B. (2001). *Intangibles: Management, measurement and reporting.* Washington, DC: Brookings Institution Press.

Lundvall, B. A., & Nielsen, P. (2007). Knowledge management and innovation performance. *International Journal of Manpower, 28*(3-4), 207–223. doi:10.1108/01437720710755218

Martins, E. C. (2000). *The influence of organizational culture on creativity and innovation in a university library.* Unpublished master's thesis, Pretoria, South Africa, University of South Africa.

Maznevski, M., & Athanassiou, N. (2007). Bringing the outside in: Learning and knowledge management through external networks. In K. Ichijo & I. Nonaka (Eds.), *Knowledge creation and management: New challenges for managers* (pp. 69-82). New York: Oxford University Press.

Meritum Project. (2002). *Guidelines for managing and reporting on intangibles.* Madrid, Spain: Fundación Aitel Móvil.

Nahapiet, J., & Ghoshal, S. (1998). Social capital, intellectual capital, and the organizational advantage. *Academy of Management Review, 23*(2), 242–266. doi:10.2307/259373

Nenonen, S. (2004). Analyzing the intangible benefits of work space. *Facilities, 22*(9-10), 233–239. doi:10.1108/02632770410555940

Nonaka, I. (1991). The knowledge-creating company. *Harvard Business Review, 69*(6), 96–104.

Nonaka, I., Krogh von, G., & Voelpel, S. (2006). Organizational knowledge creation theory: Evolutionary paths and future advances. *Organization Studies, 27*(8), 1179–1208. doi:10.1177/0170840606066312

Nonaka, I., Reinmoeller, P., & Senoo, D. (1998). The art of knowledge: Systems to capitalize on market knowledge. *European Management Journal, 16*(6), 673–684. doi:10.1016/S0263-2373(98)00044-9

Nonaka, I., Schamer, O., & Toyama, R. (2001). *Building ba to enhance knowledge creation: An innovation at large firms.* Retrieved from http://www.dialogonleadership.org/Nonaka_et_al.html

Nonaka, I., & Takeuchi, H. (1995). *The knowledge-creating company.* New York: Oxford University Press.

Nonaka, I., Toyama, R., & Byosière, P. (2003). A theory of organizational knowledge creation: Understanding the dynamic process of creating knowledge. In M. Dierkes, A. Berthoin, J. Child, & I. Nonaka (Eds.), *Handbook of organizational learning & knowledge* (pp. 491-517). New York: Oxford University Press.

OECD. (2005). *Oslo manual – guidelines for collecting and interpreting innovation data – third edition*. Paris: OECD Publishings.

Plessis, M. (2007). The role of knowledge management in innovation. *Journal of Knowledge Management, 11*(4), 20–29. doi:10.1108/13673270710762684

Roos, G., Roos, J., Dragonetti, N., & Edvinsson, L. (1997). *Intellectual capital: Navigating in the new business landscape*. New York: New York University Press.

Schultz, T. W. (1961). Investment in human capital. *The American Economic Review, 51*(1), 1–17.

Schumpeter, J. (1934). *The theory of economic development*. Cambridge, MA: Harvard University Press.

Shapiro, C., & Varian, H. (1998). *Information rules: A strategic guide to the network economy*. Boston: Harvard Business School Press.

Simons, R. (1995). *Levers of control: How managers use innovative control systems to drive strategic renewal*. Boston: Harvard Business School Press.

Simons, R. (2000). *Performance measurement and control systems for implementing strategy*. Upper Saddle River, NJ: Prentice Hall.

Solow, R. (1957). Technical change and the aggregate production function. *The Review of Economics and Statistics, 39*, 312–320. doi:10.2307/1926047

Stewart, T. A. (1997). *Intellectual capital: The new wealth of organizations*. New York: Doubleday/Currency.

Subramaniam, M., & Youndt, M. A. (2005). The influence of intellectual capital on the types of innovative capabilities. *Academy of Management Journal, 48*(3), 450–463.

Sullivan, P. H. (Ed.). (1998). *Profiting from intellectual capital: extracting value from innovation*. New York: John Wiley & Sons.

Sveiby, K. E. (1997). *The new organizational wealth: Managing and measuring knowledge-based assets*. San Francisco: Berrett-Koehler Publishers, Inc.

Teece, D. J. (2007). Explicating dynamic capabilities: The nature and microfoundations of (sustainable) enterprise performance. *Strategic Management Journal, 28*(13), 1319–1350. doi:10.1002/smj.640

Thompson, V. A. (1965). Bureaucracy and innovation. *Administrative Science Quarterly, 10*(1), 1–20. doi:10.2307/2391646

Van de Ven, A. H. (1986). Central problems in the management of innovation. *Management Science, 32*(5), 590–607. doi:10.1287/mnsc.32.5.590

Van de Ven, A. H., & Angle, H. L. (2000). An introduction to the Minnesota innovation research program. In A. H. Van de Ven, H. L. Angle, & M. Scott-Poole, (Eds.), *Research on the management of innovation: The Minnesota studies* (pp. 3-30). New York: Oxford University Press.

Wernefelt, B. (1984). A resource-based view of the firm. *Strategic Management Journal, 5*(2), 171–180. doi:10.1002/smj.4250050207

Wiig, K. (2004). *People-focused knowledge management*. Oxford, UK: Elsevier Inc.

Wold, H. (1985). Partial least squares. In S. Kotz & N. L. Johnson (Eds.), *Encyclopedia of statistical sciences* (pp. 581-591). New York: Wiley.

Youndt, M. A., Subramaniam, M., & Snell, S. A. (2004). Intellectual capital profiles: An examination of investments and returns. *Journal of Management Studies, 41*(2), 335–362. doi:10.1111/j.1467-6486.2004.00435.x

FURTHER READINGS

Davenport, T. H., Leibold, M., & Voelpel, S. (2006). *Strategic management in the innovation economy: Strategy approaches and tools for dynamic innovation capabilities*. Hoboken, NJ: Wiley.

Easterby-Smith, M., & Lyles, M. (2005). *Handbook of organizational learning and knowledge management*. Malden, MA: Blackwell Publishing.

Edvinsson, L., & Malone, M. S. (1997). *Intellectual capital: Realizing your company's true value by finding its hidden brainpower*. New York: Harper Collins Publishers, Inc.

Marr, B. (2005). *Perspectives on intellectual capital: Multidisciplinary insights into management, measurement, and reporting*. Burlington, MA: Elsevier Butterworth-Heinemann.

Nonaka, I., Kohlbacher, F., Hirata, T., & Toyama, R. (2008). *Managing flow: A process theory of the knowledge-based firm*. New York: Palgrave Macmillan.

Prusak, L., & Matson, E. (2006). *Knowledge management and organizational learning*. Oxford, UK: Oxford University Press.

Roos, G., Pike, S., & Fernström, L. (2005). *Managing intellectual capital in practice*. Burlington, MA: Elsevier Butterworth-Heinemann.

Rothberg, H. N., & Erickson, G. S. (2005). *From knowledge to intelligence: Creating competitive advantage in the next economy*. Burlington, MA: Elsevier Butterworth-Heinemann.

Teece, D. J. (2000). *Managing intellectual capital – organizational, strategy and policy dimensions*. Oxford, UK: Oxford University Press.

White, M. A., & Bruton, G. D. (2007). *The management of technology and innovation*. Mason, OH: Thomson.

APPENDIX: QUESTIONNAIRE EXCERPT

Hereafter, an excerpt of the questionnaire used for the research reported in this chapter is provided. Only questions related to the variables analyzed in this paper have been kept.

Organizational Design

1. In accordance with what criteria are organizational units defined in the top hierarchical level of your company? You may tick more than one option.
    - Functions
    - Geographic areas
    - Types of customer
    - Types of product
    - Processes
    - Projects
    - Others
2. Rate from 1 to 7 (1 = Not at all; 7 = Totally) the extent to which the following communication channels permit the flow of ideas, initiatives and points of view in a quick and fluid way:
    - Vertical communication channels (that is, communication channels between one organizational unit and the units above it or the ones that are beneath)
    - Horizontal communication channels (that is, between organizational units on the same level)
3. Rate from 1 to 7 (1 = Not at all; 7 = Totally) the extent to which:
    - The physical design of the workplace favours communication and dialogue among all members of your company.

Organizational Culture

4. Rate from 1 to 7 (1 = Not at all; 7 = Totally) to what extent is the following the case in your company:
    - There is a climate of trust
    - There is a climate of transparency
    - There is an open mentality
    - Mistakes are considered as learning opportunities
    - There is a climate of cooperation and mutual help

Hiring and Professional Development Policies

5. Rate from 1 to 7 (1 = Not at all; 7 = A great deal) to what extent do hiring and professional development policies in your company take into account the cultivation of competences linked to:
    - Creativity
    - Entrepreneurship
    - Leadership

Innovation Strategy

6.   Rate from 1 to 7 (1 = Not at all; 7 = A great deal) to what extent:
    – Top management carries out visible action to convey their commitment to innovation to the organization as a whole.
    – The company has a group of qualified people specifically devoted to facilitating the generation and implementation of new ideas.
7.   Please state weather specific policies and/or guidelines have been defined in your company as regards the following aspects:
    – Introduction of new products and/or services
    – Improvement of currently existing products and/or services
    – Introduction of new production methods and/or new methods for the provision of services, or improvement of those currently employed
    – Introduction of new logistics methods, or improvement of already existing ones
    – Introduction of new marketing methods, or improvement of those currently employed
    – Introduction of new management methods, or improvement of already existing ones
8.   For those aspects for which specific policies and/or guidelines have been defined, please state the approximate percentage of staff who know about them:
    – Less than 25%
    – 25% or more, but less than 50%
    – 50% or more, but less than 75%
    – 75% or more, but less than 100%
    – 100%

Technological Capital

9.   Rate from 1 to 7 (1 = Not at all; 7 = Totally) the extent to which your company is equipped with information and communication technologies specifically devised for:
    – The storage of organizational knowledge and its easy retrieval
    – Permitting permanent connection between all its members
    – Promoting continued action and joint work with external agents

External Structure

10.   Rate from 1 to 7 (1 = No importance; 7 = Great importance) the degree of relevance of other external agents in developing the innovation strategy of your company:
    – Customers
    – Suppliers of equipment, materials, components or software
    – Other companies belonging to the same industry
    – Other companies belonging to different industries
    – Universities and research centres

Knowledge Sharing Through Day-To-Day Management Processes

11.   Rate from 1 to 7 (1 = Not at all; 7 = A great deal) to what extent in your company:

– The strategy reflection process allows a wide set of contributions and viewpoint exchange to occur among the members of the company.

– Middle managers contribute effectively to the exchange of knowledge and information among upper and lower hierarchical levels.

– Strategy follow-up meetings based on the use of the balanced scorecard are an important point for reflection, viewpoint exchange and subsequent adoption of action.

– External agents' thoughts and viewpoints tend to be incorporated in the company's management processes.

People-Focused Knowledge Sharing

12.   Rate from 1 to 7 (1 = Not at all; 7 = Very high) the degree of adoption in your company of the following initiatives that favour the exchange of knowledge and experiences among its members:
   – Communities of practice and/or meetings according to fields of interest
   – Forums
   – Storytelling and/or lessons learned and/or best practice collection and diffusion
   – Coaching and/or mentoring
   – Employee functional rotation
   – Employee external mobility

13.   Rate from 1 to 7 (1 = Not at all; 7 = A great deal):

– The extent to which the company develops different initiatives (meetings, conferences, workshops, etc.) that attempt to promote reflection and exchange of knowledge and experiences with all its external agents.

ICT-Based Knowledge Sharing

14.   Rate from 1 to 7 (1 = Not at all; 7 = A great deal) the extent to which the following computer tools are used in your company as a means of sharing knowledge (not the mere fact that they exist, but rather that they are actually used for such purpose):
   – Email
   – On-line discussion forums and/or blogs
   – Intranet
   – Extranet
   – Groupware tools
   – On-line knowledge repositories

New Idea Generation Process

15. In terms of the last five years, rate from 1 to 7 the extent to which you agree or disagree with the following statements about your company (1 = Totally disagree; 7 = Totally agree):
    – We have identified numerous opportunities for incremental improvement.
    – We have identified numerous opportunities for radical innovation, or innovation in terms of the development of totally new products, processes or management methods.
    – We have identified plenty of alternative and new uses for already-available technologies.
    – The new idea generation process has been managed in a conscious and effective way.
    – We have been able to clearly distinguish which of the new opportunities identified had a greater potential for development.

Innovation Project Management

16. In terms of the last five years, rate from 1 to 7 the extent to which you agree or disagree with the following statements about your company (1 = Totally disagree; 7 = Totally agree):
    – We have a method that really facilitates the management of innovation projects.
    – We have been able to reuse the knowledge acquired from innovation projects carried out in the past.
    – Innovation projects have been suitably coordinated.
    – The allocation of roles in innovation projects carried out in cooperation has been the best it could be.

Timeliness and Cost Efficiency

17. In terms of the last five years, rate from 1 to 7 the extent to which you agree or disagree with the following statements about your company (1 = Totally disagree; 7 = Totally agree):
    – Incremental innovation projects carried out have been finished within envisaged deadlines.
    – Radical innovation projects carried out have been finished within envisaged deadlines.
    – Incremental innovation projects carried out have met budgeted costs.
    – Radical innovation projects carried out have met budgeted costs.

Business Competitiveness

18. In terms of the last five years, rate from 1 to 7 the extent to which you agree or disagree with the following statements about your company (1 = Totally disagree; 7 = Totally agree):
    – Incremental innovation projects carried out have shown expected results.
    – Radical innovation projects carried out have shown expected results.
    – Innovation results have had a very positive impact on the company's income statement.
    – Innovation results have had a very positive impact on the company's competitive position.
    – Innovation results have allowed the company to grow and improve its market share.

Chapter 16
Overcoming Reticence to Aid Knowledge Creation Between Universities and Business:
A Case Reviewed

Elly Philpott
University of Bedfordshire, UK

John Beaumont-Kerridge
University of Bedfordshire, UK

ABSTRACT

This chapter argues the case for a proactive process to facilitate knowledge creation between universities and small to medium size enterprises (SMEs). Cultural issues dictating reticence of engagement are discussed as well as the inhibitors that prevent the free interchange of knowledge. The chapter shows how reticence can be overcome by serving the needs of both parties and how knowledge created through successful interaction can be measured. The knowledge creation process itself is analysed in the context of Nonaka's SECI model. The chapter concludes with recommendations for the reader on areas for public investment to enhance the knowledge transfer process and provides lessons learned for the measurement of knowledge transfer at these interfaces. The outcomes are of value to those interested in the continuing applicability of Nonaka's work outside of the heavy industrial context as well as to those interested in the traditional problems associated with knowledge transfer between universities and SMEs.

INTRODUCTION

This chapter's objectives are to convey to the reader, the current issues around culture and process relating to proposed knowledge transfer activities between universities and SMEs; to review a case of successful knowledge transfer activity and to suggest

areas in which future improvement activities can be made which will help reticent parties move to a successful knowledge transfer.

In an environment where access to knowledge is promoted by government (Lambert 2003) but where senior managers in the public and private sector are encouraged to recognise and protect their tacit assets (UK Intellectual Property Office 2008), a dichotomy of reality is emerging between

DOI: 10.4018/978-1-60566-790-4.ch016

the economic needs of government and business and the needs of universities to grow and protect their tacit knowledge in order to compete amongst themselves. Kutinlahti (2005) found that the major challenge that universities face was the integration and simultaneous accomplishment of their knowledge creation, knowledge dissemination and knowledge exploitation functions.

In an environment where universities are encouraged to aspire to research excellence and thereby compete with peers, to spin out their own businesses where it is advantageous to do so and to work with small businesses to help them innovate, effective processes for selecting businesses with whom to work have never been more important.

Section 1 describes the political background to the current emphasis on business-university engagement. Section 2 describes the cultural theory that applies in this context; Section 3 describes the theory of innovation and knowledge management and how this relates to university-SME interaction. The work of Nonaka is overviewed to understand whether this existing model of knowledge creation is apt for this circumstance. Section 4 describes a real case of successful university – SME engagement and proposes a model for successful university – SME interaction that can be used to maximise the benefits of sharing tacit knowledge while retaining and growing independent competitive position. Section 5 concludes with a discussion of lessons learned from a three year project which has attempted to reconcile the views and working practices of universities working together – each exhibiting its own culture and priorities – and that of SMEs wishing to both access and benefit from tacit knowledge of academics. Conclusions are drawn on the appropriateness of using Nonaka's framework in this juxtaposed cultural context, and anomalies are discussed.

BACKGROUND

In 2003 the United Kingdom (UK) Government's Lambert report purported:

"It is clear that much more needs to be done to persuade business of the economic benefits to be gained from innovation, and of working in collaboration with university departments to achieve this goal. This applies especially to [Small to medium sized Enterprises] (SMEs), which have few resources to risk on reaching out to find new ways of developing products and services." (Lambert 2003, 142)

The UK Department of Trade and Industry (DTI) responded to Lambert describing how companies had reported that support for innovation was patchy and inconsistent; confusing; lacking in specialist advice (innovation, design and marketing); bureaucratic and long-winded; and remote. This represented a challenge to the author. Firstly to overcome the perceived level of existing service; secondly to identify companies that could benefit from university help, and thirdly the engagement process – access - itself.

It was clear from the outset that both sides had reservations in working together. Career academics were often adverse to entrepreneurial opportunities preferring to engage with other academics and students as opposed to business. There was an errant scepticism around what Duberley, Cohen et al. (2007) describe as the 'triple helix' of university-industry-government in that it had been associated with significant reductions in government funding and an increased emphasis on adopting a more 'entrepreneurial' approach. Duberley, Cohen et al. explain that this approach emphasises the generation of research income, greater collaboration with industry and a strong focus on outputs. They explain that in the past university science departments were able to rely heavily on non-output specific funding and that financial support is now more focused and output driven, strictly geared to meet national priorities while being more closely monitored. This represents a problem for academics and university – SME knowledge transfer activities. Without third party funding to the university it is difficult to justify the transaction cost of working with SMEs and difficult to measure the outcomes for SMEs as a dependent variable of university input.

The work to address these issues in the context of academics working with external SMEs, although practically based, also raised academic questions in terms of Nonaka's Theory of Knowledge Creation, specifically in terms of how the Socialisation -Externalisation-Combination-Internalisation (SECI) model related to knowledge creation across boundaries, where reticence existed on both sides. In this case, the boundary between a university and a SME. Further, it invited investigation into whether stages of the SECI process could be quantified in terms of tangible outputs like knowledge transfer activities. Finally, it also brought into question whether Nonaka's work was an appropriate tool from which to gain insight at UK universities boundaries.

CULTURAL DIFFERENCES BETWEEN UNIVERSITIES AND SMALL BUSINESSES

Hofstede (1991) describes organisational cultures as phenomena per se, different in many respects from national cultures. He describes an organisation as a social system of a different nature than a nation if only because the organisation's members usually have a certain influence in their decision to join, and are only involved during working hours, and may one day leave it again.

Campbell and Kleiner (1997) describe culture in an organisation as a self -reinforcing set of beliefs, attitudes and behaviours. They go on to say that spontaneous, futile attempts to change culture will undoubtedly fail unless the old values, beliefs and rewards are no longer being encouraged, enforced and rewarded.

Brown (1998) lists 14 different definitions of culture. Each of the definitions uses culture as a descriptor of an entity at any particular point in time, sculptured by the past, operating in the present and evolving in the future.

Trompenaars and Hampden-Turner (1997) describe culture in general as consisting of three layers:

- Explicit culture consisting of the observable realities, e. g. language and structures
- Norms and values, where norms are described as the mutual sense a group has of what is right and wrong and values which define good and bad
- The third 'core' layer is comprised of assumptions about existence. Assumptions about existence are derived from past and present experience of problems to be solved.

They argue that organizational culture or functional culture is nothing more than the ways in which groups have organized to solve the problems presented to them. Of all the definitions found, the Trompenaars and Hampden-Turner definition seemed the most recognisable to the author. Observable realities manifest themselves at universities as 'academic language', and hierarchical structures. Norms and values manifest as the ethos of academic rigour and excellence so evident in many university mission statements, while assumptions about existence include the gravitation to peer-review for all things and the need to contribute to the existing body of knowledge in all practices.

In order to understand academic culture and thereby understand reticence to engage with external businesses we need to understand all three layers in terms of the traditional university context. The traditional context for academics has been that in order to progress they need to serve three sets of customers: their university superiors, degree candidates and other academics external to their institution. The problems solved have traditionally been related to serving these three types of customer.

Academic language and structure, norms and values have evolved within an environment where all are engaged in reconciling the demands of teaching with those of obtaining research funding to allow the ongoing participation in research activity. Scott (2003) lists critical inquiry, disinterested science, intellectual freedom and a commitment to truthful knowledge as traditional academic values.

Trompenaars and Hampden-Turner tell us that values determine the definition of good and bad and are therefore closely related to the ideals shared by a group. Traditionally, academics have served the public and the advancement of knowledge. This has been the ideal and by default deemed good. The addition of enforced entrepreneurship or an expectation that academic efforts will service the needs of profit-motivated business is abhorrent to many academics: it is not desired nor aspired to.

In asking academics as individuals to serve external businesses we are in effect introducing a forth customer. This has implications for existing language and structure, norms and values and problems to be solved. In short, to engage successfully, we are suggesting a shift in culture. The literature tells us that we are doomed to fail unless we stop encouraging, enforcing and rewarding old values, beliefs and rewards.

The SME culture is very different to that of the academic culture. Senior personnel within small companies are driven by the need to keep the company viable and to make profit by the most efficient means necessary e.g., growth, divestiture, and reciprocal arrangements with others. Academics do not generally have profit making as a goal. SMEs deal with suppliers and custom-

ers in power based relationships and are generally myopic in their perception of acquiring knowledge to innovate. Cash flow within a company of this type dictates whether innovation activities occur. Business language, structure, norms and values are often sector-specific and dictated by whether the people in the participant company are project orientated, self-empowered or lean. Product and service focussed companies will also vary in the time taken to respond to their own markets and hence the urgency with which problems must be solved will differ too.

To engage with universities, SMEs must have a specific need. Engaging a university as a supplier of services is probably the most familiar route for them because SMEs are used to dealing with suppliers. Engaging a university as a partner is less familiar. A supplier-customer relationship has a power component in the form of financial control. Payment is contingent upon outcomes coming to fruition. And here lies another problem. The work that universities undertake does not always result in positive outcomes. Indeed, universities pride themselves on reporting valid outcomes as opposed to positive ones. 'Truthful knowledge' as defined by Scott pervading in this instance.

For a SME to engage with a university requires a specific need and sufficient cash flow to engage and utilise the outcomes. Problems often need to be solved quickly. Ironically, the implication from the literature is that where this activity is a success a new hybrid culture will be created due to the evolution of joint language, structure, norms and values as well as the combined experience of problem solving gained. Such successes may then well perpetuate other engagements because of a common culture. These requirements demand that the university academics and SMEs need to be matched very carefully to marry their very specific needs at any point in time.

The UK Confederation of British Industry (CBI) (CBI 2001) reports the more general benefits of industry and university partnering for industry as:

Benefiting from new ideas

Thinking longer term

Going global

Outsourcing

Complementing the company's skill base

Taking a multi-disciplinary approach

Harnessing public funds

Reducing risk

Complementing the company's physical resource base

Recruitment made easy

For a university to engage with a SME there must be a heuristic interest which is greater than the culture change required to serve a fourth type of customer. This can be in the form of additional funding to pursue research interests; the addition of empirical research opportunities over and above those currently available; or by the provision of dissemination channels which are otherwise unavailable to the academic. The CBI reports the more general benefits to a university are:

Improving market awareness

Enriching teaching programmes

Maintaining research momentum

Applying knowledge

Complementing the university's skills base

Learning business processes

Harnessing private and public funds

Building on excellence and reputation

Complementing the university's physical resource base

Sourcing job opportunities

It is clear then that for such a relationship to work there must be a clear outcome for both sides in terms of measurable output. On a case-by-case basis, both parties need to mitigate the time of engagement against opportunity costs elsewhere. This requires a clear, 'explicit' outcome for each, which can be used by the SME to further its business aims and by the university to demonstrate both activity and that activities are justified for reasons commensurate with university strategy. The problems for the university are that with the exception of 'harnessing public funds' the benefits are often soft and difficult to quantify. For this reason, the measurement of activity is often chosen as the more appropriate approach, the softer benefits being implicit within the activities themselves.

INNOVATION, KNOWLEDGE MANAGEMENT AND SMES

The Oslo Manual developed jointly by Eurostat and the Organisation for Economic Co-operation and Development (OECD) is the foremost international source of guidelines for the collection and use of data on innovation activities in Europe. This document currently proposes the following definition of innovation:

"An innovation is the implementation of a new (for the enterprise) solution aiming at enhancing its competitive position, its performance, or its know-how".

(Organisation for Economic Co-operation and Development 2007)

This definition allows for innovation in technological and non-technological companies and accommodates product, service and business process innovation. The implementation of new solutions may require the active use of knowledge within the company or the acquisition of knowledge from outside the company. Innovation implies that new knowledge is created, and that the new knowledge created should add value to the company either directly through increased competitive position, through its performance or through its know-how. As know-how can be both explicit and tacit, it is perhaps the most elusive element to manage and particularly to source.

Therefore, to achieve an innovative outcome; and thereby one that will enhance a SMEs competitive position, a SME needs to know a number of things. Firstly, – how does it compare with its competitors / peers? In what areas does it underperform? Finally, if it does not have resource in-house it needs to obtain information on where external help and knowledge is available.

In the context where universities are potential suppliers of innovation services, the questions for universities at this juncture are: What does the SME need? What does it want? How can this fit with known research outcomes, ongoing research and teaching requirements or provide additional dissemination or funding opportunities?

Today, knowledge and the capability to create and utilize knowledge are considered to be the most important source of a firm's competitiveness (Nonaka and Toyama 2003). Davenport and Prusak (1998) showed that external sources (customers, market surveys, etc.) of knowledge were essential element for firms. However access to tacit and explicit knowledge outside of the company is often necessary if firms are to bring products rapidly to market or to customise offerings to customer needs.

Lambert (2003) stated that individual companies might not have the time or capacity to find out which of the many university research departments around the country are doing work that is relevant to their needs. This problem applies especially to SMEs and is all the more important because SMEs can be quickly disadvantaged in a market where competitors have access to knowledge that is otherwise precluded to them.

Here we consider how knowledge management relates to any prospective relationship between a SME and a university. In 1995 Nonaka and Takeuchi popularised their SECI model, which focussed on the movement of knowledge between tacit and explicit states through the four processes of socialisation, externalisation, combination and internalisation. This work was developed through the study of innovation practices in Japanese

manufacturing processes, which were evidently culturally and geographically specific. Since then, their work has been applied, validated and critiqued in many different business and public environments and used widely to give structure to the processes around knowledge creation. The cultural differences between universities and SMEs coupled with the physical problems of overcoming interfaces ensure that transaction costs for such knowledge transfer will be high. However, if we consider how SECI might be applied around this interface the strengths of SECI may provide us with insights in areas otherwise missed.

The next section describes the development and application of a dyadic tool and set of processes that facilitates the creation of knowledge within small companies and at universities, while allowing individual companies and university departments to service their own needs and control the flow of tacit to explicit knowledge. The tool allows SMEs to source knowledge at universities, while allowing universities to select SMEs with whom to work based on innovation potential. Both parties then use the knowledge created; SMEs to form explicit knowledge to problem solve or innovate, universities to improve the interface; to inform ongoing research and to highlight new research directions.

DEVELOPMENT, APPLICATION AND TEST OF AN INNOVATION ENGAGEMENT TOOL

Universities have traditionally embarked on engagement with business in a 'research push' mode. This is where the university drives the research activities. A number of innovation models have actively been applied by organisations in the public sector in this mode in order to knowledge-transfer innovation expertise to small firms. These include publications intended for the business market, networking events combining research academics and companies in related fields, 'speed dating', on-line tools for common communication areas, and targeted workshops etc.

A problem for universities has always been the costs of promoting these relatively new services to SMEs and interacting with local companies while maintaining research kudos and momentum. Universities have tried a number of methods in the past. These methods have included direct mailing, TV advertising, radio advertising and marketing through partner organisations. Judging from the recent DTI input to the Lambert report however, one can conclude that these methods have had limited success.

The problem with this approach is that the clients' needs are not understood before the first meeting and hence resource is expended with little guarantee that any of the companies has a prospect of ever working with the university. In truth, there is little understanding of their market.

There is however an alternative way of working – 'research pull'. In this mode, the SME dictates the research agenda effectively acting as the customer in a supplier-customer relationship. The problem with this mode in practice is that SMEs often find it difficult to articulate research requirements in language that academics will understand and be able to relate to current knowledge, research interests and funding opportunities.

Our conclusion based on these findings was that a new process of engagement was needed to understand SMEs' needs and match this to university needs and funding opportunities before first academic contact was actually made. The universities needed to be more proactive in going out and finding the companies whose innovation needs they could meet before expending valuable resource; thereby allowing assessment of internal tacit knowledge in terms of what needed to be made explicit. We realised that we needed to sell the 'knowledge offering' to SMEs in order to overcome perceptions and experiences, and to reach those who had never perceived a university as a supplier of services before. The approach would be to:

- Conduct a pilot project which would involve the innovation profiling of companies prior to first contact;
- Select companies for direct contact based on whether the university could meet its need; then to
- Mould a package specifically for the business based on the services and infrastructure already in place between the universities

The nature of the relationship, once dialogue was established would then depend upon there being sufficient funding sources for the relationship to go ahead. These sources could be from the university, from the SME, or from external funding sources. The relationship could then be one of research pull or research push, depending upon the demands of the funding source.

SME: University Knowledge Creation

An online tool was subsequently created and tested using staff from 5 universities, Business Development Officers from each institution and a user group. Functionality, clarity of question and aesthetics were investigated with each. User feedback in these areas needed to be reconciled with the equivalent need to maintain question integrity in order to ensure that the econometric model used to profile companies remained valid.

The process created around the tool needed to ensure that both parties would gain benefit from the activity whether the relationship came to fruition or not. The SME would gain access to appropriate innovation help, and the universities establish a relationship that would complement and inform ongoing research. Figure 1 illustrates the tool's use in the context of creating knowledge at both the university and at the SME. Table 1 shows the process of engagement and how this relates to knowledge creation.

Figure 1. Illustrating the tool's use in the context of creating knowledge at both the universities and at the SMEs (© 2008, Inderscience. Used with permission)

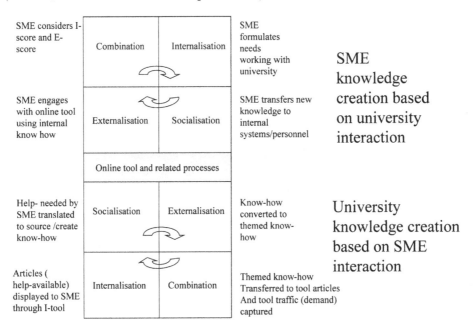

Tool Performance Testing

The effectiveness of the tool and its application would be measured by the knowledge transfer activities between the SMEs and the universities. For purposes of measurement, knowledge transfer activities were defined as:

- Undergraduate placement
- Post graduate placement
- Course attendance
- Subsidised programmes e.g., Knowledge Transfer Partnerships (KTP)
- Attendance at events, e.g. special interest groups, town and gown
- Consultancy
- Research

Table 1. Showing the (6Is) process of engagement and how it relates to Knowledge Creation

Process step	SECI	Activity description at SME	Activity description at university
Identify			Targeted marketing
Induce Individualize	E – Articulating tacit knowledge through dialogue and reflection C – Systemizing and applying explicit knowledge and information	E - SME engages with online tool using internal know how, the SME gets benchmark score and sign posting to help needed C–SME considers I-score, E-score and sign posting given.	I- Articles (help available) displayed to SME through I-tool
Instigate Initiate Innovate	I – learning and acquiring new tacit knowledge in practice S – Sharing and creating tacit knowledge through direct experience	I-SME formulates needs and works with university S- SME transfers new knowledge to internal systems / personnel	S – Help needed data used to create / source know-how at universities E–Know-how converted to themed know-how C – Themed know-how transferred to tool articles

(Key – SECI refers to Nonaka's Socialisation, Externalisation, Combination, and Internalisation Model of Knowledge Creation)

It was recognised that other types of knowledge transfer may be initiated through the process and these will be discussed in the Conclusion.

Results of Pilot

Within a 6-month pilot period, 7000 companies were contacted by mail and invited to use the tool. 37 manufacturing companies used the tool; submitted Innovation profiles; and were sign posted to university help. University-employed intermediaries approached 20 companies. Of these companies, 7 were not interested in engaging with the universities directly; however, 14 continued through the process. The knowledge created at the universities and SMEs by using the tool enabled a number of knowledge transfer activities.

The knowledge transfer opportunities identified were principally at the Internalisation and Socialisation stages for SMEs and ranged from attendance at university - hosted events; case study collaboration; consultancy opportunities; student placement, facilities use, and Knowledge Transfer Partnerships (KTPs). A number of supplementary activities were also identified outside the initial definition of knowledge transfer activities and these are discussed in the next section. .

A recent review of Innovation Management Consultancy throughout the European Union identifies this innovation tool amongst the top 15 innovation tools in Europe (Diedrichs, Engel et al. 2006)

DISCUSSION

Amongst UK universities there is currently a growing emphasis on what has been labelled 'third stream funding' or commercial income, which can sit alongside research and teaching. In this research we have addressed the reticence that many small businesses have for approaching universities and that held by individual academics associated with realizing academic benefit from such interactions.

In considering the cultural differences between the two bodies we have been able to isolate the needs of both parties and thereby understand the circumstances under which successful knowledge transfer might take place.

An innovation survey tool has been designed to provide an initial step to encourage companies in the region to consider communicating with their local universities and to simultaneously provide a mechanism by which universities can select SMEs as partners. The tool provides the participating universities with an understanding of a SME's innovation profile allowing internal knowledge management in terms of packaging existing know-how. Further interaction that occurs following the use of the tool allows knowledge creation to take place on both sides allaying to a degree, the reticence with which academics often enter into these types of activities. From this starting point it has been possible for universities (and academics therein) to engage knowledgeably and voluntarily with SMEs, to capture specific business needs and to offer appropriate responses, while engaging fully in the tacit to explicit side of the knowledge creation process. Philpott and Bevis (2005) and Philpott (2008) describe the detail of tool design and development as well as the outcomes for the SMEs and academics involved.

As the profiling reflects both the needs of the SME and the strengths of the universities, this particular internet-enabled model for engaging in innovation opportunities sidesteps the weaknesses identified in the university sector of patchy and inconsistent services. Companies who only use the innovation tool on-line, without immediate intermediary follow up; gain the added value of innovation benchmarking. They gain an indication of their own innovation potential and are signposted to other sources of support. In terms of mutual knowledge creation, both parties still benefit. The use of intermediaries however, does at this stage appear to help the knowledge creation process and result in knowledge transfer activities.

The experience in the East of England has

been that voluntary engagement by businesses and university academics with the innovation tool is producing a valuable dataset of information about the regional SME community, from skills needs to specific innovation opportunities. Being able to measure a need is enabling the universities to better plan their provision of services for SMEs.

CONCLUSION

The innovation profiling developed can be applied to any region where regional economic priorities are known and where local universities have explicit expertise or where tacit knowledge is available and volunteered. The I-score mechanism itself is based on OECD-recognized questions. Use of a similar process would allow universities in other regions to provide "easier access to knowledge", to identify innovation opportunities and to focus finite translation resources on these opportunities.

In terms of outcomes and the ability SECI to accurately reflect the knowledge creation process, the knowledge created and subsequent knowledge transfer activities undertaken appear to stem mainly from the Internalisation and Socialisation stages at SMEs and universities. However, the cultural issues entrenched with both sides are only resolved if the university has already gone through a process of internalization, whereby it decides which of its tacit knowledge it will make explicit. The SME needs to have gone through a contextualisation process where it sees itself in a wider context e.g., where it has identified that it needs external help, has access to finance and has started to look for funding and know how available.

This is an important finding in that it informs the next level of IT systems integration opportunities, e.g., integrating SME internal knowledge management systems with those of the universities may well yield greater operational efficiencies, knowledge creation and subsequent knowledge

transfer activities. The insight provided by this work in terms of the theory of knowledge creation generates further research questions in terms of where public funds should be targeted to promote SME-Uni interaction, while encouraging universities to embark on cultural change. Further, it informs where systems developers should be working to remove SME-university transaction costs. In real terms target areas should be:

Internalisation at SME
Provide processes that help SMEs formulate their needs
Socialisation at Universities
Provide processes that flag local business needs within a university
Contextualisation at SME
Provide processes that allow SMEs to see themselves in a wider context e.g., hard economic benchmarking, and have this related to specific types of help available e.g., product /service development, production control, marketing.
Internalisation at Universities
Provide processes that consolidate, compile and review expertise on offer to SMEs.

Many existing knowledge transfer offices at universities remain firmly in the 'research push' mode failing to match the needs of internal academics and external SMEs. When working with SMEs the funding source dictates the mode of working so there is little point expending university effort in research push activities until funding sources are identified and secured. There is then a reason to introduce funding awareness at both the contextualisation stage for the SME and at the internalization stage for the universities. Systems that do this in synchrony for both universities and SMEs would allow the maximum benefit.

The knowledge transfer metrics used were as follows: Undergraduate placements that occurred, Post graduate placements that occurred; Course attendance increased; Subsidised programmes e.g.,

Knowledge Transfer Partnerships (KTP) began; Attendance at events increased, e.g. special interest groups, town and gown; Consultancy started; Research started. However a number of supplementary activities have also been recognized which have developed spontaneously by virtue of the interaction e.g., SMEs joining virtual networks, SMEs engaging with course validation, and 'in-kind' involvement in research projects where no payment exchanges hands. These activities were often unrelated to the initial inquiries and as such need to be recognised as secondary or 'mini-seci' activities. This phenomena has theoretical semblance with the work of Snowden (2002) which looked to advance knowledge management theory by embracing the paradoxical nature of knowledge as both a thing and a flow. While we have recognized the tacit to explicit flows of knowledge in the model developed having started with the SME going through a process of externalisation to 'problem-state'. The model as it stands fails to recognize knowledge as a thing emanating from interaction with informal networks also at play. Snowden describes the importance of informal networks in organizations. In attempting to relate SECI to the tool developed we have been unable to describe the self-propagating knowledge flows that were seeded by the use of the tool itself. This may either be a shortcoming of the SECI model itself or a failure on our part to recognize the variety of metrics needed to describe activities at these types of interfaces. Researchers aiming to replicate these activities may wish to consider multiple dimensions to SECI or consider applying wider metrics to the knowledge flows. Those looking at the paradoxical nature of knowledge and the most efficient use of knowledge for competitive advantage would do well to embrace all identifiable forms of value- adding activities.

FUTURE RESEARCH DIRECTION

The innovation tool and processes therein are currently being developed for use with regional development bodies to aid the benchmarking of innovation activities in local SMEs. The tool can be used over time to understand the progress made by SMEs following a variety of public interventions. The tool's use for innovation benchmarking has also been of interest to public bodies in other European countries. Use of the tool by SMEs in 'innovation follower' countries allows them to effectively benchmark themselves against SMEs in an 'innovation leader' country – the UK. Development of the tool and the research required is both market-driven in terms of possible application and fundamental in terms of ensuring that the econometric models within the tool reflect the best national data available, and that additional knowledge 'flagging' tools are needed by both universities and SMEs. In general research and development of the tool will take four avenues:

The first is the customisation of the tool for application in different geographies. This activity is dependent upon interest from potential users who can use the tool to benchmark current innovation performance and seek help, or to benchmark over time to look at the value of public intervention.

The second is the customisation of the mapping of economic indicators to likely problems being experienced by SMEs and then for signposting to expertise required. This is largely a maintenance function and will require ongoing research as available expertise changes, as problems generated by the market change and as the interplay of econometric indicators creates new variables autonomously.

The third is the maintenance of the econometric models that sit within the tool itself. These are data-derived and hence maintenance of the data set over time may expose changes to relevant coefficients within the models generated.

The fourth research direction is also fundamental in that while a variety of IT solutions are available that seek to address Internalisation at the SME and University and Socialisation at a University, the process of Contextualisation for the SME is still not addressed. The process of relating a company's hard economic indicators to likely problems and then to help available is still largely a tacit process, conducted here through a workshop of experts and in society by a myriad of expensive consultants who themselves are vulnerable to ageing knowledge. The most important research hereafter is therefore the packaging of this knowledge in a way that is cost effective, easy to use and sustainable.

REFERENCES

Brown, A. (1998). *Organisational culture*. London: Financial Times Pitman.

Campbell, S., & Kleiner, B. H. (1997). New developments in re-engineering organisations. *Work Study*, *46*(3), 99–103. doi:10.1108/00438029710162953

CBI. (2001). *Partnerships for research and innovation between industry and universities: A guide to better practice*. London: Confederation of British Industry

Davenport, T. H., & Prusak, L. (1998). *Working knowledge. How organisations manage what they know*. Boston, MA: Harvard Business School Press.

Diedrichs, E., Engel, K., et al. (2006). *European innovation management landscape - IMPROVE: Assessment of current practice in innovation management consultancy* (Europe INNOVA Paper No 2). Augsberg, Germany: European Commission Directorate General Enterprise and Industry.

Duberley, J., & Cohen, L. (2007). Entrepreneurial academics: Developing scientific careers in changing university settings. *Higher Education Quarterly*, *61*(4), 479–497. doi:10.1111/j.1468-2273.2007.00368.x

Hofstede, G. (1991). *Cultures and organisations-software of the mind: Intercultural co-operation and its importance for survival*. New York: McGraw-Hill International (UK) Ltd.

Kutinlahti, P. (2005). *Universities approaching market: Intertwining scientific and entrepreneurial goals*. Helsinki, Finland: Faculty of Social Sciences of the University of Helsinki.

Lambert, R. (2003). *Lambert review of business-university collaboration: Final report*. London: HM Treasury.

Nonaka, I., & Toyama, R. (2003). The knowledge-creating theory revisited: Knowledge creation as a synthesising process. *Knowledge Management Research & Practice*, *1*, 2–10. doi:10.1057/palgrave.kmrp.8500001

Organisation for Economic Co-operation and Development. (2007). *The measurement of scientific and technological activities: Proposed guidelines for collecting and interpreting technological innovation data - the Oslo manual*. European Commission and Eurostat.

Philpott, E. (2008). Identifying innovation opportunities – using the Internet to match universities with SMEs. *International Journal of Knowledge Management Studies*, *2*(3), 285–303. doi:10.1504/IJKMS.2008.018793

Philpott, E., & Bevis, K. (2005). Detecting innovation opportunities: The development of an online innovation tool and process for university - business engagement. In *Proceedings of the ISPIM 2005*, Porto, Portugal.

Scott, P. (2003). Challenges to academic values and the organisation of academic work in a time of globalisation. *Higher Education in Europe, 28*(3), 295–306. doi:10.1080/0379772032000119937

Snowden, D. (2002). Complex acts of knowing: Paradox and descriptive self-awareness. *Journal of Knowledge Management, 6*(2), 100–111. doi:10.1108/13673270210424639

Trompenaars, F., & Hampden-Turner, C. (1997). *Riding the waves of culture: Understanding cultural diversity in business.* London: Nicholas Brealy Publishing Ltd.

UK Intellectual Property Office. (2008). *Intellectual property explained.* Retrieved October 2008, from http://www.ipo.gov.uk/whatis.htm

ADDITIONAL READINGS

Athreye, S., & Keeble, D. (2000). *Sources of increasing returns and regional innovation in the UK* (Cambridge Working Paper No. 158). Cambridge, UK: ESRC Centre for Business Research, University of Cambridge.

Cooke, P. (2004). The role of research in regional innovation systems: New models meeting knowledge economy demands. *International Journal of Technology Management, 28*(3/4/5/6), 507-533.

Cosh, A., & Hughes, A. (2002). *Innovation activity and performance in UK SMEs, British Enterprise in transition: Growth, innovation and public policy in the small and medium sized enterprise sector 1994 - 1999.* Cambridge, UK: Centre for Business Research.

Cosh, A. D., & Hughes, A. (1998). *Enterprise Britain: Growth, innovation and public policy in the small and medium sized enterprise sector 1994-97.* Cambridge, UK: ESRC Centre for Business Research.

Criscuolo, C., & Haskel, J. (2002). *Innovations and productivity growth in the UK.* London: UCL, CeRiBA, University of London.

Dodgson, M., & Bessant, J. (1996). *Effective innovation policy: A new approach.* London: International Thomson Business Press

DTI. (2002). *Enterprise for all.* UK: HMSO.

Ford, D., & McNiven, V. (2001). *Manufacturing industry in the Eastern Region: An analysis of support, needs and provision* (A report for the East of England Development Agency, Institute for Manufacture).

Geroski, P. (1994). *Market structure, corporate performance and innovative activity.* Oxford, UK: Clarendon Press.

Griffith, R. S. Redding, et al. (1998). *Productivity growth in OECD industries: Identifying the role of R&D, skills and trade.* London: Institute of Fiscal Studies.

Hollanders, H. (2002). *2002 European innovation scoreboard: Technical paper no 4 indicators and definitions.* European Commission.

Jones, O., & Tang, N. (2000). Innovation in product and process: The implications for technology strategy. *International Journal Manufacturing Technology and Management, 1*(4/5), 465–477.

Kalantaridis, C., & Pheby, J. (1999). Process of innovation among manufacturing SMEs: The experience of Bedfordshire . *Entrepreneurship and Regional Development, 11*, 57–78. doi:10.1080/089856299283290

Keeble, D. (1996). *Small firms, innovation and regional development in Britain in the 1990s* (ESRC CBR Working paper wp42).

Kleinknecht, A. (1987). Measuring R&D in small firms: How much are we missing. *The Journal of Industrial Economics, 36*, 253–256. doi:10.2307/2098417

Lefebvre, E., & Lefebvre, L. A. (2002). Innovative capabilities as determinants of export performance and behaviour: A longitudinal study of manufacturing SMEs. In A. Kleinknecht & P. Mohnen (Eds), *Innovation and firm performance: Econometric explorations of survey data*. London: MacMillan.

Neely, A., & Filippini, R. (2001). A framework for analysing business performance, firm innovation and related contextual factors: Perceptions of managers and policy makers in two European regions. *Integrated Manufacturing Systems, 12*(2), 114–124. doi:10.1108/09576060110384307

Neely, A., & Hii, J. (1999). *Innovative capacity of firms in East of England: Actions and performance*. UK: East of England Development Agency, Cranfield School of Management.

Compilation of References

Aboody, D., & Lev, B. (2001). *The productivity of chemical research & development* (Working paper). New York: New York Stern University, Stern School of Business.

Adair, W. L., Okumura, T., & Brett, J. M. (2001). Negotiation behavior when culture collide: The Unites States and Japan. *The Journal of Applied Psychology, 86*(3), 371–385. doi:10.1037/0021-9010.86.3.371

Adam, D. (2006). Can planting trees really give you a clear carbon conscience? *The Guardian*. Retrieved from http://www.guardian.co.uk/environment/ 2006/oct/07/climatechange.climatechangeenvironment

Adamides, E., & Karacapalidis, N. (2006). Information technology support for the knowledge and social processes of innovation management. *Technovation, 26*, 50–59. doi:10.1016/j.technovation.2004.07.019

Adams, S. (1995). The corporate memory concept. *The Electronic Library, 13*(4), 309–312. doi:10.1108/eb045380

Agrawal, A. (2001). University-to-industry knowledge transfer: Literature review and unanswered questions. *International Journal of Management Reviews, 3*(4), 285–302. doi:10.1111/1468-2370.00069

Ahteela, R., Blomqvist, K., & Puumalainen, K. (in press). Linking organizational culture and trust to organizational innovativeness. *Creativity and Innovation Management*.

Akrivos, C., Ladkin, A., & Reklitis, P. (2007). Hotel managers' career strategies for success. *International Journal of Contemporary Hospitality Management, 19*(2), 107–119. doi:10.1108/09596110710729229

Alas, R., & Vadi, M. (2006). The impact of organisational culture on organisational learning and attitudes concerning change from an institutional perspective. *International Journal of Strategic Change Management, 1*(1), 155–170. doi:10.1504/IJSCM.2006.011109

Alavi, M. (1997). *KPMG Peat Marwick U.S.: One giant brain*. Boston: Harvard Business School.

Alavi, M., & Leidner, D. (2001). Review: Knowledge management and knowledge management systems: Conceptual foundations and research issues. *MIS Quarterly, 25*(1), 107–136. doi:10.2307/3250961

Alavi, M., Kayworth, T. R., & Leidner, D. E. (2006). An empirical examination of the influence of organizational culture on knowledge management practices. *Journal of Management Information Systems, 22*(3), 191–224. doi:10.2753/MIS0742-1222220307

Allee, V. (1997). *The knowledge evolution: Expanding organizational intelligence*. Boston: Butterworth-Heinemann.

Allee, V. (2003). *The future of knowledge: Increasing prosperity through value networks*. Burlington, MA: Elsevier Science.

Allen, S. (2006). *Geography and economy*. Oxford, UK: Oxford University Press.

Allen, T. D. (2003). Mentoring others: A dispositional approach. *Journal of Vocational Behavior, 62*(1), 134–154. doi:10.1016/S0001-8791(02)00046-5

Allen, T. D., & Eby, L. T. (2004). Factors related to mentor reports of mentoring functions provided: Gender and relational characteristics. *Sex Roles*, *50*(1-2), 129–139. doi:10.1023/B:SERS.0000011078.48570.25

Allen, T. D., Poteet, M. L., & Burroughs, S. M. (1997). The mentor's perspective: A qualitative inquiry and future research agenda. *Journal of Vocational Behavior*, *51*(1), 70–89. doi:10.1006/jvbe.1997.1596

Allen, T. D., Poteet, M. L., & Russell, J. E. A. (1998). Attitudes of managers who are more or less career plateaued. *The Career Development Quarterly*, *47*(2), 159–172.

Allen, T. J. (1970). Communication networks in R&D laboratories. *R & D Management*, *1*(1), 14–21. doi:10.1111/j.1467-9310.1970.tb01193.x

Allen, T. J. (1977). *Managing the flow of technology: Technology transfer and the dissemination of technological information within the research and development organization*. Cambridge, MA: MIT Press.

Allen, T. J., & Cohen, S. I. (1969). Information flow in research and development laboratories. *Administrative Science Quarterly*, *14*(1), 12–19. doi:10.2307/2391357

Alley, D., & Crimmins, E. (2007). The demography of aging and work. In K. S. Shultz & G. A. Adams (Eds.), *Aging and work in the 21st century* (pp. 7-23). Mahwah NJ: Lawrence Erlbaum Associates.

Allio, M. K. (2004). Family businesses: Their virtues, vices and strategic paths. *Strategy and Leadership*, *32*(4), 24–33. doi:10.1108/10878570410576704

Allweyer, T. (1998). Modellbaslertess wissensmanagement. *IM Information Management and Consulting*, *13*(1), 37–45.

Almeida, P., & Phene, A. (2004). Subsidiaries and knowledge creation: The influence of the MNC and host country on innovation. *Strategic Management Journal*, *25*, 847–864. doi:10.1002/smj.388

Almeida, P., Anupama, P., & Grant, R. M. (2003). Innovation and knowledge management: Scanning, sourcing and integration. In M. Easterby-Smith & M. A. Lyles (Eds.), *Blackwell handbook of organizational learning and knowledge management* (pp. 356-371). Malden, MA: Blackwell Publishing.

Almeida, P., Song, J. Y., & Grant, R. M. (2002). Are firms superior to alliances and markets? An empirical test of cross-border knowledge building. *Organization Science*, *13*(2), 147–161. doi:10.1287/orsc.13.2.147.534

Aloni, M. (1985). Patterns of information transfer among engineers and applied scientists in complex organizations. *Scientometrics*, *8*(5/6), 279–300. doi:10.1007/BF02018054

Altshuller, G. (1996). *And suddenly the inventor appeared: TRIZ, the theory of inventive problem solving*. Worcester, MA: ICAL Innovation Center.

Alvesson, M., & Kärreman, D. (2001). Odd couple: Making sense of the curious concept of knowledge management. *Journal of Management Studies*, *38*(7), 995–1008. doi:10.1111/1467-6486.00269

Alvesson, M., & Willmott, H. (1992). *Critical management studies. London*. London: Sage.

Amabile, T. M. (1988). A model of creativity and innovation in organizations. In B. M. Staw & L. L. Cummings (Eds.), *Research in organizational behavior vol. 10* (pp. 123-167). Greenwich, CT: JAI Press.

Amabile, T. M., Conti, R., Coon, H., Lazenby, J., & Herron, M. (1996). Assessing the work environment for creativity. *Academy of Management Journal*, *39*(5), 1154–1184. doi:10.2307/256995

Ambos, B., & Schlegelmilch, B. B. (2008). Innovation in multinational firms: Does cultural fit enhance performance? *Management International Review*, *48*(2), 189–206. doi:10.1007/s11575-008-0011-2

Andersen, A., & The American Productivity and Quality Center. (1996). *The knowledge management assessment tool* [white paper].

Anderson, J. R. (2000). *Cognitive psychology and its implications* (5th ed.). New York: Worth.

Anderson, P. (1993). Toward exemplary research in the management of technology - an introductory essay. *Journal of Engineering and Technology Management*, *10*, 7–22. doi:10.1016/0923-4748(93)90056-O

Andrews, K. M., & Delahaye, B. L. (2000). AT influences on knowledge processes in organizational learning: The psychosocial filter. *Journal of Management Studies, 37*(6), 797–810. doi:10.1111/1467-6486.00204

Ankers, P., & Brennan, R. (2002). Managerial relevance in academic research: An exploratory study. *Marketing Intelligence & Planning, 20*(1), 15–21. doi:10.1108/02634500210414729

Anon. (2000). How to be an e-manager? *The Economist, E-Management Survey,* 50-52.

Appleyard, M. M. (1996). How does knowledge flow? Interfirm patterns in the semiconductor industry. *Strategic Management Journal, 17,* 137–154.

Aramburu, N., Sáenz, J., & Rivera, O. (2006). Fostering innovation and knowledge creation: The role of management context. *Journal of Knowledge Management, 10*(3), 157–168. doi:10.1108/13673270610670920

Ardichvili, A., Maurer, M., Li, W., Wentling, T., & Stuedemann, R. (2006). Cultural influences on knowledge sharing through online communities of practice. *Journal of Knowledge Management, 10*(1), 94–107. doi:10.1108/13673270610650139

Argote, L., & Ingram, P. (2000). Knowledge transfer a basis for competitive advantage in firms. *Organizational Behavior and Human Decision Processes, 82*(1), 150–169. doi:10.1006/obhd.2000.2893

Argote, L., Beckman, S. L., & Epple, D. (1990). The persistence and transfer of learning in industrial settings. *Management Science, 36,* 140–154. doi:10.1287/mnsc.36.2.140

Argyris, C., & Schön, D. A. (1978). *Organizational learning: A theory of action perspective.* Reading, MA: Addison-Wesley.

Argyris, C., & Schön, D. A. (1996). *Organizational learning II: Theory, method, and practice.* Reading, MA: Addison-Wesley.

Armagan, S., & Ferreira, M. P. (2005). The impact of political culture on firms' choice of exploitation-exploration internationalization strategy. *International Journal of Cross Cultural Management, 5*(3), 275–291. doi:10.1177/1470595805058791

Armstrong, J. S., & Sperry, T. (1994). Business school prestige-research versus teaching. *Interfaces, 24,* 13–43. doi:10.1287/inte.24.2.13

Aryee, S., Chay, Y. W., & Chew, J. (1996). The motivation to mentor among managerial employees. *Group & Organization Management, 21*(3), 261–277. doi:10.1177/1059601196213002

Ashkanasy, N. M., Wilderom, C. P. M., & Peterson, M. F. (Eds.). (2000). *The handbook of organizational culture and climate.* Thousand Oaks, CA: Sage.

Astrachan, J. H., & Shanker, M. C. (2006). Family businesses' contribution to the US economy: A closer look. In P. Z. Poutziouris, K. X. Smyrnios, & S. B. Klein (Eds.), *Handbook of research on family businesses.* Cheltenham, UK: Edward Elgar.

Astrachan, J. H., Keyt, A., Lane, S., & McMillan, K. (2006). Generic models for family business boards of directors. In P. Z. Poutzioris, K. X. Smyrnios, & S. B. Klein (Eds.), *Handbook of research on family businesses.* Cheltenham, UK: Edward Elgar.

Augier, M., & Teece, D. J. (2005). An economics perspective on intellectual capital. In B. Marr (Ed.), *Perspectives on intellectual capital* (pp. 3-27). Burlington, MA: Elsevier Butterworth Heinemann.

Australian Bureau of Statistics. (2007). *NT at a glance.* Retrieved August 10, 2008, from http://www.abs.gov.au

Awazu, Y. (2007). Managing knowledge within and across geographic borders: The role of culture. *Knowledge and Process Management, 14*(3), 145–147. doi:10.1002/kpm.288

Back, A., von Krogh, G., Seufert, A., et al. (2005). *Putting knowledge networks into action.* Berlin, Germany: Springer Verlag.

Badawy, M. K. (1996). A new paradigm for understanding management of technology: A research agenda for 'technocologists'. *International Journal of Technology Management, 12*(5/6), 717–732.

Ball, C. (1990). *More means different: Widening access to higher education*. London: RSA.

Baltes, P. B., & Baltes, M. M. (1990). Psychological perspectives on successful aging: The model of selective optimization with compensation. In P. B. Baltes & M. M. Baltes (Eds.), *Successful aging: Perspectives from the behavioral sciences* (pp. 1-34). New York: Cambridge University Press.

Barclay, D., Higgins, C., & Thompson, R. (1995). The partial least squares (PLS) approach to causal modeling: Personal computer adoption and use as an illustration. *Technological Studies, 2*(2), 285–309.

Barnes, T., Pashby, I., & Gibbons, A. (2002). Effective university-industry interaction: A multi-case evaluation of collaborative R&D projects. *European Management Journal, 20*(3), 272–285. doi:10.1016/S0263-2373(02)00044-0

Barnes-Farrell, J. L., & Mathews, R. A. (2007). Age and work attitudes. In K. S. Shultz & G. A. Adams (Eds.), *Aging and work in the 21st century* (pp. 139-162). Mahwah NJ: Lawrence Erlbaum Associates.

Barney, J. (1991). Firm resources and sustained competitive advantage. *Strategic Management Journal, 17*(1), 99–120.

Barney, J. B. (1991). Looking inside for competitive advantage. *Academy of Management Executive, 9*(4), 49–61.

Barth, M. C., McNaught, W., & Rizzi, P. (1993). Corporations and the aging workforce. In P. H. Mirvis (Ed.), *Building the competitive workforce: Investing in capital for corporate success* (pp. 156-200). New York: John Wiley & Sons.

Barton, L. D. (1995). *Wellsprings of knowledge*. Boston: Harvard Business School Press.

Bates, T. (1997, June). *Restructuring the university for technological change*. Paper presented at The Carnegie Foundation for the Advancement of Teaching, What Kind of University, London, GB.

Baumeister, R. F., & Tice, D. M. (1986). Four selves, two motives, and a substitute process self-regulation model. In R. F. Baumeister (Ed.), *Public self and private self* (pp. 63-74). New York: Springer-Verlag.

BBC. (2006). *Hypocrisy claim over Cameron bike*. Retrieved from http://news.bbc.co.uk/2/hi/uk_news/politics/4953922.stm

Beehr, T. A., & Bowling, N. A. (2002). Career issues facing older workers. In D. C. Feldman (Ed.), *Work careers: A developmental perspective* (pp. 214-241). San Francisco: Jossey-Bass.

Begoña Lloria, M. (2008). A review of the main approaches to knowledge management. *Knowledge Management Research & Practice, 6*, 77–89. doi:10.1057/palgrave.kmrp.8500164

Bell DeTienne, K., Dyer, G., Hoopes, C., & Harris, S. (2004). Toward a Model of effective knowledge management and directions for future research: Culture, leadership, and CKOs. *Journal of Leadership & Organizational Studies, 10*(4), 26–43. doi:10.1177/107179190401000403

Bendt, A. (2000). *Wissenstransfer in multinationalen unternehmen*. Wiesbaden, Germany: Gabler Verlag.

Berman Brown, R., & Woodland, M. J. (1999). Managing knowledge wisely: A case study in organisational behaviour. *Journal of Applied Management Studies, 8*(2), 175–198.

Bernard, A., & Tichkiewitch, S. (2008). Methods and tools for effective knowledge life-cycle-management. Berlin, Germany: Springer Verlag.

Bernus, P., & Fox, M. (2005). *Knowledge sharing in the integrated enterprise*. New York: Springer Verlag.

Berry, J. W. (2001). A psychology of immigration. *The Journal of Social Issues, 57*(3), 615–631. doi:10.1111/0022-4537.00231

Berwick, D. (1996). A primer on leading the improvement of systems. *BMJ (Clinical Research Ed.), 132*, 619–622.

Bhagat, R. S., Kedia, B. L., Harveston, P. D., & Triandis, H. C. (2002). Cultural variations in the cross-border transfer of organizational knowledge: An integrative framework. *Academy of Management Review, 27*(2), 204–221. doi:10.2307/4134352

Bijker, W. (1995). *Bikes, bakelite, and bulbs: Steps toward a theory of socio-technical change.* Cambridge, MA: MIT Press.

Bijker, W., Pinch, T., & Hughes, T. (Eds.). (1987). *The social construction of technological systems: New directions in the sociology and history of technology.* Cambridge, MA: MIT Press.

Biloslavo, R. (2006). *Strateški management in management spreminjanja.* Koper, Slovenia: Fakulteta za management.

Biloslavo, R., & Trnavčevič, A. (2007). Knowledge management audit in a higher educational institution: A case study. *Knowledge and Process Management, 14*(4), 275–286. doi:10.1002/kpm.293

Bilson, A. (1997). Guidelines for a constructivist approach: Steps toward the adaptation of ideas from family therapy for use in organization. *Systems Practice, 10*(2), 154–177. doi:10.1007/BF02557914

Bilson, A. (2007). Promoting compassionate concern in social work: Reflections on ethics, biology and love. *British Journal of Social Work, 37*(8), 1371–1386. doi:10.1093/bjsw/bcl060

Birdir, K. (2002). General manager turnover and root causes. *International Journal of Contemporary Hospitality Management, 14*(1), 43–47. doi:10.1108/09596110210415123

Birkinshaw, J. (2001). Why is knowledge management so difficult? *Business Strategy Review, 12*(1), 11–18. doi:10.1111/1467-8616.00161

Bitkom. (2007). *Trends im wissensmanagement 2007 bis 2011.* Frankfurt, Germany: KnowTech 2007.

Blackler, F. (1995). Knowledge, knowledge work and organizations: An overview and interpretation. *Organization Studies, 16*, 1021–1046. doi:10.1177/017084069501600605

Blackler, F. H. M. (1995). Knowledge, knowledge work and organizations: An overview and interpretation. *Organization Studies, 16*(6), 1021–1046. doi:10.1177/017084069501600605

Blackmore, A. (2004). Improving the use of know-how in organisations by recognising enablers and contributors. *Journal of Knowledge Management, 8*(2), 112–113. doi:10.1108/13673270410529154

Bloor, G., & Dawson, P. (1994). Understanding professional culture in organizational context. *Organization Studies, 15*(2), 275–295. doi:10.1177/017084069401500205

Bodrow, W., & Bergmann, P. (2003). *Wissensbewertung in unternehmen.* Berlin, Germany: Erich Schmidt Verlag.

Boisot, M. (1987). *Information and organisations: The manager as anthropologist.* London: Fontana/Collins.

Boisot, M. (1994). *Information and organization: The manager as anthropologist.* London: Harper and Collins.

Boisot, M. (1995). *Information space: A framework for learning in organizations.* London: Routledge.

Boisot, M. (1995). Is your firm a creative destroyer? Competitive learning and knowledge flows in the technological strategies of firms. *Research Policy, 24*, 489–506. doi:10.1016/S0048-7333(94)00779-9

Boisot, M. (1998). *Knowledge assets: Securing competitive advantage in the information economy.* Oxford, UK: Oxford University Press.

Bollinger, A. S., & Smith, R. D. (2001). Managing organizational knowledge as a strategic asset. *Journal of Knowledge Management, 5*(1), 8–18. doi:10.1108/13673270110384365

Bollisani, E. (Ed.). (2008). *Building the knowledge society on the Internet: Sharing and exchanging knowledge in networked environments.* Hershey, PA: Information Science Reference.

Bond, P. L. (2000). Knowledge and knowing as structure: A new perspective on the management of technology for the knowledge based economy. *Int. J. of Technology Management, 20*(5/6/7/8), 528-544.

Bond, P. L. (2002). *Conversations with organisations and other objects. Featuring a mujician, two bears, and two ceramic pots.* Paper presented at the Art of Management and Organisation Conference, King's College, London.

Bond, P. L. (2003). The biology of technology: An exploratory essay. *Knowledge, Technology, and Policy, 16*(3), 125–142. doi:10.1007/s12130-003-1036-2

Bond, P. L. (2004). Maturana, technology, and art: Is a biology of technology possible? *Cybernetics & Human Knowing, 11*(2), 49–70.

Bond, P. L. (2004). Communities of practice and complexity: Conversation and culture. *AMED's Organisations & People Journal, 11*(4).

Bond, P. L. (2005). *The emergence of complex emotioning innovating and polytechnical systems. An essay on the biology of technology.* Paper presented at Conference on Complexity and Society, University of Liverpool, Liverpool, UK.

Bond, P. L. (2006). Emotioning, foundational knowledge and enterprise creation. *Organisation and People, 13*(1), 42–49.

Bonn, M. A., & Forbringer, L. R. (1992). Reducing turnover in the hospitality industry: An overview of recruitment, selection and retention. *International Journal of Hospitality Management, 11*(1), 47–63. doi:10.1016/0278-4319(92)90035-T

Bontis, N. (1996). There's a price on your head: Managing intellectual capital strategically. *Business Quarterly,* (Summer).

Bontis, N. (1999). Managing organizational knowledge by diagnosing intellectual capital: Framing and advancing the state of the field. *International Journal of Technology Management, 18*(5-8), 433–462. doi:10.1504/IJTM.1999.002780

Bopry, J. (2005). Levels of experience: An exploration for learning design. *Educational Media International, 42*(1), 83–89. doi:10.1080/09523980500116688

Borgatti, S. P., & Cross, R. (2003). A relational view of information seeking and learning in social networks. *Management Science, 49*(4), 432–445. doi:10.1287/mnsc.49.4.432.14428

Bornemann, M., & Sammer, M. (2002). *Anwendungsorientiertes wissensmanagement.* Wiesbaden, Germany: Deutscher Universitätsverlag.

Böschen, S., Schneider, M., & Lerf, A. (2004). *Handeln trotz nichtwissen. vom umgang mit chaos und risiko in politik, industrie und wissenschaft.* Frankfurt, Germany: campus.

Bosi, M., & Mercado-Martinez, F. (2004). *Pesquisa qualitativa de serviços de saúde.* Rio de Janeiro, Brazil: Vozes.

Boyd, R., & Richerson, P. J. (1996). Why culture is common but cultural evolution is rare. *Proceedings of the British Academy, 88*, 77–93.

Boyle, D. P. (1999). The road less traveled: Cross-cultural, international experiential learning. *International Social Work, 42*(2), 201–214. doi:10.1177/002087289904200208

Braganza, A., & Mollenkramer, G. J. (2002). Anatomy of a failed knowledge management initiative: Lessons from PharmaCorp's experiences. *Knowledge and Process Management, 9*(1), 23–33. doi:10.1002/kpm.130

Bråsjö, E., & Blomqvist, P. (2006). *Swedish strengths in the environmental industry.* Stockholm: Kungl. Ingenjörsvetenskapsakademien (IVA).

Breuker, J., & Van de Velde, W. (1994). *CommonKADS library for expertise modelling: Reusable problem solving components.* Amsterdam: IOS Press.

Brey, P. (1999). Philosophy of technology meets social constructivism. *Techne, 2*(3/4).

Bright, M. I. (2005). Can Japanese mentoring enhance understanding of Western mentoring? *Employee Relations, 27*(4/5), 325–339. doi:10.1108/01425450510605679

Broadbent, M. (1998). The phenomenon of knowledge management: What does it mean to the information profession? *Information Outlook, 2*(5), 23–36.

Bröchner, J., Rosander, S., & Waara, F. (2004). Cross-border post-acquisition knowledge transfer among construction consultants. *Construction Management and Economics, 22,* 421–427. doi:10.1080/0144619042000240003

Brooke, L., & Taylor, P. (2005). Older workers and employment: Managing age relations. *Ageing and Society, 25,* 415–429. doi:10.1017/S0144686X05003466

Brooking, A. (1997). The management of intellectual capital. *Journal of Long Range Planning, 30*(3), 364–365. doi:10.1016/S0024-6301(97)80911-9

Brown, A. (1998). *Organisational culture.* London: Financial Times Pitman.

Brown, J. S., & Duguid, P. (1991). AT organizational learning and communities of practice: Toward a unified view of working, learning, and innovation. *Organization Science, 2*(1), 40–57. doi:10.1287/orsc.2.1.40

Brown, W., & Karagozoglu, N. (1989). Systems model of technological innovation. *IEEE Transactions on Engineering Management, 36*(1). doi:10.1109/17.19977

Bryant, S. (2005). The impact of peer mentoring on organizational knowledge creation and sharing: An empirical study in a software firm. *Group & Organization Management, 30*(3), 319–338. doi:10.1177/1059601103258439

Bryceson, K. (2007). The online learning environment: A new model using social constructivism and the concept of 'Ba' as a theoretical framework. *Learning Environments Research, 10*(3), 189–206. doi:10.1007/s10984-007-9028-x

Bryceson, K. (2007). SECI, BA, ESCI and VAG: Linking models of knowledge acquisition, elearning and online immersive worlds to create an innovative learning environment. In G. Richards (Ed.), *Proceedings of the World Conference on E-Learning in Corporate, Government, Healthcare, and Higher Education 2007* (pp. 2365-2372). Québec, Canada: AACE.

Buckley, P. J., & Carter, M. J. (1999). Managing cross-border complementary knowledge: Conceptual development in business process approach to knowledge management in multinational firms. *Int. Studies of Mgt. & Org., 29*(1), 80–104.

Buckley, P. J., Carter, M. J., Clegg, J., & Tan, H. (2005). Language and social knowledge in foreign-knowledge transfer to China. *International Studies of Management & Organization, 35*(1), 47–65.

Buckley, P. J., Clegg, J., & Tan, H. (2006). Cultural awareness in knowledge transfer to China – The role of *guanxi* and *mianzi. Journal of World Business, 41,* 275–288. doi:10.1016/j.jwb.2006.01.008

Buckley, W. (1968). Society as a complex adaptive system. In Open System Group (Eds.), *Systems behaviour.* London: Open University/Harper and Row.

Bukh, P. N., & Johanson, U. (2003). Research and knowledge interaction: Guidelines for intellectual capital reporting. *Journal of Intellectual Capital, 4*(4), 576–587. doi:10.1108/14691930310504572

Bukowitz, W. R., & Williams, R. L. (2000). *The knowledge management fieldbook.* London: Pearson Education Limited.

Burt, R. S., & Schott, T. (1985). Relation contents in multiple networks. *Social Science Research, 14,* 287–308. doi:10.1016/0049-089X(85)90014-6

Butler, R. (1998). Seasonality in tourism: Issues and implications. *Tourism Review, 53*(3), 18–24. doi:10.1108/eb058278

Cabrera-Suarez, K., De Saa-Perez, P., & Garcia-Almeida, D. (2001). The succession process from a resource- and knowledge-based view of the family firm. *Family Business Review, 14*(1), 37–46. doi:10.1111/j.1741-6248.2001.00037.x

Calori, R., Lubatkin, M., Very, P., & Veiga, J. F. (1997). Modelling the origins of national-bound administrative heritages: A historical institutional analysis of French and British firms. *Organization Science, 8*(6), 681–696. doi:10.1287/orsc.8.6.681

Cameron, K. S., & Freeman, S. J. (1991). Cultural congruence, strength, and type: Relationships to effectiveness. *Research in Organizational Change and Development, 5*, 23–58.

Cameron, K. S., & Quinn, R. E. (1999). *Diagnosing and changing organizational culture*. Reading, MA: Addison-Wesley, Inc.

Campbell, S., & Kleiner, B. H. (1997). New developments in re-engineering organisations. *Work Study, 46*(3), 99–103. doi:10.1108/00438029710162953

Cantwell, J. (2005). Innovation and competitiveness. In J. Fagerberg, D. C. Mowery, & R. R. Nelson, (Eds.), *The Oxford handbook on innovation* (pp. 543-567). New York: Oxford University Press.

Capelli, P. (2003). Will there really be a labor shortage? *Organizational Dynamics, 32*(3), 221–233. doi:10.1016/S0090-2616(03)00034-2

Capos, C. (2008). *The currency of favours* (James Westphal interview). Retrieved from http://www.bus.umich.edu/NewsRoom/ArticleDisplay.asp?news_id=12754

Capra, F. (1996). *The web of life*. London: Harper Collins.

Capra, F. (2001). *The hidden connections. A science for sustainable living*. London: Harper Collins.

Carbery, R., & Garavan, T. N. (2003). Predicting hotel managers' turnover cognitions. *Journal of Managerial Psychology, 18*(7), 649–679. doi:10.1108/02683940310502377

Carley, K., & Krackhardt, D. (2001). *A typology for network measures for organizations*. Retrieved August 10, 2008, from http://www.casos.cs.cmu.edu/bios/carley/working_papers.php

Carr-Chellman, A. A. (Ed.). (2005). *Global perspectives on e-learning: Rhetoric and reality*. Thousand Oaks, CA: Sage.

Carson, D. (2008). The 'blogosphere' as a market research tool for tourism destinations: A case study of Australia's NT. *Journal of Vacation Marketing, 14*(2), 111–119. doi:10.1177/1356766707087518

Carson, D., & Macbeth, J. (Eds.). (2005). *Regional tourism cases: Innovation in regional tourism*. Altona, Australia: Common Ground Publishing.

Carson, D., Boyle, A., & Hoedlmaier, A. (2007, March). *Plan or no plan? The flexibility of backpacker travel in Australia*. Paper presented at CAUTHE 2007, Australia.

Caspers, R., Bickhoff, N., & Bieger, T. (2004). *Interorganisatorische wissensnetzwerke*. Berlin, Germany: Springer Verlag.

Castells, M. (2000). *The rise of the network society*. Oxford, UK: Blackwell Publishing.

Castro, L., & Toro, M. A. (2004). The evolution of culture: From primate social learning to human culture. *Proceedings of the National Academy of Sciences of the United States of America, 101*(27), 10235–10240. doi:10.1073/pnas.0400156101

CBI. (2001). *Partnerships for research and innovation between industry and universities: A guide to better practice*. London: Confederation of British Industry

CEN. (2004). *European guide to good practice in knowledge management - part 1: Knowledge management framework*. CEN Workshop Agreement, European Committee For Standardization, Management Centre.

CEN. (2004). *European guide to good practice in knowledge management - part 2: Organizational culture*. CEN Workshop Agreement, European Committee For Standardization, Management Centre.

CEN. (2004). *European guide to good practice in knowledge management - part 3: SME implementation*. CEN Workshop Agreement, European Committee For Standardization, Management Centre.

CEN. (2004). *European guide to good practice in knowledge management - part 4: Guidelines for measuring KM*. CEN Workshop Agreement, European Committee For Standardization, Management Centre.

CEN. (2004). *European guide to good practice in knowledge management - part 5: KM terminology.* CEN Workshop Agreement, European Committee for Standardization, Management Centre.

Center for Research into the Older Worker (CROW). (2004). *Job transitions* (Briefing Paper 3). Centre for Research into the Older Workforce: University of Surrey.

Chai, K. H. (1998). *Managing knowledge in organizations: A literature review and a preliminary conceptual model* (Working paper series). Cambridge, UK: Cambridge University, Manufacturing and Management Center, Engineering Department, Cambridge.

Chambon, M. (2005). How to look modest in an organization: Supervisors' perceptions of subordinates' account for success. *Psychologie du Travail et des Organisations, 11*(3), 151–164. doi:10.1016/j.pto.2005.07.003

Chang, H.-C., & Holt, R. (1994). A Chinese perspective on face as inter-relational concern. In S. Ting-Toomey (Ed.), *The challenge of facework: Cross-cultural and interpersonal issues.* Albany, NY: State University of New York.

Chang, K., & Lu, L. (2007). Characteristics of organizational culture, stressors and wellbeing: The case of Taiwanese organizations. *Journal of Managerial Psychology, 22*(6), 549–598. doi:10.1108/02683940710778431

Chapman, J. A., & Lovell, G. (2006). The competency model of hospitality service: Why it doesn't deliver. *International Journal of Contemporary Hospitality Management, 18*(1), 78–88. doi:10.1108/09596110610642000

Chatman, J. A., & Barsade, S. G. (1995). Personality, organizational culture, and cooperation: Evidence from a business simulation. *Administrative Science Quarterly, 40*(3), 423–443. doi:10.2307/2393792

Chatti, M. A., Klamma, R., Jarke, M., & Naeve, A. (2007, July). *The Web 2.0 driven SECI model based learning process.* Paper presented at the 7th IEEE International Conference on Advanced Learning Technologies (ICALT 2007), Niigata, Japan.

Chaudhry, A. S., & Higgins, S. (2003). On the need for a multi disciplinary approach to education for knowledge management. *Library Review, 52*(1-2), 65–69. doi:10.1108/00242530310462134

Child, J. (994). *Management in China during the age of reform.* Cambridge, UK: Cambridge University Press.

Chin, W. W. (2003). A permutation procedure for multi-group comparison on PLS models. In M. Vilares, M. Tenenhaus, P. Coelho, V. Exposito, & A. Morineau (Eds.), *PLS and related methods: Proceedings of the PLS'03 International Symposium.*

Chin, W. W., & Frye, T. (2003). *PLS-graph version 3.00.* Houston, TX: University of Houston.

Chin-Loy, C. (2003). *Assessing the influence of organizational culture on knowledge management success.* Unpublished doctoral dissertation, The Wayne Huizeng School of Business and Entrepreneurship, Nova Southeastern University, Florida.

Cho, S., & Woods, R. H., SooCheong, J., & Mehmet, E. (2006). Measuring the impact of human resource management practices on hospitality firms' performances. *International Journal of Hospitality Management, 25*(2), 262–277. doi:10.1016/j.ijhm.2005.04.001

Choi, B., & Lee, H. (2003). An empirical investigation of KM styles and their effect on corporate management. *Information & Management, 40*(5), 179. doi:10.1016/S0378-7206(02)00060-5

Christiansen, J. A. (2000). *Building the innovative organization: Management systems that encourage innovation.* New York: St. Martin's Press.

Chubb, J. E., & Moe, T. M. (1990). *Politics, markets and America's schools.* Washington: The Brookings Institution.

CIC. (2003). *Intellectus model: Measurement and management of intellectual capital* (Intellectus Document No. 5). Madrid, Spain.

Clark, B. R. (Ed.). (1984). *Perspectives on higher education: Eight disciplinary and comparative views.* Berkeley, CA: University of California Press.

Clark, T. (1990). International marketing and national character: A review and proposal for an integrative theory. *Journal of Marketing*, 66–79. doi:10.2307/1251760

Cloete, M., & Snyman, R. (2003). The enterprise portal: Is it knowledge management. *Aslib Proceedings*, *55*(4), 234–242. doi:10.1108/00012530310486593

Clutterbuck, D., & Megginson, D. (2005). *Making coaching work: Creating a coaching culture*. London: Chartered Institute of Personnel and Development.

Coca Cola. (2008). *Regional and local foundations*. Retrieved from http://www.thecoca-colacompany.com/citizenship/foundation_local.html

Coffey, R., Richards, J., Remmert, C., Leroy, S., Schoville, R., & Baldwin, P. (2005). An introduction to critical paths'. *Quality Management in Health Care*, *1*, 46–55.

Cohen, D., & Prusak, L. (2004). *In good company: How social capital makes organizations work*. Boston, MA: Harvard Business School Press.

Cohen, I. J. (1989). *Structuration theory: Anthony Giddens and the constitution of social life*. London: Macmillan.

Cohen, W. M., & Levinthal, D. A. (1990). Absorptive capacity: A new perspective on learning and innovation. *Administrative Science Quarterly*, *35*, 128–152. doi:10.2307/2393553

Collins English dictionary (4th ed.). (1998). Glasgow, Scotland: Harper Collins.

Cook, K. S., & Rice, E. (2003). Social exchange theory. In *Handbook of social psychology*. New York: Springer Verlag.

Cooper, C. (2006). Knowledge management and tourism. *Annals of Tourism Research*, *33*(1), 47–64. doi:10.1016/j.annals.2005.04.005

Cooper, D. (2001). Innovation and reciprocal externalities: Information transmission via job mobility. *Journal of Economic Behavior & Organization*, *45*, 403–425. doi:10.1016/S0167-2681(01)00154-8

Cotton, J. L., & Turtle, J. M. (1986). Employee turnover: A meta analysis and review of implications for research. *Academy of Management Review*, *11*, 55–70. doi:10.2307/258331

Craig, C. S., & Douglas, S. P. (2006). Beyond national culture: Implications of cultural dynamics for consumer research. *International Marketing Review*, *23*(3), 322–342. doi:10.1108/02651330610670479

Cranwell-Ward, J., Bossons, P., & Gover, S. (2004). *Mentoring: A Henley review of best practice*. Basingstoke, UK: Palgrave Macmillan.

Critchley, R. K. (2004). *Doing nothing is not an option: Facing the imminent labor crisis*. Mason, OH: Thomson South-Western.

Cross, R., & Baird, L. (2000). Technology is not enough: Improving performance by building organizational memory. *Sloan Management Review*, *41*(3), 69.

Cross, R., Borgatti, S., & Parker, A. (2001). Beyond answers: Dimensions of the advice network. *Social Networks*, *23*, 215–235. doi:10.1016/S0378-8733(01)00041-7

Crossan, M., Lane, H., & White, R. (1999). An organizational learning framework: From intuition to institution. *Academy of Management Review*, *24*(3), 522–537. doi:10.2307/259140

Cummings, J. L., & Teng, B. S. (2003). Transferring R&D knowledge: The key factors affecting knowledge transfer success. *Journal of Engineering and Technology Management*, *20*(1), 30–68. doi:10.1016/S0923-4748(03)00004-3

Cummings, J. N. (2004). Work groups, structural diversity, and knowledge sharing in a global organization. *Management Science*, *50*(3), 352–264. doi:10.1287/mnsc.1030.0134

Cyert, R. M., & Goodman, P. S. (1997). Creating effective university-industry alliances: An organizational learning perspective. *Organizational Dynamics*, *25*(4), 45–57. doi:10.1016/S0090-2616(97)90036-X

Czaja, S., & Sharit, J. (1993). Age differences in the performance of computer-based work. *Psychology and Aging*, *8*(1), 59–67. doi:10.1037/0882-7974.8.1.59

Daft, R. L., & Lengel, R. H. (1986). Organizational information requirements, media richness and structural design. *Management Science, 3*, 554–571. doi:10.1287/mnsc.32.5.554

Daghfous, A. (2003). Uncertainty and learning in university-industry knowledge transfer projects. *Journal of American Academy of Business, 3*(1/2), 145–151.

Dalkir, K. (2005). *Knowledge management in theory and practice.* Oxford, UK: Elsevier Inc.

Dalton, D. R., & Krackhardt, D. M. (1983). The impact of teller turnover in banking: First appearances are deceiving. *Journal of Bank Research, 14*(3), 184–192.

Dalton, G. W., Thompson, P. H., & Price, R. L. (1977). The four stages of professional careers: A new look at performance by professionals. *Organizational Dynamics, 6*(1), 19–42. doi:10.1016/0090-2616(77)90033-X

Darling, N., Hamilton, S., Tokoyama, T., & Matuda, S. (2002). Naturally occurring mentoring in Japan and the United States: Social roles and correlates. *American Journal of Community Psychology, 30*(2), 245–271. doi:10.1023/A:1014684928461

Darr, E. D., Argote, L., & Epple, D. (1995). The acquisition, transfer, and depreciation of knowledge in service organizations: Productivity in franchises. *Management Science, 41*(11), 1750–1762. doi:10.1287/mnsc.41.11.1750

Darwin, A. (2004). Characteristics ascribed to mentors by their protégés. In D. Clutterbuck & G. Lane (Eds.), *The situational mentor: An international review of competencies and capabilities in mentoring* (pp. 29-41). Aldershot, UK: Gower.

Davenport, T. H. (2007). Information technologies for knowledge management. In K. Ichijo & I. Nonaka (Eds.), *Knowledge creation and management: New challenges for managers* (pp. 97-117). New York: Oxford University Press.

Davenport, T. H., & Prusack, L. (1998). *Working knowledge: How organizations manage what they know.* Boston: Harvard Business School Press.

Davenport, T. H., & Prusak, L. (1997). *Information ecology: Mastering the information and knowledge environment.* New York: Oxford University Press.

Davenport, T., & Prusak, L. (2003). *What's the big idea?* Boston: Harvard Business School Press.

Davey, J. (2003). Opportunity or outrage? Redundancy and educational involvement in mid-life. *Journal of Education and Work, 16*(1), 87–102. doi:10.1080/1363908022000032902

Davey, J., & Cornwall, J. (2003). *Maximising the potential of older workers* (NZiRA Future Proofing New Zealand Series). Wellington, New Zealand: New Zealand Institute for Research on Ageing.

Davies, D., Taylor, R., & Savery, L. (2001). The role of appraisal, remuneration and training in improving staff relations in the Western Australian accommodation industry: A comparative study. *Journal of European Industrial Training, 25*(7), 366–373. doi:10.1108/EUM0000000005837

Davies, J., Duke, A., & Sure, Y. (2004). OntoShare-an ontology-based knowledge sharing system for virtual communities of practice. *Journal of Universal Computer Science, 10*(3), 262–283.

Davila, T., Epstein, M. J., & Shelton, R. (2006). *Making innovation work: How to manage it, measure it, and profit from it.* Upper Saddle River, NJ: Pearson Education.

Dawson, R. (2000). *Developing knowledge-based client relationship: The future of professional services.* Boston: Butterworth-Heinemann.

De Long, D. W., & Fahey, L. (2000). Diagnosing cultural barriers to knowledge management. *The Academy of Management Executive, 14*(4), 113–127.

De Long, D. W., & Fahey, L. (2000). Diagnosing cultural barriers to knowledge management . *The Academy of Management Executive, 14*(4), 113–128.

Deakins, D., Ishaq, M., Whittam, G., & Wyper, J. (2008). Diversity in ethnic minority businesses in rural and urban localities. *International Journal of Entrepreneurship and Small Business, 7*(3).

Deal, T. E., & Kennedy, A. A. (1982). *Corporate cultures.* Reading, MA: Addison-Wesley.

Declercq, G. V. (1981). A third look at the two cultures: The new economic responsibility of the university. *International Journal of institutional Management in Higher Education, 5*(2), 117-122.

Deem, R. (2003). Gender, organizational cultures and the practices of manager-academic in UK universities. *Gender, Work and Organization, 10*(2), 239–259. doi:10.1111/1468-0432.t01-1-00013

Deery, M. A., & Shaw, R. N. (1997). An exploratory analysis of turnover culture in the hotel industry in Australia. *International Journal of Hospitality Management, 16*(4), 375–392. doi:10.1016/S0278-4319(97)00031-5

DeGraaf, J., Wann, D., & Naylor, T. H. (2001). *Affluenza: The all-consuming epidemic.* San Francisco: Berrett, Kohler Publishers Inc.

Dekkers, R. (2005). *(R)Evolution.* New York: Springer Verlag.

DeLong, D. W. (2004). *Lost knowledge: Confronting the threat of an aging workforce.* NewYork: Oxford University Press.

DePaulo, B. (1992). Nonverbal behaviour and self-presentation. *Psychological Bulletin, 111*, 203–243. doi:10.1037/0033-2909.111.2.203

Despres, C., & Chauvel, D. (1999). Knowledge management(s). *Journal of Knowledge Management, 3*(2), 110–120. doi:10.1108/13673279910275567

Dhaliwal, S., & Kangis, P. (2006). Asians in the UK: Gender, generations and enterprise. *Equal Opportunities International, 25*(2), 92–108. doi:10.1108/02610150610679529

Diamond, J. (2008). *What's your consumption factor?* Retrieved August 3, 2008, from http://www.nytimes.com/2008/01/02/opinion/02diamond.html

Dickson, T. J., & Huyton, J. (2008). Customer service, employee welfare and snowsports tourism in Australia. *International Journal of Contemporary Hospitality Management, 20*(2), 199–214. doi:10.1108/09596110810852177

Diedrichs, E., Engel, K., et al. (2006). *European innovation management landscape - IMPROVE: Assessment of current practice in innovation management consultancy* (Europe INNOVA Paper No 2). Augsberg, Germany: European Commission Directorate General Enterprise and Industry.

Dixon, N. (2000). *Common knowledge. How companies thrive by sharing what they know.* Cambridge, MA: Harvard Business School Press.

Donald, M. (1993). Précis of origins of the modern mind: Three stages in the evolution of culture and cognition. *The Behavioral and Brain Sciences, 16*(4), 737–791.

Donaldson, L. (2001). Reflections on knowledge and knowledge-intensive firms. *Human Relations, 54*(7), 955–963. doi:10.1177/0018726701547008

Doney, P. M., Cannon, J. P., & Mullen, M. R. (1998). Understanding the influence of national culture on the development of trust. *Academy of Management Review, 23*(3), 601–620. doi:10.2307/259297

Dosi, G., Nelson, R. R., & Winter, S. G. (2000). *The nature and dynamics of organizational capabilities.* New York: Oxford University Press.

Droege, S. B., & Hoobler, J. M. (2003). Employee turnover and tacit knowledge diffusion: A network perspective. *Journal of Managerial Issues, 15*(1), 50.

Drory, A., & Zaidman, N. (2007). Impression management behaviour: Effects of the organizational system. *Journal of Managerial Psychology, 22*(3), 290–308. doi:10.1108/02683940710733106

Drucker, P. (1994). The age of social transformation. [from http//www.providersedge.com/docs/leadership_articles/Age_of_Social_Transformation.pdf]. *Atlantic Monthly, 274*(5), 53–80. Retrieved March 2, 2007.

Drucker, P. (2001). *The essential Drucker: Selections from the management works of Peter F. Drucker.* New York: Harper Business.

Drucker, P. F. (1991). The new productivity challenge. *Harvard Business Review, 69*, 69–76.

Drucker, P. F. (1992). The new society of organizations. *Harvard Business Review, 70*(5), 95–104.

Drucker, P. F. (1993). *Post capitalist society.* New York: Harper-Business.

Drucker, P. F. (1995). The network society. *International forum on information and documentation, 20*(1), 5-7.

Druker, P. F. (1998). The coming of the new organisation. *Harvard Business Review,* •••, 1–21.

Drummond, J., Silva, E., & Coutinho, M. (2002). *Medicina baseada em evidências: Novo paradigma assistencial e pedagógico.* São Paulo, Brazil: Atheneu.

DTi Small Business Service. (2006). *Annual small business survey.* London: DTi.

Duberley, J., & Cohen, L. (2007). Entrepreneurial academics: Developing scientific careers in changing university settings. *Higher Education Quarterly, 61*(4), 479–497. doi:10.1111/j.1468-2273.2007.00368.x

Dussauge, P., Hart, P., & Ramanantsoa, B. (1992). *Strategic technology management.* Chichester, UK: John Wiley and Sons.

Dychtwald, K., Erickson, T. J., & Morison, R. (2006) *Workforce crisis: How to beat the coming shortage of skills and talent.* Boston: Harvard Business School Press.

Dyer, W. G. Jr. (1998). Culture and continuity in family firms. *Family Business Review, 1*(1), 37–50. doi:10.1111/j.1741-6248.1988.00037.x

Easterby-Smith, M., Lyles, M. A., & Tsang, E. W. K. (2008). Inter-organizational knowledge transfer: Current themes and future perspectives. *Journal of Management Studies, 45*(4), 677–690. doi:10.1111/j.1467-6486.2008.00773.x

Eckhardt, G. M., & Houston, M. J. (2002). Cultural paradoxes reflected in brand meaning: McDonald's in Shanghai, China. *Journal of International Marketing, 10*(2), 68–82. doi:10.1509/jimk.10.2.68.19532

Eden, C., & Ackermann, F. (1998). *Making strategy: The journey of strategic management.* London: Sage Publications.

Edvinsson, L., & Malone, M. (1997). *Intellectual capital: Realizing your company's true value by finding its hidden brainpower.* New York: Harper Business.

Edvinsson, L., & Richtner, A. (1999). *Words of value – giving words to IC.* Skandia.

Edvinsson, L., & Sullivan, P. (1996). Developing a model for managing intellectual capital. *European Management Journal, 14*(4), 356–364. doi:10.1016/0263-2373(96)00022-9

Edwards, J. S., & Kidd, J. B. (2003). Knowledge management sans frontiers. *The Journal of the Operational Research Society, 54*(2), 130–139. doi:10.1057/palgrave.jors.2601419

Ehms, K., & Langen, M. (2003). *Holistic development of knowledge management with KMMM.* Positioning Paper on Workshop Bewertung von Wissensmanagement projekten.

Eisenhardt, K. M. (1999). Strategy as strategic decision making. *Sloan Management Review, 40*(3), 65–73.

Eisenhardt, K. M., & Martin, J. A. (2000). Dynamic capabilities: What are they? *Strategic Management Journal, 21*(10-11), 1105–1121. doi:10.1002/1097-0266(200010/11)21:10/11<1105::AID-SMJ133>3.0.CO;2-E

Ekman, P., & Davidson, J. (Eds.). (1994). *The nature of emotion: Fundamental questions.* New York: Oxford University Press.

Ekman, P., & Friesen, W. V. (1971). Constants across cultures in the face and emotion. *Journal of Personality and Social Psychology, 17*, 124–129. doi:10.1037/h0030377

Ellul, J. (1964). *The technological society* (J. Wilkinson, Trans.). New York: A.A. Knopf.

Elmuti, D., Abebe, M., & Nicolosi, M. (2005). An overview of strategic alliances between universities and corporations. *Journal of Workplace Learning, 17*(1/2), 115–129. doi:10.1108/13665620510574504

Epple, D., Argote, L., & Devadas, R. (1991). Organizational learning curves: A method for investigating intra-plant transfer of knowledge acquired through learning by doing. *Organization Science*, *2*(1), 58–70. doi:10.1287/orsc.2.1.58

Erickson, G. S., & Rothberg, H. N. (2002). B2B Internet applications: Strategic considerations. *Competitiveness Review*, *12*(2), 57–63.

Erikson, E. H. (1963). *Childhood and society* (2nd ed.). New York: Norton.

Eun, J. H., Lee, K., & Wu, G. (2006). Explaining the *university-run enterprises* in China: A theoretical framework for university-industry relationship in developing countries and its application to China. *Research Policy*, *35*, 1329–1346. doi:10.1016/j.respol.2006.05.008

European Commission. (2003). *Green paper entrepreneurship in Europe*. Brussels, Belgium: Commission of the European Communities.

European Commission. (2006). *RICARDIS: Reporting intellectual capital to augment research, development and innovation in SMEs*. Brussels, Belgium.

Fagerberg, J. (2005). Innovation: A guide to the literature. In J. Fagerberg, D. C. Mowery, & R. R. elson (Eds.), *The Oxford handbook on innovation* (pp. 1-26). New York: Oxford University Press.

Fairtrade Foundation. (2008). *About fairtrade towns*. Retrieved from http://www.fairtrade.org.uk/get_involved/campaigns/fairtrade_towns/about_fairtrade_towns.aspx

Family Business Network International. (2008). Retrieved from http://www.fbn-1.com

Faulconbridge, J. (2006). Stretching tacit knowledge beyond a local fix? Global spaces of learning in advertising professional service firms. *Journal of Economic Geography*, *6*(4), 517–540. doi:10.1093/jeg/lbi023

Feldman, D. C. (1999). Toxic mentors or toxic protégés? A critical re-examination of dysfunctional mentoring. *Human Resource Management Review*, *9*(3), 247–278. doi:10.1016/S1053-4822(99)00021-2

Fiddler, L. (2000). *Facilitators and impediments to the internal transfer of team-embodied competences in firms operating in dynamic environments*. Unpublished doctoral dissertation, Boston University, Boston.

Finkelstein, L. M., Allen, T. D., & Rhoton, L. A. (2003). An examination of the role of age in mentoring relationships. *Group & Organization Management*, *28*(2), 249–281. doi:10.1177/1059601103028002004

Fischer, M. M. (2001). Innovation, knowledge creation and systems of innovation. *The Annals of Regional Science*, *35*(2), 199–216. doi:10.1007/s001680000034

Florida, R. (2002). *The rise of the creative class*. New York: Basic Books.

Foos, T., Schum, G., & Rothenberg, S. (2006). Tacit knowledge transfer and the knowledge disconnect. *Journal of Knowledge Management*, *10*(1), 6–18. doi:10.1108/13673270610650067

Ford, D. P., & Chan, Y. E. (2003). Knowledge sharing in a multicultural setting: A case study. *Knowledge Management Research and Practice*, *1*, 11–27. doi:10.1057/palgrave.kmrp.8499999

Fortes, J., & Adler, L. (1994). *Becoming a scientist in Mexico: The challenges of creating a scientific community in an underdeveloped country*. University Park, PA: The Pennsylvania State University Press.

Fraccaroli, F., & Depolo, M. (2008). Careers and aging at work. In N. Chmiel (Ed.) *An introduction to work and organizational psychology: A European perspective* (pp. 97-118). Malden, MA: Blackwell.

Frappaulo, C., & Toms, W. (1997). Knowledge management: From terra incognita to terra firma. In J. W. Cortada & J. A. Woods (Eds.), *The knowledge management yearbook 1999–2000*. Boston: Butterworth Heinemann.

Friedman, T. L. (1999). *The Lexus and the olive tree*. New York: Farrar, Straus and Giroux.

Friedman, V. J., Lipshitz, R., & Overmeer, W. (2003). Creating conditions for organizational learning. In M. Dierkes, A. Berthoin, J. Child, & I. Nonaka (Eds.), *Handbook of organizational learning & knowledge* (pp. 757-774). New York: Oxford University Press.

Fu, P. P., Tsui, A. S., & Dess, G. G. (2006). The dynamics of *guanxi* in Chinese high-tech firms: Implications for knowledge management and decision making. *Management International Review, 46*(3), 277–305. doi:10.1007/s11575-006-0048-z

Fukugawa, N. (2005). Characteristics of knowledge interactions between universities and small firms in Japan. *International Small Business Journal, 23*(4), 379–401. doi:10.1177/0266242605054052

Furst, S. A., Reeves, M., & Rosen, B. (2004). Managing the life cycle of virtual teams. *The Academy of Management Executive, 18*(2), 6–20.

Gamble, P. R., & Blackwell, J. (2001). *Knowledge management: A state of the art guide.* London: Kogan Page Lim.

Gangestad, S. W., & Snyder, M. (2000). Self-monitoring: Appraisal and reappraisal. *Psychological Bulletin, 126,* 530–555. doi:10.1037/0033-2909.126.4.530

Garud, R., & Nayyar, P. R. (1994). Transformative capacity: Continual structuring by intertemporal technology transfer. *Strategic Management Journal, 15,* 365–385. doi:10.1002/smj.4250150504

Gassmann, O., & Han, Z. (2004). Motivations and barriers of foreign R&D activities in China. *R & D Management, 34*(4), 423–437. doi:10.1111/j.1467-9310.2004.00350.x

Gayle, D. J., Tewarie, B., & White, A. Q. (2003). *Governance in the twenty-first-century university: Approaches to effective leadership and strategic management: ASHE-ERIC higher education report.* San Francisco: Jossey-Bass.

Gehle, M. (2006). *Internationales wissensmanagment.* Wiesbaden, Germany: Deutscher Universitätsverlag.

Geisler, E. (2008). *Knowledge and knowledge systems: Learning from the wonders of the mind.* Hershey, PA: IGI Publishing.

Geng, Q., Townley, C., Huang, K., & Zhang, J. (2005). Comparative knowledge management: A pilot study of Chinese and American universities. *Journal of the American Society for Information Science and Technology, 56*(10), 1031–1044. doi:10.1002/asi.20194

Gergen, J. (1991). *The saturated self.* New York: Basic Books.

Getz, D., Carlson, J., & Morrison, A. (2004). *The family business in tourism and hospitality.* Wallingford, UK: CABI Publishing.

Ghoshal, S., & Bartlett, C. A. (1988). Creation, adaptation and diffusion of innovations by subsidiaries of multinational corporations. *Journal of International Business Studies,* (Fall): 365–388. doi:10.1057/palgrave.jibs.8490388

Giddens, A. (1998). *The third way. The renewal of social democracy.* Cambridge, UK: Polity Press.

Giddens, A. (2006). We should ditch the green movement: The climate change debate is too important to be left in the hands of those who are hostile to science and technology. *The Guardian.* Retrieved from http://www.guardian.co.uk/commentisfree/2006/nov/01/post561

Gilad, B., & Gilad, T. (1998). *Business intelligence systems: A new tool for competitive advantage.* Chicago, IL: AMACOM.

Gilbert, J. (2005). *Catching the knowledge wave? The knowledge society and the future of education.* Wellington, New Zealand: NZCer Press.

Gille, B. (Ed.). (1986). *The history of techniques - volume 1.* Montreux, Switzerland: Gordon and Breach.

Gille, B. (Ed.). (1986). *The history of techniques - volume 2.* Montreux, Switzerland: Gordon and Breach.

Giroux, H. A. (2003). The corporate university and the politics of education. *Revista Praxis, 2,* 22-31. Retrieved June 15, 2007, from http://www.revistapraxis.cl/ediciones/numero2/giroux_praxis_2.htm

Gladstein, D., & Quinn, J. (1985). Making decisions and producing action: The two faces of strategy. In J. M. Pennings et al. (Eds.), *Organizational strategy and change.* San Francisco: Jossey-Bass Inc.

Glasersfeld, E. v. (1995). *Radical consructivism: A way of knowing and learning.* London: Falmer Press.

Glisby, M., & Holden, N. J. (2003). Contextual constraints in knowledge management theory: The cultural embeddedness of Nonaka's knowledge-creating company. *Knowledge and Process Management, 10*(1), 29–36. doi:10.1002/kpm.158

Goddard, A. (1998). Facing up to market forces. *Times Higher Education Supplement, 13*, 6–7.

Gold, A. H., Malhotra, A., & Segars, A. H. (2001). Knowledge management: An organizational capabilities perspective. *Journal of Management Information Systems, 18*(1), 185–214.

Goodman, E. A., Zammuto, R. F., & Gifford, B. D. (2001). The competing values framework: Understanding the impact of organizational culture on the quality of work life. *Organization Development Journal, 19*(3), 58–67.

Gopalakrishnan, S., & Santoro, M. D. (2004). Distinguishing between knowledge transfer and technology transfer activities: The role of key organizational factors. *IEEE Transactions on Engineering Management, 51*(1), 57–69. doi:10.1109/TEM.2003.822461

Goranzon, B., Ennals, R., & Hammeron, M. (2005). *Dialogue, Skill and tacit knowledge.* West Sussex, UK: Wiley & Sons.

Gordon, R. A. (1996). Impact of ingratiation on judgments and evaluations: A meta-analytic investigation. *Journal of Personality and Social Psychology, 71*(1), 54–70. doi:10.1037/0022-3514.71.1.54

Götz, K. (2002). *Wissensmanagement - zwischen wissen und nichtwissen.* Mering, Germany: Hampp Verlag.

Gourlay, S. (2004). *The SECI model of knowledge creation: Some empirical shortcomings.* Retrieved October 16, 2008, from http://kingston.eprints.org/2291/1/Gourlay%202004%20SECI.pdf

Gourlay, S. (2006). Towards conceptual clarity for 'tacit knowledge': A review of empirical studies. *Knowledge Management Research and Practice, 4*(1), 60–69. doi:10.1057/palgrave.kmrp.8500082

Granose, C. S. (2007). Gender differences in career perceptions in the people's republic of China. *Career Development International, 12*(1), 9–14. doi:10.1108/13620430710724802

Granovetter, M. S. (1973). The strength of weak ties. *American Journal of Sociology, 78*(6), 1360–1380. doi:10.1086/225469

Grant, R. M. (1996). Prospering in dynamically-competitive environments: Organizational capability as knowledge integration. *Organization Science, 7*(4), 375–387. doi:10.1287/orsc.7.4.375

Grant, R. M. (1996). Toward a knowledge-based theory of the firm. *Strategic Management Journal, 17*, 109–122. doi:10.1002/(SICI)1097-0266(199602)17:2<109::AID-SMJ796>3.0.CO;2-P

Grant, R. M. (1997). The knowledge-based view of the firm: Implications for management practice. *Long Range Planning, 30*(3), 450–454. doi:10.1016/S0024-6301(97)00025-3

Grant, R. M. (1998). *Dirección estratégica.* Madrid, Spain: Civitas.

Grant, R. M., & Baden-Fuller, C. (1995). A knowledge-based theory of inter-firm collaboration. In *Academy of Management Best Papers Proceedings* (pp. 17-21).

Grant, R. M., & Baden-Fuller, C. (2004). A knowledge accessing theory of strategic alliances. *Journal of Management Studies, 41*(1), 62–84. doi:10.1111/j.1467-6486.2004.00421.x

Green Marketing Conference. (2008). *Grange City Hotel.* Retrieved from http://www.haymarketevents.com/conferenceDetail/278

Grey, J. H., & Densten, I. L. (2005). Towards an integrative model of organizational culture and knowledge management. *International Journal of Organisational Behaviour, 9*(2), 594–603.

Griffin, D., Shaw, P., & Stacey, R. (1999). Knowing and acting in conditions of uncertainty: A complexity perspective. *Systemic Practice and Action Research, 12*(3), 295–309. doi:10.1023/A:1022403802302

Griliches, Z. (1995). R&D and productivity: Econometric results and econometric and measurement issues. In P. Stoneman (Ed.), *Handbook of the economics of innovation and technological change.* Malden, MA: Blackwell Publishing.

Gross, J. L., & Yellen, J. (2006). *Graph theory and its applications.* Boca Raton, FL: Chapman & Hall/CRC.

Gu, S.-L., & Lundvall, B. -Å. (2006). Policy learning as a key processes in the transformation of the Chinese innovation systems. In B.-Å. Lundvall, et al. (Eds.), *Asia's innovation systems in transition.* Cheltenham, UK: Edward Elgar.

Guan, J. C. (2005). Collaboration between industry and research institutes/universities on industrial innovation in Beijing, China. *Technology Analysis and Strategic Management, 17*(3), 339–353. doi:10.1080/09537320500211466

Gudykunst, W. B., & Ting-Toomey, S. (1988). *Culture and interpersonal communication.* Newbury Park, CA: Sage.

Gummer, J., & Goldsmith, Z. (2007). *Blueprint for a green economy. A report to the shadow cabinet.* Quality of Life Policy Group. Retrieved July 21, 2008, from www. qualityoflifechallenge.com/documents/fullreport-1.pdf

Gunther, R. (2007). No longer a stepchild: How the management field can come into its own. *Academy of Management Journal, 50*(6), 1365–1378.

Gupta, A. K., & Govindarajan, V. (2000). Knowledge flows within multinational corporations. *Strategic Management Journal, 21*, 473–496. doi:10.1002/(SICI)1097-0266(200004)21:4<473::AID-SMJ84>3.0.CO;2-I

Gupta, A. K., & Govindarajan, V. (2000). Knowledge management's social dimension: Lessons from Nucor Steel. *Sloan Management Review, 42*(1), 71–81.

Gupta, A. K., Smith, K. G., & Shalley, C. E. (2006). The interplay between exploration and exploitation. *Academy of Management Journal, 49*(4), 693–706.

Gupta, B., Iyer, L. S., & Aronson, J. E. (2000). Knowledge management: Practices and challenges. *Industrial Management & Data Systems, 100*(1), 17–21. doi:10.1108/02635570010273018

Guptill, J. (2005). Knowledge management in health care. *Journal of Health Care Finance, 31*, 10–14.

Gurria, A. (2008). *Competition brings prosperity* [Presentation to OECD Competition Committee]. Retrieved July 21, 2008, from http://www.oecd.org/document/3/0,3343

Gustavs, J., & Clegg, S. (2005). Working the knowledge games? Universities and corporate organizations in partnership. *Management Learning, 36*(1), 9–30. doi:10.1177/1350507605049900

Habberston, T. G., & Pistrui, J. (2004). *A model for strategic dialogue, establishing congruency in your mindset and methods.* Paper Presented at FBN-IFERA (International Family Enterprise Research Academy) Conference, Jonkoping, Sweden.

Habberston, T. G., & Williams, M. L. (1999). A resourced-based framework for assessing the strategic advantages of family firms. *Family Business Review, 12*(1), 1–22. doi:10.1111/j.1741-6248.1999.00001.x

Habberston, T. G., Williams, M. L., & MacMillan, I. (2003). Familieness: A unified systems theory of family business performance. *Journal of Business Venturing, 18*(4), 451. doi:10.1016/S0883-9026(03)00053-3

Habberston, T. G., Williams, M., & MacMillan, I. C. (2006). A unified systems perspective of family firm performance. In P. Z. Poutziouris, K. X. Smyrnios, & S. B. Klein (Eds.), *Handbook of research on family businesses.* Cheltenham, UK: Edward Elgar.

Hagen, R. (2002). Globalization, university transformation and economic regeneration. A UK case study of public/private sector partnership. *International Journal of Public Sector Management, 15*(2), 204–218. doi:10.1108/09513550210423370

Hall, A., Melin, L., & Nordqvist, M. (2006). Understanding strategizing in the family business context. In P. Z. Poutziouris, K. X. Smyrnios, & S. B. Klein (Eds.), *Handbook of research on family businesses.* Cheltenham, UK: Edward Elgar.

Hall, D. T., & Mirvis, P. H. (1995). The new career contract: Developing the whole person at midlife and beyond. *Journal of Vocational Behavior, 47*(3), 269–289. doi:10.1006/jvbe.1995.0004

Hall, E. T. (1976). *Beyond culture.* New York: Doubleday.

Hall, R. E. (1993). Macro theory and the recession of 1990-1991. *The American Economic Review, 83*(2), 275–279.

Halliday, D., Resnick, R., & Walker, J. (2007). *Fundamentals of physics.* New York, Wiley & Sons.

Hamel, G. (1991). Competition for competence and inter-partner learning within international strategic alliances. *Strategic Management Journal, 12,* 83–103. doi:10.1002/smj.4250120908

Hamel, G., & Prahalad, C. K. (1994). *Competing for the future.* Boston: Harvard Business School Press.

Hamilton, C., & Denniss, R. (2005). *Affluenza: When too much is never enough.* Crows Nest, Australia: Allen and Unwin.

Handy, C. (1993). *Understanding organizations* (4th ed.). London: Penguin Books.

Hankin, H. (2005). *The new workforce: Five sweeping trends that will shape your company's future.* New York: AMACOM.

Hansen, M. T. (1999). The search-transfer problem: The role of weak ties in sharing knowledge across organization subunits. *Administrative Science Quarterly, 44*(1), 82. doi:10.2307/2667032

Hansen, M., Nohria, N., & Tierney, T. (1999). What's your strategy for managing knowledge? *Harvard Business Review,* (March-April): 106–116.

Hansotia, B. J. (2003). Bridging the research gap between marketing academics and practitioners. *Journal of Database Marketing & Consumer Strategy Management, 11*(2), 114–120. doi:10.1057/palgrave.dbm.3240212

Hansson, F. (2007). Science parks as knowledge organizations – the "ba" in action? *European Journal of Innovation Management, 10*(3), 348–366. doi:10.1108/14601060710776752

Harding, R. (2006). *Family business specialist summary.* GEM Consulting for the Institute of Family Business

Harkins, P., Carter, L. L., & Timmins, A. J. (2000). *Linkage Inc.'s best practices in knowledge management and organizational learning handbook: Case studies instruments models research.* Lexington, MA: Linkage Incorporated.

Harorimana, D. (2007). Boundary spanners and networks of knowledge: Developing a knowledge creation and transfer model. In D. Remenyi (Ed.), *Proceedings of the Academic Conferences International* (pp. 430-435).

Harorimana, D. (2008). *An investigation into the role of gatekeepers in the knowledge transfer process: A study based on manufacturing high tech industries, financial and R&D Firms.* Unpublished doctoral thesis, Nottingham Trent University and Southampton Solent University, Southampton, UK

Harorimana, D. (2008). Leading firms as knowledge gatekeepers in a networked environment. In E. Bollisani (Ed.), *Building the knowledge society on the Internet: Sharing and exchanging knowledge in networked environments* (pp. 260-281). Hershey, PA: Information Science Reference.

Harorimana, D. (2008). Understanding the role of knowledge gatekeepers in knowledge identification, translation and transfer process: Some empirical evidences. In *Proceedings of the European Conference on Knowledge Management,* Southampton Solent University.

Harrington, B., & Hall, D. T. (2007). *Career management & work-life integration: Using self-assessment to navigate contemporary careers.* Thousand Oaks, CA: Sage.

Hartman, S. J., & Yrle, A. C. (1996). Can the hobo phenomenon help explain voluntary turnover? *International Journal of Contemporary Hospitality Management, 8*(4), 11–16. doi:10.1108/09596119610119930

Hasu, M., Helle, M., & Kerosuo, H. (2005). *Ethnography in expansion – emergent trends and future challenges.*

Paper presented at the First ISCA Congress, Seville.

Hatch, M., & Schultz, M. (1997). Relations between culture, identity and image. *European Journal of Marketing, 31*(5/6), 356–365. doi:10.1108/eb060636

Hedge, J. W., Borman, W. C., & Lammlein, S. E. (2006). *The aging workforce: Realities, myths, and implications for organizations*. Washington, DC: American Psychological Association.

Hedlund, G., & Nonaka, I. (1993). Models of knowledge management in the West and Japan. In P. Lorange, B. Chakravarthy, J. Roos, & A. van Der Ven (Eds.), *Implementing strategic processes: Change, learning and cooperation*. Oxford, UK: Blackwell Business.

Heikkinen, J., Blomqvist, K., & Hong, J. Z. (2007). *Ba for knowledge creation in Sino-Western university-industry collaboration*. Paper presented in the Conference of EBRF 2007 - Research Forum to Understand Business in Knowledge Society, Agora - Jyväskylä, Finland.

Heinen, S. J., & O'Neill, C. (2000). Managing talent to maximise performance. *Employment Relations Today, 31*(2), 67–82. doi:10.1002/ert.20018

Heisig, P. (2000). Process modelling for knowledge management. In *Proceedings of the EKAW Workshop on Common Approaches on Knowledge Management, 12th International Conference on Knowledge Engineering and Knowledge Management*.

Helfat, E., Finkelstein, S., Mitchell, W., Peteraf, M. A., Singh, H., Teece, D. J., & Winter, S. G. (2007). *Dynamic capabilities: Understanding strategic change in organizations*. Malden, MA: Blackwell Publishing.

Hermans, H. J. M., & Kempen, H. J. G. (1998). Moving cultures: The perilous problems of cultural dichotomies in a globalizing society. *The American Psychologist, 53*(10), 1111–1120. doi:10.1037/0003-066X.53.10.1111

Hermans, J., & Castiaux, A. (2007). Knowledge creation though university/industry collaborative research projects. [Retrieved from http://www.ejkm.com]. *Electronic Journal of Knowledge Management, 5*(1), 43–54.

Hernández, R., Fernández, C., & Baptista, P. (2003). *Metodología de la investigación*. Mexico City, Mexico: McGraw-Hill Interamericana.

Herschbach, D. R. (1995). Technology as knowledge: Implications for instruction. *Journal of Technology Education, 7*(1), 14–24.

Herschbach, D. R. (1996). Defining technology education. *The Journal of Technology Studies, 22*(2), 6–9.

Herschbach, D. R. (1997). From industrial arts to technology education: The eclipse of purpose. *The Journal of Technology Studies, 23*(2), 20–28.

Higgins, M. C., & Kram, K. E. (2001). Reconceptualizing mentoring at work: A developmental network perspective. *Academy of Management Review, 26*(2), 264–289. doi:10.2307/259122

Hildreth, P. M., & Kimble, C. (2002). The duality of knowledge. *Information Research, 8*(1). Retrieved August 15, 2008, from http://informationr.net/ir/8-1/paper142.html

Hinkin, T. R., & Tracey, J. B. (2000). The cost of turnover. *The Cornell Hotel and Restaurant Administration Quarterly, 41*(3), 14–21.

Hislop, D. (2005). *Knowledge management in organizations*. Oxford, UK: Oxford University Press.

Hjalager, A. M., & Andersen, S. (2001). Tourism employment: Contingent work or professional career? *Employee Relations, 23*(2), 115–129. doi:10.1108/01425450110384165

Hocking, J. B., Brown, M., & Harzing, A. (2007). Balancing global and local strategic contexts: Expatriate knowledge transfer, applications, and learning within a transnational organization. *Human Resource Management, 46*(4), 513–533. doi:10.1002/hrm.20180

Hoe, S. L. (2006). Tacit knowledge, Nonaka and Takeuchi SECI model and informal knowledge processes. *International Journal of Organization Theory and Behavior, 9*(4), 490–502.

Hofstede, G. (1980). *Culture's consequences: International differences in work-related values*. Beverly Hills, CA: Sage Publications.

Hofstede, G. (1991). *Culture and organizations: Software of the mind*. New York: McGraw-Hill.

Hofstede, G. (1997). *Cultures and organizations: Software of the mind: Intercultural cooperation and its importance for survival*. New York: McGraw-Hill.

Hofstede, G., & Bond, M. (1988). The Confucian connection: From cultural roots to economic growth. *Organizational Dynamics, 16*(4), 4–21. doi:10.1016/0090-2616(88)90009-5

Hohl, A., & Tisdell, C. (1995). Peripheral tourism: Development and management. *Annals of Tourism Research, 22*(3), 517–534. doi:10.1016/0160-7383(95)00005-Q

Holden, N. (2001). Knowledge management: Raising the spectre of the cross-cultural dimension. *Knowledge and Process Management, 8*(30), 155. doi:10.1002/kpm.117

Holden, N. J. (2002). *Cross-cultural management: A knowledge management perspective*. Harlow, UK: Pearson Education.

Holden, N., & Von Kortzfleisch, H. F. O. (2004). Why cross-cultural knowledge transfer is a form of translation in more ways than you think. *Knowledge and Process Management, 11*(2), 127–136. doi:10.1002/kpm.198

Hollander, E. P. (1958). Conformity, status, and idiosyncrasy credit. *Psychological Review, 65*, 117–127. doi:10.1037/h0042501

Holsapple, C. W., & Joshi, K. D. (1999). Description and analysis of existing knowledge management frameworks. In *Proceedings of the 32nd Hawaii International Conference on System Sciences*.

Holsapple, C. W., & Joshi, K. D. (1999). Knowledge selection: Concepts, issues, and technologies. In J. Liebowitz (Ed.), *Handbook on knowledge management*. Boca Raton, FL: CRC Press.

Holsapple, C. W., & Joshi, K. D. (2004). A formal knowledge management ontology: Conduct, activities, resources, and influences. *Journal of the American Society for Information Science and Technology, 55*(7), 593–612. doi:10.1002/asi.20007

Holsapple, C. W., & Joshi, K. D. (2004). Exploring primary activities of the knowledge chain. *Knowledge and Process Management, 11*(3), 155–174. doi:10.1002/kpm.200

Holsapple, C. W., & Joshi, K. D. (2005). Exploring secondary activities of the knowledge chain. *Knowledge and Process Management, 12*(1), 3–31. doi:10.1002/kpm.219

Holsapple, C. W., & Singh, M. (2001). The knowledge chain model: Activities for competitiveness. *Expert Systems with Applications, 20*, 77–98. doi:10.1016/S0957-4174(00)00050-6

Hong, J. Z., & Engeström, Y. (2004). Changing communication principles between Chinese managers and workers: Confucian authority chains and *guanxi* as social networking. *Management Communication Quarterly, 17*, 552–585. doi:10.1177/0893318903262266

Hong, J. Z., Kianto, A., & Kyläheiko, K. (2008). Moving culture and the creation of new knowledge and dynamic capabilities in emerging markets. *Knowledge and Process Management, 15*(3), 196–202. doi:10.1002/kpm.310

Hong, J., Heikkinen, J., & Niemi, M. (2007). Collaborative knowledge creation and innovation between MNCs and Chinese universities, In B. Martins & D. Remenyi (Eds.), *Proceedings of the 8th European Conference on Knowledge Management, 1* (pp. 486-449). Barcelona, Spain: Consorci Escola Industrial de Barcelona.

Horng, D., & Hsueh, C. (2005). How to improve efficiency in transfer of scientific knowledge from university to firms: The case of universities in Taiwan. *Journal of American Academy of Business, Cambridge, 7*(2), 187–190.

House, R. J., Hanges, P. J., Javidan, M., Dorfman, P. W., & Gupta, V. (2004). *Culture, leadership, and organizations: The GLOBE study of 62 societies*. Thousand Oaks, CA: Sage.

Howard, L. W. (1998). Validating the competing values model as a representation of organizational cultures. *The International Journal of Organizational Analysis, 6*(3), 231–250. doi:10.1108/eb028886

HSBC. (2008). *Global website*. Retrieved from http://www.hsbc.com

Huang, K. T. (1997). Capitalizing collective knowledge for winning, execution and teamwork. *Journal of Knowledge Management, 1*(2). doi:10.1108/EUM0000000004590

Huff, L., & Kelley, L. (2003). Levels of organizational trust in individualist versus collectivist societies: A seven-nation study. *Organization Science, 14*(1), 81–90. doi:10.1287/orsc.14.1.81.12807

Huggins, R., Demirag, M., & Ratcheva, V. I. (2007). Global knowledge and R&D foreign direct investment flows: Recent patterns in Asia Pacific, Europe, and North America. *International Review of Applied Economics, 21*(3), 437–451. doi:10.1080/02692170701390437

Hummert, M. L., Garstka, T. A., Ryan, E. B., & Bonneson, J. L. (2004). The role of age stereotypes in interpersonal communication. In J. F. Nussbaum & J. Coupland (Eds.), *Handbook of communication and aging research* (pp. 91-114). Mahwah, NJ: Lawrence Erlbaum Associates.

Ichijo, K. (2007). Enabling knowledge-based competence of a corporation. In K. Ichijo & I. Nonaka (Eds.), *Knowledge creation and management: New challenges for managers* (pp. 83-96). New York: Oxford University Press.

Ichijo, K., Krogh, G., & Nonaka, I. (1998). Knowledge enablers. In G. Von Krogh, J. Roos, & D. Kleine (Eds.), *Knowing in firms*. London: SAGE Publications.

Ilgen, A. (2001). *Wissensmanagement im großanlagenbau. Ganzheitlicher ansatz und empirische prüfung.* Wiesbaden, Germany: Deutscher Universitätsverlag.

Ingersoll-Dayton, B., & Saengtienchai, C. (1999). Respect for the elderly in Asia: Stability and change. *International Journal of Aging & Human Development, 48*(2), 113–130.

Inkpen, A. (2008). Knowledge transfer and international joint ventures: The case of Nummi and General Motors. *Strategic Management Journal, 29*, 447–453. doi:10.1002/smj.663

Institute for Family Business. (2008). *The UK family business sector: An Institute for Family Business report.* Capital Economics Institute for Family Business. (2007). *Key facts on the UK family business economy, fact sheet.* London: The Institute for Family Business.

ISO. (2007). *Discover ISO - who standards benefit*. Retrieved December 2007, from http://www.iso.org

Jackson, C., Colquitt, J. A., Wesson, M., & Zapata-Phelan, C. (2006). Psychological collectivism: A measurement validation and linkage to group member performance. *The Journal of Applied Psychology, 91*(4), 884–899. doi:10.1037/0021-9010.91.4.884

James, O. (2007). *Affluenza*. London: Vermillion.

Jarvenpaa, S. L., & Staples, S. D. (2001). Exploring perceptions of organizational ownership and expertise. *Journal of Management Information Systems, 18*(1), 151–184.

Järvilehto, T. (1998). The theory of the organism-environment system: I. Description of the theory. [from http://wwwedu.oulu.fi/homepage/tjarvile]. *Integrative Physiological and Behavioral Science, 33*, 321–334. Retrieved March 2006. doi:10.1007/BF02688700

Järvilehto, T. (1998). The theory of the organism-environment system: II. Significance of nervous activity in the organism-environment system. [from http://wwwedu.oulu.fi/homepage/tjarvile]. *Integrative Physiological and Behavioral Science, 33*, 335–343. Retrieved March 2006. doi:10.1007/BF02688701

Järvilehto, T. (1999). The theory of the organism-environment system: III. Role of efferent influences on receptors in the formation of knowledge. [from http://wwwedu.oulu.fi/homepage/tjarvile]. *Integrative Physiological and Behavioral Science, 34*, 90–100. Retrieved March 2006. doi:10.1007/BF02688715

Järvilehto, T. (2000). Feeling as knowing: Emotion as reorganization of the organism-environment system. *Consciousness & Emotion, 1*(2), 53-65. Retrieved March 2006, from http://wwwedu.oulu.fi/homepage/tjarvile

Järvilehto, T. (2000). The theory of the organism-environment system: IV. The problem of mental activity and consciousness. [from http://wwwedu.oulu.fi/homepage/tjarvile]. *Integrative Physiological and Behavioral Science, 35*, 35–57. Retrieved March 2006. doi:10.1007/BF02911165

Jennewein, K. (2005). *Intellectual property management.* Heidelberg, Germany: Physica Verlag.

Jennex, M. (Ed.). (2005). *Case studies in knowledge management.* Hershey, PA: Idea Group Publishing.

Jennex, M., Olfman, L., & Pituma, P. (1998). An organizational memory information systems success model: An extension of DeLone and McLean's I/S success model. In *Proceedings of the 31ˢᵗ Annual Hawaii International Conference on System Sciences.*

Jischa, M. F. (2008). Management trotz nichtwissen. In A. von Gleich & S. Gößling-Reisemann (Eds.), *Industrial ecology* (pp. 271-283). Wiesbaden, Germany: Vieweg+Teubner.

Johannessen, J. A., Olsen, B., & Lumpkin, G. T. (2001). Innovation as newness: What is new, how new, and new to whom? *European Journal of Innovation Management, 4*(1), 20–31. doi:10.1108/14601060110365547

Johannessen, J., Olaisen, J., & Olsen, B. (2001). Mismanagement of tacit knowledge: The importance of tacit knowledge, the danger of information technology and what to do about it. *International Journal of Information Management, 21*, 3–20. doi:10.1016/S0268-4012(00)00047-5

Johnson, B., Lorenz, E., & Lundvall, B.-Å. (2002). Why all this fuss about codified and tacit knowledge? *Industrial and Corporate Change, 11*(2), 245–262. doi:10.1093/icc/11.2.245

Johnson, J., & Paper, D. J. (1998). An exploration of empowerment and organizational memory. *Journal of Managerial Issues, 10*(4), 503.

Johnson, V., & Peppas, S. C. (2003). Crisis management in Belgium: The case of Coca Cola. *Corporate Communications: An International Journal, 8*(1), 18–22. doi:10.1108/13563280310458885

Johnson, W. H. A., & Johnson, D. A. (2004). Organisational knowledge creating processes and the performance of university-industry collaborative projects. *International Journal of Technology Management, 27*(1), 93–114. doi:10.1504/IJTM.2004.003883

John-Steiner, V. (2000). *Creative collaboration.* New York: Oxford University Press.

Johnston, S., & Paladino, A. (2007). Knowledge management and involvement in innovations in MNC subsidiaries. *Management International Review, 47*(2), 281–302. doi:10.1007/s11575-007-0016-2

Jolliffe, L., & Farnsworth, R. (2003). Seasonality in tourism employment: Human resource challenges. *International Journal of Contemporary Hospitality Management, 15*(6), 312–316. doi:10.1108/09596110310488140

Jones, O. (2003). Competitive advantage in SMEs: Towards a conceptual framework. In O. Jones & F. Tilley (Eds.), *Competitive advantage in SMEs.* Chicester, UK: Wiley.

Joseph, M. F. (2001). Key issues in knowledge management. *Knowledge and Innovation: Journal of the Knowledge Management Consortium International, 1*(3), 231–250.

Joynt, P., & Warner, M. (1996). *Managing across cultures.* London: Thomson Business Press.

Kachra, A., & White, R. (2008). Know-how transfer: The role of social, economic/competitive and firm boundary factors. *Strategic Management Journal, 29*, 425–445. doi:10.1002/smj.668

Kagiticibasi, C. (1997). Individualism and collectivism. In J. W. Berry, M. H. Segall, & C. Kagiticibasi (Eds.), *Handbook of cross-cultural psychology* (pp. 1-50). Needham Heights, MA: Allyn & Bacon.

Kakabadse, N. K., Kouzmin, A., & Kakabadse, A. (2001). From tacit knowledge to knowledge management:

Leveraging invisible assets. *Knowledge and Process Management*, *8*(3), 137–154. doi:10.1002/kpm.120

Kalla, H. K. (2005). Integrated internal communications: A multidisciplinary perspective. *Corporate Communications: An International Journal*, *10*(4), 302–314. doi:10.1108/13563280510630106

Kankanhalli, A., & Tan, B. C. (2004). A review of metrics for knowledge management systems and knowledge management initiatives. In *Proceedings of the 37th Hawaii International Conference on System Sciences.*

Karatepe, O. M., & Kilic, H. (2007). Relationships of supervisor support and conflicts in the work-family interface with the selected job outcomes of frontline employees. *Tourism Management*, *28*(1), 238–252. doi:10.1016/j.tourman.2005.12.019

Karatepe, O. M., & Uludag, O. (2008). Affectivity, conflicts in the work-family interface, and hotel employee outcomes. *International Journal of Hospitality Management*, *27*(1), 30–41. doi:10.1016/j.ijhm.2007.07.001

Kauffman, N. (1987). Motivating the older worker. *SAM Advanced Management Journal*, *52*(2), 43–48.

Kayes, D. C., Kayes, A., & Yamazaki, Y. (2005). Essential competencies for cross-cultural knowledge. *Journal of Managerial Psychology*, *20*(7), 578–589. doi:10.1108/02683940510623399

Ketchen, D., Thomas, J., & Mcdaniel, R. (1996). Process, content and context: Synergistic effects on organizational performance. *Journal of Management*, *22*, 231–257. doi:10.1016/S0149-2063(96)90048-3

Kets de Vries, M. F. R., & Carlock, R. S. with Florent-Treacy, E. (2007). *Family business on the couch.* Chichester, UK: Wiley.

Khavul, S., Bruton, G. D., Zheng, C. C., & Wood, E. (2007). Learning during and after internationalization by entrepreneurial firms from emerging economies. *Academy of Management Proceedings*, 1-6.

Kianto, A. (2007). What do we really mean by the dynamic dimension of intellectual capital? *International Journal of Learning and Intellectual Capital*, *4*(4), 342–356. doi:10.1504/IJLIC.2007.016332

Kidwell, J. J., Vander Linde, K. M., & Johnson, S. L. (2000). Applying corporate knowledge management practices in higher education. *EDUCAUSE Quarterly*, *23*(4), 28–33.

Kilmann, R. H., & Saxton, M. J. (1983). *Kilmann-Saxton cultural gap survey.* Pittsburgh, PA: Organization Design Consultants.

Kim, D., & Lannon, C. P. (1994). *A pocket guide to using archetypes.* Waltham, MA: Pegasus Communications Inc.

Kim, U., & Yamaguchi, S. (1995). Cross-cultural research methodology and approach: Implications for the advancement of Japanese social psychology. *Research in Social Psychology*, *10*, 168–179.

Kim, Y. G., Yu, S. H., & Lee, J. H. (2003). Knowledge strategy planning: Methodology and case. *Expert Systems with Applications*, *24*, 295–307. doi:10.1016/S0957-4174(02)00158-6

King, W. R. (2007). A research agenda for the relationships between culture and knowledge management. *Knowledge and Process Management*, *14*(3), 226–236. doi:10.1002/kpm.281

Klingenberg, B., & Watson, K. (2003). Problem analysis: Intellectual property exchange between two partner companies - an application of the theory of constraints thinking processes. In E. Omojokun (Ed.), *Proceedings of the 33rd Annual Meeting of the Southeast Decision Sciences Institute,* Williamsburg, VA (pp. 112-114).

Kluckhohn, F. R., & Strodtbeck, F. L. (1961). *Variations in value orientations.* Evanston, IL: Row, Peterson and Company.

Ko, D. G., Kirsch, L. J., & King, W. R. (2005). Antecedents for knowledge transfer from consultants to clients in enterprising system implementations. *MIS Quarterly*, *29*, 59–85.

Kochan, F. K., & Pescarelli, P. T. (2003). Culture, context, and issues of change related to mentoring programs and relationships. In F. K. Kochan & P. T. Pescarelli (Eds.) *Global perspectives on mentoring: Transform-*

ing contexts, communities, and cultures (pp. 417-428). Greenwich, London: Information Age.

Kodama, M. (2003). Knowledge creation through the synthesizing capability of networked strategic communities: Case study on new product development in Japan. *Knowledge Management Research & Practice, 1*, 77–85. doi:10.1057/palgrave.kmrp.8500012

Kodama, M. (2005). New knowledge creation through dialectical leadership: A case of IT and multimedia business in Japan. *European Journal of Innovation Management, 8*(1), 31–55. doi:10.1108/14601060510578565

Kogut, B., & Zander, U. (1996). What firms do? Coordination, identity, and learning. *Organization Science, 7*(5), 502–518. doi:10.1287/orsc.7.5.502

Kohlbacher, F., & Krähe, M. O. B. (2007). Knowledge creation and transfer in a cross-cultural context – empirical evidence from Tyco Flow Control. *Knowledge and Process Management, 14*(3), 169–181. doi:10.1002/kpm.282

Kolb, D. A. (1984). *Experiental learning: Experience as the source of learning.* Englewood Cliffs, NJ: Prentice Hall.

Koschatzky, K. (2002). Networking and knowledge transfer between research and industry in transition countries: Empirical evidence from Slovenian innovation system. *The Journal of Technology Transfer, 27*(1), 27–38. doi:10.1023/A:1013192402977

Kotabe, M., Dunlap-Hinckle, D., & Mishra, H. (2007). Determinants of cross national knowledge transfer and its effect on firm performance. *Journal of International Business Studies, 38*, 259–282. doi:10.1057/palgrave.jibs.8400261

Kotabe, M., Martin, X., & Domoto, H. (2003). Gaining knowledge from vertical partnerships: Knowledge transfer, relationship duration and supplier performance improvement in the U.S. and Japanese automotive industries. *Strategic Management Journal, 42*, 293–316. doi:10.1002/smj.297

Kotter, J. P., & Heskett, J. L. (1992). *Corporate culture and performance.* New York: The Free Press.

Krackhardt, D., & Porter, W. E. (1985). When friends leave: A structural analysis of the relationship between turnover and stayers attitudes. *Administrative Science Quarterly, 30*, 242–261. doi:10.2307/2393107

Krackhart, D., & Porter, W. E. (1986). The snowball effect: Turnover embedded in communication networks. *The Journal of Applied Psychology, 71*(1), 50–55. doi:10.1037/0021-9010.71.1.50

Kram, K. E. (1985). *Mentoring process at work: Developmental relationships in organizational life,* Glenview, IL: Scott, Foresman.

Kransdorff, A., & Williams, R. (2000). Managing organizational memory (OM): The new competitive imperative. *Organization Development Journal, 18*(1), 107.

Kroes, P. (1998). Technological explanations: The relation between structure and function of technological objects. *Philosophy and Technology, 3*(3).

Krome-Hamilton, M. (2005/2006). The transformation of heterogenous individual learning into organizational knowledge: A cognitive perspective. *International Journal of Knowledge . Culture and Change Management, 5*, 59–68.

Krugman, P. (1991). Increasing returns and economic geography. *The Journal of Political Economy, 99*(3), 483–499. doi:10.1086/261763

Kubeck, J. E., Delp, N. D., Haslett, T. K., & McDaniel, M. A. (1996). Does job-related training performance decline with age? *Psychology and Aging, 11*(1), 92–107. doi:10.1037/0882-7974.11.1.92

Kubota, H., & Nishida, T. (2003). Channel design for strategic knowledge interaction. In . *Proceedings of the KES, 2003*, 1037–1043.

Kucza, T. (2001). *Knowledge management process model.* Technical Research Centre of Finland, Finland: VTT Publications 455.

Kuhlin, B., & Thielmann, H. (2005). *Real-time enterprise in der praxis.* Berlin, Germany: Springer Verlag.

Kuhn, T. S. (1972). *The structure of scientific revolutions.* Chicago: University of Chicago Press.

Kurman, J. (2001). Self-enhancement: Is it restricted to individualistic cultures? *Personality and Social Psychology Bulletin, 27*(12), 1705–1716. doi:10.1177/01461672012712013

Kutinlahti, P. (2005). *Universities approaching market: Intertwining scientific and entrepreneurial goals.* Helsinki, Finland: Faculty of Social Sciences of the University of Helsinki.

Kvist, A., & Klefsjo, B. (2006). Which service quality dimensions are important in inbound tourism?: A case study in a peripheral location. *Managing Service Quality, 16*(5), 520–537. doi:10.1108/09604520610686151

Kwan, P., & Walker, A. (2004). Validating the competing values model as a representation of organizational culture through inter-institutional comparisons. *Organizational Analysis, 12*(1), 21–37. doi:10.1108/eb028984

Ladkin, A., & Juwaheer, T. D. (2000). The career paths of hotel general managers in Mauritius. *International Journal of Contemporary Hospitality Management, 12*(2), 119–125. doi:10.1108/09596110010309925

Lahaie, D. (2005). The impact of corporate memory loss: What happens when a senior executive leaves? *Leadership in Health Services, 18*(3), 35–48. doi:10.1108/13660750510611198

Lai, P. C., & Baum, T. (2005). Just-in-time labour supply in the hotel sector: The role of agencies. *Employee Relations, 27*(1), 86–102. doi:10.1108/01425450510569328

Lam, A. (1997). Embedded firms, embedded knowledge: Problems of collaboration and knowledge transfer in global cooperative ventures. *Organization Studies, 18*(6), 973–996. doi:10.1177/017084069701800604

Lambert, R. (2003). *Lambert review of business-university collaboration: Final report.* London: HM Treasury.

Lambooy, J. G. (2004). The transmission of knowledge, emerging networks, and the role of university: An evolutionary approach. *European Planning Studies, 12*(5), 643–657. doi:10.1080/0965431042000219996

Lamond, D. (2003). The value of Quinn's competing values model in an Australian context. *Journal of Managerial Psychology, 18*(1), 46–59. doi:10.1108/02683940310459583

Latour, B. (1987). *Science in action.* Cambridge, MA: Harvard University Press.

Laudon, K., & Laudon, J. (1999). *Management information systems-organization and technology in the networked enterprise.* Englewood Cliffs, NJ: Prentice Hall.

Lave, J., & Wenger, E. (1991). *Situated learning legitimate peripheral participation.* Cambridge, UK: Cambridge University Press.

Laverde, G. P. (2003). *Administração hospitalar.* Rio de Janeiro, Brazil: Guanabara Koogan.

Law, J. (1987). Technology and heterogeneous engineering: The case of the Portuguese expansion. In W. Bijker, T. Pinch, & T. Hughes (Eds.), *The social construction of technological systems: New directions in the sociology and history of technology.* Cambridge, MA: MIT Press.

Law, J. (2000). *Objects, spaces, others.* Retrieved March 30, 2006, from http://www.comp.lancaster.ac.uk/sociology/soc027jl.html

Law, J., & Singleton, V. (2000). *This is not an object.* Retrieved March 30, 2006, from http://www.comp.lancs.ac.uk/sociology/soc032jl.html

Lawson, S. (2003). *Examing the relationship between organizational culture and knowledge management.* Unpublished doctoral dissertation, The Wayne Huizenga School of Business and Entrepreneurship, Nova Southeastern University, Florida.

Lawton, G. (2001). Knowledge management: Ready for prime time? *IEEE Computer, 34*(2), 12–14.

Leary, M. R., & Kowalski, R. M. (1990). Impression management: A literature review and two-component model. *Psychological Bulletin, 107*(1), 34–47. doi:10.1037/0033-2909.107.1.34

Lee, C. K., Foo, S., & Goh, D. (2006). On the concept and types of knowledge. *Journal of Information & Knowledge Management, 5*(2), 151–163. doi:10.1142/S0219649206001402

Lee, C., & Moreo, P. J. (2007). What do seasonal lodging operators need to know about seasonal workers? *International Journal of Hospitality Management, 26*(1), 148–160. doi:10.1016/j.ijhm.2005.11.001

Lee, D. S., Lim, G. H., & Lim, W. S. (2003). Family business succession: Appropriation risk and choice of successor. *Academy of Management Review, 28*(4), 657–666.

Lee, E. (1966). A theory of migration. *Demography, 3*, 47–57. doi:10.2307/2060063

Lee, Y. S. (1996). Technology transfer and the research university: A search for the boundaries of university-industry collaboration. *Research Policy, 25*, 843–863. doi:10.1016/0048-7333(95)00857-8

Lee-Ross, D. (1998). Comment: Australia and the small to medium-sized hotel sector. *International Journal of Contemporary Hospitality Management, 10*(5), 177–179. doi:10.1108/09596119810227703

Leigh, T. W., & Summers, J. O. (2002). An initial evaluation of industrial buyers' impressions of salespersons' nonverbal cues. *Journal of Personal Selling & Sales Management, 22*(1), 41–53.

Leiponen, A. (2006). Managing knowledge for innovation: The case of business-to-business services. *Journal of Product Innovation Management, 23*(3), 238–258. doi:10.1111/j.1540-5885.2006.00196.x

Lembke, G. (2005). *Wissenskooperation in wissensgemeinschaften*. Wiesbaden, Germany: LearnAct.

Leonard, D., & Swap, W. (2005). *Deep smarts: How to cultivate and transfer enduring business wisdom*. Boston: Harvard Business School Press.

Leonard-Barton, D. (1988). Implementation as mutual adaptation of technology organisation. *Research Policy, 17*, 251–267. doi:10.1016/0048-7333(88)90006-6

Leonard-Barton, D., & Sensiper, S. (1998). The role of tacit knowledge in group innovation. *California Management Review, 40*(3), 112–134.

Leung, K., Bhagat, R. S., Buchan, N. R., Erez, M., & Gibson, C. B. (2005). Culture and international business: Recent advances and their implications for future research. *Journal of International Business Studies, 36*, 357–378. doi:10.1057/palgrave.jibs.8400150

Lev, B. (2001). *Intangibles: Management, measurement and reporting*. Washington, DC: Brookings Institution Press.

Levine, A. E. (2000, October 7). The future of colleges: 9 inevitable changes. *Chronicle of Higher Education*.

Levinson, D. J., Darrow, C. N., Klein, E. B., Levinson, M. H., & McKee, B. (1978), *The seasons of a man's life*. New York: Alfred A. Knopf.

Lewin, R., & Regine, B. (1999). *The soul at work: Unleashing the power of complexity science for business success*. London: Orion.

Li, J. D. (2005). *A study on R&D collaboration between MNCs and Chinese universities* (in Chinese). Unpublished master's thesis, Tsinghua University, China.

Li, J., & Zhong, J. (2003). Explaining the growth of international R&D alliances in China. *Managerial and Decision Economics, 24*, 101–115. doi:10.1002/mde.1079

Li, M., & Gao, F. (2003). Why Nonaka highlights tacit knowledge: A critical review. *Journal of Knowledge Management, 7*(4), 6–14. doi:10.1108/13673270310492903

Li, S., & Scullion, H. (2006). Bridging the distance: Managing cross-border knowledge holders. *Asia Pacific Journal of Management, 23*, 71–92. doi:10.1007/s10490-006-6116-x

Liden, R. C., & Mitchell, T. R. (1988). Ingratiatory behaviour in organizational settings. *Academy of Management Review, 13*, 572–587. doi:10.2307/258376

Liebowitz, J. (2000). *Building organizational intelligence*. Boca Raton, FL: CRC Press.

Lienhard, J. H. (2000). *The engines of our ingenuity. An engineer looks at technology and culture.* New York: Oxford University Press.

Lin, L. (2005). *Study on the university-enterprise knowledge alliance based on the theory of knowledge activity system* (in Chinese). Unpublished doctoral dissertation, Dalian University of Technology: Dalian.

Linde, C. (2001). Narrative and social tacit knowledge. *Journal of Knowledge Management, 5*(2), 160–171. doi:10.1108/13673270110393202

Lindqvist, J., Blomqvist, K., & Saarenketo, S. (2007). The role of sales subsidiary in MNC innovativeness - Explorative study and emerging issues on knowledge transfer. In R.R. Sinkovics and M. Yamin (Eds), *Anxieties and Management Responses in International Business.* Houndmills, Basingstoke, UK: Palgrave MacMillan.

Lippman, S. A., & Rumelt, R. P. (1982). Uncertain imitability: An analysis of interfirm differences in efficiency under competition. *The Bell Journal of Economics, 13*(2), 418–439. doi:10.2307/3003464

Lissack, M., & Roos, J. (1999). *The next common sense.* London: Nicholas Brealey.

Liu, X., & Shaffer, M. (2005). An investigation of expatriate adjustment and performance: a social capital perspective. *International Journal of Cross Cultural Management, 5*(3), 235–254. doi:10.1177/1470595805058411

Livingstone, D. W., & Sawchuck, P. H. (2004). *Hidden knowledge.* Aurora, Ontario: Garamond.

Lopez -Martinez, E. et al. (1994). Motivations and obstacles to university-industry coop eration (UIC): A Mexican case. *R & D Management, 24*(2), 17.

Luby, A. (1999). Accrediting teaching in higher education – voices crying in the wilderness. *Quality Assurance in Higher Education, 7*(4), 216–223. doi:10.1108/09684889910297721

Lucas, L. (2006). The role of culture on knowledge transfer: The case of the multinational corporation. *The Learning Organization, 13*(3), 257–275. doi:10.1108/09696470610661117

Lucas, R. (1993). Making a miracle. *Econometrica, 61*(2), 251–272. doi:10.2307/2951551

Lueddeke, G. (1998). UK higher education at a crossroads: Reflections on issues and practice in teaching and learning. *Innovations in Education and Training International, 35*(2), 108–116.

Lumsden, C. J., & Wilson, E. O. (1981). *Genes, mind, and culture: The coevolutionary process.* Cambridge, MA: Harvard University Press.

Lundvall, B., & Nielsen, P. (2007). Knowledge management and innovation performance. *International Journal of Manpower, 28*(3/4), 207–223. doi:10.1108/01437720710755218

Lundvall, B.-Å., & Johnson, B. (1994). The learning economy. *Journal of Industry Studies, 2*, 23–42.

Luo, Y. D. (1997). *Guanxi:* Principles, philosophies, and implications. *Human Systems Management, 16*(1), 43–51.

Luu, N., Wykes, J., Williams, P., & Weir, T. (2001). *Invisible value: The case for measuring and reporting intellectual capital.* Canberra, Australia: Commonwealth of Australia, Department of Industry Science and Resources.

Lynch, R. (2006). *Corporate strategy.* Harlow, UK: Pearson Education Ltd.

Lynn, M. (2002). Turnover's relationships with sales, tips and service across restaurants in a chain. *International Journal of Hospitality Management, 21*(4), 443–447. doi:10.1016/S0278-4319(02)00026-9

MacHatton, M. T., & Dyke, T. V. (1997). Selection and retention of managers in the US restaurant sector. *International Journal of Contemporary Hospitality Management, 9*(4), 155–160. doi:10.1108/09596119710185837

Maier, R. (2002). *Knowledge management systems: Information and communication technologies for knowledge management.* Berlin, Germany: Springer-Verlag.

Maier, R. (2002). State-of-practice of knowledge management systems: Results of an empirical study. *Upgrade, 3*(1), 15–23.

Maier, R., & Remus, U. (2003). Implementing process-oriented knowledge management strategies. *Journal of Knowledge Management, 7*(4), 62–74. doi:10.1108/13673270310492958

Malone, M. (1997). New metrics for a new age. *Forbes Magazine, 7.*

Manley, H. (1996). Hospitality head hunting. *Australian Hotelier,* 8-11.

Manville, B., & Foote, N. (1996). Strategy as if knowledge mattered. *FastCompany, 2,* 66-68. Retrieved February 1, 2008, from http://www.fastcompany.com/magazine/02/stratsec.html

March, J. G. (1991). Exploration and exploitation in organizational learning . *Organization Science, 2*(1), 71–86. doi:10.1287/orsc.2.1.71

March, J. G. (1999). The pursuit of organizational intelligence. MA: Blackwell Publishers Inc.

Marhuenda, F., Martinez, I., & Navas, A. (2004). Conflicting vocational identities and careers in the sector of tourism. *Career Development International, 9*(3), 222–244. doi:10.1108/13620430410535832

Markus, H., & Kitayama, S. (1991). Culture and self: Implications for cognition, emotion, and motivation. *Psychological Review, 98,* 224–253. doi:10.1037/0033-295X.98.2.224

Marra, M. (2004). Knowledge partnerships for development: What challenges for evaluation? *Evaluation and Program Planning, 27*(2), 151–160. doi:10.1016/j.evalprogplan.2004.01.003

Martin, E. (2004). Who's kicking whom? Employees' orientations to work. *International Journal of Contemporary Hospitality Management, 16*(3), 182–188. doi:10.1108/09596110410531177

Martin, J. S., & Marion, R. (2005). Higher education leadership roles in knowledge processing. *The Learning Organization, 12*(5), 140–151. doi:10.1108/09696470510583520

Martins, E. C. (2000). *The influence of organizational culture on creativity and innovation in a university library.* Unpublished master's thesis, Pretoria, South Africa, University of South Africa.

Marwick, A. (2001). Knowledge management technology. *IBM Systems Journal, 40*(4).

Marx, K. (1861). *Economic manuscripts of 1861-63. Part 3. Relative surplus value division of labour and mechanical workshop. Tool and machinery.* Retrieved April 2005, from http://www.marxists.org

Matthews, K., & Harris, H. (2006). Maintaining knowledge assets. In J. Mathew, J. Kennedy, L. Ma, & A. Tan (Eds.), *Engineering asset management.* London, Springer Verlag.

Maturana, H. (1997). *Metadesign.* Retrieved August 1, 2005, from http://www.inteco.cl

Maturana, H., & Varela, F. (1980). *Autopoiesis and cognition: The realization of the living.* Dordrecht, The Netherlands: D. Reidel.

Maturana, H., & Varela, F. (1992). *The tree of knowledge: The biological roots of human understanding.* Boston: Shambhala.

Maturana, H., Mpodozis, J., & Lettelier, J. C. (1995). Brain, language and the origin of human mental functions. *Biological Research, 28,* 15–26.

Maurer, T. J. (2007). Employee development and training issues related to the aging workforce. In K. S. Shultz & G. A. Adams (Eds.), Aging and work in the 21st century (pp. 163-178). Mahwah, NJ: Lawrence Erlbaum Associates.

Maurer, T. J., Weiss, E. M., & Barbeite, F. G. (2003). A model of involvement in work-related learning and development activity: The effects of individual, situational, motivational, and age variables. *The Journal of Applied Psychology, 88*(4), 707–724. doi:10.1037/0021-9010.88.4.707

Maznevski, M., & Athanassiou, N. (2007). Bringing the outside in: Learning and knowledge management through external networks. In K. Ichijo & I. Nonaka (Eds.), *Knowledge creation and management: New challenges for managers* (pp. 69-82). New York: Oxford University Press.

Maznevski, M., & Chudoba, K. (2000). Bridging space over time global virtual team dynamics and effectiveness. *Organization Science, 11*(5), 473–492. doi:10.1287/orsc.11.5.473.15200

McAdam, R., & McCreedy, S. (1999). The process of knowledge management within organizations: A critical assessment of both theory and practice. *Knowledge and Process Management, 6*(2), 101–113. doi:10.1002/(SICI)1099-1441(199906)6:2<101::AID-KPM53>3.0.CO;2-P

McAdam, R., & Reid, R. (2001). SME and large organization perceptions of knowledge management: comparisons and contrasts. *Journal of Knowledge Management, 5*(3), 231–241. doi:10.1108/13673270110400870

McAdam, R., Mason, B., & McCrory, J. (2007). Exploring the dichotomies within the tacit knowledge literature: Towards a process of tacit knowing in organizations. *Journal of Knowledge Management, 11*(2), 43–59. doi:10.1108/13673270710738906

McCabe, V. S., & Savery, L. K. (2007). "Butterflying" a new career pattern for Australia? Empirical evidence. *Journal of Management Development, 26*(2), 103–116. doi:10.1108/02621710710726026

McCann, R. M., & Giles, H. (2006). Communication with people of different ages in the workplace: Thai and American data. *Human Communication Research, 32*(1), 74. doi:10.1111/j.1468-2958.2006.00004.x

McDermott, R. (1999). Why information technology inspired cannot deliver knowledge management? *California Management Review, 41*(4), 103–117.

McElroy, M. (2002). *The new knowledge management, complexity, learning, and sustainable innovation.* Burlington, England: Butterworth-Heineman.

McGregor, J., & Gray, L. (2002). Stereotypes and older workers: The New Zealand experience. *Social Policy Journal of New Zealand, 18*, 163–177.

McInerney, C. (2002). Hot topics: Knowledge management – a practice still defining itself. *Bulletin of the American Society for Information Science, 28*(3), 14–15. doi:10.1002/bult.235

McInerney, C. R., & Mohr, S. (2007). Trust and knowledge sharing in organizations: Theory and practice. In C. R. McInerney & R. E. Day (Eds.), *Rethinking knowledge management: From knowledge objects to knowledge processes* (pp. 65-86). New York: Springer.

McLoughlin, H., & Thorpe, R. (1993). Action learning - a paradigm in emergence: The problems facing a challenge to traditional management education and development. *British Journal of Management, 4*, 19–27. doi:10.1111/j.1467-8551.1993.tb00158.x

McMillan, E. (2004). *Complexity, organizations and change.* London: Routledge.

McPherson, M. (2008). *Older workers: Employers speak out.* Auckland, New Zealand: Equal Employment Opportunities Trust (EEO).

Megginson, D., & Clutterbuck, D. (2006). Creating a coaching culture. *Industrial and Commercial Training, 38*(5), 232–237. doi:10.1108/00197850610677670

Mendola, M. (2006). *Rural out-migration and economic development at origin. What do we know?* (Sussex Migration Working Paper N.40). Retrieved August 10, 2008, from http://dipeco.economia.unimib.it/persone/mendola/CV-07BICOC.pdf

Menon, A., Dekker, R., Oosterhof, J., & Oppelland, H. (1998). *Creating tomorrow's business: Managing knowledge.* Rotterdam, The Netherlands: Learning Center for Strategy and Entrepreneurship „le manageur".

Mentzas, G., Apostolou, D., Abecker, A., & Young, R. (2003). *Knowledge asset management: Beyond the process-centred and product-centred approaches.* London: Spinger-Verlag.

Meritum Project. (2002). *Guidelines for managing and reporting on intangibles.* Madrid, Spain: Fundación Aitel Móvil.

Mertins, K., Alwert, K., & Heisig, P. (2005). Wissensbilanzen. Berlin, Germany: Springer Verlag.

Mertins, K., Heisig, P., & Vorbeck, J. (2001). *Knowledge management. Best practices in Europe.* Berlin, Germany: Springer.

Meyer, H. D. (2002). The new managerialism in education management: Corporatization or organizational learning? *Journal of Educational Administration, 40*(6), 534–551. doi:10.1108/09578230210446027

Meyer, J. W. (1977). The effect of education as an institution. *American Journal of Sociology, 83*(1), 55–77. doi:10.1086/226506

Meyerson, D., & Martin, J. (1987). Cultural change: An integration of three different views. *Journal of Management Studies, 24*(6), 623–647. doi:10.1111/j.1467-6486.1987.tb00466.x

Michailova, S., & Hutchings, K. (2006). National cultural influences on knowledge sharing: A comparison of China and Russia. *Journal of Management Studies, 43*(3), 383–405. doi:10.1111/j.1467-6486.2006.00595.x

Middlehurst, R., & Woodfield, S. (2006). Quality review in distance learning: Policy and practice in five countries. *Tertiary Education and Management, 12*(4), 37–58. doi:10.1007/s11233-005-4072-5

Miesing, P., Kriger, M. P., & Slough, N. (2007). Towards a model of effective knowledge transfer within transnational: The case of Chinese foreign invested enterprises. *The Journal of Technology Transfer, 32*, 109–122. doi:10.1007/s10961-006-9006-y

Millard, D. E., Tao, F., & Doody, K. (2006). The knowledge life cycle for e-learning. *International Journal of Continuing Engineering Education and Lifelong Learning, 16*(1), 110–121. doi:10.1504/IJCEELL.2006.008921

Milman, A. (2003). Hourly employee retention in small and medium attractions: The central Florida example. *International Journal of Hospitality Management, 22*, 17–35. doi:10.1016/S0278-4319(02)00033-6

Mingers, J. (1989). An introduction to autopoiesis: Implications and applications. *Systems Practice, 2*(2), 569–584. doi:10.1007/BF01059497

Mingers, J. (1991). The cognitive theories of Maturana and Varela. *Systems Practice, 4*(4), 319–338. doi:10.1007/BF01062008

Mingers, J. (1996). A comparison of Maturana's autopoietic social theory and Giddens' theory of structuration. *Systems Research, 13*(4), 469–482. doi:10.1002/(SICI)1099-1735(199612)13:4<469::AID-SRES81>3.0.CO;2-I

Mintzberg, H. (1983). *Structure in fives: Designing effective organizations.* Englewood Cliffs, NJ: Prentice-Hall.

Mintzberg, H. (1987). The strategy concept I: Five ps for strategy. *California Management Review,* (Fall).

Mintzberg, H. (2007). *Tracking strategies... toward a general theory.* New York: Oxford University Press.

Miroschedji, S. A. (2002). *Globale unternehmens-und wertschöpfungsnetzwerke.* Wiesbaden, Germany: Deutscher Universitäts-Verlag.

Mittleton-Kelly, E. (1997). *Complex adaptive systems in an organisational context.* Paper presented at the British Academy of Management Conference, London.

Mohsin, A. (2003). Backpackers in the NT of Australia - motives, behaviours and satisfactions. *International Journal of Tourism Research, 5*(2), 113–131. doi:10.1002/jtr.421

Mohsin, A. (2003). Service quality assessment of restaurants in Darwin, NT, Australia. *Journal of Hospitality and Tourism Management, 10*(1), 12–23.

Mohsin, A. (2005). Service quality assessment of 4-star hotels in Darwin, NT, Australia. *Journal of Hospitality and Tourism Management, 12*(1), 25–36.

Moitra, D., & Kumar, K. (2007). Managed socialization: How smart companies leverage global knowledge. *Knowledge and Process Management, 14*(3), 148–157. doi:10.1002/kpm.278

Möller, K., & Svahn, S. (2004). Crossing East-West boundaries: Knowledge sharing in intercultural business networks. *Industrial Marketing Management, 33*, 219–228. doi:10.1016/j.indmarman.2003.10.011

Montepare, J. M., & Zebrowitz-McArthur, L. A. (1988). Impressions of people created by age-related qualities of their gaits. *Journal of Personality and Social Psychology, 55*, 547–556. doi:10.1037/0022-3514.55.4.547

Moore, F. (2006). Strategy, power and negotiation: Social control and expatriate managers in a German multinational corporation. *International Journal of Human Resource Management, 17*(3), 399–413. doi:10.1080/09585190500521359

Moorman, C., & Miner, A. S. (1997). The impact of organizational memory on new product performance and creativity. *JMR, Journal of Marketing Research, 34*(1), 91. doi:10.2307/3152067

Moorman, R. H., & Blakely, G. L. (1995). Individualism collectivism as an individual difference predictor of organizational citizenship behavior. *Journal of Organizational Behavior (1986-1998), 16*(2), 127.

Morrison, A. (2008). Gatekeepers of knowledge within industrial districts: Who they are, how they interact. *Regional Studies, 42*(6), 817–835. doi:10.1080/00343400701654178

Mowday, R. T. (1981). Viewing turnover from the perspective of those who remain: The relationship of job attitudes to attributions of the causes of turnover. *The Journal of Applied Psychology, 66*(1), 120–123. doi:10.1037/0021-9010.66.1.120

Mowday, R., Steers, R., & Porter, L. (1982). *Employee-organization linkages.* New York: Academic Press.

Mu, J., Peng, G., & Love, E. (2008). Interfirm networks, social capital, and knowledge flow. *Journal of Knowledge Management, 12*(4), 86–100. doi:10.1108/13673270810884273

Nahapiet, J., & Ghoshal, S. (1998). Social capital, intellectual capital, and the organizational advantage. *Academy of Management Review, 23*(2), 242–266. doi:10.2307/259373

Nahapiet, J., Gratton, L., & Rocha, H. O. (2005). Knowledge and relationships: When cooperation is the norm. *European Management Review, 2*(1), 3. doi:10.1057/palgrave.emr.1500023

Nenonen, S. (2004). Analyzing the intangible benefits of work space. *Facilities, 22*(9-10), 233–239. doi:10.1108/02632770410555940

Neu, D., Silva, L., & Ocampo-Gomez, E. (2007). Diffusing financial practices in Latin America higher education understanding the intersection between global and influence and local context. *Accounting, Auditing & Accountability Journal, 21*(1), 49–77. doi:10.1108/09513570810842322

Neustadt, R. E., & May, E. R. (1986). *Thinking in time: The uses of history for decision-making.* New York: The Free Press.

New Zealand Department of Labour. (2004). *Future of work.* Retrieved April 1, 2006, from http://www.dol.govt.nz/futureofwork/workforce-ageing.asp

Newell, S. (2005). Knowledge transfer and learning: Problems of knowledge transfer associated with trying to short-circuit the learning cycle. *Journal of Information Systems and Technology Management, 2*(3).

Newell, S., & Swan, J. (2000). Trust and inter-organizational networking. *Human Relations, 53*(10), 287–328.

News, B. B. C. (2003). *India to test Coca-Cola sludge.* Retrieved from http://news.bbc.co.uk/2/hi/south_asia/3133259.stm

News, B. B. C. (2003). *Indian colas 'not unsafe'.* Retrieved from http://news.bbc.co.uk/2/hi/south_asia/3126519.stm

News, B. B. C. (2004). *Coke recalls controversial water.* Retrieved from http://news.bbc.co.uk/1/hi/business/3550063.stm

News, B. B. C. (2005). *Indian Coca-Cola protest to go on.* Retrieved from http://news.bbc.co.uk/1/hi/world/south_asia/4603511.stm

Ng, S. I., Lee, J. A., & Soutar, G. N. (2006). Are Hofstede's and Schwartz's value frameworks congruent? *International Marketing Review, 24*(2), 164–180. doi:10.1108/02651330710741802

Nicholson, N. (2005). Family ties – binding, bonding or breaking? *Families in Business,* (March-April): 80.

Nickols, F. W. (2000). The knowledge in knowledge management. In J. W. Cortada & J. A. Woods (Eds.),

The knowledge management yearbook 2000-2001 (pp. 12-21). Boston: Butterworth-Heinemann.

Nisbett, R. E. (2003). *The geography of thought: How Asians and Westerners think differently... and why.* New York: The Free Press.

Nisbett, R. E., Peng, K., Choi, I., & Norenzayan, A. (2001). Culture and systems of thought: Holistic vs. analytic cognition. *Psychological Review, 108*(2), 291–310. doi:10.1037/0033-295X.108.2.291

Nishida, T. (1987). Local traditions and cultural transmission. In B. B. Smuts, D. L. Cheney, R. M. Seyfarth, R. W. Wrangham, & T. T. Struhsaker (Eds.), *Primate societies.* Chicago: University of Chicago Press.

Nishida, T. (2002). A traveling conversation model for dynamic knowledge interaction. *Journal of Knowledge Management, 6*(2), 124–134. doi:10.1108/13673270210424657

Nishida, T. (Ed.). (2000). *Dynamic knowledge interaction.* Boca Ranton, FL: CRC Press.

Nonaka, I. (1991). The knowledge-creating company. *Harvard Business Review, 69*(3), 96–104.

Nonaka, I. (1994). A dynamic theory of organizational knowledge creation. *Organization Science, 5*(1), 14–37. doi:10.1287/orsc.5.1.14

Nonaka, I. (2007). The knowledge-creating company. *Harvard Business Review, 85*(7/8), 162–171.

Nonaka, I., & Konno, I. (1998). The concept of 'Ba': Building a foundation for knowledge creation. *California Management Review, 40*(3), 40–54.

Nonaka, I., & Takeuchi, H. (1995). *The knowledge-creating company: How Japanese companies create the dynamics of innovation.* Oxford, UK: Oxford University Press.

Nonaka, I., & Toyama, R. (2003). The knowledge-creating theory revisited: Knowledge creation as a synthesizing process. *Knowledge Management Research & Practice, 1*(1), 2–10. doi:10.1057/palgrave.kmrp.8500001

Nonaka, I., Krogh von, G., & Voelpel, S. (2006). Organizational knowledge creation theory: Evolutionary paths and future advances. *Organization Studies, 27*(8), 1179–1208. doi:10.1177/0170840606066312

Nonaka, I., Krogh, G. V., & Aben, M. (2001). Making the most of your company's knowledge: A strategic framework. *Long Range Planning, 34*, 421–439. doi:10.1016/S0024-6301(01)00059-0

Nonaka, I., Reinmoeller, P., & Senoo, D. (1998). The art of knowledge: Systems to capitalize on market knowledge. *European Management Journal, 16*(6), 673–684. doi:10.1016/S0263-2373(98)00044-9

Nonaka, I., Schamer, O., & Toyama, R. (2001). *Building ba to enhance knowledge creation: An innovation at large firms.* Retrieved from http://www.dialogonleadership.org/Nonaka_et_al.html

Nonaka, I., Toyama, R., & Byosière, P. (2001). A theory of organizational knowledge creation: Understanding the dynamic process of creating knowledge. In M. Dierkes, A. Berthoin Antal, J. Child, & I. Nonaka (Eds.), *Handbook of organizational learning and knowledge* (pp. 491-517). Oxford, UK: Oxford University Press.

Nonaka, I., Toyama, R., & Konno, N. (2000). SECI, ba and leadership: A unified model of dynamic knowledge creation. *Long Range Planning, 33*, 5–34. doi:10.1016/S0024-6301(99)00115-6

Nonaka, I., Toyama, R., & Nagata, A. (2000). A firm as a knowledge-creating entity: A new perspective on the theory of the firm. *Industrial and Corporate Change, 9*(1), 1–20. doi:10.1093/icc/9.1.1

Nonaka, I., Von Krogh, G., & Voepel, S. (2006). Organizational knowledge creation theory: Evolutionary paths and future advances. *Organization Studies, 27*, ll79–ll1208. doi:10.1177/0170840606066312

Nussbaum, J. F., & Baringer, D. K. (2000). Message production across the lifespan: Communication and aging. *Communication Theory, 8*, 1–26.

O'Dell, C., & Grayson, C. J. (1998). If only we knew what we know: Identification and transfer of internal best practices. *California Management Review, 40*(3), 154–170.

O'Dell, C., & Grayston, C. J. (1998). *If only we knew what we best know: The transfer of internal knowledge and best practice.* New York: The Free Press.

O'Donohue, S. J. (2000). *A Canterbury employers' perspective on the aging workforce and the use of flexible work options for older workers.* Palmerston North, New Zealand: Master of Business Studies, Massey University.

OECD. (1999). *The knowledge-based economy a set of facts and figures.* Paris: OECD.

OECD. (2005). *Oslo manual – guidelines for collecting and interpreting innovation data – third edition.* Paris: OECD Publishings.

OECD. (2006). *Live longer, work longer: Executive summary.* Paris: OECD.

OECD. (2007). *Education and training policy: No more failures ten steps to equity in Education.* Paris: OECD.

Oliver, M. (2005). McLibel. *The Guardian.* Retrieved from http://www.guardian.co.uk/news/2005/feb/15/food.foodanddrink

Organisation for Economic Co-operation and Development. (2007). *The measurement of scientific and technological activities: Proposed guidelines for collecting and interpreting technological innovation data - the Oslo manual.* European Commission and Eurostat.

Ortmann, G., & Sydow, J. (2001). *Strategie und strukturation.* Wiesbaden, Germany: Gabler Verlag.

Palmer, R. J., Welker, R. B., Campbell, T. L., & Magner, N. R. (2001). Examining the impression management orientation of managers. *Journal of Managerial Psychology, 16*(1), 35–49. doi:10.1108/02683940110366588

Palmisano, J. (2008). A motivational model of knowledge sharing. In F. Burstein & C. W. Holsapple (Eds.), *Handbook on decision support systems 1.* Berlin, Germany: Springer Verlag.

Pan, S. L., & Scarbough, H. (1999). Knowledge management in practice: An exploratory case study. *Technology Analysis and Strategic Management, 11*(3), 359–374. doi:10.1080/095373299107401

Parise, S., Cross, R., & Davenport, T. H. (2006). Strategies for preventing a knowledge loss crisis. *Sloan Management Review, 47*(4).

Park, H., Ribiere, V., & Schulte, W. D. (2004). Critical attributes of organizational culture that promote knowledge management technology implementation success. *Journal of Knowledge Management, 8*(3), 106–117. doi:10.1108/13673270410541079

Park, S. H., & Luo, Y. (2001). *Guanxi* and organizational dynamics: Organizational networking in Chinese firms. *Strategic Management Journal, 22,* 455–477. doi:10.1002/smj.167

Parker, R., & Rea, L. (2000). *Metodologia de pesquisa: Do planejamento à execução.* São Paulo, Brazil: Pioneira.

Parkes, L. P., Bochner, S., & Schneider, S. K. (2001). Person-organisation fit across cultures: An empirical investigation of individualism and collectivism. *Applied Psychology: An International Review, 50*(1), 81–108. doi:10.1111/1464-0597.00049

Parsloe, E., & Wray, M. (2002). *Training mentors is not enough: Everything else schools and districts need to do.* Thousand Oaks, CA: Corwin Press.

Pauleen, D. J. (Ed.). (2007). *Cross-cultural perspectives on knowledge management.* Westport, CT: Libraries Unlimited.

Paulhus, D. (1982). Individual differences, self presentation and cognitive dissonance: Their concurrent operation in forced compliance. *Journal of Personality and Social Psychology, 43*(4), 838–852. doi:10.1037/0022-3514.43.4.838

Pecchioni, L. L., Ota, H., & Sparks, L. (2004). Cultural issues in communication and aging. In J. F. Nussbaum & . J. Coupland (Eds.), *Handbook of communication and aging research* (pp. 91-114). Mahwah, NJ: Lawrence Erlbaum Associates.

Peltokorpi, V. (2006). Japanese organizational behaviour in Nordic subsidiaries: A Nordic expatriate perspective. *Employee Relations, 28*(2), 103–118. doi:10.1108/01425450610639347

Perkmann, M., & Walsh, K. (2006). *Relationship-based university-industry links and open innovation: Towards a research agenda* (AIM Research Working Paper Series, 041-July-2006). Loughborough University.

Peroune, D. (2007). Tacit knowledge in the workplace: The facilitating role of peer relationships. *Journal of European Industrial Training, 31*(4), 244–258. doi:10.1108/03090590710746414

Persson, O. (1981). Critical comments on the gatekeeper concept in science and technology. *R & D Management, 11*(1), 37–40. doi:10.1111/j.1467-9310.1981.tb00447.x

Pessacq, R. A., Iglesias, O., & Willis, E. (2004). *Hacia un nuevo paradigma en la relación Universidad-Empresa.* Buenos Aires, Argentina: IV CAEDI: Cuarto Congreso Argentino de Enseñanza de la Ingeniería.

Peters, T. (1992). *Liberation management.* New York: Pan Books.

Petrash, G. (1996). Dow's Journey to a Knowledge Value Management Culture. *European Management Journal, 14*(4), 365–373. doi:10.1016/0263-2373(96)00023-0

Pettigrew, A. (1979). On studying organizational cultures. *Administrative Science Quarterly, 24*, 570–581. doi:10.2307/2392363

Pettigrew, A., & Whipp, R. (1994). Managing the twin processes of competition and change – the role of intangible assets. In P. Lorange, B. Chakravarthy, J. Roos, & A. Van de Ven (Eds.), *Implementing strategic processes: Change, learning and cooperation.* Cambridge, MA: Blackewell Business.

Pfeffer, J. (2007). A modest proposal: How we might change the process and product of managerial research. *Academy of Management Journal, 50*(6), 1334–1345.

Pfeffer, J., & Fong, C. T. (2002). The end of business school? Less success that meets the eye. *Academy of Management Learning & Education, 1*, 78–95.

Pfeffer, J., & Sutton, R. I. (2003). *The knowing-doing gap.* Boston: Harvard Business School Press.

Philpott, E. (2008). Identifying innovation opportunities – using the Internet to match universities with SMEs. *International Journal of Knowledge Management Studies, 2*(3), 285–303. doi:10.1504/IJKMS.2008.018793

Philpott, E., & Bevis, K. (2005). Detecting innovation opportunities: The development of an online innovation tool and process for university - business engagement. In *Proceedings of the ISPIM 2005*, Porto, Portugal.

Pillania, R. K. (2005). New knowledge creation scenario in India industry. *Global Journal of Flexible Systems Management, 6*(3&4), 49–57.

Pinch, S., Henry, N., Jenkins, M., & Tallman, S. (2003). From industrial districts to knowledge clusters a model of knowledge dissemination and competitive advantage in industrial agglomerations. *Journal of Economic Geography, 31*, 665–682.

Pineda, J. L., & Zapata, L. E. (2007). From universities to corporations: Determining factors in the diffusion and adoption of knowledge. In *Proceedings of the 8th European Conference on Knowledge: Vol. 2.* (pp. 788-793). England: Academic Conferences International.

Pires, G., Stanton, J., & Ostenfeld, S. (2006). Improving expatriate adjustment and effectiveness in ethnically diverse countries: Marketing insights. *Cross Cultural Management, 13*(2), 156–170. doi:10.1108/13527600610662339

Pistrui, D., Huang, W. V., Welsh, H. P., & Jing, Z. (2006). Family and cultural forces: Shaping entrepreneurship and SME development in China. In P. Z. Poutziouris, K. X. Smyrnios, & S. B. Klein (Eds.), *Handbook of research on family businesses.* Cheltenham, UK: Edward Elgar.

Pitt, J. (1999). *Thinking about technology.* New York: Seven Bridges Press.

Pittaway, L., Thorpe, R., Holte, R., & Macpherson, A. (2005). *Knowledge within small and medium sized firms: A systematic review of the evidence* (Lancaster University Management School Working Paper 2005/020).

Pizam, A., & Thornburg, S. W. (2000). Absenteeism and voluntary turnover in Central Florida hotels: A pilot study. *International Journal of Hospitality Management, 19*, 211–217. doi:10.1016/S0278-4319(00)00011-6

Plessis, M. (2007). The role of knowledge management in innovation. *Journal of Knowledge Management, 11*(4), 20–29. doi:10.1108/13673270710762684

Polanyi, M. (1967). *The tacit dimension.* New York: Doubleday.

Ponzi, L., & Koenig, M. (2002). Knowledge management: Another management fad? *Information Research, 8*(1). Retrieved August 15, 2004, from http://informationr.net/ir/8-1/paper145.html

Poon, A. (1993). *Tourism, technology and competitive strategies.* UK: C.A.B International.

Popadiuk, S., & Choo, C. W. (2006). Innovation and knowledge creation: How are these concepts related? *International Journal of Information Management, 26*(4), 302–312. doi:10.1016/j.ijinfomgt.2006.03.011

Popper, K. (1994). *The myth of the framework: In defence of science and rationality.* London: Routledge.

Pór, G. (1995). The quest for collective intelligence. In K. Gozdz (Ed.), *Community building – renewing spirit & learning in business.* San Francisco: Sterling & Stone.

Porschen, S. (2008). *Austausch impliziten erfahrungswissens.* Wiesbaden, Germany: Verlag für Sozialwissenschaften.

Porter, M. E. (1990). *The competitive advantage of nations.* London: Macmillan.

Porter, M. E., & van der Lind, C. (1995). Towards a new conception of the environment-competitiveness relationship. *The Journal of Economic Perspectives, 9*, 97–118.

Poulston, J. (2008). Hospitality workplace problems and poor training: A close relationship. *International Journal of Contemporary Hospitality Management, 20*(4), 412–427. doi:10.1108/09596110810873525

Poutziouris, Z. P., Smyrnios, K. X., & Klein, B. S. (Eds.). (2006). *Handbook of research on family business.* Cheltenham, UK: Edward Elgar.

Poyago-Theotoky, J., Beath, J., & Siegel, D. S. (2002). Universities and fundamental research: Reflections on the growth of university-industry partnerships. *Oxford Review of Economic Policy, 18*(1), 10. doi:10.1093/oxrep/18.1.10

Prahalad, C. K., & Hamel, G. O. (1990). The core competence of the corporation. *Harvard Business Review, 68*, 79–91.

Probst, G. J. B., Raub, S., & Romhardt, K. (2006). *Wissen managen.* Wiesbaden, Germany: Gabler Verlag.

Provonost, P., Nolan, T., Zegwe, S., Miller, M., & Rubin, H. (2004). How can clinicians measure safety and quality in acute care. *Lancet, 363*, 1061–1067. doi:10.1016/S0140-6736(04)15843-1

Prusak, L. (2001). Where did knowledge management come from? *IBM Systems Journal, 40*(4).

Quinn, J. B. (1992). *Intelligent enterprise.* New York: Free Press, New York.

Quinn, R. E. (1988). *Beyond rational management: Mastering the paradoxes and competing demands of high performance.* San Francisco: Jossey-Bass.

Quinn, R. E., Cameron, K. S., DeGraff, J., & Thakor, A. V. (2006). *Competing values leadership: Creating value in organizations.* Cheltenham, UK: Edward Elgar Publishing, Inc.

Quintas, P., Lefrere, P., & Jones, G. (1997). Knowledge management: A strategic agenda. *Journal of Long Range Planning, 30*(3), 385–391. doi:10.1016/S0024-6301(97)90252-1

Ragins, B. R., & Cotton, J. L. (1993). Gender and willingness to mentor in Organizations. *Journal of Management, 19*(1), 97–111. doi:10.1177/014920639301900107

Ragins, B. R., & Scandura, T. A. (1994). Gender differences in expected outcomes of mentoring relationships. *Academy of Management Journal, 37*(4), 957–971. doi:10.2307/256606

Ragins, B. R., & Scandura, T. A. (1999). Burden or blessing? Expected costs and benefits of being a mentor. *Journal of Organizational Behavior, 20*(4), 493–509. doi:10.1002/(SICI)1099-1379(199907)20:4<493::AID-JOB894>3.0.CO;2-T

Ramasamy, B., Goh, K. W., & Yeung, M. C. H. (2006). Is *guanxi* (relationship) a bridge to knowledge transfer? *Journal of Business Research, 59*, 130–139. doi:10.1016/j.jbusres.2005.04.001

Rammert, W. (1999). Relations that constitute technology and media that make a difference: Toward a social pragmatic theory of technicisation. *Techne, Journal of Philosophy and Technology, 4*(3). Retrieved March 1999, from http://scholar.lib.vt.edu/ejournals/SPT/v4n3/pdf/

Randeree, E. (2006). Knowledge management: Securing the future. *Journal of Knowledge Management, 10*(4), 145–156. doi:10.1108/13673270610679435

Rao, A., Schmidt, S. M., & Murray, L. H. (1995). Upward impression management: Goals, influence strategies, and consequences. *Human Relations, 48*, 147–167. doi:10.1177/001872679504800203

Rastogi, P. N. (2000). Knowledge management and intellectual capital - the new virtuous reality of competitiveness. *Human Systems Management, 19*(1), 15–39.

Reed, R., & DeFillippi, R. J. (1990). Causal ambiguity, barriers to imitation, and sustainable competitive advantage. *Academy of Management Review, 15*(1), 88–102. doi:10.2307/258107

Rees, J. (2008). *Notes from summary of issues raised at ECKM 08.* Reading, UK: Academic Conference Ltd.

Reid, R. S., & Adams, J. S. (2001). Human resource management – a survey of practices within family and non-family firms. *Journal of European Industrial Training, 25*(6), 310–320. doi:10.1108/03090590110401782

Reid, R., & Harris, R. I. D. (2004). *Family-owned SME growth in Scotland: A comparison with the UK* (Report to Scotecon).

Remus, U. (2002). *Prozessorientiertes wissensmanagement. Konzepte und modellierung.* Unpublished doctoral dissertation, Universitat Regensburg, Wirtschaftswissenschaftliche Fakultät.

Reuters. (2007). *Prince Charles shows of smaller carbon footprint.* Retrieved from http://www.reuters.com/article/environmentNews/idUSL2691546320070626

Reynolds, M. (2004). Churchman and Maturana: Enriching the notion of self-organization for social design. *Systemic Practice and Action Research, 17*(6).

Ribière, V., & Sitar, S. A. (2003). Critical role of leadership in nurturing a knowledge-supporting culture. *Knowledge Management Research & Practice, 1*, 39–48. doi:10.1057/palgrave.kmrp.8500004

Rice, J. L., & Rice, B. S. (2005). The applicability of the SECI model to multi-organisational endeavours: An integrative review. *International Journal of Organisational Behaviour, 9*(8), 671–682.

Richardson, J., & McKenna, S. (2006). Exploring relationships with home and host countries: A study of self-directed expatriates. *Cross Cultural Management, 13*(1), 6–22. doi:10.1108/13527600610643448

Rigby, D. (2001). Management tools and techniques: A survey. *California Management Review, 43*(2), 139–160.

Roberts, J. (2000). From know-how to show-how? Questioning the role of information and communication technologies in knowledge transfer. *Technology Analysis and Strategic Management, 12*(4), 429–443. doi:10.1080/713698499

Robins, G., & Pattison, P. (2006). *Multiple networks in organizations. Australian Defence Science and Technology Organisation (DSTO).* Retrieved August 10, 2008, from http://www.sna.unimelb.edu.au/publications/publications.html

Rokeach, M. (1973). *The nature of human values.* New York: Free Press.

Rolland, N., & Chauvel, D. (2000). Knowledge transfer in strategic alliances. In Ch. Depres & D. Chauvel (Eds.), *Knowledge horizons, the present and the promise of knowledge management.* MA: Butterworth-Heinemann.

Rollett, H. (2003). *Knowledge management: Processes and technologies*. Boston: Kluwer Academic Publishers.

Roos, J., Roos, G., Edvinsson, L., & Dragonetti, N. (1997). *Intellectual capital: Navigating in the new business landscape*. London: Macmillan Press.

Rose, R. A. (1988). Organizations as multiple cultures: A rules theory analysis. *Human Relations, 41*(2), 139–170. doi:10.1177/001872678804100204

Rosemann, M. a. (2000). Structuring and modeling knowledge in the context of enterprise resource planning. In *Proceedings of the Pacific Asia Conference on Information Systems,* Hong Kong, China.

Rosenfeld, P., Giacalone, R. A., & Riordan, C. A. (1995). *Impression management in organizations: Theory, measurement, practice*. London: Routledge.

Roth, J. (2003). Enabling knowledge creation: Learning from an R&D organization. *Journal of Knowledge Management, 7*(1), 32–48. doi:10.1108/13673270310463608

Rothberg, H. N. (1997). Fortifying competitive intelligence systems with shadow teams. *Competitive Intelligence Review, 8*(2), 3–11. doi:10.1002/cir.3880080204

Rothberg, H. N., & Erickson, G. S. (2002). Competitive capital: A fourth pillar of intellectual capital? In N. Bonits (Ed.), *Proceedings of the World Congress on Intellectual Capital Readings* (pp. 94-113). Woburn, MA: Elsevier Butterworth-Heinemann.

Rothberg, H. N., & Erickson, G. S. (2005). *From knowledge to intelligence: Creating competitive advantage in the next economy*. Woburn, MA: Elsevier Butterworth-Heinemann.

Rothwell, W. J., Sterns, H. L., Spokus, D., & Reaser, J. M. (2008). *Working longer: New strategies for managing, training, and retaining older employees*. New York: AMACOM.

Rousseau, D. (1995). *Psychological contracts in organizations: Understanding written and unwritten agreements*. Thousand Oaks, CA: Sage.

Rowley, G., & Purcell, K. (2001). "As cooks go, she went": Is labour churn inevitable? *International Journal of Hospitality Management, 20*(2), 163–185. doi:10.1016/S0278-4319(00)00050-5

Rowley, J. (2000). Is higher education ready for knowledge management? *International Journal of Educational Management, 14*(7), 325–333. doi:10.1108/09513540010378978

Roy, A., & Gupta, R. K. (2007). Knowledge processes in small manufacturing: Re-examining Nonaka and Takeuchis' model in the Indian context. *Journal of Entrepreneurship, 16*(1), 77–93. doi:10.1177/097135570601600104

Ruggles, R. (1998). The state of the notion: Knowledge management in practice. *California Management Review, 40*(3), 80–89.

Rulke, D. L., Zaheer, S., & Anderson, M. H. (2000). Sources of managers' knowledge of organizational capabilities. *Organizational Behavior and Human Decision Processes, 82*(1), 134–149. doi:10.1006/obhd.2000.2892

Ryan, L. (2007). Developing a qualitative understanding of university-corporate education partnerships. *Management Decision, 45*(2), 153–160. doi:10.1108/00251740710727214

Ryan, R. M., & Deci, E. L. (2002). Overview of self-determination theory: An organismic dialectical perspective. In E. L. Deci & R. M. Ryan (Eds.), *Handbook of self-determination research* (pp. 3-33). Boydell & Brewer.

Ryle, G. (1949). *The concept of mind*. Chicago, IL: University of Chicago.

Saari, T., Laarni, J., Ravaja, N., Kallinen, K., & Turpeinen, M. (2004). Virtual ba and presence in facilitating learning from technology mediated organizational information flows. In *Presence 2004, Proceedings of the Seventh Annual International Workshop* (pp. 133-140). Retrieved August 12, 2008, from http://www.temple.edu/ispr/prev_conferences/proceedings/2004/Saari,%20Laarni,%20Ravaja,%20Kallinen,%20Turpeinen.pdf

Sackett, D. (2003). *Medicina baseada em evidências: Prática e ensino*. São Paulo, Brazil: Artmed.

Sackman, S. A. (1991). *Cultural knowledge in organisations –exploring the collective mind*. London: SAGE Publications.

Sackmann, S. A. (1991). *Cultural knowledge in organizations: Exploring the collective mind*. Newbury Park, CA: Sage.

Saint-Onge, H. (1996). Tacit knowledge: The key to the strategic alignment of intellectual capital. *Strategy and Leadership*, (March/April): 10–14. doi:10.1108/eb054547

Sallis, E., & Jones, G. (2002). *Knowledge management in education: Enhancing learning & education*. London: Kogan Page.

Santoro, M. (2006). Self-interest assumption and relational trust in university-industry knowledge transfer. *IEEE Transactions on Engineering Management*, *53*(3), 335–347. doi:10.1109/TEM.2006.878103

Santoro, M. D., & Gopalakrishnan, S. (2000). The institutionalization of knowledge transfer activities within industry-university collaborative ventures. *Journal of Engineering and Technology Management*, *17*, 299–319. doi:10.1016/S0923-4748(00)00027-8

Saxenian, A. L. (1994). *Regional advantage: Culture and competition in Silicon Valley and Route 128*. Cambridge, MA: Harvard University Press.

Scarborough, H. (1996). *Business process re-design: The knowledge dimension*. Retrieved from http://bprc.warwick.ac.uk/rc-rep-8.1

Scarborough, H., & Corbett, J. M. (1992). *Technology and organization*. London: Routledge.

Scarbrough, H. (2001). Knowledge management, HRM and the innovation process. *International Journal of Manpower*, *24*(5), 501–516. doi:10.1108/01437720310491053

Schartinger, D. (2002). Knowledge interactions between universities and industry in Austria: Sectoral patterns and determinants. *Research Policy*, *31*, 303–328. doi:10.1016/S0048-7333(01)00111-1

Schein, E. H. (1984). Coming to a new awareness of organizational culture. *Sloan Management Review*, *25*(2), 3–16.

Schein, E. H. (1985). How culture forms, develops, and changes. In R. Kilman, M. J. Saxton, et al. (Eds.), *Gaining control of the corporate culture* (pp. 17-43). San Francisco: Jossey-Bass.

Schein, E. H. (1985). *Organizational culture and leadership: A dynamic view*. San Francisco, CA: Jossey-Bass.

Schein, E. H. (1992). *Organizational culture and leadership*. San Francisco: The Jossey-Bass Inc.

Schein, E. H. (1996). Culture: The missing concept in organization studies. *Administrative Science Quarterly*, *41*(2), 229–240. doi:10.2307/2393715

Schein, E. H. (1996). Three cultures of management: The key to organizational learning. *Sloan Management Review*, *38*(1), 9–20.

Schlenker, B. R. (1980). *Impression management: The self-concept, social identity, and interpersonal relations*. Monterey, CA: Brooks/Cole.

Schmidt, S. M., & Kipnis, D. (1984). Managers' pursuit of individual and organizational goals. *Human Relations*, *37*, 781–794. doi:10.1177/001872678403701001

Schreiber, G. A., de Hoog, R., Shadbolt, N., Van de Velde, W., & Wielinga, B. (1999). *Knowledge engineering and management: The CommonKADS methodology*. Cambridge, MA: The MIT Press.

Schreyögg, G., & Kliesch, M. (2005). *Dynamic capabilities and the development of organizational competencies* (Discussion Papers No. 25/05). Berlin: Freie Universität Berlin.

Schultz, T. W. (1961). Investment in human capital. *The American Economic Review*, *51*(1), 1–17.

Schumann, C.-A., & Tittmann, C. (2007). Multilevel cross-linking and offering of organisational knowledge. In B. Martins & D. Remenyi (Eds.), *Proceedings of the 8th European Conference on Knowledge Management, ECKM2007*, Barcelona, Spain (pp. 878-883).

Schumann, C.-A., Tittmann, C., & Tittmann, S. (2008). Merger of knowledge network and users support for lifelong learning services. In M. Kendall & B. Samways (Eds.), *Learning to live in the knowledge society.* Berlin, Germany: Springer Verlag.

Schumpeter, J. (1934). *The theory of economic development.* Cambridge, MA: Harvard University Press.

Schumpeter, J. A. (1947). *Capitalism, socialism and democracy.* New York: Harper and Brothers.

Schwartz, S. H. (1992). Universals in the content and structure of values: Theoretical advances and empirical tests in 20 countries. In M. Zanna (Ed.), *Advances in experimental social psychology* (Vol. 25, pp. 1-65). New York: Academic Press.

Schwartz, S. H. (1994). Beyond individualism/collectivism: New cultural dimensions of values. In U. Kim, H. C. Triandis, C. Kagitcibasi, S. C. Choi, & G. Yoon (Eds.), *Individualism and collectivism: Theory, method, and applications* (pp. 85-119). Thousand Oaks, CA: Sage.

Schwartz, S. H., & Bilsky, W. (1987). Toward a psychological structure of human values. *Journal of Personality and Social Psychology, 53*, 550–562. doi:10.1037/0022-3514.53.3.550

Schwartz, S. H., & Bilsky, W. (1990). Toward a theory of the universal content and structure of values: Extensions and cross-cultural replications. *Journal of Personality and Social Psychology, 58*, 878–891. doi:10.1037/0022-3514.58.5.878

Schwartz, S. H., Melech, G., Lehmann, A., Burgess, S., Harris, M., & Owens, V. (2001). Extending the cross-cultural validity of the theory of basic human values with a different method of measurement. *Journal of Cross-Cultural Psychology, 32*(5), 519–542. doi:10.1177/0022022101032005001

Scott, P. (2003). Challenges to academic values and the organisation of academic work in a time of globalisation. *Higher Education in Europe, 28*(3), 295–306. doi:10.1080/0379772032000119937

Scottish Executive Annual Survey of Small Businesses. (2003). *Final report enterprise and lifelong learning.*

Scottish Executive Annual Survey of Small Businesses. (2005). *Final report enterprise and lifelong learning.*

Scottish Executive. (2004). *The framework for economic development in Scotland.* Scottish Executive.

Scottish Government. (2007). *The government economic strategy.* The Scottish Government, Edinburgh, Scotland.

Scottish Government. (2008). *Annual survey of small business opinions 2006.* Scottish Government.

Seaman, C., Graham, S., & Falconer, P. (2007). *Family businesses in Scotland: In pursuit of a national strategy for local solutions.* Paper Presented at "Bridging Cultures' Confronting Theory and Practice in Family Business,' Lancaster University Management School.

Seaman, C., Graham, S., & Falconer, P. (2009). Exploring Scottish family businesses: Economy, geography and community. *International Journal of Entrepreneurship and Small Business, 7*(3).

Seigel, D. S., Waldman, D. A., Atwater, L. E., & Link, A. N. (2003). Commercial knowledge transfers from universities to firm: Improving the effectiveness of university-industry collaboration. *Journal of High Technology Research, 14*, 111–133. doi:10.1016/S1047-8310(03)00007-5

Selmer, J. (2006). Adjustment of business expatriates in greater China: A strategic perspective. *International Journal of Human Resource Management, 17*(12), 1994–2008.

Selmer, J., Chiu, R. K., & Shenkar, O. (2007). Cultural distance asymmetry in expatriate adjustment. *Cross Cultural Management, 14*(2), 150–160. doi:10.1108/13527600710745750

Selznick, P. (1957). *Leadership in administration: A sociological interpretation.* New York: Harper and Row.

Senge, P. (1990). *The fifth discipline: The art and practice of the learning organisation.* London: Random House.

Senge, P. M. (2006). *The fifth discipline: The art & practice of the learning organization.* New York: Currency Doubleday.

Serban, A. M., & Luan, J. (Eds.). (2002). *Knowledge management: Building a competitive advantage in higher education* (New Directions for Institutional Research, No. 113). San Francisco: Jossey-Bass.

Seufert, A., Von Krogh, G., & Bach, A. (1999). Towards knowledge networking. *Journal of Knowledge Management, 3*(3), 180–190. doi:10.1108/13673279910288608

Sewell, N. (1997). Continuous quality improvement in acute health care, creating a holistic and integrated approach. *International Journal of Health Care Quality Assurance, 10*, 20–26. doi:10.1108/09526869710159598

Shaffer, M. A., Harrison, D. A., Gregersen, H., Black, J. S., & Ferzandi, L. A. (2006). You can take it with you: Individual differences and expatriate effectiveness. *The Journal of Applied Psychology, 91*(1), 109–125. doi:10.1037/0021-9010.91.1.109

Shahnawaz, M. G., & Bala, M. (2007). Exploring individualism-collectivism in young employees of new organizations. *Journal of Indian Psychology, 25*(1-2), 24–40.

Shanker, M. C., & Astrachan, J. H. (1996). Myths and realities: Family businesses contribution to the U.S. economy. A framework for assessing business statistics. *Family Business Review, 9*(2), 107–119. doi:10.1111/j.1741-6248.1996.00107.x

Shapiro, C., & Varian, H. (1998). *Information rules: A strategic guide to the network economy*. Boston: Harvard Business School Press.

Sharimllah Devi, R., Chong, S. C., & Lin, B. (2007). Organizational culture and KM processes from the perspective of an institution of higher learning. *Int. Journal of Management Education, 1*(1/2), 57–79.

Sharma, P. (2006). An overview of the field of family business studies: Current status and directions for the future. In P. Z. Poutziouris, K. X. Smyrnios, & S. B. Klein (Eds.), *Handbook of research on family businesses*. Cheltenham, UK: Edward Elgar.

Shaw, P. (2002). *Changing conversations in organizations: A complexity approach to change*. London: Routledge.

Shenhar, A. J., van Wyk, R., Steganovic, J., & Gaynor, G. (2005). *Technofact: Toward a fundamental entity of technology - a new look at technology and MOT*. Retrieved December 2005, from http://howe.stevens.edu/CTMR/WorkingPapers/WP2005/index.html

Shimanoff, S. B. (1994). Gender perspectives on facework: Simplistic stereotypes vs. complex realities. In S. Ting-Toomey (Ed.), *The challenge of facework: Cross-cultural and interpersonal issues* (pp. 159-207). Albany, NY: State University of New York Press.

Shimoni, T., Ronen, S., & Roziner, I. (2005). Predicting expatriate adjustment: Israel as a host country. *International Journal of Cross Cultural Management, 5*(3), 293–312. doi:10.1177/1470595805060812

Silverthorne, C. P. (2005). *Organizational psychology in cross-cultural perspective*. New York: New York University Press.

Simonin, B. (1999). Transfer of marketing know-how in international strategic alliances: An empirical investigation of the role and antecedents of knowledge ambiguity. *Journal of International Business Studies, 30*(3), 463–490. doi:10.1057/palgrave.jibs.8490079

Simonin, B. L. (1999). Ambiguity and the process of knowledge transfer in strategic alliances. *Strategic Management Journal, 20*(7), 595–623. doi:10.1002/(SICI)1097-0266(199907)20:7<595::AID-SMJ47>3.0.CO;2-5

Simons, R. (1995). *Levers of control: How managers use innovative control systems to drive strategic renewal*. Boston: Harvard Business School Press.

Simons, R. (2000). *Performance measurement and control systems for implementing strategy*. Upper Saddle River, NJ: Prentice Hall.

Smirnov, A., Pashkin, M., Chilov, N., & Levashova, T. (2004). Knowledge logistics in information grid environment. *Future Generation Computer Systems, 20*, 61–79. doi:10.1016/S0167-739X(03)00165-1

Snowden, D. (2002). Complex acts of knowing: Paradox and descriptive self-awareness. *Journal of Knowledge Management, 6*(2), 100–111. doi:10.1108/13673270210424639

Snyder, M. (1974). Self-monitoring of expressive behaviour. *Journal of Personality and Social Psychology, 30*(4), 526–537. doi:10.1037/h0037039

Sojka, J. Z., & Tansuhaj, P. (1995). Cross-cultural research: A twenty-year review. *Advances in Consumer Research. Association for Consumer Research (U. S.),* 461–474.

Solow, R. (1957). Technical change and the aggregate production function. *The Review of Economics and Statistics, 39,* 312–320. doi:10.2307/1926047

Spencer, J. W. (2003). Firm's knowledge-sharing strategies in the global innovation system: Empirical evidence from the flat panel display industry. *Strategic Management Journal, 24,* 217–233. doi:10.1002/smj.290

Spender, J. C. (2003). Knowledge fields: Some post 9/11 thoughts about the knowledge-based theory of firm. In C. W. Holsapple (Ed.), *Handbook on knowledge management—knowledge matters* (pp. 59–71). Berlin, Germany: Springer-Verlag.

Spender, J.-C. (1992). Limits to learning from the West. *The International Executive, 34,* 389–410.

Spender, J.-C. (1996). Making knowledge the basis of a dynamic theory of the firm. *Strategic Management Journal, 17,* 45–62.

Spender, J.-C. (1998). The dynamics of individual and organizational knowledge. In C. Eden & J.-C. Spender (Eds.), *Managerial and organizational cognition theory, methods and research.* London: SAGE Publications.

Spender, J.-C., & Grant, R. (1996). Knowledge and the firm: Overview. *Strategic Management Journal, 17,* 5–9.

Spurlock, M. (Director). (2004). *Supersize me* [Motion picture]. USA: Samuel Goldwyn Films.

Srikanthan, G., & Dalrymple, J. F. (2002). Developing a holistic model for quality in higher education. *Quality in Higher Education, 8*(2), 215–224. doi:10.1080/1353832022000031656

Sriramesh, K., & Vercic, D. (2001). International public relations: A framework for future research. *Journal of Communication Management, 6*(2), 103–117. doi:10.1108/13632540210806973

Stacey, R. D., Griffin, D., & Shaw, P. (2000). *Complexity and management: Fad or radical challenge to systems thinking?* London: Routledge.

Stahl, G. K., & Caligiuri, P. (2005). The effectiveness of expatriate coping strategies: The moderating role of cultural distance, position level, and time on the international assignment. *The Journal of Applied Psychology, 90*(4), 603–615. doi:10.1037/0021-9010.90.4.603

Starbuck, W. H. (1992). Learning by knowledge intensive firms. *Journal of Management Studies, 29*(6), 713–740. doi:10.1111/j.1467-6486.1992.tb00686.x

Stark, J. (2007). *PLM enabling global products.* London: Springer Verlag.

Starkey, K., & Tempest, S. (2005). The future of the business school: Knowledge challenges and opportunities. *Human Relations, 58*(1), 61–82. doi:10.1177/0018726705050935

Staw, B. M. (1980). Rationality and justification in organizational life. In B. M. Staw & L. L. Cummings (Eds.), *Research in organizational behavior* (Vol. 2, pp. 45-80). Greenwich, CT: JAI.

Steier, L. (2001). Variants of agency contracts in family financed ventures as a continuum of familial altruistic and market rationalities. *Journal of Business Venturing, 18*(5), 597–618. doi:10.1016/S0883-9026(03)00012-0

Stein, E. W. (1995). Organizational memory: Review of concepts and recommendations for management. *International Journal of Information Management, 15*(1), 17. doi:10.1016/0268-4012(94)00003-C

Stenmark, D. (2001). Leveraging tacit organizational knowledge. *Journal of Management Information Systems, 17*(3), 9–24.

Stepek, M., & Laird, M. (2007). *SFBA strategy: A discussion document.* Scottish Family Business Association.

Stephens, G. K., Bird, A., & Mendenhall, M. E. (2002). International careers as repositories of knowledge: A new look at expatriation. In D. C. Feldman (Ed.), *Work careers: A developmental perspective* (pp. 257-320). San Francisco: Jossey-Bass.

Sterns, H. L., & Dorsett, J. G. (1994). Career development: A lifespan issue. *Experimental Aging Research, 20*(4), 257–264. doi:10.1080/03610739408253975

Sterns, H. L., & Doverspike, D. (1989). Aging and the training and learning process in organizations. In I. L. Goldstein & R. Katzell (Eds.), *Training and development in work organizations.* (pp. 299-332). San Francisco: Jossey-Bass.

Sterns, H. L., & Miklos, S. M. (1995). Aging worker in a changing environment: Organizational and individual issues. *Journal of Vocational Behavior, 47*, 248–268. doi:10.1006/jvbe.1995.0003

Stewart, F., & Samman, E. (2006). Human development: Beyond the human development index. *Journal of Human Development, 7*(3), 323–358. doi:10.1080/14649880600815917

Stewart, T. A. (1997). *Intellectual capital: The new wealth of organizations.* New York: Doubleday/Currency.

Steyn, G. M. (2004). Harnessing the power of knowledge in higher education. *Education, 124*(4), 615–631.

Strack, R., Baier, J., & Fahlender, A. (2008). Managing demographic risk. *Harvard Business Review,* (February): 119–128.

Subramaniam, M., & Youndt, M. A. (2005). The influence of intellectual capital on the types of innovative capabilities. *Academy of Management Journal, 48*(3), 450–463.

Sullivan, P. H. (Ed.). (1998). *Profiting from intellectual capital: extracting value from innovation.* New York: John Wiley & Sons.

Sveiby, K. (1998). Intellectual capital: thinking ahead. *Australian CPA, June,* 18-22.

Sveiby, K. E. (1997). *The new organizational wealth: Managing and measuring knowledge-based assets.* New York: Berrett-Kohler.

Swan, J. A., Scarbrough, H., & Preston, J. (1999). Knowledge management – the next fad to

Swap, W., Leonard, D., Shields, M., & Abrams, L. (2001). Using mentoring and storytelling to transfer knowledge in the workplace. *Journal of Management Information Systems, 18*(1), 95–114.

Sydow, J. (2006). *Management von netzwerkorganisationen.* Wiesbaden, Germany: Gabler Verlag.

Syed-Ikhsan, S. O. S., & Rowland, F. (2004). Knowledge management in a public organization: A study on the relationship between organizational elements and the performance of knowledge transfer. *Journal of Knowledge Management, 8*(2), 95–111. doi:10.1108/13673270410529145

Szulanski, G. (1995). Unpacking stickiness: An empirical investigation of the barriers to transfer best practice inside the firm. *Academy of Management Journal, 38*, 437–441.

Szulanski, G. (1996). Exploring internal stickiness: Impediments to the transfer of best practice within the firm. *Strategic Management Journal, 19*, 27–44.

Szulanski, G. (2000). The process of knowledge transfer: A diachronic analysis of stickiness. *Organizational Behavior and Human Decision Processes, 82*(1), 9–27. doi:10.1006/obhd.2000.2884

Szulanski, G. (2003). *Sticky knowledge: Barriers to knowing in the firm.* London: SAGE.

Szulanski, G., & Jensen, R. (2004). Stickiness and the adaptation of organizational practices in cross-boarder knowledge transfers . *Journal of International Business Studies, 34*(6), 508–523.

Szulanski, G., & Jensen, R. J. (2006). Presumptive adaptation and the effectiveness of knowledge transfer. *Strategic Management Journal, 27*(10), 10. doi:10.1002/smj.551

Takeuchi, H., & Nonaka, I. (Eds.). (2004). *Hitotsubashi on knowledge management.* Singapore: John Wiley & Sons.

Takeutchi, H. (1998). *Beyond knowledge management: Lessons from Japan.* Retrieved January 15, 2005, from http://www.sveiby.com/articles/LessonsJapan.htm

Tannenbaum, S., & Alliger, G. (2000). *Knowledge management: Clarifying the key issues.* Paper presented at the IHRIM.

Taylor Small, C., & Tatalias, J. (2000). *Knowledge management model guides KM process.* Retrieved April 7, 2002, from http://www.mitre.org/news/the_edge/april_00/small.html

Taylor, (1997)... *International Journal of Technology Management, 11*(3), 385–391.

Teece, D. J. (1998). Capturing value from knowledge assets: The new economy, markets for know-how, and intangible assets. *California Management Review, 40*(3), 55–79.

Teece, D. J. (2007). Explicating dynamic capabilities: The nature and microfoundations of (sustainable) enterprise performance. *Strategic Management Journal, 28*(13), 1319–1350. doi:10.1002/smj.640

Teece, D. J., Pisano, G., & Shuen, A. (1997). Dynamic capabilities and strategic management. *Strategic Management Journal, 18*, 509–533. doi:10.1002/(SICI)1097-0266(199708)18:7<509::AID-SMJ882>3.0.CO;2-Z

Telegraph. (2008). *Green grows the value so when you go eco-friendly.* Retrieved from http://www.telegraph.co.uk/property/main.jhtml?xml=/property/2004/06/26/prgre26.xml

Thompson, V. A. (1965). Bureaucracy and innovation. *Administrative Science Quarterly, 10*(1), 1–20. doi:10.2307/2391646

Thorelli, H. B. (1986). Networks: Between markets and hierarchies. *Strategic Management Journal, 7*(1), 37–51. doi:10.1002/smj.4250070105

Thornton, B., Audesse, R. J., Ryckman, R. M., & Burckle, M. J. (2006). Playing dumb and knowing it all: Two sides of an impression management coin. *Individual Differences Research, 4*(1), 37–45.

Tian, Y. (2006). Communicating with local publics: A case study of Coca Cola's Chinese website. *Corporate Communications: An International Journal, 11*(1), 13–22. doi:10.1108/13563280610643516

Timmerman, G., & Bajema, C. (1999). Incidence and methodology in sexual harassment research in northwest Europe. *Women's Studies International Forum, 22*(6), 673–681. doi:10.1016/S0277-5395(99)00076-X

Timo, N. (2001). Lean or just mean? The flexibilisation of labour in the Australian hotel industry. *Research in the Sociology of Work, 10*, 287–309. doi:10.1016/S0277-2833(01)80030-3

Ting-Toomey, S. (1999). *Communicating across cultures.* New York: Guilford.

Ting-Toomey, S. (Ed.). (1994). *The challenge of facework: Cross-cultural and interpersonal issues.* Albany, NY: State University of New York.

Tippins, M. (2003). Implementing knowledge management in academia: Teaching the teachers. *International Journal of Educational Management, 17*(7), 339–345. doi:10.1108/09513540310501021

Tiwana, A. (2000). *The knowledge management toolkit: Practical techniques for building a knowledge management system.* Upper Saddle River, NJ: Prentice Hall.

Tremblay, P. (2005). Learning networks and tourism innovation in the top end. In D. Carson & J. Macbeth (Eds.), *Regional tourism cases: Innovation in regional tourism* (pp. 53-59). Australia: Common Ground Publishing Pty Ltd.

Trevinyo-Rodriguez, R. N., & Tapies, J. (2006). Effective knowledge transfer in family firms. In P. Z. Poutziouris, K. X. Smyrnios, & S. B. Klein (Eds.), *Handbook of research on family business.* Cheltenham, UK: Edward Elgar.

Triandis, H. C. (1989). The self and social behaviour in differing cultural contexts. *Psychological Review, 96*, 506–520. doi:10.1037/0033-295X.96.3.506

Triandis, H. C. (1995). *Individualism and collectivism.* Boulder, CO: Westview Press.

Triandis, H. C., & Gelfand, M. (1998). Converging measurement of horizontal and vertical individualism and collectivism. *Journal of Personality and Social Psychology, 74*, 118–128. doi:10.1037/0022-3514.74.1.118

Trompenaars, F., & Hampden-Turner, C. (1997). *Riding the waves of culture: Understanding cultural diversity in business.* London: Nicholas Brealy Publishing Ltd.

Tsai, W. (2001). Knowledge transfer in intraorganizational networks: Effects of network position and absorptive capacity on business unit innovation and performance. *Academy of Management Journal, 44*(5), 996–1004. doi:10.2307/3069443

Tsoukas, H. (2003). Do we really understand tacit knowledge? In M. Easterby-Smith & M. A. Lyles (Eds.), *The Blackwell handbook of organizational learning and knowledge management* (pp. 410-427). Malden, MA: Blackwell.

Tsoukas, H., & Vladimirou, E. (2003). What is organizational knowledge? *Journal of Management Studies, 38*(7), 973–993. doi:10.1111/1467-6486.00268

Tsui, E. (2000). Exploring the KM toolbox. *Knowledge Management, 4*(2), 11–14.

Tylor, E. B. (1871). *Primitive culture: Researches into the development of mythology, philosophy, religion, art and custom, vol. 1.* London: John Murray.

Uhlander, L. M., & Habberson, T. (2005). *Family influence, strategy, and innovation in family firms: Application of the DSP-"f" model in an exploratory four country investigation.* Paper Presented at FBN-IFERA (International Family Enterprise Research Academy) Conference, Barcelona, Spain.

UK Intellectual Property Office. (2008). *Intellectual property explained.* Retrieved October 2008, from http://www.ipo.gov.uk/whatis.htm

Valera, G. (2006). The higher educational system in Mexico at the threshold of change. *International Journal of Educational Development, 26*, 52–66. doi:10.1016/j.ijedudev.2005.07.012

Van de Ven, A. H. (1986). Central problems in the management of innovation. *Management Science, 32*(5), 590–607. doi:10.1287/mnsc.32.5.590

Van de Ven, A. H., & Angle, H. L. (2000). An introduction to the Minnesota innovation research program. In A. H. Van de Ven, H. L. Angle, & M. Scott-Poole, (Eds.), *Research on the management of innovation: The Minnesota studies* (pp. 3-30). New York: Oxford University Press.

van der Spek, R., & Spijkervet, A. (1997). Knowledge management: Dealing intelligently with knowledge. In J. Liebowitz & L. Wilcox (Eds.), *Knowledge management and its intergrative elements.* New York: CRC Press.

Van Dyne, L., Vandewalle, D., Kostova, T., Latham, M. E., & Cummings, L. L. (2000). Collectivism, propensity to trust and self-esteem as predictors of organizational citicenship in a non-work setting. *Journal of Organizational Behavior, 21*, 3–23. doi:10.1002/(SICI)1099-1379(200002)21:1<3::AID-JOB47>3.0.CO;2-6

Van Wyk, R. J. (2002). Technology: A fundamental structure. *Knowledge, Technology, and Policy, 15*(3).

van Wyk, R. J. (2004). *A credo for MOT.* Retrieved August 2004, from http://iamot.org/homepage/ACRE-DOFORMOT-2004.pdf

Varela, F. (1979). *Principles of biological autonomy.* New York: Elsevier (North-Holland).

Vatter, W. J. (1947). *The fund theory of accounting and its implications for financial reports.* Chicago, IL: The University of Chicago Press.

Vaugeois, N., & Rollins, R. (2007). Mobility into tourism: Refuge employer? *Annals of Tourism Research, 34*(3), 630–648. doi:10.1016/j.annals.2007.02.001

Venzin, M., Krogh, G. v., & Roos, J. (1998). Future research into knowledge management. In G. v. Krogh, J. Roos, & D. Kleine (Eds.), *Knowing in firms, understanding, managing and measuring knowledge.* London: SAGE Publications.

Viale, R., & Pozzali, A. (2007). Cognitive aspects of tacit knowledge and cultural diversity. In L. Magnani

& P. Li (Eds.), *Model-based reasoning in science, technology, and medicine* (pp. 229-244). Heidelberg, Germany: Springer.

Vilela, B. B., González, J. A. V., Ferrín, P. F., & del Río Araújo, M. L. (2007). Impression management tactics and affective context: Influence on sales performance appraisal. *European Journal of Marketing, 41*(5-6), 624–639. doi:10.1108/03090560710737651

Völker, R., Sauer, S., & Simon, M. (2007). *Wissensmanagement im innovationsprozess*. Heidelberg, Germany: Physica-Verlag.

Von Hippel, E. (1994). 'Sticky information' and the locus of problem solving: Implications for innovation. *Management Science, 40*(4), 429–439. doi:10.1287/mnsc.40.4.429

Von Krogh, G. (1998). Care in knowledge creation. *California Management Review, 40*(3), 133–153.

von Krogh, G., Back, A., & Enkel, E. (2007). *Knowledge networks for business growth*. Berlin, Germany: Springer.

Von Krogh, G., Ichijo, K., & Nonaka, I. (2000). *Enabling knowledge creation: How to unlock the mystery of tacit knowledge and release the power of innovation*. Oxford, UK: Oxford University Press.

Von Krogh, G., Nonaka, I., & Aben, M. (2001). Making the most of your company's knowledge: A strategic framework. *Long Range Planning, 34*(4), 421–439. doi:10.1016/S0024-6301(01)00059-0

von Zedtwitz, M. (2007). *Innovation in China – from an R&D perspective*. Presentation in Lotus Flower Day, VTT Espoo.

Vonk, R. (1998). The slime effect: Suspicion and dislike of likeable behaviour toward superiors. *Journal of Personality and Social Psychology, 74*(4), 849–864. doi:10.1037/0022-3514.74.4.849

Vonk, R. (2002). Self-serving interpretations of flattery: Why ingratiation works. *Journal of Personality and Social Psychology, 82*(4), 515–526. doi:10.1037/0022-3514.82.4.515

Voronov, M., & Singer, J. (2002). The myth of individualism-collectivism: A critical review. *The Journal of Social Psychology, 142*(4), 461–480.

Walsh, J. P. (1995). Managerial and organizational cognition: Notes from a trip down memory lane. *Organization Science, 6*(3), 280–321. doi:10.1287/orsc.6.3.280

Walsh, J. P., & Ungson, G. R. (1991). Organizational memory. *Academy of Management Review, 16*(1), 57–91. doi:10.2307/258607

Wang, Y., & Lu, L. (2007). Knowledge transfer through effective university-industry interactions: Empirical experiences from China. *Journal of Technology Management in China, 2*(2), 119–133. doi:10.1108/17468770710756068

Ward, J. L. (1987). *Keeping the family business healthy*. San Francisco: Jossey-Bass.

Wartofsky, M. (1979). *Models: Representation and scientific understanding*. Dordrecht, The Netherlands: Reidel.

Watson, T. (1994). *In search of management: Culture, chaos and control in managerial work*. London: International Thomson Business Press.

Wayne, S. J., & Liden, R. C. (1995). Effects of impression management on performance ratings: A longitudinal study. *Academy of Management Journal. Special Issue: Intra- and Interorganizational Cooperation, 38*(1), 232-260.

Weber, F., Wunram, M., Kemp, J., Pudlatz, M., & Bredehorst, B. (2002). Standardisation in knowledge management – towards a common KM framework in Europe. In *Towards Common Approaches & Standards in KM, Proceedings of the UNICOM Seminar*, London.

Weggeman, M. (1997). *Kennismanagement, inrichting es besturing vas kennisintensieve organisaties*. Schiedam, The Netherlands: Scriptum management.

Wegner, D. (1987). Transactive memory: A contemporary analysis of group mind. In B. Mullen & G. Goethals (Eds.), *Theories of group behavior* (pp. 185-208). New York: Springer.

Weick, K. E. (1976). Educational organizations as loosely coupled systems. *Administrative Science Quarterly, 21,* 1–19. doi:10.2307/2391875

Weick, K. E. (1995). *Sensemaking in organizations.* London: SAGE Publications.

Weir, D., & Hutchings, K. (2005). Cultural embeddedness and contextual constraints: Knowledge sharing in Chinese and Arab cultures. *Knowledge and Process Management, 12*(2), 89–98. doi:10.1002/kpm.222

Wenger, E. (1998). Communities of practice: Learning as a social system. *Systems thinker, 9*(5).

Wenger, E. (2004). Knowledge management as a doughnut: Shaping your knowledge strategy through communities of practice. *Ivey Business Journal, 2004*(January/February). Retrieved August 12, 2008, from http://www.iveybusinessjournal.com/view_article.asp?intArticle_ID=465

Wenger, E. C. (1998). *Communities of practice: Learning, meaning and identity.* New York: Cambridge University Press.

Wernefelt, B. (1984). A resource-based view of the firm. *Strategic Management Journal, 5*(2), 171–180. doi:10.1002/smj.4250050207

Westhead, P., & Cowling, M. (1997). Performance contrasts between family and non-family unquoted companies in the UK. *International Journal of Entrepreneurial Behaviour & Research, 3*(1), 30–52. doi:10.1108/13552559710170892

Westphal, J. D., & Stern, I. (2006). The other pathway to the boardroom: Interpersonal influence behaviour as a substitute for elite credentials and majority status in obtaining board appointments. *Administrative Science Quarterly, 51*(2), 169–204. doi:10.2189/asqu.51.2.169

Westphal, J. D., & Stern, I. (2007). Flattery will get you everywhere (especially if you are a male Caucasian): How ingratiation, boardroom behaviour, and demographic minority status affect additional board appointments at U.S. companies. *Academy of Management Journal, 50*(2), 267–288.

Wheatley, M. J. (1992). *Leadership and the new science: Learning about organization from an orderly universe.* San Francisco: Berrett-Koehler.

Wheatley, M. J., & Kellner-Rogers, M. (1996). *A simpler way.* San Francisco: Berrett-Koehler.

White, J., & Weathersby, R. (2005). Can universities become true learning organizations? *The Learning Organization, 12*(3), 292–298. doi:10.1108/09696470510592539

Whittington, R. (2006). Completing the practice turn in strategy research. *Organization Studies, 27,* 613–634. doi:10.1177/0170840606064101

Wickramasinghe, N. (2006). Knowledge creation: A meta-framework. *International Journal of Innovation and Learning, 3*(5), 558–573.

Wiig, K. (2004). *People-focused knowledge management.* Oxford, UK: Elsevier Inc.

Wiig, K. M. (1993). *Knowledge management foundations: - Thinking about thinking – how people and organizations create, represent and use knowledge.* Arlington, TX: Schema Press.

Wiig, K. M. (1997). Knowledge management: An introduction and perspective. *The Journal of Knowledge Management*, September, *1*(1), 6-14.

Wiig, K. M. (1997). Knowledge management: Where did it come from and where will it go? *Expert Systems with Applications, 13*(1), 1–14. doi:10.1016/S0957-4174(97)00018-3

Wiig, K. M. (1999). What future knowledge management users may expect. *Journal of Knowledge Management, 3*(2), 155–165. doi:10.1108/13673279910275611

Wildes, V. J. (2007). Attracting and retaining food servers: How internal service quality moderates occupational stigma. *International Journal of Hospitality Management, 26*(1), 4–19. doi:10.1016/j.ijhm.2005.08.003

Wildner, S., Lehner, F., & Lehmann, H. (2007). Holistic approaches and standardisation as measures for broader adoption of KM in practice. In B. Martin & D. Remenyi (Ed.), *ECKM 2007 8th European Conference on Knowl-*

edge Management 2007, Volume Two (pp. 1107-1114). Academic Conferences Limited.

Wilkens, U., Menzel, D., & Pawlowsky, P. (2004). Inside the black-box: Analysing the generation of core competencies and dynamic capabilities by exploring collective minds. *An Organisational Learning Perspective. Management Review, 15*(1), 8–26.

Williams, C. (2007). Transfer in context: Replication and adaptation in knowledge transfer relationships. *Strategic Management Journal, 28*, 867–889. doi:10.1002/smj.614

Williams, J. D., Han, S.-L., & Qualls, W. J. (1998). A conceptual model and study of cross-cultural business relationships. *Journal of Business Research, 42*, 135–143. doi:10.1016/S0148-2963(97)00109-4

Wilson, D. A. (1996). *Managing knowledge.* Oxford, UK: Butterworth Heinnmann.

Wilson, T. (2002). The nonsense of knowledge management. *Information Research, 8*(1).

Wilson, T. D. (2002). The nonsense of knowledge management. *Information Research, 8*(1). Retrieved February 6, 2003, from http://InformationR.net/ir/8-1/paper144.html

Wind, J., & Main, J. (1999). *Driving change.* New York: The Free Press.

Winter, S. G. (2000). The satisfying principle in capability learning. *Strategic Management Journal, 21*, 981–996. doi:10.1002/1097-0266(200010/11)21:10/11<981::AID-SMJ125>3.0.CO;2-4

Wit, B., & Meyer, R. (1998). *Strategy: Process, content, context.* London: International Thomson Business Press.

Wold, H. (1985). Partial least squares. In S. Kotz & N. L. Johnson (Eds.), *Encyclopedia of statistical sciences* (pp. 581-591). New York: Wiley.

Woods, E., & Sheina, M. (1999). *Knowledge management: Building the collaborative enterprise* (Report). London: Ovum Ltd.

Woods, R., Heck, W., & Sciarini, M. (1998). *Turnover and diversity in the lodging industry.* American Hotel Foundation.

Yamazaki, Y. (2005). Learning styles and typologies of cultural differences: A theoretical and empirical comparison. *International Journal of Intercultural Relations, 29*(5), 521–548. doi:10.1016/j.ijintrel.2005.07.006

Yamazaki, Y., & Kayes, D. C. (2007). Expatriate learning: Exploring how Japanese managers adapt in the United States. *International Journal of Human Resource Management, 18*(8), 1373–1395.

Yin, R. K. (2003). *Case study research: Design and methods.* (3rd ed.). Thousand Oaks, CA: Sage.

Youndt, M. A., Subramaniam, M., & Snell, S. A. (2004). Intellectual capital profiles: An examination of investments and returns. *Journal of Management Studies, 41*(2), 335–362. doi:10.1111/j.1467-6486.2004.00435.x

Yurke, B., & Denker, J. S. (1984). Quantum network theory. *Physical Review A., 29*(3), 1419–1437. doi:10.1103/PhysRevA.29.1419

Zack, M. H. (1999). Developing a knowledge strategy. *California Management Review, 41*(3), 125–146.

Zack, M. H. (1999). Managing codified knowledge. *Sloan Management Review, 40*(4), 45–59.

Zahra, S. A., Klein, S. B., & Astrachan, J. H. (2006). Epilogue: Theory building and the survival of family firms – three promising research directions. In P. Z. Poutziouris, K. X. Smyrnios, & S. B. Klein (Eds.), *Handbook of research on family businesses.* Cheltenham, UK: Edward Elgar.

Zammuto, R. F., Gifford, G., & Goodman, E. A. (1999). Managerial ideologies, organisation culture and the outcomes of innovation: a competing values prospective. In N. Ashkanasy, C. Wilderon, & M. Peterson (Eds.), *The handbook of organisational culture and climate* (pp. 263-280). Thousand Oaks, CA: Sage Publications.

Zander, U., & Bruce, K. (1995). Knowledge and the speed of transfer and imitation of organizational capabilities:

An empirical test. *Organization Science*, *6*(1), 76–92. doi:10.1287/orsc.6.1.76

Zander, U., & Kogut, B. (1995). Knowledge and the speed of transfer and imitation of organizational capabilities: An empirical test. *Organization Science*, *6*(1), 76–92. doi:10.1287/orsc.6.1.76

Zapata, L. E. (2004). *Los determinantes de la generación y la transferencia del conocimiento en pequeñas empresas de tecnologías de la información en Barcelona*. Unpublished doctoral dissertation, Universidad Autónoma de Barcelona, Barcelona.

Zappia, C. A. (2000). The private sector and public higher education. *Perspectives, 38*(5). Retrieved June 15, 2007, from http://www.historians.org/perspectives/issues/2000/0005/0005spl5.cfm

Zeleny, M., & Hufford, K. D. (1992). The application of autopoiesis in systems analysis: Are autopoietic systems also social systems? *International Journal of General Systems*, *21*, 145–160. doi:10.1080/03081079208945066

Zemke, R., Raines, C., & Filipczak, B. (2000). *Generations at work: Managing the clash of veterans, boomers, xers, and nexters in your workplace*. New York: AMACOM.

Zhang, H. Q., & Wu, E. (2004). Human resources issues facing the hotel and travel industry in China. *International Journal of Contemporary Hospitality Management, 16*(7), 424–428. doi:10.1108/09596110410559122

Zhu, Z. (2004). Knowledge management: Towards a universal concept or cross-cultural contexts? *Knowledge Management Research & Practice, 2*, 67–79. doi:10.1057/palgrave.kmrp.8500032

Zhuge, H. (2002). A knowledge flow model for peer-to-peer team knowledge sharing and management. *Expert Systems with Applications*, *23*(1), 23–30. doi:10.1016/S0957-4174(02)00024-6

Zhuge, H. (2006). Knowledge flow network planning and simulation. *Decision Support Systems*, *42*(2), 571–592. doi:10.1016/j.dss.2005.03.007

Zhuge, H., Guo, W., & Li, X. (2006). The potential energy of knowledge flow. *Concurrency and Computation*, *19*(15), 2067–2090. doi:10.1002/cpe.1143

Zopiatis, A., & Constanti, P. (2007). Human resource challenges confronting the Cyprus hospitality industry. *EuroMed Journal of Business*, *2*(2), 135–153. doi:10.1108/14502190710826022

Zukin, S., & Maguire, J. S. (2004). Consumers and consumption. *Annual Review of Sociology*, *30*, 173–197. doi:10.1146/annurev.soc.30.012703.110553

About the Contributors

Deogratias Harorimana, a proud British-Rwandan completed his PhD in Knowledge Management around the topic of the Role of Gatekeepers in the Knowledge creation and Transfer Process at Southampton Solent University and Nottingham Trent University following an earlier undergraduate at Southampton Solent University-then, called Southampton institute. As I was editing this book, I became the Deputy Chief Executive Officer (CEO) in charge of Human Capital and Institutional Development within the newly created Rwanda Development Board (RDB). Key responsibilities there include (a) instituting mechanisms of increasing National Expertise and Capacity and (b) Instituting mechanisms of evaluating and monitoring services rendered by foreign National to Rwanda by developing knowledge transfer strategy as well as the monitoring mechanism for the country. (c) Further responsibilities include developing national institutions' capacity and instituting mechanisms that support the development of the public and private sector partnership. Reporting to the president of Rwanda, His Excellency Paul Kagame; Rwanda Development Board employs more than 700 employees and it was inspired by the Economic Development Board (EDB) of Singapore. It has the mission of fast racking the development of Rwanda beyond aid. RDB was created from merging seven other existing agencies, namely former Rwanda Investment and Export promotion (RIEPA), Rwanda office of Tourism and Conservation (ORTPN), The Human and Institution Development Agency (HIDA), Rwanda Information Technology Authority (RITA), Centre for Business Registration, The Centre for Support to Small and Medium Enterprises in Rwanda (CAPMER), Rwanda Environment Management Agency (REMA); its division for Environmental Impact Assessment and the Secretariat for Privatisation. Previously I was a lecturer on Knowledge and competitiveness, information management at Southampton Solent University (UK). Prior to that, Deo worked in the Viva Group in its arm of healthcare insurance. I was chair of the Royal Geographical Society of Great Britain research group (Post Graduate Forum) since 2006. I became a committee member on the Research and Higher Education Division of the Society in 2007. In 2006, I became an Executive committee member (ACL Ltd)   and programme co-chair for the 9th European Conference on Knowledge Management (Southampton, UK). I have published books, journal articles and I regularly speak on internationally respected academic and practitioner's knowledge management conferences in the area of knowledge management in general, particularly on knowledge networks, knowledge gatekeepers, Identity and culture, Impact of culture on knowledge transfer and indigenous knowledge management.

* * *

Nekane Aramburu is a PhD in Economics and Business Administration and faculty member of the Organization and Business Policy Department of ESTE School of Management (University of Deusto, Spain). Her teaching areas are: Business Organization, Organizational Change, Organizational Learning, Knowledge Management and Innovation, and her current research focus is on the last three domains. Her research work has been published in specialized journals such as the Journal of Knowledge Management, The Learning Organization and the Journal of Intellectual Capital. She has collaborated in different research projects with diverse institutions which are focused on the aforementioned areas, such as the Knowledge Cluster of the Basque Region (Spain) and the Research Centre on the Knowledge Society (CIC–Autonomous University of Madrid, Spain). Finally, she is a connection member of the Society for Organizational Learning (SOL), an international network in the field of Organizational Learning promoted by Peter Senge.

Dr. Roberto Biloslavo is an associate professor in the fields of Management, Knowledge Management, and Strategic Management at the University of Primorska, Faculty of Management Koper. He is currently in a position of Vice-Rector for Study. His work experience includes the development of executive information systems, marketing and leading small business systems. His research work focuses on knowledge management, strategic decision-making, organizational culture, and strategic management of professional service firms and SMEs.

Peter Bond has enjoyed a varied career in the private and public sectors, industry and commerce, and ten years in academia (1990-2000) as Head of Technology Management Group at Liverpool John Moores University and Director of Studies for Manufacturing and Technology Management (John Moores and University of Liverpool). He has advised local economic development agencies on technology and enterprise support policy and acted as a consultant, coach and mentor, and as business analyst with a venture capital provider. His first consultancy and advisory business was established in 1989. Learning Futures (Consulting) was created in 2004. He adheres strongly to the belief that learning is the primary source of organizational performance improvement and competitiveness, and is a committed systems thinker. He has published several articles and papers on the nature of technology and on the application to organization development of the work of biologists and cyberneticians Humberto Maturana and Francisco Varela. He is currently exploring the connections between Maturana and Varela's theory of the biology of cognition and Robin Dunbar's Social Brain Hypothesis as possible elements of a new approach to improving organizational performance.

Christopher D. B. Burt (PhD. Canterbury) is an Associate Professor of Industrial and Organizational Psychology at the University of Canterbury. His current research centers on employee recruitment issues. As well as research on recruitment, he is conducting work on the relationship between trust and safety, and the influence of organizational context on time management outcomes. He has published over 40 papers in various international journals.

A/Prof Dean Carson, Associate Professor Dean Carson is the Head of Population Studies at Charles Darwin University. He has twenty years experience researching human mobility, with a focus on tourism. Dean has conducted research in regional and remote contexts across Australia, and published widely on how information and communications technologies help regional areas manage mobile populations. Dean took up his current role at the end of 2007, with the specific charter to develop theoretical models of the emergence of population dynamics in remote Australia.

Kalotina Chalkiti, PhD Candidate Kalotina Chalkiti investigates staff turnover in the Australian accommodation sector. Her work looks at how hospitality businesses that operate in dynamic labour environments can remain both operational and competitive. She contributes to academic discourse by researching turnover from a qualitative perspective aiming to draw out the knowledge management and social networking effects staff turnover has on remaining employees. She is supervised by researchers from both Charles Darwin University (Australia) and the University of Melbourne (Australia); while sustains active co-authorship ties with researchers from the University of the Aegean (Greece). Her work has been published in international peer reviewed scientific journals (e.g. Advances in Hospitality and Leisure, Current Issues in Tourism) co-authored with exceptional researchers from both Greece and Australia. Her research interests are social networks, knowledge sharing and staff turnover in hospitality businesses located in remote and peripheral tourism destinations.

Yanqing Duan, PhD, is a Professor of Information Systems at The University of Bedfordshire Business School. Her principal research interest is how the emerging Information and Communication Technologies (ICT) can be effectively used in, and their impact on, supporting decision making, facilitating knowledge transfer, and improving skills development. This research focus is reflected in the context of ICT-based knowledge management and transfer, use of intelligent systems in supporting organizational and individual decision making, Small to Medium Sized Enterprises' (SMEs) adoption of e-commerce/e-business, and web-based training systems for SMEs. She has co-ordinated many research projects funded by the European Commission and published over one hundred papers in journals, books and international conference proceedings.

Annette H. Dunham is a Doctoral candidate in Industrial and Organizational Psychology at the University of Canterbury, where she is investigating the relationship between organizational memory and mentoring variables, including the willingness to mentor, and expected costs and benefits of mentoring. Her research interests include organizational learning and development, and a life span approach to the career, with particular interest in issues surrounding mid-to-late career.

Cláudio Reis Gonçalo is an associate professor of Management at the University of the Sinos Valley - UNISINOS, São Leopoldo, Brazil. He holds an MBA in Management Science from Federal University of the Rio Grande do Sul, and a PhD in Production Engineering from Federal University of Santa Catarina on which he started being a fellow researcher at Monash University in the Knowledge Management Research Program, School of Information System, Melbourne, Australia. He has extensive experience of management in the sector of Electric Services before joining the research work in the academe profession. He served as assistant director for UNISINOS being responsible for the research projects in the latest two years, including 200 projects in the 20 doctoral programs. He coordinates a research project in the health care management field on which different hospitals of Brazil participate and can access the performance measures in the hospital organizational sector, facilitating the actions of management improvements based on other hospitals' managerial outcomes. His current research interests include organizational services strategy, knowledge management, organizational behavior in relation to information development and performance improvement.

Stuart Graham is a Senior Lecturer in the School of Business, Enterprise and Management at Queen Margaret University in Edinburgh. Prior to this current position he held academic teaching/

research and management posts in a number of other UK university business schools and management centres. Before pursuing a career in higher education, he gained considerable business and management experience working within both multinational corporations and the SME sector, including family businesses. The management and operational practices adopted by family orientated businesses has become a key research interest, particularly in respect to their approach to strategy formulation and ongoing development.

Markus Haag holds a BA in Information Management from Stuttgart School of Media, Germany, and an MA in Intercultural Communication from the University of Bedfordshire, UK. His areas of interest are international information management, knowledge management, knowledge organization, cross-cultural psychology, the effective use of media in a multicultural setting and cross-cultural differences in e-learning. He was a researcher at KIeM Institute for Intercultural Management, Values and Communication at Konstanz University of Applied Sciences, Germany, and is a PhD researcher at the Centre for Research in ICT Business Applications, University of Bedfordshire. He is investigating knowledge development processes and learning outcomes in e-learning from a cross-cultural and personal value perspective.

Ms. Johanna Heikkinen is currently working as a service manager for a consulting company specializing on change management, coaching and project management and its subsidiary that is a fast growing, already leading open source company in Finland. In her previous work at Technology Business Research Center at Lappeenranta University of Technology she concentrated on studying the establishment of the relationships and the evolution of the collaboration between MNCs and Chinese universities. Her theoretical interest lied on the evolution of Ba and development of absorptive capacity in cross-cultural university-industry collaboration.

Dr. Jianzhong Hong is a senior lecturer of knowledge management in the School of Business at Lappeenranta University of Technology. He is docent of psychology particularly in cross-cultural research in Department of Psychology at University of Joensuu. His articles have appeared in several international journals, including those in the areas of Psychology, Education and Management. His prime teaching is related to organizational learning and competence development, and his current research focuses on the impact of culture on cross-border knowledge interaction and collaborative innovation.

Jacques Edison Jacques is a medical professional specialized in Clinical and Cardiology Services. He holds two MBA: the MBA of Production Enginnering in integrated system of hospital costs at Federal University of Rio Grande do Sul, Brazil and the MBA of Management in knowledge management in hospitals at UNISINOS – University of Sinos Valley, São Leopoldo, Brazil. He was a lecturer at UNISINOS in the hospital management. He served as consultant of hospital management for Emergency Hospitals. He was the Coordinator during 10 years of the Intensive Treatment Unit of the well-known hospital in specialized care treatment, Porto Alegre, Brazil (Hospital Mãe de Deus). His current research interest is knowledge management, hospital costs and strategic management in hospitals.

Caroline Kamau obtained her PhD in Social Psychology in 2005 at the University of Kent in Canterbury, England, where she had obtained a BSc (Hons) in Psychology with Clinical Psychology in 2001. During her PhD, Caroline was also a Fellow (now alumnus) of the International Graduate College (based in Jena, Germany), which is an association of group process researchers in Europe. After working as a postdoctoral research associate in the Kent Department of Psychology until 2006, exploring intergroup evaluations of compunction emotions, Caroline taught General Psychology at Florida State University's London centre. In 2007 she joined Southampton Solent University, UK, as a Lecturer in Psychology and is based in the School of Human Sciences. Caroline conducts both experimental and applied social psychology research and is a member of the International Association for Cross-Cultural Psychology. Caroline's research interests include group processes, in particular social identity strategies, the severe initiation effect, compunction emotions (i.e. guilt or shame) in intergroup contexts, cross-national comparisons of group phenomena, group decision-making in industry, impression management strategies, and related aspects of experimental as well as applied social psychology.

John Beaumont Kerridge is the Sub Dean for Quality Enhancement for the Business School at the University of Bedfordshire and also teaches marketing and e-business related subjects. His doctorate from the Middlesex University in 2001, focused upon Market Orientation and Service Quality whilst his Masters in management studies (marketing option) was gained at the University of Greenwich in 1985. Prior to this, his B.Sc. in Biological Chemistry was awarded in 1975 from the University of Essex. He joined the University in 1988 as a senior lecturer in marketing, and has also been a Principal Teaching Fellow since 1999. Teaching and research areas include: Marketing, E Business Management, Internet Marketing Management, and Brand Management.

Dr. Beate Klingenberg is Assistant Professor of Management at Marist College, with a focus on Operations Management and Decision Sciences, and the Director of the Master of Science in Technology Management Program. Her areas of research expertise include knowledge management in technology transfer settings, environmental management and financial performance of firms as well as operations management issues in real estate. Her publications appear in academic as well as practitioner publications. Beate's credentials include a Master in Chemistry and Ph.D. in Physical Chemistry (both University of Erlangen-Nuernberg, Germany) as well as an MBA from Marist College. Furthermore, she has extensive industry experience in technology transfer and project management.

Epaminondas Koronis has obtained his PhD from University of Warwick, UK, where he is currently an associate fellow while he is the Director and MBA Coordinator of the Business School of Mediterranean University College, Greece. He is working as a business consultant, he is a partner of Reputation Lab Ltd, a research and consultancy firm, and is a member of board of several firms. His research interests involve the nature and challenges of knowledge, crises and reputation management in organizations.

Brian Mathews, B.Tech MBA PhD, is Professor of Marketing and Head of Department of Marketing and Entrepreneurship at the University of Bedfordshire Business School. His research career has spanned more than a quarter of a century and in that time he has published more than 130 research papers and journal articles in both leading academic journals (e.g. Industrial Marketing Management, International Journal of Research in Marketing) and those with a greater practitioner focus (e.g. the TQM Magazine). His early research focused on sales forecasting but developed into more interdisciplinary areas, including issues of service quality and SME internationalisation and more recently applications of knowledge management.

Elly Philpott is a Senior Research Fellow at the University of Bedfordshire, a visiting lecturer at the University of Hertfordshire UK and the visiting lecturer at the Cracow University of Technology. She has a BSc in Physical Science, a Masters in IT for Manufacture and a PhD in Concurrent Engineering and Design Ethos. Elly has worked in international supply chain management in the telecommunications sector and with various aerospace and automotive OEMs to improve new product introduction processes. More recently, Elly has been engaged in the support of UK SMEs. She is currently involved in regional and European innovation projects and consults on projects with the aim of improving processes of knowledge exchange between universities and small businesses. Teaching responsibilities have included Quality, Concurrent Engineering, Supply Chain Management, Knowledge Management, Design Tools and Techniques, and E-business. Her current research interests include holistic approaches to business strategy, knowledge transfer and the implementation of innovation in small companies.

Dr. Jose L. Pineda is an assistant professor at the Department of Marketing, within the Business School of the Tecnológico de Monterrey, Monterrey Campus, in Mexico. His experience in mass media includes a term as a journalist and cartoonist in newspapers. In radio and television he has produced and conducted several shows within promotional strategies for non-profit institutions. He has been involved in the management of public relations events for academic institutions. As a full time professor, his teaching activities are related to advertising, marketing communications and business ethics. He was awarded a PhD from the Universitat Autonoma de Barcelona and his research interests have been focused on mass media consumption and domestication of new technologies, and recently on the impact of the academic research in the business practice, e-mail: jlpineda@itesm.mx

Dr. Stavros T. Ponis is a Lecturer in the Section of Industrial Management and Operations Research of National Technical University Athens (NTUA) where he is teaching a number of courses in a graduate and post graduate level (Supply Chain Management, E-Commerce and Management of Information Systems among others). Dr. Ponis is also an expert reviewer for the European Community, the General Secretariat of Research and Development and the Greek Information Society S.A.. His current research interests and publications move around the areas of Supply Chain Management and Supporting Technologies, Knowledge Management for Empowering Supply Chain Effectiveness and Performance and Supply Chain Risk Management.

Mojca Prevodnik is a teaching assistant in Strategic Management and Management Decision Making. Her area of expertise is general management and leadership, knowledge management, and sport management. She has completed Master degree in Entrepreneurship at the University of Ljubljana, Faculty of Economics. She joined the University of Primorska, Faculty of Management in autumn 2003 having previously spent four years in a small firm as a marketing executive. Through this work, she developed an interest in organizational processes. Currently she is a PhD candidate at the University of Primorska.

Dr. Jacobo Ramirez (Doctor of Business Administration, U. of Newcastle upon Tyne, England in collaboration with Grenoble School of Management, France) is professor of Human Resource Management at the Tecnológico de Monterrey (Mexico). Dr. Ramirez holds the research Chair in European Studies. Currently, Dr. Ramirez is Assistant Professor at the Copenhagen Business School (CBS), Copenhagen,

Denmark, where he is attached to the graduate program on cross-cultural management. His current research focuses on cross-cultural studies of the formulation and impact of human resource strategy in workplaces, e-mail: jrn@itesm.mx.

Olga Rivera is Professor of Organization and Business Policy at ESTE School of Management (University of Deusto, Spain). She has been a member of the Steering Group of the Knowledge Cluster of the Basque Region and now she conducts the Business Competitiveness and Regional Development course in the Basque Country. This course has been designed by Professor Michael E. Porter of Harvard University. Her research focus is currently on Organizational Learning, Knowledge Management and Innovation. Her research work has been published in several international journals, such as the Journal of Knowledge Management, The Learning Organization and the Journal of Intellectual Capital.

Dr. Helen N. Rothberg is a Professor of Strategic Management, School of Management, Marist College, Poughkeepsie, NY, and has been the principal consultant for HNR Associates "a network of knowledge" since 1987. Her noted specialty is in the fields of knowledge management and competitive intelligence. Her publications appear in both academic and practitioner publications. Her co-authored book with G. Scott Erickson: "Knowledge to Intelligence: Building Advantage in the Next Economy", was published by Butterworth-Heinemann, 2005. Helen's credentials include an MBA from Baruch College, CUNY, and M.Phil. from City University Graduate Center, and a Ph.D. in Business specializing in both Organization and Policy Studies from the City University Graduate Center, NY.

Josune Sáenz is a PhD in Economics and Business Administration and faculty member of ESTE School of Management (University of Deusto, Spain). She is also a senior researcher at Orkestra, the Basque Institute of Competitiveness, which belongs to the network of Institutes associated with Harvard University's Institute for Strategy and Competitiveness. She specializes in Management Accounting and Strategic Management Control, and her research focus is currently on Knowledge Management, Intellectual Capital, and Innovation. Her research work has been published in several international journals, such as the Journal of Intellectual Capital, the Journal of Knowledge Management, The Learning Organization and the International Journal of Learning and Intellectual Capital.

Mrs. Mia Salila works as project manager in The Linde Group, a world leading gases and engineering company. Her project is about integrating country specific information in local languages into a crossnational intranet tool. Previously she worked as project manager in Technology Business Research Centre at Lappeenranta University of Technology. The project's aim was to understand, model and measure the critical factors for collaborative innovation and networked R&D. She was then in charge of managerialization of the research results, and she also assisted in the research work.

Christian-Andreas Schumann, born 1957 in Chemnitz (Germany), studied Industrial Engineering at the 'Chemnitz University of Technology' (CUT), doing his first doctor's degree in 1984 and second doctor's degree in 1987. He was appointed associate professor for plant planning and information processes at CUT in 1988. In 1994 he became professor for business and engineering information systems at the 'University of Applied Sciences Zwickau'. Since March 2003 he is dean of the faculty 'Business and Man-agement Sciences' at Zwickau. Currently he is also director of the 'Centre for New Forms of Education' and director of the 'Central German Academy of Further Education'.

Claire Seaman, Now a senior lecturer based in the School of Business, Enterprise and Management at Queen Margaret University in Edinburgh, Claire developed an interest in family businesses by a somewhat circuitous route! Originally a researcher in agriculture, the businesses involved tended to be family owned and run. Working as Knowledge Transfer Partnerships manager alongside a role running the Scottish Centre for Enterprise and Ethnic Business research, she developed projects with businesses as diverse as food manufacturing companies and funeral directors but one common factor became clear - the family component tended to be a major influence on the business but only half-acknowledged! Thus was a research interest born, which now forms the basis for an active research area and a direct link to the teaching being developed within Queen Margaret University.

Dipl.-Inform. Claudia Tittmann, born in 1972, studied from 1992 to 1996 information sciences with economics at the University of Applied Sciences Zwickau, worked from 1996 to 1997 at the data-service department in the bank *Sparkasse Zwickau*. Since 1997 she is busy at the University of Applied Sciences Zwickau with information and knowledge management systems and also works on research projects. Additionally she works on receiving a doctor's degree in the domain of knowledge management.

George Vagenas is a Mechanical Engineer of the National Technical University of Athens (NTUA), specialized in Industrial Engineering. He is also a Doctoral Researcher in the Sector of Industrial Management and Operational Research of the NTUA's Mechanical Engineering School. His current research interests include the areas of Supply Chain Management and Knowledge Management, with an emphasis on Web based technological support.

Dr. Laura Zapata-Cantú (Doctor of Business Administration, U Autónoma de Barcelona) is professor of Management at Tecnológico de Monterrey (Mexico). Among her research interests are: knowledge management in small and medium enterprises, intellectual capital and organizational learning. She has presented her research work at national and international conferences. Since 2006, she is a member of Mexico's National Researcher's System, e-mail: laura.zapata@itesm.mx.

Index

A

absorptive capacity 136, 148, 151, 412
academic journal 143, 144
actor-network theory 109
adaptability 203, 218, 219
architectural knowledge. *See* knowledge, composites of
Australian hospitality industry 203, 204, 205,
    206, 376, 211, 212, 224, 225, 226, 227,
    376, 380, 394, 397, 398, 411
autopoietic theory 115. *See also* cognition, biology of

B

Ba concept 93, 94
business consulting 134, 135, 137, 139, 140,
    141, 143, 147, 148
business learning 231, 241, 244, 245, 247

C

career contracts 252, 267, 268, 269, 271, 386
Chief Knowledge Officer 12
clinical guidelines 181, 186. *See also* medical protocols
cognition, biology of 109, 115, 121, 125, 126,
    132,
cognitive barriers 181, 182, 183, 184
cognitive constructions 181
collaborative knowledge creation (CKC) 295,
    296, 297, 302, 303, 304, 308, 310, 311
communities of practice (CoPs) 87, 105, 379
competitive advantage 203, 204, 210, 217,
    220, 221, 229, 252, 253, 254, 255, 256,
    261, 263, 264, 267, 268, 269, 270
complex adaptive system 120, 128, 129, 375.

See also living system
complex system. *See* living system
component knowledge. *See* knowledge, composites of
contextualised information. *See* knowledge
continuing education 134, 141, 143, 147, 148
corporate ethics 73
corporate memory 272, 393. *See also* organizational memory
cross-cultural contexts 285
cross-cultural knowledge absorption competencies 286
cross-cultural knowledge transfer 277, 290,
    292, 388
cross-cultural models of engagement 280
cross-cultural settings 287
cross-cultural training 60, 61, 70, 71, 72, 79
cultural barriers 48, 52, 53, 57
cultural knowledge 60, 69, 70, 79
cultural situatedness 26, 27, 34, 36, 41
cultural space 118, 119, 120, 122, 124, 125,
    127
culture 49, 50, 52, 53, 54, 55, 56, 57, 378, 397,
    153, 154, 256, 261, 263, 264, 265, 267,
    269, 270, 273
culture, academic 357, 358
culture, functional 296, 298, 299, 357
culture, national 26, 27, 28, 36, 37, 39, 41, 42,
    298, 299, 304, 306, 309, 310, 311, 314,
    378, 380
culture, organizational 26, 27, 29, 36, 37, 38,
    39, 41, 42, 43, 46, 62, 67, 68, 69, 79, 80,
    369, 152, 153, 371, 154, 155, 156, 157,
    158, 376, 159, 377, 384, 171, 172, 173,
    174, 175, 176, 393, 177, 401, 406, 298,
    299, 305, 309, 311, 313, 314, 357